Lecture Notes in Computer Science 12786

More information about this subseries at http://www.springer.com/series/7409

Qin Gao · Jia Zhou (Eds.)

Human Aspects of IT for the Aged Population

Technology Design and Acceptance

7th International Conference, ITAP 2021
Held as Part of the 23rd HCI International Conference, HCII 2021
Virtual Event, July 24–29, 2021
Proceedings, Part I

 Springer

Editors
Qin Gao
Tsinghua University
Beijing, China

Jia Zhou
Chongqing University
Chongqing, China

ISSN 0302-9743 ISSN 1611-3349 (electronic)
Lecture Notes in Computer Science
ISBN 978-3-030-78107-1 ISBN 978-3-030-78108-8 (eBook)
https://doi.org/10.1007/978-3-030-78108-8

LNCS Sublibrary: SL3 – Information Systems and Applications, incl. Internet/Web, and HCI

This Springer imprint is published by the registered company Springer Nature Switzerland AG
The registered company address is: Gewerbestrasse 11, 6330 Cham, Switzerland

Foreword

Human-Computer Interaction (HCI) is acquiring an ever-increasing scientific and industrial importance, and having more impact on people's everyday life, as an ever-growing number of human activities are progressively moving from the physical to the digital world. This process, which has been ongoing for some time now, has been dramatically accelerated by the COVID-19 pandemic. The HCI International (HCII) conference series, held yearly, aims to respond to the compelling need to advance the exchange of knowledge and research and development efforts on the human aspects of design and use of computing systems.

The 23rd International Conference on Human-Computer Interaction, HCI International 2021 (HCII 2021), was planned to be held at the Washington Hilton Hotel, Washington DC, USA, during July 24–29, 2021. Due to the COVID-19 pandemic and with everyone's health and safety in mind, HCII 2021 was organized and run as a virtual conference. It incorporated the 21 thematic areas and affiliated conferences listed on the following page.

A total of 5222 individuals from academia, research institutes, industry, and governmental agencies from 81 countries submitted contributions, and 1276 papers and 241 posters were included in the proceedings to appear just before the start of the conference. The contributions thoroughly cover the entire field of HCI, addressing major advances in knowledge and effective use of computers in a variety of application areas. These papers provide academics, researchers, engineers, scientists, practitioners, and students with state-of-the-art information on the most recent advances in HCI. The volumes constituting the set of proceedings to appear before the start of the conference are listed in the following pages.

The HCI International (HCII) conference also offers the option of 'Late Breaking Work' which applies both for papers and posters, and the corresponding volume(s) of the proceedings will appear after the conference. Full papers will be included in the 'HCII 2021 - Late Breaking Papers' volumes of the proceedings to be published in the Springer LNCS series, while 'Poster Extended Abstracts' will be included as short research papers in the 'HCII 2021 - Late Breaking Posters' volumes to be published in the Springer CCIS series.

The present volume contains papers submitted and presented in the context of the 7th International Conference on Human Aspects of IT for the Aged Population (ITAP 2021) affiliated conference to HCII 2021. I would like to thank the Co chairs, Qin Gao and Jia Zhou, for their invaluable contribution in its organization and the preparation of the Proceedings, as well as the members of the program board for their contributions and support. This year, the ITAP affiliated conference has focused on topics related to designing for and with older users, technology acceptance and user experience of older users, use of social media and games by the aging population, as well as applications supporting health, wellbeing, communication, social participation and everyday activities.

I would also like to thank the Program Board Chairs and the members of the Program Boards of all thematic areas and affiliated conferences for their contribution towards the highest scientific quality and overall success of the HCI International 2021 conference.

This conference would not have been possible without the continuous and unwavering support and advice of Gavriel Salvendy, founder, General Chair Emeritus, and Scientific Advisor. For his outstanding efforts, I would like to express my appreciation to Abbas Moallem, Communications Chair and Editor of HCI International News.

July 2021   Constantine Stephanidis

HCI International 2021 Thematic Areas and Affiliated Conferences

Thematic Areas

- HCI: Human-Computer Interaction
- HIMI: Human Interface and the Management of Information

Affiliated Conferences

- EPCE: 18th International Conference on Engineering Psychology and Cognitive Ergonomics
- UAHCI: 15th International Conference on Universal Access in Human-Computer Interaction
- VAMR: 13th International Conference on Virtual, Augmented and Mixed Reality
- CCD: 13th International Conference on Cross-Cultural Design
- SCSM: 13th International Conference on Social Computing and Social Media
- AC: 15th International Conference on Augmented Cognition
- DHM: 12th International Conference on Digital Human Modeling and Applications in Health, Safety, Ergonomics and Risk Management
- DUXU: 10th International Conference on Design, User Experience, and Usability
- DAPI: 9th International Conference on Distributed, Ambient and Pervasive Interactions
- HCIBGO: 8th International Conference on HCI in Business, Government and Organizations
- LCT: 8th International Conference on Learning and Collaboration Technologies
- ITAP: 7th International Conference on Human Aspects of IT for the Aged Population
- HCI-CPT: 3rd International Conference on HCI for Cybersecurity, Privacy and Trust
- HCI-Games: 3rd International Conference on HCI in Games
- MobiTAS: 3rd International Conference on HCI in Mobility, Transport and Automotive Systems
- AIS: 3rd International Conference on Adaptive Instructional Systems
- C&C: 9th International Conference on Culture and Computing
- MOBILE: 2nd International Conference on Design, Operation and Evaluation of Mobile Communications
- AI-HCI: 2nd International Conference on Artificial Intelligence in HCI

List of Conference Proceedings Volumes Appearing Before the Conference

http://2021.hci.international/proceedings

7th International Conference on Human Aspects of IT for the Aged Population (ITAP 2021)

Program Board Chairs: **Qin Gao**, *Tsinghua University, China*, **and Jia Zhou, *Chongqing University, China***

- Bessam Abdulrazak, Canada
- Inês Amaral, Portugal
- Panagiotis Bamidis, Greece
- Alan H. S. Chan, China
- Alex Chaparro, USA
- Honglin Chen, China
- José Baptista Coelho, Portugal
- Fausto Colombo, Italy
- Loredana Ivan, Romania
- Hirokazu Kato, Japan
- Chaiwoo Lee, USA
- Jiunn-Woei Lian, Taiwan
- Hai-Ning Liang, China
- Eugene Loos, Netherlands
- Yan Luximon, Hong Kong
- Lourdes Moreno, Spain
- Sergio F. Ochoa, Chile
- Peter Rasche, Germany
- Marie Sjölinder, Sweden
- Patrice Terrier, France
- Wang-Chin Tsai, Taiwan
- Ana Veloso, Portugal
- Nadine Vigouroux, France
- Tingru Zhang, China
- Yuxiang (Chris) Zhao, China

The full list with the Program Board Chairs and the members of the Program Boards of all thematic areas and affiliated conferences is available online at:

http://www.hci.international/board-members-2021.php

HCI International 2022

The 24th International Conference on Human-Computer Interaction, HCI International 2022, will be held jointly with the affiliated conferences at the Gothia Towers Hotel and Swedish Exhibition & Congress Centre, Gothenburg, Sweden, June 26 – July 1, 2022. It will cover a broad spectrum of themes related to Human-Computer Interaction, including theoretical issues, methods, tools, processes, and case studies in HCI design, as well as novel interaction techniques, interfaces, and applications. The proceedings will be published by Springer. More information will be available on the conference website: http://2022.hci.international/:

General Chair
Prof. Constantine Stephanidis
University of Crete and ICS-FORTH
Heraklion, Crete, Greece
Email: general_chair@hcii2022.org

http://2022.hci.international/

Contents – Part I

Technology Acceptance and User Experience Studies

Aging and Social Media

Contents – Part II

Supporting Health and Wellbeing

Supporting Communication, Social Participation and Everyday Activities

Designing for and with Older Users

Elderly, ICTs and Qualitative Research: Some Methodological Reflections

Simone Carlo[✉] and Francesco Bonifacio

Università Cattolica del Sacro Cuore, Milan, Italy
{simone.carlo,francesco.bonifacio}@unicatt.it

Abstract. The study of the use of media by the elderly has been producing an ever-increasing number of social researches. ICTs are seen by many as tools for a more actively facing ageing processes. Moreover, due to the reduction of the age-related digital divide, older adults represent an interesting type of users. From this standpoint, social researchers have been increasingly investigating older adults' uses and non-uses of ICTs, both with quantitative and qualitative methods, online and offline tools.

Starting from the presentation of three empirical studies carried out by the Università Cattolica del Sacro Cuore (Italy) between 2013 and 2020, the following paper aims to reflect on limits and opportunities offered by different research designs in this field of studies. To this purpose, we provide an overview on methods adopted in order to grasp the relationship between the elderly and technologies in complex and articulated social contexts. Furthermore, we will reflect on future lines of inquiry in this field of research, advocating for a greater interdisciplinarity in ageing studies as well as underlining the benefits offered by ethnographic methods and overall qualitative research. Finally, we sketch potential issues referring to the future of empirical research on the elderly in the upcoming years of the post-pandemic era.

Keywords: Elderly · Methods · ICTs · Domestication · Research design

1 Introduction and Objectives

The ageing of society raises serious challenges in terms of social sustainability, which concerns politics and public health but also families and caregivers [1]. From a policy-oriented perspective, ICTs are expected to reduce the welfare spending due to ageing processes, and to improve older adults' social inclusion [2]. Still, while the increasing digitisation of care is portrayed as a source of opportunities, it also entails critical issues, especially for older adults who are not adequately equipped and trained to use digital devices [3]. From this standpoint, understanding the current state of ICTs (Information Communication Technologies) domestication by older adults and their concrete uses of digital technologies has become crucial [4]. Many studies have addressed these issues, adopting both quantitative (statistical, demographic, etc.) and qualitative methods; the latter are the focal point of this paper. Studies oriented toward the development of

© Springer Nature Switzerland AG 2021
Q. Gao and J. Zhou (Eds.): HCII 2021, LNCS 12786, pp. 3–20, 2021.
https://doi.org/10.1007/978-3-030-78108-8_1

products and services dedicated to older adults tend to include them into the research design, together with doctors and caregivers [5, 6]. Others employ methods to engage elderly people more effectively [7]. Drawing on participatory research designs, such studies consider the active inclusion of older adults as the best way to fully explore their difficulties in adopting ICTs in their daily life [8, 9]. Many studies follow this direction, using various methods such as interviews [10], focus groups, ethnographies [11], or more holistic multi-methodological approaches [12]. In particular, ethnographic and qualitative interviews seem useful to investigate older adults' everyday life, and to explore the "taken for granted" knowledge related to ordinary ICTs-based practices [13]. In order to rationalise some methodological issues concerning the growing literature in this field of research, this paper provides a comparative summa of the empirical results obtained by using various approaches.

Starting from the presentation of three studies carried out by the Università Cattolica del Sacro Cuore (Italy) between 2013 and 2020, the paper presents limits and opportunities of different methodological approaches applied to the study of the use of ICT by senior citizens. To this purpose, we will reflect on broader differences between qualitative and quantitative designs of research. We will focus on different strategies of recruitment in terms of openness and flexibility of the research design, critically addressing the researcher's position. We will discuss the intertwined relationship between the construction of the research object and its empirical investigation, stressing the contingent efficacy of various methodological tools. Furthermore, we will reflect on future lines of inquiry in this field of research, advocating for a greater interdisciplinarity in ageing studies as well as remarking the benefits offered by ethnographic methods and overall qualitative research. Finally, we will sketch potential issues referring to the future of empirical research on the elderly in the upcoming years of the post-pandemic era, paying particular attention to context-related issues (e.g. the role of domestic settings of research).

2   The Combination of Quantitative and Qualitative Research: Active Ageing and the Role of ICTs (2013–2014)

AGE GROUP	65+
SAMPLING	Probabilistic+non-probabilistic
DATA COLLECTION	Structured interviews+Ethnographic observations and Biographical interviews

2.1   Structure of the General Research

The first research whose methodological structure we want to illustrate took place in the years 2013–2014.

As part of a wider research project regarding Italian adult generations, a multidisciplinary team from Università Cattolica del Sacro Cuore (Milan, Italy) composed by sociologists, psychologists, media and communication experts and demographers launched a complex investigation combining the generational approach with media use analysis.

The research, entitled "I don't want to be inactive: the lengthening of life, a challenge for generations, an opportunity for the society", lasted two years and investigated the opportunities offered by life lengthening according to an active ageing perspective. It consists of a survey and several researches conducted by using qualitative and ethnographic methods.

2.2 Quantitative Research

The survey was conducted (between December 2013 and January 2014) through face-to-face questionnaires administered to a statistically representative national sample of 900 Italian seniors aged between 65 and 74 years old (selected by using a random and proportional criterion stratified by region and by the size of place of residence, built in two-stage sampling).

The sample was extracted from the electoral lists of 91 municipalities for a total of 1600 elderly people between 65 and 74 years of age, after having carried out a stratification of the reference population by region and by size of the municipality of residence. The selection of such a large number was made necessary by the constraints of non-replacement of the sample imposed by the methodology itself, also taking into consideration cases of refusal of the interview, wrong address, unavailability or illness. At the end of the sampling process, it was possible to obtain a sample of 900 units (Error sample: 3%; confidence error: 0.05%).

As mentioned, for the sampling process we chose to build the sampling lists starting from the electoral lists, in line with a consolidated tradition in quantitative research processes [14]. In Italy, electoral constituency represents the only source accessible to universities and research institutes that safely guarantees a full coverage of the country. In this case, however, the reference population was made up of the elderly who had the right to vote and not of the senior population present on the territory. Other solutions were discarded as less rigorous from a methodological point of view, although the limit remained of not being able to know the opinion of foreigners, largely absent from the electoral lists due to the existing restrictions to the right of passive and active electorate (also local) for non-Italian citizens. This limit, which is extremely serious in case of researches involving groups of younger age (among which the percentage of foreigner non-voting resident is high), has a lesser impact when the research concerns the elderly. The number of foreign seniors present in Italy is so modest[1] that their exclusion is methodologically insignificant in the case of a quantitative research on representative samples. Given the narrowness of the reference group [15], opinions, values, and experiences of foreign elderly residing in Italy can be effectively investigated even with non-probabilistic samplings.

The questionnaire collected data such as information about family and intergenerational relationships (size of personal network), health status, leisure time and cultural

---

[1] The number of foreigners over 60 represents 8.8% of the total number of foreigners residing in Italy [14].

consumption, use of new technologies, any past or present connection to the business world, participation to any kind of voluntary or socio-political activities, the reaction to the current economic and financial crisis, social capital and social solidarity, family network and friendship (forms of exchange and support), orientation toward intergenerational relationships such as fairness between generations, values, representation of the elderly condition, and finally the economic status of respondents.

As regards media use by the younger elderly the questionnaire aimed to investigate technological devices, time spent and preferred time for using PCs and the Internet, ways to implement said use, types of activities carried out while doing so, manners of learning how to use PCs, online services and the Internet, reasons for using the Internet, use of and attitudes toward health technologies.

The questionnaire was very long and dense, so it was decided to discard the hypothesis of a CATI but rather to administer the questionnaire to the participants' homes. To do this, a partner company was activated in the cities included in the sample. Their team was responsible for going directly door-to-door (without notice, landline numbers not having been provided) in order to either carry out the interview or to make a later appointment.

Despite the use of local operators with a great knowledge of both the territory and the resident families, the level of refusal was high (900 interviews completed against a total of 1600 contacts made). As regards the interviews, given their large number the central research team did not have the opportunity to properly supervise their management: unfortunately this remains a very strong limit of quantitative research, made even more evident in the case of a research concerning the elderly, where the delicate nature of the sample and the general difficulty in training all the interviewers in the area in depth represent a challenge.

A second important limit is the impossibility of collecting data on the daily and social contexts in which the research is carried out: possible observations and notes on the over 900 houses visited have been absent. On this last point, the possibility of a questionnaire to be filled out by the interviewees about their experience could be a good strategy to retrieve useful information for research.

2.3 Qualitative Research: In-Depth Interviews

Starting from the results of the questionnaire, OssCom then carried out, in May 2014, 20 unstructured and in-depth interviews with older people aged 65–74, all ICTs users. In the second part of the research we investigated how media and ICTs consumption is spatially and temporally located and how these media uses and routines are shared within the household and are enabled by processes of domestication [16]. The interviews aimed to understand the moral economies of the household and the processes of use and symbolic appropriation of media and ICTs in the everyday family life. The interviews were held within the residential areas of the interviewees in order to better investigate the size of domestic contexts, in coherence with the theoretical and methodological approach of studies on the domestication of media and ICTs and in continuity with previous research in the field of media studies and the elderly [17].

The sample was chosen based on family income, age of the elderly, family composition, geographical context (big or small city of northern Italy).

The finding of the subjects to be interviewed was carried out through a specialised marketing and research company. At the end of the interview, the interviewees received a gift voucher worth €40. The selection of elderly people previously included in lists of subjects interested in being interviewed has:

- made the retrieval quick (all 20 subjects were found in 15 days) in 15 days
- ensured accuracy and seriousness in the interviewees, in the management of appointments, in schedule, in communication
- made the procurement company "guarantor" of both the seriousness of the participants and the truthfulness of the personal information provided (age, technological equipment, habits of use, family unit composition); the interviewers, thanks to their legitimacy, were able to access without resistance and with the maximum serenity and freedom of movement the homes of the elderly

The use of a procurement company has also shown some limits:

- in some cases a certain "artificiality" or "professionalism" emerged in the responses of the elderly, being the interviewers subjects with an already established experience in research and/or marketing interviews and who in some situations seem to have given the answer they thought was "right" and that they thought the researcher would like to receive
- in some cases the elderly felt the urge to appear more passionate than they actually were about digital means, as if to show to the reference company and to the interviewer that they had deserved to be picked in a search for "digital elderly"
- presumably the elderly in contact with procurement companies showed a higher level of education, income and social capital than the elderly outside these networks, and this represents a very risky bias

As regards the way the interviews were led, the ethnographic approach and the domestic context allowed a positive relationship to be built between the elderly interviewed and the (young) interviewer.

As emphasized by Hammersley and Atkinson [18], listening, observing, and gathering the greatest amount of information about the daily life of the elderly and the context of their responses is fundamental for understanding the world of the respondents. Discursiveness, i.e. the narrative construction of one's own biography (on the use of the media) is an essential element in the research activity.

Even with the limitations entailed by the "professionalised" context of the retrieval and interview process, the research made possible to enter the "world" of the elderly participants as opposed to just listen to their words. Obviously, as Manderson et al. [19] suggest, the more "intense" the relationship becomes, the more the interviewer's age, gender and social class is involved in influencing said relationship. In truth, the use of young interviewers would seem to have facilitated the establishment of a relationship of confidence similar to that of grandfather-grandchild, where the elderly felt less judged about certain behaviours considered in a negative light (for example laziness, the fault of not being "active seniors") and at the same time more open to confessing to some technical difficulties experienced when using ICTs. The in-depth interviews offered the opportunity to better understand the contexts of use of digital media. Thanks to the exploratory opportunity provided by the ethnographic survey, unexpected themes and elements emerged during the interview in comparison to those outlined during the quantitative phase and the questionnaire: the risks associated with the use of ICTs, the difficulties that have brought ICTs into family and couple life, in some cases the perception of the worst aspects of everyday life after the adoption of ICTs. It is as if the connection created between interviewer and interviewee had offered the opportunity to go beyond the rhetorical discourses on the positive impact of ICTs in people's daily lives, and to better investigate the hurdles linked to an innovation that is not necessarily the bearer of positive news.

In order to study the computer skills and online activities of the subjects, the interview checked the availability to the interviewee of computer and smartphone possessed, used under the interviewer's supervision and observation. However, this type of sessions proved to be somehow "unnatural". Sometime they favoured the emergence of a "non-equal" power relationship between the elderly (generally with lower digital skills) and the researcher [20]. The interviewer placed himself in a position of power (thanks to the greater technical skills owned) with respect to the elderly, who in some cases felt that their ability to use technologies, their choice of services used and the contents enjoyed were "under judgment". For example, in the interviews there were no references to the use of questionable contents (sex, eroticism, vulgar videos, gambling) that other quantitative researches have highlighted as being important also for the elderly users.

Finally, the study of domestic contexts allowed the collection of interesting ethnographic notes on the organisation of spaces, which were useful for a classification of the houses and the rethinking of the interior with respect to the presence in the domestic nucleus of ICTs (Figs. 1 and 2).

Fig. 1. "When I use it I put it on the kitchen table, the rest of the time I have made space in a cupboard that has become a sort of workstation, complete with printer, modems and paper, so when I close it you can't see anything and my wife doesn't complain." (M, 70, GC)

Fig. 2. "Cleaning up, I leave the second tablecloth on so that I put the computer on top of it and I don't scratch the table." (F, 72, PC).

The relationship of confidence created during the interview between interviewer and interviewee made it possible to access, even with a certain simplicity, the elderly's online social network: the interviewee ended up offering an exchange of contacts on Facebook, thus providing the opportunity, not foreseen first and therefore unexpected, to conduct a post-interview web ethnography. The web ethnography of the elderly's social profiles added further interesting data and elements for the researchers that helped contextualize the profile of the elderly investigated. On the latter point, however, an ethical doubt remains: the trust received during the interview is transformed into a bond of friendship (albeit virtual) created with the aim of adding a piece of investigation and research not previously agreed upon and lacking clear boundaries [21]. This is a recurring ethical dilemma related to shadowing researches which in particular arises in the studies focused on users, like the elderly, with low digital skills and a limited awareness of the risks associated with the use of social media (such as those related to privacy or the sharing of sensitive information) [22].

MAIN INSIGHTS

The mix of quantitative and qualitative methods allows to study both the macro and micro context

---

Professional recruitment (qualitative part) saved time. Yet, it found subjects accustomed to being interviewed by researchers

---

Ethnographic observations give access to the immediacy of older adults' house and daily life

---

3   An International Qualitative Research: Grannies on the Net (2017)

AGE GROUP	65+
SAMPLING	Non-probabilistic
DATA COLLECTION	Focus groups

3.1   The General Research Structure

The second research whose methodological structure we want to illustrate took place in 2017 in Milan (Italy). The "Understanding the Role of Internet Communication Technologies (ICTs) in Family Relationships with Grandparents" project aimed to understand how grandmothers use Facebook and digital devices (computers, laptops, tablets, smartphones).

A crucial importance was given to the role played by the intergenerational and intragenerational relations in shaping the media use and the learning style of the elderly. This research wanted to specifically investigate:

- The relationships supposedly in place between the grandmothers and the children/grandchildren, with the aim of understanding the dynamics involved in their intergenerational exchange and how grandmothers experience the use of Internet as a tool to facilitate the communication with younger family members.
- The possible existing relationships between the grandmothers and their friends, with the aim of understanding the dynamics surrounding intergenerational and intragenerational exchange, and how grandmothers experience the use of Internet as a tool for communication and entertainment and leisure activities with friends.

Researchers implemented the project in collaboration with an international network of professionals (from Canada, Romania, Peru, Israel, Italy, Spain, and Colombia) coordinated by Shannon Hebblethwaite at the Department of Applied Human Sciences of Concordia University, Montreal, Canada. The research was funded by the Social Sciences and Humanities Research Council of Canada and by the centres of research/departments participating in the network (for Italy OssCom – the research centre on media and communication of Università Cattolica).

The coordination saw the sharing of research objectives, research protocols, retrieval processes, gatherings from the focus groups and finally analysis protocols.

3.2   Qualitative Research: Focus Groups

For the aforementioned research, the focus group was considered to be the most suitable tool in order to reach the predetermined cognitive objectives. The use of this method allowed the researchers "to observe a large amount of interaction on a topic in a limited period of time" [23] and to experience the participants' natural vocabulary on the topic. Interaction, one of the most distinctive features of this method, is important, as it leads to "a relatively spontaneous response" and produces a "fairly high level of participant involvement" [23, p. 10]. The "friendliness" of this methodology with respect to its participants, "who typically enjoy their interactions together" [23, p. 18], also makes it particularly suitable for the specific age group taken into consideration. Moreover, the focus group method activates social interactions that stress shared experiences and allow mutual recognition among members of the same generation.

Data were collected through four focus groups - each lasting approximately 2 h - that took place in February and March 2017 in Milan, Italy.

We recruited 28 Italian women, first via a snowball approach through acquaintances and then in collaboration with two local associations of the elderly. In particular, along the process of finding and selecting possible participants, we culled participants from Milan's University of the Third Age and from a leisure association (attended not exclusively by the elderly) based in a suburban neighbourhood of Milan.

The researchers organised information sessions during the activities of the association's Milan's University of the Third Age in order to promote the initiative. Throughout these sessions, the elderly's adhesions were collected and contact details were gathered for any prospective subsequent adhesions.

The involvement of such associations was very efficient in terms of reaching and informing a large number of elderly people in the shortest time possible. On the other hand, however, it mixed in the research elderly people with an atypical profile, characterised by high social, cultural and economic capital (see below). In general, the snowball sampling has collected the adhesion of very similar profiles of elderly people, all expressing a strong homophilia, often belonging to the same social context (if not explicitly acquaintances and friends): the non-probabilistic sampling does obviously not aim to represent the entire variety of the elderly population, but a certain heterogeneity would be considered necessary. To foster the latter, it was decided to reach out to two associations with profoundly different characteristics: the University of the Third Age based in the city centre of Milan and a neighbourhood association located in the outskirts of the same city. The subjects thus found were then combined within the focus groups.

We prepared the way for the focus group with brief telephone calls between each elderly participant and one of the researchers. The purpose of these calls was to have prior knowledge of the grandmother in question and to check – through a closed questionnaire – if she had the characteristics (age, family situation, computer skills) required in order to be part of the focus group. Selection criteria were: being 65 years of age or older, a grandmother and a frequent user (at least twice a week) of at least one digital device among the following: computer, laptop, tablet, and smartphone. Participants were born between 1936 and 1952 (the average age was 72, with a minimum of 65 and a maximum of 81) and all resided in Milan; for the majority, they acknowledged their daily use of either desktop or laptop computers, as well as smartphones. On the whole, the sample turned out to be very homogeneous, made up of well-educated middle and middle-upper class women. Most of them were involved in community activities around Milan. This peculiarity of the sample was not the result of a particular selection in the recruitment phase, during which no restriction was placed on socioeconomic or sociocultural status.

The researchers rather considered this uniformity as the consequence of the spread of ICTs among older women in Italy, which, as we have previously seen [24], still tends to favour people with a high economic, cultural, and social standing. Therefore, the members of the focus group show characteristics that are consistent with the relatively small and privileged segment of older female ICTs users in Italy, being thus very relevant in order to understand their appropriation dynamics.

We organised two focus groups at the University and two others at the associations. The University meetings were carried out in a more formal environment than the associations' ones; nevertheless, no substantial differences emerged in the management and trend of the focuses. The chatting progressing at a natural pace and a certain inclination in the "grandmothers" for speaking and narrating made the conversations extremely fluid and all participants, even if with due differences, actively contributed to the exchange (Fig. 3).

Fig. 3. Focus group N1 at Università Cattolica del Sacro Cuore

Each focus group was led by a pair of researchers, one in charge of moderating the discussion while the other was making a videotape and taking notes on the most significant interactions. After the warm-up phase, the researcher investigated the participants' initial approach to the use of ICTs, discovering when and how the grandmothers learned it and for which reasons. Then participants were asked to describe ICTs and their risks and benefits in the users' everyday lives. A second section focused on how they communicate with their families in comparison to how they communicate with their friends and acquaintances, and on difficulties faced when using ICTs with these different types of people. The final section encouraged the participants to declare what they would change about these technologies and what they reckon is the "correct and appropriate use" of ICTs. During the focus groups, information was collected about family relationships and individual memories, including very personal and familiar situations for some of the interviewees (such as their relationship with children and grandchildren). All the material recorded in Italian was transcribed and translated into English by the researchers in order to support a cross-cultural comparison of data within the international framework of the project. Lastly, all transcripts were analysed by using video writing programs to facilitate a qualitative thematic text analysis and the coding and comparison in accordance to the constant comparative method [25].

MAIN INSIGHTS
Recruiting through associations of seniors saved time but found seniors markedly more active, well-off, healthy than average
The focus group among grandmothers made it natural and simple to manage the speech and debate, stimulating the creation of an atmosphere of confidence and friendly
The collection of video materials during the focus made the non-verbal reactions of the grandmothers "visible" during the debate

4   Harvest - Castel Del Monte (2020)

AGE GROUP	65+
SAMPLING	Open, non-probabilistic
DATA COLLECTION	Community-based ethnography (Biographical interviews + participant observations)

4.1   Structure of the General Research

The last research we discuss in this paper unfolded in 2019/2020 within the project *Harvest: eHealth and Ageing in Rural Areas: Transforming Everyday Life, Digital Competences, and Technology*. Due to the geographical isolation and depopulation that characterise several areas of Central Italy, remote contexts are often indicated as the intended privileged beneficiaries of the digitalisation of health and bureaucratic services. In an attempt to bring such policy-oriented considerations into a concrete reality, we settled the research in a small village called Castel del Monte, located in the Apennine Mountains, with less than 500 resident citizens and a high average age. Through a community-based study we meant to observe whether a circumscribed context, characterised not only by geographical constraints but also by a peculiar socioeconomic organisation and consolidated social routines, shows specific patterns of domestication when it comes to digital technologies. If, according to Soja [26], age and technology are culturally influenced, the place where a research is set should be taken into account, thus questioning how situated cultural beliefs related to old age and technology shape ICTs uses, competences and meanings. The importance of the contexts of reception has been recognised since the ethnographic tradition of audience studies. In particular, the approach to the domestication of media [27] has acknowledged the symbolic as well as the physical dimension of the household (its *moral economy*), remarking "how the uses of technologies are shaped by the exigencies of their" local "environment" [28]. The ubiquitous nature of contemporary digital devices and services dictates to look beyond the domestic context of adoption, and to grasp practices and places where use and consumption occur. In this case, the relevance of domestic uses of ICTs represents an outcome of our empirical investigation, rather than being the analytical premise for the construction of our research object. Nevertheless, this leaves new analytical issues open.

4.2 Constructing the Research Object

In line with media scholar's plea to decentre media from our research objects (among many: [29–33]) we have framed ICTs uses as activities embedded in broader practices, which may not be primarily media-oriented. Before addressing ICTs appropriation by older adults, our leading question was: "what does ageing mean in this context?". Such wide premise has required an initial analytical effort to identify which portions of reality were relevant to our specific research interest [34]. Accordingly, in a first exploratory phase we aimed to identify which contextual dimensions may have informed our understanding of older villagers' everyday life. To do this, we organised a multi-sited ethnography [35] in the locations where most of sociality occurs (bar, main square, food stores, pharmacy), and shadowing sessions with available subjects in different social occasions (Fig. 4).

Fig. 4. Participant observation in a bar

These observations have been enriched by a series of interlocutory interviews with privileged witnesses, such as the mayor and the pharmacist, who helped us reconstructing the socioeconomic history of the village and its current administrative features, paying particular attention to the spread of internet infrastructures and to the available access to healthcare services. By integrating the theoretical framework that guided the research design, the information gathered in this phase has affected the subsequent steps: the choice and structuring of the interview outline and the construction of the sample.

4.3 Constructing the Interview Outline

The choice of the biographical interview as our main investigative tool is justified by the exploratory approach of the research and by a theoretical perspective that frames ageing as a process of embodiment of age [36]. By comparing the past to the present, biographical interviews enable the subject to give an account of their individual experience in terms of ageing-related changes. [37]. In addition to theoretical-conceptual dimensions [38], the information obtained in the pre-field phase and during our initial exploratory observations has been translated into empirical dimensions of interest. Then both have been ordered into a highly-structured interview outline. The standard interview began with a generic input: "I would like you to tell me about your daily day in this village, starting from wherever you want", and then proceeded with non-directive verbal inputs from the researcher. The intrinsic openness of such interview mode meant that the dimensions contained within the outline were not always touched by the interviewee's story. On the other hand, this allowed the researcher to enrich the track after each interview with the addition of emerging and hitherto ignored empirical categories. For example, after completing a few interviews we observed that people who had always lived in the village and those who moved back there in their adulthood used to focus their biographical account on quite different life issues (e.g. family, work, community, etc.). They disclosed different motivations for living in the village and a varying social networks composition. They also showed different uses of ICTs and of the meanings attached to them, and such dimension influenced the following recruitment.

Social representativeness is indeed an important criterion also in ethnographic approaches: not in statistic terms but in thematic ones. Grasping unexpected dimensions of interest enabled us to enrich our established understanding of ageing processes, and to relate ICTs domestication to various biographical patterns. In this instance, empirical information advised us to recruit more returning migrants, thus achieving a greater social representativeness.

4.4 Advantages of Flexibility

Setting an ethnographic system of research offers benefits in terms of flexibility [38]. For example, a progressive analysis of the interviews allows to formulate preliminary interpretations and to refine the further collection of empirical material. In this case, observations of initial participants enabled us to also identify *context-related* dimensions of interest. For example, hiking practices emerged as a habit rooted within most of the villagers' everyday lives, and some of them were also observed monitoring their performances with fitness apps. In this vein, we included outdoor activities as a thematic area in our interview outline. Then, during the interview, we noted how people charged it with different meanings: older adults with cardiac problems invested mountain walking with health-related concerns, while others considered it mainly as a leisure activity. Accordingly, the use of fitness apps achieved specific roles and meanings too (Fig. 5).

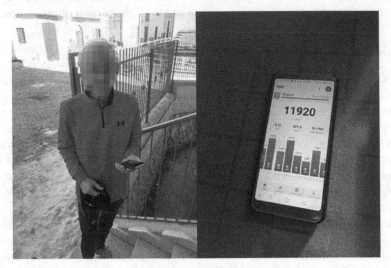

Fig. 5. Shadowing session

First, it is important to note that by adopting an explorative approach we could have identified devices (e.g. the smartwatch) and uses that would probably have remained hidden to a more directive investigation. In fact, a flexible research design allows researchers to adjust possible analytical oversights while constructing the research object. Secondly, by addressing outdoor activities – and not the use of fitness apps – as a thematic area of interest, we were able to grasp a practice-situated understanding of ICTs use. Overcoming interpretations in terms of users' adoption/resistance, we appreciated how ICTs are meaningfully incorporated into practices which, as in this case, are not primarily media-based, rather than into others. This allowed us to question ICTs use in terms of change or *remediation* [39] of pre-existent everyday habits – e.g. providing walking activities with data-driven information.

MAIN INSIGHTS

Open and flexible recruitment allows to adjust the sample in accordance with the emerging theory and contextual specificities

---

Biographical interviews enable to capture changes related to aging processes

---

Ethnographic observations give access to the immediacy of older adults' experience

---

5   What's Next: Concluding Remarks for Future Research

The methodological reflection advanced in this paper must be contextualised with respect to two broad aspects: the increasing pervasive mediatization and the evolution of media research. Due to the former, the presence of digital media in everyday lives has become ubiquitous and hardly capturable both spatially and temporally [40]. Despite an initial delay, such process has been involving also older people. Indeed, quantitative research has pointed out that age-related digital divide has been shrinking, at least in terms of access of digital technologies [41], while qualitative studies have been addressing increasingly nuanced uses of ICTs by older adults. Coming to the second aspect, the plea of important media scholars to decentre media from our research objects seems having acknowledged such socio-technical transformations. Our empirical investigations, here reported chronologically, have also gradually integrated these insights into research designs.

From this standpoint, a final provocative consideration may be: what is still urgent about studying older adults as a specific group of ICTs users? If they increasingly incorporate digital media into their everyday practices, what should social scientists question more about this issue?

Now, while addressing something as the use of ICTs by the elderly seems quite naïve, it seems urgent to focus on what is *elderly* about *the elderly use of ICTs*. The term as such is even much debated, where someone prefer to talk about older people, older adults or senior citizens [42]. Maybe due also to the quantitative roots of this sub-disciplinary field, being old has been often defined by the mere belonging to a certain age cohort, which usually starts at 65 years old [39]. Of course, the research on age-related digital divide has remarked that economic and cultural factors shape a more faceted reality beyond the monolithic elderly cohort. Yet, a theoretical reflection on the meaning of elderly is quite missing. In this vein, a greater interdisciplinary dialogue between ageing studies and media studies seems required. Instead of interviewing older adults as users of a certain digital service, a theoretical reflection on concepts as ageing and elderly would provide media scholars with newer heuristic tools to grasp how ICTs affect the aging processes.

In methodological terms, ethnographic approaches are particularly suitable. In the last research mentioned, we accounted for the construction of our research object as a result of the ongoing dialogue between theoretical categories and empirical dimensions emerging from the field. As Cardano observes [43], ethnographic research lies on sensitizing concepts [44] in opposition to operatively defined concepts that are typical of the variable-based research. The adoption of biographical interviews, together with the ongoing data analysis during the field-phase, enabled us to find unexpected features challenging our initial theoretical premises. In such dialectical opposition between empirical findings and researchers' expectations, we believe, lies the richness of qualitative research. While it does not aim at a statistical comparability of results [38], it provides sophisticated tools in order to grasp how contextual beliefs related to age and technologies may shape ICTs domestication among older adults.

Lastly, a reflection on the turbulent times we are experiencing. The Covid-19 pandemic has also affected the way social research is carried out [45]. In particular, these effects have concerned - and will concern for a long time - the ways of implementing social research with the elderly, which are the individuals most affected by the current disease and the focus of several efforts for their protection that have isolation and reduction of social contacts as consequences.

Doubts therefore emerge about the possibility of using ethnographic methods to study the elderly in the future as it has been done up until now.

On the one hand, at the moment restrictions due to the Covid-19 pandemic make the access into "homes" and places frequented by the elderly prohibited, difficult and problematic also for the foreseeable future. For example, how long will it take before the elderly willingly welcome a stranger into their house, meeting them freely and occupying their private spaces?

On the other hand, technology-mediated research and digital ethnography (as a substitute for offline ethnography) show many limits [46]. In particular, digital ethnography profoundly changes the research context with elderly people (often not very digitalised), especially when it comes to addressing a "non-media centric" understanding of their ICTs domestication.

Therefore, social researchers are critically challenged to not rely only on technology-mediated methods but to find suitable tools, despite the post-pandemic era, to continue studying the elderly and their use of digital technologies of communication in their living context.

Acknowledgments. Research entitled "I don't want be inactive: the lengthening of life, a challenge for generations, an opportunity for the society" (Sect. 2), was funded by Università Cattolica del Sacro Cuore (Italy).

Research entitled "Understanding the Role of Internet Communication Technologies (ICTs) in Family Relationships with Grandparents" (Sect. 3) was funded by Social Sciences and Humanities Research Council of Canada and by the centres of research/departments involved in the network (for Italy, OssCom – the research centre on media and communication of Università Cattolica).

Research "Harvest: eHealth and Ageing in Rural Areas: Transforming Everyday Life, Digital Competences, and Technology" (Sect. 4) is funded by Joint Programming Initiative (JPI) "More Years, Better Lives" (Third Call). The third Joint Transnational Call, launched in December 2016, is entitled "Ageing and Place in a digitising world", Joint Programming Initiative "More Years, Better Lives" (JPI MYBL) is supported by J-Age II. J-Age II is funded by Horizon2020, the EU Framework Programme for Research and Innovation, under Grant Agreement nr 643850.

References

1. Balachandran, A., de Beer, J., James, K.S., van Wissen, L., Janssen, F.: Comparison of population ageing in Europe and Asia using a time-consistent and comparative ageing measure. Ageing Health **32**, 340–351 (2020). https://doi.org/10.1177/0898264318824180
2. European Commission: Overview of the European strategy in ICT for Ageing Well, p. 8 (2010). https://tinyurl.com/y6da94o2
3. Blažič, B.J., Blažič, A.J.: Overcoming the digital divide with a modern approach to learning digital skills for the elderly adults. Educ. Inf. Technol. **25**(1), 259–279 (2019). https://doi.org/10.1007/s10639-019-09961-9
4. Colombo, F., Aroldi, P., Carlo, S.: "Stay Tuned": the role of ICTs in elderly life. Stud. Health Technol. Inform. **203**, 145 (2014)
5. Tanner, D.: Co-research with older people with dementia: experience and reflections. J. Ment. Health **21**, 296–306 (2012). https://doi.org/10.3109/09638237.2011.651658

6. Martins, L., Baptista, J., Arezes, P.: Research methods applied to studies with active elderly: a literature review. In: Di Bucchianico G., Kercher P. (eds.) Advances in Design for Inclusion. Advances in Intelligent Systems and Computing. Springer, Cham (2016). https://doi.org/10.1007/978-3-319-41962-6_38
7. Holroyd-Leduc, J., Resin, J., Ashley, L., Barwich, D., Elliott, J., Huras, P., et al.: Giving voice to older adults living with frailty and their family caregivers: engagement of older adults living with frailty in research, health care decision making, and in health policy. Res. Involvement Engage. **2**, 1–19 (2016). https://doi.org/10.1186/s40900-016-0038-7
8. Fernández-Ardèvol, M., et al.: Methodological strategies to understand smartphone practices for social connectedness in later life. In: Zhou, J., Salvendy, G. (eds.) HCII 2019. LNCS, vol. 11593, pp. 46–64. Springer, Cham (2019). https://doi.org/10.1007/978-3-030-22015-0_4
9. Demirbilek, O., Demirkan, H.: Universal product design involving elderly users: a participatory design model. Appl. Ergon. **35**, 361–370 (2004). https://doi.org/10.1016/j.apergo.2004.03.003
10. Robertson, L., Hale, B.: Interviewing older people; relationships in qualitative research. Internet J. Allied Health Sci. Pract. **9**, 1–8 (2011)
11. Endter, C.: Design for elderly – a meeting point for ethnography and usability. I-Com **15**, 17–26 (2016). https://doi.org/10.1515/icom-2016-0005
12. Schilling, I., Gerhardus, A.: Methods for involving older people in health research—a review of the literature. Int. J. Environ. Res. Pub. Health (2017). https://doi.org/10.3390/ijerph14121476
13. Colombo, F., Aroldi, P., Carlo, S.: "I use it correctly!": the use of ICTs among Italian grandmothers in a generational perspective. Hum. Technol. **14**, 343–365 (2018). https://doi.org/10.17011/ht/urn.201811224837
14. Lanzetti, C.: Come Ridurre L'errore Di «Non-Risposta» Nei Campioni Probabilistici: La Pratica Tradizionale E Il Modello Gallup Evs. Stud. Sociol. **53**(2), 187–200 (2015)
15. ISTAT: Cittadini Non Comunitari In Italia 2019 (2020). https://www.istat.it/it/archivio/249445
16. Hirsch, E., Silverstone, R. (eds.): Consuming Technologies: Media and Information in Domestic Spaces, 1° edizione. Routledge, London; New York (1992)
17. Haddon, L.: Social exclusion and information and communication technologies: lessons from studies of single parents and the young elderly. New Media Soc. **2**(4), 387–406 (2000)
18. Hammersley, M., Atkinson, P.: Ethnography: Principles in Practice. Psychology Press (1995)
19. Manderson, L., Bennett, E., Andajani-Sutjahjo, S.: The social dynamics of the interview: age, class, and gender. Qual. Health Res. **16**(10), 1317–1334 (2006). https://doi.org/10.1177/1049732306294512
20. Russell, C.: Interviewing vulnerable old people: ethical and methodological implications of imagining our subjects. J. Ageing Stud. **13**(4), 403–417 (1999). https://doi.org/10.1016/s0890-4065(99)00018-3. PMID: 14626238
21. Bart, J.: Ethical issues in shadowing research. Qual. Res. Organ. Manage. Int. J. **9** (2014). https://doi.org/10.1108/QROM-09-2012-1099
22. Yadlin-Segal, A., Tsuria, R., Bellar, W.: The ethics of studying digital contexts: reflections from three empirical case studies. Hum. Behav. Emerg. Technol. **2** (2020). https://doi.org/10.1002/hbe2.183
23. Morgan, D.L.: Focus Groups as Qualitative Research. Sage (1996)
24. Colombo, F., Aroldi, P., Carlo, S.: New elders, old divides: ICTs, inequalities and well-being amongst young elderly Italians. Comunicar **23**(45), 47–55 (2015)
25. Glaser, B., Strauss, A.: The Discovery of Grounded Theory: Strategies for Qualitative Research. Sociology Press, Mill Valley (1967)

26. Soja, E.: Information and communication technology in active and healthy ageing: exploring risks from multi-generation perspective. Inf. Syst. Manage. **34**(4), 320–332 (2017). https://doi.org/10.1080/10580530.2017.1366217
27. Hirsch, E., Silverstone, R.: Consuming Technologies: Media and Information in Domestic Spaces, 1 edizione. Routledge, London; New York (1992)
28. Silverstone, R., Morley, D.: Media Audiences Communication and Context: Ethnographic Perspectives on the Media Audience, pp. 163–176. Routledge (2002)
29. Couldry, N.: Theorising media as practice. Soc. Semiot. **14**(2), 115–132 (2004). https://doi.org/10.1080/1035033042000238295
30. Couldry, N.: Theorising Media and Practice, NED-New edition, 1. Berghahn Books (2010)
31. Krajina, Z., Moores, S., Morley, D.: Non-media-centric media studies: a cross-generational conversation. Eur. J. Cult. Stud. **17**(6), 682–700 (2014). https://doi.org/10.1177/1367549414526733
32. Morley, D.: For a materialist, non—media-centric media studies. Telev. New Media **10**(1), 114–116 (2009). https://doi.org/10.1177/1527476408327173
33. Tosoni, S., Ridell, S.: Urban communication research\ de-centering media studies, verbing the audience: methodological considerations concerning people's uses of media in urban space. Int. J. Commun. **10** (2016)
34. Jensen, K. B.: The Qualitative Research Process, pp. 279–296. Routledge (2013)
35. Marcus, G.E.: Ethnography in/of the world system: the emergence of multi-sited ethnography. Ann. Rev. Anthropol. **24**, 95–117 (1995)
36. Tulle, E.: Ageing, The Body and Social Change: Running in Later Life. Palgrave Macmillan UK (2008)
37. Bichi, R.: L'intervista biografica, Vita e Pensiero (2007)
38. Sacchetti, F.: Processi di categorizzazione in etnografia. Il ruolo degli impliciti e delle categoria ex ante. Bonanno, Acireale (2014)
39. Lanzara, G.F.: Remediation of practices: how new media change the ways we see and do things in practical domains. First Monday (2010). https://doi.org/10.5210/fm.v15i6.3034
40. Deuze, M.: Media life and the mediatization of the lifeworld. In: Hepp, A., Krotz, F. (eds.) Mediatized Worlds, pp. 207–220. Palgrave Macmillan UK, London (2014). https://doi.org/10.1057/9781137300355_12
41. Hunsaker, A, Hargittai, E.: A review of Internet use among older adults. New Media Soc. **20**(10), 3937–3954 (2018). https://doi.org/10.1177/1461444818787348.
42. Avers, D., et al.: Use of the term "Elderly". J. Geriatr. Phys. Ther. **34**(4), 153–154 (2011)
43. Cardano, M.: Etnografia e riflessività. Le pratiche riflessive costrette nel binario del discorso scientifico, Rassegna italiana di sociologia **42**, 173–204 (2001). https://doi.org/10.1423/2564
44. Blumer, H.: Symbolic Interactionism; Perspective and Method. Prentice-Hall, Englewood Cliffs (1969)
45. Deslandes, S., Coutinho, T.: Social research in digital environments in COVID-19 times: theoretical and methodological notes. Cadernos De Saúde Pública **36**(11) (2020). https://doi.org/10.1590/0102-311X00223120
46. Vittadini, N., Carlo, S., Gilje, O., Laursen, D., Murru, M.F., Schrøder, K.: Multi-Method and innovative approaches to researching the learning and social practices of young digital users. Int. J. Learn. Media **4**, 47–55 (2012)

Exploring User Opinion on the Benefits of Cognitive Games Through an Online Walkthrough and Interview

Kyle Harrington[1,2] , Michael P. Craven[1,3](✉) , Max L. Wilson[4] ,
and Aleksandra Landowska[4]

[1] NIHR MindTech MedTech Co-operative, The Institute of Mental Health,
University of Nottingham Innovation Park, Nottingham, UK
{Kyle.Harrington,Michael.Craven}@nottingham.ac.uk
[2] Division of Psychiatry and Applied Psychology, University of Nottingham, Nottingham, UK
[3] Bioengineering Research Group, Faculty of Engineering, University of Nottingham,
Nottingham, UK
[4] Mixed Reality Lab, School of Computer Science, University of Nottingham, Nottingham, UK
{Max.Wilson,Aleksandra.Landowska}@nottingham.ac.uk

Abstract. Online walkthrough interviews were conducted via internet video-calling, which formed part of wider Patient and Public Involvement activities investigating perceptions of digital and gamified cognitive assessment and training/coaching applications. Participants were invited to play a series of mobile mini-games which have been developed for the purposes of training of executive functions and the assessment of memory, whilst verbalizing their thought processes, using a process based on the Think-Aloud Protocol and Cognitive Walkthrough principles, before concluding with a semi-structured interview. The enquiry was particularly interested in wider motivational aspects surrounding these technologies, including identifying potential barriers to engagement and facilitators of adoption. In general, there was broad acceptance of digital cognitive assessments and training, although issues of data handling and trust were raised by participants. Several usability issues were also captured.

Keywords: User-centered design · Evaluation · Pervasive healthcare

1 Introduction

In recent years there has been a growing interest in the application of digital technologies designed to promote healthy lifestyles; particularly in the prevention, management, and mitigation of dementia and within the context of applications designed to protect cognitive health more generally [1–4]. Robert et al. [5] highlight the importance of serious games for dementia, suggesting uses such as rehabilitation, stimulation, and treatment, as well as providing the capability to monitor the disease severity and progression. However, there are still open research questions about the effectiveness and uptake of such interventions [6, 7]. Likewise, there are still complex and unresolved issues surrounding

© Springer Nature Switzerland AG 2021
Q. Gao and J. Zhou (Eds.): HCII 2021, LNCS 12786, pp. 21–32, 2021.
https://doi.org/10.1007/978-3-030-78108-8_2

digital cognitive interventions and cognitive assessments and their acceptance to people living with dementia and their carers [8, 9].

As part of a European collaboration Alzheimer's Disease Detect and Prevent that is investigating the design, effectiveness, and suitability of cognitive (also termed 'brain') training/coaching and memory assessment games for people at risk of dementia [10], we are conducting a series of patient and public involvement (PPI) activities for the purposes of understanding user requirements, improving usability of the software and to guide future trials with end-users. This work is being conducted in addition to in-house usability testing to investigate the broader determinants of adherence and overall perceptions of the specific software, as well as people's perceptions of the utility of serious gaming for dementia. As these aspects are relatively under-explored, we are seeking to explore user opinion on motivation, adherence, and trust.

2 Background

2.1 Dementia, Persuasive and Serious Gaming

Persuasive games are a form of 'serious game' designed to change human behaviors or attitudes, often within a public health context [11]. Persuasive technologies may provide additional functionality which make behavior change easier and may be better able to use cues to engender trust, therefore supporting engagement and subsequent behavior change [12].

Games aimed at reducing the public risk of dementia and helping those with dementia to mitigate and manage the symptoms are becoming increasingly commonplace. Some of these games have been specifically designed with dementia-related issues in mind or are aimed at cognitive health of older adults more broadly, whilst others may have been developed for other purposes or audiences but offer relevant experiences.

Dementia games may have preventative, rehabilitative or informative purposes, in addition to their entertainment value. In a systematic literature review, McCallum and Boletsis [13] identified research studies of games related to dementia and mild cognitive impairment, including games with a physical component. They note that many of the games which have been evaluated for their benefits within the dementia population were actually developed for the "typical user" and that despite the fact that these games may not necessarily meet all of the requirements of people living with dementia-related conditions, these applications were widely used amongst the elderly and those with cognitive impairments. McCallum and Boletsis [13] suggest that physical-based games may help to improve the mobility of people living with dementia and other games were also shown to provide benefits to cognition. They also note that there may be emotional benefits to playing certain games, but caution that many games suffer from usability problems which impede or discourage usage for dementia-related populations. Finally, they highlight that bone fide games tend to place more of a focus on the emotional and social aspects of play, which may lead to higher engagement than the more therapy-based cognitive training programs.

Similarly, digital gaming for community dwelling older adults is seen to promote life-long learning, optimize mental, physical and social stimulation and foster independence [14].

Fanfarelli [15] argues that although some studies seem to show positive results for dementia-related games, these have primarily been low sample size pilot studies, or studies which fail to examine whether improvements in games can have real-world transferrable benefits. Overall, they conclude that the field is in the early stages of research and lacks the evidence base which would be necessary to implement these games with confidence. It is suggested that future studies should enlist larger samples of participants and consider outcome measures applicable to the lived experience of users.

However, evidence is emerging demonstrating measurable improvements in certain cognitive domains following game-based brain training in older populations. A systematic literature review and meta-analysis conducted by Wang et al. [16] revealed that game-based cognitive training software significantly improved executive functions such as processing speed, selective attention and short-term memory. Wang et al. identified 15 randomized control trials utilizing game-based brain training interventions for populations of community dwelling adults aged 60 and above, representing a total sample size of 759. However, the reported quality of the evidence of the three primary outcome measures was judged to range between low and very low, further emphasizing the need for high quality clinical trials in this area.

Robert et al. [5] highlight the importance of serious games for dementia, suggesting uses such as rehabilitation, stimulation, treatment and monitoring. Through stakeholder workshops attended by healthcare professionals, technology companies, family association representatives and IT experts, attendees discussed the numerous items discovered from a preliminary literature review and were asked to prioritize them, as well as to propose new ideas. Serious games can enhance motivation, positive mood and improve assessment and facilitate independent practice and self-assessment. Serious games may have advantages over standardized cognitive assessments as the person is less focused on the fact they are being 'tested', which may be distressing to some people. They may also have built-in social elements to facilitate interactions among peers; both by having people physically co-present or online and connected via remote locations. On the other hand, unfamiliarity with the technology could be a barrier to engagement for some people.

2.2 Motivation and Engagement

Motivation is identified as a key aspect of cognitive gaming, and one that needs further attention in research [17]. Motivation is often considered to be comprised of two aspects; intrinsic and extrinsic [18]. Intrinsic motivations are those motivations which are directly related to the task; the activity is performed for its own sake, because it is rewarding. Game-based mechanics may contribute towards fostering intrinsic motivations, through interactions, progressions, and contextualization; and this could give players a sense mastery, autonomy and competence [17]. Some have argued that performance feedback is a primary source of motivation for the player [19], others have suggested the use of affective computing models to increase the adoption and effectiveness of cognitive assistive technologies for people with dementia [20].

Extrinsic motivation are those motivations which are external to the task, for example, the potential cognitive health benefits conferred such as dementia risk reduction [21].

Mishra, Anguera and Gazzaley argue that whilst intrinsic motivation may be important for cognitive games, engagement with even very enjoyable games may wane over time, suggesting the need for independent and externally motivating factors, which may include the adoption of motivational frameworks, goal-setting, and habit formation [22].

More generally, there is a clear and established link between learning outcomes and motivations in traditional educational settings [23]. However, in a cognitive training study which varied gamified and motivational features between two cognitive training programs, there were no statistically significant group differences between those that had undertaken training with gamified elements and those who had completed similar training with less gamification [24]. Despite this, those who completed the gamified training exerted more effort in training, improved more, and enjoyed the training more. The relationship between game mechanics, motivation, and improvements in following cognitive training is not well-understood. Engagement and motivation may have more of an impact outside of laboratory settings, where a person is engaging in an activity of their own volition and for a potentially longer, undetermined period.

2.3 Perceptions About Cognitive Screening

A systematic literature review investigating people's attitudes about cognitive screening for dementia concluded that screening raises complex issues around preference and choice for both clinicians and the public and suggested that clear communication is a vital part of patient acceptance of testing that could otherwise lead to confusion or a misunderstanding of results [25]. Furthermore, patients may find tests to be strenuous or stressful, due to a perceived pressure to perform well which could be addressed by managing expectations, clear explanation beforehand, and a debrief afterwards.

Other studies have suggested that being healthier (taking fewer medications) was associated with less willingness to accept dementia screening [26]. Conversely, those who perceive themselves as more susceptible to illness, and those who experiencing cognitive difficulties have been shown to be more likely to accept cognitive screening [27].

Stigma may also play a part in the acceptability of cognitive screening. People who have had experience in caring for people living with dementia are less likely to be accepting of screening technology and more likely to perceive it as inducing suffering than their non-caregiving counterparts, despite there being no difference between the two groups about the perceived benefits [26].

It is suggested that those living in rural areas may be at particular risk of developing Alzheimer's, being undiagnosed and being at risk of a higher rate of falls and unintentional harm [28]. Therefore, this is a population which may significantly benefit from prompt cognitive screening. This finding is also supported by a meta-analysis conducted by Lang et al. who investigated the determinants of undetected dementia.

In light of the Coronavirus pandemic, many countries have had to adopt to remote and online services in lieu of otherwise routine checkups [29], encouraging a heightened interest in the area. In a recent qualitative study involving interviews with 148 Indian physicians, a prominent theme was that Tele-health was the future of dementia care [30]. However, those interviewed stated multiple challenges, some felt unable to build therapeutic rapport or struggled to apply traditional psychometric scales over the phone and video. Gamified cognitive training and monitoring may help to overcome issues faced when access to clinicians is scarce and may also provide support in addition to the unique benefits discussed earlier.

3   Method

Drawing influence from the Think-Aloud Protocol [10] and Cognitive Walkthrough principles [11], we designed an interview procedure in which participants played a series of mini-games designed to assess and train various components of cognition, whilst verbalizing their cognitive process. In total, the interview consisted of participants completing four mini-games before being presented with results which reflect their relative performance in the different cognitive domains (see Fig. 1). After the mini-games, interviewees were asked broad questions about their views of technology to assess and train cognition in order to reduce the risk and manage the symptoms of dementia.

We are currently conducting interviews with a small number of people over the age of 45 with no diagnosis of cognitive impairment and are reporting here on the first three interviews conducted to date (February 2021). This work is complementary to and followed focus groups, conducted in 2019 and reported on elsewhere [9], in which we invited people living with dementia and carers to discuss a range of similar issues.

Because of restrictions placed upon UK universities and society during the Coronavirus pandemic, these interviews are now being conducted remotely via Microsoft Teams video conference calling (see Fig. 1). We modified our procedure to split the interview session into two separate one-hour sessions which allowed for additional opportunities to resolve any technical problems which might arise during the installation of third-party software on participants' personal devices, and reduced the demand placed on participants. Participants were recruited using word of mouth and email campaigns, and organization of the interview sessions was arranged via email. In the two sessions, participants were called on Microsoft Teams on a desktop PC whilst they used the app in front of the camera in such a way that the interviewer could see the screen at times and guide the interviewee through the gameplay before proceeding to the questions at the end, as shown in Fig. 1. The typical interview procedure for the first session consisted of 15 min for introduction, information and consent, followed by approximately 10 min of software installation, 20 min of cognitive assessment games, and finishing with 10 min of an initial semi-structured interview. The second session involved approximately 20–25 min of cognitive assessment, followed by approximately 20–25 min of a second semi-structured interview before conclusion and debrief.

During the interviews, several probes were used during the cognitive assessment phase, to ensure that participants were verbalizing their thought process "Please keep saying what you are thinking" and to elicit their understanding of the task requirements, "What are you being asked to do?".

In addition, probing questions which formed part of the semi-structured interview process included questions such as "What do you think the purpose of the mini-game was?", "Is this something that you would do in your everyday life?" and "Do you think this application would be of benefit to you?".

Ethical approval for the original protocol as well as the amendment suitable for a fully online method was granted by the Faculty of Medicine and Health Sciences Research Ethics Committee (Approval number: 333–1906).

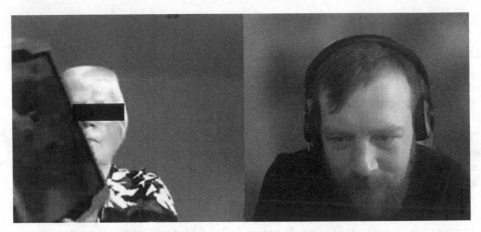

Fig. 1. Illustration of online video call with participant and researcher

4 Results

Initial findings from the three interviews conducted so far show that the mobile software application was well-received, and participants could imagine using these types of cognitive training and assessment games in their everyday life. Participants indicated a general interest in using these types of applications, if it could be shown to be of some benefit to them.

Table 1 shows the results from the main session divided into motivations, capabilities, concerns and usability.

Overall, participants were well-motivated to engage in these types of activities and participants also mentioned that their own personal routines often included word and number puzzles, as well as more typical video games. Two of the participants also commented on the satisfaction of seeing self-improvement in the games that they already played (crosswords and strategy games), and in the case of the latter, they said that the in-game rewards for good performance kept them engaged; an example of intrinsic motivation.

In general, participants were unsure whether dementia could be prevented or whether anything could be done at the present to lessen the severity of possible dementia symptoms at some point in the future. Despite this, participants linked the concepts of engaging with cognitively stimulating activities with good brain health and had an implicit understanding of the importance of maintaining this, including conceptualizing cognitive training as "mental exercise". This finding is supported by the associated focus groups research conducted previously [9]. These are all extrinsic motivations.

Table 1. Summary of Results

Theme	Example	Detail
Motivations	Fit of the App with personal routines	Already play puzzles on similar devices
	Importance of Cognitive Health	Participants aware of the importance of maintaining good cognitive health through cognitively stimulating activities
	Like the idea of competing against one's self and objective measures of improvement	Several participants mentioned that they like to see improvements when they play games or learn new skills. Personal high scores, etc
	Unsure of life-expectancy	One participant said that he had a family history of heart problems and was unsure of his life expectancy. This meant that they were unsure they would reach an age to be at risk of dementia
	Unsure of whether the risk can be reduced	Several participants were unsure whether the risk of dementia could be lessened
Capabilities	Find learning new things difficult	Participants claimed that they are not used to learning new skills and find it more difficult to do so with age
Concerns	Use of feedback in the games	May cause unnecessary anxiety How can the cognitive domain be improved? Can it be improved?
	Data handling	Participants concerned that their data may be used in ways they have not agreed to
Usability	Instructions	Game starting before task was fully understood
	Interaction	Confusion of drag versus point-and-click
	Affordances	Confusion over targets vs distractors in visual search task Confusion with symbols used in planning task

One participant commented that they thought cognitive health would be increasingly important as life expectancy increased, with a growing number of people becoming at risk of acquiring dementia. Another participant spoke of a family history of heart disease and did not necessarily expect to reach an age where they would be at risk of dementia. This meant that they saw little reason to undertake activities to reduce the risk of dementia. Participants were open to the possibility of cognitive training and cognitive assessments to form part of routine healthcare.

"I don't know, it depends if there's something I could do about it. It's hard to say, isn't it? I mean, if I was to get dementia in twenty years, I'd be lucky if I lived twenty years" – Participant #3.

Whilst participants liked the fact that individual tests could target specific cognitive domains, concerns were raised about the feedback of cognitive assessments, which may cause unnecessary anxiety for people concerned about their cognition. One participant commented that they would like their scores to be shown against average scores for that age bracket but suggested that being presented with a below average score might be disappointing for some people. The participant commented that whilst it might motivate some people to work on the areas of cognition that they are less proficient in, it could deter or demotivate others.

Another participant commented that when being presented with a score for a certain cognitive domain, it is important that the cognitive domain is understood, and that the person knows, in very concrete terms, how they might improve their score in the future.

"Do we want the scores back?... Some people might really want to. But some people who are fearful like me, fearful of the dementia, actually, I'm happy not to know...but actually I could imagine some people really, really want to know" - Participant #1.

One participant commented on the presentation of problems, suggesting that they preferred very visual problems such as map reading and spatial transformations above word-based memory problems, they liked the idea of cognitive tasks which related to real-world activities but commented that abstract tasks (such as word or symbol recall) would be less enjoyable.

Broader issues relating to cognitive training and assessments were also discussed and participants were invited to make suggestions and recommendations. Participants commented on the presentation of results and expressed concern about who would have access to the results of these cognitive tests and how they could be used. Whilst participants were made aware of their anonymity in our research, their concern was that if cognitive tests became more widely accepted, a growing number of people would want access to the results and may use them in ways the participants had not agreed to (for example, health insurers or governmental departments like the Department for Work and Pensions that make decisions about access to welfare benefit payments).

"I think the main thing is, it would have to be secure and you'd have to be comfortable it wasn't being shared. I don't think I'd be too comfortable about sharing it". – Participant #2.

Whilst usability of individual functions or games within the app was not the direct focus of this enquiry, we observed more specific perceptions about some of the cognitive assessments. For instance, one task was specially designed to evaluate working memory deficits. The task involved participants remembering a series of intentionally difficult to verbalize objects, followed by a distractor task, then a recall task and finally, dragging the recalled object to the position onscreen where it was first seen. The target objects were designed to be difficult to verbalize and so the design utilized small constellations of stars. However, one participant attempted to name these shapes in order to facilitate recall. The participant stated that they did better in shapes which they could assign a name to. In another example, the participant misunderstood the control mapping of the task on the touch screen, which caused a mismatch between expected and observed behavior, and led to the participant underperforming in the assessment.

5 Discussion

Whilst cognitive training and at-home cognitive assessments are becoming increasingly popular research topics and have promising real-world practical applications, there are still several barriers to adoption, including ambiguity around the potential benefit for the person being assessed [31]. Interventions designed to form part of a person's daily routine need to ensure that there is involvement from patients and the public in the testing and evaluation of cognitive technologies; this is likely to facilitate better uptake and ensure that the application is being used as intended [32]. Similarly, there are open questions about whether cognitive training increases the subjective well-being in older adults, over and above more traditional leisure time activities [33]. Interviewees in our study were able to articulate knowledge and opinion about the trajectory of dementia and more broadly about health in aging although it was apparent from the one comment about cardiovascular health that there was lack of knowledge about the vascular dimension of dementia risk. Preferences for particular types of game were apparent as well as preferences for gamification mechanisms, such as rewards. Participants were able to identify possible demotivating factors in gamification for themselves or potential for this in others. Personalization was also explicitly mentioned, with people expressing the desire to have custom training programs. Participants raised concerns about privacy, security and the handling of data, as well as complex issues about autonomy and self-mastery [34]. Research into assistive technologies for people living with or at risk of cognitive impairment needs to further explore the consequences of technology in relation to quality of live, digital rights and overall wellbeing to facilitate better usability and acceptability [35].

Overall, participants enjoyed the games, and of those interviewed so far, all had either experience playing computer games, or paper-based puzzles (crosswords, Sudoku, other video games). However, it was clear that in some instances, the participants struggled to think their way through the problems (designed to evaluate their working memory, planning, etc.) whilst verbalizing their thought process. Think-aloud protocols can reveal insights about information which is being actively processed in working memory, but high cognitive load (as in this case) may hinder the verbalization process and as such the procedure can only offer a partial glimpse into cognition. [36]

Whilst we designed prompts in our interview script to remind participants to keep talking, it was clear during the interviews that too many prompts would interrupt participants' thought process and impact upon their performance. This may present unique challenges to using 'Think-Aloud' inspired protocols during tasks specifically designed to test the maximum limits of certain cognitive domains. Other studies using methodology inspired by Think-Aloud Protocols have also identified similar methodological issues, such as a higher level of guidance required, and the unfeasibility of asking participants to verbalize their thoughts whilst reading [37]. Alternative approaches to more typical Think-Aloud protocols have employed retrospective think-aloud procedures, sometimes called 'virtual revisits' [38] and this has been shown to be useful in areas where the Think-Aloud protocol impacted upon task-performance [39]. However, the focus of our work was to explore motivational issues surrounding the use and adoption of cognitive training technologies with experienced participants, and we were less interested in the specific usability issues encountered by participants. A more appropriate use of participant time was the exploration and discussion of broader motivational issues, such as what value participants thought it might have to them personally, and whether or not they would consider using cognitive training games in their everyday lives.

Conducting these interviews during national lockdown restrictions presented a variety of challenges to research. We found it more difficult overall to recruit participants for online studies than in previous similar projects. In part this is because we were unable to provide mobile devices for those who did not have devices compatible with the software. Conducting this study remotely also meant that in addition to a compatible mobile device, participants also needed access to another device with a camera to conduct the interview.

Whilst these challenges were not insurmountable, they forced us to change our initial methodology to ensure that participants were adequately supported during remote interviews. For instance, splitting the interview over two consecutive days gave us more opportunity to resolve any technical issues and ensured that participants did not feel too overwhelmed or unduly burdened.

6 Conclusion

Motivational aspects of cognitive gaming are still an under-researched area, but in light of the globally aging population and increased burden on healthcare services; there is an increasing focus on technology used to support people living with dementia, and to encourage lifestyle changes to reduce lifetime risk [40]. However, various questions remain about privacy and utility of such interventions, and these may be potential barriers to wider adoption. Patient and Public Involvement, as well as research exploring broader perceptions of cognitive technologies may help to overcome barriers to adoption, and improve engagement with training and assessment regimes; improving overall outcomes and reducing the strain on healthcare services.

Acknowledgements. Funding was provided by the European Commission Horizon 2020 EIC-FTI-2018–2020 grant no. 820636, coordinated by Brain+ ApS (Denmark). The research reported in this paper was also supported by the NIHR MindTech MedTech Co-operative and the NIHR Nottingham Biomedical Research Centre. The views represented are the views of the authors alone and do not necessarily represent the views of the Department of Health and Social Care in England, the NHS, or the NIHR.

References

1. Ben-Sadoun, G., Manera, V., Alvarez, J., Sacco, G., Robert, P.: Recommendations for the design of serious games in neurodegenerative diseases. Front. Aging Neurosci. **10**, 13 (2018)

2. Bhavnani, S.P., Narula, J., Sengupta, P.P.: Mobile technology and the digitization of healthcare. Eur. Heart J. **37**(18), 1428–1438 (2016)
3. Cudd, P., Bolton, E., Gallant, Z., Greasley, P.: The person living with dementia, their carer and their digital technology. J. Assitive Technol. **33**, 610–615 (2013)
4. Gibson, G., Dickinson, C., Brittain, K., Robinson, L.: The everyday use of assistive technology by people with dementia and their family carers: a qualitative study. BMC Geriatr. **15**(1), 89 (2015)
5. Robert, P., et al.: Recommendations for the use of Serious Games in people with Alzheimer's Disease, related disorders and frailty. Front. Aging Neurosci. **6**, 54 (2014)
6. Simons, D.J., et al.: Do "brain-training" programs work? Psychol. Sci. Pub. Interest **17**(3), 103–186 (2016)
7. Harvey, P.D., McGurk, S.R., Mahncke, H., Wykes, T.: Controversies in computerized cognitive training. Bio. Psychiatry Cogn. Neurosci. Neuroimaging **3**(11), 907–915 (2018)
8. Meiland, F., et al.: Technologies to support community-dwelling persons with dementia: a position paper on issues regarding development, usability, effectiveness and cost-effectiveness, deployment, and ethics. J. Rehabil. Assitive Technol. **4**, e1 (2017)
9. Harrington, K., Craven, M.P., Wilson, M.L., Landowska, A.: Exploring user expectations of brain-training and coaching technologies for cognitive health. In: Kurosu, M. (ed.) HCII 2020. LNCS, vol. 12183, pp. 49–60. Springer, Cham (2020). https://doi.org/10.1007/978-3-030-49065-2_4
10. Alzheimer's Disease Detect and Prevent: 12 Feb 2021 (2021). https://www.addp.eu/
11. Orji, R., Vassileva, J., Mandryk, R.L.: Modeling the efficacy of persuasive strategies for different gamer types in serious games for health. User Model. User-Adap. Inter. **24**(5), 453–498 (2014). https://doi.org/10.1007/s11257-014-9149-8
12. Berkovsky, S., Freyne, J., Oinas-Kukkonen, H.: Influencing individually: fusing personalization and persuasion. ACM Trans. Comput.-Hum. Interact. **2**, 1–8 (2012)
13. McCallum, S., Boletsis, C.: Dementia games: a literature review of dementia-related serious games. In: Ma, M., Oliveira, M.F., Petersen, S., Hauge, J.B. (eds.) Serious Games Development and Applications. SGDA 2013. Lecture Notes in Computer Science, vol 8101. Springer, Berlin, Heidelberg (2013). https://doi.org/10.1007/978-3-642-40790-1_2
14. Cutler, C., Hicks, B., Innes, A.: Does digital gaming enable healthy aging for community-dwelling people with dementia? Games Cult. **11**(1–2), 104–129 (2015)
15. Fanfarelli, J.R.: Games and dementia: evidence needed. In: Ferguson, C.J. (ed.) Video Game Influences on Aggression, Cognition, and Attention, pp. 163–171. Springer, Cham (2018)
16. Wang, G., Zhao, M., Yang, F., Cheng, L.J., Lau, Y.: Game-based brain training for improving cognitive function in community-dwelling older adults: a systematic review and meta-regression. Arch. Gerontol. Geriatr. **92**, 104260 (2021)
17. Craven, M.P., Fabricatore, C.: Game features of cognitive training. In: 2016 International Conference on Interactive Technologies and Games (ITAG), Nottingham, UK, pp. 42–49 (2016)
18. Lepper, M.R., Corpus, J.H., Iyengar, S.S.: Intrinsic and extrinsic motivational orientations in the classroom: age differences and academic correlates. J. Educ. Psychol. **97**(2), 184 (2005)
19. Corbalan, G., Kester, L., van Merriënboer, J.J.G.: Dynamic task selection: effects of feedback and learner control on efficiency and motivation. Learn. Instr. **19**(6), 455–465 (2009)
20. Robillard, J.M., Hoey, J.: Emotion and motivation in cognitive assistive technologies for dementia. Computer **51**(3), 24–34 (2018)
21. Kim, S., Sargent-Cox, K., Cherbuin, N., Anstey, K.J.: Development of the motivation to change lifestyle and health behaviours for dementia risk reduction scale. Dement. Geriatr. Cogn. Disord. Extra **4**(2), 172–183 (2014)
22. Mishra, J., Anguera, J.A., Gazzaley, A.: Video games for neuro-cognitive optimization. Neuron **90**(2), 214–218 (2016)

23. Liu, O.L., Bridgeman, B., Adler, R.M.: Measuring learning outcomes in higher education: motivation matters. Educ. Res. **41**(9), 352–362 (2012)
24. Mohammed, S., et al.: The benefits and challenges of implementing motivational features to boost cognitive training outcome. J. Cogn. Enhancement **1**(4), 491–507 (2017). https://doi.org/10.1007/s41465-017-0047-y
25. Martin, S., et al.: Attitudes and preferences towards screening for dementia: a systematic review of the literature. BMC Geriatr. **15**(1), 66 (2015)
26. Boustani, M.A., et al.: Caregiver and noncaregiver attitudes toward dementia screening. J. Am. Geriatr. Soc. **59**(4), 681–686 (2011)
27. Krohne, K., Slettebø, Å., Bergland, A.: Cognitive screening tests as experienced by older hospitalised patients: a qualitative study. Scand. J. Caring Sci. **25**(4), 679–687 (2011)
28. Mattos, M.K., Snitz, B.E., Lingler, J.H., Burke, L.E., Novosel, L.M., Sereika, S.M.: Older rural-and urban-dwelling Appalachian adults with mild cognitive impairment. J. Rural Health **33**(2), 208–216 (2017)
29. Fisk, M., Livingstone, A., Pit, S.W.: Telehealth in the context of COVID-19: changing perspectives in Australia, the United Kingdom, and the United States. J. Med. Internet Res. **22**(6), e19264 (2020)
30. Banerjee, D., Vajawat, B., Varshney, P., Rao, T.: Perceptions, experiences and challenges of physicians involved in dementia care during the COVID-19 lockdown in India: a qualitative study. Front. Psych. **11**, 1494 (2020)
31. Fowler, N.R., et al.: Effect of patient perceptions on dementia screening in primary care. J. Am. Geriatr. Soc. **60**(6), 1037–1043 (2012)
32. Hassan, L., Swarbrick, C., Sanders, C., Parker, A., Machin, M., Tully, M.P., Ainsworth, J.: Tea, talk and technology: patient and public involvement to improve connected health 'wearables' research in dementia. Res. Involvement Engage. **3**(12) (2017)
33. Bureš, V., Čech, P., Mikulecká, J., Ponce, D., Kuca, K.: The effect of cognitive training on the subjective perception of well-being in older adults. PeerJ **4**, e2785 (2016)
34. Bennett, B.: Technology, ageing and human rights: challenges for an ageing world. Int. J. Law Psychiatry **66**, 101449 (2019)
35. Holthe, T., Halvorsrud, L., Karterud, D., Hoel, K.-A., Lund, A.: Usability and acceptability of technology for community-dwelling older adults with mild cognitive impairment and dementia: a systematic literature review. Clin. Interv. Aging **13**, 863–886 (2018)
36. Jääskeläinen, R.: Think-aloud protocol. In: Handbook of Translation Studies, vol. 1, pp. 371–374 (2010)
37. Cotton, D., Gresty, K.: Reflecting on the think-aloud method for evaluating e-learning. Br. J. Edu. Technol. **37**(1), 45–54 (2006)
38. Beach, P.: Self-directed online learning: a theoretical model for understanding elementary teachers' online learning experiences. Teach. Teach. Educ. **61**, 60–72 (2017)
39. van den Haak, M., De Jong, M., Jan Schellens, P.: Retrospective vs. concurrent think-aloud protocols: testing the usability of an online library catalogue. Behav. Inf. Technol. **22**(5), 339–351 (2003)
40. Woodward, M., Brodaty, H., Budge, M., Byrne, G., Farrow, M., Flicker, L., Hecker, J., Velandai, S.: Dementia risk reduction: The evidence: Alzheimer's Australia, Paper 13, September 2007

Review of Remote Usability Methods for Aging in Place Technologies

Irina Kondratova[1]($\boxtimes$) (iD), Helene Fournier[2] (iD), and Keiko Katsuragawa[3] (iD)

[1] Human-Computer Interaction, Digital Technologies Research Centre, National Research
Council Canada, Fredericton, Canada
Irina.Kondratova@nrc-cnrc.gc.ca

[2] Human-Computer Interaction, Digital Technologies Research Centre, National Research
Council Canada, Moncton, Canada
Helene.Fournier@nrc-cnrc.gc.ca

[3] Human-Computer Interaction, Digital Technologies Research Centre, National Research
Council Canada, Waterloo, Canada
Keiko.Katsuragawa@nrc-cnrc.gc.ca

Abstract. This paper reports on the study of best practices in evaluation methodologies for aging in place technologies, and analyses their feasibility in a pandemic environment. The pandemic situation, with various physical distancing restrictions in place, especially for vulnerable older adults, has increased the importance of deploying health monitoring and social interaction technologies for aging in place. The pandemic also made it more difficult for researchers and developers of technologies to evaluate the usability of home health monitoring technologies. Existing technology evaluation methods mostly involve laboratory and home technology usability evaluations that could be problematic during physical distancing restrictions, and are not well suited for rapid evaluation of health monitoring technologies. The increasing trend in virtual doctor and health professional visits puts additional pressure to speed up innovation for home health and wellness monitoring and communication technologies without increasing risks for vulnerable populations. Researchers observed challenges with performing HCI research with older adults in a pandemic situation, including challenges with participant recruitment, obtaining informed consent for the study, shipping technology to the willing participants, assessing the ability of older adults to set up both digital health technology and remote usability tools, and research data collection. The need for low cost, low risk, easy to use and privacy-preserving usability evaluation methods and tools for home health monitoring is growing rapidly, and new remote usability evaluation methods and tools will add to the growing arsenal of digital technologies used in the public health response to COVID-19 and beyond.

Keywords: Aging in place · Usability evaluation methods · Remote usability evaluation · Home health monitoring

Q. Gao and J. Zhou (Eds.): HCII 2021, LNCS 12786, pp. 33–47, 2021.
https://doi.org/10.1007/978-3-030-78108-8_3

1 Introduction

This paper reports on the study of existing best practices in usability evaluation methodologies and tools for aging in place technologies, and analyses their feasibility in a pandemic situation. Older adults (=65 years of age), particularly with comorbidities, are at an increased risk of severe COVID-19 [1, 2]. Physical distancing and self-isolation mitigate the risk of exposure to the virus, however, the lack of timely health care access and the increased susceptibility to social isolation and loneliness is associated with poor physical and mental health outcomes for older adults [3]. Assistive technologies, home health monitoring, and social interaction technologies help to create safer, positive, personalized environments for older adults aging in place with virtual access to a healthcare professional and a social support network for companionship [4].

The COVID-19 pandemic has made it more difficult for researchers and developers of digital health and aging in place technologies to test usability [5]. Existing technology evaluation methods primarily involve traditional face-to-face laboratory and at home usability evaluations that frequently are problematic during restrictive pandemic conditions, and are not well suited for rapid evaluations of home health monitoring technologies. An increasing trend in virtual doctor and health professional visits [6] puts significant pressure on technology developers to speed up innovation for home health and wellness monitoring and communication technologies without increasing risks for vulnerable populations. The need for low cost, low risk, easy to use, and privacy-preserving usability evaluation tools for home health monitoring and aging in place technologies is growing rapidly. New usability testing methods and tools will add to the growing arsenal of digital technologies for the public-health response to COVID-19 [7].

2 Usability Evaluation for Aging in Place Technologies

The COVID-19 pandemic situation, with physical and social distancing restrictions in place, especially relevant for vulnerable older adults, has emphasized the importance of deploying health monitoring and social interaction technologies for aging in place. Research demonstrates that older adults are "intrinsically motivated" by technology that promotes autonomy [3]. Older adults' acceptance and perceptions around assistive technologies are influenced by individual factors such as gender, experience, attitude towards technology, and education [8, 9]. Additionally, factors such as accessibility and availability of assistance, support and guidance from family or social network, can either positively or negatively affect acceptance and perceptions around assistive technologies for aging in place [8].

Currently, the design and development of home health management technologies are mostly based on the requirements of social and caregiving environments, rather than the needs and preferences of older adult users. This creates a significant disconnect between functionalities, intrinsic motivations and expected benefit, and could have detrimental effects on user acceptance [8, 10]. In the next sections of the paper, we provide an account of the most commonly used usability evaluation methods and tools, including remote usability testing, and assess their fit for evaluation of home health monitoring and aging in place technologies (in a pandemic environment).

2.1 Methods of Usability and User Experience Analysis

Researchers have reviewed the state of the art methods that are used to evaluate usability and user experience (UX) of medical products, devices and medical technologies [11] and identified the following methods commonly used to test usability in the field of medicine (see Table 1).

Table 1. Methods for usability/UX analysis in medicine (based on [11])

Method of analysis	Description
Questionnaire	The questionnaire involves a series of questions for the user
Observation	A qualitative method, involves a researcher observing user interactions with the device, product or system
Manual review of literature	A literature review involves the collection and analysis of research on the topic of interest
Interview	The interview is a research method where users are asked questions by the researcher
Focus-group interview	In a focus-group interview, a group of people is asked about the medical device and their opinion concerning the interface under study. This method is interactive, and the participants can discuss any topics with each other
Benchmarking testing	Benchmark testing involves testing the components and system to evaluate the performance characteristics of the subject
Heuristic evaluation	The heuristic evaluation is applied in usability research for understanding problems in the user-interface design, it is normally done by a researcher or an expert
Think-aloud protocol	The think-aloud protocol allows collecting data for improving the design of a medical device. The main distinguishing feature of this method is the ability to evaluate participants' thinking according to their speech during the solving of specified problems. There is no attempt to interpret their feelings, actions, and words
Cognitive walkthrough	The cognitive-walkthrough method is applied in usability evaluation for interactive medical systems. It focuses on new users and their opinions regarding the ease of task implementation

Some of the traditional usability/UX testing methods listed in Table 1 lend themselves well in a pandemic environment, and some are difficult to perform during physical distancing restrictions, especially for vulnerable user populations. Gupta [5] lists several human factors methods as suitable for medical product design evaluation during development cycles in COVID-19 pandemic environment (see Table 2). The majority of testing methods listed in Table 2 do not involve users and could be carried out during the pandemic. Other usability testing methods, such as interviews via telephone, video and remote testing do involve users, however, they could be carried out remotely via telephone, video, or online. While being low risk for users, these methods have their challenges: "…recruitment of representative users, shipment of study materials to participants, and the safety of participants given the absence of the moderator in the vicinity of participants, and challenges in remote observation. These methods can still be carried out, although the outcomes may not be as rich and insightful as conducting face-to-face usability testing" [5]. Examples of usability evaluation methods that could be safely utilized during the pandemic include heuristic evaluations by experts, data from previous technology evaluations and manufacturers, online surveys with users and remote testing methods [12].

Table 2. Human factors activities suitable for product design cycles in a pandemic environment (based on [5])

Human factors activities	Human factors methods
User insight research	Desk-based research Interviews via telephone and video
Preliminary analysis	Task analysis Investigation of known use problems with similar products User related risk assessment
Concept evaluation	Expert review Heuristic analysis Remote testing
Formative evaluations	Expert review Heuristic analysis Remote testing (challenging for physical interaction)
Validation testing	Remote testing (challenging to justify to regulators)

It is evident from Table 2 that remote testing in medicine and medical devices is considered to be somewhat challenging for both, physical interaction testing and for the final validation testing for medical devices. Additionally, technology developers in the medical device industry have serious doubts that medical device user testing sessions could be converted to online methodologies, including audio and video connection. Some have concerns [12] that the adoption of online methods will not produce the level of insights required to objectively map critical use errors to root cause, and that without this mapping, which is normally provided via lab-based user testing, the remote user testing will be a waste of time and resources. Instead, it is suggested to introduce widespread utilization of the heuristics analysis and other expert testing methods in the design process, and especially in cases where the lab-based evaluation is not a viable option.

Other researchers [13] who reviewed and compared remote usability evaluation methods to the commonly used laboratory usability evaluation methods, came to more positive conclusions on the viability of remote usability testing for medical devices.

They identified some remote usability testing methods comparable to traditional lab-based testing methods. The next section of the paper lists common remote usability evaluation methods and compares them to other tools.

2.2 Remote Usability Testing Methods

Remote usability testing denotes a usability testing setup where "the evaluators are separated in space and/or time from users" [14]. The idea of conducting usability tests remotely emerged about twenty years ago and has been studied empirically since then, with many researchers and even software organizations employing remote methods to evaluate technologies with users. The remote usability methods could be synchronous or asynchronous. Researchers [13] conducted a review of the methods for remote usability testing. Their findings are summarized in Table 3.

Table 3. Remote usability testing methods (based on [13]).

Activities	Synchronous methods		Asynchronous methods		
	Usability evaluation	Usability inspection	Self-administered web study	Self-reporting of critical incident	Logged use pattern
Text communication	X	X	X	X	
Questionnaire or multiple choice	X	X	X	X	X
Post-test interview			X		
Workflow logging	X	X			X
Screenshot (still image)	X	X			
Live observation	X				
Audio communication	X	X		X	
Video capture of the screen	X	X		X	
Video capture of face	X				

The next section of the paper will focus on the most commonly used remote usability testing methods, including their pros and cons.

2.3 Methods Commonly Used for Remote Usability Testing

Synchronous Remote Usability Testing. Most synchronous methods allow for conducting remote usability testing by simulating a conventional laboratory-based think-aloud test, with researchers using video and audio connections that could be combined with remote desktop sharing with users [15]. The advantages of synchronous methods include cost efficiency, a diverse pool of suitable test users, and identification of the same number or sometimes even more problems as a conventional face-to-face usability test. The disadvantages of the synchronous remote usability evaluation method include more time needed to build trust between a researcher and a user; longer hardware/software setup time, and potential for significant difficulties to re-establish the test setup if there is a malfunction in the hardware or software [15]. For example, the synchronous remote usability setup was used by researchers to evaluate the home-based telemedicine system [16]. The study used two laptop computers with web cameras, one for the participant and one for the researcher. Participants were also provided with headphones, a microphone, and a printed clinical scenario, and researchers were able to evaluate four telemedicine systems with users via this setup.

Asynchronous Remote Usability Testing. The asynchronous remote usability evaluation methods put the majority of the effort on the users since in this case it is the users who carry the software and device setup and maintenance, including setting up the software and devices used to conduct remote usability testing. The asynchronous methods are considered to be more efficient since they can relieve expert evaluators from a considerable amount of work, and enable the collection of user data from a large number of participants. However, these methods are more burdensome and time-consuming for the users. The asynchronous methods tend to identify fewer usability problems, and the users frequently have difficulties with providing a usable categorization of the usability problems [13].

   While being more time-consuming to set up and conduct, synchronous remote usability testing methods have the potential to be utilized more widely to test health monitoring technologies in a pandemic situation. For example, researchers [13] conducted an empirical comparison of three methods for remote usability testing versus a conventional laboratory-based think-aloud method. The three remote methods tested were a remote synchronous condition, where testing was conducted in real-time, but the test monitor was separated spatially from the test subjects, and two remote asynchronous conditions, where the test monitor and the test subjects were separated both spatially and temporally. The results of the evaluation demonstrated that the remote synchronous method was virtually equivalent to the conventional laboratory think-aloud method.

3   Remote Usability Testing for Aging In Place Technologies

Usability evaluation methods that are being used by medical technology designers during the COVID-19 pandemic include heuristic evaluations by experts, data from previous technology evaluations and manufacturers, online surveys with users, and remote usability tools [5, 12, 17, 18]. Within the aging in place technology design and evaluation cycle, some aspects of technology design such as understanding users, needs analysis for both older adults and caregivers, concept generation and prototyping [5] certainly could be conducted with minimal end-user involvement, especially for at-risk vulnerable older adults. Additionally, some remote usability methods might not be suited well for home technology evaluations with older adults in a pandemic situation with physical distancing measures in place. This section of the paper presents our analysis of the applicability of various methods for remote usability testing in situations when physical distancing policies are in place, like during the COVID-19 pandemic (Table 4).

Table 4. Pros and cons of common remote usability evaluation methods when physical distancing policies are in place

Method	Pros	Cons
Text communication	Synchronous/asynchronous; compatible with physical distancing; cost-efficiency	Requires users to have internet or mobile phone connectivity; does not provide rich information; does not prevent dishonesty, personalization absence, and individual interpretation
Questionnaire or multiple choice	Synchronous/asynchronous; compatible with physical distancing; cost-efficiency; scalability; anonymity; no pressure; quick results	Requires users to have internet or mobile phone connectivity if performed online; requires shipment and collection of questionnaires, if done on paper; does not prevent dishonesty; no personalization; and allows for individual interpretation of answers
Interview	Synchronous only; compatible with physical distancing, if online or via phone	More expensive than questionnaire; interviewer bias; more time needed to conduct and set up
Workflow logging	Synchronous/ asynchronous; does not require set up by the user; detects use patterns; compatible with physical distancing	Requires users to have internet or mobile phone connectivity to download logging results; does not capture the full context of use

(*continued*)

Table 4. (*continued*)

Method	Pros	Cons
Screenshot (still image)	Synchronous, could be done asynchronously by prompting the user to take screenshots during use or in case of a critical incident; compatible with physical distancing	Requires users to have internet or mobile phone connectivity; does not capture the full context of use; requires certain abilities/technology skills if the user/caregiver is involved; privacy and security considerations
Live observation	Synchronous, could be done asynchronously with user consent; compatible with physical distancing	Requires users to have internet or mobile phone connectivity; requires user/caregiver to have a certain level of abilities/technology skills; privacy and security considerations
Audio communication	Synchronous, could be done asynchronously with the user reporting a critical incident; compatible with physical distancing	Does not capture the context of use; does not provide rich information, time-consuming
Video capture of the screen	Synchronous, could be done asynchronously with the user reporting a critical incident; compatible with physical distancing	Requires users to have internet or mobile phone connectivity; requires user/caregiver to have certain abilities/technology skills; privacy and security considerations
Video capture of face	Synchronous, could be done asynchronously with user consent; compatible with physical distancing	Requires users to have internet or mobile phone connectivity; requires user/caregiver to have certain abilities/technology skills; privacy and security considerations

Despite significant benefits that could be obtained by using remote usability methods for evaluation of home health monitoring technologies, the major challenge is that remote usability evaluation of aging at home technology prototypes, excluding expert reviews and heuristic evaluations, need to be conducted with the intended technology users and need to deploy some remote evaluation tools, which could be problematic, considering overall challenges for HCI research methods with older adults. In the next section of the paper, we will elaborate on the challenges of performing HCI research with older adults in general, and in a pandemic situation.

3.1   Challenges and Limitations for Evaluation of Home Health Monitoring Technology with Older Adults

Based on our recent research project on the adoption of home monitoring technologies by older adults, we compiled the list of features and functionalities that are common across home health monitoring and telehealth management solutions:

- Contact management and videoconferencing: each end-user can manage a list of contacts, which may include friends and family members, as well as their family physician. These contacts form a circle of caregivers, who can access the system from their own devices and communicate with the senior, as well as receive valuable information about the senior's well-being and notification in case of need. Audio and videoconferencing features allow seniors to remain in contact with their families and peers. This type of service promotes social engagement, which can help seniors who live in isolation and may be struggling with loneliness, boredom and depression. In case of emergency, the end-user can also make an emergency call and request medical assistance.
- Information and entertainment features, including date, time, weather, music channels and games.

Mastering the above-mentioned complex features of a home health management system requires a substantial set of technical and cognitive skills from the older adult users or caregivers, and suggests a need for extensive usability testing for the home health monitoring technology applications. Additionally, it has been proven, that many existing HCI usability testing methods could be challenging to apply with vulnerable older adults as intended technology users. Some common challenges that researchers should be prepared for when doing HCI research with older adults include the following [9, 10, 19–21]:

- Recruitment challenges

- Participant recruitment tends to be difficult because those who are willing to volunteer are younger, healthier and with better social networks than those who are not;
- Older persons, particularly those aged 85 and older, are less likely to participate in surveys and more likely to provide incomplete surveys when they do participate;
- Many older participants might not live close to research institutions.

- Experimental challenges

- Older adults have a wider range of educational levels, with a significant proportion having low literacy;
- Lack of formal educational qualifications means that it cannot be assumed that older adults will be familiar with experimental techniques: it is important to make it explicit, for example, that silence and concentration are expected during certain parts of an experiment;

- Older individuals have relatively high rates of cognitive impairment, which sometimes limits their ability to provide meaningful information;
- Aging is associated with changes in characteristics such as visual and auditory perception, fine motor control and some aspects of memory and cognition, influencing participants' ability to, for example, read or hear experimental instructions, use a mouse, or remember steps through an interface.

• Mobility and illness challenges

- Some older adults may experience temporary or permanent mobility difficulties that might adversely affect their physical ability to participate in a research project, for example, operations with significant implications for mobility, such as joint replacements, are more commonly carried out on older people;
- People living with significant illnesses such as cancer, diabetes and cardiovascular disease tend to be older.

• Technological challenges

- Challenges and frustration with new technology make older adults unsure of their ability to use it, leaving them unmotivated to even try;
- A significant gap exists between the potential benefits offered by digital technologies and the barriers that plague older adults in the adoption of these technologies;
- A key barrier to wider adoption of technology by older adults is the "top-down" design process that is used in creating aging in place technology;
- The current assistive technology design process is based on 'technologists' or geriatricians' preconceptions of what older adults need with little consideration of user perspectives and preferences or their real-world constraint;
- Increasing technology literacy of older adults can provide meaningful improvements in helping these users interact more successfully with technology;
- There is a need to educate technology creators about older adults to increase "aging literacy" of technology developers.

Considering the numerous challenges that aging in place technology researchers and designers deal with every day in designing and evaluating digital technologies for older adults and the difficulties with technology adoption by older adults, it is of most importance to develop a co-design process that involves both, technology developers and older adults in the assistive technology development and evaluation process, especially if it does incorporate technology education as a component to increase "tech literacy" [10]. Some additional challenges with usability testing with older adults could arise in a pandemic situation, and are discussed in the next section of the paper.

3.2 Challenges with Usability Testing for Home Health Monitoring Technologies During the Pandemic

The short time since the start of the COVID-19 pandemic did not allow researchers to study in-depth and to develop better usability testing methods and tools to evaluate usability and user experience of home health monitoring technologies that can work well under physical distancing restrictions. While remote usability testing has been previously extensively used to evaluate mobile medical applications and web-based medical applications (Gupta, Suresh, 2020), the use of remote testing for physical medical devices, including home health monitoring technology and devices, has been limited. During the COVID-19 pandemic, performing remote usability testing has become even more challenging (Gupta, Suresh, 2020), including concerns with:

- Challenges with user recruitment;
- Delivery of multiple cameras and device prototypes to participants;
- Having reliable internet or Wi-Fi connection at user homes;
- User's physical and cognitive capabilities to set up the web conferencing and cameras;
- User's ability to use a web conferencing platform to interact with the researchers;
- The ability of the moderator to run the interviewer's script over the web conference without compromising the natural flow of the use process and without being too intrusive and leading;
- The ability of the observer to capture all the nuances of the use process including the subtle use errors and difficulties;
- Handling device prototypes after the study;
- Assuring data security, confidentiality, and participant safety.

In our research, we also observed some challenges with performing usability research with older adults in a pandemic situation. The following section of the paper reflects on our recent research experience in conducting human factors research with older adults during the COVID-19 pandemic.

3.3 Technology Acceptance Research for Virtual Care and Home Health Monitoring During the Pandemic

Our recent exploratory study with older adults focused on technology acceptance in the context of home health monitoring and telehealth management, including technologies to support aging in place. In particular, we looked at a "typical homecare solution" to gain insights into how seniors' attitudes and experiences related to home health monitoring and telehealth have changed since the pandemic. For the study, a researcher has conducted interviews from December 2020 to January 2021 with a sample of seniors, who previously received a tablet and a smartwatch, as part of a pilot study on home health monitoring and telehealth management in the province of New Brunswick (Atlantic Canada). The Atlantic provinces are expected to see the highest increase in their proportion of seniors in Canada by 2026 [22].

For the study, we invited six seniors to participate in an interview with a researcher on the phone, to share their experiences with a home health care solution, including their use of key features and functionalities of the application, their lived experience since the pandemic, and challenges in living independently. The study was approved by the National Research Council Canada's Research Ethics Board following strict protocols for consent, and for conducting open-ended interviews by phone under the ongoing pandemic, given restrictions on face-to-face interactions with vulnerable populations.

The study participants included both females and males, ranging in age from 66 to 92 years of age, all college or university-educated, with the highest level of education starting at the Ph.D. level, followed by Masters and a College degree. They were all vulnerable senior adults with various medical needs that require home health monitoring. All participants (but one) use computing devices regularly, for work or leisure, some even own multiple mobile devices and smartwatches. While a detailed description of the study and the findings is outside the scope of this paper and will be the subject of a future paper, some of the findings of the study, that reveal senior adults' lived experiences since the pandemic, are relevant to this paper and demonstrate a profound need for more social and home technology support required for vulnerable senior adults living at home during pandemic (see Table 5).

Table 5. Older adults' lived experience during the COVID-19 pandemic

- All seniors experienced fear, anxiety and stress;
- Some seniors countered the negative impact of the pandemic with increased activity and fitness tracking (e.g., using a smartwatch to track steps taken, level of activity, walking distance, heart rate, and sleep patterns);
- Many not see their physician since the beginning of a pandemic (e.g., blood work for chronic conditions not done during pandemic restrictions);
- Some seniors would like to consult virtually if that were an option, not aware if their physician offers a virtual care;
- Common lack of awareness of what services are available, and where to get information.

During our study on technology acceptance with older adults we experienced some common challenges of human factors research during the pandemic:

- Challenges with accessing older adults at home to recruit for the study;
- Front line health care workers that work with vulnerable seniors are busy with addressing the COVID-19 situation and have little time to participate/contribute/ or help with participant recruitment;
- The process of obtaining participant consent had to be modified due to ongoing COVID-19 restrictions including no face-to-face interactions, therefore digital consent was obtained, and interviews were conducted strictly by phone.

Our study revealed that older adults have increased demands for home health monitoring, virtual care, and social interaction technologies during the pandemic, and, at the same time, it is more difficult for researchers and developers of assistive technologies to test and improve the usability of these technologies, and, consequently, assure better technology adoption by senior adults. More research and development is needed to develop better usability research methodologies for aging in place technologies that will facilitate technology adoption by both, older adults, and healthcare practitioners. The final section of our paper will provide an insight into our future technology research and development with a focus on the needs of older adults aging at home.

4   Conclusions – Research and Technology Development Opportunities

The review of usability and user experience testing methods available for testing aging in place and home health monitoring technologies with older adults, including remote usability testing methods, highlights the importance of using the most appropriate usability testing methods and demonstrates the lack of appropriate remote usability testing tools for a pandemic situation. Improving HCI research methods and tools for conducting usability research with older adults will be the focus of our future research, focusing especially on improving remote usability testing methods and tools for home health monitoring technologies. In collaboration with healthcare researchers and home health management developers, we will develop novel research methodologies and usability evaluation tools for aging in place digital technologies, with a focus on health and chronic disease management tools. The aim is to improve the health and wellbeing of older adults, promote aging in place, and reduce avoidable hospitalizations with the help of digital health technologies.

Our current study of existing best practices in evaluation methodologies and tools for evaluating technology for aging at home and their feasibility in the context of COVID-19, reported in this paper, will be supplemented with follow up research on needs analysis with health monitoring technology companies and healthcare partners, complemented with surveys with older adults. Research results will lead to the development of guidelines and evaluation methods that are suitable for low cost, rapid, at-home technology evaluations intended for older adults, with minimal physical contact and with integrated privacy-preserving techniques. The evaluation tools we aim to develop will be suitable for HCI evaluation of other types of aging in place technologies, including personal health, safety, mobility, and communication technologies.

References

1. Shahid, Z., et al.: COVID-19 and older adults: what we know. J. Am. Geriatr. Soc. **68**, 926–929 (2020). https://doi.org/10.1111/jgs.16472
2. Zhou, F., et al.: Clinical course and risk factors for mortality of adult inpatients with COVID-19 in Wuhan, China: a retrospective cohort study. Lancet **395**, 1054–1062 (2020). https://doi.org/10.1016/S0140-6736(20)30566-3
3. Leigh-Hunt, N., et al.: An overview of systematic reviews on the public health consequences of social isolation and loneliness. Pub. Health **152**, 157–171 (2017). https://doi.org/10.1016/j.puhe.2017.07.035
4. Fournier, H., Kondratova, I., Molyneaux, H.: Designing digital technologies and safeguards for improving activities and well-being for aging in place. In: Stephanidis, C., Antona, M., Gao, Q., Zhou, J. (eds.) HCII 2020. LNCS, vol. 12426, pp. 524–537. Springer, Cham (2020). https://doi.org/10.1007/978-3-030-60149-2_40

5. Gupta, S.P.: Human Factors Engineering (HFE) During COVID-19 Pandemic (2020). https://www.mddionline.com/human-factors/human-factors-engineering-hfe-during-covid-19-pandemic

6. Koonin, L.M., et al.: Trends in the use of telehealth during the emergence of the COVID-19 pandemic — United States, January–March 2020. MMWR. Morb. Mortal. Wkly. Rep. **69**, 1595–1599 (2020). https://doi.org/10.15585/mmwr.mm6943a3

7. Budd, J., et al.: Digital technologies in the public-health response to COVID-19. Nat. Med. **26**, 1183–1192 (2020). https://doi.org/10.1038/s41591-020-1011-4

8. Cahill, J., McLoughlin, S., O'Connor, M., Stolberg, M., Wetherall, S.: Addressing issues of need, adaptability, user acceptability and ethics in the participatory design of new technology enabling wellness, independence and dignity for seniors living in residential homes. In: Zhou, J., Salvendy, G. (eds.) ITAP 2017. LNCS, vol. 10297, pp. 90–109. Springer, Cham (2017). https://doi.org/10.1007/978-3-319-58530-7_7

9. Offermann-van Heek, J., Gohr, S., Himmel, S., Ziefle, M.: Influence of age on trade-offs between benefits and barriers of AAL technology usage. In: Zhou, J., Salvendy, G. (eds.) HCII 2019. LNCS, vol. 11592, pp. 250–266. Springer, Cham (2019). https://doi.org/10.1007/978-3-030-22012-9_19

10. Wang, S., et al.: Technology to support aging in place: older adults' perspectives. Healthcare. **7**, 60 (2019). https://doi.org/10.3390/healthcare7020060

11. Bitkina, O.V., Kim, H.K., Park, J.: Usability and user experience of medical devices: An overview of the current state, analysis methodologies, and future challenges. Int. J. Ind. Ergon. **76**, 102932 (2020). https://doi.org/10.1016/j.ergon.2020.102932

12. Mauro, C.L.: Medical Device Usability Testing In The Age Of COVID-19 (2020). https://www.meddeviceonline.com/doc/medical-device-usability-testing-in-the-age-of-covid-0001

13. Andreasen, M.S., Nielsen, H.V., Schrøder, S.O., Stage, J.: What happened to remote usability testing?: An empirical study of three methods. In: Conference on Human Factors in Computing Systems, pp. 1405–1414 (2007). https://doi.org/10.1145/1240624.1240838.

14. Castillo, J.C., Hartson, H.R., Hix, D.: Remote usability evaluation: can users report their own critical incidents? In: CHI 98 Conference Summary on Human Factors in Computing Systems, pp. 253–254 (1998). https://doi.org/10.1145/286498.286736

15. Dray, S., Siegel, D.: Remote possibilities? International usability testing at a distance. Interactions **11**, 10–17 (2004). https://doi.org/10.1145/971258.971264

16. Agnisarman, S.O., Chalil Madathil, K., Smith, K., Ashok, A., Welch, B., McElligott, J.T.: Lessons learned from the usability assessment of home-based telemedicine systems. Appl. Ergon. **58**, 424–434 (2017). https://doi.org/10.1016/j.apergo.2016.08.003

17. Chidambaram, S., Erridge, S., Kinross, J., Purkayastha, S.: Observational study of UK mobile health apps for COVID-19. Lancet Digit. Heal. **2**, e388–e390 (2020). https://doi.org/10.1016/S2589-7500(20)30144-8

18. Manta, C., Jain, S.S., Coravos, A., Mendelsohn, D., Izmailova, E.S.: An evaluation of biometric monitoring technologies for vital signs in the era of Covid-19. Clin. Transl. Sci. 1–11 (2020). https://doi.org/10.1111/cts.12874

19. Dickinson, A., Arnott, J., Prior, S.: Methods for human-computer interaction research with older people. Behav. Inf. Technol. **26**, 343–352 (2007). https://doi.org/10.1080/01449290601176948

20. Neumann, P.J., Araki, S.S., Gutterman, E.M.: The use of proxy respondents in studies of older adults: lessons, challenges, and opportunities. Geriatrics (1984). https://doi.org/10.1111/j.1532-5415.2000.tb03877.x

21. Tacken, M., Marcellini, F., Mollenkopf, H., Ruoppila, I., Széman, Z.: Use and acceptance of new technology by older people. Findings of the international MOBILATE survey: 'Enhancing mobility in later life.' Gerontechnology 3 (2005). https://doi.org/10.4017/gt.2005.03.03. 002.00

22. Kembhavi, R.: Canadian Seniors : A Demographic Profil (2012). https://www.elections.ca/res/rec/part/sen/pdf/sen_e.pdf

Application of Sustainability Design Method for Well-Being Design

Yi Li[✉]

Beijing Institute of Technology, Zhuhai, China

Abstract. Product manufacturing (SDM) with sustainable design as the core concept is designed and manufactured by optimizing the product life cycle model through the concept of sustainable development. The aging of the population has caused a series of social problems, such as old-age care, medical care and health care, which need to be deeply studied in various fields of society [1]. This paper will discuss the use cases of elderly products, taking lifting bath accessories as an example. Find out the weight factors and influence of design and implementation in the whole life cycle of the product, and play a positive role in product design optimization, especially in application and experience [2]. Based on the background of limited application of this method in non-material design of service types such as welfare design, driven by the concept of sustainable design, the whole life cycle of development, operation, production, use and product is developed through the concept of sustainable ecological design. Prove the case study and application value in the development of such products.

Keywords: Sustainable design · Well-being design · Product and service design · Product life cycle

1 Introduction

Sustainable product system design can be simply divided into three types: product-oriented services, result-oriented services, and user-oriented services. (unep, 2002) technology life cycle costs and their potential volatile organic compound emissions were the main factors in the analysis. Katchasuwanmanee (2016) developed an intelligent energy production management system to simulate the relationship between energy flow, work flow and heating data flow and the thermal effect and correlation analysis between ventilation and air-conditioning systems. Simulation results show that the fuzzy control algorithm can reduce the energy consumption of the manufacturing system. Evans et al. (2017) developed a sustainable business model to analyze the value networks of economic, environmental and social mobility and the challenges of business model innovation to sustainability. Wang (2016) developed a sustainable project quality management cycle called accountability, predictability, balance, and policy cycle (APBP). To control sustainable systems, you need to understand their accountability, predictability, and balance between policies. These methods and tools can serve as reference for the sustainability of product manufacturing and new product development (Fig. 1).

© Springer Nature Switzerland AG 2021
Q. Gao and J. Zhou (Eds.): HCII 2021, LNCS 12786, pp. 48–60, 2021.
https://doi.org/10.1007/978-3-030-78108-8_4

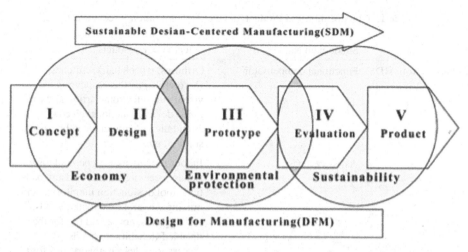

Fig. 1. Sustainable Design-Centered Manufacturing (SDM).

Product design methods that focus on the product life cycle and methods that can provide life-cycle information support to continuously optimize the life cycle, the pathways and effects of product support services, and life-cycle cost concepts and analysis tools [3]. In the product life cycle, it includes market demand analysis, Design, development, manufacture, circulation, use and invalidation That is, tbasic attributes of the product, environmental attributes, effective use of resources, manufacturing, business strategy and life cycle cost factors.

2   Ancillary Products for the Elderly

2.1   Development Trend of Assistive Devices for the Elderly

In the face of the globalization trend of population aging, the original rehabilitation aids can no longer meet the severe situation in the future [4]. Only the further development of rehabilitation aids can keep up with the pace of the times, and intelligence, modularization and integration are becoming the development direction of rehabilitation aids. Rehabilitation aids are suitable for the elderly, disabled, sick and wounded [5]. In this field, the boundaries of these three categories of people are not distinct and often intersect with each other. For example, some elderly people also have some physical disabilities, and some injured patients are also elderly people. So they are collectively referred to as dysfunction in the field of rehabilitation aids [6]. According to the definition of the International Organization for Standardization (ISO-9999: 1992), rehabilitation aids refer to products, appliances, equipment or technical systems that can effectively prevent, compensate, monitor and mitigation [6]. The main service objects of rehabilitation aids are the elderly, the disabled, the sick and wounded, and so on. Using science and technology to make them return to life, participate in social activities, and play an important role in the independent life of people with special needs [7]. Internationally, rehabilitation aids are divided into 11 main categories, 135 subcategories, 741 branches and tens of thousands of varieties [8] (Table 1).

Table 1. Classification and Product Table of Rehabilitation Accessoriest.

Domain Name	Subdomain Name	Selected key products
Rehabilitation AIDS	Functional compensator	Orthoses, wheelchairs, crutches, Decorative prostheses, hearing aids, visual aids, electronic artificial throat, guide device, functional electrical stimulation equipment, cerebral palsy support, etc.
	Assistive devices	Indoor moving aids, upper and lower Ladder accessories, anti-bedsore pads, two-stool dysfunction monitoring and nursing devices, toilet/bathing aids, walking aids, household life for the disabled Rehabilitation aids Accessories, learning/work aids for the disabled, home monitoring system, rehabilitation devices for disabled human dysfunction, etc.
	Functional training equipment	Home physiotherapy/physical therapy equipment, vocational skills training equipment, disability sports function evaluation system, elderly behavior training system, rehabilitation training equipment for patients with intellectual disabilities, etc.

2.2   China's Aging Characteristics and Product Demand

China's aging population is special, according to the relevant departments of research, by 2020, the number of elderly people aged 60 and over in our country has reached 248 million, accounting for more than 17% of the total population (CBS2020), Among them, 80 years old and older people will exceed 30 million. After 2021 will enter the accelerated aging development stage. The number of people aged 60 and over is expected to exceed 400 million by 2050, including 80 years and older The number of elderly people will also reach 95 million. By the end of 2020, China's disabled population was 33 million, accounting for 19 percent of the total number of elderly people. With the trend of population aging, the proportion of the elderly with disabilities will increase further, and the 2030 is expected to reach about 50 million.

Nowadays, China has started a relatively late research on assistive devices used by the elderly disabled [9]. Most of the existing products are produced in Japan and Europe and the United States. However, these products have high prices, high requirements for supporting equipment, difficult W purchase and use by ordinary family W and pension institutions.

The object of the study of the auxiliary bath apparatus for the severely disabled is the disabled elderly, who generally have no physical and limb movement and can not complete their daily life without the help of people or accessories [10, 11]. The basic purpose of product design is to meet the functional requirements of the product, strength requirements, reliability, stability requirements, aesthetic requirements and economic requirements as follows:

1. Product functional requirements: any product must first meet the design functional requirements. For the disabled elderly, it is necessary to satisfy the movement of the transfer device, the safe docking between the transfer device and the bathtub the meaning and the lifting back, the curved leg, the massage effect in the bathtub and so on [12].
2. Strength requirements: Strength requirements are the basic requirements to ensure the normal operation of the product. Product design needs to ensure the overall strength requirements of each component and assembly [13, 14].
3. Reliability and stability requirements: since the design product of the assistive bath equipment for the severely disabled is for the disabled and the mobility of the disabled is limited, it is necessary to ensure the stability of the product and the safety and reliability of the parts and components in the process of using the product [15].
4. Aesthetic requirements: the whole bath equipment system needs to consider certain aesthetic value, in addition to the appearance of proportional coordination, shape selection to avoid the shape that may cause accidental injury, but also to consider the transfer device, bathtub, under frame color matching [16].
5. Economic requirements; any product should be designed to take into account the economy of the product. While meeting the above product performance requirements, by reducing resource consumption, parts modular processing, mechanism optimization design to reduce production costs and other ways to improve the economy of products, enhance the cost-performance ratio of products, enhance the popularity of products, so that more disabled patients can enjoy quality services [17].

3 Design Process of Auxiliary Bath Apparatus for Heavy Impaired Elderly

3.1 Case Study on the Product Development of Elderly Bath Auxiliary

The project includes four phases of sustainable manufacturing. The details of the design phase, goals, activities, and schedules are shown in Table 2.

In the first phase of the project, the design team focuses on understanding market demand through investigation and research. Details of activities at this stage include research on similar products in the market and their manufacturability, and definition of product availability, such as environmental conditions, user definition and operational concept formation, and final summary of sample construction: effective solution to the monotony of existing products, functional design operations are not friendly, physical decline, physical function aging reduces action and operational ability, product pursuit of function is not enough to pay attention to the mental mood of the elderly, resulting in psychological rejection and use of rehabilitation equipment is not high [18].

Table 2. Gantt chart of new product development

phase	Goal	Activ ities	1	2	3	4	5	6	7	8	9	10	11	12
Concept genera-tion	Market sursey	Design for manu-facturing	■	■	■									
Prototype	Design architec-ture	Manufacturing for design				■	■	■	■					
Assessment	Product specifi-cations	Life cycle analysis									■	■		
Production	Final product	Sustainable manu-facturing											■	■

Table 3. KPIs for the final product of Elderly Bath Accessories

Image	Concise	Simple, neat shape
	Innovative	Unique, trendy, and novel shape
	Visual entirety	Harmonious shape, with a unified, congenial sense of coordination
Elements	Exterior contours	Exterior visible contours have unified entirety, consistent with the principles of formation (balance, proportion, rhyme/rhythm, contrast, and blending) and principles of gestalt (proximity, similarity, closure, continuity, and regularity)
	Size	Defining the quality of exterior contours and perceiving the object's existence (for example, the actual size of the appearance of the object)
	Appearance color	Hue, saturation, and brightness shown by the object, such as color plan
Value	Design style	Product appearance enhancing users' tast
	Product features	Product appearance representing product features
	Popularity	Dynamic course of being widely welcomed by consumers
Attraction	Semantic interpretation	Significant modeling illustration
	Functional orientation	Appearance showing strong functional appeal
	Pleasure	Modeling bringing people pleasure

According to the classification of key performance indicators developed by sustainable design [19], performance analysis is carried out from modeling images, element applications, value embodiments and attracting attention, as shown in Table 3.

After decomposing the total function of demand into a series of functional elements, [20] the principle scheme of each functional element can be determined, and the functional element can be obtained Solution is to find the technical entity that completes the function element. The idea of solving the function element can be expressed as: function - working principle - work Energy carrier.

After the functional element solution is obtained, the morphological matrix method is used to combine the functional element solution to form the total system [21]

The original understanding of the function. Morphological matrix method is a method to solve the combination of system-receiving and programmed functions [22]. It is an advanced method the basic way of mechanical system innovation is to obtain a variety of feasible schemes, and the best scheme can be obtained by screening and evaluation [23]. Factors and morphology are the two key concepts in the morphological matrix method. Factors refer to each component of a mechanical product Yes, and form refers to the solution of each function. The morphological matrix method is generally expressed in tables, such as Table 4.

Table 4. Morphological matrix

Functional element		Functional meta-analysis		
F1	F11	F21	...	F1
F2	F12	F22	...	F1
F3	F13	F32	...	F1
...	...	...	...	...
Fi	Fi1	Fi2	...	Fin
...	...	...	...	...
Fm	Fm1	Fm2	...	Fmn

A system solution is obtained by taking a solution from each functional element for organic combination N can be obtained at most A formula such as formula

$$ZN = n_1 \times n_2 \times n_3 \ldots n_i, \ldots \times n_m$$

The m is the number of functional elements and the ni is the number of i functional element solutions.

3.2 Programme Evaluation and Decision-Making

The design process is the innovation process from divergence to convergence, and the scheme evaluation is to compare and evaluate the value of each scheme [24]. Decision is to choose the best plan according to the goal and make the final decision.

Decisions should be based on the design's own characteristics and follow the following principles:

(1) System principles. From a system point of view, any scheme is a system, which can be described and decided by various performance indicators [25]. We should take the overall goal of the whole project as the core consideration to achieve the total enterprise Body best decision.

(2) Principle of feasibility. Decision-making should take into account not only the need but also the possibility of estimating both the advantages and the disadvantages Element, make decision have feasibility.

(3) Principle of satisfaction. Because of the complexity of the design work, there is no perfect design in the design, so we can only choose the phase among many schemes a satisfactory plan.

(4) Feedback principle. Whether the decision is correct or not should be checked by practice, adjusted in time according to the feedback information in the process, and made the correct decision.

(5) Multi-programme principles. In the process of design, the design scheme is gradually concretized and the understanding is gradually comprehensive. In order to ensure the quality, the design scheme is designed Stage, choose several schemes to develop at the same time, know that each scheme can be divided into advantages and disadvantages before making decisions [26].

3.3 Evaluation Objective Tree

Programme evaluations should take into account a wide range of factors, including technical, economic and social factors, so that multiple evaluations occur Evaluation objectives, and the importance of each goal is different, generally using weighting coefficient and target tree for comprehensive evaluation [27].

The target tree is based on the principle of system decomposition, Decompose the total target into sub-goals at all levels according to the inverted tree, The final sub-goal is the final evaluation goal [28]. The evaluation target tree is shown in Fig. 2, Z of which is the overall objective; Z1, Z2,…,Zn as a primary sub-goal; Z11, Z12,…, Znn as a secondary sub-goal; Ziii, Zii2,…,Znnn for Level 3 sub-goals, such as Fig. 2.

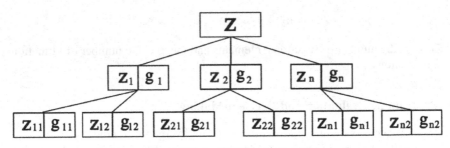

Fig. 2. Evaluation objectives tree

According to the principle of systematicness and feasibility of program evaluation decision-making, this bath accessory focuses on technical index Consider workability, processability and serviceability; focus on cost in terms of economic indicators Factors; in the social indicators focus on energy conservation [29], environmental protection and aesthetic factors, the final evaluation objectives are: working performance, processing technology, maintenance, life, cost, appearance and environmental protection [30, 31]. Due to evaluation objectives versus end product. According to the experience, the weight of technical index is 0.6, the weight of economic index is 0.2, and the weight of social index is 0.2, in which the working performance, processing technology, maintenance and life index weight of the technical index are 0.15, respectively, after. The cost weight of economic index is 0.2, the appearance and environmental protection weight of social index is 0.1, formed Fig. 3.

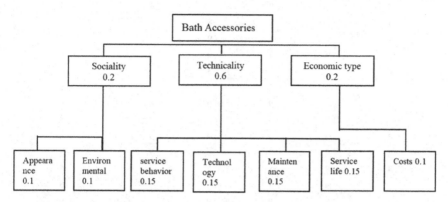

Fig. 3. Weight of scheme evaluation system

4 Product Design Evaluation of Bath Accessories

4.1 Setting Evaluation Objectives

(1) According to the previous section, the final evaluation objectives are: working performance, processing technology, maintenance, life, of production Z, of evaluation objective matrix established for this [32], appearance and environmental protection, the formula is as follows

$$Z = [Z_1 Z_2 Z_3 Z_4 Z_5 Z_6 Z_7]$$

(2) Determine the weighting factors for each evaluation objective. The weighted coefficients corresponding to each evaluation objective are 0.15, 0.15, 0.15, 0.15, 0.2, 0.1, 0.1, Forming G of weighted coefficient matrix, For example:

$$G = [g_1 g_2 g_3 g_4 g_5 g_6 g_7]$$

$$G = [0.15\ 0.15\ 0.15\ 0.15\ 0.2\ 0.1\ 0.1]$$

(3) Score each evaluation target to form a scoring matrix

According to the price target, the final 36 schemes are evaluated, and the scores of each scheme are as follows (Table 5):

A target evaluation matrix W formed is:

Table 5. Program scores

Order number	Performance	Processing Technology	Maintenance	Service life	Cost	Appearance	Environmental protection
1	4	9	9	9	9	8	9
2	4	8	8	8	7	9	8
3	4	9	9	9	9	8	8
4	4	9	7	9	7	9	9
5	4	8	8	8	7	9	8
6	4	9	7	9	7	8	8
7	4	8	9	9	8	9	9
8	4	8	8	8	7	9	8
9	4	9	9	9	9	8	8
10	4	9	7	9	7	9	9
11	4	8	8	8	7	9	8
12	4	9	7	9	7	8	8
13	4	9	9	9	9	9	9
14	4	8	8	8	7	9	8
15	4	9	9	9	7	8	8
16	4	9	7	8	7	9	9
17	4	8	8	9	8	9	8
18	4	9	7	9	7	8	8
19	9	9	9	9	9	9	9
20	8	8	9	9	7	9	8
21	9	9	7	8	7	8	8
22	8	9	8	9	7	9	9
23	9	8	9	9	9	9	8
24	9	9	8	8	7	8	8
25	8	9	9	9	9	9	9
26	8	8	7	9	7	9	8
27	9	9	8	8	7	8	8
28	8	9	7	9	7	9	9
29	9	8	8	9	9	9	8
30	8	9	7	8	7	8	8
31	8	9	9	9	9	9	9
32	9	8	8	9	7	9	8
33	8	9	9	8	7	8	8
34	9	9	7	9	7	9	9
35	9	8	8	8	9	9	8
36	8	9	7	9	7	8	8

$$W = \begin{matrix}
W_1 \\ W_2 \\ W_3 \\ W_4 \\ W_5 \\ W_6 \\ W_7 \\ W_8 \\ W_9 \\ W_{10} \\ W_{11} \\ W_{12} \\ W_{13} \\ W_{14} \\ W_{15} \\ W_{16} \\ W_{17} \\ W_{18} \\ W_{19} \\ W_{20} \\ W_{21} \\ W_{22} \\ W_{23} \\ W_{24} \\ W_{25} \\ W_{26} \\ W_{27} \\ W_{28} \\ W_{29} \\ W_{30} \\ W_{31} \\ W_{32} \\ W_{33} \\ W_{34} \\ W_{35} \\ W_{36}
\end{matrix}
\begin{bmatrix}
4 & 9 & 9 & 9 & 9 & 8 & 9 \\
4 & 8 & 8 & 8 & 7 & 9 & 8 \\
4 & 9 & 9 & 9 & 9 & 8 & 8 \\
4 & 9 & 7 & 9 & 7 & 9 & 9 \\
4 & 8 & 8 & 8 & 7 & 9 & 8 \\
4 & 9 & 7 & 9 & 7 & 8 & 8 \\
4 & 8 & 9 & 9 & 8 & 9 & 9 \\
4 & 8 & 8 & 8 & 7 & 9 & 8 \\
4 & 9 & 9 & 9 & 9 & 8 & 8 \\
4 & 9 & 7 & 9 & 7 & 9 & 9 \\
4 & 8 & 8 & 8 & 7 & 9 & 8 \\
4 & 9 & 7 & 9 & 7 & 8 & 8 \\
4 & 9 & 9 & 9 & 9 & 9 & 9 \\
4 & 8 & 8 & 8 & 7 & 9 & 8 \\
4 & 9 & 9 & 9 & 7 & 8 & 8 \\
4 & 9 & 7 & 8 & 7 & 9 & 9 \\
4 & 8 & 8 & 9 & 8 & 9 & 8 \\
4 & 9 & 7 & 9 & 7 & 8 & 8 \\
9 & 9 & 9 & 9 & 9 & 9 & 9 \\
8 & 8 & 9 & 9 & 7 & 9 & 8 \\
9 & 9 & 7 & 8 & 7 & 8 & 8 \\
8 & 9 & 8 & 9 & 7 & 9 & 8 \\
9 & 8 & 9 & 9 & 9 & 9 & 8 \\
9 & 9 & 8 & 8 & 7 & 8 & 8 \\
8 & 9 & 9 & 9 & 9 & 9 & 9 \\
8 & 8 & 7 & 9 & 7 & 9 & 8 \\
9 & 9 & 8 & 8 & 7 & 8 & 8 \\
8 & 9 & 7 & 9 & 7 & 9 & 9 \\
9 & 8 & 8 & 9 & 9 & 9 & 8 \\
8 & 9 & 7 & 8 & 7 & 8 & 8 \\
8 & 9 & 9 & 9 & 9 & 9 & 9 \\
9 & 8 & 8 & 9 & 7 & 9 & 8 \\
8 & 9 & 9 & 8 & 7 & 8 & 8 \\
9 & 9 & 7 & 9 & 7 & 9 & 9 \\
9 & 8 & 8 & 8 & 9 & 9 & 8 \\
8 & 9 & 7 & 9 & 7 & 8 & 8
\end{bmatrix}$$

(5) Solving the Weighted Value Matrix R

The R of weighted score matrix R = WGT obtained in MATLAB according to formula, Ri of each component($1 \leq i \leq 36$) The following Table 6

(6) Best Selection Scheme

According to the principle of selection, the scheme with the highest value of people is the best scheme, Table 6 shows scheme 19 (F11-F21-F32-F41-F51-F61-F71). Because of the maximum R value, it is the best scheme, that is, the horizontal drive adopts manpower, the horizontal shift adopts wheel, the vertical lift drive adopts motor, the vertical drive adopts gear, the vertical shift adopts shift, in attitude adjustment adopts manpower. Gear is used in attitude adjustment [33].

Table 6. Ri weighted score

Scheme number	Weighted score	Scheme number	Weighted score	Scheme number	Weighted score	Scheme number	Weighted score
1	8.15	10	7.55	19	9	28	8.3
2	7.3	11	7.3	20	8.05	29	8.05
3	8.05	12	7.35	21	8.65	30	7.95
4	7.55	13	8.25	22	8.3	31	8.85
5	7.4	14	7.3	23	8.05	32	8.05
6	7.35	15	8.05	24	7.95	33	8.65
7	7.9	16	7.55	25	8.5	34	8.3
8	7.3	17	7.3	26	8.05	35	8.05
9	8.05	18	7.35	27	8.65	36	7.95

5 Conclusion

China's current aging trend is increasing, the number of the elderly and the disabled is increasing, the nursing workload of the disabled and the disabled is becoming more and more heavy, the traditional nursing work mode is not enough to solve this problem, and it is more and more urgent to upgrade the nursing products [34]. Based on the sustainable design method, according to the requirements of the use of the auxiliary equipment for functional rehabilitation of the disabled and the principles of product design [35], the design flow chart of the auxiliary bath for the disabled is established, the design ideas are straightened out and the best design scheme is finally obtained.

References

1. Zhihong, L.: Analysis of the essence and characteristics of population aging. Popul. Overaging Sci. Res. Ageing (2), 3–10 (2013)
2. Fang, Y.T.: Analysis of spatial characteristics and related factors of urban aging population data in China. J. Urban Plann. **211**(6), 5–66 (2013)
3. Jian, L., Hui, L., Lifeng, L., et al.: Analysis on the safety design of rehabilitation aids. Packaging, 65–68 (2012)
4. United Nations. World Population Ageing: 1950–2050 [EB/OL]. http://www.un.org/chinese/esa/ageing/trends.htm
5. National Bureau of Statistics of the People's Republic of China. Statistical Bulletin on the Development of Aging (2010). http://www.mps.gov.cn/n16/n1947768/n1950060/3331458.html
6. Kuicheng, L., Haiyan, C., Xiaoyan, L., et al.: Investigation on the application of rehabilitation aids in patients with severe dysfunction. China Rehabilitation **28** (2013)
7. Xiangying, Z.: Design of Bath Accessories for Heavy Impaired Persons. Transfer Device Tianjin: Tianjin University of Science and Technology (2012)
8. Guerra-Zniga, M., Cardemil-Morales, F., Albertz-Arévalo, N.: Explanations for the non-use of hearing aids in a group of older adults. a qualitative study. Acta Otorrinolaringol. Esp. **65**(1), 8–14 (2014)

9. Lifeng, L.: Discussion on Inclusive Products and Frontier Technology in Rehabilitation Accessories China Social Daily **11**(4), 003 (2013)
10. Chen, P.-T., Hsieh, H.-P.: Personalized mobile advertising: its key attributes trends, and social impact. Technol. Forecast. Soc. Change, 543–557 (2012)
11. Hung, L.-p.: A personalized recommendation system based on product taxonomy for one-to-one marketing online. Expert Syst. Appl. **29**, 383–392 (2005)
12. Moon, J., Chadee, D., Tikoo, S.: Culture, product type, and price influences on consumer purchase intention to buy personalized products online. J. Bus. Res. **61**, 31–39 (2008)
13. Jimenez-Diaz, I., Zafra-Gomez, A., Ballesteros, O.: Analytical methods for the determination of personal care products in human samples: an overview. Talanta **129**, 448–458 (2014)
14. Chowdhury, A., Karmakar, S., Reddy, S.M.: Usability is more valuable predictor than product personality for product choice in human-product physical interaction. Int. J. Ind. Ergon. **44**, 697–705 (2014)
15. Lee, H.C., Lee, J.M., Seo, J.H.: Design and improvement of product using intelligent function model based cost estimating. Expert Syst. Appl. **38**, 3131–3141 (2011)
16. Valckenaers, P., Germain, B.S., Verstraete, P.: Intelligent products: Agere versus Essere. Comput. Ind. **60**, 217–228 (2009). https://doi.org/10.1016/j.compind.2008.12.008
17. Assari, P., Adibi, H., Dehghan, M.: The numerical solution of weakly singular integral equations based on the meshless product integration (MPI) method with error analysis. Appl. Numer. Math. **81**, 76–93 (2014). https://doi.org/10.1016/j.apnum.2014.02.013
18. Brackea, S., Inoueb, M., Ulutasc, B.: CDMF-RELSUS concept: reliable and sustainable products - influences on design, manufacturing, layout integration and use phase. Proc. CIRP **15**, 8–13 (2014)
19. Zhang E. Theory and Methods of Modern Design, vol. 6. Science and Technology Press, Beijing (2007)
20. Heintz, J., Belaud, J.-P., Pandya, N.: Computer aided product design tool for sustainable product development. Comput. Chem. Eng. **71**, 362–376 (2014)
21. Wang, H., (Kevin) Rong, Y., Li, H.: Computer aided fixture design: recent research and trends. Comput. -Aided Des. **42**, 1085–1094 (2010)
22. Gao Weiguo, X., Yanshen, C.Y.: Generalized modular design principle and method. J. Mech. Eng. **43**(6), 48–54 (2007)
23. Zhang, Yu.: Research into the engineering application of reverse engineering technology. J. Mater. Process. Technol. **139**, 472–475 (2003)
24. Kharmanda, G., Ibrahim, M.-H., Abo Al-kheer, A.: Reliability-based design optimization of shank chisel plough using optimum safety factor strategy. Comput. Electron. Agric. **109**, 162–171 (2014)
25. Vardarlier, P., Vural, Y., Birgiin, S.: Modelling of the strategic recruitment process by axiomatic design principles. Proc. Soc. Behav. Sci. **150**, 374–383 (2014). https://doi.org/10.1016/j.sbspro.2014.09.031
26. Albers, A., Wagner, D., Kern, L.: Adaption of the TRIZ method to the development of electric energy storagesystems. Proc. CIRP **21**, 509–514 (2014). https://doi.org/10.1016/j.procir.2014.02.060
27. Lordelo, A.D.S., Fazzolari, H.A.: On interval goal programming switching surface robust design for Integral Sliding Mode Control. Control Eng. Pract. **32**, 136–146 (2014). https://doi.org/10.1016/j.conengprac.2014.07.010
28. Xingguo, M.: A Study on Some Key Theoretical Issues in Product Systemic Design. Northeast University, Shenyang (2010)
29. Enriquez, A.H., Binns, M., Kim, J.-K.: Systematic retrofit design with Response Surface Method and process integration techniques: a case study for the retrofit of a hydrocarbon fractionation plant. Chem. Eng. Res. Des. **92**, 2052–2070 (2014). https://doi.org/10.1016/j.cherd.2014.02.030

30. Jinyong, Y.: Generalized positioning expression of product function in conceptual design. Process. Mech. Des. **31**(6), 6–12 (2014)
31. Burattini, C., Bisegna, F., Gugliermetti, F.: A new conceptual design approach for habitative space modules. Acta Astronaut. **97**, 1–8 (2014). https://doi.org/10.1016/j.actaastro.2013.12.008
32. Freitas, F.A., Leonard, L.J.: Maslow's hierarchy of needs and student academic success. Teach. Learn. Nurs. **6**, 9–13 (2011). https://doi.org/10.1016/j.teln.2010.07.004
33. Duncan, M.K.W., Blugis, A.: Maslow's needs hierarchy as a framework for evaluating hospitality houses' resources and services. J. Pediatr. Nurs. **26**, 325–331 (2011). https://doi.org/10.1016/j.pedn.2010.04.003
34. Xidong, C., Xiaodong, Z., Xiaoqiu, F.: Development and application of finite element method. China Manuf. Informatization **39**(11), 6–8 (2010)
35. Gangtian, L.: Ergonomics, pp. 26–32. Peking University Press, Beijing (2012)

Co-designing with Senior Citizens: A Systematic Literature Review

Sónia Machado[(⊠)] ⓘ, Liliana Vale Costa ⓘ, and Óscar Mealha ⓘ

DigiMedia, Department of Communication and Art, University of Aveiro, Aveiro, Portugal
{scsm,lilianavale,oem}@ua.pt

Abstract. The past few years have seen an increasing dependence on the use of Information and Communication Technologies and never had the design of age-friendly technologies been so important as nowadays, given the ageing population. Indeed, most of the software development projects designed for senior citizens rely on the designers' assumptions of the users' cognitive models, presenting the risk of falling into stereotypes and leading to products that end up not being used, which reinforces the need to involve older adults in the co-design process. This review of studies published in the last six years in the Scopus, Web of Science, and Google Scholar databases aims to understand the effectiveness of the application of co-design techniques in senior citizens. One hundred and forty-six eligible articles from a sample of 534 met inclusion criteria. Focus groups, Questionnaires, Low-fidelity/Paper Prototyping; Scenario-building, and Cultural Probes have been the most used techniques applied in this age segment. A set of recommendations was formulated such as the need to explain the technological terms prior to creative activities, involving the creation of technological artifacts and devoting time to create a sense of trust with the participants.

Keywords: Co-design · Senior citizens · Systematic literature review

1 Introduction

The proportion of the global population aged 60 and over has been growing faster than any other age segment over the past years [1]. People not only tend to live longer and actively in older age but also with higher physical and mental capabilities [2]. This increasing population age and recent advancements in Information and Communication Technologies (ICT) have also led to an overly dependence on the end-users' digitally-mediated interactions with the environment [3]. However, there is a general disengagement with online activities from older generations [4], aggravating the gap between older and younger adults in terms of ICT usage [2]. Czaja and colleagues [2] present possible reasons for the gap's persistence, such as: Income disparities; perception of the need to use technology; and the difficulties in its use. The aging process carries both physiological and psychological impairments that also make technology harder to use [2], and such impairments require the user's context to be prioritized over technology [5]. Most software development projects rely on the designers' assumptions of the users'

© Springer Nature Switzerland AG 2021
Q. Gao and J. Zhou (Eds.): HCII 2021, LNCS 12786, pp. 61–73, 2021.
https://doi.org/10.1007/978-3-030-78108-8_5

cognitive models with the risk of homogenizing the aging experience and falling under stereotypes [6]. By falling into these preconceived notions, some of these projects end up disregarding the needs of senior citizens and, subsequently, not being used by them [7]. A co-design approach could be, therefore, used in order to come up with products that senior citizens would use, *i.e.* the participation of senior citizens in the technology development process that may facilitate the identification of their wishes, abilities, and resources [5], and the end-users' engagement in co-design sessions are also very likely to impact their unique and added-value experiences [8] with the product use [9].

The aim of this review is to gain further insights into the recent trends (last six years) of co-design techniques used involving senior citizens. This paper starts by defining co-design, followed by the explanation of the procedures to carry out the literature search, criteria selection, data extraction, and management. Then, the results are presented, in which the applied co-design techniques are further detailed.

1.1 Co-design Definition and Domain

In 1970, co-design (referred to as Participatory Design) was first acknowledged as a workplace democracy movement that emerged [10–12], counting with the involvement, active participation, and collaboration of different entities in the design process, such as researchers, designers, developers, potential customers, and users [10, 13]. The three main reasons for involving stakeholders and interfering with the design process, as mentioned by Reddy and colleagues [14], were: (1) bring relevance to the User Experience Research [14, 15] by early meeting the end-user's context, users' needs with the product or service features, and subsequently, decreasing the probability of failure and the adjacent costs and efforts [16]; (2) provide stakeholders a sense of ownership and accountability of product design and development [14, 15]; and (3) strengthen the gap between social networks and community involvement through the collaboration and contact among all the stakeholders and the organizations [10, 17]. This co-design experience also allows designers to anticipate the end-users' unmet and unrecognized needs with previous assumptions of their behaviors and cognitive models [12].

Moreover, different co-design techniques can be used depending on the time of the development life cycle, the participants involved and purpose, and the appropriate group sizes for practice [18]. Sanders and Stappers [19] mention four main phases of the design research process, in which those techniques were the most included: pre-design, generative, evaluative, and post-design. The purpose of pre- and post-design is to understand people's experiences in the context of their past, present, and future lives (*e.g.*, survey and questionnaires; interviews and focus groups; cultural probes). During the design research phase, the designer/researcher prepares participants for the co-design activities while creating empathy with them. In the generative research phase, aiming for future scenarios of use and exploration of the design space, participants generate ideas, insights, and concepts to be designed and/or developed (*e.g.*, low-fidelity and paper prototyping, scenarios, card sorting). The evaluative phase allows assessing the effectiveness of products, spaces, systems, or services (*e.g.*, user evaluation). In this phase, the identification of possible problems occurs.

2   Method

The present study was conducted using a qualitative approach and following the Preferred Reporting Items for Systematic Reviews and Meta-Analyses (PRISMA) guidelines [20]. Figure 1. Presents a PRISMA flow diagram with the study selection results.

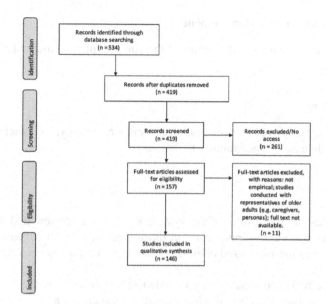

Fig. 1. PRISMA flow diagram.

The inclusion criteria used to select candidate articles were: (a) being peer-reviewed articles published between 2015 and 2020; (b) target the group of senior citizens and involve them in the design process. Exclusion criteria included non-English or non-Portuguese articles, duplicated ones, or/and with no full access,

To select the eligible articles, titles, and abstracts were screened and, then, the articles full texts were read. The conducted search yielded potentially 534 eligible studies (as shown in Fig. 1), 297 from Web of Science, 208 from Scopus, and 29 from Google Scholar, leaving 146 eligible articles. In addition, publications that only covered co-design with caregivers or that were centered on attempts to construct personas based on the user's cognitive model were also excluded.

2.1   Literature Search

Articles from Jan 2015 to March 2020 were searched using the databases Scopus, Web of Science and Google Scholar. The Google Scholar database was searched in order to include "grey literature"- i.e. white papers with examples of market-oriented techniques that might fall out of the scope of commercial academic publishers [21]. The search was limited to the last six years to understand the most recent developments in the field.

The following search terms were used to conduct the search: "co-design" OR "participatory design" OR "collaborative design" AND ("senior" OR "senior citizen" OR elder OR "older adult"). The search terms on the database Scopus and Web of Science were search at the title, abstract and keywords. At the Google Scholar database, to limit the results, the terms were only search on the study title.

2.2 Data Extraction and Management

Fully read articles were analyzed in terms of the aim, sample and methods/instruments used in each study.

2.3 Risk of Bias

The systematic literature review was conducted by one researcher, and other researchers were consulted in case of uncertainties to discuss.

3 Results

This section presents the results of the systematic literature review and the description of different techniques approached in those studies, as well as their results, in order to understand the most used co-design techniques in the last six years, and their effectiveness.

Some of the reviewed studies only included senior citizens as their target group. However, some studies focused on other related users such as caregivers, health staff, other family members, among others (e.g. [22–24]). Hence, the activities conducted with these other groups were not considered as they were out of this research scope. In addition, senior citizens of diverse backgrounds were included, *i.e.* adult learners (e.g. [25]); adults living in care homes (e.g. [26]), having some sort of health issue like cognitive impairments and hearing difficulties (e.g. [27]), or having low income and limited education (e.g. [28]), among others. It is worth noting that senior citizens do not form an homogeneous group since the aging process is not the same for everyone and leads to different physiological, psychological, and social changes [2].

Different co-design techniques were presented on the eligible articles, being most of them qualitative. Most studies were conducted in the form of group workshops/co-design sessions (n = 64) (e.g. [29–32]) and the following techniques are the most common among the studies were: interviews (n = 68) (e.g. [33–36]); focus groups (n = 30) (e.g. [37–39]); questionnaire surveying (n = 18) (e.g. [40–43]) and questionnaires administration (n = 22) (e.g. [44–46]); low-fidelity and paper prototyping (n = 21); and activities involving scenario building (n = 15), often combined with personas creation (n = 8) (*e.g.* [47]; and storytelling (see [25]). Card sorting games (n = 13) (*e.g.* [30, 48]; and cultural probes (n = 10) (*e.g.* [49, 50]). Furthermore, it was noted that some studies combine the previously mentioned co-design techniques with others. As an example, Muriana and Hornung [51] make use of collages, storytelling, interaction with a paper prototype and an interactive prototype, and user evaluation, in order to better understand how to properly engage senior citizens on the construction of a low-fidelity prototype.

Analyzing the literature review sample, most workshops and co-design sessions were conducted in group settings with small groups of participants (e.g. [52, 53]), often dividing the study sample. Furthermore, while most of the analyzed studies concentrate on one of the phases of product development, some studies engage the senior citizens throughout all the phases (e.g. [54]).

This subsection presents an overview of the previously mentioned co-design techniques, describing the different phases of the design research process that those techniques were most applied, as well as different modes of participation, described in the previous section, that were used to engage senior citizens.

Focus Groups and Interviews

The purpose of focus groups is to reunite users in group settings to evaluate products and to discuss them in a group [55]. The designer's role in the focus group is not to participate in the discussion directly, but to provide inputs for the topics that are to be discussed by the participants [55]. According to Schuler & Namioka [55], the use of co-design techniques in focus groups has been adopted by researchers in order to generate comments on their work, and get further insights into a certain concept or technology [55].

Interviews can be either unstructured, semi-structured or structured. Analyzing the results of the systematic literature review, and even though some studies do not specify the type of interview that was conducted, most of the studies seem to have conducted semi-structured interviews (e.g. [56, 57]). In a semi-structured interviews, the interviewer has a series of open guiding questions about the topics of the study matter, and gives the participants freedom to discuss and debate them, directing and guiding the interview to its guidelines every time the participants move away from the topic and asks them questions at the right time [58].

Questionnaires

According to Schuler and Namioka [55], questionnaire surveying involves administering a standard questionnaire to potential or existing users with the intention of determining users' preferences. Questionnaires allow the quantification of a large number of data and correlation analysis. It can be especially useful to carry out an analysis of social phenomena that are hardly quantified and underexplored [58].

Eighteen of the analyzed studies apply surveys, either as the only technique (see [59]), or combined with other co-design techniques such as focus groups (see [40]) and were mostly used at the early stages of co-design. Moreover, an account of 22 studies uses questionnaires in the research (e.g. [36, 37, 41]).

Low-fidelity and Paper-Prototyping

Prototypes are physical manifestations of ideas or concepts [19]. They represent a widespread design technique, particularly in software development, enabling designers and end-users to communicate and eventually agree about the features of a product [11]. They vary from rough (giving the overall idea - as paper prototypes) to finished (resembling the actual result) [19]. Paper prototyping is a method to brainstorm, design, create, test, and communicate user interfaces [60–62]. End-users work with materials they are familiar with such as papers, pencils, and sticky notes [60–62]. This technique does not require high budgets and as much development time as computer prototyping [60, 61]. Therefore, developers are more willing to accept changes to the design [61].

However, based on the reviewed studies - *e.g.* [60], Muriana and Horning [51], and Ventura and Talamo [11] studies, there has been some difficulty in engaging senior citizens with paper-prototyping, as they cannot see it being a real application or service. Interactive prototypes are a better solution to solve that problem even though there can be fewer idea contributions and suggestions for changes [60].

Scenarios, Personas and Storyboards

A persona is a fictional character who represents the ideal user and helps designers envision and considerate the users' perspective in the development process [63]. Most personas are often complemented with scenarios [64]. A scenario refers to a short story that contains information that connects the product/service requirements with the persona's goals, desires, and behaviors in certain contexts and situations [65, 66]. Rosson and Carroll [67] described four kinds of scenarios that designers can use in the development of a software application in different design phases: Analysis phase - designers study the current practices of stakeholders (1), and perform field studies to generate problem scenarios (2); and Design phase - designers use activity scenarios to introduce concrete ideas about how the user's requirements can be met (3), and create information design scenarios (4), which specify the representations of task's objects and actions that will help users to perceive, interpret and make sense of the proposed functionalities.

A storyboard is a series of drawings or images that represent envisioned scenarios on how an interface would be used to accomplish a particular task [62]. According to [68], stories and storyboards can anchor design in the end-use; promote innovation by capturing real problems; convey the functionality of a proposed solution, product, or service; help people to understand how they could incorporate new technology in their working practices; among others [65].

By engaging senior citizens in scenario activities in order to gain insights on how senior citizens plan their budget, Maqbool and Munteanu [69] results showed that participants had difficulties envisioning a scenario they thought that would be unrealistic.

Card Sorting Games

Card sorting consists in giving co-design sessions participants' a pack of cards with a concept associated to each card. It is often conducted in groups as it has the advantage of being quicker to carry out and allow more elaborated results gained through the group dynamics [70]. By carrying out card sorting activities, the concepts are tangible for the co-design sessions, and participants interact with and create discussion around these concepts [42].

Different card sorting games were spotted in the analyzed studies. Harrington and colleagues [71] use card sorting to label images on given cards. Nevay and Lim [72], use a card sorting exercise to understand the participants preferences. Also, Nevay and Lim [72], and Harrington and colleagues [71] draw attention that card sorting games can contain blank cards, in order to encourage participants to prompt ideas and personalize the cards. For transforming a card sorting activity in wearables prototypes, Nevay and

Lim [72] (p. 3), noted that "participants commented that the incorporation of blank cards was useful to capture any 'missing' items or design components."

Cultural Probes
Cultural Probes consist of self-documentation materials, created by Designers and sent to the end-users with the task of documenting their everyday life or aspects of it [19, 73]). Cultural Probes are sent as an individual task, often with little or no guidance, and after completed, they are returned to who sent them out [19]. Materials given in cultural probes are diverse, such as diaries, cameras, packages of maps, and games [19, 73, 74]. Those materials were originally designed to provoke inspirational responses from senior citizens in diverse communities, as part of a strategy of pursuing experimental design, on an urge to design for unfamiliar groups [74].

As an example, [75] make use of a cultural probe pack, constituted by a large wallet with the following materials: mood board and stickers to quickly indicate positive/negative experiences for each day; a scrapbook and glue sticks to do a collage activity of the articles read or noticed; a disposable camera to capture storytelling, and lastly, a notebook for senior citizens to express their thoughts. The authors state that raw data such as photos and videos of users in their homes and individual stories and quotes can be a good way to create empathy and personal connections to the users' experiences. However, [76]' results have shown that activities in which postcards were given to the participants as materials of cultural probes, senior citizens were less comfortable with showing their photos and were more likely to show their postcards.

4 Discussion

The findings of this review suggest that senior citizens are engaged in a vast variety of co-design techniques, being the main co-design techniques applied in the last six years: (1) Focus groups and interviews; (2) Questionnaires; (3) Low-fidelity and Paper-prototyping; (4) Scenarios, Personas and Storyboards; and (5) Cultural probes.

Based on the vast number of co-design techniques applied, and the heterogeneity of participants make a comparison of the best co-design techniques for older adults hard to make. However, some "good practices" and general observations can be made. When analyzing the results of the mentioned techniques, some senior citizens showed difficulties in creative activities, such as prototypes creation and evaluation, concerned with new technology adoption. Since senior citizens might not be familiar with technologies, it is important to explain the concept of the type of technology that is being tested or created in order to better perceive it and to be able to fully collaborate in it. Some studies included a technology introduction before the co-design activities. Clear guidance and explanation of the activities' goals can also foster the participants' engagement and interest. Furthermore, some studies engaged senior citizens in multiple co-design techniques. This can be a good way to ensure that every participant contributes to the co-design process, considering that senior citizens represented in the analyzed studies have different skills and psychological/physiological needs and capabilities.

In terms of the depth of user involvement during the product phases, this was also variable during the studies. Many studies referred to engage senior citizens in co-design processes but there were a lack of involvement or explanation of the conducted activities, sometimes referring only a small part of a continuous co-design process which difficulted the overall analysis of results. It was noted that a product would benefit from the involvement of the senior citizen during all stages of the conceptualization, design and development, although it cannot be taken for granted. Kopeć and colleagues [77], for example, engage senior citizens in a hackathon, working together with designers. The results of the study showed that senior citizens felt isolated and deserted by designers and only one group of senior citizens were fully involved in a in every stage of product development, leading to a successful product and win the hackathon.

Moreover, despite the techniques conducted, researchers should invest in creating an informal relationship with the participants (see [78]), building a non-hierarchical relationship with them to build a sense of trust (see [79]). Likewise, the categorization of the participants 'older', 'elder', etc. should be avoided as well as a different treatment in relation to younger age groups.

5 Conclusions

There is a need to (re)invent some of the design methods and workflows to match the products' features to senior citizens' context, especially in a digital era. Co-design can be an efficient solution to include this often-excluded population. In the analyzed studies, it was noticeable that some authors only referred "co-design" and often failed to apply co-design techniques at the different phases of product development. Efforts should be made to engage this target group in the co-design sessions and evaluate its impact on product development.

Acknowledgements. This work was supported by the research project SEDUCE 2.0 - Use of Communication and Information in the miOne online community by senior citizens. This project is funded by FCT – Fundação para a Ciência e a Tecnologia, I.P., COMPETE 2020, Portugal 2020 and European Union, under the European Regional Development Fund, POCI-01-0145-FEDER-031696 SEDUCE 2.0.

References

1. WHO: Active ageing: a policy framework. Adv. Gerontol. 11, 7–18 (2003)
2. Czaja, S.J., Boot, W.R., Charness, N., Rogers, W.A.: Designing for Older Adults (2019). https://doi.org/10.1201/b22189
3. Davison, R., Sia, S.K., Dong, X.Y.: Introduction to the special issue on information systems in China (2008). https://doi.org/10.1111/j.1365-2575.2008.00307.x
4. Neves, B.B., Franz, R.L., Munteanu, C., Baecker, R.: Adoption and feasibility of a communication app to enhance social connectedness amongst frail institutionalized oldest old: an embedded case study. Inf. Commun. Soc. **21**, 1681–1699 (2018). https://doi.org/10.1080/1369118X.2017.1348534
5. Pearson, J., Walsh, N., Carter, D., Koskela, S., Hurley, M.: Developing a web-based version of an exercise-based rehabilitation program for people with chronic knee and hip pain: a mixed methods study. JMIR Res. Protoc. **5**, (2016). https://doi.org/10.2196/resprot.5446

6. Vines, J., Pritchard, G., Wright, P., Olivier, P., Brittain, K.: An age-old problem: examining the discourses of ageing in HCI and strategies for future research. ACM Trans. Comput. Interact. **22**, 2 (2015). https://doi.org/10.1145/2696867

7. Brandt, E., Binder, T., Malmborg, L., Sokoler, T.: Communities of everyday practice and situated elderliness as an approach to co-design for senior interaction. In: ACM International Conference on Proceeding Series, pp. 400–403 (2010). https://doi.org/10.1145/1952222.195 2314

8. Wiklund, S., Cecilia, A., Åsa, B., Nilsson, W., Normark, J.: Participatory design of user interfaces for senior people's active aging (2018)

9. Mathis, E.F., Kim, H.L., Uysal, M., Sirgy, J.M., Prebensen, N.K.: The effect of co-creation experience on outcome variable. Ann. Tour. Res. **57**, 62–75 (2016). https://doi.org/10.1016/j.annals.2015.11.023

10. Muller, M.J., Kuhn, S.: Participatory design. Commun. ACM **36**, 24–28 (1993). https://doi.org/10.1145/153571.255960

11. Ventura, S., Talamo, A.: Simpler is better? Analysis of a codesign session with elders. Soc. Semiot. **26**, 111–127 (2016). https://doi.org/10.1080/10350330.2015.1075777

12. King, A.P.: Co-designing mobile collection points with older persons to promote green attitudes and practices in Hong Kong. Des. J. **22**, 1675–1686 (2019). https://doi.org/10.1080/146 06925.2019.1595000

13. Sanders, E.B.-N., Stappers, P.J.: Co-creation and the new landscapes of design. CoDesign **4**, 5–18 (2008). https://doi.org/10.1080/15710880701875068

14. Reddy, A., Lester, C.A., Stone, J.A., Holden, R.J., Phelan, C.H., Chui, M.A.: Applying participatory design to a pharmacy system intervention. Res. Soc. Adm. Pharm. **15**, 1358–1367 (2019). https://doi.org/10.1016/j.sapharm.2018.11.012

15. Burns, K.E.A., Jacob, S.K., Aguirre, V., Gomes, J., Mehta, S., Rizvi, L.: Stakeholder engagement in trial design: survey of visitors to critically ill patients regarding preferences for outcomes and treatment options during weaning from mechanical ventilation (2016). https://doi.org/10.1513/annalsats.201606-445oc

16. Steen, M., Manschot, M., de Koning, N.: Benefits of co-design in service design projects. Int. J. Des. **5**(2), 53–60 (2011)

17. Jagosh, J., et al.: Uncovering the benefits of participatory research: implications of a realist review for health research and practice (2012). https://doi.org/10.1111/j.1468-0009.2012.006 65.x

18. Yamauchi, Y.: Participatory design. In: Ishida, T. (ed.) Field Informatics, pp. 123–138. Springer, Berlin, Heidelberg (2012). https://doi.org/10.1007/978-3-642-29006-0_8

19. Sanders, E.B.N., Stappers, P.J.: Probes, toolkits and prototypes: Three approaches to making in codesigning. CoDesign **10**, 5–14 (2014). https://doi.org/10.1080/15710882.2014.888183

20. PRISMA: PRISMA - Transparent Reporting of Systematic Reviews and Meta-analyses. http://www.prisma-statement.org/documents/PRISMA2009 checklist.doc

21. Haddaway, N.R., Collins, A.M., Coughlin, D., Kirk, S.: The role of google scholar in evidence reviews and its applicability to grey literature searching. PLoS ONE **10**, (2015). https://doi.org/10.1371/journal.pone.0138237

22. Sadler, E., Sarre, S., Tinker, A., Bhalla, A., McKevitt, C.: Developing a novel peer support intervention to promote resilience after stroke. Heal. Soc. Care Commun. **25**, 1590–1600 (2017). https://doi.org/10.1111/hsc.12336

23. Chui, M.A., Stone, J.A., Holden, R.J.: Improving over-the-counter medication safety for older adults: a study protocol for a demonstration and dissemination study. Res. Soc. Adm. Pharm. **13**, 930–937 (2017). https://doi.org/10.1016/j.sapharm.2016.11.006

24. Raju, D.: Participatory Design for Creating Virtual Environments (2018). https://doi.org/10.1145/3297121.3297129

25. Righi, V., Sayago, S., Rosales, A., Ferreira, S.M., Blat, J.: Co-designing with a community of older learners for over 10 years by moving user-driven participation from the margin to the centre. CoDesign **14**, 32–44 (2018). https://doi.org/10.1080/15710882.2018.1424206

26. Campos, J.C., Abade, T., Silva, J.L., Harrison, M.D.: Supporting the design of an ambient assisted living system using virtual reality prototypes. In: Cleland, I., Guerrero, L., Bravo, J. (eds.) Ambient Assisted Living. ICT-Based Solutions in Real Life Situations (IWAAL 2015). Lecture Notes in Computer Science, vol. 9455, pp. 49–61. Springer, Cham (2015). https://doi.org/10.1007/978-3-319-26410-3_6

27. Nielsen, A.C., Rotger-Griful, S., Kanstrup, A.M., Laplante-Lévesque, A.: User-innovated eHealth solutions for service delivery to older persons with hearing impairment. Am. J. Audiol. **27**, 403–416 (2018). https://doi.org/10.1044/2018_AJA-IMIA3-18-0009. LK - https://ari zona-primo.hosted.exlibrisgroup.com/openurl/01UA/01UA?&sid=EMBASE&issn=155891 37&id=doi:10.1044%2F2018_AJA-IMIA3-18-0009&atitle=User-Innovated+eHealth+Sol utions+for+Service+Delivery+to+Older+Persons+With+Hearing+Impairment&stitle=Am+ J+Audiol&title=American+journal+of+audiology&volume=27&issue=3&spage=403& epage=416&aulast=Nielsen&aufirst=Annette+Cleveland&auinit=A.C.&aufull=Nielsen+A. C.&coden=&isbn=&pages=403-416&date=2018&auinit1=A&auinitm=C

28. Lee, H.R., et al.: Steps toward participatory design of social robots: mutual learning with older adults with depression. In: 2017 12th ACM/IEEE International Conference on Human-Robot Interaction (HRI), pp. 244–253 (2017)

29. Kim, S., Fadem, S.: Communication matters: exploring older adults' current use of patient portals. Int. J. Med. Inform. **120**, 126–136 (2018). https://doi.org/10.1016/j.ijmedinf.2018. 10.004

30. Tsekleves, E., Bingley, A.F., Luján Escalante, M.A., Gradinar, A.: Engaging people with dementia in designing playful and creative practices: co-design or co-creation? Dementia **19**, 915–931 (2020). https://doi.org/10.1177/1471301218791692

31. Veloso, A., Costa, L.: Social network games in an ageing society: co-designing online games with adults aged 50 and over. In: 2015 10th Iberian Conference on Information Systems and Technologies (CISTI), pp. 1–6 (2015). https://doi.org/10.1109/CISTI.2015.7170613

32. Martin-Hammond, A., Vemireddy, S., Rao, K.: Engaging older adults in the participatory design of intelligent health search tools. In: Proceedings of the 12th EAI International Conference on Pervasive Computing Technologies for Healthcare, pp. 280–284. Association for Computing Machinery, New York, NY, USA (2018). https://doi.org/10.1145/3240925.324 0972

33. Amado, P., Vale Costa, L., Veloso, A.I.: Methods and strategies for involving older adults in branding an online community: the miOne case study. In: Zhou, J., Salvendy, G. (eds.) Human Aspects of IT for the Aged Population. Social Media, Games and Assistive Environments (HCII 2019). Lecture Notes in Computer Science (Lecture Notes in Artificial Intelligence and Lecture Notes in Bioinformatics), vol. 11593, pp. 3–19. Springer, Cham (2019). https://doi.org/10.1007/978-3-030-22015-0_1

34. Malmborg, L., Grönvall, E., Messeter, J., Raben, T., Werner, K.: Mobilizing senior citizens in co-design of mobile technology. Int. J. Mob. Hum. Comput. Interact. **8**, 42–67 (2016). https://doi.org/10.4018/IJMHCI.2016100103

35. Brookfield, K., Scott, I., Tinker, A., Thompson, C.W.: Perspectives on "novel" techniques for designing age-friendly homes and neighborhoods with older adults. Int. J. Environ. Res. Public Health. **17** (2020). https://doi.org/10.3390/ijerph17051800

36. Harrington, C.N., Wilcox, L., Connelly, K., Rogers, W., Sanford, J.: Designing health and fitness apps with older adults: Examining the value of experience-based co-design (2018). https://doi.org/10.1145/3240925.3240929

37. Doppler, J., Gradl, C., Sommer, S., Rottermanner, G.: Improving user engagement and social participation of elderly people through a TV and tablet-based communication and entertainment platform. In: Miesenberger, K., Kouroupetroglou, G. (eds.) Computers Helping People with Special Needs (ICCHP 2018). Lecture Notes in Computer Science (Lecture Notes in Artificial Intelligence and Lecture Notes in Bioinformatics), vol. 10897, pp. 365–373. Springer, Cham (2018). https://doi.org/10.1007/978-3-319-94274-2_51

38. Caravau, H., Silva, T., Silva, V.: Interrupt emission or ask if TV viewer wants to see. In: 2017 12th Iberian Conference on Information Systems and Technologies (CISTI), pp. 1–6 (2017). https://doi.org/10.23919/cisti.2017.7975753

39. Juel, W.K., et al.: SMOOTH robot: design for a novel modular welfare robot. J. Intell. Robot. Syst. Theor. Appl. **98**, 19–37 (2020). https://doi.org/10.1007/s10846-019-01104-z

40. Mehrotra, S., et al.: Embodied conversational interfaces for the elderly user (2016). https://doi.org/10.1145/3014362.3014372

41. Orzeszek, D., et al.: Beyond participatory design: Towards a model for teaching seniors application design (2017)

42. Kim, S., Fadem, S.: Communication matters: exploring older adults' current use of patient portals. Int. J. Med. Inform. **120**, 126–136 (2018). https://doi.org/10.1016/j.ijmedinf.2018. https://doi.org/10.004

43. Li, C.: The design of a system to support storytelling between older adults living in a nursing home and their children. Des. J. **23**, 153–163 (2020). https://doi.org/10.1080/14606925.2019.1697585

44. Volkmann, T., Sengpiel, M., Karam, R., Jochems, N.: Age-appropriate participatory design of a storytelling voice input in the context of historytelling (2019). https://doi.org/10.5220/0007729801040112

45. Gomes, C.A., Ferreira, S., Gouveia, T., Rito, P., Morais, N., Sousa, B.: Intergenerational participatory design: Contributions to the development of an app (2018). https://doi.org/10.1109/siie.2018.8586739

46. Silva, T., Caravau, H., Reis, L., Campelo, D.: Interrupt the TV emission: usage evaluation in real context. In: 2018 13th Iberian Conference on Information Systems and Technologies (CISTI), pp. 1–6 (2018). https://doi.org/10.23919/cisti.2018.8399378

47. Cahill, J., McLoughlin, S., Wetherall, S.: Lived experience, stakeholder evaluation and the participatory design of assisted living technology. Stud. Health Technol. Inform. **242**, 64–71 (2017). https://doi.org/10.3233/978-1-61499-798-6-64

48. Wiklund-Axelsson, S., Björklund, C., Wikeberg-Nilsson, Å., Normark, J.: Health Cloud: Participatory Design of User Interfaces for Senior People's Active Aging. Luleå University of Technology (2017)

49. Wiklund Axelsson, S., Wikberg-Nilsson, Å., Melander Wikman, A.: Sustainable lifestyle change-participatory design of support together with persons with obesity in the third age. Int. J. Environ. Res. Public Health. **13**, 1248 (2016). https://doi.org/10.3390/ijerph13121248

50. Panek, P., et al.: On the prototyping of an ICT-enhanced toilet system for assisting older persons living independently and safely at home (2017). https://doi.org/10.3233/978-1-61499-759-7-176

51. Muriana, L.M., Hornung, H.: Towards participatory prototyping with older adults with and without cognitive impairment: challenges and lessons learned. In: Bernhaupt, R., Dalvi, G., Joshi, A., K. Balkrishan, D., O'Neill, J., Winckler, M. (eds.) Human-Computer Interaction - INTERACT 2017 (INTERACT 2017). Lecture Notes in Computer Science, vol. 10513, pp. 344–363. Springer, Cham (2017). https://doi.org/10.1007/978-3-319-67744-6_23

52. King, A.P.: Participatory design with older adults: exploring the latent needs of young-old and middle-old in daily living using a universal design approach. In: Di Bucchianico, G. (ed.) Advances in Design for Inclusion, pp. 149–160. Springer, Cham (2020). https://doi.org/10.1007/978-3-030-20444-0_15

53. Baker, S., Waycott, J., Carrasco, R., Hoang, T., Vetere, F.: Exploring the design of social VR experiences with older adults. In: Proceedings of the 2019 on Designing Interactive Systems Conference, pp. 303–315. Association for Computing Machinery, New York, NY, USA (2019). https://doi.org/10.1145/3322276.3322361

54. Hu, L., Dong, H.: Designing poker time: older people as fixpartners in a co-design process. In: Zhou, J., Salvendy, G. (eds.) Human Aspects of IT for the Aged Population. Design for Aging (ITAP 2016). Lecture Notes in Computer Science (Lecture Notes in Artificial Intelligence and Lecture Notes in Bioinformatics), vol. 9754, pp. 13–22. Springer, Cham (2016). https://doi.org/10.1007/978-3-319-39943-0_2

55. Schuler, D., Namioka, A.: Participatory Design: Principles and Practices (1993)

56. Jaakola, H., Ekstrom, M., Guilland, A.: Changing Attitudes Towards Seniors as Learners. Creating an Understanding of Seniors as Digital Storytellers. (2015)

57. Huisman, E., Appel-Meulenbroek, R., Kort, H.: A structural approach for the redesign of a small-scale care facility as a guideline for decision-makers. Intell. Build. Int. **12**, 32–43 (2020). https://doi.org/10.1080/17508975.2018.1493569

58. Quivy, R., Campenhoudt, L. Van, Marques, J.M., Mendes, M.A.: Manual de Investigação em Ciências Sociais (1992)

59. Goeman, D., et al.: Optimising health literacy and access of service provision to community dwelling older people with diabetes receiving home nursing support. J. Diab. Res. **2016**, 2483263 (2016). https://doi.org/10.1155/2016/2483263

60. Duh, E.S., Guna, J., Pogačnik, M., Sodnik, J.: Applications of paper and interactive prototypes in designing telecare services for older adults. J. Med. Syst. **40**, 1–7 (2016). https://doi.org/10.1007/s10916-016-0463-z

61. Osman, A., Baharin, H., Ismail, M.H., Jusoff, K.: Paper Prototyping As A Rapid Participatory Design Technique. Comput. Inf. Sci. **2**, 53–57 (2009). https://doi.org/10.5539/cis.v2n3p53

62. Snyder, C.: Paper Prototyping—The Fast and Easy Way to Design and Refine User Interfaces List of Figures Introduction Case Studies Thinking About Prototyping Making a Paper Prototype Planning a Usability Study with a Paper Prototype Ta (2003)

63. Grudin, J., Pruitt, J.: Personas, Participatory Design and Product Development: An Infrastructure for Engagement, pp. 144–152. PDC (2002)

64. Maa, S., Buchmuller, S.: The crucial role of cultural probes in participatory design for and with older adults. I-Com **17**, 119–135 (2018). https://doi.org/10.1515/icom-2018-0015

65. Valaitis, R., et al.: Health TAPESTRY: co-designing interprofessional primary care programs for older adults using the persona-scenario method. BMC Fam. Pract. **20**, 1–11 (2019). https://doi.org/10.1186/s12875-019-1013-9

66. Saurer, B.R., Mueller-Gorchs, M., Kunze, C.: Scenario-based Design of an ICT platform for mobile information services in ambulatory care nursing. Stud. Health Technol. Inform. **146**, 64–68 (2009). https://doi.org/10.3233/978-1-60750-024-7-64

67. Rosson, M.B., Carroll, J.M.: Usability Engineering: Scenario-Based Development of Human-Computer Interaction. Academic Press (2002)

68. Gruen, D.: Storyboarding for design: an overview of the process. Collab. User Exp. Tech. Rep. 00, 7 (2000)

69. Maqbool, S., Munteanu, C.: Understanding older adults' long-term financial practices: challenges and opportunities for design. In: Extended Abstracts of the 2018 CHI Conference on Human Factors in Computing Systems, pp. 1–6. Association for Computing Machinery, New York, NY, USA (2018). https://doi.org/10.1145/3170427.3188677

70. Pazart, L., et al.: "Card sorting": a tool for research in ethics on treatment decision-making at the end of life in Alzheimer patients with a life threatening complication. BMC Palliat. Care. **10**, 2–7 (2011). https://doi.org/10.1186/1472-684X-10-4

71. Harrington, C.N., Borgos-Rodriguez, K., Piper, A.M.: Engaging low-income african american older adults in health discussions through community-based design workshops. In: Proceedings of the 2019 CHI Conference on Human Factors in Computing Systems, pp. 1–15. Association for Computing Machinery, New York, NY, USA (2019). https://doi.org/10.1145/3290605.3300823

72. Nevay, S., Lim, C.S.C.: The role of co-design in wearable adoption for mobility study (2015). https://doi.org/10.1201/b18293-22

73. Jarke, J., Gerhard, U.: Using probes for sharing (tacit) knowing in participatory design: facilitating perspective making and perspective taking. I-Com 17, 137–152 (2018). https://doi.org/10.1515/icom-2018-0014

74. Gaver, B., Dunne, T., Pacenti, D.: Design: cultural probes. ACM Interact. 6, 21–29 (1999). https://doi.org/10.1145/291224.291235

75. Shore, L., Kiernan, L., DeEyto, A., Connolly, A., White, P.J.: Older Adult Insights for Age Friendly Environments, Products and Service Systems. Int. J. Technol. Des. Educ. 23, 40–58 (2018)

76. Nicol, E., Komninos, A., Dunlop, M.D.: A participatory design and formal study investigation into mobile text entry for older adults. Int. J. Mob. Hum. Comput. Interact. 8, 20–46 (2016). https://doi.org/10.4018/IJMHCI.2016040102.oa

77. Kopeć, W., Balcerzak, B., Nielek, R., Kowalik, G., Wierzbicki, A., Casati, F.: Older adults and hackathons: a qualitative study. Empir. Softw. Eng. 23, 1895–1930 (2018). https://doi.org/10.1007/s10664-017-9565-6

78. Hornung, D., Müller, C., Shklovski, I., Jakobi, T., Wulf, V.: navigating relationships and boundaries: concerns around ICT-uptake for elderly people. In: Proceedings of the 2017 CHI Conference on Human Factors in Computing Systems, pp. 7057–7069. Association for Computing Machinery, New York, NY, USA (2017). https://doi.org/10.1145/3025453.3025859

79. Raber, C., et al.: Emily Carr University Zeitgeist program. In: Brankaert, R., IJsselsteijn, W. (eds.) Dementia Lab 2019. Making Design Work: Engaging with Dementia in Context. D-Lab 2019. Communications in Computer and Information Science, vol. 1117, pp. 62–70. Springer, Cham (2019). https://doi.org/10.1007/978-3-030-33540-3_6

Design for Ageing in Place in Isolated Contexts: A Methods Literature Review

Carla Resendiz-Villasenor[1](✉) ⓘ, Farzad P. Rahimian[1] ⓘ, Phillippa Carnemolla[2] ⓘ, Sergio Rodriguez[1] ⓘ, and Nashwan Dawood[1] ⓘ

[1] Teesside University, Middlesbrough TS1 3BX, UK
c.resendizvillasenor@tees.acuk
[2] University of Technology Sydney, Sydney 2007, NSW, Australia

Abstract. Ageing in place is one of the answers to the changing needs of older global demographics. After evaluating alternatives for ageing in place, the effects of the COVID-19 pandemic lockdowns and the challenges of living in remote contexts, the need to integrate a Human-Centered Design approach to increase the usability of the Built Environment became evident. This literature review describes different methods and instruments that can be used for data collection in the context of a Human-Centered Design process for the built environment. Contributions of this research include the application of a user-centered theory of the built environment focused on the user experience.

Keywords: Human-Centered Design · Ageing in place · Older people · Usability

1 Introduction

1.1 Healthy Ageing

Statistics show how a large number of the global population is getting older. By 2050 more than two billion people will be over 60 years old, compared with one billion in 2020 [1]. In the United Kingdom, by 2043, more than 10 million households will be headed by someone aged 65 or more, increasing the numbers of 2016 by 54% [2]. Specifically in Scotland, in 2019, reports showed the demographic age shift, increasing by 31% the group of people aged 75 or more, while on the other hand, the population group aged 0–15 decreased by 8% [3].

The Healthy Life Expectancy (HLE) refers to the number of years a person will enjoy good health. The gap between Life Expectancy and Healthy Life Expectancy is getting bigger, and the HLE projection for Scottish people shows that males born in 2015–2017 can expect to spend 62.3 years of good health, and for females the number is 62.6 years, variations are mainly defined by gender and access to services [3]. This projection suggests that people might struggle with health issues for about 15 to almost 20 years, and explains why there is an interest on focusing on healthy ageing.

However, healthy ageing is a concept that needs clarification. For many years, the MacArthur Model of Successful Ageing was used as a reference to determine the quality

© Springer Nature Switzerland AG 2021
Q. Gao and J. Zhou (Eds.): HCII 2021, LNCS 12786, pp. 74–87, 2021.
https://doi.org/10.1007/978-3-030-78108-8_6

of the ageing process. The model considers three aspects: low risk of disease, maintenance of high mental and physical function and continued engagement with life [4]. Healthy ageing is defined by the World Health Organization (WHO), as 'the process of maintaining the functional ability that enables wellbeing in older age'. An individual achieves functional ability by an intrinsic capacity (physical and mental health) and their environment (extrinsic factors) [5]. Healthy ageing frequently associated with the concept of "wellbeing", other sources [6] align with the WHO describing it as the balance point between resources and challenges faced by the individual.

1.2 Wellbeing and the Built Environment

Wellbeing is a complex and non-static perception, there are several affirmations in literature that agree it can be achieved despite illness, successfully managing health conditions, and executing most activities independently [6–8]. Nevertheless, this balancing act frequently gets impacted by housing characteristics. The House of Commons [9] lists housing characteristics that affect older people's wellbeing, such as low quality, unadapted, hazardous, poorly heated and poorly insulated accommodations. The Centre for Ageing Better adds other features such as small room sizes, steep stairs, baths rather than showers and steps outside as some common problems with mainstream housing [10] Some consequences of poor housing can be: reduced mobility, depression, chronic and acute illness, falls, social isolation, loneliness and depression [3]. Appropriate housing should enable users in several ways, keeping them warm, safe and healthy, close to their social circle and allowing them to execute activities they consider important [10], support them in living independently, and reduce the need for social care [11–13].

There is a trend on housing policies to focus on ageing-in-place [14–16] as a response to the increase in older demographics which has been explained previously, and also to the fact that only few homes have accessibility features. Specifically in the U.K. only 7% of the house stock includes accessible characteristics (level access and accessible threshold, W.C. at entrance level, wide doors and circulation space for wheelchairs) [10]. The National Health Service (NHS) [17] offers a support program for older adults to adjust their properties and allow them to stay at home for longer and increase their independence. Modifications can go from adding grab rails to fitting a stairlift. This type of policy focuses on retrofitting a segment of the other 93% properties.

2 Background

2.1 Alternatives for Ageing in Place

The alternatives for ageing in place can be determined by users age, level of independence and level of care needed, and different options vary from general needs to specialized solutions [18, 19], a comparison is shown in Fig. 1.

The alternatives which not consider age restrictions and that promote user independence (Adapted Housing, Lifetime Homes, Future Proofed Homes and Wheelchair Homes) will be described next.

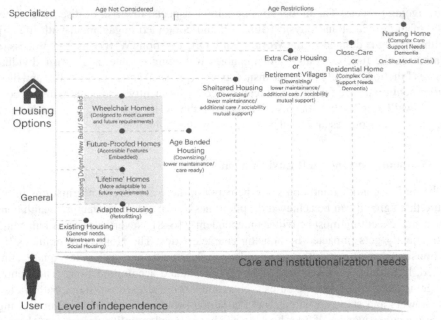

Fig. 1. Comparison of alternatives for ageing in place, according to the level of specialization of housing and user's age, level of independence, and need for care. Based on [18, 19]

Adapted Housing. Modifications to the Built Environment, or Home Adaptations (HA), have been studied thoroughly [10, 11, 14, 20–29]. HA apply to existing housing, and can be classified as minor (i.e. additional grabrails in stairs and bathroom, installing shower seat) or significant (i.e. installation of stairlift, replacing bath with shower). Other authors [14] classify them in more specific categories: the sense of being at home, usability and safety. Most longitudinal studies present positive results, i.e. Carnemolla and Bridge [24] measured the impact of this type of H.A. on older people's wellbeing. They found that improving accessibility led to a 40% increase in Health-Related Quality of Life.

On the other hand, on occasions users delay H.A. installation because are perceived as "stigmatizing associations with decline and vulnerability" [23, 26], often causing H.A. product acceptance until reaching a crisis point. Other literature [30] based on phenomenological methods, describes new discoveries of inconsistent and unintended uses for H.A. products after immersing into users B.E. with novel approaches. These polarized results in H.A. use present the need of a Human Centered approach while planning and performing changes to the B.E.

For some users, transforming their B.E. is not a viable alternative, and moving to other alternatives to age in place might be the only option. A study by Age Scotland [31] on the Orkney Islands describes how older people use government programs to adapt their houses to increase comfort. Subjects were asked about their current and future housing plans, showing that 61% do not intend to move in the future. Only 11% have considered moving because their facilities are perceived as unsuitable (high running costs and single level property is preferred). Other studies show that most of the respondents don't want to move due to getting older, only relocating voluntarily when downsizing or convenience reasons [7, 32] and the action can be taken after crisis situation (i.e. increased frailty, reduced mobility, etc.) or planning ahead proactively[19].

Lifetime Homes. Refers to a design guide [33] that complements (and enhances) the Building Regulations [34] and increases the building's adaptability. The aim is to improve the user experience while facing challenges of different moments in life, i.e. using the entrance of a dwelling with a pushchair or with a walking aid. The design principles can be applied to communal residences or single-family dwellings. Some initiatives like HOME (Housing Made for Everyone) advocate for including these guides as basic standards[35] for new-build housing.

Future-Proof Homes. This concept refers to houses designed to be easily adaptable to changes in user's needs, some features might be embedded from the planning stage [19].

Wheelchair Homes. These homes follow the Approved Document M2-Part 3 of the Building Regulations [36] to allow a wheelchair maneuvering through all the living spaces without. The focus is on describing minimum spaces, widths of doors, height of working spaces and sockets, storage and accessible layouts.

After describing the non-age-restrictive alternatives for ageing in place to promote independence, it's also necessary to add that BE theories include other aspects as well, such as location [26].

2.2 Remote and Isolated Contexts

When evaluating and designing the BE, the physical environment is framed by multiple levels: Immediate surroundings, neighborhood and community [19, 26, 37, 38]. In some cases, integrating the three levels can be challenging. The context of this research is in the north of Scotland, which is described as one of the most remote and sparsely populated parts of the United Kingdom [39]. One of the consequences of geography is isolation from various service provisions, especially healthcare. The study 'Scotland's Wellbeing' shows the perception of the quality of public services such as transport and health services has been decreasing in rural areas [40]. Other sources mention that "older people in rural areas are more likely to experience ill-health conditions caused by poorer housing conditions", frequently facing fuel poverty, with properties that are difficult to maintain and with inefficient heating [41]. This situation was foreseen since 2011, when the Strategy for Housing Scotland's Older People was published [42] and dictating "should be accessible and adaptable and meet the needs of older people", considering the lack of availability of suitable housing for older people in remote and rural areas. The strategy remarks on the importance of new build to meet the needs of an ageing population, and specifies that new options to have an increased potential of accommodating people with mobility needs.

After the previous description, it can be suggested that some characteristics of remote living can be comparable with recent lockdown living. With increased time at home due to COVID – 19 Pandemic, the relationship between users and the B.E. has changed dramatically [43–45]. Elderly and disabled people have suffered consequences of not living in a place that suits their needs while spending more (if not all) time indoors emphasized good and bad aspects of B.E. where people live [44, 46]. Quoting a segment of an article related to the effect of the pandemic in social experiences "As we navigate through life, much of what fulfils us are the bonds we create with other people, and more often than not, those bonds materialize through physical interactions." [47] It became apparent that housing solutions must consider social connections even in remote or isolated contexts.

2.3 Best Practices and Local Considerations

The framework for dimensions and features to be taken into account when designing a B.E. to age in place, are described in the Building Regulations [34]. However other resources of additional information, such as the National Design Guide [48] defines "well designed" homes as functional, accessible, sustainable, and providing internal environments and external spaces that support their users' health and wellbeing. The 'Housing our ageing population' reports [41, 49, 50] encourage the industry to introduce 'care ready' features in houses, integrating new home technologies, keeping users connected and increasing their sense of autonomy. Also, they provide design principles and rural proof principles to be considered while designing the B.E., i.e. generous internal space standards to allow overnight visitors/carers, adaptability and 'care aware' design which is digitally/technology enabled.

For local considerations, the Design Brief for building Homes for the Highlands [51] is referenced, even though the audience for the publication are Affordable Housing Providers, it includes information like heating systems requirements, use of supplementary low or zero carbon technologies, and considerations for diverse needs (inclusive design for sight loss, hearing loss, limited mobility and dementia).

Despite the best practices and local considerations mentioned, technologies and care ready features do not offer specific information on which technologies should be taken into account. Studies about smart homes and IoT for older people have categorized technologies according to Activities of Daily Living (ADLs) [52]. The categories are safety, health and nutrition, physical activity, personal hygiene and care, social engagement and leisure.

2.4 Usability at Home

Usability happens with every user-product interaction. According to the Draft of BS ISO 15928-7 [53], usability is the characteristic of the built environment to be used by everybody in convenience and safety. The draft also describes the dwelling's performance, which is defined as the behavior of houses related to users' needs. This approach of defining usability needs to be differentiated from accessibility. While accessibility is based on objective information, usability is loaded with subjective perceptions [20].

Usability evaluation has been thoroughly explored in the area of Human-Computer Interaction, in the field of the Built Environment has been explored on to evaluate interface design (i.e. of service controls) and to assess the risks on existing housing to prescribe minor or major home adaptations.

2.5 Human-Centered Design

The National House Building Council Foundation [54] framed the question: "Could well designed, stylish and safe homes suited to downsizing or single person occupancy become a more common new house type within 20 years?" This research focuses on the residential BE as a product. The so-called "industrial house" [55] has been present since early 20th century [56] and has become an alternative to an increased housing shortage in several countries [57, 58]. The industrial house concept is related to the Offsite Manufacturing (OSM) process, which refers to producing construction elements in a factory facility or other controlled environment [59].

OSM process requires adding value by integrating stakeholders in the design stage [57], which is one of the benefits of applying human-centered Design (HCD). References for HCD process and tools are explained by Maguire [60], Bowmast and Tait [61] and ISO 13407 standard on human-centered design [62, 63].

Currently, there are only a few pieces of literature available regarding HCD applied to the B.E., most of the theory is applied to Healing Environments [29] or adaptations to homes for rehabilitation [64]. Some authors [65, 66] suggest that the construction sector lacks the use of Human Factors and HCD fundamentals. Agee, Gao [67] recently published a paper regarding a framework to consider HCD the BE; however, their outcomes are related to smart interfaces at home.

This research aims to answer the question: which HCD methods for data collection can be employed to integrate users' inputs when selecting and prioritizing features and technologies to age in place?

3 Methodology

A literature review took place online in scientific databases, analyzing peer-reviewed journal articles and conference papers involving Human-Centered Design methods for data collection applied to the BE, and related to ageing in place, usability or assistive technologies.

The methods and instruments identified were analyzed by type of user, type of data collected and elements considered (Fig. 2).

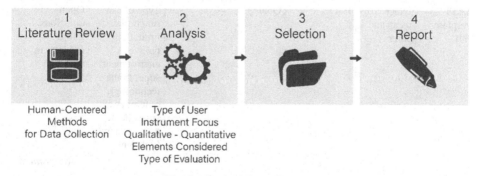

Fig. 2. Methodology diagram.

Methods and tools were selected according to relevant elements and finally reported as part of a new framework of design for the BE.

4   Results

The result of the methods and instruments are described in this section. After reviewing 43 journal papers, 8 were selected. The criteria for selection of instruments was the detail of description for application, focus related to the aspects of BE for ageing in place (home adaptations, wellbeing, independence) or assistive technologies. Specifically for quantitative data instruments, validity and refinement was also considered.

All the methods and instruments included demographic and background data; this feature is not included in Table 1 to avoid repetition. The first column refers to the name of the instrument or tool; the second one describes the type of user or the focus of the application. The third column defines if the data collected is qualitative or quantitative. The fourth column enlists the elements considered by the method or tool, and the last column provides a reference to the authors.

Table 1. Analysis of methods for data collection.

Name of instrument	Type of user	Instrument focus	Qualitative/Quantitative	Elements considered	Type of evaluation
UIMH survey [20, 21, 27]	Older and disabled user	HA	Quant	Activity aspects, personal and social aspects and physical environmental aspects	Usability Scale
USAE survey [68]	Older users	Technologies	Quant	Mobile phone use frequency and usability, social activity, environmental awareness	Usability Scale
HAST template [69]	Older users and carers	HA	Qual	Type of care, functional limitations, built environment, smart home technology, outcomes of smart home tech., general highlights	Open questions, guide answers in template

(*continued*)

Table 1. (*continued*)

Name of instrument	Type of user	Instrument focus	Qualitative/Quantitative	Elements considered	Type of evaluation
Board interactive interview [70]	Not age related. Early adopters and early majority technology users	Technologies	Qual	Temporal approach (different times of a day), activities, control devices, appliances, features and interaction styles	Open questions, descriptive interactions
MoCA [27]	Older users	HA	Quant	Cognitive assessment (short-term memory, visuospatial abilities, executive functions, attention, concentration, working memory, language and orientation in time and place)	Test/Scores
ADL staircaise [27]	Older users	HA	Quant	Independent living assessment (feeding, mobility, using the toilet, dressing, bathing, cooking, transportation, shopping, and cleaning, and shows how independent the individual is in these situations	Independence Scale

(*continued*)

Table 1. (*continued*)

Name of instrument	Type of user	Instrument focus	Qualitative/Quantitative	Elements considered	Type of evaluation
Service controls interfaces usability tool [71]	Not age related. Users of heating systems	Technologies	Quant	Cognition, physical ergonomics and Affordances	Yes/No/I don't know answers
Lived experience method	Older and disabled users	HA	Qual	HA, process of getting the HA, analysis of before and after HA, other users of the HA and further adaptations	Semi Structured interviews and Wearable camera use

In order to understand how housing characteristics and technologies can help the users achieve functional ability, a model was developed based on HAST model (Human/Activity/Space/Technology) [25] and the Just Living Target Model [19]. The resultant model together with the methods selected are described in Fig. 3 (Table 2).

Fig. 3. HCD model to design homes for ageing in place in isolated contexts.

This review demonstrates that methods are available to obtain qualitative and quantitative data from users for interventions in the BE and to evaluate and increase its usability. As well as its application to technologies that promote independence and connection and engagement with the community.

Adding users input to the equation for designing new residential houses, together with best practices, lessons learned from HA, additional to the Building Regulations, can have a positive impact on users everyday lives. Improving the levels of wellbeing of users while increasing their independence and reducing the need for extra care (Fig. 4).

Table 2. Methods selection

Focus	Aspects to understand	Methods selected
Main user (A)	Wellbeing (functional ability and physical and mental capacity)	MoCA [27] ADL Staircaise [27]
Home (Residential BE) (B) and activities of daily living (ADL's) (C)	Usability of Areas, elements (furniture, adaptations, appliances, technologies, etc.)	HAST Template [69] Board Interactive Interview [70]
Community (D)	Accessibility (physical and virtual), Care (self, informal and formal) and engagement with the community	USAE Survey [68]

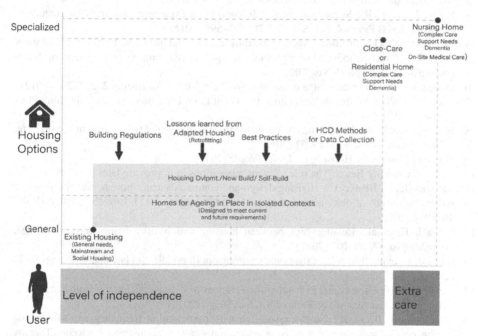

Fig. 4. Integration of methods and instruments in the HCD process to develop homes for ageing in place in isolated contexts.

5   Conclusion

As mentioned before in this paper, the UK is facing the challenge of having almost all of the housing stock inaccessible or with hazard conditions, when in the other hand the population is getting older with changing needs. Designers, developers and professionals of the BE, as well as other stakeholders, should use available methods to consider real needs of users, as well as considering best practices instead of only the minimum standards. This integration could help avoid usability nightmares (or psychopathologies) as the ones mentioned by Norman in his book The Design of Everyday Things [72].

The impact of this review is expected to be applied to help provide brighter scenarios in the future, where people can find the balance for wellbeing while at home for as long they might need to (such as in lockdowns) and for as long as they prefer to.

Acknowledgements. This research is part of a Knowledge Transfer Project between Norscot Joinery, Teesside University and Innovate UK.

References

1. World Health Organization, Decade of healthy ageing: baseline report. Geneva (2020)
2. Office for National Statistics, National population projections: 2018-based (2019)
3. Age UK, Later Life in the United Kingdom. Age UK (2019)
4. Rowe, J., Kahn, R.: Successful aging 2.0: conceptual expansions for the 21st century. J. Gerontol. Ser. B Psychol. Sci. Soc. Sci. **70**, 593–596 (2015)
5. World Health Organization. Ageing: Healthy ageing and functional ability, 26 October 2020. https://www.who.int/westernpacific/news/q-a-detail/ageing-healthy-ageing-and-functional-ability. Accessed 15 Nov 2020
6. Dodge, R., et al.: The challenge of defining wellbeing. Int. J. Wellbeing **2**, 222–235 (2012)
7. Ansari, L.: When We're 64: Your Guide to a Great Later Life. Bloomsbury Publishing PLC, London (2019)
8. Ball, M., Nanda, A.: Household attributes and the future demand for retirement housing. Int. J. Hous. Mark. Anal. **6**(1), 45–62 (2013)
9. House of Commons, Housing for Older People (2018)
10. Centre for Ageing Better, The role of home adaptations in improving later life (2017)
11. Carnemolla, P., Bridge, C.: Housing design and community care: how home modifications reduce care needs of older people and people with disability. Int. J. Env. Res. Public Health **16**, 1951 (2019)
12. Oswald, F., et al.: Relationships between housing and healthy aging in very old age. Gerontologist **47**, 96–107 (2007)
13. Oswald, F., et al.: The role of the home environment in middle and late adulthood, pp. 7–24 (2006)
14. Devlin, A.S.: Environmental Psychology and Human Well-Being: Effects of Built and Natural Settings. Elsevier Science & Technology, San Diego (2018)
15. Thordardottir, B., et al.: Factors associated with participation frequency and satisfaction among people applying for a housing adaptation grant. Scandinavian J. Occup. Therapy **23**(5), 347–356 (2016)
16. Luther, A., et al.: Identifying and validating housing adaptation client profiles - a mixed methods study. Disab. Rehabil. **42**(14), 2027–2034 (2020)
17. NHS UK. Home adaptations, 8 August 2018. https://www.nhs.uk/conditions/social-care-and-support-guide/care-services-equipment-and-care-homes/home-adaptations/29. Accessed 29 June 2020
18. DWELL Designing for Wellbeing in Environments for Later Life, Designing with Downsizers (2016)
19. Dickson, C., Hailey, D.: Just Living (2017)
20. Fänge, A., Iwarsson, S.: Accessibility and usability in housing: construct validity and implications for research and practice. Disab. Rehabil. **25**(23), 1316–1325 (2003)

21. Fänge, A., Iwarsson, S.: Changes in accessibility and usability in housing: an exploration of the housing adaptation process. Occup. Therap. Int. **12**(1), 44–59 (2005)
22. Iwarsson, S., Isacsson, Å.: Housing standards, environmental barriers in the home and subjective general apprehension of housing situation among the rural elderly. Scandinavian J. Occup. Therap. **3**, 52–61 (2009)
23. Bailey, C., et al.: "What? That's for old people, that." home adaptations, ageing and stigmatisation: a qualitative inquiry. Int. J. Environ. Res. Public Health **16**(24), 4989 (2019)
24. Carnemolla, P., Bridge, C.: Accessible Housing and Health-Related Quality of Life: Measurements of Wellbeing Outcomes Following Home Modifications. Arch Net-IJAR, vol. 10 (2016)
25. Carnemolla, P.: Ageing in place and the internet of things – how smart home technologies, the built environment and caregiving intersect. Vis. Eng. **6** (2018)
26. Brookfield, K., et al.: Perspectives on "Novel" techniques for designing age-friendly homes and neighborhoods with older adults. Int. J. Env. Res. Public Health **17**(5), 1800 (2020)
27. Boström, L., et al.: Health-related quality of life among people applying for housing adaptations: associated factors. Int. J. Env. Res. Public Health **15**(10), 2130 (2018)
28. Kylén, M., et al.: Home and health in the third age - methodological background and descriptive findings. Int. J. Env. Res. Public Health **11**(7), 7060–7080 (2014)
29. Kylén, M., et al.: The importance of the built environment in person-centred rehabilitation at home: study protocol. Int. J. Env. Res. Public Health **16**(13), 2409 (2019)
30. Wilson, G., et al.: The hidden impact of home adaptations: using a wearable camera to explore lived experiences and taken-for-granted behaviours. Health Soc. Care Commun. **27**(6), 1469–1480 (2019)
31. Muncie, S.: Older People and Housing. Age Scotland Orkney, Edinburgh (2019)
32. Hollinghurst, J., et al.: Do home modifications reduce care home admissions for older people? A matched control evaluation of the Care & Repair Cymru service in Wales. Age Ageing **49**(6), 1056–1061 (2020)
33. Lifetime Homes, Lifetime Homes Design Guide. Bracknell, Berkshire: IHS BRE Press (2011)
34. HM Government, Approved Document M. Category 2. Accessible and Adaptable Dwellings. 2015 Edition (2015)
35. HOME Coalition, HOME: Housing Made For Everyone Vision (2019)
36. HM Government, Approved Document M. Category 3. Wheelchair User Dwellings (2015)
37. Shin, J.-H.: Listen to the elders: design guidelines for affordable multifamily housing for the elderly based on their experiences. J. Housing Elderly **32**(2), 211–240 (2018)
38. Burton, E.J., Mitchell, L., Stride, C.B.: Good places for ageing in place: development of objective built environment measures for investigating links with older people's wellbeing. BMC Publ. Health **11**(1), 839 (2011)
39. National Records of Scotland. Highland Council Area Profile, 16 July 2020. https://www.nrs cotland.gov.uk/files/statistics/council-area-data-sheets/highland-council-profile.html
40. Scottish Government: Scotland's Wellbeing – Delivering the National Outcomes. The National Performance Framework Team, Edinburgh (2019)
41. Porteus, J.: Rural housing for an ageing population: preserving independence. In: HAPPI 4 (2018)
42. Scottish Government, Age Home and Community - a strategy for housing Scotlands Older people 2012–2021. Edinburgh (2011)
43. IKEA, Life at Home Report 2020: The big home reboot (2020)
44. World Health Organization. Older people & COVID-19 (2021). https://www.who.int/teams/social-determinants-of-health/demographic-change-and-healthy-ageing/covid-19. Accessed 9 Feb 2021

45. Office for National Statistics. Coronavirus and how people spent their time under lockdown, 28 March to 26 April 2020 (2020). https://www.ons.gov.uk/economy/nationalaccounts/satell iteaccounts/bulletins/coronavirusandhowpeoplespenttheirtimeunderrestrictions/28marchto 26april2020. Accessed 27 May 2020
46. Centre for Ageing Better, Homes for Life (2020)
47. Sikali, K.: The dangers of social distancing: How COVID-19 can reshape our social experience. J. Commun. Psychol. **48**(8), 2435–2438 (2020)
48. Ministry of Housing: Communities & Local Government, National Design Guide. Ministry of Housing Communities and Local Government, London (2019)
49. Best, R., Porteus, J.: HAPPI 3 housing our ageing population: positive ideas. Housing Learning and Improvement Network (LIN) (2016)
50. Homes and Community Agency, Housing our Ageing Population Panel for Innovation (HAPPI). Homes and Community Agency, London (2009)
51. The Highland Council, Design Brief: Building Homes for the Highlands. Firm Foundations (2017)
52. Kon, B., Lam, A., Chan, J.: Evolution of smart homes for the elderly. In: International World Wide Web Conference. International World Wide Web Conference Committee: Perth, Australia
53. BSI., Draft BS ISO 15928-7 Houses — Description of performance. Part 7: Accessibility and usability (2020)
54. National House Building Council Foundation, Homes Through the Decades (2016)
55. Smith, R.E., Quale, J.D.: Offsite architecture: constructing the future. Taylor & Francis Group, London (2017)
56. Vogler, A.: The house as a product. In: Mick, E. (ed.) Research in Architectural Engineering Series. IOS Press (2015)
57. Deakin, M., et al.: Increasing offsite housing construction in Scotland
58. An evidence base to support new policy and systems (2020)
59. Pittini, A., et al.: The State of Housing in the EU in 2017, H. Europe (2017)
60. Goulding, J.S., Rahimian, F.P.: Offsite Production and Manufacturing for Innovative Construction: People, Process and Technology. CRC Press LLC, Milton (2019)
61. Maguire, M.: Methods to support human-centred design. Int. J. Hum Comput Stud. **55**, 587–634 (2001)
62. Bowmast, N., Tait, M.: Nick Bowmast's Userpalooza: A Field Researcher's Guide. Nick Bowmast (2018)
63. ISO. ISO 13407:1999 Human-centred design processes for interactive systems (2020). https://www.iso.org/standard/21197.html.. Accessed 7 July 1999
64. ISO. ISO 9241-210:2019 Ergonomics of human-system interaction — Part 210: Human-centred design for interactive systems (2019). https://www.iso.org/standard/77520.html. Accessed 7 July 2020
65. Dovjak, M., Shukuya, M., Krainer, A.: User-centred healing-oriented conditions in the design of hospital environments. Int. J. Env. Res. Public Health **15**(10), 2140 (2018)
66. Agee, P., et al.: Toward a user-centered built environment. Sci. Technol. Built Environ. **26**(9), 1163–1164 (2020)
67. Vischer, J.C.: Towards a user-centred theory of the built environment. Build. Res. Inf. **36**(3), 231–240 (2008)
68. Agee, P., et al.: A human-centred approach to smart housing. Build. Res. Inf. **49**(1), 84–99 (2021)
69. Briede-Westermeyer, J.C., et al.: Mobile phone use by the elderly: relationship between usability, social activity, and the environment. Sustainability **12**(7), 2690 (2020)

70. Bittencourt, M.C., do Valle Pereira, V.L.D., Júnior, W.P.: The usability of architectural spaces: objective and subjective qualities of built environment as multidisciplinary construction. Procedia Manufact. **3**, 6429–6436 (2015)
71. Coskun, A., Gul, K., Bostan, I.: Is smart home a necessity or a fantasy for the mainstream user? a study on users' expectations of smart household appliances. Int. J. Des. **12**(1) (2018)
72. Baborska-Narożny, M., Stevenson, F.: Service controls interfaces in housing: usability and engagement tool development. Build. Res. Inf. Int. J. Res. Dev. Demonstr. **47**(3), 290–304 (2019)
73. Norman, D.A.: The Design of Everyday Things. Basic Books (2002)

Older Adults "Jump" into coDesiging a Digital Game: A Field Study

Liliana Vale Costa[1]([✉]) [iD], Ana Isabel Veloso[1] [iD], Liliana Sousa[2] [iD],
Michael Loizou[3] [iD], and Sylvester Arnab[3] [iD]

[1] DigiMedia, Department of Communication and Art, University of Aveiro, Aveiro, Portugal
{lilianavale,aiv}@ua.pt

[2] CINTESIS, Department of Education and Psychology, University of Aveiro, Aveiro, Portugal
lilianax@ua.pt

[3] Disruptive Media Learning Lab, Coventry University, Coventry, UK
{ab8703,aa8110}@coventry.ac.uk

Abstract. The aim of this paper is to contribute to establishing practices to involve adults aged 50 and over in the design of digital games within the paradigm of active ageing. This paper focuses on a component of a larger project entitled SERIOUS-GIGGLE integrated in the SEDUCE 2.0 research that enabled to develop the digital game JUMP that goes beyond illness recovery or skill maintenance, addressing active ageing. Using a Participatory Action Qualitative Research that deployed 64-session group discussions and participant observation of 33 learners at a Portuguese University of the Third Age, the necessary course of actions to involve the end-users in game design were identified. Results suggest four phases: 1. Validate the content and the materials that will be used during coDesign with experts in the area, using the Delphi method; 2. Carry out the activities in the end-user's places; 3. Design the game tool based on the end-users' context and the content validated by the experts during the previous phases; and 4. Validate the game-based product with the end-users. Literature is still scarce in giving standards for designing digital games for active ageing and most of the solutions on the market tend to focus on health and rehabilitation rather than on other dimensions, such as security and social participation.

Keywords: coDesign · Security · Social participation · Action Qualitative Research · Digital game

1 Introduction

The global ageing population has brought to the fore a renewed interest in identifying a set of strategies for increasing the participation of older adults in society [1–8]. In fact, the current framework of active ageing is launched by the World Health Organization [9], defined as the process of optimizing opportunities for health, participation, and security in order to enhance the quality of life as people age. The concept was further refined in 2010 with the addition of opportunities for lifelong learning to the definition [10], and a boom occurred in the development of the so-called 'technology for active

Q. Gao and J. Zhou (Eds.): HCII 2021, LNCS 12786, pp. 88–99, 2021.
https://doi.org/10.1007/978-3-030-78108-8_7

ageing' [11]. However, the current solutions in the market tend to overlook the end-user's involvement in the design process and are too much focused on health-related issues rather than embodying such important pillars of active ageing as security and participation in society [9]. The end-user's involvement in the design process is essential to understanding the context of the use of a certain technology and there is a lack of research in the use of coDesign with older adults [12]. Moreover, in the game sector, there is a need to document practices that need to be undertaken and in which phase of the product development cycle, which are relevant to build a certain empathy between the end-user and the interface and meeting the philosophy "for, with and by the users" [13].

Literature [7, 14] has shown that games can be beneficial to older adults' physical and mental health by fostering social connectedness and participation in daily life activities and contributing to neighborhood, sense of purpose, and a 'care for place' culture. Concomitantly, social disengagement is a key concern as it may affect both older adults' interpersonal activities and decisions in the political sphere [6]. Yet, in the specific case of games, coDesigning is a particular challenge because games are often considered as an art form [15] and a balance between the level of involvement of the end-users and the creativity and role of the design and development teams is needed. Literature shows that game design techniques and mechanics can be used to enable players to 'witness and experience' certain phenomenona, collect stories or/and testimonials, and present daily-life events [16, 17].

This study is part of a larger project that covers all pillars of active ageing, under the project SeriousGiggle that encompasses the development of the JUMP game, and health-related domains were reported in other publications [16, 18].

2   CoDesigning JUMP

CoDesign refers to the involvement of the end-users in the design process and may comprise the following techniques: BrainDraw and Group Elicitation Method (GEM); PICTIVE; Strategic Visioning and Future Workshops; Card Sorting; Low-tech Proto-types; Storyboarding and Scenario Building, Collaborative Analysis of Requirements and Design (CARD), and Contextual Inquiry.

The game JUMP was developed under the project SERIOUSGIGGLE integrated in the SEDUCE 2.0 research, with the purpose of encouraging a positive attitude towards the ageing process. The content covered was based on the WHO framework, being divided into the following themes: Health, Security and Participation in Society. The game premise was the following: "Sul, the city's fisherman, is tired of getting stuck to a routine that he never got used to. Depressed and isolated, Sul has to face the storyteller Nubel, who forces him to a time travel experience, in order to recover values and significant meaning to his own life." Although the game premise was a result of the team's creative authorship, the possibility to travel to different places as game activity was based on the participants' reported favorite activity during the co-design sessions. Therefore, time-traveling encompassed the following scenarios: 1) Paris, France 1948 (Palais de Chaillot in Paris, France, 1948 – The Universal Declaration of Human Rights); 2) Hizen, Japan 1709 (Hizen Province, The Art of Being a Samurai with Physical and Cognitive

Challenges); and 3) London, England 1895 (Scenarios of malnutrition and violation of basic Human Rights).

This paper focuses on 'Paris, 1948', i.e. missions related to 'Human Security' and 'Human Rights' that were introduced in order to create awareness of the role of institutions in Human Rights, through the use of history-related symbols (*e.g.* Palais de Chaillot) (Fig. 1). It is worth mentioning that the game settings were based on the place and date when the Universal Declaration of Human Rights was adopted since adventure games with problem-solving and history-based narratives are preferred by older adult gamers [16, 18].

Fig. 1. Game setting – Paris, 1948

Therefore, this paper aims to contribute to identify a set of practices on how to involve older adults in the design of a digital game for active ageing. The focus is on the variables of security and participation in society, which are the least considered pillars of active ageing within the game area.

3   Method

In this project, a Participatory Action Qualitative Research (PAR) was adopted in order to understand the meaning of a social and mediated experience [19] that is coDesigning a digital game (JUMP) for active ageing with a focus on the variables of security and participation in society. The PAR was chosen since it embraces [20]: (a) a holistic view of the phenomenon; (b) offer multiple perspectives and sources of information, and (c) context-awareness. Therefore, this method allows us to get a comprehensible knowledge of a phenomenon for obtaining the best solution and involve the participants in a cyclical study [21]. The Ethics Committee of the University of Aveiro (Resolution n. 3/2015) has approved this study.

3.1 Preparing the Involvement of End-Users

Before involving the end-users in the design process, experts in the area validated the materials and contents for the coDesign activities, using the Delphi method. The researchers developed the materials for debating two topics with the end-users. The first topic was the sense of security (Learning goals: Describe the rights associated with Human and environmental security; Apply the strategies of security and prevention in different contexts, and Build a learning program that encourages the sense of security). The second topic was participation in society (Learning goals: Identify some projects related to participation in society through the use of Information and Communication Technologies; and Build a learning program that encourages participation in society).

The Delphi method was employed in order to discuss the content and coDesign materials with a group of four experts in a wide range of fields: Gerontology, Psychology, Education, and Social Work. The Delphi technique is used to structure group communication when dealing with a complex problem, gathering experts' information and opinions towards the modus operandi, instruments, and materials used for assessing the participants' context, and co-design activities by using a questionnaire. Experts were asked to validate the materials considering: content; sequence of contents; and questionnaires in use. After having the co-design materials and surveys validated by the group of experts, the Universities of the Third Age were contacted in order to recruit older adult learners (50+ years old), who were available to be involved in the design process of a digital game.

3.2 Recruitment of Participants

The participants in this study were selected accordingly with the following criteria: (a) aged 50+ years old; (b) know how to read and write; (c) voluntary participation, and (d) interest in learning. The initial convenience sample that was involved in the co-design sessions consisted of 37 participants. Four participants did not fit within the age bracket and three did not complete all sessions. The total of participants was 33, 51.5% females; the average age was 67 years old (SD = 7.06, minimum = 55; maximum = 82) and the majority had between 10 and 14 years of schooling.

3.3 CoDesign Sessions

The coDesign sessions were then carried out from March 2015 to December 2016, enabling us to determine the context of use beyond the content, usability and accessibility issues. The global project comprised a total of 64 sessions (160 h) (Table 1), carried out with the following purposes: (a) understand the participants' context and their perception towards ageing (sense of security and participation in society); and (b) brainstorm the functionalities of a game-based learning program for active ageing. Although the process covered all the active ageing pillars (*i.e.* health, security, and participation in society), this paper will address solely security and social participation, with the aim of affecting both older adults' interpersonal activities and decisions in the political sphere.

The sessions specifically on the topics of security and participation in society are the five and six (Table 1).

Table 1. Sessions and activities: Project SERIOUSGIGGLE – SEDUCE 2.0, game JUMP

Designation	Activities
0 [March - 26th 2015, weekly]	Building alliances with the researcher
1 [March 6th, 2015]	*Presentation of the Research Project.* Introduce the researcher, the research project, procedures, the rationale for doing research, the main goals, the topics to be drawn during the course, and the chronogram of the learning sessions
2 [March 13th, 20th 2015]	*Debate on physical exercise for active ageing.* Discuss the role of leisure and physical exercise in encouraging active ageing; Build a learning programme that encourages physical exercise
3 [April 10th, 17th 2015]	*Debate on nutrition for active ageing.* Describe the factors that influence nutrition and the consequences of malnutrition; Identify the nutrients that exist in different foods and diets; Build a learning programme that encourages healthy diets
4 [April 24th, 2015]	*Debate on cognitive* activity. Discuss the role of leisure and cognitive activity in encouraging active ageing; Build a learning programme that encourages cognitive activity
5 [May 08th, 2015]	*Debate on the sense of security.* Describe the rights associated with Human and environmental security; Apply the strategies of security and prevention in different contexts; Build a learning programme that encourages the sense of security
6 [May 15th, 2015]	*Debate on participation in society.* Identify some projects related to participation in society through the use of Information and Communication Technologies; Build a learning programme that encourages the participation in society
7 [May 22th, 2015]	*Debate on the process of* learning. Look at the different factors of the learning process; Discuss different elements of the learning programme

(*continued*)

Table 1. (*continued*)

Designation	Activities
8 [Oct 6th 2015–Dec. 6th, 13th 2016, weekly]	*Interaction with Information and Communication Technologies.* Identify the learners' needs and motivations to use and learn Information and Communication Technologies, as well as barriers

Like all sessions, these two began with a welcoming message and icebreaker questions followed by a survey or discussion towards a plan for preventing and addressing top threats to Human security. It should also be stated that the project was developed with the principle of reciprocity and collaboration, i.e. researchers and participants build an alliance and benefit from these interactions, mostly through knowledge sharing, context-aware variables, and strength of the relationships (sessions 0 and 8, Table 1).

3.4 Session 'Sense of Security'

Regarding the topic "Sense of Security", the sessions aimed to (a) identify some projects/initiatives that encourage participation in society through the use of digitally-mediated products; (b) describe the rights associated with Human and environmental security; (c) apply the strategies of security and prevention in different contexts, and (d) build a game-based learning program that creates awareness to Human threats and encourages participation in society. The topics covered were based on the definition of Active Ageing pillar "Security" (WHO 2002): the concept of Human security; types of Human security; Human rights; Human development and social intervention policies; intervention policies in the environment; intervention policies in education; and intervention policies in health. Extra classes on Information and Communication Technologies (ICT) were given in order to gain the participants' confidence and assess the participants' motivations, interaction patterns, and difficulties when using ICT.

The methods in the sessions were group discussions, using semi-structured open-ended questions to generate new insights into the design issues of a game-based approach for community engagement and security and participation in society. Participant observation was used through an observation protocol with the following structure: reference number, place, date and time, activity and goals, portraits/ description of the main actions with the participants' statements, and references to audio-visual materials/photos/documents. The participants were invited to answer a questionnaire about the perceived sense of Security and Human Rights. They were given a list of statements based on the possible threats to Human Security ascertained by the United Nations [22]. The threats are to the survival, subsistence, Human dignity, economy, environment, personal security, threats to community, and abuse of Human Rights. A 5-point Likert scale ranging from 1 (totally disagree) to 5 (totally agree) was used to rate the sentences. Beyond these specific threats, the statement "I do not feel threats to Human Security" was added in order to assess the participants' overall perception of their sense of security and reduce acquiescence bias. Globally (Table 2) participants tend to feel safe at home and have someone to help in case of illness or emergency. In terms of the group discussions, the participants had to define a plan for preventing and addressing the top threats to Human Security. The following scenario was posed: "People are not aware of their rights. As a policymaker and citizen, it is your mission to solve this problem." The participants were divided into 2 groups of 15 participants, who had about 10 min to discuss the problem and how to solve it. In addition, the following strategies were used to ensure internal validity: (a) carrying out the design session iteratively with the group; (b) peer debriefing for the content used in the sessions; and (c) triangulating multiple sources of data collected (i.e. observation field notes, survey results).

Table 2. Sessions and activities: Project SERIOUSGIGGLE – SEDUCE 2.0, game JUMP

Statements	Mean	SD
1. I feel safe in my home	4.10	0.94
2. I feel safe outside home	3.13	1.21
3. I feel discriminated against for some reason	1.94	1.35
4. I feel safe about my health	3.65	1.17
5. I feel threatened by the environment	3.31	1.20
6. I feel threatened or harassed	1.90	1.51
7. I feel pressure to practice religion	1.26	0.99
8. I feel my rights as citizen are respected	3.48	1.53
9. I have someone who can help me in case of illness or emergency	4.03	0.82
10. I do not feel threats to my Human Security	3.03	1.68

3.5 Session 'Participation in Society'

The participants were also given a list of statements with a 5-point Likert scale ranging from 1 to 5 relative to Human Rights based on the United Nations report [22] (Table 3). The rights are freedom from discrimination, freedom from violence, social security, health (healthcare), property and inheritance rights, continuing education, and participate in political and cultural decisions, to work and have access to justice.

Most of the participants feel that they have access to goods and services regardless of their age, gender or physical condition ($M = 4.3$, $SD = 0.75$) (Table 3). One of the services that they find to have access to is relative to the health sector ($M = 4.30$, $SD = 0.95$). However, they do not feel that their participation in political decisions is valued ($M = 1.73$, $SD = 1.82$).

A group discussion was carried out in this session in order to gather the participants' perspective to ways that they can participate in society through the intervention in creating solutions and awareness to Human Rights.

The group discussions were carried out in order to define a plan for addressing two out of the eight of the Millennium Development Goals and the participants chose

Table 3. Participants' perception towards Human Rights

Statements	Mean	SD
1. I have access to goods and services regardless of my age, gender or physical condition	4.30	0.75
2. I feel protected from verbal, sexual, financial, psychological abuse…	3.57	1.59
3. I feel that I have access to social protection	1.94	1.35
4. I have access to the health system	3.90	1.39
5. I feel threatened by the environment	4.30	0.95
6. I have access to learning/training initiatives	3.58	1.42
7. I feel that my participation in the political decisions is valued	1.73	1.82
8. I have access to justice and judicial remedies	2.59	2.02
9. I feel protected against material goods	3.38	1.41
10. I feel that my rights are respected	3.46	1.55

"eradicate extreme poverty and hunger" and "ensure environmental sustainability". For each goal, they decided to define: "intervention/resources", "strategies" and "impact." The participants proposed for the following strategies to overcome the goal "eradicate extreme poverty and hunger": reuse wastes; minimize social gaps; provide access to water supply; and run learning programs to manage resources.

In this process of problem-solving, participants suggest four Phases to tackle these societal problems: 1. Create awareness to Human Rights; 2. Educate to Human Rights and perceived threats to Human Security; 3. Simulate real scenarios and encourage changes in behaviors; and 4. Connect the learning content and goals to daily activities. Figure 2 shows an illustrative example of the application of problem-solving, using scenario building.

As a result, a history-based game scenario in which the Human Rights were at risk was simulated, aiming to encourage the players' action.

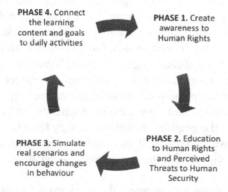

Fig. 2. Example of the application of problem-solving, using scenario building

4 Practices for CoDesigning a Digital Game on Security and Social Participation

The results of this research give two main insights: (A) Four phases of the end-user's involvement in the design process of a digitally mediated tool; and (B) Set of design recommendations to foster security and participation in society.

(A) Phases of the end-user's involvement in the design process of a digitally mediated tool.

Following the procedures undertaken in the Method section, the users' involvement in the design process of digitally-mediated tools can be divided into the following four phases:

i.   Validate the content and materials that will be used during codesign with experts in the area, using the Delphi method;
ii. Carry out the activities in the end-users' places;
iii. Design the game-based tool based on the end-users' context and the contents validated by the experts during the previous phases; and
iv. Validate the game-based product with the end-users.

(B) Set of design recommendations to foster security and participation in society.

During the phase "Validate the Game-based product with the end-users", the following design recommendations to address games that foster security and participation in society can be pointed out:

i.   Offer the possibility of using a game-based tool at home but assist the adult learners in outdoor activities, since they mainly feel safe at home;
ii. Design missions that ask the participants to act upon their environment and political decisions and increase awareness to Human Rights through visual novels. The purpose of visual novels is twofold: give a sense of purpose to the activity and create empathy with a game character to model a behaviour. Few participants felt that their participation in political decisions was valued, and self-expression should also be strengthened with the link to social media and communities;
iii. Simulate real scenarios and encourage changes in behaviour by giving it a purpose through storytelling and providing a 'witnessing experience' through the use of hints and schemas in the game scenario in which the participants have to interfere. In the participants' observation diary, the researchers note: "Relative to the game, the participants liked the graphics, narrative and they found it easier to interact with the mouse. They have also revealed that in Paris, there should be hints indicating the poster 'Human Rights' and the newspapers' seller were clickable and opened different missions.";
iv. Foster cognitive challenges to improve the participants' cognitive capacity. Their main motivation to play digital games was to train their cognitive capacity and

games should enable them to practice Problem-solving, Memory and Attention, Logic and Reaction Time. Education to Human Rights and Perceived Threats to Human Security should be performed through these cognitive challenges in the game;

v. Connect the learning content and goals to daily activities, encouraging the players' search for information, retaining information and creating awareness of non-governmental organizations' (NGOs) actions. As one participant states: "As long as the learning content is suitable for our daily lives, it is fine." The participants also suggested to establish a link between recent news and Violation of Human Rights, Petitions and Initiatives of the International Amnesty and other organisations.

Together these results provide insight into a set of practices on how to involve older adults in the design of a digital game for active ageing with a focus on the variables of security and participation in society.

5   Final Considerations

The aim of this study was to identify a set of practices on how to involve older adults in the design of a digital game for active ageing with a focus on the variables of security and participation in society. In specific, the procedures to involve the end-users in the design process of a game-based tool, and the design recommendations to foster security and participation in society in older adult learners of the Universities of the Third Age. Results suggest four phases for involving the older adults in the design process of a game-based tool: (i) validate the content and the materials that will be used during coDesign with experts in the area, using the Delphi method; (ii) carry out the activities in the end-users' places; (iii) design the game tool based on the end-users' context and the content validated by the experts during the previous phases; and (iv) validate the game-based product with the end-users.

In terms of the codesign recommendations to foster security and participation in society, results have identified the following phases that are essential to the game design process: Phase 1. Create awareness to Human Rights; Phase 2. Educate to Human Rights and perceived threats to Human Security; Phase 3. Simulate real scenarios and encourage changes in behaviours; and Phase 4. Connect the learning content and goals to daily activities. Based on these phases and the end-users' feedback on the game prototype, the following recommendations can be suggested: (a) offer the possibility of using a game-based learning programme at home but assist the adult learner in outdoor activities; (b) design missions that ask the participants to act upon their environment and political decisions; (c) simulate real scenarios and encourage changes in behaviour by giving it a purpose through storytelling and providing a 'witnessing experience'; (d) foster cognitive challenges to improve the participants' cognitive capacity; and (e) connect the learning content and goals to daily activities, encouraging the players' search for information, retaining information and creating awareness of the Non-governmental Organizations' (NGO) actions. The application of a PAR in this context differ from regular Participatory design by avoiding abstraction-related activities and low fidelity prototypes and establishing strong empathetic connections with the product/service, relying on scenario-building and contextual information.

The small sample size and the lack of an instrument to design and assess the effectiveness of digitally mediated artefacts to boost community engagement and adherence to societal initiatives make this study exploratory. Thus, further work needs to be done in order to improve the game prototype, taking into account the identified design recommendations and construct a scale for assessing its effectiveness, extend the sample and compare the results obtained with other initiatives.

Acknowledgements. This work was supported by the research project SEDUCE 2.0 - Use of Communication and Information in the miOne online community by senior citizens, which includes the SERIOUSGIGGLE project and the game JUMP. The SEDUCE 2.0 project is funded by FCT – Fundação para a Ciência e a Tecnologia, I.P., COMPETE 2020, Portugal 2020 and European Union, under the European Regional Development Fund, POCI-01-0145-FEDER-031696 SEDUCE 2.0.

References

1. Adler, G., Schwartz, J., Kuskowski, M.: An exploratory study of older adults' participation in civic action. Clin. Gerontol. **31**(2), 65–75 (2007). https://doi.org/10.1300/J018v31n02_05
2. Erlinghagen, M., Hank, K.: The participation of older Europeans in volunteer work. Ageing Soc. **26**(04), 567–584 (2006). https://doi.org/10.1017/s0144686x06004818
3. Marchand, I.: Stories of contemporary aging: An analysis of "lived" citizenship in later life. J. Gerontol. Soc. Work **61**(5), 472–491 (2018). https://doi.org/10.1080/01634372.2017.142 0001
4. Narushima, M.: A gaggle of raging grannies: the empowerment of older canadian women through social activism. Int. J. Lifelong Educ. **23**(1), 23–42 (2004). https://doi.org/10.1080/0260137032000172042
5. Noreau, L., et al.: Measuring social participation: reliability of the LIFE-H in older adults with disabilities. Disab. Rehabil. **26**(6), 346–352 (2004). https://doi.org/10.1080/096382804 10001658649
6. Strate, J.M., et al.: Life span civic development and voting participation. Am. Polit. Sci. Rev. **83**(2), 443–464 (1989). https://doi.org/10.2307/1962399
7. Tomioka, K., Kurumatani, N., Hosoi, H.: Social participation and cognitive decline among community-dwelling older adults: a community-based longitudinal study. J. Gerontol. Ser. B Psychol. Sci. Soc. Sci. (2018). https://doi.org/10.1093/geronb/gbw059
8. Wiles, J.L., Jayasinha, R.: Care for place: the contributions older people make to their communities. J. Aging Stud. **27**(2), 93–101 (2013). https://doi.org/10.1016/j.jaging.2012. 12.001
9. World Health Organization - WHO. Active aeging: a policy framework. World Health Organization, Geneva (2002)
10. Ponse to the Longevity Revolution. Rio de Janeiro: International Longevity Centre Brazil (2015)
11. Felsted, K.F., Wright, S.D.: Toward Post Ageing: Technology in an Ageing Society. Springer International Publishing, Switzerland (2014)
12. Xie, B.: Civic engagement among older Chinese internet users. J. Appl. Gerontol. **27**(4), 424–445 (2008). https://doi.org/10.1177/0733464808315292

13. Parra, C., Andrea, V.D., Giacomin, G.: Enabling community participation of senior citizens through participatory design and ICT. In: CIRN 2012 Community Informatics Conference: "Ideals meet Reality", November 2012
14. Wiles, J.L., Jayasinha, R.: Careforplace: the contributions older people make to their communities. J. Aging Stud. **27**(2), 93–101 (2013)
15. Costikyan, G.: I have no words & i must design: toward a critical vocabulary for games. In: CGDC Conference Proceedings of the Computer Games and Digital Cultures Conference, Finland (2002)
16. Costa, L.V., et al.: Games for active ageing, well-being and quality of life: a pilot study. Behav. Inf. Technol. **37**(8), 842–854 (2018). https://doi.org/10.1080/0144929x.2018.1485744
17. Werbach, K., Hunter, D.: For the Win: How Game Thinking Can Revolutionize Your Business. Wharton Digital Press, Philadelphia (2012)
18. Costa, L.V., Veloso, A.I.: "Game-based psychotherapy" for active ageing: a game design proposal in non-game context. In: TISHW 2016 - 1st International Conference on Technology and Innovation in Sports, Health and Wellbeing, Proceedings (2016). https://doi.org/10.1109/TISHW.2016.7847788
19. Silverman, D.: Doing qualitative research: A practical handbook, 4th edn. SAGE Publications Ltd, London (2013)
20. Tracy, S.J.: Qualitative Research Methods: Collecting Evidence, Crafting Analysis, Communicating Impact. Wiley, Sussex (2012)
21. McIntyre, A.: Participatory Action. SAGE Publishing, Thousand Oaks (2008)
22. United Nations: Human Development Report Published for the UN Development Programme (UNDP). Oxford University Press, New York, Oxford (1994)

Expansion of Design Thinking Method: A Case Study of a Senior-Friendly Online Survey System

Danyang Wang and Hsien-Hui Tang[✉]

National Taiwan University of Science and Technology, Taipei, Taiwan
drhhtang@gapps.ntust.edu.tw

Abstract. Facing with the aging society, more and more companies are moving their customer segments of their products and services to the elderly users, exploring their needs and pain points. The online survey is useful but relatively complex for elderly users. So, what challenges will the designers face for a senior-friendly system, and how to deal with them? This research uses the LELEHO online survey system as an example to discuss how the design thinking methods can deal with the challenges from the complex senior-friendly design in reality. The result summarized the challenges faced by designers who design for the elderly user group, and proposed strategies for the senior-friendly design based on case experience, simultaneously showed how to properly deal with it through design thinking methods. In addition, the enlightenment of this research is that when facing practical problems, design thinking should pay attention to the principle of pragmatic innovation. It is necessary to improve the design details according to the situation and cooperate with practical design methods to truly complete each level of design purpose.

Keywords: Design thinking · Senior-friendly design · Case study · Online survey

1 Introduction

With the decline of global fertility rates and the increase in human life expectancy over the past 50 years, an aging population has rapidly become a worldwide problem. By 2050, about 50% of the population of mainland China and Taiwan are projected to be over 50 years old. Facing with the aging society, it seems that we need more information from older adults to better accommodate their attitudes and preferences for various design artifacts as well as for various services that help their wellbeing. More and more companies are moving their customer segments of their products and services to the elderly users, exploring their needs and pain points.

For research the needs of people, face-to-face research methods such as interviews or focus groups are often effective ways to obtain deep insights and the contexts. However, the rapid change and heterogeneous nature of the aging population prevent these

© Springer Nature Switzerland AG 2021
Q. Gao and J. Zhou (Eds.): HCII 2021, LNCS 12786, pp. 100–113, 2021.
https://doi.org/10.1007/978-3-030-78108-8_8

methods to effectively and efficiently to explore the majority of the elderly group. Questionnaire surveys are more effective for collecting extensive user information and laying a foundation for follow-up research. With the appearance of email surveys in the 1980s and the initial application of online surveys in the 1990s, the internet revolutionized questionnaire-based research methodology [1]. Online surveys remain a critical means of collecting user information due to their low cost and high efficiency; the ease with which they can be recycled; and the possibility of accessing specific ethnic groups [2–4].

However, there is limited research in using online surveys to obtain information from elderly groups. The typical online survey platform is relatively complicated and unfriendly especially for senior users who have limited experience with information technology (IT). There are many mature online survey platforms on the market today. Commonly-used platforms in Chinese communities include Survey Monkey, Questionnaire Star, Google Forms, and Tencent Questionnaire. Unfortunately, none of these online questionnaire systems have optimized versions suitable for people with limited IT experience, so they are not friendly for senior users.

Elderly people are the least presence on the internet. This group is most affected by the digital divide, with less Internet access, knowledge, and use [5]. Usability is one of the most important factors that affect the acceptance of product and service systems by elderly users [6]. Moreover, the online survey platform is relatively complex for elderly users. So, what challenges will the designers face for establishing a senior-friendly online survey system, and how to deal with them?

Design thinking is a user-centered innovation process which helps to develop empathy with target audience. It is often used to solve unknown or complex design issues [7]. In the face of the various challenges of senior-friendly design, how design thinking methods can assist designers develop solutions to establish a senior-friendly online survey system?

This research uses the LELEHO online survey system as an example to discuss how the design thinking methods can deal with the challenges from the complex senior-friendly design in reality. While the research presents the practical value of design thinking, it also analyzes the implementation details and reflects on the revision of theory and practice. It will also help the advancement of design thinking research and has academic value. There are three research objectives:

1. Sort out the characteristics of senior-friendly design issues, and what design challenges of designers when seeking solutions;
2. Put forward suggestions for the senior-friendly design for reference in subsequent design projects, and summarize how the design thinking methods can help designers cope with design challenges;
3. Discuss how to expand the connotation of the design thinking method when entering the real field to solve practical problems for special user groups.

2 Background

This section will discuss the following questions from the elderly design and design thinking methods: 1) What are the unique needs and challenge for the senior-friendly design from the elders' physical and psychological characteristics; 2) How existing methods deal with the elderly design issues; and 3) Based on its principles and characteristics, whether the design thinking method can meet above challenges.

2.1 Design for the Elderly Users

As WHO recently pointed out, when it comes to health, there is no "typical" older person [8]. The degenerative process of physical, mental, social happen gradually along the way to getting older. Their memory and physical and mental functions are also diminishing, such as the response becomes slow [9], poor body coordination [10], and so on. These degradations significantly affect the experience of interaction with the digital device or system for the elders, namely the usability issues occur during the process. Recently research summarized the influence of aging barriers on digital computer use experienced by older adults and made a list of cognitive, physical ability, perception, and motivational aging barriers related to the usability of digital technologies [11].

Those mentioned above physical and psychological degradation of the elderly put forward higher requirements for the elderly design. For example, font size, text layout, navigation, color adaption, operation feedback, etc. [12, 13] In particular, in the online survey scenarios, the age-related limitations affect the ability of the elderly users to use smartphones or computers, including vision, hearing, cognitive and motor function limitations [14].

Based on empirical research, the National Institute of Aging (NIA) and the National Library of Medicine (NLM) developed 25 recommendations for designing a senior-friendly website [13]. The recommendations cover three topics: designing readable text, improving the user's memory and understanding of website content, and increasing the ease of navigation. In addition to web design for computers, the popularity of mobile devices has led to a growing body of academic research focused on the design of touchscreen-based smartphone interfaces. A throughout the review of studies on mobile interface design for seniors classified the information contained in guidelines and checklists into different categories, such as gesture, feedback, font size, button size, etc. [15].

Various senior-friendly design guidelines provide practical references for web and mobile interface design for elderly users. However, there are still very few exemplary cases to illustrate how to design a suitable interface that meets the usage needs of seniors. Further, Hart, Chaparro, and Halcomb [16] showed that, even if a website meets senior-friendly design guidelines and improves the success rate of a given task, it may still not promote efficiency or user preferences and satisfaction during operation. Therefore, following the design guidelines alone is insufficient for creating a truly senior-friendly user interface. Simultaneous usability testing is therefore needed to assist in design decision-making and confirm the effectiveness of the design elements. Therefore, a design method focusing on user needs and feedback, dynamic adjustment, and follow-up may be relatively more competent.

2.2 Design Thinking Method

The term Design Thinking has existed for a long time in design research. It was used to explore how designers solve wicked problems, and it is also a key issue in Design Studies. IDEO, which has been promoting design thinking for a long time, has a more comprehensive definition of it:

Design thinking is a human-centered approach to innovation that draws from the designer's toolkit to integrate the needs of people, the possibilities of technology, and the requirements for business success [17].

The understanding and interpretation of design thinking by different organizations are divided into different stages, corresponding to different research goals and design output. However, some common characteristics and principles of design thinking can be seen, such as emphasizing that design thinking is user-centric, multi-discipline collaboration, repeated iteratively through prototypes. All descriptions of the design thinking process highlight the iterative cycle for exploring design insights and guidelines: generating innovative concepts through in-depth user research, and then prototyping and testing, finally choose the best solution [18].

The origin of design thinking is not academic research or theoretical construction, but the process and experience accumulated in the actual work of design innovation. It does not provide a prescriptive model for people to follow, but a descriptive model allowing people to understand the design process in the real context. It makes a design develop from a vague concept to a clear outline of details, and stops until an ideal and feasible solution appear. Therefore, design thinking can be used as an appropriate method to explore the unknown and complex design issues, such as elderly design, and try to help designers overcome the design challenges caused by the huge cognition and experience differences between the elderly users and them.

Most of the design thinking literature is the sharing of cases, but there are few discussions on implementation details. Micheli et al. [19] analyzed 104 core articles in his systematic literature review of design thinking and deduced the eight categories of tools and ten attributes. It can be seen that the design thinking method is biased towards practice-based theories; most of the research is operated on a case study. Therefore, this research also continues the tradition of describing its different aspects based on cases to clarify the value of design thinking methods in the real context. Moreover, this study also analyzes the operational details to reflect on the revision of theory and practice of design thinking method, giving an academic value.

3 Method

The focus of this research is to present how the design thinking method can help establish a senior-friendly online survey system, and finally complete a large-scale trend survey for the elders. Qualitative case studies are a more appropriate method. Case studies have the characteristics of specificity, descriptiveness, and heuristics [20], which can present complex and dynamic facts and gain insight into the fundamental issues of the research. Based on the case in the reality, this study records and analyzes on the development of the entire project and discusses how the design thinking method play its value in senior-friendly design.

3.1 The Case of the LELEHO Online Survey

LELEHO survey is an online survey activity in Taiwan. The purpose of the survey was to collect public opinion data and provide solutions to seniors by encouraging elders to voice their needs, pain points, and expectations actively. LELEHO invited people over 50, and particularly those over 65, to participate in the survey and share it with their peers via social media. The aim was to improve seniors' future lives by building a senior-friendly society. This research chose this project reasons:

- It follows the design thinking process and method, which can be used as a complete and typical case to summarize the experience of the design thinking method applied to senior-friendly design and provide a reference for follow-up research.
- After completing the system design, many elderly users filled in the questionnaire by themselves after launch, we find it can be a successful case to analyze and summarize how to optimize a senior-friendly design through design thinking.

3.2 Design Process and Analysis

According to the research purpose, the case study divided into two-phase: first, record the overall process and details of each design stage of the case through participation; second, analyze and reflect on the various elements and critical points, then explore in depth from different perspectives: how design thinking methods can help to response challenges in real-world cases, and their value to related issues.

Among them, the design stage can be divided into three stages: problem distillation, design iteration, and practice diffusion according to the core characteristics of design thinking method, corresponding to the Inspire-Ideate-Implement proposed by IDEO [17], as shown in Fig. 1:

1. **Problem distillation:** understand users and define problems. In this stage, we need to recruit elderly users to conduct usability tests and interviews on the existing online survey system, to understand their habits of using digital devices, and the usability of the interface.

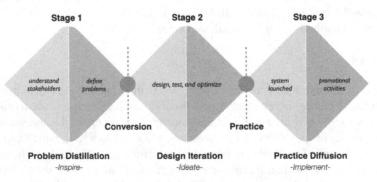

Fig. 1. The three design stages.

2. **Design iteration:** design, test, and optimize. Based on the insights of the problem distillation stage, we need to optimize the design of the existing system, make an interactive prototype, follow the principles of agile development for user testing, collect feedback, and continue to iterate.

3. **Practice diffusion:** final test and promotional activities after the system launched. On the one hand, the test results are compared with the initial system to evaluate the optimized design effect. On the other hand, summarize the future optimization direction combined with offline activities.

4 Challenges and Strategies of Senior-Friendly Design Projects

Based on the case experience of establishing a senior-friendly online survey system through design thinking, the research analyzes and summarizes how the design team uses the design thinking method to deal with the challenges brought by the complex senior-friendly design issues in the real field. The analysis resulted in the identification of three key themes: 1) gain empathy; 2) usability test method; 3) design content. Hereafter are the challenges and strategies of senior-friendly design learned by the case.

4.1 Start with Empathy

In addition to age, young designers and elderly users are also very different in physiological conditions and life experiences. Therefore, it is not easy to design products or services that truly meet the needs of elderly people [21]. The design thinking method emphasizes user-oriented and advocates that designers should explore the needs of elderly people for products and services based on empathy, which needs to be the basic work of the design and development team [17]. Based on the case, this study analyzes and summarizes two key strategies to deal with the challenge of gaining empathy: 1) First determine the target audience and its characteristics, 2) understand the real needs through user research.

Clarify the Target Audience
Clearly defining the characteristics and ranges of the target audience of the design will help to focus on the design purpose and evaluate the design results. In quantifying the indicators of user clustering, in addition to the support of the relevant literature, the actual usage condition of users is also very important.

Taking our case as an example: with reference to Chadwick-Dias et al. [22], the case identified one of the grouping axes of the user group was the experience of smart devices, as shown in Fig. 2, but how to define the baseline also needs to consider the specific situation in the social context to make dynamic adjustments, for example, in terms of experience with digital products, we found that the Taiwanese seniors used LINE as a starting point for accessing smartphones. Therefore, in the test we used "have a LINE account and can use LINE to send and receive messages to socialize" as a baseline. We classified seniors who could send and receive E-mail, do online shopping, and use cloud drives as experienced elderly users.

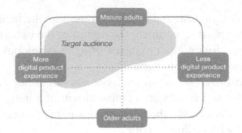

Fig. 2. Classification of elderly users and the scope of target audience.

Understand the Real Needs of Elderly Users. During the need research, the design team will also encounter the following challenges: on the one hand, the cognitive abilities of elderly users will decline along with aging, making a physical and psychological impact. it will easier for them to confine their imagination of new technologies and products to past experiences [21], making it challenging to describe future life and potential needs; on the other hand, when describing needs, they are more passive than young people and are not good at expressing their opinions. Young design teams tend to underestimate the potential challenges of elderly people in the face of new things. Therefore, user-centered is particularly important. It is necessary to incorporate real users for observation, interview, and testing at different stages of the design to continuously confirm the authenticity of user needs.

Constantly and User-Centered Usability Tests. Many seniors did not have contact with computers and networks from childhood, and as a result, they have very different operational habits than young people. Therefore, during the development of any senior-friendly design, it is necessary to involve elderly users in usability problems inquiry. Inviting the actual participation of elderly users in all stages of the design development can improve product acceptance, usefulness, information quality, and utilization [23].

Czaja et al. [21] proposed that older adults as a group tend to be more heterogeneous than younger adults. That means that older adults vary a great deal in their capabilities, limitations, and experience with technology. During the case study, we found that the diversity of the elderly is much more abundant than we think. As we do not know enough about the elderly, we need to continuously explore and confirm the needs of elderly users through user research.

Design thinking advocates the use of prototypes for testing so that users can have a real interactive experience, which can provide designers with direct behavioral feedback and help designers accurately sort out problems. However, it should be noted that When iterative design and testing in ordinary design projects, low-fidelity design prototypes can be used to bring interviewees into using context by verbal description, but elderly users have little experience with digital products. There are higher requirements for the fidelity of the test prototype. High-fidelity prototypes can provide users with a more realistic operating experience so that designers can obtain more direct feedback.

In terms of iterative design, when facing time pressure in the real context, the design team needs to react quickly and constantly modify, and make minor optimizations after each test. Therefore, it is hard to achieve a clear stage or complete iteration cycle which the theory described. This is also one of the differences between the design thinking method and its theoretical model in the context of reality.

4.2 Comprehensive Consideration of Design Contents

Salman, Ahmad, and Sulaiman [24] found that the usability problems were not only due to UI design, but some of the problems were also due to difficulties of the elderly in performing the gestures which applied to the corresponding task. Other than that, the clarity of content is also essential in a case such as the online survey system. We found that even if usability problems associated with an operation are solved, if seniors cannot understand the content, it will be a significant obstacle to their filling out the questionnaire. In other words, for the online survey system, the usability is more than the interactive level which including the user interface and gesture, sometimes the understandable content is more important.

If taking the design contents in the case corresponds to the five levels of user experience elements proposed by Garrett [25], we will find that it was essentially solving a complex user experience design problem. As shown in Fig. 3. The principles of design thinking methods play a role in different design levels. The following description is based on different user experience element levels.

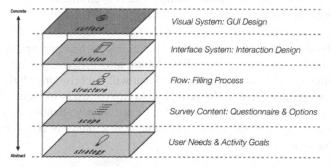

Fig. 3. Correspondence between system design content and UX elements at various levels

Strategy Level. In the early stages of design, based on the principle of user-centered, the design team conducted user interviews and usability tests to contact with real elderly users to understand their behavior and establish empathy. In addition to user needs, the team also needs to understand the goals of the activity initiators and organizers. For example, it is necessary to attract more elders to participate and voice for their future life through the meaningful questionnaire content design, and spread them to friends spontaneously, achieving the diffusion effect of "snowballing". Therefore, the design team needs to cooperate closely with the organizer or other stakeholders to clarify the right direction for subsequent system design at the initial strategy level.

Scope Level. The online questionnaire content comes from the four-year qualitative interview data related to the aging issue by the research team and has undergone modification before being converted into a questionnaire. However, there are still many problems caused by the content or improper wording in the test at different design stages. Based on the principles of design thinking of multi-discipline cooperation and rapid iteration, the design team invited experts to participate in the content's semantic test and revise the wording and adjust the content and presentation. Examples of content optimization are as below:

- Present the questionnaire in a more colloquial way;
- Give the content practical meaning. E.g. Change the "diagnosis" in the ending page to "healthy tips", and recommend related articles based on the pain points selected when the elders filled out the questionnaire.

Structure Level. The cognition of the older adult is gradually deteriorating, and the experience of using digital products is insufficient. Through multiple tests, it is found that the elders cannot read and memorize too much information at the same time, and easily disturbed by the irrelevant information. Moreover, difficulties are often encountered in inputting something. These difficulties bring higher requirements to the questionnaire filling process design. Based on prototype testing and user interviews, the questionnaire filling process has undergone several rounds of iterations. Figure 4 has shown the comparison of the filling process between the initial version and the final launched version. The core principle is not to interrupt the filling process to ensure the smooth submission of questionnaire data. Examples of process optimization are as below:

- Avoid interfering information during user operations, such as pop-ups after clicking;
- Unlock the clickable state of the next page button after swipe down to browse all the contents of the page, to avoid the question finish without browsing all the items;
- Set an encouragement page in the process and inform users of their questionnaire filling progress. The use of encouragement page should pay attention to (a) Clear text reminder to continue; (b) The number of reminders should not be too many, which will affect the flow.

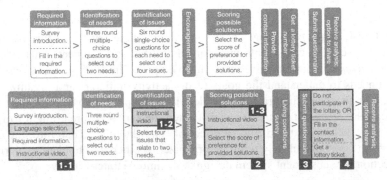

Fig. 4. Comparison of the initial and final launched version of questionnaire filling process

Skeleton Level. When using smartphones, elderly users may encounter difficulties in carrying out meticulous operations, they often repeatedly and rapidly tapped the screen with a significant force, leading to them accidentally touching other features on the page. Therefore, the complex interactive model may bring more cognitive load. Example of interaction optimization is as below:

- User operations were simplified to two simple gestures of clicking and scrolling to reduce operation difficulty.

Surface Level. As visual abilities decreased with age, the elders have higher requirements for color and contrast. They tended to pay attention to the manifest content and often avoided the content written in smaller text (such as the prompt descriptions for some questions) unless they were having difficulty with a section. Examples of optimization for Graphical User Interface are as below:

- The key visual elements are familiar to elderly users and embody a cordial feeling. The main color of the system was adjusted to warm bright orange to encourage senior users' participation.
- For consistency, all buttons were set to orange as a clickable action hint, and during operation and selection the buttons with shadows when clicked, providing clear visual feedback (Fig. 5).

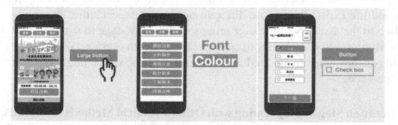

Fig. 5. Examples of optimization for Graphical User Interface (Color figure online)

5   Discussion: Expansion of Design Thinking Methods

More and more developers are using design thinking with other design and development methods, such as agile and lean [17]. As mentioned in the previous section, this research case takes the design thinking method as the basic framework. Moreover, when carrying out the system design details, it still needs to cooperate with the experience design elements to check the design rationality of each part. Besides, when the system is officially launched, how to carry out publicity and promotion in reality also should be considered in order to achieve the goal that the organizers want more elders to fill in questionnaires and widely collect feedback.

Therefore, this study believes that the good operation of innovation projects from initiation to implementation cannot be separated from the three levels of the pragmatic innovation process. Similarly, Design Council [26] has also updated its classic Double Diamond model. In addition to the design process, principles and tools, it takes cooperation between stakeholders and organizations to consider design innovation and highlights the importance of practical implementation.

Problem Distillation Stage: Combining User Needs with Stakeholder Objectives. User-centered is the core of design thinking, which operates in the real situation, while the cases with business goals need to put the stakeholder first. In the case of LELEHO design, the first thing is to determine the appropriate carrier to achieve the activity objectives of the organizer, and the second thing is to consider the unique needs of the particular user groups for the system design. In the demand study aspect, design thinking method provides the core concept, but it still needs to incorporate with specific methods to complete the analysis.

- **Organizers:** in the actual implementing cases, the organizers' goals significantly influence the select of design medium, such as design carriers and cooperation teams. In the early stage of demand study, the stakeholder meeting discussed the activity goals, technological restrictions, and cooperation methods, which had a far-reaching effect on the subsequent design and implementation.
- **Elderly users:** elder users are often regarded as homogeneous groups according to their age range. However, in fact, in addition to age differences, different physiological states and life experiences cause different needs and expectations, so we paid more attention to the diversity of the user groups in the early stage to determine the target group. Moreover, it is necessary to carry out the in-depth user interviews and usability tests to enhance empathy and reduce self-centered bias, which might result from the age differences.

Design Iteration Stage: Cooperating with Other Practical Methods for Details. The design thinking method provides the basic process of inspiration- ideation- implement for the innovation cycle in the specific design process. Furthermore, it proposes the basic principles of prototype testing, rapid iteration, and multi-discipline cooperation. However, there is a lack of specific methods in the actual design process, which needs to be combined with other practical design methods. The following are examples from the case study:

- **Usability test:** it was carried out at different design phases to find out problems in time to achieve the goal of rapid iteration. Besides, inviting the research team and technical team to participate in the test promoted the diversity of solutions.
- **Contextual design:** the case used Work Activity Note and Affinity Diagram to record and converge the usability test findings, and then translate them into design strategies.
- **Prototyping:** designers got the feedback of elderly users' operation experience through high-fidelity prototypes in the real context, to improve the effect and reliability of usability test;

- **UX elements:** this practical theory helped designers connect the design details of all levels, and inspect comprehensiveness and rationality of the system.

Practice Diffusion Stage: Getting a Higher Reaching Rate Through Offline Activities. When the online survey system is ready for feedback collection, it faces two critical problems:

- How to let more elders know about this activity;
- How to make more elders willing to spread this activity.

Because of the limitation of resources, the design cannot fully solve these two problems, especially for rural areas with underdeveloped digital technology penetration. Therefore, when the project reached the implementing and promoting level, the case conducted offline activities with the help of the organizer. The face-to-face publicity and encouragement helped the elders understand the significance of voicing for their future life through the online survey to identify the value of the LELEHO survey activity. Only in this way, the design team achieved the goal of the activity and made the survey activity spread naturally in the social circle of elders. Through the snowball effect of social media, many sectors of society and NPO participated in the activity to build a senior-friendly society in the future.

6 Conclusion

With the rapidly aging society, senior-friendly design has become an important research topic. This research backtracking the design process of the case LELEHO, and analyzes how design thinking methods can help designers' response to the design challenges posed by special user groups and complete a senior-friendly online survey system.

Past research in the field of cognitive psychology has a large number of studies exploring the various physical, psychological, and social changes brought about by aging, as well as the possible risks, obstacles and coping strategies that may be brought about in work and life, but when comes to the real field, the complex use context will bring more system problems, the results of cognitive psychology research may not be able to deal with it comprehensively.

Design thinking emphasizes observation, collaboration, visualization, user-centered and continuous innovation, providing a more flexible and systematic method to properly deal with the relationship between the context and users. This research summarized the challenges faced by designers who design for the elderly user group, and proposed strategies for the senior-friendly design based on case experience, simultaneously showed how to properly deal with it through design thinking methods.

In addition, the enlightenment of this research is that when facing practical problems, design thinking should pay attention to the principle of "pragmatic innovation". Design thinking methods provide core principles, basic frameworks, and process methods to provide the driving force for innovation. But in the process of developing specific solutions and actual implementation, it is necessary to improve the design details according to the situation and cooperate with practical design methods to truly complete each level of design purpose. This way of reflection in practice can only be accomplished through the accumulation of experience and the precipitation of knowledge through various cases, which is also the core value of this research. We believe that this type of research needs to be promoted, so that knowledge can be better used and presented in the real context, so that future research can move toward a comprehensive approach to various disciplines and contribute to society.

References

1. Schonlau, M., Ronald, Jr. D., Elliott, M.N.: Conducting Research Surveys Via E-mail and the Web. Rand Corporation, Santa Monica (2002)
2. Dommeyer, C.J., Moriarty, E.: Comparing two forms of an e-mail survey: embedded vs. attached. Int. J. Mark. Res. **42**(1), 39–50 (2000)
3. Pitkow, J.E., Recker, M.M.: Using the Web as a survey tool: results from the second WWW user survey. Comput. Netw. ISDN Syst. **27**(6), 809–822 (1995)
4. Witte, J.C., Amoroso, L.M., Howard, P.E.: Research methodology: method and representation in internet-based survey ToolsŠ mobility, community, and cultural identity in survey 2000. Soc. Sci. Comput. Rev. **18**(2), 179–195 (2000)
5. Karahasanović, A., et al.: Co-creation and user-generated content–elderly people's user requirements. Comput. Hum. Behav. **25**(3), 655–678 (2009)
6. Barnard, Y., Bradley, M.D., Hodgson, F., Lloyd, A.D.: Learning to use new technologies by older adults: Perceived difficulties, experimentation behaviour and usability. Comput. Hum. Behav. **29**(4), 1715–1724 (2013)
7. Damali, U., Miller, J.L., Fredendall, L.D., Moore, D., Dye, C.J.: Co-creating value using customer training and education in a healthcare service design. J. Oper. Manage. **47–48**(1), 80–97 (2016). https://doi.org/10.1016/j.jom.2016.10.001
8. WHO. Global age-friendly cities: a guide (2007). http://whqlibdoc.who.int/publications/2007/9789241547307_eng.pdf?ua=1. Accessed 1 Nov 2015
9. Salthouse, T.A.: The processing-speed theory of adult age differences in cognition. Psychol. Rev. **103**(3), 403 (1996)
10. Smith, M.W., Sharit, J., Czaja, S.J.: Aging, motor control, and the performance of computer mouse tasks. Hum. Factors **41**(3), 389–396 (1999)
11. Wildenbos, G.A., Peute, L., Jaspers, M.: Aging barriers influencing mobile health usability for older adults: a literature based framework (MOLD-US). Int. J. Med. Inf. **114**, 66–75 (2018)
12. Morrell, R., et al.: Older Adults and Information Technology: A Compendium of Scientific Research and Web Site Accessibility Guidelines. National Institute on Aging, Bethesda (2004)
13. National Institute on Aging/the National Library of Medicine (2001) Making your website senior friendly: A checklist
14. Balata, J., Mikovec, Z., Slavicek, T.: KoalaPhone: touchscreen mobile phone UI for active seniors. J. Multimod. User Interfaces **9**(4), 263–273 (2015)
15. Petrovčič, A., Taipale, S., Rogelj, A., Dolničar, V.: Design of mobile phones for older adults: an empirical analysis of design guidelines and checklists for feature phones and smartphones. Int. J. Hum. Comput. Interact. **34**(3), 251–264 (2018)
16. Hart, T., Chaparro, B.S., Halcomb, C.G.: Evaluating websites for older adults: adherence to 'senior-friendly' guidelines and end-user performance. Behav. Inf. Technol. **27**(3), 191–199 (2008)
17. IDEO. IDEO: Design thinking (2020). https://designthinking.ideo.com/
18. Liedtka, J.: Perspective: linking design thinking with innovation outcomes through cognitive bias reduction. J. Prod. Innovat. Manage. **32**(6), 925–938 (2015)

19. Micheli, P., Wilner, S.J.S., Bhatti, S.H., Mura, M., Beverland, M.B.: Doing design thinking: conceptual review, synthesis, and research agenda. J. Prod. Innovat. Manage. **36**(2), 124–148 (2019). https://doi.org/10.1111/jpim.12466
20. Merriam, S.B., Tisdell, E.J.: Qualitative Research: A Guide to Design and Implementation. Wiley, New York (2015)
21. Czaja, S.J., Rogers, W.A., Fisk, A.D., Charness, N., Sharit, J.: Designing for Older Adults: Principles and Creative Human Factors Approaches. CRC Press, Boca Raton (2009)
22. Chadwick-Dias, A., McNulty, M., Tullis, T.: Web usability and age: how design changes can improve performance. In: ACM SIGCAPH Computers and the Physically Handicapped, No. 73–74, pp. 30–37. ACM, November 2003
23. Roberts, D., Berry, D., Isensee, S., Mullaly, J.: Designing for the user with OVID: bridging the gap between software engineering and user interface design. (1st edn.). Macmillan Technical Publishing (1998)
24. Salman, H.M., Ahmad, W.F.W., Sulaiman, S.: Usability evaluation of the smartphone user interface in supporting elderly users from experts' perspective. IEEE Access **6**, 22578–22591 (2018)
25. Garrett, J.J.: The Elements of User Experience: User-Centered Design for the Web. 1st edn. New Riders, Indianapolis (2002)
26. DesignCouncil. What is the framework for innovation? Design Council's evolved Double Diamond (2020). https://www.designcouncil.org.uk/news-opinion/what-framework-innovation-design-councils-evolved-double-diamond. Accessed 15 Oct 2020

Designing Local Assessment Workshops and Web-Mobile Applications for Facilitating the Workshop

Based on the Schemes of Problem/Project-Based Learning (PBL) and ADDIE Model

Ken-ichiro Yabu[1], Takahiro Miura[1,2]([✉]), Tomoko Segawa[3], Yuki Murakami[3], and Tetsuya Nakahashi[3]

[1] Institute of Gerontology, The University of Tokyo, 7-3-1 Hongo, Bunkyo-ku, Tokyo 113-8656, Japan
yabu@human.iog.u-tokyo.ac.jp
[2] Human Augmentation Research Center (HARC), National Institute of Advanced Industrial Science and Technology (AIST), The University of Tokyo, c/o Kashiwa II Campus, 6-2-3 Kashiwanoha, Kashiwa, Chiba 277-0882, Japan
miura-t@aist.go.jp
[3] Hongo Ikinuki Kôbô, Bunkyo-ku, Hongo, Tokyo 113-0033, Japan

Abstract. Rapid improvements in real-world accessibility conditions have enabled greater mobility of people with disabilities as well as senior citizens. However, the most recent information on accessibility conditions in areas such as suburbs is challenging to obtain quickly because of infrequent updates of this type of information along with local information upgrades. Though volunteer groups continuously check local conditions to ensure they are safe for people with disabilities, some of them face difficulty in maintaining the accessibility of information because of the shortage of members in such groups. In this study, we firstly proposed a framework named to design an assessment workshop and its supporting application based on the schemes of Problem/Project-based learning (PBL) and the ADDIE (Analyze, design, develop, implement, and evaluate). Based on the framework, we designed the workshop sessions of local assessments and supported mobile and web applications, then preliminarily evaluated this approach's availability. The results suggested that our framework might appropriately enable facilitators to plan workshop sessions and consider how to facilitate, and also enable participants to learn the local conditions.

Keywords: Field assessment · Volunteers · Smartphones · Instructional design

1 Introduction

Smartphones with advanced accessibility features have been spreading not only to young people without disabilities but also to older adults and people with

Q. Gao and J. Zhou (Eds.): HCII 2021, LNCS 12786, pp. 114–125, 2021.
https://doi.org/10.1007/978-3-030-78108-8_9

disabilities. Since smartphones have a similar or better performance than personal computers that manufactured several years ago, many people can use advanced tools anywhere and anytime. As a result, the worldwide activation of the citizen-based scientific activity named *Citizen Science* have been emerging and dispersing [1, 2].

Our group has conducted research and development to incorporate the concept of *Citizen Science* into volunteers using mobile applications to efficiently share accessibility conditions for people with disabilities, including wheelchair users and older adults [3–5]. Though accessibility in urban areas and buildings has progressed more and more rapidly to reduce barriers of mobility for people with severe and mild physical disabilities, they have difficulty accessing the information about such accessibility conditions smoothly due to the disclosure and fragmentation of the information. We have developed an information system that allows many people to share and update the accessibility conditions. Then, several community-based volunteer groups used the smartphone-native version and web-based tool of the system for facilitating the workshop of the city walk. As a result, the developed system has contributed to the collection of accessibility information more efficiently and has enabled the participants to organize information and distribute accessibility maps more easily.

However, the methodology using such information collection tools has not been established in the context of education and workshops. In the field of education technology, most of the cases were carried out mainly in the classroom, and knowledge outside the classroom has not sufficiently obtained [6, 7]. Thus, It is necessary to establish a methodology that can balance information sharing and collaborative learning with mobile devices and apply them to educational sites and NPO activities. Notably, such methodology needs to be applied to various types of the area, target persons, and the information.

Therefore, in this paper, our objective is to develop and improve a sharing system of local information for activating assessments, increasing the accuracy of collected information, and building the methodology to continue such assessments using the system. This paper mainly reports our proof-of-concept framework that unites the designs of events, learning schemes, and applications and evaluates the scheme at the assessment activity.

2   Related Work

This section presents a study of field information collection. Holone et al. developed a prototype system to record accessibility conditions on OpenStreetMap, and evaluated it with volunteers in Oslo. The results indicated that there were issues in ensuring the quality of the information and security [8]. Goncalves et al. developed a tool to share accessibility status briefly and evaluated it in Finland [9]. They found that this tool can raise awareness of accessibility among people with disabilities. Miura et al. conducted case studies on workshops for collecting local accessibility and safety information using a smartphone application among young and older adult volunteers. They reported that the important factors included the context setting to encourage seniors to use the application, the purpose setting to promote seniors' awareness of the community contribution, and other elements regarding interfaces are important [3,4]. Ichikari et al. developed a scheme and system of virtual mapping parties, which allows various volunteers to collect information without going to the real places and with using the remote area by using VR technology [10]. Hara et al. proposed a method to check the barrier-free status based on omnispherical images in Google Street View (GSV) [11,12]. In their system, cloud workers are requested to mark the objects relates to road accessibility, such as a sign or a bus stop in the GSV environment. Based on the worker's labeling results, the system performed machine learning and automatic recognition of the objects. Sensr, proposed by Kim et al., is a collection of easy-to-use measurement and analytical functions to improve the quality of information collected by citizens, based on the Citizen Science framework [13]. Regarding other local information collection, Frommberger reported on a system for sharing information on agriculture [14], Omata et al. on local disaster prevention information [15], and Shah et al. on crime information [16].

The activities and studies described above have led to the increased sharing of information associated with various maps and locations on the Web. In addition, many volunteers have been working to improve accessibility for people with disabilities by integrating their work only or mainly on the Web. However, the construction of a methodology to encourage participants to collect information continuously has been a challenge in various cases. Moreover, the tasks for participants in the studies, as mentioned earlier, were either simple or required specialized knowledge to participate. In short, there have been few cases that have explicitly studied how to get participants to learn and summarized it as a methodology. Therefore, we decided to propose a proof-of-concept framework and conducted a feasibility study.

3   Framework to Design Workshop and Support Application

Figure 1 shows an overview of our framework to design an assessment workshop and its supporting application. The framework generally consists of two procedures: planning a workshop that considers learning elements (left part of Fig. 1) and organizing the requirements of the support application (right part of Fig. 1). The process of planning a workshop is based on the method of Problem/Project-Based Learning (PBL) [7]. In this process, workshop facilitators firstly enumerate the contents of the driving question, learning goals, collaboration, engaging in collaborative practice, leaning technology, and artifacts to structure the learning elements in the participants and what the supporting application should compensate for. Then, the application's elemental design is detailed based on the ADDIE (Analyze, design, develop, implement, and evaluate) process [17], which is a representative framework in the instructional design method. In particular, the facilitators list the elements such as analyze, design, develop, implement,

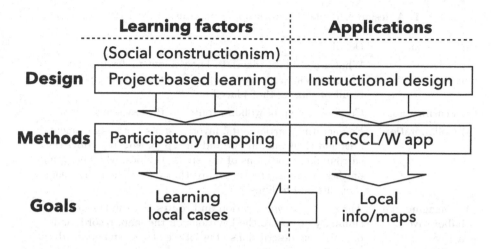

Fig. 1. Overview of the design framework of computer-supported cooperative learning/work (CSCL/W) for an assessment workshop and its supporting application

and evaluate included in the ADDIE framework to organize the functions to be satisfied by the application.

Next, the actual local information assessment is conducted based on the participatory mapping methodology derived from the participatory learning and action (PLA) [18,19]. This mapping approach attempts to gather multifaceted information by involving people with various attributes in the mapping. In order to involve participants in mapping their points of view, the workshop facilitators ask them to introduce themselves and their feelings about the area before conducting the field assessment. During these introductions, the facilitators record the places that the participants have mentioned that are memorable and refers to it when they walk around the city. Then, the facilitators decide the routes of the field assessment based on the listed places that the participants have feelings toward and the places that should be assessed (depending on the purpose). After that, the facilitators arrange the participants into groups. In the grouping of the participants, the facilitators should match the interests of each participant and also be aware of the various individual characteristics of them. This grouping could promote their motivations because the different characteristics of each participant make different contributions. Then, the facilitators ask them to walk through the assigned routes using the supporting application mentioned later. They will bring smartphones and record information about the area. After completing the assessment, the collected data are organized by these groups as their local maps, and the participants take them home as kinds of learning outcomes, which corresponds to the artifacts of the PBL.

Table 1. A design example of a workshop session using the PBL framework

PBL element	Details
(1) Driving questions	What are the best places to know about preferring the assessment area more? What arises in each participant as a result of sharing that place?
(2) Learning goals	Creating a map of walking routes in the assessment area
(3) Collaboration	Enumerating participants' favorite spots in the assessment area and then walking around the spots with recording the surrounding conditions of the spots. Besides, while mapping on these records, creating maps that reflect the individual's thoughts and feelings
(4) Engaging in collaborative practices	The phases of enumeration and routes determination and summary: To paste the locations on the map, record, and organize the descriptions. The phase of assessment: To discuss and edit pre-populated records on the mobile, enhance the understanding of the records after observing actual locations, and refine the records
(5) Learning technologies	Facilitating data recording during the assessment. Particularly, organizing these data at the phase of discussion and associating the data to the GPS coordinates to refer these data at the assessment. All records should be recorded on mobile devices and be able to be viewed on the web
(6) Artifacts	Creating a walking route map of the assessment area. During the reflection of the assessment, participants summarize what they felt

4   Case Study

4.1   Design of a Field Assessment Workshop and a Supporting Application

The workshop we designed was to create a map for participants to survive and live in a state of feeling relax within a specific area of Bunkyo-ku, Tokyo, Japan, and consisted of three sessions. The objectives of these sessions were as follows:

- To help participants to love the area
- To understand the topography of the area for promoting awareness of disaster prevention and learning how to help each other at the emergencies
- To summarize the contents of the two workshops and then create the *Ikinuki map* (*Ikinuki* have double meanings such as 'to survive' and 'to relax.')

The content of each workshop session and its supporting application are designed based on the framework described in Sect. 2. The design framework of the specific workshop content and the requirements of the application are shown in Tables 1 and 2, respectively. These tables show the design of the first

Table 2. A design example of application requirements using the ADDIE framework

ADDIE element	Details
i. Analyze	1. It is troublesome to reflect the result of route determination in the desk to the field assessment route
	2. It would be better if the participants could list the results of the assessment routes on a map
ii. Design	1. The users quickly move mapping and route information that decided at the desk to mobile. Also, the voice recognition function could be required for helping the participants input the data smoothly in the discussion
	2. The routes registered by the mobile application should be aggregated into a web-based map. This map should be printable
iii. Develop	1. We decided to use the speech recognition API of iOS
	2. We implemented synchronization and upload function of the mapping data from the mobiles to the web. We also used the browser's printing function
iv. Implement	1. The phase of enumeration and routes determination: When the participants put a sticker on the paper-based map, the facilitators find the location and records it on the mobile. The facilitators also input the participant comment as text data by using speech recognition
	2. The assessment phase: The participants edit or add information during the assessment while looking at the textual information acquired by the speech recognition
v. Evaluate	Evaluation of learning: We decided to conduct a questionnaire to evaluate the workshop's impressions and the application to facilitators and participants

workshop session. The description of the workshop procedure is designed after enumerated the items shown in Table 1 and 2. First, the workshop facilitators decide the detailed practice and coordination methods based on enumerated the driving questions and learning objectives. Then, to implement the technologies and techniques required in this process, the facilitators determine the requirements of the application to meet the items in Table 2.

4.2 Developed Applications

Figures 2 and 3 show the user interfaces of the support tool of route decision designed based on requirements described at Table 2, and the mobile data recording application for field assessment.

The tool shown in Fig. 2 helps the participants to decide assessment routes by displaying the locations introduced by them. This tool was coded in PHP 7.3 and the Google Maps JavaScript API v3, and runs on Ubuntu Linux 18.04 LTS. This tool enables users to view and edit the recorded information displayed as

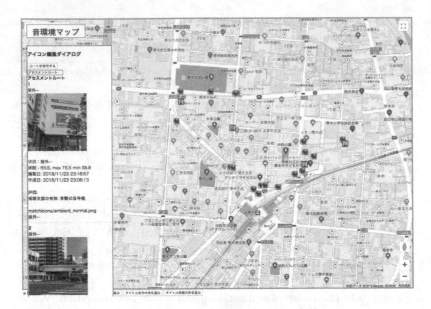

Fig. 2. The user interface of the support tool of the route decision. Green lines and blue icons represent the draft of a route and markers that mean spots to assess. (Color figure online)

Fig. 3. The user interface of the mobile data recording application for assessments. The left figure shows the map view, and the middle and right figures show the data input views.

markers on the map by using web browsers and the mobile application shown in Fig. 3 for creating the route in advance of the field assessment. It can also extract the GPS coordinates from the Exif data of photos taken by other tools and display them as the markers on the map.

Figure 3 shows the user interface of the mobile application developed for the assessment. This application consists of two views: the map view and the input view of the data. We employed Xcode 9.0–11.2 and Objective-C as an integrated development environment and programming language. This application is available on iOS devices such as the iPhone 5s–11 (OS: iOS 9.0 or later). The design of these views was developed based on the scheme of user-centered design (UCD) [20], and their objects, including button and font sizes, were designed by consulting the Apple iOS Human Interface Guidelines and a guideline for seniors proposed by Kobayashi et al. [21,22].

The map view shown in the left picture in Fig. 3 is an initial view that displays the map, current position, and markers that represent location information. The users can register new information and make modifications through this view. When a user needs to register or modify the specified conditions associated with a marker, they can do so by using the input view, the central and right pictures in Fig. 3, that transits from the map view. The input view provides a marker selection function in combination with the functionalities of reporting brief conditions, acquiring pictures, recording voice, converting textual information using speech recognition API, and entering text input. The current location is identified based on the global positioning system (GPS). The added or modified entries are accumulated in the SQLite database in the smartphone and can be output in various formats such as JSON or XML. The contents of this database can be updated in conjunction with the support tool of route decision, as shown in Fig. 2.

5 Workshop Procedure and Acquired Data

We conducted a series of three workshop sessions designed based on the framework shown in Table 1. The total number of participants was twenty-eight, including four facilitators. The assessment site was in the Hongo area, Bunkyo-ku, Tokyo, Japan.

The first session comprises an ice breaker and self-introductions of the participants, as well as an introduction of favorite spots in the assessment area. Then, the participants decided on the assessment routes by checking the spots displayed in Fig. 2, and then conducted an assessment to resister the information of these spots by using the mobile application shown in Fig. 3. Lastly, they reviewed the registered data by using the two systems.

The second session started from a mini-workshop on how to move on a wheelchair outdoors. During this workshop, the participants experienced to go through the steps, gentle/steep slopes, and ramps and then registered the path conditions with the mobile application shown in Fig. 3. After that, they joined in the successive mini-workshop about the topography of the area. They learned topography through the assembly of the cardboard dioramas of the assessment area [23].

In the third session, the facilitators distributed a summary of the results (map) of the first session to the participants. Then, the participants created their own *Ikinuki map* based on their exciting events at the series of workshops.

After completing the workshop, the facilitators reviewed their impressions based on the KPT (keep, problem, and try) framework [24]. The facilitators wrote down and arranged the items to keep (what they think to keep), items of the problem (whet they think to stop), and items to try (what they think to do anew). Notably, two of the facilitators who facilitated the second workshop session reported their subjective introspection before and after the experience of workshop facilitation. One of the two facilitators was a wheelchair user, and the other did not have any physical disabilities. They had never experienced the workshop facilitation before the workshop session.

6   Results and Discussion

This paper presents an overview of the workshop sessions' results and the introspection reviews by two facilitators.

Figure 4 shows an example of the map created through the workshop. Throughout the whole workshop sessions, the participants registered 73 entries by the applications we developed. In particular, their favorite spots included restaurants and cafes, hotels and lodges, cultural and educational facilities such as community centers, and universities. Also, there was information on difficult places for wheelchair users to go independently and their supporters to assist them.

According to the participants' feedback, the workshop and the application were useful to find information that was tailored to their needs, to walk through the route that the wheelchair users independently went though, to strengthen their attachment to the assessment area, to strike discoveries by meeting people from different characteristics. This feedbacks suggest that the workshop and supported application designed based on the proposed framework enable to collect local information such as accessibility conditions for wheelchair users and also enable participants to learn fresh perspectives. In addition to the detailed classification of the data obtained, we will analyze the participants' introspection in the future.

According to the feedback from one of the facilitators, anxiety and apologetic feelings toward others had preceded the workshop session, at the time of workshop planning. Then she had felt a sense of bargaining toward the preparation situation. After that, she took an elevated view of things, accepted the situation, and had hope for the workshop session and other facilitators. After the workshop, she also told us that after the event, she felt a sense of fulfillment, emotions, and relief and then willing to look back at the workshop session and to realize various things. Through this experience, this facilitator has acquired the initiative to organize several workshops afterward.

On the other hand, the other facilitator did not have any negative feelings about the workshop session's planning and facilitation because he had already written down his ideas before planning the workshop session. However, he was worried that he could not speak loudly or showed how to do it because of his disability. During and after the workshop session, he felt a sense of accomplishment that he could produce a vivid atmosphere by collaborating with other facilitators and the participants. However, he also mentioned that there were challenges in

Fig. 4. The example of shared information displayed on the map. Markers and balloons on the map represent the assessed spots and corresponding entries, respectively.

terms of time scheduling and ensuring safety when more people participated in this kind of workshop.

From the above, this feedbacks suggest that our framework might appropriately enable facilitators to plan workshop sessions and consider how to facilitate and also enable participants to learn the local conditions. However, how to design a framework for exact facilitation is future work.

7 Conclusion and Future Work

In this study, we firstly proposed the framework to design an assessment workshop and its supporting application. After that, we designed the series of a workshop and supporting application based on this framework, and then preliminarily evaluated the availability of this approach. Our achievements are as follows:

- We proposed the framework to design an assessment workshop and its supporting application based on Problem/Project-Based Learning (PBL) and the ADDIE (Analyze, design, develop, implement, and evaluate) approach.
- Our framework might appropriately enable facilitators to plan workshop sessions and consider how to facilitate, and also enable participants to learn the local conditions.

Our future work is as follows:

- Further analysis of the obtained data and a follow-up analysis of participants' introspection
- Planning and conducting ongoing mapping events to refine the proposed framework and design the related framework for facilitation.s

Acknowledgement. This work was supported by the SECOM Science and Technology Foundation.

References

1. Silvertown, J.: A new dawn for citizen science. Trends Ecol. Evol. **24**(9), 467–471 (2009)
2. Preece, J.: Citizen science: new research challenges for human-computer interaction. Int'l. J. Hum. Comput. Interact. **32**(8), 585–612 (2016)
3. Miura, T., Yabu, K., Ogino, R., Hiyama, A., Hirose, M., Ifukube, T.: Collaborative accessibility assessments by senior citizens using smartphone application ReAcTS (real-world accessibility transaction system). In: Proceedings of the ACM W4A 2018, p.10, April 2018. Article No. 32
4. Miura, T., et al.: Sharing real-world accessibility conditions using a smartphone application by a volunteer group. In: Miesenberger, K., Bühler, C., Penaz, P. (eds.) ICCHP 2016, Part II. LNCS, vol. 9759, pp. 265–272. Springer, Cham (2016). https://doi.org/10.1007/978-3-319-41267-2_36
5. Miura, T., et al.: Sharing accessibility information for people with disabilities: analyses of information acquired by field assessment and crowdsourcing. Trans. VRSJ **21**(2), 283–294 (2016). (in Japanese)
6. OECD Center for Educational Research and Innovation: The Nature of Learning: Using Research to Inspire Practice. OECD (2010)
7. Sawyer, R.K.: The Cambridge Handbook of the Learning Sciences, vol. 2. Cambridge Univerity Press, Cambridge (2014)
8. Holone, H., Misund, G.: People helping computers helping people: navigation for people with mobility problems by sharing accessibility annotations. In: Miesenberger, K., Klaus, J., Zagler, W., Karshmer, A. (eds.) ICCHP 2008. LNCS, vol. 5105, pp. 1093–1100. Springer, Heidelberg (2008). https://doi.org/10.1007/978-3-540-70540-6_164
9. Goncalves, J., Kostakos, V., Hosio, S., Karapanos, E., Lyra, O.: IncluCity: using contextual cues to raise awareness on environmental accessibility. In: Proceedings of the ACM ASSETS 2013, pp. 17:1–17:8 (2013)
10. Ichikari, R., Kurata, T.: Virtual mapping party: co-creation of maps for visually impaired people. J. Technol. People Disabil. **7**, 208–224 (2017)
11. Hara, K., Le, V., Froehlich, J.E.: Combining crowdsourcing and google street view to identify street-level accessibility problems. In: Proceedings of the ACM CHI 2013, pp: 631–640 (2013)
12. KHara, K., et al.: Improving public transit accessibility for blind riders by crowdsourcing bus stop landmark locations with google street view: an extended analysis. ACM Trans. Access. Comput. (TACCESS) **6**(2), 1–23 (2015)
13. Kim, S., Mankoff, J., Paulos, E.: Sensr: evaluating a flexible framework for authoring mobile data-collection tools for citizen science. In: Proceedings of the CSCW 2013, pp. 1453–1462 (2013)

14. Frommberger, L., Schmid, F., Cai, C.: Micro-mapping with smartphones for monitoring agricultural development. In: Proceedings of the ACM DEV 2013, pp, 1–2 (2013). Article No. 46

15. Omata, M., Nakamura, J., Komiya, M., Imamiya, A., Suzuki, T., Hada, Y.: Prototype of an automatic inspection map creation system interlocked with user's walking and a large information board for regional disaster prevention. Trans. VRSJ **17**(2), 111–118 (2012)

16. Shah, S., Bao, F., Lu, C.-T., Chen, I.-R.: CROWDSAFE: crowd sourcing of crime incidents and safe routing on mobile devices. In: Proceedings of the ACM GIS 2011, pp: 521–524 (2011)

17. Branch, R.M.: Instructional Design: The ADDIE Approach, vol. 722. Springer Science & Business Media, Boston (2009)

18. Chambers, R.: Revolutions in Development Inquiry. Routledge, London (2008)

19. Chambers, R.: Whose Reality Counts? Putting the First Last. Intermediate Technology Publications, London (1997)

20. Vredenburg, K., Mao, J.-Y,. Smith, P.W., Carey, T.: A survey of user-centered design practice. In: Proceedings of the ACM CHI 2002, pp. 471–478 (2002)

21. Apple iOS Human Interface Guidelines. https://developer.apple.com/ios/human-interface-guidelines/

22. Kobayashi, M., Hiyama, A., Miura, T., Asakawa, C., Hirose, M., Ifukube, T.: Elderly user evaluation of mobile touchscreen interactions. In: Campos, P., Graham, N., Jorge, J., Nunes, N., Palanque, P., Winckler, M. (eds.) INTERACT 2011, Part I. LNCS, vol. 6946, pp. 83–99. Springer, Heidelberg (2011). https://doi.org/10.1007/978-3-642-23774-4_9

23. Cardboard Diorama Disaster Prevention Class. https://www.bosai-diorama.or.jp/english/

24. Kinoshita, F.: Practices of an agile team. In: Proceedings of the IEEE Agile 2008 Conference, pp. 373–377 (2008)

Interface Adaption to Elderly Users: Effects of Icon Styles and Semantic Distance

Kairu Zhao[✉], Xiaochun Wang, and Linyao Bai

Beijing University of Posts and Telecommunications, Beijing, China

Abstract. Elderly users constitute the fastest expanding user group of the Internet and smart devices. However, there is a lack of research on the adaptation of user interfaces with regard to the elderly. This study focused on icons, which are widely used in today's user interfaces but often lack proper design. The purpose of this study was to determine how different icon design strategies affect the user experience of older adults. We mainly studied two factors which were icon style and semantic distance, and investigated their influence on older users with different levels of smart phone using experience in terms of identification performance and subjective preference through a set of experiments and interviews. Results showed that both icon style and semantic distance significantly affected the preferences and performance of elderly adults. Interestingly, the experienced participants showed an overall better performance than inexperienced ones, which indicated that older users can adapt to simplified and abstract icons to a certain extent through learning and frequent use of smart devices; however, more careful design considerations are necessary to achieve a better user experience.

Keywords: Interface adaptation · Icon design · UI design · Age-related preference

1 Introduction

1.1 Problems Encountered by Elderly Users of Smart Devices

With rapid economic and technological development, the elderly are increasingly becoming a major user group of smart devices. The number of older users of mobile Internet currently exceeds 50 million in China, and is still rapidly increasing. Meanwhile, elderly people aged over 60 will soon constitute one-third of the labour force in many countries, and are also the fastest-growing computer and Internet user group (Wagner et al. 2014). However, research on the theory and practice of adapting human-computer interfaces to older users is still limited (Vines et al. 2015), despite the adaptation of interfaces, especially personalization, being a widely recognized issue in design (Arazy et al. 2015). The inability of the elderly to use smart devices as skilfully as most young users is primarily attributed to age-related cognitive and physical impairment. Although such changes may have been observed at a young age, it is particularly significant among older adults (Salthouse 2012). As people age, the decline in the ability of visual perception, selective

© Springer Nature Switzerland AG 2021
Q. Gao and J. Zhou (Eds.): HCII 2021, LNCS 12786, pp. 126–141, 2021.
https://doi.org/10.1007/978-3-030-78108-8_10

attention, and semantic memory results in slow processing of new information, especially visual information (Ganor and Te'eni 2016), which affects their understanding and learning of interactive interfaces. Consequently, older users tend to find it difficult to understand the concepts of menus and hierarchies (Ziefle and Bay 2004), as well as metaphors, such as windows and forms (Dickinson et al. 2005).They are also unable to adapt to complex and precise interactive operations like scrolling, dragging, dropping (Hawthorn 2003), and double clicking (Dickinson et al. 2005) due to a decline in physical abilities. Therefore, high costs are incurred toward helping the elderly learn and adapt to smart device interfaces.

1.2 Influence of Icon Design on User Experience

The graphical user interface (GUI) is still the dominant form of interface applied to most today's smart devices. Moreover, icons, typically in the form of small photographs representing specific functions, are widely used in GUIs as a control and information transmission mechanism. The use of icons in interfaces can reduce users' cognitive load and perceived system complexity (Goonetilleke et al. 2001). Small changes in the usability of icons have the potential to significantly improve user experience with computers and mobile devices (Gatsou et al. 2012). Nowadays, icons used in smart device interfaces cannot undergo the same rigorous testing process as those used in public signs due to the high frequency of market updates; further, during their design, more emphasis is often placed on visual presentation rather than usability. As a result, users may struggle or be unable to understand the meanings of icons encountered during everyday use – a problem that is particularly pronounced among older users with cognitive decline.

Five cognitive attributes of icons have been widely discussed in research on icon identification: familiarity, concreteness, complexity, meaningfulness and semantic distance (Gatsou et al. 1999). Compared with physical attributes, such as icon size and text font, cognitive attributes have a greater impact on icon identification and constitute up to 69% of the variance seen in performance (Isherwood et al. 2007). Familiarity is a description of the user's past experience, and reflects the frequency of an icon encountered by the user; concreteness is used to describe the extent to which an icon depicts real-world objects; complexity refers to the amount of detail in an icon; meaningfulness describes the amount of useful information contained in an icon; and semantic distance refers to the closeness of the relationship between an icon itself and the function it represents. Studies have shown that these five attributes are not independent with each other. Concreteness is strongly correlated with meaningfulness, familiarity (Mcdougall et al. 1999; McDougall et al. 2000), and complexity (García et al. 1994). Among these five attributes, concreteness and complexity describe the morphological characteristics and determine the style of the icon, while semantic distance describes the relationship between an icon and its representing function (McDougall and Isherwood 2009).

Research on icon style mainly focuses on the two distinct strategies of flat and skeuomorphic. Compared with skeuomorphic icons, flat icons are usually more abstract and simplified, which means they have a lower degree of concreteness and complexity. Icons used in early electronic product interfaces were usually in the skeuomorphic style, simulating objects in the real world by metaphor, as well as strategies like shadows, gradients, 3D perspective, and realistic textures. However, flat design is currently more common in interface design. It was first widely used in the UI design of the Windows Phone 7 launched in 2010 and attracted extensive attention from the design community (Burmistrov, Tatiana & Anna 2015); three years later, it was fully applied in the IOS 7 smart-phone operating system introduced by Apple. The flat style has a high degree of abstraction and generality, and mainly depicts the general image rather than the fine details. Meanwhile, the common three-dimensional elements used in skeuomorphic style are eliminated, making the overall visual appearance of the interface more concise and unified. The flat design, together with its modern aesthetic concept, was soon widely favoured by both designers and users.

On the other hand, flat design has been under heated debate for a long time. Some earlier studies noted that the over-simplification of flat icons may cause a reduction in usability. Compared with abstract icons, concrete icons can provide higher recognition accuracy and shorter response time (Rogers and Oborne 1987; Stammers and Hoffman 1991; Stotts 1998). In visual search tasks, Burmistrov (2015) found that subjects spent twice as much time finding flat icons as they did for skeuomorphic icons. In addition, flat icons caused higher cognitive load for participants. Comparative studies among different age groups indicated that the influence of icon style was related to subject age. The increased level of detail is more helpful to the elderly than to the young, indicating that the elderly seemed to rely more on the detailed information in skeuomorphic icons than young adults (Leung et al. 2011; Mertens and Schlick 2011; Schroder and Ziefle 2008). Moreover, some other studies have noted that older users tend to show a preference for skeuomorphic icons over flat ones (Backhaus et al. 2018; Cho and Kwon 2015; Tu and Ho 2018).

1.3   A Gradually Blurred Boundary Between Flat and Skeuomorphic Design

The flat design has evolved for ten years, starting from the release of Windows Phone 7 in 2010. In recent years, some new trends have emerged in UI design. Many newly developed design languages are no longer confined to flat design principles, and seek more diversified design elements as a supplement on the basis of simple form. Thus, they can avail of many elements as opposed to in flat design, such as spatial relationship and realistic texture, which are often seen in skeuomorphic icons. The introduction of these new strategies has made today's user interfaces more diversified and personalized. Material Design introduced by Google is a good example because it cannot be simply classified as flat design. Material Design proposed the concept of a "z-axis" in the UI interface, providing the two-dimensional user interface a spatial metaphor. On this basis, Material Design also drew on other metaphors in physical reality, such as texture, light and shadow, acceleration, and paper simulation, making it easier for users to understand. Similarly, the Fluent Design System, a new design language by Microsoft, also contains many elements beyond the category of flat design. Figure 1 shows some of the official example icons published by Microsoft. Similar to the "z-axis" of Material Design, Microsoft introduced the concept of "depth" in UI design to enhance the spatial effects of icons. Besides, Microsoft has proposed four more design principles: light, motion, material, and scale, among which the light and material principles advocate the simulation of object states in the real physical world. Hence, newer strategies no longer only emphasize simplicity; rather, they focus more on the physical world, trying to create a more intuitive interactive experience through natural and familiar design elements.

Fig. 1. Official icon examples of fluent design system from Microsoft.

In this paper, we term this new trend 'semi-skeuomorphic design'. It inherits the simple and modern language of flat design but has more diversity in its methods. It does not completely exclude elements related to the real physical world, but in contrast, manages to apply and arrange them appropriately with the aim of enhancing the visual appeal and usability of the interface as a whole.

On the one hand, there has been a gradual reduction in the competition between flat and skeuomorphic design, and some new styles that draw on the advantages of both have begun to emerge. On the other hand, the penetration rate of smart devices among elderly users is increasing rapidly. Their experience and usage frequency of smart devices have been significantly improved compared with the past. In this context, it is necessary to conduct more targeted research to include the trends of style evolution and sharp rise of user base in the research scope.

Thus, the purpose of this study was to determine how different icon design strategies affect the user experience of older adults. Icon style was considered as an independent variable and defined as flat, semi-skeuomorphic, or skeuomorphic according to the degrees of concreteness and complexity, which are two strongly correlated factors. Although semantic distance, as a vital cognitive attribute, does not correlate with concreteness and complexity, it may have a great influence on the results of the study. Therefore, the semantic distance was considered as another independent variable. Finally, the level of user experience was considered as the third independent variable of this study.

In sum, this study mainly focused on two factors: icon style and semantic distance, and investigated their influence on older users in terms of icon identification and preference. Smart-phones were recognized as representatives of smart devices, and a comparative study was conducted between two groups of older users with different levels of smartphone-usage experience (one with no experience and the other with rich experience) to observe the influence of increased experience on the results.

2   Method

This study comprised three stages. First, the researchers collected a large number of icons and invited elderly adults to participate in sorting icons for the experiment. In the second stage, a lab-controlled experiment was conducted, and the data were analysed in SPSS (Statistical Product and Service Solutions from IBM). Subsequently, a set of post-task interviews were conducted at the third stage to further understand the thoughts of the participants with respect to different icons and the problems and doubts that they encountered during the experiment to supplement the experimental results.

2.1 Preparation of Testing Icons

We collected 202 icons that corresponded to common functions from the interfaces of smart phones and web pages. First, three designers were required to classify these icons by style; this was primarily achieved according to the degree of concreteness and complexity, which were strongly correlated. Icons with a very high or very low degree of concreteness and complexity were classified into the skeuomorphic and flat groups, respectively; however, icons with a moderate degree of concreteness and complexity, a highly generalized form, but with realistic colours, textures, and shadows were classified into the semi-skeuomorphic group. The three designers first classified all the icons independently and then reached a consensus through discussion and negotiation on divergent opinions.

Icons were then classified according to semantic distance. Twelve participants were recruited to rate their perceived semantic distance of icons; six participants were designers and the remaining participants were adults aged over 60. Researchers first introduced the concept of semantic distance to each participant in detail and further explained it through a case introduction. Then, participants were required to rate the semantic distance for each icon according to their own judgment. The score was given on a five-point Likert scale, with point one indicating a very far semantic distance and point five indicating a very close one.

Two levels, "far" and "close", were set for the semantic distance variable. In each style group, eight icons with the highest scores and another eight with the lowest scores were selected and sorted into six groups (a total of 48 icons) (Fig. 2) as materials to use in the experiment, while the rest of them were used as interference items.

Fig. 2. Icon examples of six different groups.

2.2 Participants

Twenty-four elderly subjects participated in this study and were divided into two groups according to their experience of using smart phones, namely: the inexperienced group (subjects who had never used smart phones) and the experienced group (those who used smart phones every day for more than one year). The age distribution of the two groups of subjects is shown in Table 1. A t-test was conducted to compare the mean age of the two groups, and no significant difference was found (t(22) = 0.44, p = 0.40); thus, the influence of age on the experimental results could be excluded.

Table 1. Age distribution of participants

	Min	Max	Mean	Std. deviation
Experienced (12)	58	80	69.67	8.34
Inexperienced (12)	60	83	71.08	7.38

2.3 Design of Experiment

The mixed design method was used both in the identification experiment and preference evaluation. There were two within-subjects variables (icon style and semantic distance) and one between-subjects variable (smart-phone experience).

Ganor and Te'eni (2016) divided the icon recognition process into two steps: visual search and icon identification. Visual search refers to the subjects' active browsing of the visual environment and searching for a specific icon among distractors, whereas icon recognition refers to identifying the content of the icon and analysing its corresponding function or name via referential connections stored in long-term memory.

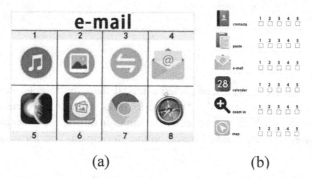

(a)   (b)

Fig. 3. Testing tools: (a) interface of icon identification test and (b) part of the icon list used in the preference evaluation test.

The identification test in this study followed this theory. In each task, participants were presented with eight icons and a function description at the same time (Fig. 3(a)), and they were required to pick out the specific icon matching the function description as quickly as possible. Among the eight icons, the target icon was selected from experimental materials in the first stage, and the remaining seven were regarded as interference items. Each participant was required to complete 48 such tasks one by one (i.e., repeated 8 times on each of the 6 independent variable combinations). The 48 tasks were arranged in such an order that icons in six groups were displayed in turn, whereas the target icon appeared at a random place. The average response time for the subjects to complete a task (i.e., successfully identify the target icon) and the identification accuracy for each icon group were recorded as indicators of performance and analysed in SPSS.

A preference evaluation test was then conducted after the identification experiment. Participants were shown a list of 48 icons selected in the first stage with function descriptions on their sides (Fig. 3(b)), and were required to rate the extent to which they like the design of each icon through a 5-point Likert scale with 1 indicating extreme dislike and 5 indicating extreme like. The rating results from both participant groups were collected and analysed in SPSS.

In summary, all the variables and their evaluation methods in this study are listed in Table 2.

Table 2. Variables in this study

Independent variables	Style (3 levels)	Semantic distance (2 levels)	Experience (2 levels)
Name of levels	Flat/semi-skeuomorphic/skeuomorphic	Far/close	Inexperienced/experienced
Dependent variables	Performance		Preference
Measuring index	Accuracy/response time		5-point Scale

2.4 Interview

Semi-structured interviews were conducted after all the experiments were finished to further understand the participants' subjective feelings towards different types of icon designs as well as any problems and doubts encountered during the experiment. A series of open-ended questions were asked based on the participants' performance during the test, such as:

"What aspect of the icon confused you and did not allow you to identify it?"

"If you don't agree that this icon can represent this function, could you please try to sketch out an icon that in your opinion is more proper?"

"Why do you think this icon can represent this function properly, and what elements of the icon gave you hints?"

"Why did you give this icon a low preference rating and what part did you dislike?"

The interviews acted as a supplement to the experiment and also helped to explain the results of the data analysis more effectively.

3 Results and Discussion

3.1 Performance

Three-way ANOVA was conducted to examine the effects of the design style, semantic distance, and smart phone experience on the icon identification accuracy of participants. Mauchly's test showed that the assumption of sphericity was not violated ($X2(2) = 3.942$, $p = 0.139$). The results are shown in Table 3. First, there were significant main effects of icon style ($F(2, 44) = 36.343$, $p < 0.001$), semantic distance ($F(1, 22) = 197.813$, $p < 0.001$), and experience ($F(1, 22) = 77.216$, $p < 0.001$). This indicates that icons with a close semantic distance are easier to recognize, and experienced participants were able to correctly identify more icons in the test. Multiple comparisons among three levels of design style were then conducted by the Fisher least significant difference (LSD) test. The results (Table 3) show that the flat icons were significantly less correctly identified than the semi-skeuomorphic and skeuomorphic ones; however, there was no significant difference between the impacts of semi-skeuomorphic and skeuomorphic icons. This indicates that the loss of details and visual clues in flat icons may lead to a reduction in usability.

Table 3. Effects of style, semantic distance, and smart-phone experience on identification accuracy.

Items of ANOVA	SS	df	MS	F	p
style	68.097	2	34.049	36.343	0.000*
semantic distance	212.674	1	212.674	197.813	0.000*
experience	79.507	1	79.507	77.216	0.000*
style*experience	6.347	2	3.174	3.387	0.043*
semantic distance*experience	12.840	1	12.840	11.943	0.002*
style*semantic distance	4.264	2	2.132	2.098	0.135
style*semantic distance*experience	11.347	2	5.674	5.582	0.007*
Multiple comparisons	*Mean difference*		*Std. Error*		*p*
flat vs. semi-skeuomorphic	−1.479		0.221		0.000*
flat vs. skeuomorphic	−1.438		0.152		0.000*
semi-skeuomorphic vs. skeuomorphic	0.042		0.213		0.847

Moreover, interactions between style and experience ($F(2, 44) = 3.387$, $p = 0.043$), semantic distance and experience ($F(1, 22) = 11.943$, $p = 0.002$), and design style, semantic distance, and experience ($F(2, 44) = 5.582$, $p = 0.007$) were observed.

Figure 4(a) depicts the interaction between style and experience, which indicates that experienced participants had an overall better performance towards the identification of icons of all three styles; however, they seemed to be most adapted to semi-skeuomorphic icons in terms of accuracy, while inexperienced participants reached the highest accuracy with skeuomorphic icons. This indicates that as icons get more complex and concrete, the increase of details and visual cues may effectively help inexperienced subjects to make the right decision; however, it somehow adversely impacted the performance of those participants having rich smart phone experiences.

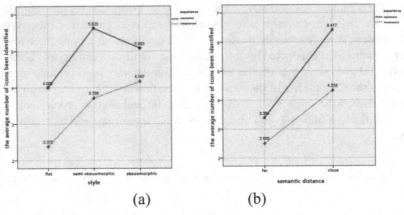

(a)   (b)

Fig. 4. (a) Interaction between style and experience. (b) Interaction between semantic distance and experience.

It was noted in previous literature that the increase in the complexity of icons could have two conflicting effects. On the one hand, the increased complexity gives an icon more details and visual clues, which help to make the icon more concrete (García et al. 1994), more similar to familiar objects, and thus easier to understand (Lloyd-Jones and Luckhurst 2002; Lloyd-Jones and Nettlemill 2007). On the other hand, high complexity may bring higher cognitive load to users, which may negatively affect their efficiency in icon identification (Humphreys et al. 1988; Ellis and Morrison 1998; Alario et al. 2004; Schroder and Ziefle 2008). Therefore, it is necessary to felicitously control the amount of details involved when designing icons. Furthermore, Moyes and Jordan (1993) pointed out that the advantage of concrete icons over abstract ones was significant when they were first encountered; however, once users had already learned the meanings of icons and with an increase in their experience, the advantage of concrete icons diminished (McDougall et al. 1998, 2000; Stammers and Hoffman 1991). This is in line with the results of the experiment. For experienced participants, too many details may even have negative effects, while it is still necessary for inexperienced participants to exploit this extra information to complete the tasks.

The interaction between semantic distance and experience (shown in Fig. 4(b)) indicates that the changes in semantic distance had a greater impact on the experienced subjects; that is to say, a close semantic distance could bring about a greater improvement in identification accuracy for them, and it seems that they can better take advantage of the semantic distance improvement in icon design to achieve a significantly better performance than those of the inexperienced participants.

Regarding response time, three-way ANOVA was conducted, and the assumption of sphericity was not violated ($X2(2) = 0.280$, $p = 0.869$). The results (Table 4) indicate that style ($F(2, 44) = 16.013$, $p < 0.001$), semantic distance ($F(1, 22) = 63.613$, $p < 0.001$), and experience ($F(1, 22) = 59.036$, $p < 0.001$) all had main effects on the participant response time; however, no interaction was observed. Fisher LSD test was then conducted to compare the three levels of design style. The results (Table 4) indicate that experienced participants were able to correctly identify icons in significantly less time. A close semantic distance could significantly reduce response time, and flat icons caused significantly longer response time than those observed for the semi-skeuomorphic and skeuomorphic icons; no significant difference was found between the impacts of semi-skeuomorphic and skeuomorphic icons. This is basically consistent with the research results of Burmistrov (2015), which claimed that when performing visual search tasks, it takes a longer time for participants to identify flat icons than that required to identify icons with more traditional styles; further, he claimed that flat designs caused higher cognitive loads.

Table 4. Effects of style, semantic distance, and smart-phone experience on response time.

Items of ANOVA	SS	df	MS	F	p
style	71.933	2	35.966	16.013	0.000*
semantic distance	186.368	1	186.368	63.613	0.000*
experience	207.408	1	207.408	59.036	0.000*
style*experience	1.343	2	0.672	0.299	0.743
semantic distance*experience	0.131	1	0.131	0.045	0.835
style*semantic distance	11.619	2	5.809	3.045	0.058
style*semantic distance*experience	6.290	2	3.145	1.648	0.204
Multiple comparisons	*Mean difference*		*Std. Error*		*p*
flat vs. semi-skeuomorphic	0.975		0.305		0.004*
flat vs. skeuomorphic	1.726		0.291		0.000*
semi-skeuomorphic vs. skeuomorphic	0.752		0.321		0.029

3.2 Preference

Three-way ANOVA was conducted and the assumption of sphericity was not violated (X2(2) = 2.991, p = 0.224). The main effects of style, semantic distance, and experience were observed, and then a Fisher LSD test was conducted to compare the three levels of design style. The results (Table 5) indicate that icons with close semantic distance were rated significantly higher in terms of preference than those with far semantic distances (F(1, 22) = 25.894, p < 0.001), and participants' experience could also affect their preference. Experienced participants tended to give generally higher marks than those of the inexperienced ones (F(1, 22) = 17.287, p < 0.001). Style was also a critical factor (F(2, 44) = 23.649, p < 0.001). According to the results of the LSD test, the subjects' preferences for semi-skeuomorphic and skeuomorphic icons were significantly higher than those of the flat icons, while no significant difference was found between the impact of semi-skeuomorphic and skeuomorphic design on the preference rating.

Table 5. Effects of style, semantic distance, and smart-phone experience on preference rating.

Items of ANOVA	SS	df	MS	F	p
style	19.645	2	9.823	23.649	0.000*
semantic distance	20.062	1	20.062	25.894	0.000*
experience	16.168	1	16.168	17.287	0.000*
style*experience	1.944	2	0.972	2.340	0.108
semantic distance*experience	0.293	1	0.293	0.379	0.545
style*semantic distance	2.053	2	1.026	1.928	0.157
style*semantic distance*experience	0.209	2	0.104	0.196	0.823
Multiple comparisons	*Mean difference*		*Std. Error*		*p*
flat vs. semi-skeuomorphic	−0.695		0.145		0.000*
flat vs. skeuomorphic	−0.849		0.141		0.000*
semi-skeuomorphic vs. skeuomorphic	−0.154		0.105		0.158

3.3 Interview

Semi-structured interviews were conducted after the experiments. According to the participants' performance, we asked a series of open questions to further understand their feelings and views towards different icon design strategies. The findings were as follows:

First, icon identification is closely related to the activation and extraction of long-term memory (Ganor and Te'eni 2016). The experienced participants were able to retrieve and activate useful information from their long-term memories of the physical world as well as smartphone using (virtual world) experience to complete identification tasks, while the inexperienced ones relied more on their memories of only the physical world. For example, 83.33% (10 people) of the participants in the experienced group could correctly identify the icon shown in Fig. 5(a), which represents the function of contacts. However, only 33.33% (4 people) of the inexperienced participants identified it. Through the interview, we found that participants who failed to identify the icon did not manage their contacts with a notebook in their daily lives, as depicted in Fig. 5(a). In contrast, they claimed that they did not have many regular contacts; therefore, they tended to print or transcribe their contacts on a piece of paper in a large font and place it right next to the phone or stick it on the wall. On the other hand, the participants with rich smart phone experience were already accustomed to organizing and managing their contact information through the contacts app or other social media apps, such as Wechat on their phone. Therefore, when asked what clues in this icon helped them to correctly identify it, most of the experienced participants claimed that the shape of a portrait profile on the cover played the major role, because it was similar to the corresponding icons in their mobile phones (Fig. 5(b)). In contrast, the inexperienced participants who were able to identify the icon (4 people) claimed that the notebook-like form provided the main clue because they had the experience of recording their contacts in a notebook, and they thought the profile shape on the cover was just a decoration.

(a)   (b)

Fig. 5. (a) Contacts icon used in this study and (b) the contacts icon in Wechat.

Secondly, the ability of the participants to understand the meanings of the icons affected their preference. In the interview, most participants claimed that when giving preference marks, they usually compared the function description to the icons with their own opinions. Clearly understandable icons were rated more favourably, while those that caused confusions were given lower ratings even if they were more aesthetically pleasing. This partially explains the fact that the results of the preference test are consistent with the results of the performance test. In other words, icons that brought about better performance also obtained higher degrees of preference. Furthermore, some participants argued that the reason why they did not like the flat icons was the monotonous colour schemes; this is because to pursue a simple visual impression, flat icons often use large blocks of colours with few details, layers, and brightness changes. In the interview, participants expressed their criticism of this "dull and tedious" style, especially for the black and white flat icons. In contrast, they preferred icons in "lively and vivid" colours, which are more commonly used in semi-skeuomorphic and skeuomorphic icons.

Finally, in the interview, some experienced subjects expressed the difficulty encountered in identifying the parts of the skeuomorphic icons because the icons were "so complex that careful observation was needed to identify the details clearly; otherwise they could not understand the meanings of the icons". This is consistent with the results that the identification accuracy of experienced participants for skeuomorphic icons decreased to a lower level than that observed for semi-skeuomorphic icons. A typical example is the icon shown in Fig. 6(a), representing the function of remote control. Only 41.67% (5 people) of the experienced participants could correctly identify it. During the interview, we further communicated with these subjects, asking for their opinions on how to depict the icon of remote control function more properly and encouraging them to sketch out their creative ideas. As shown in several representative sketches (Fig. 6(b, c, d)), participants tried to depict the function with some simpler and less three-dimensional elements, and they represented the abstract infrared signal with a variety of shapes. These sketches were more similar to the icon styles in smart phones they use every day, which indicated that these elderly participants with rich smart phone using experience have adapted to a relatively simple icon style to some extent, and the icons with too much detail may lead to confusion.

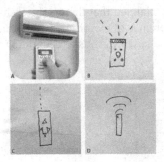

Fig. 6. (a): Remote control icon used in this study; (b)(c)(d): participants' sketches of their own ideas.

4   Conclusion

In this study, we investigated how different icon design styles and semantic distances affect the icon identification and preference of older users with different levels of smart phone experience. The results can provide references and guidelines for current user interface design practice. In terms of style, we proposed the concept of semi-skeuomorphic design, according to the current UI design trend and newly emerged design languages, and we compared it with the flat design and skeuomorphic design that have long been under debate.

First, as a vital cognitive attribute, semantic distance had significantly influenced the subjects' recognition and preference for icons. The icons with a close semantic distance were easier to understand for older users, as reflected in the higher identification accuracy and lower response time. Regarding accuracy, the impact of semantic distance was influenced by the level of experience of the participants. Those with rich smart phone experience tended to be more sensitive to the improvement in semantic distance and could better exploit the resulting increase in usability to achieve greater improvement in identification accuracy. Meanwhile, participants also preferred icons with close semantic distance due to usability advantages.

Second, the design style of icons significantly affect icon recognition and preference. Semi-skeuomorphic and skeuomorphic icons led to better performance than flat icons in terms of identification accuracy and response time. Participants also showed greater preference for these two styles. In most cases, no significant difference was found between the influence of semi-skeuomorphic and skeuomorphic icons. However, the interaction between style and experience indicated that icon style influenced participants with different levels of experience in different patterns. As icon style became increasingly concrete and complex, inexperienced participants could exploit these increased details and clues to achieve higher identification accuracy. However, experienced participants were hindered by the overuse of details. Further, in the interviews, consistent opinions were expressed and a few more concise and abstract icon sketches were created by the experienced participants as alternatives to the original icon that caused confusion for them in the identification experiment. We presume that this was related to frequent use over long periods. The accumulation of experience made them more familiar and comfortable with the common icon styles in current smart phone interfaces.

In summary, elderly people can nowadays adapt to smart phone interfaces to a certain extent via learning and frequent use, and compared with inexperienced older users, those . with rich smart phone experience have higher capability to correctly identify icons of all three design styles. However, more careful consideration from the designer's perspective is still necessary to achieve better user experience for older adults.

In the process of icon design for older users, on the one hand, semantic distance should be considered, and designers should select objects or concepts closely related to the representing function of the icon to make it as appropriate as possible. On the other hand, the icon style is a vital factor that should be properly understood and controlled to avoid excessive simplification or lack of details and visual clues, both of which will reduce the usability of icons. Appropriate arrangement of shadow, perspective, texture, and other details that simulate the physical world can make icons more easily identifiable by older adults. Meanwhile, the fine details and vivid colours rendered by these elements could also gain more preference from them. Skeuomorphic icons seem to be more suitable for novice older users because rich details and concrete forms can help them understand and learn the use of smart devices more efficiently during an early stage. With the increase of experience, semi-skeuomorphic style would be more in line with older users' cognitive habits because the relatively simple and concise form can enhance interaction efficiency in frequent use for long periods.

One limitation of this study is that only Chinese elderly users participated. Therefore the influence of cultural backgrounds was neglected and the results may not be valid among elderly users from other nations. Moreover, interfaces of smart devices consist of a variety of design elements, including icons, menus, navigation, images, and text. An efficient and easy-to-use interface requires a reasonable and systematic combination of all these factors. Therefore in future research, we will focus on more systematic interaction interface design, and consider the interaction experience of the elderly in real scenarios. Comparative study between subjects of different cultural backgrounds is also necessary.

Acknowledgment. This work was supported by Beijing Municipal Social Science Foundation [Grant No. 17YTB011] and Social Science Foundation of Ministry of Education of China [Grant No. 18YJA760053].

References

Alario, F.X., Ferrand, L., New, M.L.B., Frauenfelder, U.H., Segui, J.: Predictors of picture naming speed. Behav. Res. Methods Instru. Comput. **36**(1), 140–155 (2004)

Arazy, O., Nov, O., Kumar, N.: Personalityzation: UI personalization, theoretical grounding in HCI and design research. AIS Trans. Hum. Comput. Interact. **7**(2), 43–69 (2015)

Backhaus, N., Trapp, A.K., Thüring, M.: Skeuomorph Versus Flat Design: User Experience and Age-Related preferences. In: Marcus, A., Wang, W. (eds.) DUXU 2018. LNCS, vol. 10919, pp. 527–542. Springer, Cham (2018). https://doi.org/10.1007/978-3-319-91803-7_40

Burmistrov, I., Zlokazova, T., Izmalkova, A., Leonova, A.: Flat design vs traditional design: comparative experimental study. In: INTERACT 2015 - 15th IFIP TC 13 International Conference (2015)

Cho, M., Kwon, S., Na, N., Lee, K.P., Suk, H.J.: The elders preference for skeuomorphism as app icon style. In: Proceedings of the 33rd Annual ACM Conference Extended Abstracts on Human Factors in Computing Systems, pp. 899–904 (2015)

Dickinson, A., Newell, A.F., Smith, M.J., Hill, R.L.: Introducing the Internet to the over-60 s: developing an email system for older novice computer users. Interact. Comput. **17**(6), 621–642 (2005)

Ellis, A.W., Morrison, C.M.: Real age-of-acquisition effects in lexical retrieval. J. Exp. Psychol. Learn. Memory Cogn. **24**(2), 515–523 (1998)

Findlater, L., Froehlich, J.E., Fattal, K., Wobbrock, J.O., Dastyar, T.: Age-related differences in performance with touchscreens compared to traditional mouse input. In: Proceedings of the SIGCHI Conference on Human Factors in Computing Systems, pp. 343–346. ACM (2013)

García, M., Badre, A.N., Stasko, J.T.: Development and validation of icons varying in their abstractness. Interacti. Comput. **6**(2), 191–211 (1994)

Ganor, N., Te'eni, D.: Designing interfaces for older users: effects of icon detail and semantic distance. AIS Trans. Hum. Comput. Interact. **8**(1), 22–38 (2016)

Gatsou, C., Politis, A., Zevgolis, D.: The importance of mobile interface icons on user interaction. Int. J. Comput. Sci. Appl. **9**(7), 92–107 (2012)

Goonetilleke, R.S., Shih, H.M., On, H.K., Fritsch, J.: Effects of training and representational characteristics in icon design. Int. J. Hum Comput Stud. **55**, 741–760 (2001)

Hawthorne, D.: How universal is good design for older users? In: Conference on Universal Usability. ACM (2003)

Humphreys, G.W., Riddoch, M.J., Quinlan, P.T.: Cascade processes in picture identification. Cogn. Neuropsychol. **5**, 67–104 (1988)

Isherwood, S.J., Mcdougall, S.J.P., Curry, M.B.: Icon identification in context: the changing role of icon characteristics with user experience. Hum. Factors **49**(3), 465–476 (2007)

Leung, R., McGrenere, J., Graf, P.: Age-related differences in the initial usability of mobile device icons. Behav. Inf. Technol. **30**(5), 629–642 (2011)

Lloyd-Jones, T.J., Luckhurst, L.: Effects of plane rotation, task, and complexity on recognition of familiar and chimeric objects. Mem. Cogn. **30**(4), 499–510 (2002)

Lloyd-Jones, T.J., Nettlemill, M.: Sources of error in picture naming under time pressure. Mem. Cogn. **35**(4), 816–836 (2007)

Moyes, J., Jordan, P.W.: Icon design and its effect on guessability, learnability, and experienced user performance. People Comput. **8**, 49–60 (1993)

McDougall, S.J., Curry, M.B., de Bruijn, O.: Understanding what makes icons effective: how subjective ratings can inform design. In: Hanson, M. (ed.) Contemporary Ergonomics, pp. 285–289. CRC Press, Boca Raton (1998)

Mcdougall, S.J.P., Curry, M.B., Bruijn, O.D.: Measuring symbol and icon characteristics: norms for concreteness, complexity, meaningfulness, familiarity, and semantic distance for 239 symbols. Behav. Res. Methods Instru. Comput. **31**(3), 487–519 (1999)

McDougall, S.J., de Bruijn, O., Curry, M.B.: Exploring the effects of icon characteristics on user performance: the role of icon concreteness, complexity, and distinctiveness. J. Exp. Psychol. Appl. **6**(4), 291 (2000)

Mcdougall, S., Isherwood, S.: What's in a name? the role of graphics, functions, and their inter-relationships in icon identification. Behav. Res. Methods Instru. Comput. **41**(2), 325–336 (2009)

Mertens, A., Koch-Körfges, D., Schlick, C.M.: Designing a user study to evaluate the feasibility of icons for the elderly. In: Mensch & Computer 2011: überMEDIEN|ÜBERmorgen. München: Oldenbourg Verlag, pp. 79–83 (2011)

Rogers, Y., Oborne, D.J.: Pictorial communication of abstract verbs in relation to human–computer interaction. Br. J. Psychol. **78**(1), 99–112 (1987)

Salthouse, T.: Consequences of age-related cognitive declines. Ann. Rev. Psychol. **63**(1), 201–226 (2012)

Schröder, S., Ziefle, M.: Effects of icon concreteness and complexity on semantic transparency: younger vs. older users. In: Miesenberger, K., Klaus, J., Zagler, W., Karshmer, A. (eds.) ICCHP 2008. LNCS, vol. 5105, pp. 90–97. Springer, Heidelberg (2008). https://doi.org/10.1007/978-3-540-70540-6_12

Stammers, R.B., Hoffman, J.: Transfer between icon sets and ratings of icon concreteness and appropriateness. In: Paper presented at Proceedings of the Human Factors and Ergonomics Society Annual Meeting. SAGE Publications, New York (1991)

Stotts, D.B.: The usefulness of icons on the computer interface: effect of graphical abstraction and functional representation on experienced and novice users. In: Paper presented at Proceedings of the Human Factors and Ergonomics Society Annual Meeting, vol. 42, no. 5, pp. 453–457. SAGE Publications, New York (1998)

Tu, Y.-L., Ho, C.-H.: The cognition of the elderly on the icons of smart phones. KEER 2018. AISC, vol. 739, pp. 612–621. Springer, Singapore (2018). https://doi.org/10.1007/978-981-10-8612-0_64

Vines, J., Pritchard, G., Wright, P., Olivier, P., Brittain, K.: An age-old problem: examining the discourses of ageing in HCI and strategies for future research. ACM Trans. Comput. Hum. Interact. **22**(1) (2015)

Wagner, N., Hassanein, K., Head, M.: The impact of age on website usability. Comput. Hum. Behav. **37**, 270–282 (2014)

Ziefle, M., Bay, S.: Mental models of a cellular phone menu. comparing older and younger novice users. In: Brewster, S., Dunlop, M. (eds.) Mobile HCI 2004. LNCS, vol. 3160, pp. 25–37. Springer, Heidelberg (2004). https://doi.org/10.1007/978-3-540-28637-0_3

Technology Acceptance and User Experience Studies

Determining Possible Risks of Introducing Socially Assistive Robots with Mobility Functions to Aged Care Facilities

Tomoya Hattori[1], Mio Nakamura[1], Kazuki Kawamura[2], and Misato Nihei[1]([✉])

[1] The University of Tokyo, Chiba, Japan
{1926146171,mnihei,nakamura.mio}@edu.k.u-tokyo.ac.jp
[2] Softbank Robotics Co. Ltd, Tokyo, Japan
kazuki01.kawamura@g.softbank.co.jp

Abstract. If introduced into aged care facilities, socially assistive robots (SARs) with mobility functions will expand the applications of robotics through their ability to take on new tasks, specifically, actively approaching residents and patrolling. However, because the residents of aged care facilities in Japan are frail, and more than 90% of them have dementia, robots with mobility functions must be introduced carefully. The purpose of this study is to investigate the possible risks of introducing SARs with mobility functions into aged care facilities. Consequently, online semi-structured interviews were conducted with staff of nine elderly care facilities, and cases highlighting the characteristic behaviors of older people with dementia were collected and analyzed. Based on the results, we present the possible risks of introducing SARs with mobility functions into aged care facilities and proposed countermeasures.

Keywords: Socially assistive robot · Risk assessment · Dementia

1 Introduction

Japan has the world's highest life expectancy, with a reported aging rate of 28.4% in 2019; the aging rate is the ratio of the population of older people (above 65) to the total population. However, the declining birthrate and rapidly aging population presents some peculiar social issues, such as an increase in the number of older people that require nursing care and a shortage in nursing care personnel. Consequently, toward achieving a human-centered society that aims to achieve both economic development and solutions to social issues through a system that integrates cyberspace (virtual space) and physical space (real space), the Cabinet Office has proposed the Society 5.0 in the Fifth Science and Technology Basic Plan. In this plan, the possibility of solving social problems related to nursing care through robotics was previously envisioned [1]. In particular, socially assistive robots (SARs) offer a variety of benefits to older people, such as providing opportunities for conversation, improving quality of life, and maintaining cognitive functions [2, 3]. In an experiment in which a number of SARs were introduced

Q. Gao and J. Zhou (Eds.): HCII 2021, LNCS 12786, pp. 145–155, 2021.
https://doi.org/10.1007/978-3-030-78108-8_11

into an aged care facility, the quality of life of approximately one-third of the subjects improved [4]. However, most of the SARs currently used in aged care facilities are installed in a specific location, such as the corner of a shared space, and long-term experiments have shown that users become bored with the SARs and stop approaching them, resulting in a decrease in the frequency of use [5].

In a related study, an SAR with mobility functions was introduced into an aged care facility, and a method whereby the SAR approaches the user to initiate conversation was proposed (approach behavior, hereinafter referred to as APB). Owing to the use of the APB method, the rate of successfully initiating a conversation with older people, who were not generally actively conversing with the SAR, increased, demonstrating the usefulness of SARs with mobility functions [6].

However, because many residents in aged care facilities are frail, the risk of injury through contact should be minimized. In addition, as more than 90% of the patients have dementia [7], it is necessary to develop risk assessment guidelines that consider unexpected behaviors caused by the peripheral symptoms of patients with dementia when introducing SARs with mobility functions into nursing homes. Although there have been studies on risk assessment frameworks for older people with dementia [8], to date, there are no guidelines for risk assessment when introducing SARs with mobility functions to aged care facilities.

Based on this background, the purpose of this study is to develop a risk assessment guideline for when introducing SARs with mobility functions into aged care facilities. The study was performed as follows. First, we conducted semi-structured interviews in aged care facilities to analyze the behavior of older people with dementia and collect data on related behavioral cases. Then, from the data obtained through the interviews, we classified the behaviors of older people with dementia and the caregivers' responses to them, extracted items that are applicable to interacting with SARs with mobility functions, and established guidelines for risk assessment based on those items.

2 Method

2.1 SAR

The SAR with the mobility function envisioned in this study is Pepper (Softbank Robotics Co., Ltd.), shown in Fig. 1. Pepper is 121-cm tall, approximately the same height as a child, making it easy for older residents and caregivers to recognize and notice its approach. In addition, Pepper is equipped with a mobility function—three omni-wheels—at its lower end. It can move and talk remotely via Bluetooth. In the future, it is envisioned that it will be equipped with functions such as autonomous driving, remote control, and obstacle detection. Therefore, it would be possible to avoid contact between the robot and older residents in small shared spaces and minimize the risk of injury. Further, the robot will be able to communicate automatically and remotely, and talk and respond according to the situation.

Currently, many of the SARs installed in Japanese aged care facilities through government projects are not mobile; hence, they are stationary when conducting conversations. Typical examples are Paro (ND Software Co., Ltd.) and Palro (Fujisoft Co., Ltd.), shown in Figs. 2 and 3, respectively.

Fig. 1. Pepper

Fig. 2. Paro

Fig. 3. Palro

2.2 Risk Assessment

The risks referred to in this study are the possible injuries and mental anxiety of the residents arising from the failure of SARs with mobility functions upon their introduction into aged care facilities. Risk assessment refers to the entire process, including risk identification, analysis, and evaluation. The extent to which risks can be foreseen is an important factor in minimizing residual risks. There are four safety standards for risk assessment that apply to machines with mobility functions (including carts, electric wheelchairs, etc.) [9].

- Standard A: Assessment Standard ISO14121
- Standard B: System Safety Standard ISO13849
- Standard B: Standard for Functional Safety IEC61508
- Standard C: Standard for Life Support Robots ISO13482

The constraints in this study include the following two factors concerning spatial conditions and interpersonal relationships:

- Spatial conditions of barrier-free, indoor aged care facilities (including day services and group homes)
- The interpersonal relationship between Pepper, older people, with and without dementia, care staff, and administrators

Because many older people with dementia are included in the situations covered by this study, semi-structured interviews were conducted with professionals in aged care facilities to establish the reactions and behaviors of older people with dementia toward SARs with mobility function, which are mainly caused by their symptoms.

2.3 Interviews with Aged Care Facilities

Participants. The recruitment of survey targets was conducted using the opportunity recruitment method. Various facility types were selected. The interviewees included a variety of professionals, including caregivers who routinely work with people with dementia and facility administrators. The target facilities were welfare facilities for older people (special nursing homes, health care facilities for older people, group homes, short-stay homes, and small-scale multifunctional in-home care facilities). The interviewees included nursing and medical staff and management personnel from each of the nine facilities considered. The basic information on the facilities is summarized in Table 1.

Table 1. Basic information on the facilities whose personnel were interviewed

No.	Type of facility	Number of residents	Average age of residents	Ratio of male to female residents
1	Group home	9	-	0:10
2	Health care facilities for older people	100	85	3:7
3	Special nursing homes/group home	39/18	88.9/88.1	1:3/1:8
4	Special nursing homes/short-stay	60/10	85	1:4
5	Fee-based nursing homes	–	85	1:2
6	Special nursing care/nursing home/day-care service	60/50/20	Range of age 80–95/75–95	1:4/1:3
7	Small-scale multifunctional in-home care/group home	15/6	90	0:10/1:2
8	Day-care service	30	82	1:9
9	Special nursing homes	75	86.7	1:9

Interview Method. Semi-structured interviews were conducted using an interview guide via online videoconferencing. The data acquired using the interview guide included basic information, such as facility type and size, characteristics of residents, ratio of males to females, percentage of people with dementia, number of people using wheelchairs and equipment, and age range. Questions pertaining to the introduction of robots included, "Have you ever been introduced to a robot, and if so, what kind?", "How did residents react to and behave toward the robots?", and "What kind of SAR safety functions do you think are necessary?" Other questions pertained to unexpected behaviors of people with dementia toward objects in the facility other than robots (TVs, sensors, cupboards, desks, stuffed animals, and dolls) and the facility's response to such behaviors. The final set of questions pertained to the unexpected behaviors of people with dementia toward facility staff and visitors. Facilities that had never introduced robots were asked how they thought people with dementia would respond to robots, whether they would like to introduce robots, and what safety-related functions did they think were necessary.

Analysis and Ethics. A verbatim transcript was created from the data of the recorded interviews, and each statement was labeled. We also analyzed (1) the behavior of older people with dementia toward objects (excluding robots), (2) the behavior of older people with dementia, and (3) the behavior of older people with dementia toward robots.

This research was approved by the University of Tokyo's Ethical Review Committee (Demonstration Experiment of a Communication Robot with Mobility Functions in Nursing Care Settings (5), Project No. 20-267).

2.4 Results

Behavior of Older People with Dementia toward Objects. The behavior of older people with dementia toward various "objects" installed in the facility were extracted from the interview. Noted typical behavior included "unplugging the TV (ID001-14)," "stripping a part of the floor (ID004-14)," and "collecting toilet paper (ID007-4)". In this section, we categorize the interview data into target "objects," "behaviors," and "factors."

These "objects", "behaviors", and "factors" are listed in Table 2. There were 29 types of objects, 22 types of behaviors, and seven types of factors. However, even the facility staff did not know all the possible factors, and in the survey, "banging on walls", "knocking over desks," "disassembling remote controls and beds," "pulling and breaking nurse call buttons and door handles," "eating different foods," and "collecting things (including things that do not belong to him/her)" were mentioned as behaviors specific to dementia, but no clear causes were provided.

The actions noted to be associated with the behaviors include "unplug," "wash," "hit," "knock down," "saw wrong," "eat (parts)," and "disassemble (or try to disassemble)." These actions were cited as risks that could damage equipment or affect the residents' own health. Conversely, positive behaviors (emotional changes), such as calming down and caring, were also noted. The causes could generally be explained by the core and peripheral symptoms of dementia (behavioral and psychological symptoms in dementia (BPSD)). In many cases, staff immediately intervened to limit the impact of highly destructive behaviors such as eating disorders or violence. Conversely, for less urgent behaviors, most of the subjects interviewed stated that they would not intervene; rather, they would subtly distract the patient, if necessary.

Table 2. Classification of behaviors of older people with dementia toward objects

Objects	Actions	Factors
Emergency lamp	Press a button	· Concerned about light
Photo	Gather	· Mistake it for something else
Sensor	Wash	· Misunderstand others and
Mirror	Eat	acquaintances
TV	Unplug	· Concerned about fragile parts
Fireplace	Saw wrong	· Feel lonely
Air conditioner	Put hands in	· Think they have been called
Baby doll	Collect	· Hallucination
Air purifier	Put in garbage	(7 types)
Vacuum cleaner	Defecate	
Humidifier	Talk to	
Floor	Calm down	
Trash can	Care	
Wall	Sleep together	
Desk	Throw	
Remote controller	Hit	
Bed	Peel off	
Nurse call	Knock down	
Door handle	Disassemble	
Room light	Push	
Soap	Pull	
Wrinkled sheet	Tuck away	
Toothpaste	(22 types)	
Outlet		
Soil in vase		
Tissue		
Toilet paper		
Facility items		
Other people's things		
(29 types)		

Behavior Analysis of Older People with Dementia. The results of the interviews—including experiences related to the behaviors of people with dementia, support to deal with them, and the assumptions of caregivers—were extracted and categorized by behavior. The causes of the behaviors were categorized into core and peripheral symptoms of dementia.

The interviews revealed that there were 35 cases of behaviors that caused problems for caregivers in residential and day-care facilities for older people with dementia. These included nine cases of verbal abuse and violent behavior, eight cases of misrecognition and delusion, five cases of malacia, three cases of abnormal behavior due to anxiety, three cases of desire to return home, two cases of wandering and related behaviors, two cases of auditory hallucinations, two cases of persistent verbal behavior, and one case of crashing into a window. The summary of the causes of the behaviors and the facilities' response measures is presented in Table 3.

Table 3. Causes of behavior of people with dementia toward others and facility support

Symptoms	Number of symptoms	Behaviors	Number of behavior	Type of Support	Support
Excitement	9	Thoughtless words	4	Environmental support	Keep seats apart
				Human support	Intermediation
					Listening
					Interview with family
		Violent behaviors	5	Environmental support	Keep seats apart
				Human support	Intermediation
					Communicating in writing
				Pharmacotherapy	Medication adjustment
Delusion	7	Misrecognition	7	Human support	Supervision (If there is no effect on health)
Allotments	5	Misrecognition	5	Human support	Supervision (If there is no effect on health)
				Environmental support	Getting rid of the object
Desire to go home	3	Anxiety	3	Human support	Let them do some tasks
				Pharmacotherapy	Medication adjustment
Roaming	2	Escape	1		
		Lost	1		
Defect of memory	2	Thoughtless words	2	Human support	Listening
Delusion of victimization	1	Misrecognition	1		
Hallucination		Misrecognition	1		
Auditory hallucination		Misrecognition	1		
Decline in spatial cognition	1	Collision	1		

Verbal abuse and violent behavior were the most common factors that caused concern for caregivers. Caregivers' responses to these verbal and violent behaviors included environmental interventions, such as changing the seating arrangement and keeping a distance from the patient, as well as social interventions, such as mediation between conflicting parties, calming the patient down verbally, organizing meetings with family members to change the patient's mood, and adjusting medication via therapy.

Caregivers' responses to misrecognition or delusion were adjusted for each specific case. However, generally, they did not intervene, especially if there was no danger of injury, and preserved the patient's dignity by simply supervising. In the case of malacia, environmental support was provided, such as removing items that posed a danger to the patient and supervising the patients to ensure their safety. For thirty-two cases, peripheral symptoms were indicated to be the main factor, whereas three cases were presumed to be caused by core symptoms, indicating that the majority of behaviors were caused by peripheral symptoms. The most common responses by nursing staff were environmental, such as consideration of seating arrangements, exclusion from the field of vision, and creation of relaxing environments, followed by the use of human support, such as mediation, listening, and supervision. It was not confirmed whether the responses pertained to the peripheral or core symptoms.

Behavior of Older People with Dementia toward Robots We conducted interviews on the behavior of people with dementia toward communication robots and nursing care robots. Facilities that had experience with robots were asked to respond based on their actual experiences with the robots. Conversely, facilities that had no experience with robots were asked to draw on their imagination to anticipate the possible risks. In the facilities surveyed, three types of robots had been previously introduced, namely Pepper, Paro, and Palo, as described in Subsect. 2.1.

It was discovered through the survey that, after introducing the robots, facilities put up signs, such as, "Please stay away from the robots," to ensure safe use, had staff members nearby for supervision at all times, and stored them out of reach when they were not in use.

Positive impressions of the robot were found to be the result of the robot being an object that attracts attention or sparks curiosity. The interview respondents also interpreted some kind of stimulation as a good response, such as the fact that they were able to have a conversation, that they tried to communicate, or that people who tended to be quiet or withdrawn started to talk actively. Conversely, negative impressions of the robot included mismatches between the cognitive functions of the user and robot, with results such as eventual boredom with the robot, difficulty in conversation timing, and the robot being insufficient for people with relatively strong cognitive functions. In addition, there were some interactions that contrasted the positive experiences, such as handling the robot roughly, being afraid of it, or receiving limited response from it.

Based on the data from the interview survey, we classified the possible risks of introducing SARs with mobility functions into three categories: user-side physical risk, SAR-side physical risks, and risks that induce mental anxiety in users. For each of these, we further classified the risks into nine, five, and three categories, respectively. The opinions of each group are summarized in Table 4.

Table 4. Classification of risks posed by behaviors of older people with dementia toward SARs

User-side physical risks	SAR-side physical risks	Risks that cause mental anxiety in users
· Contact, Conflict with SAR · Trapped underneath a fallen SAR · Injury from lifting SAR · Lean on SAR and fall down together · Fall down because of being surprised by a call from behind · Fall down because of being surprised by oncoming SAR · Eat parts of SAR · Induce unnecessary behavior in users (e.g. Stand up) · Follow SAR (9 types)	· Contact, Conflict with users · Beaten by users · Lifted by users · Taken down by users · Fed by users (5 types)	· Dependence on SAR · Visual illusion induced by SAR · Spoken to by SAR when not feeling well (3 types)

3 Formulation of Risk Assessment

Based on the analysis of the interviews, we organized the possible incidents that may occur when older people with dementia use or encounter a situation where a SAR with mobile functions is used and summarized them, as summarized in Table 5. The possible risks and corresponding countermeasures are listed in the left and right columns of the table, respectively.

Table 5. Risk assessment

Possible risks	Countermeasures
【Move function】 (1) SAR falls down during movement · Trapped underneath a fallen SAR · Lean on SAR and fall down together · Injury from lifting SAR (2) Contact or collision with moving SAR (3) Fall down without contact with SAR · Fall down because of being surprised by a call from behind · Fall down because of being surprised by oncoming SAR (4) Wander around with SAR · Wander around the facility with SAR · Follow SAR · Attempt to get out of the facility · Take SAR somewhere else	【Countermeasures by equipment and functions】 · Increase the base of support of SAR or lower the center of gravity (1) · Make sure that SAR is alerted when it is about to fall down or when it is subjected to an external force (1) · Reduce SAR's movement speed (1) (2) · Detect obstacles to prevent contact or collision (2) · Talk to users before approaching them (3) · Do not talk to the person from behind (3) · Limit the SAR's movement range (4) 【Countermeasures by environment】 · Limit the distance between SAR and the person with dementia (1) (2) 【Countermeasures by people】 · Proximal monitoring by caregivers (1) (2) (4) · The caregiver moves with SAR and the person with dementia. (4)

4 Conclusion

To study the characteristics of the behavior of older people with dementia in determining the possible risk associated with introducing SAR with mobility functions into aged care facilities, online semi-structured interviews were conducted with facility operators and staff members of nine aged care facilities. The items extracted for "behaviors of older people with dementia toward objects" were as follows: objects (29 types), behaviors (22 types), and factors (seven types). For "behavior of people with dementia toward robots," the following items were extracted: user-side physical risks (nine types), SAR-side physical risks (five types), and risks of causing mental anxiety to users (three types). In addition, these results were summarized, and the possible risks were extracted in terms of factor-related, behavior-related, and structure/shape-related risks. As for the "behavior of dementia patients," the characteristics were extracted from the perspective of peripheral and core symptoms, which were assumed from when the robot was introduced to the facility.

Finally, we organized these items and classified the countermeasures to the possible risks of introducing SARs with mobility function into measures by equipment and function, environment, and people.

Acknowledgments. We would like to thank the participants of the interviews for their cooperation. This research was supported by AMED, under Grant Number JP 19he2002016.
We would like to thank Editage (www.editage.com) for English language editing.

References

1. Ministry of economy, trade and industry: Japan's Robot Strategy 2015 (2015)
2. Nihei, M., et al.: Change in the relationship between the elderly and information support robot system living together. In: HCI International 2017 (2017)
3. Igarashi, T., Nihei, M., Nakamura, M., Obayashi, K., Masuyama, S., Kamata, M.: Socially assistive robots influence for elderly with cognitive impairment living in nursing facilities: micro observation and analysis. In: 15th AAATE Conference (2019)
4. Japan Agency for Medical Research and Development: Project to Promote the Development and Introduction of Robotic Devices for Nursing Care (2017)
5. Nakamura, M., Kato, N., Kondo, E., Inoue, T.: Verification of effectiveness of introducing communication robots in residential facilities for the elderly. In: The 11th Conference on Rehabilitation Engineering and Assistive Technology Society of Korea 2017 (2017)
6. Nihei, M., Nakamura, M., Ikeda, K., Kawamura, K., Yamashita, H., Kamata, M.: Approaching behavior analysis for improving a mobile communication robot in a nursing home. In: HCI International 2020 -Late Breaking Papers: Universal Access and Inclusive Design, pp. 679–688 (2020)
7. Ministry of Health, Labor and Welfare, Status of users of long-term care 9 July 2020. https://www.mhlw.go.jp/toukei/saikin/hw/kaigo/service16/dl/kekka-gaiyou_05.pdf
8. Lee, L., et al.: Person-centered risk assessment framework: assessing and managing risk in older adults living with dementia. Neurodegen. Dis. Manage. **9**(1) (2019)
9. Hirukawa: "Safety Technology for Life Support Robots" (2010). https://www.ipa.go.jp/files/000004101.pdf

Older People as Early Adopters and Their Unexpected and Innovative Use of New Technologies: Deviating from Technology Companies' Scripts

Eugène Loos[1]([⊠]), Alexander Peine[2], and Mireia Fernandéz-Ardèvol[3]

[1] Utrecht University School of Governance, Utrecht University, Utrecht, The Netherlands
e.f.loos@uu.nl
[2] Copernicus Institute of Sustainable Development, Utrecht University, Utrecht, The Netherlands
a.peine@uu.nl, lbm.neven@avans.nl
[3] Internet Interdisciplinary Institute (IN3), Universitat Oberta de Catalunya/Open University of Catalonia, Barcelona (Catalonia), Spain
mfernandezar@uoc.edu

Abstract. Technology companies, when considering the design of their products or services, tend to configure users by scripting appropriate user interactions with their technology. Older users are often seen as laggards who take no part in innovation processes. The scripts for technology use planned by technology companies rarely take older users into account. Hence the role of older adults in participating in innovation processes, challenging scripts and reconfiguring technologies has not been well researched. We present four cases in which the role of older adults in innovation processes is examined: as early adopters (case 1); in playing an active role in deviating from technology companies' scripts (cases 2 and 3); or in clarifying these scripts (case 4). Finally, we present our conclusions and implications for future innovative practices, focusing on the importance for technology companies not only to involve younger, but also older people when designing new technologies with underlying scripts that are useful in their everyday life.

Keywords: Older people · Early adopters · New technologies · Unexpected use · Innovative use · Technology companies · Scripts · Configuring users · Reconfiguring technologies · Adoption · Appropriation · Repossession

1 Introduction

In the innovation diffusion literature, older people, if considered at all, are typically positioned as laggards, i.e., old age is often associated with an increased propensity not, or only reluctantly, to adopt new technologies [1]. Despite the relative absence of empirical evidence supporting this viewpoint, widespread stereotypes would have it that older people cannot be early adopters of new technologies. This paper will present four counter-intuitive examples that challenge the assumption that older people are laggards

© Springer Nature Switzerland AG 2021
Q. Gao and J. Zhou (Eds.): HCII 2021, LNCS 12786, pp. 156–167, 2021.
https://doi.org/10.1007/978-3-030-78108-8_12

who are the last to follow technology companies' planned scripts, and only doing so long after new technologies have been adopted by young users. We agree with Pinch [2, p. 247] who argues that:

> "Woolgar [3] has shown how designers actively" "configure" users, and Akrich [4] has argued that the appropriated user interaction with a technology is "scripted" into its design. Users in turn, can challenge such scripts and reconfigure technologies (Latour [5], Akrich [4]). (...) Historians have studied how users come up with (...) completely new uses for technologies. Douglas [6] drew attention to the role of amateurs operators in the history of radio, Fischer [7] and Martin [8] have shown how rural women first used the telephone for extended conversations rather than simply short business calls, and Kline and Pinch [9] documented the use of the automobile as a stationary source of power rural in the rural United States."

As far as we know, the role of older adults in challenging scripts and reconfiguring technologies through unexpected and innovative uses has not been very well researched. For this reason, we present four cases showing that older people can and do play an active role in deviating from technology companies' scripts.

The first case presents the history of the e-bike [10, 11] and the involvement of older customers who were anything but laggards. Secondly, we present a case describing the strategic use of deliberate missed calls by older people in Barcelona (Catalonia). The third case presents the development of the "Are you okay today" app by an 83-year-old man as part of the innovative start-up-plus program created by the Dutch knowledge centre, Leyden Academy on Vitality and Ageing. The fourth case is about the experiences of a 75-year-old woman who took part in testing the use of Google speakers, another initiative of the Leyden Academy on Vitality and Ageing. This resulted in a how-to guide for other older users, enabling other older users to make use of this new technology in such a way that it fit their everyday life needs. This shows what can happen when older people are given a voice in innovation processes.

Finally, we will present our conclusions and implications for future innovative practices, focusing on the importance for technology companies to involve older people when designing new technologies with underlying scripts that are useful for their everyday life. In our opinion, beyond adoption, appropriation – which happens when users make a technology their own – becomes relevant as a source of innovation. Bar et al. [12] argue that "appropriation challenges the initial power structure embedded in a technology, fostering new practices and new technological implementations." [12, p. 619]. The appropriation model they propose has three steps: "technology evolution [is] a three-stage cyclical process of adoption, appropriation, and repossession" [12, p. 624]. Users drive adoption – and further appropriation – and providers react by reclaiming the resulting innovations. Repossession modes include, on the one hand, learning from final users' practices to embed them into successive iterations of the product/service; and on the other hand, to block or suppress an innovation that technology companies and providers find too antagonistic. Under this perspective, the four cases discussed here illustrate how older people's everyday life needs may be taken into account for a more nuanced, richer evaluation of innovation processes.

2 Method

We generate insights into the unexpected and innovative use of new technologies by older people on the basis of three research projects that were initiated and conducted by the authors of this paper. We draw on these cases to reflect on older people as early adopters and their unexpected and innovative use of new technologies. For more details on the methods, we refer to Sect. 3.1 for case 1, Sect. 3.2 for case 2, and Sect. 3.3 for cases 3 and 4.

3 Cases

3.1 E-bike

In the literature on innovation diffusion – a notion famously introduced and elaborated by Rogers [1] – age is a contested topic. According to the theory of innovation diffusion, acceptance and use of a new technology is driven by social contagion – a notion that Rogers developed, having been heavily influenced by French sociologist Tarde [13] (see also [14]). This implies that *early adopters* – individuals who are particularly quick to embrace a new technology even before its usability and usefulness have been demonstrated - serve as important initiators of innovation diffusion. In the prolific literature on innovation diffusion, the defining characteristics of early adopters remain somewhat ambiguous. Uncertainty abounds regarding the extent to which these characteristics must be empirically determined per case (i.e., they are characteristics manifesting in specific human-machine relations), or whether they are generic traits of certain socio-demographic groups. In this latter view, which arguably is the most influential in industry discourses on innovation diffusion, early adopters are often said to be highly educated, venturesome, have a high exposure to diverse media channels, be socially well connected, and so forth [15]. Empirical studies that link age to different adopter characteristics are inconsistent [1]. It is therefore all the more interesting that studies that describe adopter categories in terms of generic traits of individuals generally associate older age with late adoption or with being a laggard [16, 17]. To the degree that innovation diffusion theory has found its way into marketing textbooks and popular business vernacular, this stance has contributed to the widespread and ageist assumption that older people are an adopter group of low interest for the diffusion and use of new technologies [10].

Against this background, the history of the electric bicycle, or simply e-bike, is an interesting one. In the Netherlands, sales of e-bikes outnumbered those of regular bikes in 2019 [18], and e-bikes are now used across all age groups, including, to a growing extent, secondary school students. E-bikes these days come in many varieties, but they are generally sleek and only distinguishable from normal bikes by a fairly inconspicuous battery underneath the luggage rack. They also come in more expensive and more sportive variants that carry more obvious signifiers of battery and motor assistance.

However, closer examination of the rise of the e-bike and the diffusion of this technology over the past 10–15 years reveals that this popularity was a later development. In the early 2000s, E-bikes tended to be clunky, with glaringly conspicuous electric assistance systems. They were quite obviously useful only to those requiring assistance and no longer able to ride a regular bike. Older people were among the first group of adopters [11], which meant that during the 2000s, the dominant users of e-bikes were older people, with whom they became strongly associated. How then to explain why the diffusion of e-bike usage did not end with this age group, but instead spread to become popular among Dutch bicyclists of all ages? And what role did the older early adopters play in this process of innovation diffusion?

These are questions that the second co-author of the present paper addressed in a 2017 study, during which 17 qualitative interviews were conducted with nearly all Dutch manufacturers of e-bikes [10]. The study focussed particularly on the manufacturers' recollections of the diffusion history of e-bikes, and how they related features of certain e-bike designs to the use practices of various age groups throughout this history. From these recollections, it became apparent that manufacturers frequently related the early adoption of e-bikes to an imaginary of the fourth age [19]. In their stories of the early days of e-bikes, they coupled the clunkiness of e-bike designs to the vulnerabilities of old age. As one of our respondents explained about the first e-bike designs (original quotes in Dutch, translated to English by A.P.):

"When we began, it was meant as a successor to the Spartamet [a bike with a gasoline auxiliary engine]; this was thus a target group of individuals that wanted to continue riding a bicycle, but needed a little bit of assistance. Hence, it was the somewhat older target group. A fairly old target group. That's where the success of the electric bike began." (R1)

But back then, it was anything but obvious that e-bike use would further diffuse among older and younger age groups. This became clear from the more ageist language used by other respondents in their description of the early adopters of e-bikes, as illustrated by the following quotes:

"(…) the first bikes that were electric were all for old geezers. Those that rode them were all old geezers. That's what it was associated with. [...] 'And what will the neighbors think' – that was the impression given by one of those things [*early e-bikes*]." (R2)

"In the beginning, the target group was disabled persons; one could not imagine a normal human being …an able-bodied person riding an electrical bike – insane by definition." (R3)

These recollections demonstrate that "fourth age" users – as some of the respondents explicitly called them – were not a preferred group of e-bike users. In particular, they were not deemed to be promising early adopters, because they would simply not have the contagion potential to initiate a broader uptake of e-bikes. On the contrary, many respondents noted that older adopters became the target group for the early e-bikes precisely because these early designs were not attractive to those not in dire need of assistance. Even for these e-bike manufacturers, it was difficult, at least initially, to recognize that older people could be innovative and potentially influential adopters of this new technology. Although older people were the first to adopt the use of e-bikes, it was difficult for the manufacturers to view them as *early adopters* and they consequently continued to refer to them as laggards.

In practice, however, these imagined fourth age users turned out to be something quite different. As our respondents frequently remarked, these early users of e-bikes indeed had a need for assistance, but they also – probably less surprisingly than our respondents were prepared to admit – had a keen interest in image and appearance, as well as in adding a little extra range to their existing bicycling practices. In reality, the imagined fourth age cyclists turned out to be solidly embedded in the cultural field of the third age [19]. One of our respondents succinctly described how he eventually recognized that older people, contrary to the stereotypes expressed above, formed a diverse group:

"Actually, those that consider themselves to still be a little bit young. That's really nice, it's not just the one type. Well, some bikes do actually look like, almost, revalidation exercise bikes, but that's not what they want. (…) This 84-year-old man told us' this morning I played tennis' (…) wow, fantastic. So, in that respect, old people are all seen far too often as, well the stereotypical image, but there is an unbelievable diversity [in this group]." (R4)

Statements like these illustrated how early contact with older clients led to a shift in the way this specific target group was perceived by the manufacturers, evoking an imaginary of the third age as an explanation for the further diffusion of the e-bike. Instead of focusing solely on aged, enfeebled bodies, to whom clunky designs would not matter, e-bike manufacturers started to address old age in terms of more complicated and diverse configurations of evolving disabilities, economic prosperity, recreational practices and an interest in combining assistance with a sportive appearance:

"I would say, the people that are close to retirement. Who are entering the third phase, or whatever it is called (…). Those that still cycle in pairs. They are the baby boomers, right? The people who have just retired and who have money –they need to have that –, and who have time, because they want to enjoy. That's a really nice group. All happy people." (R4)

Hence, in the early days of the technology, contrary to what many had taken for granted, actual in-the-flesh older people indeed turned out to be inspiring early adopters, who enabled e-bike designs to evolve from conspicuous mobility assistive devices to assistive devices that were not obviously recognizable as such. The very visible and clumsy battery and motors of the first e-bikes became focal areas of development, as even these older users indicated they would prefer smaller batteries and motors, that did not turn e-bikes into signifiers of vulnerabilities and disabilities. In the recollections of the manufacturers, the cultural field of the third age turned out to be much more conducive to the diffusion of e-bikes than the imaginary of the fourth age. In that sense, and in the view of the e-bike manufacturers, older people thus metamorphosed from a distinctly unpromising group of laggards into an attractive early adopter market that became an important playing field for new e-bike designs.

What this case clearly demonstrates is the extent to which widely held beliefs about older people in relation to technology are still fraught with ageist stereotypes. In the case of the e-bike, these stereotypes turned out to be misleading; e-bike manufacturers, on encountering real-life older people, were quite surprised about the diversity of this group, which, over time, led them to question their own stereotypes. They encountered a considerable number of unexpected use practices, among which an interest in image and appearance, the importance of recreational use, a keen interest in gadgetry (and the spending power to indulge this interest) and an enthusiasm for sheer speed and battery power. Over time, they grew to appreciate these unexpected use practices as a resource which could be leveraged for new e-bike designs catering to a complicated configuration of evolving vulnerabilities with recreational, sports and social practices.

3.2 The Dynamics of Deliberate Missed Calls in Barcelona

This case focuses on older individuals (aged 60 and over). The research project aimed at a qualitative exploration of the relationship between older individuals and mobile telephones and the way mobile phones were appropriated (or not) by these older users. This research project was led by the third co-author, who used a qualitative approach that involved conducting semi-structured interviews in Barcelona in the period between 2010 and 2011. The 53 participants included 33 women and 20 men aged between 60 and 93. Some 25 respondents were found to rely on missed calls, i.e., short signal calls that are not intended to be answered. Missed calls emerged as an innovative practice attached to the mobile phone in the early 2000s [20–23]. As summarized in the paper [24, p. 286] on which this section is based:

"Deliberate missed calls [DMC] constitute a communication practice per se that is linked to the economic rationale of maximizing communication while minimizing the related costs. A DMC is a message that goes in one direction; it might therefore involve a certain degree of uncertainty because there is no feedback from the receiver. In this sense, it is a more limited form of communication than a voice call or SMS. The full use and exact meaning of DMC communication is linked to the ability to screen incoming calls. In addition, a DMC can have several meanings, or no meaning at all, since it is just a ring call. For this reason, prior agreement as to what a sent message means becomes very important. Given that DMCs are not intended to be answered, they constitute a zero-cost form of communication [as no call is effectively set up]."

In the present case, it was explored how older individuals used missed calls, something not usually analyzed from the perspective of the older people themselves. A relevant finding [24, p. 293] was that:

"Seniors using DMC in the sample correspond to a diversity of profiles, from sophisticated users who utilize deliberate missed calls to make the most of communications through their mobile phones, to one (…) user who just follows basic instructions because she is almost illiterate and barely knows how to use the phone. These results are in line with the fact that DMC use is widespread among different social strata, as well as among different age groups and genders [25, 26] in societies where it is a significant practice, as in Catalonia. Most of all, when DMC responds to a previously agreed behavior, participant seniors enthusiastically explain how they use them. This attitude challenges the idea that older people are passive users of mobile phones who "tend to use the technology only when there is no alternative communication method" [27, p. 891]."

Of interest here is the fact that DMCs became part of some seniors' everyday communication practices. Most commonly, they used DMCs with close relatives, which tended to be either their spouse or their children and, although less often, the grandchildren. In some cases, they also relied on DMCs with peers– although that appeared to be less common.

Within the family or with friends, the most common use of DMCs was micro-coordination, or "the nuanced management of social interactions" [28, p. 70]:

"Yesterday, for example, my wife said: Send me a missed call and I'll hurry up if I haven't finished yet." (Man, 69 years old)

"I make a lot of missed calls. If I arrange to meet a friend, when I leave the house, I give her a missed call." (Woman, 66)

DMCs were also a way to transfer the cost of communication to the wealthier communicant. As before, the meaning of the call must be agreed upon in advance. In some cases, children would send DMCs to their parents to get a callback, as one 68-year-old woman reported. On other occasions, the children would assume the cost of the call:

"I send [my son] missed calls and he calls me back ... because it costs him nothing [as he has a flat rate] and (...) maybe otherwise I would have to pay. (Woman, 62)

[My son] says 'Look, so you don't have to pay so much', (...) send me a missed call." (Woman, 76)

Also, participants with a flat-rate contract were happy to assume the cost of voice calls. One participant used a variation of a DMC to avoid instructing those who call her. To save her callers money, she showed "an innovative behavior that takes full advantage of her flat-rate subscription in a context in which most subscriptions are billed per minute of consumed airtime." [24, p. 293]:

"[I pick up the phone and say] hang up; I'll call you back. [Because] they already know why I'm doing that." (Woman, 66)

The study was conducted during a period when missed calls were a prevalent practice. Yet, at the time of this paper's writing, the popularity of DMCs had fallen in Barcelona, as mobile phone flat-rates had since become pervasive. The communication goals sought using DMCs could now be achieved via WhatsApp messages or voice calls, which are more precise and do not increase the final bill. In fact, one participant had already reported using WhatsApp with her daughter in 2011, although this was not a feasible method of communication with peers at the time. However, in low-income contexts and among adults who have pre-paid subscriptions, deliberate missed calls (DMC) remain a zero-cost form of communication that is (still) commonly used to keep the phone bill down (e.g., [22, 29, 30]), also among older individuals –see [31] for the case of Lima (Peru).

Bar et al. [12] argued that DMCs constitute an example of appropriation that challenges the initial scripts imagined by mobile phone operators. The struggle for control (over the costs of a service) led to the use of a zero-cost communication service in the form of deliberate missed calls. It is an unexpected and innovative use that reduces the operators' benefits, as no voice call is set up. In contexts where voice calls are perceived as being too expensive, DMCs rely upon two main features. First, the caller ID identification, available on all mobile phones by default. Second, the fact that mobile phones, which are personal, portable and pedestrian [32], are perceived as a tool for micro-coordination. In terms of Bar and colleagues' theoretical framework [12], flat rates can be understood as mobile phone companies' response to DMCs –at least in part. The flat rate as a post-paid contract commits the consumer to permanent, monthly expenses that might be higher than a pre-paid subscription. However, a flat rate enables users to gain control over their costs in a way a pre-paid subscription does not. Most consumers, therefore, do switch to different, albeit more expensive plans that allow the use of mobile data in a safer way than pre-paid subscriptions.

Yet by looking at particular practices of older individuals – in this case, the deliberate use of missed calls to communicate, a practice that runs directly counter to the planned scripts set up by mobile phone operators –it is possible to understand the richness and diversity of digital practices at any age. Clearly, innovation adoption is not static in old age: DMCs were shown first to be used with relatives and later with peers, as well. Then, as usage-based charges increasingly gave way to flat rate plans, the practice was eventually abandoned.

All in all, designers should approach old age as another period of life during which innovation in digital practices (also) occurs. Such appropriations of products not only evolve, but are relevant to explore.

3.3 Stimulating Innovative Practices for Older People by the Leyden Academy on Vitality and Ageing

The Leyden Academy on Vitality and Ageing (https://www.leydenacademy.nl/home-en/) is a Dutch knowledge institution with a clear mission: to increase knowledge about ageing and vitality, and to make this knowledge accessible to policymakers, healthcare providers and the general public in order to improve the quality of life of older people. One of the programs developed by Leyden Academy was called Start-up Plus, and directed at senior entrepreneurs:

> "Most start-up courses target and are tailored to young entrepreneurs. Given our increasing number of healthy life years, however, more and more seniors are considering a second career and wish to create start-ups, which is shown to be beneficial for wellbeing and health. With Start-up Plus, we will train them to start their own businesses in healthy living and active ageing. Participants in this free course do not require any background knowledge, but we will select participants on the basis of their motivation. In eight weeks, they will follow an adaptive, individual learning pathway and learn essentials about entrepreneurship. We will provide individual coaching through face to face and virtual meetings, as well as expert interviews. (…)" https://www.leydenacademy.nl/start-up-plus-for-senior-entrepreneurs/)

As one of the participants in the Start-up Plus program for senior entrepreneurs, 83-year-old Han developed an app called "Are you okay today". The first author of this paper conducted an interview with him (December, 3, 2020) to find out more about how this came about. During that interview, Han explained that his son Thijs had told him that he wanted to keep an eye on him. Thijs didn't want his father, who lived alone, to run the risk of not being able to warn anybody, for example, if he should experience a fall. Han told his son that, although he understood his son's worries, he did not want to install a home camera surveillance system, nor was he prepared to wear a device with an alarm button. They discussed their concerns, and, as both had a technical background and had worked – or in the case of Thijs, worked - in technology, were able to come up with an innovative solution; one that guaranteed Thijs would be warned if something happened with his dad and that Han's life wouldn't be impacted by having to install a video monitoring system. The two brainstormed together and came up with the idea for the app. Han then field-tested a prototype of the "Are you okay today" app at 100 locations in the Netherlands for a period of three months. The app is linked to a smart meter (an electronic device that records information such as consumption of electric energy that electricity suppliers are currently installing in a growing number of Dutch households) in the home of the older person. The script of the smart meter, as planned by the energy supplier, is that the recorded information is communicated to the consumer, allowing her or him to gain insight into their energy consumption behavior, as well as to the electricity supplier, allowing the electricity supply to be monitored and facilitating the billing process. Clearly, Han has deviated - in an unexpected and innovative way - from the electricity supplier's script in reconfiguring this technology for a new use fully adapted to his needs, finding an unobtrusive way to alert a relative or a friend that an older person at home alone may be in need of help. Han explained how his app works:

> "It is based on my electricity consumption. I developed a self-learning system that registers the electricity consumption pattern of my household's devices. After three weeks, the system has 'learned' the pattern of my electricity use. In the event of a deviation from this pattern, the system initiates a phone call: not to my son Thijs, which would be an intrusion of my privacy, but to me. If I fail to answer, then something is wrong and the system calls Thijs."

A deviation in the average pattern of electricity consumption - Han developed an algorithm for this – will therefore trigger the smartphone app to call him and ask: "Are you OK today?". Should the older person using the app fail to respond to the smartphone call, the warning system is activated and a relative or friend is then alerted through a phone call. Han is now looking for commercial partners to introduce his app to the market. He sees this as a promising unobtrusive technological alert device for older people and their relatives and friends that works by following a script that deviates from yet at the same time builds on the script originally planned by the electricity supplier.

Another example from the Leyden Academy on Vitality and Ageing is that of 75-year-old Mary, who, after participating in a Google speakers user test session, decided to develop a guide for other older users showing how to install the device and how to use it. Her aim was to enable them to take advantage of this new technology in such a way that it fit their daily life needs. The point here is that Mary did not wish to deviate from the Google speakers' scripts as planned by Google. On the contrary, as part of the older user group, she created a language that addressed a specific target group (older people) for this new technology; a target group that is usually ignored by technology companies. In this way, she created visibility for older users of the technology and debunked the myth that older people are unable to learn how to use a new technology script independently:

> "[I developed a little user guide] with tips and showing the order of steps to be taken. You need to explain how to install the device first, and what you need in order to be able to do this. And you need to give examples of the purposes you can use it for, and that you can use your voice."

4   Conclusions and Implications for Future Innovative Practices

According to Pinch [2], designers tend to configure users [3] by scripting appropriate user interaction with a technology into the design of their products [4]. We agree with Pinch [2, p. 247] that "users, in turn, can challenge such scripts and reconfigure technologies [4, 5]". In this paper, we have introduced examples of older people cast in the role of early adopters, rather than laggards, in product innovation (case 1: e-bike); older people as innovative mobile phone users (case 2: deliberate missed calls); innovative older individuals able to reconfigure technology by deviating from planned scripts (case 3: innovative unobtrusive App Are you OK today); or innovating through the development of a user guide for Google speakers, thus helping older people learn how to use a new technology script independently by showing them how to install the device and how to use it (case 4: a user guide for Google speakers developed by an older person for older persons).

The main conclusion is, therefore, that older individuals are able to learn and innovate when it comes to using new technologies. However, for older people, getting stakeholders - such as technology companies - to hear their voice is another challenge. Many stakeholders are unaware that older people have a voice – and quite often, the realization that, not only do they have a voice, but that they also wish to be heard never dawns at all.

A final point we would like to make for future innovative practices is the need to involve users (younger and older ones) at an early stage in the design process, to avoid having designers create products and services that are designed for a projected user [4] without regard for the reality of the actual users' context. The pitfall of I-methodology, described by Akrich [33, p. x, 32] as the "reliance on personal experience, whereby the designer replaces his professional hat that by that of the layman", should be avoided. Importantly, technology companies should adopt a co-design approach when developing new technologies, involving both younger and older users to ensure the underlying scripts fulfil the needs of all users in the future use of these new technologies. One way to do this would be through the organization of focus groups [34–37].

Acknowledgements. This paper is part of the research project BConnect@Home (https://www. jp-demographic.eu/wp-content/uploads/2017/01/BCONNECT_2017_conf2018_broc hure.pdf), funded by the JTP 2017 - JPI More Years, Better Lives (Grant Agreement 363850) - the Netherlands, ZONMW (Project 9003037411). We thank Utrecht University School of Governance master student Teun Soederhuizen for transcribing the interviews for cases 3 and 4. We would also like to thank Vivette van Cooten and Louis Neven for contributions to the conception, design and data collection of the e-bike study revisited in Sect. 3.1.

References

1. Rogers, E.M.: Diffusion of Innovations. Free Press, New York (2003)
2. Pinch, T.: Giving birth to new users: how the minimoog was sold to rock and roll. In: Oudshoorn, N., Pinch, T. (eds.) How users matter: the co-construction of users and technology (inside technology), pp. 247–270. MIT Press, Cambridge (2003)
3. Woolgar, S.: Configuring the user: the case of usability trials. In: Law, J. (ed.) A Sociology of Monsters. Routledge, Abingdon (1991)
4. Akrich, M.: The de-scription of technical objects. In: Bijker, W., Law, J. (eds.) Shaping Technology/Building Society, pp. 205–224. MIT Press, Cambridge, Mass (1992)
5. Latour, B.: Science in Action: How to Follow Scientists and Engineers Through Society. Harvard University Press, Cambridge, Mass (1987)
6. Douglas, S.J.: Inventing American Broadcasting. 1899–1922. John Hopkins University Press,, California (1987)
7. Fischer, C.S.: America Calling: A Social History of the Telephone to 1940. University of California Press California (1992)
8. Martin, M.: "Hello Central?": Gender, Technology and the Culture in the Formation of Telephone Systems. McGill-Queens University Press (1991)
9. Kline, R., Pinch, T.: Users as agents of technological change: the Social construction of the automobile in the United States. Technol. Cult. **37**(4) 763–795 (1996). https://doi.org/10.2307/3107097
10. Peine, A., Van Cooten, V., Neven, L.: Rejuvenating design: bikes, batteries, and older adopters in the diffusion of e-bikes. Sci. Technol. Hum. Values **42**(3), 429–459 (2017). https://doi.org/10.1177/0162243916664589
11. Wolf, A., Seebauer, S.: Technology adoption of electric bicycles: a survey among early adopters. Transp. Res. Part A: Policy Pract. **69**, 196–211 (2014) https://doi.org/10.1016/j.tra.2014.08.007
12. Bar, F., Weber, M.S.F., Pisani, F.: Mobile technology appropriation in a distant mirror: baroquization, creolization, and cannibalism. New Media Soc. **18**(4), 617–636 (2016). https://doi.org/10.1177/1461444816629474
13. Tarde, G.: The Laws of Imitation. Henry Holt and Company, New York (1903)
14. Latour, B.: Gabriel Tarde and the end of the social. In: Joyce, P. (ed.) The Social in Question: New Bearings in History and the Social Sciences, pp. 117–132. Routledge, London and New York (2002)
15. Greenhalgh, T., Robert, G., Macfarlane, F., Bate, P., Kyriakidou, O., Peacock, R.: Storylines of research in diffusion of innovation: a meta-narrative approach to systematic review. Soc. Sci. Med. **61**, 417–430 (2005). https://doi.org/10.1016/j.socscimed.2004.12.001
16. Szmigin, I., Carrigan, M.: The older consumer as innovator: does cognitive age hold the key? J. Mark. Manage. **16**, 505–527 (2000). https://doi.org/10.1362/026725700785046038
17. Arts, J.W.C., Frambach, R.T., Bijmolt, T.H.A.: Generalizations on consumer innovation adoption: a meta-analysis on drivers of intention and behavior. Int. J. Res. Mark. **28**, 134–144 (2011). https://doi.org/10.1016/j.ijresmar.2010.11.002
18. Bovag. https://www.bovag.nl/nieuws/verkoop-elektrische-fietsen-blijft-groeien. Accessed on 14 Dec 2020
19. Gilleard, C., Higgs, P.: The fourth age and the concept of a 'social imaginary': a theoretical excursus. J. Aging Stud. **27**, 368–376 (2013). https://doi.org/10.1016/j.jaging.2013.08.004
20. Kasesniemi, E.L.: Mobile Messages. Young People and a New Communication Culture. Tampere University Press, Tampere (2003)
21. Oksman, V., Turtiainen, J.: Mobile communication as a social stage: meanings of mobile communication in everyday life among teenagers in Finland. New Media Soc. **6**(3), 319–339 (2004). https://doi.org/10.1177/1461444804042518

22. Castells, M., Fernández-Ardèvol, M., Linchuan Qiu, J., Sey, A.: Mobile Communication and Society: A Global Perspective. The MIT Press, Cambridge, MA (2008)

23. Donner, J.: The rules of beeping: exchanging messages via intentional "missed calls" on mobile phones. J. Comput.-Med. Commun. **13**(1), 1–22 (2007). https://doi.org/10.1111/j. 1083-6101.2007.00383.x

24. Fernández-Ardèvol, M.: Deliberate missed calls: a meaningful communication practice for seniors?". Mob. Media Commun. **1**(3), 285–298 (2013). https://doi.org/10.1177/205015791 3493624

25. Fjuk, A., Furberg, A., Geirbo, H.C., Helmersen, P.: New artifacts–new practices: putting mobile literacies into focus. Digital Kompetanse: Nordic J. Digital Literacy **1**(3), 21–38 (2008)

26. Sivapragasam, N., Zainudeen, A., Ratnadiwakara, D.: Hit me with a missed call: the use of missed calls at the bottom of the pyramid. Presented at 3rd Communication Policy Research South Conference (CPRsouth3), Beijing, China (2008). Retrieved from http://papers.ssrn.com/sol3/papers.cfm?abstract_id=1572282

27. Kurniawan, S.: Older people and mobile phones: a multi-method investigation. Int. J. Hum.-Comput. Stud. **66**(12), 889–901 (2008). https://doi.org/10.1016/j.ijhcs.2008.03.002

28. Ling, R.: The Mobile Connection: the Cell Phone's Impact on Society. Morgan Kaufmann Publishers, San Francisco, CA (2004)

29. Donner, J.: The rules of beeping: exchanging messages via intentional 'missed calls' on mobile phones. J. Comput. Commun. **13**(1), 1–22 (2007). https://doi.org/10.1111/j.1083-6101.2007.00383.x

30. Wamala, C.: I Have to Give an 'I Can' attitude: gender patterns in beeping Practices. Sage Open **3**(1), 1–11 (2013). https://doi.org/10.1177/2158244013477101

31. Fernández-Ardèvol, M.: One phone, two phones, four phones: Older women and mobile telephony in Lima, Peru. In: Larsson, C.W. and Stark. L. (eds.) Gendered Power and Mobile Technology: Intersections in the Global South, pp. 93–107. Routledge, London (2019)

32. Ito, M., Okabe, D., Matsuda, M.: Personal, Portable, Pedestrian: Mobile Phones in Japanese life. The MIT Ptress, Cambridge, MA (2005)

33. Akrich, M.: User representations: practices, methods and sociology. In: Rip, A., Misa, T. J., and Schot, J. (eds.) Managing Technology in Society. The Approach of Constructive Technology Assessment, pp. 167–184. Pinter, London (1995)

34. Essén, A., Östlund, B.: Laggards as innovators? Old users as designers of new services and service systems. Int. J. Des. **5**(3,0) 89–98 (2011)

35. Östlund, B.: The benefits of involving older people in the design process. In: Zhou, J., Salvendy, G. (eds.) ITAP 2015. LNCS, vol. 9193, pp. 3–14. Springer, Cham (2015). https://doi.org/10.1007/978-3-319-20892-3_1

36. Fischer, B., Östlund, B.: Technology development with older people: the role of "unfettered design". In: Gao, Q., Zhou, J. (eds.) HCII 2020. LNCS, vol. 12207, pp. 18–33. Springer, Cham (2020). https://doi.org/10.1007/978-3-030-50252-2_2

37. Östlund, B., et al.: Using academic work places to involve older people in the design of digital applications. presentation of a methodological framework to advance co-design in later life. In: Gao, Q., Zhou, J. (eds.) HCII 2020, LNCS, vol. 12207, pp. 45–58. Springer, Cham (2020). https://doi.org/10.1007/978-3-030-50252-2_4

Remote User Testing for an Age-Friendly Interface Design for Smart Homes

Adriana Marques da Silva[1]($\boxtimes$), Hande Ayanoglu[1,2]($\boxtimes$), and Bruno Silva[2,3]

[1] IADE, Universidade Europeia, Av. D. Carlos I, 4, 1200-649 Lisbon, Portugal
hande.ayanoglu@universidadeeuropeia.pt
[2] UNIDCOM/IADE, Av. D. Carlos I, 4, 1200-649 Lisbon, Portugal
bruno.silva@universidadeeuropeia.pt
[3] Instituto de Telecomunicações, Departamento de Informática, Universidade da Beira Interior, Rua Marquês d'Ávila e Bolama, 6201-001 Covilhã, Portugal

Abstract. The age group of 65 years has been described as the fastest growing demographic in the world. As life expectancy increases, older adults prefer to remain independent at home. Smart Home systems and Assistive Technologies have been developed to enable older adults to live in their own homes as they age, enhancing safety, independence and quality of life. Although considerable Smart Home mobile applications exist focused on older adult's wellbeing, they still face considerable challenges in usability, feasibility and accessibility regarding design of interfaces. There is a gap in recent research on evaluation of User Interface (UI) designed or adapted to address older adults needs and abilities. The paper takes part of an ongoing project evaluation stage, for a smart home and health monitoring system, applied in two stages: (i) heuristic evaluation and (ii) remote user testing. The main objective of the paper is to focus on the second evaluation stage, that took place with end users, applying unmoderated remote usability testing, due to Covid-19 pandemic. According to the System Usability Scale (SUS) and Net Promoter Score (NPS) techniques it could be able to quantify the users experience and measure the level of satisfaction related to the smart home and health monitoring system. The SUS results identified that the system's usability was considered acceptable with a final score of 65,6. It was concluded that the unmoderated test with a SUS post-questionnaire can be a complex method to apply with older adults. The SUS questionnaire could lead to mistakes and misinterpretation, some contradictory results could be related to this complexity among older adults, and this could lead to a major impact on overall SUS scores. In addition, the NPS metric was identified as not the appropriate to measure user satisfaction with a small sample of users as SUS technique. It is concluded that findings should be supported by applying individual moderated tests with more end users to provide insights to designers and developers to create more usable interfaces to address the needs and abilities of the older adults.

Keywords: Smart home · Age-friendly design · User interface design · Remote user testing

© Springer Nature Switzerland AG 2021
Q. Gao and J. Zhou (Eds.): HCII 2021, LNCS 12786, pp. 168–182, 2021.
https://doi.org/10.1007/978-3-030-78108-8_13

1 Introduction

This paper takes part of an ongoing project that aims to design and evaluate age-friendly user interface design for a smart home and health monitoring system that increases independence of older adults, by enabling them to age in their own homes. On the ongoing project the evaluation was applied in two stages, (i) Heuristic Evaluation and (ii) Remote User Testing. In the first evaluation, experts identified the potential usability problems through task analysis that could impact the experience of older adults as they interact with the UIs [1]. In the second evaluation stage, a design review was applied on the prototype regarding the problems identified on the first stage to test with end-users. The objective of this paper is to focus on the second evaluation stage, that took place with the end users, applying unmoderated remote usability testing due to Covid-19 pandemic. By incorporating User-Centered evaluation methods (i.e., User Testing), it is possible to assess the usability with older adults and to obtain more detailed users' feedback to improve the usability of a smart home system by applying SUS and NPS techniques.

The ongoing project will propose a system design that explores daily activities by monitoring, predicting and reminding functionalities, aiming for comfort and independent living for older adults ageing at home. The system is based on pressure, motion, temperature and air quality sensors that monitor the daily activities of the user and send the information to the system hub. The collected data will set alarms and reminders to assist older adults and their caregivers in predicting, preventing or providing emergency support. The project aims to take into consideration age-friendly design guidelines of a mobile application to address older adults' users [2]. The proposed system is composed of three interactive interfaces: Smart TV app, home hub tablet and smartphone app, to work as a personal assistant at home. In this paper, the smartphone application interfaces were evaluated with end users to apply the findings on the other system interfaces.

In 2019, as reported by the United Nations [3], the range of 65 years of age was identified as the world fastest-growing population. Therefore, by 2050, is projected that the share of older adults population will reach 28.7% of the total population in the European Union [4]. As life expectancy increase, most of older adults prefer to remain independently in their own places. [5] The concept of ageing at home enable older adults to live in their own homes as they age despite health and mobility changes [6]. As life expectancy grows, in many countries the older adults' population is retiring later in life [7]. Therefore, it is important not to stereotype the ageing population based on common perceptions and assumptions when developing comprehensive and accessible solutions. This outdated stereotypes for older adults' lifestyle and behavior limits the comprehension of their problems and the development of innovative opportunities for the ageing population needs [8]. A new perspective should be taken into consideration for the future ageing population. This emphasizes the importance of ageing research, especially innovative solutions (i.e., smart home systems and assistive technologies) that have significant potential to empower older adults to remain independent, safe and comfortable at home. The smart home concept can be defined as a lifestyle support that represents a house installed with sensors and control devices connected through a communication network [9]. It empowers the users to remotely control household appliances and it can provide comfort, security, convenience and energy efficiency. A smart home environment aims to assist and support residents to feel more comfortable, safe and independent at their home, using monitoring, warning and remote controlling integrated systems [10]. Smart and assistive technologies can provide older adults self-care, relieve caregivers support and also supply new opportunities for personalized healthcare monitoring [8]. Moreover, it can offer constant health and safety management enhancing their convenience and comfort in their daily activities [9]. This innovative technology can have a great impact to improve quality of life and encourage independent living at home so older adults can achieve long and healthy life [11].

Smart home systems have been highly increased to facilitate assisted living and health monitoring so older adults can live independently in their home, and also improve the relationship and proximity with their families and caregivers [12]. Currently, a large number of existing mobile applications are focused on health monitoring and assistive living; though, most of the existing systems have not been developed or adapted enough to older adults needs and abilities [13]. In this sense, the older adults still face considerable challenges in usability, feasibility and accessibility among User Interfaces (UIs), such as small fonts, low color contrasts and complex interactions [13]. It is essential to take into consideration the natural ageing declines that can potentially impact their experience with the technology and provide them accessible age-friendly products and services [13], [14]. Technologies, tools and devices, when properly designed to address older adults' abilities, needs and preferences, can empower their sense of wellness and independence. Once they are introduced to the basic functions, they feel included to the technology, and interested in and curious about smart devices that can enhance their daily activities [13]. Although, when they can't adapt or understand those tools and devices it can cause the sense of frustration and isolation [15, Chap. 21].

There are significant studies [2, 16, 17] about the natural ageing, cognitive, sensitive and motoric declines and how it affects the older adults learning process and experience when navigating on the web or using mobile applications. Some cognitive abilities, such as vocabulary, can be resilient to an aging brain and sometimes even improve with age. However, other abilities, such as conceptual reasoning, memory, and processing speed, decline gradually over the years. On the other hand, some activities can be associated with high cognitive function in older adults, such as intellectual engaging activities (e.g., doing puzzles, reading, using a computer, playing musical instruments), physical activities and social engagement [18]. Ageing behavior process can be hard to generalize. It always depends on the context living of the older adult. Although, to assist the development of age-friendly products and services, there is a slightly gap on recent research on usability heuristics for UIs to address older adults needs, abilities and limitations [19]. Age-friendly design aims to help older adults read, notice, scan and understand the information displayed on the interface. Age-friendly guidelines would not only help older adults, but would also be more user friendly for all users [2]. Developing an age friendly system design, to a complex smart home and health monitoring system, enables the opportunity to increase the adoption of assistive technologies by older adults. As the older adult's population increases, they turn to be potential beneficiaries of digital products. The age-friendly design should go further off accessibility, it should also make the technology attractive, powerful, easy and enjoyable to use [2].

Usability is a key aspect of the multidisciplinary field of Human Computer Interaction (HCI) to ensure the ease of use of a system, tool or device. When designing and building interactive systems the user should be first priority. It is about to understand human capabilities and limitations [20]. In many UI designs, with low contrast colors, small fonts, small targets, it can make it difficult for older adults easily use and accept mobile technologies and other smart devices [2]. Among current studies of heuristic evaluation of mobile applications to support older adults' users, Silva et al. [21] identified a research gap of appropriate heuristics to evaluate smartphone applications to be suitable and inclusive for such user groups. In this sense, this paper shows results of a heuristic evaluation that identified potentially usability problems which could be faced by older adults when interacting with a smartphone app for Smart Home.

2 Methodology

User testing is the key component of usability testing. It can include observation, user satisfaction and interviews [22]. It is the most suitable evaluation for testing prototypes and working systems. The goal is to determine how usable a product is. Planning a user testing is crucial to understand which tasks are important for the product and for the user to test it. To perform a user testing session, tasks should be planned in advance, such as the performance measures. The session includes recording data using a combination of video and interaction, and it is recommended to perform the test in controlled ambient to avoid user distractions [22].

The initial intention on user testing was to conduct individual moderated sessions, with screen video recording to use this resource to measure tasks performing and allow detailed analyses of users' difficulties and feedback. However, due to COVID-19 pandemic, the individual moderated sessions could not be applied.

In order to perform the usability tests, the procedure had to be modified to remote and non-moderated tests to attend the social isolation protocol due to COVID-19. Yet, due to the limitations of remote accessible usability tools, the test could not be recorded.

The non-moderated tests were applied using the System Usability Scale and Net Promoter Score techniques to measure user's satisfaction when interacting with the smart home and health monitoring system prototype. According to Tullis & Stetson, 2004, applying the SUS questionnaire with a small sample of users (8–12 users) is it possible to measure the perceived usability of the system and to get 75% accuracy on usability assessment of how users get to see the product prototype.

As part of the User Centered methodology, after the design review on the interactive prototype, individual usability tests were applied to assess its usability with older adults and to obtain more detailed users' feedback. Through usability testing it could be possible to analyze the interactions and reactions of the older adults with the prototype. While performing the respective tasks it could be possible to perceive its usability and the relevance of the features presented in the system [22].

2.1 Participants

9 older adults age between 55 and 69 years of age (mean = A, SD = B) participated voluntarily to the study. Five participants were between 65 to 69 years of age, two participants were between 55 to 59 and two from 60 to 64 years of age. As home

aggregates, 4 participants live alone, two of them live in two people, and others three live in 4 people or over at home. All the participants agreed to participate voluntarily and anonymously.

2.2 Procedure

The procedure was published online. Each user received the usability test evaluation sheet with the instructions and list of tasks with the links for each task to perform on the interactive prototype. Same tasks of the heuristic evaluation, except one, were performed on the user testing. The exception task is the one that is related to humidity on smart home features was replaced by the health-related feature "Energia ativa" [1]. The change was done as health was identified more important than smart home features in the Heuristic Evaluation. The procedure was done in three stages:

(i) **Briefing Stage.** In this stage the description and objective of the project was sent to the users with the detailed information about the goals and procedure of the user testing.

(ii) **Task Performing.** In this second stage the users performed tasks according to the scenarios provided on the document to find if they could complete and understand each given task. For each task, it was given a link to assess the prototype. This could help the users to not get lost during the non-moderated test. The flow of each task is shown in Figs. 1, 2, 3, 4, 5, 6, 7 and 8.

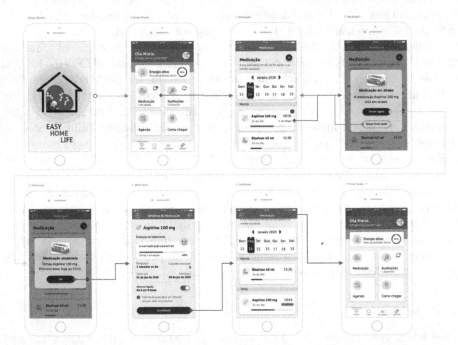

Fig. 1. User Task 1. Check medication. Imagine that you want to check your medications and make sure they are on time.

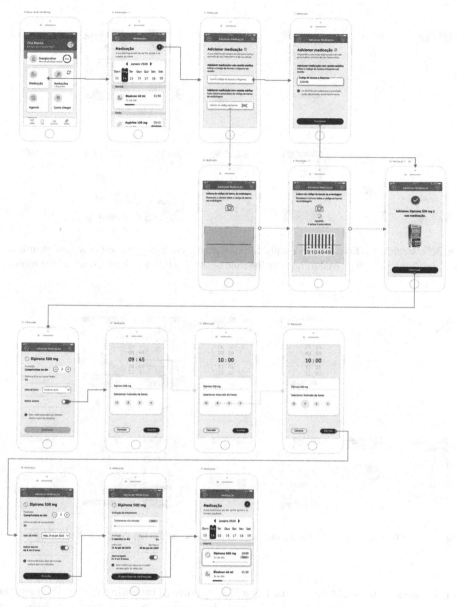

Fig. 2. User flow of Task 2. Add medication. You will start a new treatment with Dipyrone 500 g and want to add to your medication reminder list, starting at 10am, to take every 8 h.

(iii) **Evaluation stage.** In this stage, the users evaluated the prototype evaluation according to the System Usability Scale (SUS) and Net Promoter Score (NPS) questionnaire to quantify the users experience on product satisfaction. The SUS, developed by John Brooke in 1996 [24], is a 10 items questionnaire using a 5-point Likert scale numbered from 5 (as "Strongly agree") to 1 (as "Strongly disagree") and, if any item

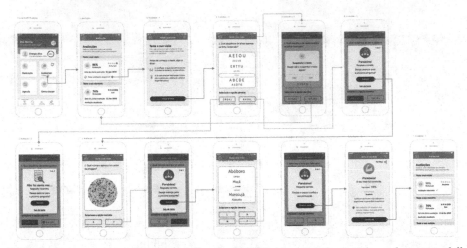

Fig. 3. User flow of Task 3. Check daily exercise activities. You want to know how your daily exercise routine is going. And to Identify the time of the day that you have exercised the most.

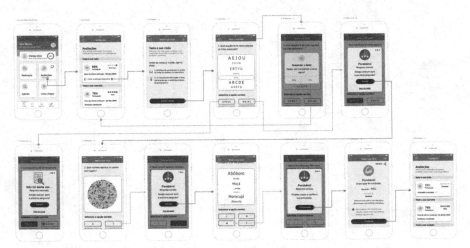

Fig. 4. User flow of Task 4. Consult your health checkups. And keep your health checkup ratings up to date.

gets no answer, it should be assigned as a 3 (the center of the rating scale). The original SUS 10 items list were developed in English, however, as the prototype was developed in Portuguese and tested with native Portuguese language users, it was translated to fit user's context.

Fig. 5. User flow of Task 5. Adjust lights. And imagine that you are sitting in your living room and want to make the lights more comfortable to watch a movie or TV.

Fig. 6. User flow of Task 6. Control windows. As it is a cold day outside, you want to close the living room windows without getting up there.

The NPS technique is a method to measure users' satisfaction level related to a product, service or company [25]. NPS is a single question method to categorize the users or customers according to their answer to the question: "On a zero-to-ten scale, how likely is it that you would recommend us (or this product/service/brand) to a friend or colleague?" [26]. If they respond from 9–10 rating (extremely likely to recommend) they are categorized as "Promoters", on a 7–8 rating, they are "Passives", and from 0–6 (extremely unlikely to recommend) they are considered "Detractors". After NPS, an open-ended follow-up question enabled users to give their feedback to the given rating.

Fig. 7. User flow of Task 7. Control temperature. Still a cold day, you want to adjust the temperature of your whole house to warm up to 25°.

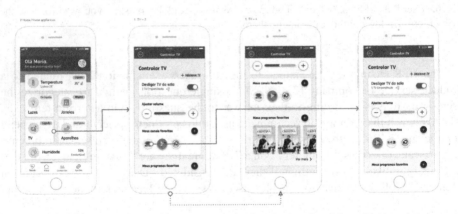

Fig. 8. User flow of Task 8. Control TV. You want to watch a movie, and you have to change your TV channel to RTP.

3 Results and Discussion

The data were reported quantitively on SUS measure and NPS score and qualitatively evaluated the correlation of the open-end question to the rating applied. After receiving the SUS results, to calculate each item's score contribution the range would scale from

0 to 4 [27]. For positively worded items (1, 3, 5, 7 and 9), the score contribution is the scale position minus 1. For negatively worded items (2, 4, 6, 8 and 10), it is 5 minus the scale position. To reach the overall SUS score, multiply the sum of the item score contributions by 2.5. Then, SUS scores scales from 0 to 100 [27]. To obtain the final NPS score, then subtract the percentage of detractors from the percentage of promoters [25].

Nine participants performed the given tasks on the interactive prototype and answered the SUS questionnaire. 3 participants scored over 80 points, 2 participants scored over 70 points while 4 participants had lower scores between 37,5 and 57,5 (see Fig. 9). Although, on the final SUS score the total average score was 65,6. According to Bangor et al. [28] the score 65,6 can be considered as a marginal high acceptable rate on acceptability ranges, as it is shown on Fig. 10. The main goal of alternating positive and negative items on SUS method is to control willing response bias and not to have the impression that the user is forced to respond only for positive feedbacks [29]. However, Sauro and Lewis [29] identified that despite the advantages in alternation items that can be safer against serial extreme responders - participants who respond all high or all low ratings - it can lead users to misinterpretation and mistakes, especially for remote usability testing. Users can misinterpret when responding to negatively items reversing responses from negative to positive and they could accidentally agree with a negative statement when they mean to disagree.

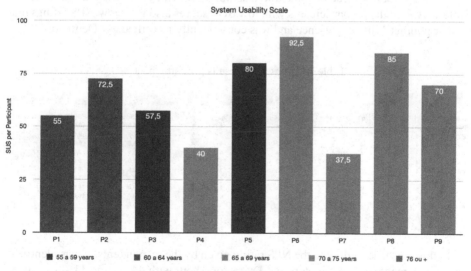

Fig. 9. SUS individual results

The NPS score can categorize the respondents into three groups that have typically different attitudes and behaviors: Promoters, Passives and Detractors [26]. Promoters are the users who respond the NPS questionnaire with a nine or a ten score. They have the potential to be loyal users and can offer constructive feedbacks and suggestions. Passives are the ones who give a seven or an eight. They tend to be passively satisfied

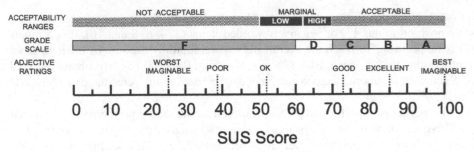

Fig. 10. SUS acceptability range

with the product/service/company but are not properly the loyal ones. And finally, the Detractors are the ones who give a rating of six or below. Their score can represents disaffection and disappointment, and they tend to share the bad experience with friends, family and colleagues [26].

According to Brooke (2013) [27], there could be a relationship between SUS and NPS scores. When users rate a system with a SUS score around 82 (±5), they also tend to be a "Promoter" [27]. Although, between four "Promoters" identified, only one scored a SUS rating over 80, others two scored over 70 and actually one "Promoter" scored 55. One of the participants was categorized as "Passive", however scored a SUS rating of 92,2. Finally, four "Detractors" identified scored between 37,5 to 57,5, as presented in Table 1. Although, the participants with low SUS scores also gave low NPS ratings due to their poor usability experience and was consequently identified as "Detractors".

Table 1. User testing results per participant

SUS Calculation														
Participant	q1	q2	q3	q4	q5	q6	q7	q8	q9	q10	SUS Score	Age	NPS	NPS classification
P1	5	4	4	5	5	4	5	4	5	5	55,0	60 a 64	10,0	Promoter
P2	5	4	4	2	3	3	5	3	5	1	72,5	60 a 64	9,0	Promoter
P3	4	2	4	5	5	2	3	4	4	4	57,5	55 a 59	5,0	Detractors
P4	3	4	4	4	2	4	5	4	2	4	40,0	65 a 69	2,0	Detractors
P5	4	4	5	1	4	3	5	1	4	1	80,0	55 a 59	6,0	Detractors
P6	4	1	5	1	5	3	5	1	5	1	92,5	65 a 69	8,0	Passives
P7	2	4	1	4	2	2	4	4	4	4	37,5	65 a 69	3,0	Detractors
P8	5	3	4	2	5	1	5	1	5	3	85,0	65 a 69	10,0	Promoter
P9	5	4	4	4	5	2	5	4	4	1	70,0	65 a 69	10,0	Promoter
Average											65,6			

In this sense, according to the NPS rating given by the respondents, it was identified the same percentage of Promoters and Detractors, both with 44%. And 11% was identified as Passives. To calculate the final NPS score it should subtract the percentage of Promoters from the percentage of Detractors (illustrated in Fig. 11) [25]. Regarding the same percentage of Promoters and Detractors, the final result lead to 0.

In the open-ended follow-up optional question, 3 participants gave their feedback about their rating:

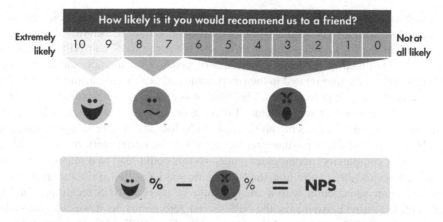

Fig. 11. How to accurate the NPS according to Reichheld and Markey [26]

P1: "*It seems to make it practical to manage the house, my daily routine, my obligations and commitments. It pleases me the possibility to be in touch with others that can help me in an emergency with one click.*"

P3: "*A 'hitech' house. It's still very expensive.*"

P6: "*Interactivity, ease of use, usefulness.*"

According to users' feedback, the system was identified as an interactive, useful and practical tool to manage daily activities at home. Also, one of them gave a positive feedback about the emergency support feature. This feature was not mentioned on the list of tasks, however, as it was given the link of the high-fidelity prototype the participants explored other active features. It might show some curiosity and interest about the related feature. Another participant mentioned that smart home is still perceived as an expensive system.

Through the usability testing with the SUS, it was identified that the system's usability was considered acceptable on the score range. On the other hand, the NPS results shows that it might not be the appropriate metric to measure user satisfaction with the same small sample of users as SUS technique. Hence that, this study showed that non-moderated remote tests with older adults can be a complex method to apply. Based on the fact that the SUS questionnaire could lead to mistakes and misinterpretation, some contradictory results could be related to this complexity among older adults with no preview experience in usability studies [29]. Also, Sauro and Lewis [29] highlights the disadvantages when applying negative and positive items in usability questionnaires, such as SUS, using non-moderated remote tests because it is more difficult to correct possible mistakes participants make, and this could lead to a major impact on overall SUS scores.

4   Conclusions and Future Work

This paper presents the user testing stage from an ongoing project that aims to design and develop a smart home and health monitoring system for older adults, to enable them ageing independent in their own homes.

The objective of this paper is to focus on the user testing stage in the ongoing project, that took place with the end users, applying unmoderated remote usability testing.

As part of the UCD methodology, in user testing, the SUS and NPS techniques were applied to quantify the users experience on product satisfaction and to measure user's level of satisfaction related to the smart home and health monitoring system. The SUS results identified that the system's usability was considered acceptable with a final score of 65,6. However, it was concluded that the unmoderated test with a SUS post-questionnaire can be a complex method to apply with older adults. The SUS questionnaire could lead to mistakes and misinterpretation, and some contradictory results could be related to this complexity among older adults, so this could lead to a major impact on overall SUS scores [29]. In addition, the NPS metric was identified as not the appropriate to measure user satisfaction with a small sample of users as SUS technique. In this small sample of nine participants, the NPS scored zero points, as it was identified the same percentage of Detractors and Promoters (d%-p% = NPS) [25]. It was concluded that the NPS did not provide relevant information for this study. It could be applied other technique to measure the level of users' satisfaction within the related prototype. Regarding the open-ended questions, users considered the system practical, easy to use and useful to support daily activities. Also demonstrated interest on the emergency support feature, considered important to be easily in touch with relatives when needed, though, it is still perceived as an expensive system.

As future work, moderated usability tests should be applied with target users. The same high-level prototype should be used to assess its usability and acceptance to compare with the current SUS score result. The moderated individual tests could provide more detailed feedback of the main difficulties of older adults when interacting with the user interfaces. And also, individual and moderated sessions could minimize misunderstandings and misinterpretations of the SUS questionnaire. Furthermore, the other interfaces of the smart home and health monitoring system, such as user interfaces of the Smart TV App and the home hub tablet will be designed following the user evaluation and user testing findings. According to this iterative design process, it could improve the acceptance and usefulness of assistive systems among older adults. The intention is to provide insights for designers and developers to create design more usable interfaces to address the needs and abilities of the fast-growing older adult's population.

Acknowledgement. The study was supported by UNIDCOM under a grant from the Fundação para a Ciência e Tecnologia (FCT) No. UIDB/00711/2020 attributed to UNIDCOM – Unidade de Investigação em Design e Comunicação, Lisbon, Portugal. The study was also partially supported by the Instituto de Telecomunicações and funded by FCT/MCTES through national funds and when applicable co-funded EU funds under the project UIDB/EEA/50008/2020.

References

1. Marques da Silva, A., Ayanoglu, H., Silva, B.M.C.: An age-friendly system design for smart home: findings from heuristic evaluation. In: Stephanidis, C., Antona, M., Gao, Q., Zhou, J. (eds.) HCII 2020. LNCS, vol. 12426, pp. 643–659. Springer, Cham (2020). https://doi.org/10.1007/978-3-030-60149-2_48

2. Johnson, J., Finn, K.: Designing User Interfaces for an Aging Population. Elsevier (2017). https://doi.org/10.1016/C2015-0-01451-4
3. United Nations: World Population Prospects 2019: Highlights, no. (ST/ESA/SER.A/423) (2019)
4. Eurostat, "Ageing Europe," Luxembourg (2019)
5. Xu, L., Fritz, H.A., Shi, W.: User centric design for aging population: early experiences and lessons. In: Proceedings of the 2016 IEEE 1st International Conference on Connected Health: Applications, Systems and Engineering Technologies. CHASE 2016, pp. 338–339 (2016). https://doi.org/10.1109/CHASE.2016.65
6. Carnemolla, P.: Ageing in place and the internet of things – how smart home technologies, the built environment and caregiving intersect. Vis. Eng. **6**(1) (2018). https://doi.org/10.1186/s40327-018-0066-5
7. Nielsen, J.: Usability for Senior Citizens: Improved, But Still Lacking (2013). https://www.nngroup.com/articles/usability-seniors-improvements/. Accessed on 03 Oct 2019
8. World report on Ageing And Health Summary (2015)
9. Marikyan, D., Papagiannidis, S., Alamanos, E.: A systematic review of the smart home literature: a user perspective. Technol. Forecast. Soc. Change **138**(2017), 139–154 (2019). https://doi.org/10.1016/j.techfore.2018.08.015
10. Liu, L., Stroulia,, E., Nikolaidis, I., Miguel-Cruz, A., Rios Rincon, A.: Smart homes and home health monitoring technologies for older adults: a systematic review. Int. J. Med. Inform. **91**, 44–59 (2016). https://doi.org/10.1016/j.ijmedinf.2016.04.007
11. Alaa, M., Zaidan, A.A., Zaidan, B.B., Talal, M., Kiah,, M.L.M.: A review of smart home applications based on internet of things. J. Netw. Comput. Appl. **97**, 48–65 (2017). https://doi.org/10.1016/j.jnca.2017.08.017
12. Alsinglawi, B., Nguyen, Q.V., Gunawardana, U., Maeder, A., Simoff, S.: RFID systems in healthcare settings and activity of daily living in smart homes: a review. E-Health Telecommun. Syst. Netw. **06**(01), 1–17 (2017). https://doi.org/10.4236/etsn.2017.61001
13. Kalimullah, K., Sushmitha, D.: Influence of design elements in mobile applications on user experience of elderly people. Procedia Comput. Sci. **113**, 352–359 (2017). https://doi.org/10.1016/j.procs.2017.08.344
14. Petrovčič, A., Rogelj, A., Dolničar, V.: Smart but not adapted enough: heuristic evaluation of smartphone launchers with an adapted interface and assistive technologies for older adults. Comput. Human Behav. **79**, 123–136 (2018). https://doi.org/10.1016/j.chb.2017.10.021
15. Barney, K.F., Perkinson, M.A.: Occupational Therapy With Aging Adults. Elsevier Inc, St. Louis, Missouri (2016)
16. Pericu, S.: Designing for an ageing society: products and services. Des. J. **20**(sup1), S2178–S2189 (2017). https://doi.org/10.1080/14606925.2017.1352734
17. Czaja, S.J., Boot, W.R., Charness, N., Rogers, W.A., Arthur, D.F.: Designing for Older Adults Principles and Creative Human Factors Approaches, 2nd edn. CRC Press, Boca Raton (2009)
18. Harada, C.N., Natelson Love, M.C., Triebel, K.L.: Normal cognitive aging. Clin. Geriatric Med. **29**(4), 737–752 (2013). https://doi.org/10.1016/j.cger.2013.07.002
19. Salman, H.M., Wan Ahmad, W.F., Sulaiman, S.: Usability evaluation of the smartphone user interface in supporting elderly users from experts' perspective. IEEE Access **6**, 22578–22591 (2018). https://doi.org/10.1109/ACCESS.2018.2827358
20. Dix, A., Finlay, J., Abowd, G.D., Beale, R.: Human Computer Interaction-Lab, 3rd edn. Pearson Education, London (2004)
21. Silva, P.A., Holden, K., Jordan, P.: Towards a list of heuristics to evaluate smartphone apps targeted at older adults: a study with apps that aim at promoting health and well-being. In: Proceedings of the Annual Hawaii International Conference on System Sciences, vol. 2015, pp. 3237–3246 (2015)

22. Rogers, Y., Preece, J., Sharp, H.: Interaction Design - beyond human-computer interaction. Interact. Comput. New Paradig. 227–254 (2002)
23. Tullis, T.S., Stetson, J.N.: A comparison of questionnaires for assessing website usability. Usability Prof. Assoc. Conf. **1**, 1–12 (2004)
24. Brooke, J.: SUS - A 'quick and dirty' usability scale. Digit. Equip. Corp. **15**(8), 41–47 (1986)
25. Reichheld, F.F.: The one number you need to grow. Harv. Bus. Rev. **81**(12), 9 (2003)
26. Reichheld, F., Markey, R.: The Ultimate Question 2.0 - How Net Promoter Companies Thrive in a Customer-Driven World (2011)
27. Brooke, J.: SUS - a retrospective. J. Usability Stud. **8**(2), 29–40 (2013)
28. Bangor, A., Staff, T., Kortum, P., Miller, J., Staff, T.: Determining what individual SUS scores mean: adding an adjective rating scale. Determining what individual SUS scores mean: adding an adjective rating scale. J. Usability Stud. Arch. **4**(3), 114–123 (2009)
29. Sauro, J., Lewis, J.R.: When designing usability questionnaires, does it hurt to be positive?. In: Proceedings of the 2011 Annual Conference on Human Factors in Computing Systems, pp. 2215–2223 (2011)

An Empirical Study on the Elderly Visual Pleasure Experience Design Elements Based on Perceptual Cognitive Characteristics Measure and Analysis

Delai Men[✉] and Mingyi Wang

School of Design, Guangzhou Higher Education Mega Centre, South China
University of Technology, Panyu District, Guangzhou 510006, P. R. China
mendelai@scut.edu.cn

Abstract. Nowadays, the research of aging design relationship the relationship between design and the elderly's visual perception has been widely concerned by scholars all over the world. However, as As the elderly grow older, changes in their eye physiological characteristics directly affect their visual habits visual perception. At present, For this topic of its research, there is still a lack of relevant reference data to support design strategy development for the elderly. Especially, there is no clear test tool for the For e-media experience of the Chinese elderly.

The aim of this study is to improve the aging design experience, enhance the visual recognition and discover the visual pleasure elements of the elderly, and sort out the relationship between the visual changes of the elderly and the applicability of the design elements. This study mainly adapted uses mobile terminal based test tool to measure the elderly's visual preference and objective attraction, in order to find the consistency of subjective and objective visual experience.

Through the analysis of the test results, the objective response and subjective preference of the elderly to visual elements have obvious differences. By comparing existing data, using SPSS quantitative and qualitative comprehensive analysis, we sort out the differences in the subjective and objective reflections of the elderly. Combining interviews and observation methods, mainly from the four dimensions of color, font, typography, and synthesize, we construct aging design strategies that meet the physiological and psychological needs of the elderly and their pleasure. The contributions of this research i.e.: (1) developed a e-media testing tool for measuring the visual preference and objective response of the elderly, the data and analysis results are conducive to the formulation of aging appropriate design strategy; (2) used qualitative and quantitative analysis of information and data to form a cross-cutting and empirical comprehensive research method innovation; (3) The research conclusion can be used as a reference for the future visual design of the elderly and supplement the existing e-media experience research.

Keywords: Visual test cards for the elderly · Visual pleasure range · Design strategy suitable for aging

© Springer Nature Switzerland AG 2021
Q. Gao and J. Zhou (Eds.): HCII 2021, LNCS 12786, pp. 183–202, 2021.
https://doi.org/10.1007/978-3-030-78108-8_14

1   Introduction

1.1   The Growth of the Elderly Population

Population aging has become a global problem and challenge. The United Nations World Health Organization (who) defines an aging society as a society in which more than 7% of the population is over 65 years old. At present, the aging of population has become a worldwide problem. Serrano et al. [1] predicted the global population in 2050, and believed that the structure of population growth will change fundamentally, and the age composition presents an inverted pyramid. According to the survey conducted by the Central Intelligence Agency (CIA) in 2010, the proportion of elderly people over 65 in Japan and the United States is more than 23%, and that in Europe is more than 17.9% [2]. In China, according to the sixth national census data, Chinese mainland population over 60 years old account for 13.26% of the total population. By 2050, China's elderly population over 65 will reach a peak of 437 million, and the proportion of the elderly population will reach 21.83% [3]. In this case, it is more important and urgent to pay attention to the relationship between the perceptual changes of the elderly and the design:

1.2   Visual Degenerative Changes in the Elderly

Based on the previous survey of this study, the questionnaire shows that more than 65% of the elderly people in the test questionnaire show that they see objects a little fuzzy or fuzzy.

The retinal imaging of the elderly degenerates, and the level of the visual system will drop sharply. Even some 70-year-olds have their vision reduced to only 0.7 due to various eye diseases, and their color discrimination ability is also lower than 25%–40%. Teenagers, at the same time, the ability to distinguish colors is 25%–40% lower than that of youth on average. The visual decline of the elderly often includes three aspects [4]:

(1) Dark adaptation: Dark adaptation refers to the process of moving from the bright place to the dark place, and the visual perception gradually improves. As age increases, the length of time needed for dark adaptation and the final level of perception that can be achieved gradually change. When the age increases by 13 years, the speed of dark adaptation decreases by 0.3 units, that is, the brightness of the target must be increased twice to be seen by the dark adapted eyes.

(2) Color perception: Old people often see colored objects as faded. Because the lens turns yellow and filters out short-wave light, blue and green, and purple fade the most, and red fade the least.

(3) Eye adjustment ability: The adjustment ability of the eyes is mainly manifested in the ability to distinguish the relative position of near and far objects, that is, distance perception or depth perception, and the ability to distinguish movement and speed of objects, that is, movement perception. According to research, there is no change in distance perception between the ages of 25 and 45, but it decreases rapidly after the age of 45.

1.3   Experience Barriers in Product Design for the Elderly

With the development of the times, products used by the elderly have gradually increased, and the form of products has also expanded from physical products to virtual products. Elderly people are basically divided into two types when using existing products commonly used in daily life. One is electronic products, and the other is household appliances.

Based on the preliminary survey of this study, in the questionnaire, the elderly people spend more than 60% of the time in contact with electronic devices (phones, computers, TVs, tablet computers, etc.) for more than 2 h. It can be seen that it is quite common for the elderly to use electronic products with screens, but the elderly are prone to frustration when using modern life products. The rapid development of the modern Internet, on the one hand, has resulted in rapid product iteration, rapid increase and change in the relationship between functions and product levels, and increased learning and use costs for the elderly; On the other hand, there are very few design specifications and products designed for the elderly in daily life [5]. The only remaining electronic products for the elderly often ignore the physical and psychological status of the elderly, and most of them are nested on the basis of existing products to delete functions or blindly enlarge fonts and pictures to lose their aesthetics.

In terms of structural design and material selection of household appliances, there are many designs specifically for the elderly. But this is not enough. In terms of structure and material, these improvements for the elderly are mostly for practicality. However, with the development of the times, we must pay more attention to what kind of design is a combination of mental comfort and physical practicality for the elderly [6]. What kind of color the elderly prefer in the design, and what kind of material will cause the elderly to feel more comfortable, this should be discussed in the future, rather than just focusing on the description of strong or non-slip.

1.4   For the Lack of Visual Testing Tools for the Elderly

The existing tools related to the elderly vision test are mostly derived from medicine and sociology, often through the exploration of the eye structure of the elderly or the social preferences of the elderly. Visual testing tools for the elderly that designers can refer to are relatively missing. In the field of design, there is no comparison of subjective and objective test results on the perception and cognition of the elderly. Designers mostly rely on observation to push the needs of the elderly. This has caused many physical products and Internet products to ignore the real needs of the elderly, so it is imperative to design test materials based on multimedia visual perception for the elderly [7]. Men (2010) based on the physiology and psychology of the elderly, developed a visual test tool for the pleasure experience of the elderly, and carried out the systematic development of paper test materials and test materials based on eye trackers, and a comparative analysis of subjective and objective reflections Define the positive visual experience (PVE) elements of the elderly [8]. This research focuses on the visual experience of electronic media products for the elderly. On the basis of the previous research, we will continue to in-depth and develop the positive visual experience of the elderly in electronic media based on the development needs of the times.

2   Research Design

2.1   Research Methods

This research uses the following methods for research:

(1) Literature analysis method: through literature analysis, sort out the overall characteristics of the elderly's progressive visual changes and the impact on physiology, psychology and behavior, and find the perceptual obstacles to design elements and the factors that lead to negative experiences.
(2) Questionnaire survey method: through questionnaire surveys, information such as statistics, basic needs, cognitive characteristics, and emotional reactions of elderly individuals are obtained.
(3) Interview method: in-depth interviews with elderly individuals. Deeply explore the awareness and needs of the elderly for the visual experience of the existing products; conduct expert consultation to obtain the expert's understanding of the aging design and the visual adaptability of the elderly, as well as consultation on the research experience.
(4) Test method: Use the questionnaire star platform to conduct subjective evaluation and objective response tests on design elements to obtain statistical data.

In the implementation of the above research methods, standard operating procedures (SOP) and social science research norms are formulated. The experiment ensures the standardization of data collection under the condition of obtaining the authorization of the informant of the investigator.

2.2   Participants

We recruited 50 participants for the study, 29 of whom were women and 21 were men, with an age range of 60–80 years. Participants are recruited through relatives and friends. The purpose is to test the preferences of visual elements in electronic products, and to determine candidates based on their age. Participants must be over 60 years old. The reason is that according to international regulations, people over 65 years old are determined to be old, but because the research content involves electronic products, the habits of using electronic products will continue for some time in the future. The research should be forward-looking, so elderly people in the 60–65 age group are included in the research category.

2.3   Test Tool Development

Element definition and selection: In the selection of test elements, five aspects are preliminarily drawn up and designed: color, text, graphics, typesetting, and synthesis. Colors are divided into hue preference, color contrast preference, purity preference, purity contrast preference, brightness preference, and brightness contrast preference; text is divided into font preference, font size preference, kerning preference, and line spacing preference; Graphics are divided into shape preference, size preference, and expression preference.

Typesetting is divided into typographic focus area, contrast preference and comprehensive typographic preference; comprehensively divided into material preference and comprehensive preference. In the selection of elements, these five aspects are expanded from the five most common elements used in electronic products for the elderly. From specific colors, text, graphics to overall typographic, and finally to comprehensive experience, there is a clear internal logic, that is, from the micro to the macro, it contains the visual influence factors of the elderly electronic products. Others, such as perspective, light and shadow, are not highly related to the design of electronic products, so they are not within the scope of this test.

Each individual test is divided into two parts, the most comfortable visually and the favorite visually. By cross-comparing each element in two directions, the visual pleasure factors of the elderly can be obtained if the results are consistent; follow-up discussion is needed to analyze the reasons for inconsistent results. This method is based on the analysis of the most favorite and most comfortable visual elements in the vision of the elderly to analyze the intersections. This is the most suitable part of electronic products in the life of the elderly, that is, the element of pleasant visual experience for the elderly. The entire test material is an extended design of the test material made by Professor Mendelai in 2011, but the difference is that this test is aimed at the electronic product experience of the elderly (Table 1).

Table 1. Select element logic and reason

Select element logic (paper size is iPad Pro 2018, size 834 * 1194)				Reasons for selection
Color	Hue preference	RGB color system as the standard, color selection. RGB color system as the standard, color selection	The selection logic is RGB three values, respectively select 255, 128, 0 values for combination (excluding the case of the same three values) to form a total of 12 color blocks	According to the characteristics of RGB hue, 12 color blocks are selected
	Lightness preference		The selection logic is RGB three values, R value increases from 0 to 250 in 25 units, GB value is 0, forming a total of 11 color blocks	According to the characteristics of RGB lightness color value, 11 color blocks are selected

(*continued*)

Table 1. (*continued*)

Select element logic (paper size is iPad Pro 2018, size 834 * 1194)				Reasons for selection
	Purity preference		The selection logic is three RGB values, and the three RGB values increase from 0 to 250 in 25 units at the same time, forming a total of 11 color blocks	According to the characteristics of RGB purity color value, 11 color blocks are selected to transition from red to black
	Hue preference		The contrast logic is RGB values, which are 255 and 0 in turn to form six color blocks (excluding the case of the same three values), and cross contrast to form 15 groups of contrast graphics with two color blocks in each group	Because the test color block should not be too many, so select one of the color blocks with characteristics for comparison
	Brightness contrast preference		The contrast logic is RGB value, R value increases from 0 to 250 in 50 units, GB value is 0, forming 15 groups of contrast graphics with two color blocks in each group	

(*continued*)

Table 1. (*continued*)

Select element logic (paper size is iPad Pro 2018, size 834 * 1194)			Reasons for selection
	Purity comparison preference		The selection logic is three RGB values, and the three RGB values increase from 0 to 250 at the same time in 50 units, forming 15 groups of contrast graphics with two color blocks in each group	
Text	Font preference	Choose song style, bold style, regular script, Pingfang style, round style, Hanyi Xiaoli style, Yuwei style, Yu Youren style	On the basis of regular script, running script and cursive script, the more commonly used fonts are selected
	Font size preference	The font size is 24/28/32/36/40px	The selected font size is the common font size of text and subtitle in the existing new media
	Line space preference	The font size is 24px, and the font spacing is 0, 50, 100, 150, 200 units	Select the line spacing as the more commonly used word spacing in the existing new media.
	Kerning spacing preference	Select the bold and thin type, the font size is 24px, and the line spacing is 24, 29, 36, 43, 48 (the font size is 1/1.2/1.5/1.8/2 times, rounded)	Select line spacing as the common line spacing in the existing new media.
Graphical	Shape preference	Square, triangle, circle, rounded square, rounded triangle, ellipse, diamond, Pentagon, rounded Pentagon, crescent, star, star, heart, irregular	Common shape, change of fillet and irregular shape
	Size preference	Select 7 circles whose diameter increases from 0 to 350px in 50px	Common graphic sizes

(*continued*)

Table 1. (*continued*)

Select element logic (paper size is iPad Pro 2018, size 834 * 1194)			Reasons for selection
		Form preference	Choose realistic, abstract, geometric, ink, flat, paper-cut form of rose pattern	The commonly used cash forms in graphic display of the elderly
Typographic	Typographic focus contrast preference	On the 135 * 240 white module, 67.5 * 120, 126 * 120 and 67.5 * 231 black blocks (simulating visual center) are selected to form the composition of upper, middle and lower, left, middle and right in turn, with a total of 15	The typographic includes almost all types of typographic area comparison
	Comprehensive typographic preference	Using small cages to wrap words and pictures, 12 vertical plates of oblique composition, up-down composition, left-right composition, diagonal composition and quadrangle composition of pictures and words, and two horizontal plates of left-right composition of pictures and words are formed	Xiaolongbao is a common food in the life of the elderly, and its typographic is changed according to its posters
Comprehensive	Material preference	Metal, glass, wood, stone, ceramic, plastic, cloth are divided into smooth, rough, rough three grades, a total of 21	It includes the materials that the elderly often contact with, and is divided into three levels according to the roughness, which makes a more detailed analysis of the elderly's material visual preference
	Comprehensive preference	Taking the kettle as an example, four traditional, modern and future kettles were selected, with a total of 12 kettle shapes	Kettle as the most common daily necessities in the life of the elderly, compared with other products, it has rich material changes and color choices

2.4 Test Steps

(1) The purpose of pilot testing is to establish which environment is more conducive to the final test. After analyzing the preliminary test results, determine the final environment required for the test.
(2) Find suitable subjects and make sure that they have no eye diseases that affect the test results.
(3) Issuing questionnaires: There are two situations: online and offline. After issuing the recovery questionnaire offline, some supplementary interviews were conducted.
(4) Analyze the data of the elderly visual preference questionnaire and the possible reasons for the results.
(5) Output the conclusions of the elderly visual preference questionnaire and product design strategies for the elderly in the future.

2.5 Pilot Testing

Five people are selected as the pre-test, the purpose is to test the test environment and the elderly's ability to understand the subject. The test content is as follows: (4) Analyze the data of the elderly visual preference questionnaire and the possible reasons for the results (Table 2).

Table 2. Pilot test

	Test ahead select element	Reason	Conclusion
Background color and color reading comfort	Place the RGB color ring on a black background with 100%–0% (10% is a ladder) transparency	Determine which grayscale is suitable for testing color reading comfort	100% transparency black (i.e. white) for color reading comfort
Background brightness and text reading comfort (black)	Place the black "rolling Yangtze River flowing east" on the black background with 100%–0% (10% is a ladder) transparency in square font	Determine which gray level is suitable for testing the reading comfort of black text	100% transparency black (i.e. white) is suitable for black text reading comfort test
Background brightness and text reading comfort (white)	Place the white "rolling Yangtze River flowing east" on the black background with 100%–0% (10% is a ladder) transparency in square font	Determine which gray level is suitable for testing white text reading comfort	10% transparency black is suitable for white text reading comfort test

(*continued*)

Table 2. (*continued*)

	Test ahead select element	Reason	Conclusion
Text size and reading comfort	Choose the 24/28/32/36/40px Pingfang font of Linjiangxian: rolling the Yangtze River eastward	It is feasible to determine the text size suitable for testing text reading comfort	Feasible
Text spacing and reading comfort	Choose the 28px Pingfang font 1/1.2/1.5/1.8/2 line spacing of Linjiangxian, rolling the Yangtze River East	It is feasible to determine the text space suitable for testing text reading comfort	Feasible

After the preliminary test, it can be basically determined that in the subsequent test, the background color of 100% transparency black (i.e. white) can be applied to almost all test scenarios.

3 Data Collection and Analysis

3.1 Data Collection

Five people are selected as the pre-test, the purpose is to test the test environment and the elderly's ability to understand the subject. The test content is as follows: (4) Analyze the data of the elderly visual preference questionnaire and the possible reasons for the results.

(1) All subjects are required to use Apple products throughout the test process, and the brightness should be adjusted to the maximum under good light conditions.
(2) Test online and use questionnaire star as a platform
(3) Before performing visual element related tests, subjects were asked to fill in gender, age group, physical condition, naked eyesight, whether there is eye disease, the city where they are, are engaged in or have been engaged in the industry, daily contact with electronic devices (mobile phones), Computer, TV, tablet computer, etc.) time period.
(4) Sop: In the process of testing visual elements, the subject clicked on the page to zoom in, then clicked to return to the original state, and then slide down the bottom to select.
(5) After the questionnaire distribution test, a total of 50 valid data were collected, and 50 were valid.

The 17 individual items were tested, and each item was tested in two parts: the favorite and the most comfortable.

Cross-analysis is carried out for gender. Due to the large amount of data, data with a single difference of more than 15% between men and women is mainly selected for separate analysis. The percentage of cross-analysis is the proportion of the gender selected by the single option to the total number of elderly people of that gender (Table 3).

Table 3. Statistics of test results: the proportion of the elderly visual preference was the highest

	Visual favorite		Visual comfort	
	Content	Proportion	Content	Proportion
Hue preference	Red ff0000	22%	Blue 0080ff	20%
Hue preference	Red ff0000 and green 00ff00	18%	Blue 00ffff and blue 0000ff	14%
Purity preference	Red fa0000	22%	Red fa0000	20%
Purity comparison preference	Fa0000 and c80000	18%	Fa0000 and c80000	20%
Lightness preference	7D7D7D	18%	7D7D7D	20%
Brightness contrast preference	000000And C8	14%	969696And C8	16%
Font preference	Yu Wei's simplified running script	30%	Circle - simple	22%
Font size preference	40	60%	40	58%
Pitch preference	200	44%	200	48%
Line spacing preference	1.8 times	46%	1.8 times	46%
Shape preference	Right circle	18%	heart-shaped	20%
Size preference	6	28%	5	34%
Form preference	Realism, paper cutting, traditional Chinese painting	20%	Realism	30%
Typographic focus on regional contrast preference	Half points center up and down - half points center left and right	28%	Half point up and down Center - all left and right center	20%
Comprehensive Typographic preference	Top, middle and bottom composition	18%	Top, middle and bottom composition	24%
Material preference	Wood (medium rough), stone (medium rough), silk (with luster), leather (with dark flowers)	10%	Leather (with dark flowers)	18%

(continued)

Table 3. (*continued*)

	Visual favorite		Visual comfort	
	Content	Proportion	Content	Proportion
Comprehensive preference	Black and silver metal plastic modern hot water kettle	20%	White glass plastic modern hot water kettle	18%

In view of the consistent subjective and objective feelings, follow-up analysis is carried out. Take color preference as an example, focus on analysis. The follow-up analysis is too long, so we don't put too much analysis data.

3.2   Color

It is divided into hue preference, color contrast preference, purity preference, purity contrast preference, lightness preference and lightness contrast preference (Figs. 1 and 2).

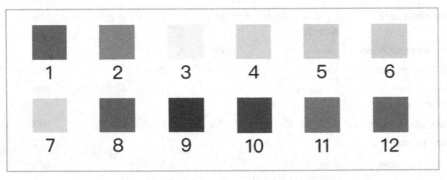

Fig. 1.   Color selection 1–12 in the hue preference test. (Color figure online)

In the hue preference test, when the subjects were asked about their favorite hue, the ratio of No. 1 red (#FF0000) was 22.00%, far exceeding the second (14%) No. 8 blue (#0080FF) ;However, the color preference test looks at the most comfortable item for the testees, the 8 blue (#0080FF) has 20% of people choose, while the 1 red (#FF0000) only 8% of the people choose.

According to the query data, the visual impact of the red No. 1 (#FF0000) is very strong. Red is a very strong color, and it can form a strong contrast with many colors. Physiologically, red is a color that has a great influence on human heartbeat and blood circulation. Red is easy to promote the secretion of adrenaline and dopamine, making people excited, excited, and nervous, but it is also a color that easily causes visual fatigue and mental fatigue. As for No. 8 blue (#0080FF), many elderly people don't like blue, probably because blue has melancholic properties. But at the same time, it also has the

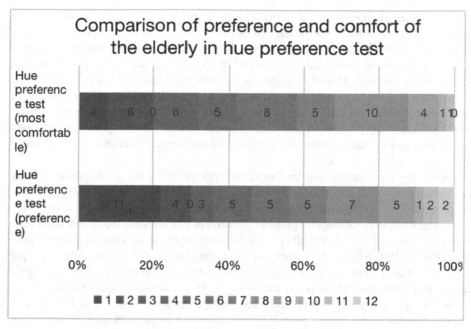

Fig. 2. Comparison of preference and comfort of the elderly in hue preference test

effect of calming and calming the nerves [9]. Most hypnosis uses blue lights to imitate the flickering of physiological frequencies. Therefore, the elderly think that No. 8 blue (#0080FF) is the most comfortable color that looks.

In the preference of hue contrast, 18% of the elderly chose red (# ff0000) and green (# 00ff00) as their visual favorite colors, while 14% of the elderly chose blue (# 00ffff) and blue (# 0000ff) as their visual most comfortable colors. Although red and green are not suitable for matching in traditional Chinese concepts, only from the perspective of favorite colors, the most elderly people choose red (# ff0000) and green (# 00ff00), which is also because the combination of red and green forms the most striking contrast. The most comfortable looking combination is blue (# 00ffff) and blue (# 0000ff), which is also similar to the above hue preference. Because of the sedative effect of blue, for the elderly, the contrast between the two kinds of blue is not strong, and both of them have the effect of calming the nerves, so they look most comfortable [10]. In addition, it is worth mentioning that among the elderly people who choose blue (# 00ffff) and blue (# 0000ff) as "the most comfortable color to look at", men are 16.91% higher than women, which may be because men prefer blue in traditional gender concepts.

Among purity preferences, red (#FA0000) is the most loved and most comfortable color, Compared with the color that gradually tends to black, red (#FA0000) is the most positive red color among all options. The elderly insisted on the choice consistent with their hue preference and chose the red with the purity closest to true red. At the same time, pure black (#000000) is 15.6% higher for men than women in the most favorite option.

In the purity comparison preference test, the contrast between red (#C80000) and red (#FA0000) is considered to be the favorite and most comfortable purity comparison by nearly 20% of the elderly. Among them, this option is the most comfortable choice Middle-aged women and elderly people are 18.07% higher than men. The feature of this option is that red (#FA0000) is the "most authentic" red, and red (#C80000) and red (#FA0000) have the lowest purity contrast among all the options. The second most favorite and most comfortable purity comparison is the contrast between pure black (#000000) and red (#FA0000). Compared with other options, the two purity comparisons ranked first and second have the characteristics of the largest or smallest comparison of the two purity comparisons.

In the lightness preference test, medium gray (#7D7D7D), as the same favorite and most comfortable color, was chosen by nearly 20% of the elderly. Among them, the proportion of female elderly in the most comfortable option is 18.07% higher than Male. The RGB value of medium gray (#7D7D7D) is 125, which is the closest half of the total RGB value of 255 among all options. In addition, the RGB value of medium gray (#646464) is 100. Among the favorite options, the choice of male and elderly people is 23.81% higher than that of females, which is also a medium-to-medium grayscale option. Regularly, the elderly prefer medium gray that is not too bright or dark.

In the lightness contrast preference test, the percentages of the most favorite and favorite options of the elderly over 10% chose the colors gray (#C8C8C8) and black (#000000)/grey (#C8C8C8) and gray (# 969696). Among them, gray (#C8C8C8) is a gray with RGB values of 200, which is composed of 33.33% red, 33.33% green and 33.33% blue, which is a relatively bright medium gray; black (#000000) is pure black; and gray (#969696) is a color whose RGB value is 150, which has the closest contrast relationship with gray (#C8C8C) color composition in the brightness of gray.

3.3 Text

Divided into font preference, font size preference, kerning preference, kerning preference, each item has been tested in two parts: favorite and most comfortable.

Among the font preferences, 30% of the elderly like Yuwei's calligraphy in Simplified Chinese script, but 22% of the elderly who seem to be the most comfortable voted for Yuanti.

This data is more in line with the prediction, because compared to the black, regular script, cursive script and official script, the running script is both artistic and recognizable; Yuanti is chosen as the most comfortable font. The reason may be that it is a variant of the black body. The gestures are more uniform and slender, which is easier to read, and the corners are handled very smoothly. In the process of cross-analysis with gender, it is found that the selection of Yuwei calligraphy running script simplified as the favorite item is 22.17% higher than that of women in middle-aged men and elderly people, and Pingfang font is 20.19% higher than that of men in middle-aged and elderly women as the most favorite item.

In the font size preference selection, the elderly choose the most favorite and the most comfortable ones are 40 font sizes. The elderly in the two options are close to 60% of the total number. In the kerning preference choice, nearly half of the elderly choose double kerning as the favorite and the most comfortable. But this does not mean that older people prefer 40px font size and 200 unit kerning space. With the increase of font size and kerning, the number of elderly people in these two tests gradually increased. Since 40px font size and 200 unit kerning are the largest font sizes and kerning among all options, this only shows that older people prefer relatively large fonts and kerning. In addition, the percentage of older females who choose 36-point fonts in the "Choose your favorite item in the font size preference test" is 16% higher than that of males. Women prefer relatively large font sizes than men, but not too large.

In line spacing preference, more than 40% of the elderly choose 1.8 times the line spacing as their favorite and look the most comfortable, which is different from the kerning and font size. The largest line spacing option is 2 times the line spacing. Among them, choosing 2 times the row spacing as the favorite row spacing is about 25.62% higher for men and elderly people than women, but in the favorite options of 1.8 times and 1.5 times the row spacing, women and elderly people are 21.84% and 15.93% higher than men respectively; And in the choice of 1.8 line spacing of about 20% higher than the older women as seems most comfortable spacing than men. This shows that in the line spacing preference, the elderly prefer relatively large line spacing, but when too large line spacing affects reading, female elderly prefer relatively moderate line spacing, and male elderly prefer larger line spacing.

3.4   Graphics

Divided into shape preference, size preference, expression preference, each item has been tested in two parts: favorite and most comfortable.

The top three most popular shapes in shape preference are circle (18%), heart shape (14%), crescent shape (14%); The top three figures that look the most comfortable are heart-shaped (20%), crescent-shaped (12%), and round (12%). Among them, it is worth mentioning that in the heart shape as the favorite and most comfortable-looking figure, the elderly females are 15.93% and 18.07% higher than the males respectively; And men regard rounded squares as the most comfortable figure that looks 19.05% higher than women.

From the above data, it can be seen that round, heart and crescent shapes are the three most popular shapes for the elderly. We specifically analyze that the center shape and crescent shape are shapes with beautiful meanings, and have meanings such as warmth and brightness; while the circle seems to be the simplest geometric figure, but the earliest circle originated from the observation of the sun and the fifteenth lunar calendar. For the moon, the good impression given by this round shape may already exist in people's subconscious mind, so we can also understand that the elderly like shapes with beautiful meanings. Cross-analysis with gender shows that older men prefer round and rounded squares, while women prefer heart shapes.

The most popular size preference is size 6 (350px), while size 5 (300px) looks the most comfortable. Based on this, it can be inferred that the elderly like to have relatively large graphics in the screen.

In terms of expression style, among the six selected forms, realistic, paper-cut, and traditional Chinese painting accounted for 20% of the most popular options, while the most comfortable-looking ones belonged to realism, accounting for 30%. However, in the data analysis, among the favorite forms of expression, male elderly prefer abstract style and paper-cut style (higher than women 21.67% and 11.33% respectively), while female elderly prefer concrete style and traditional Chinese painting style (higher than male 21.52% and 5.09% respectively). This can make older men like more abstract styles, such as abstraction and paper-cutting; older women like more concrete styles, such as realistic and traditional Chinese painting styles.

3.5 Typographic

Divided into typographic focus area comparison preference and comprehensive typography preference, each item has been tested in two parts: favorite and most comfortable.

In the preference of typographic focus area comparison, the No. 6 "half up and down-half left and right centered" option is the most favorite, accounting for 28%, followed by the No. 8 "half up and down-full left and right distance centered", accounting for 20%. Among the most comfortable options, 20% of the elderly chose No. 8 "half up and down-full left and right centered", followed by 18% chose No. 6 "half up and down-half left and right centered". It can be analyzed that the elderly like to center the typesetting. Compared with the left and right center, the elderly pay more attention to the top and bottom center, so the most important content needs to be placed in the top and bottom center. Among older men, 21.67% higher than women think that No. 6 "half up and down-half left and right centered" is the favorite typographic focus area, so male elderly people prefer more concentrated attention areas than women (Fig. 3).

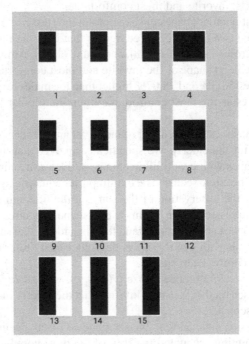

Fig. 3. Typographic focus area comparison preference icon

In the comprehensive typographic preferences, "top, middle, bottom composition, picture bottom" accounted for 18% and 24% of favorite and most comfortable. That is to say, the typographic that most elderly people like with the text on the top and the pictures on the bottom is in line with people's habit of reading text and pictures from top to bottom. At the same time, 19.05% and 23.81% of elderly males think that the picture is on the top and the text is on the bottom as the favorite composition and the most comfortable composition. And 34.48% of female elderly think that the text is on the top and the picture is on the bottom as the most comfortable typographic. But the tilt as "about placing images on the corner" or overly full composition "put the four corners of the picture" type of typographic chosen people is minimal. Therefore, in order to facilitate the elderly to read, try to avoid being overfull or oblique.

3.6 Comprehensive

Divided into material preference and comprehensive preference, each item has been tested in two parts: favorite and most comfortable.

In the material preference, wood (medium rough), stone (medium rough), silk (with luster), leather (with dark pattern) are the most popular choices, and 18% of the elderly choose leather (with dark pattern) as the most comfortable. Few elderly people choose the roughest grade in the material selection, and most prefer medium roughness. Regarding the favorite material, male elderly people who like silk (with luster) and leather (with shadow) are 15.6% higher than women.

In the comprehensive preference test taking the hot water kettle as an example, 20% of the elderly chose the black and silver metal plastic modern hot water kettle as their favorite, and 18% of the elderly chose the white glass plastic modern hot water kettle as the most comfortable one. Although there are differences in color and material, they are basically modern-style hot water kettles made of plastic materials. Since the two styles of traditional and future appear less frequently in the elderly, this also verifies the conclusions in the above-mentioned form of expression. What elderly people like and adapt most is that they will not be too abstract in the future, nor are they blindly traditional styles, but practical and common styles.

4 Propose for the Elderly Visual Pleasure Experience Design Elements

Through the above analysis, we can sort out product design improvement strategies for the elderly based on the above classification. The test uses a test line is because before Professor Mende to paper and eye test basis, so this is in order to meet future needs of older mobile terminal and an electronic medium and using this test. The following provides a reference for the visual characteristics and improved experience of the elderly adapted to the design of electronic media products.

4.1 Color Strategy

From a color perspective, red and blue are the most popular colors among the elderly. Red has the lowest frequency in the visible light band. The low frequency of red means its long wavelength, and the longest red wavelength means that it has the strongest diffraction ability and the strongest ability to traverse obstacles. Red is also an urgent color, which means that red has a warning or promotional effect in product design related to the elderly in many cases. The most comfortable color for the elderly is azure (also the most positive blue, also known as "soothing color"). This color has a good calming effect and is suitable for relatively large backgrounds in products. Let the elderly have a better space to relieve energy. In addition, men prefer blue, while women prefer red. Therefore, when designing for different groups of people, you should pay attention to their color preferences, and you can also design different theme styles.

In the hue preference, the combination of red and green has a very prominent effect. When there is a need to be highlighted in the design, you can use the contrast of different brightness and purity of red and green to achieve a harmonious effect. The similar color contrast in the blue series has a better soothing effect, so you can use the contrast of similar colors in the blue series in places such as design relaxation, transition and background.

With regard to purity preference, older people prefer colors with higher or lower purity, such as red and black. At the same time, black is obviously more popular with men in terms of purity preference. This may be because black can be regarded as without any visible light entering the visual range, so it does not appear to be strongly irritating. For men, they have weaker visual perception capabilities than women, so they look black more comfortable.

Among the purity comparison preferences, the more similar purity comparison or the maximum purity comparison are favored by the elderly. Both red and black are strong colors, and when put together, black can be used as a buffering effect; while the contrast of the internal purity of the red series appears to have a more lively and joyous atmosphere.

In lightness preference, the elderly prefer medium gray, RGB is 128, also known as "absolute neutral gray", achieving color balance. In the preference for gray scale contrast, the elderly tend to be based on medium gray, with relatively small gray scale contrast and maximum gray scale contrast (i.e., contrast with black) compared with medium gray. Therefore, in the gray scale, too bright gray scale should be used as little as possible to increase the tiredness of reading for the elderly.

4.2 Text Strategy

In font preference, the elderly prefer calligraphy and round. Among them, calligraphy is a typeface with both practicality and artistry, but its scope of application is not recommended for large-scale use of small print on a page. Because the cultural level and life background of the elderly are different, the recognition of calligraphy is not uniform, so calligraphy is more suitable for the big characters or decoration of the title. As a regular font, Yuanti is horizontal and vertical, straight and clear, with corners, it can be used as a large-area font for the elderly to read. In addition, Pingfang fonts are very popular among female senior citizens, so you can consider using Pingfang fonts when designing for female senior citizens.

In terms of font size preference and kerning preference, older people like the largest font and kerning, which shows that older people need larger fonts and kerning because of the physiological degenerative changes in their eyes. But at the same time, it should be noted that the kerning preferred by women among the elderly is to keep it as beautiful as possible, rather than enlarge it intentionally.

In line spacing preference, the elderly like 1.8 times the line spacing. Perhaps the speed and degenerative physiological changes related to older women, they refer 1.5 and 1.8 times kerning, while older men prefer the double word distance.

4.3 Graphics Strategy

Among the shape preferences, round, heart and crescent shapes are the favorites of the elderly. Compared with other shapes in the experiment content, such as rhombus and pentagon, these three shapes are more beautiful, quiet and warm. At the same time, elderly women prefer heart-shaped and crescent-shaped shapes, and men prefer shapes such as round and rounded square shapes, indicating that women prefer shapes with specific images, while men prefer regular, stable and meaningless shapes.

In the size preference, the elderly like to have relatively large graphics in the screen. The larger the graphics, the easier it is for the elderly to recognize them. However, attention should be paid to the typographic of the typographic and the typesetting strategy is used to match the size of the elderly.

In terms of expression, male elderly people prefer abstract and paper-cut styles. These two styles are relatively simple and have more white space. Female elderly people like figurative and traditional Chinese painting styles. These two styles are more clear and easy to identify. In the actual design and application, design corresponding icons or pictures for the elderly, pay attention to the specific preferences of the audience and the matching degree of the design content, and select the appropriate style for design.

4.4 Typographic

In Typographic typographic strategy, the typographic area of concern for the elderly is different, areas of concern elderly men relatively smaller, often from top to bottom about half points in the vertical version of the core area, while relatively larger area of women concerned, is up and down A horizontal area in the center. Therefore, in the design, the most core content should be placed in the top and bottom center as much as possible, and even the left and right should be more centered, so that the elderly can grasp the key information in the first time.

Among comprehensive typographic preferences, top-middle-bottom composition is the most popular. The text on the top and the picture on the bottom make it easier for the elderly to recognize the main content of the poster. Compared with the horizontal composition, the elderly like the vertical composition with the text and picture centered. For many of the common oblique composition and the four-corner composition will not be more attractive to the elderly, and will cause the elderly to feel unbalanced and over-full of oppression.

4.5 Comprehensive Strategy

In terms of material preference, the elderly do not visually like textures that look too delicate or too rough. The leather, wood, and stone they like have a slight texture.

Therefore, in the process of designing products for the elderly, with appropriate bumps and textures, it is more natural and real for the elderly.

In the comprehensive test taking the electric kettle as an example, the fusion of plastic, metal and glass materials is the most popular among the elderly. Moreover, overly traditional styles and future styles are not popular. Practical and common simple styles are most suitable for the elderly, without too much color. Therefore, in the product, black, silver, and pure white can all be used as a good matching color.

5 Conclusions and Recommendations

The contribution of this research lies in the development of a new media pleasure visual test tool for the elderly based on the first generation of test tools by Professor Mendela, and the test corresponding to the visual experience of the elderly. The data obtained is optimized and the test results are cross-analyzed. It can provide a reference for design decisions that are suitable for aging to enhance the positive visual experience of the elderly. At the same time, the research results are universal and can be used in various visual tests, and the results are realiable and repeatable.

Acknowledgment. This work was supported by Project of Research Planning Foundation on Humanities and Social Sciences of the Ministry of Education of China (19YJA760043).

Disclosure Statement. No potential conflict of interest was reported by the author(s).

References

1. Serrano, J.P., Latorre, J.M., Gatz, M.S.: Promoting the welfare of older adults in the context of population aging. Gerontol. **54**(5), 733–740 (2014). https://doi.org/10.1093/geront/gnu010
2. Gardner, L., Powell, L., Page, M.: An appraisal of a selection of products currently available to older consumers. Appl. Ergon. **24**(1), 35–39 (2013). https://doi.org/10.1016/0003-6870(93)90158-6
3. Yin, L., Wu, F.: Inclusive design for elderly users. Packag. Eng. **14**, 128–131 (2015)
4. Lin, N., Zhe, L., Jinsong, Z.: Applying contrast sensitivity analyzer to evaluate the visual quality of cataract patients. Biomed. Eng. Clin. **13**(5), 425–430 (2009). https://doi.org/10.29011/ORRT-138.100038
5. Wang, T.: Analysis of the emotional needs of the elderly and the corresponding design problems. Art Des. (Theory) **2**(07), 169–171(2009)
6. Meng, F., Jiang, X.: On the inspiration of the psychological needs of the elderly on design. Popular Liter. Art (13), 6 (2012)
7. Yang, Z.: Review on the research of character, color and layout design for the elderly. Decoration **05**, 86–87 (2012)
8. Men, D.: An Investigation into the Positive Visual Experience Design for the Elderly. De Montfort University, England (2016)
9. Zhu H., Zhang Y.: Research on color psychology based on experimental psychology. China Packag. Indus. (07), 48–51 (2008)
10. Zhang, W.: On the associative meaning of color words. Lang. Teach. Res. **03**, 112–122 (1988)
11. Zhang, Y., Meng, J.: Form perception and psychology in visual art. Packag. Eng. **04**, 203–204 (2004)

Lesson Learned from the Cases Utilizing Information Systems in Support Sites for Seniors in Japan

Helping Caregivers on Information Sharing by ICT and Seniors on Vitalizing Their Life by IoT

Takahiro Miura[1,2(✉)], Ryogo Ogino[2,3], Akiko Nishino[2,4], Ken-ichiro Yabu[5], Mari Kimata[2,6], Junichiro Okata[7], and Tohru Ifukube[5]

[1] Human Augmentation Research Center (HARC), National Institute of Advanced Industrial Science and Technology (AIST), 6-2-3 Kashiwanoha, Kashiwa, Chiba 277-0882, Japan
miura-t@aist.go.jp
[2] Institute of Gerontology, The University of Tokyo, Tokyo, Japan
[3] Graduate School of Teacher Education, Saga University, Saga, Japan
[4] Graduate School of Engineering, The University of Tokyo, Tokyo, Japan
[5] Research Center for Advanced Science and Technology, The University of Tokyo, Tokyo, Japan
[6] Kawasaki City College of Nursing, Kawasaki, Japan
[7] School of Business Administration, Meiji University, Tokyo, Japan

Abstract. The shortage of human resources to support the pre-frail and frail older adults is a critical issue. As such, supporting them using various information and communication technology (ICT) and internet of things (IoT), including monitoring systems, communication robots, and nursing-care information systems, has been increasingly demanded. Although studies regarding these have increased, their actual usages in care and support corporations have not been widely implemented. In this study, we aim to collect the remarkable cases that improve the work in such corporations using information systems in community-based care and then to summarize the implications of ICT and IoT for supporting the pre-frail and frail older adults. First, we conducted on-site and interview surveys of twelve domestic cases and clarified various needs and usages. Then, we summarized the needs of ICT and IoT in the perspective of supporting older adults and caregivers. After that, as notable examples, we introduced the use of information-sharing systems in some corporations, and also mentioned a workshop where sensors originally used to monitor the older adults were used to create opportunities for motivating them to rethink their way of living.

Keywords: Interview survey · Case study · Nursing-care sites · Groupware · IoT-based workshop

© Springer Nature Switzerland AG 2021
Q. Gao and J. Zhou (Eds.): HCII 2021, LNCS 12786, pp. 203–212, 2021.
https://doi.org/10.1007/978-3-030-78108-8_15

1   Introduction

The aging rate in Japan reached 28.7% in 2020, and it is expected that the working population will continue to decline [4]. Moreover, most seniors in Japan are not certified as requiring nursing support or care, and many want to participate in society [1]. Therefore, maintaining and improving their physical and mental functions is an essential issue for enhancing society's vitality. In addition to various types of care support for seniors certified as requiring nursing support or care, employment and volunteer support for active seniors have increased as current support measures [6–8,11,12,14,16].

Under these circumstances, the shortage of human resources to support pre-frail and frail seniors has become a critical issue. Thus, there is an increasing need for alternative support using various information and communication technology (ICT) and internet of things (IoT), including monitoring systems, communication robots, and nursing-care information systems [2,3,13,17–19]. To this end, Nakamura et al. reported a case study of the introduction of a communication robot into a care facility [15]. Ito et al. proposed interaction-based sensing as a framework for monitoring seniors who live independently through human-agent interaction [9]. Kamesawa et al. conducted an interview survey on the acceptance and practical use of monitoring systems in nursing homes [10], reporting that although the introduction of the sensor initially caused a temporary increase in nighttime patrols, the information obtained from the tuned monitoring system reduced excessive nursing care and led to the securing of care receivers private areas. Even though such case studies have increased globally, the actual situation of such usages has not been widely implemented.

Therefore, this study collects the remarkable cases that improve the work in care and support corporations using information systems in community-based care and then summarizes the implications of ICT and IoT for the support of older adults with various health conditions. First, we conducted on-site and interview surveys of twelve domestic cases and clarified various needs and usages. Then, as notable examples, we introduce the use of information-sharing systems in a hospital, a nursing home, and a workshop where sensors originally used to monitor seniors were used to create opportunities for motivating them to rethink their way of living.

The research questions for this study are as follows:

Q1. What are the needs of the information system in organizations engaging in care and support for seniors?
Q2. What are the actual use cases of the information system in the organizations, and what kind of benefits do the systems actually provide?

2   Method

Based on the design framework of holistic multiple case study [5,20], we conducted a series of on-site interview surveys at twelve corporations that support and care for seniors in Japan, illustrated in Tables 1 and 2. These corporations include four incorporated medical institutions, three incorporated nonprofit

Table 1. Overview of the corporations that we interviewed. Date format is year/month/day. We conducted on-site interviews at No. 1–11, and a remote interview at No. 12. In the case of interviews with subsidiary corporations, (p) is appended to the parent corporation.

No.	Date to interview	Corporation type or parent organization ((p) added)	Number of interviewees	Interviewees' position
1	2019/06/08	Incorporated nonprofit organization	1	Directive
2	2019/06/08	Limited company	1	Directive
3	2019/09/03	Interconnected organization	2	Directive/manager
4	2019/09/24	Incorporated nonprofit organization	1	Directive
5	2019/09/26	Incorporated foundations or association	1	Directive
6	2019/10/29–30	Incorporated foundations or association	2	Directive/manager
7	2019/11/06	Incorporated nonprofit organization	1	Directive
8	2020/02/19	Incorporated medical institution (p)	1	Manager
9	2020/02/19	Incorporated medical institution (p)	1	Directive
10	2020/02/20	Incorporated medical institution (p)	1	Manager
11	2020/02/20	Incorporated foundations or association (p)	1	Manager
12	2020/02/25	Incorporated medical institution	1	Directive

Table 2. Sizes of the corporations along with the services and activities they provide. We determined the status of services and activities based on interview data.

No.	Number of staff (full/part-time)	Number of bases	Services and activities			
			Medical treatment	Nursing care	Lifelong learning	Regional exchange
1	Approx. 30	3		✓		✓
2	>1000	>100		✓		✓ (partially)
3	5–10	2			✓	✓
4	Approx. 150	4		✓	✓	✓
5	1–5	1		✓	✓	
6	Approx. 30	3	✓ (in the past)	✓		
7	Approx. 50	3		✓		✓
8	1–5	1	✓	✓		✓
9	1–5	1	✓	✓		✓
10	1–5	1		✓		✓
11	1–5	1			✓	✓
12	Approx. 40	1	✓			✓

organizations, three incorporated foundations or associations, one limited company, and one interconnected organization. The interview participants mainly included representatives of the corporations and managers.

The reason for this research design is to extract remarkable efforts of the entire organization for helping seniors rather than those of individuals belonging to the organization. Further, the reason for selecting these twelve sites is that these corporations have been featured in newspaper and research articles as remarkable cases, and No. 8–11 have also been recommended as remarkable cases by a local government.

Table 3. Overview of the semi-structured interview items.

No.	Question
Q1	Do you have any difficulties or capabilities in transferring and sharing information on work, project philosophy, skills, etc. within your organization? For example, what kind of methods do you employ for meetings and communication?
Q2	What are the complicated tasks that you have to perform even in the shortage of human resources? What do you think should be automated among them?
Q3	If you use an ICT/IoT system to support your work, could you tell us how effective the system has been, and what you think still needs to be improved?
Q4	Please tell us about any other activities using the ICT/IoT system

We employed a semi-structured interview paradigm to determine the needs of such corporations regarding information-sharing methods and contents and the support they would like to receive with information systems. Moreover, when the respondents actually used the information system, we asked them how they used it. Table 3 is the overview of the interview items. At least two of the authors were present during the interviews. The interviews lasted approximately one to four hours.

The interview data were recorded on an IC recorder (SONY ICD-PX470F) and then transcribed separately. These text data were briefly reviewed by four researchers regarding the case study methodology, and then one of the authors coded using NVivo (QSR International) to form categories. At that time, we first added codes such as "support needs by ICTs" and "practical usages of ICTs and IoTs" to the relevant part of interview texts and then classified them as findings after additionally coding their specific needs and uses. Then, these findings were double-checked among the authors.

3   Findings

In this article, we mainly mention the overview of the needs and usages of the work supports by ICTs and IoTs. Then, as examples of the practical use of such systems, in this study, describe two cases of information sharing within the facility and one case of IoT sensor application to a workshop. Summarizing other topics including collaboration and coordination among relevant organizations and individuals will be future work.

3.1   Support Needs by ICTs

From the interviews, we identified the following needs for support using the information system.

- Information sharing on the status of seniors in need of support and care (No. 3, 6, and 9)
- Information on community resources for recreation planning (No. 2)

- Support for creating work shifts and place use schedules (No. 6, and 10)
- Automation of standardized paperwork, i.e. care records, and its summarization (No. 3, and 6)
- Converting handwritten maps into digital information (No. 1)

First, concerning the method for sharing information on the status of the seniors in need of support and care, there was a demand for recording changes in the predicting physical and mental conditions of seniors participating in seminars for the residents (No. 3). According to the participants, this is because the organizations that do not have medical or nursing-care functions themselves would like to use this information as preliminary material for introducing seniors to such organizations. Similar needs were listed by medical institutions, but the purpose of information collection was different; it was mainly to examine care methods for target seniors (No. 6 and 9).

Another need for information on the use of local resources, especially in planning recreational activities, came up (No. 2). Particularly, since staff members at the company do not consolidate contact and service information on private business owners, companies, etc., such listings may sometimes be meaningful to make planning and implementation smoother.

As ICT support for time scheduling, there were comments on the efficient preparation of work shifts (No. 6) and the assistance in creating a schedule for the use of the community exchange center (No. 10). In particular, when creating work shifts, the participant mentioned that the desirable interaction should be possible on a smartphone or tablet so that many staff members can easily use the system and make shift decisions by looking at a calendar while making voice calls (No., 6).

There was a need for automation of standardized office work, including care reports and its summary creation. One of the opinions indicated the requirement for a system that can robustly recognize speech even when the user speaks with unique habits and dialects, so as to improve the efficiency of caregivers in describing the care and physical condition of the patients (No. 6). Also, they suggested that summarizing this information may lead to a more efficient transfer of information.

In addition, in case No. 1, we found a need to convert handwritten maps of local resources and people who can provide support into digital form. However, to meet such needs, it is essential to consider the handling of personal information.

3.2   Information-Sharing ICT Systems in the Corporations

For information sharing within and outside of the institution, some of the organizations employed groupware (No. 3, 7, and 12), and one of the participating institutions (No. 4) shared information by holding general meetings or subcommittees to share plans and reports based on a fixed elaborated format. Of these cases, No. 4, 7, and 12 generally had more staff (30 or more) or more facilities (3 or more) than the other facilities. Regardless of the small-scale organization, No. 3 had a large number of collaborating companies and local organizations (60 or more).

First, the three cases that used business groupware were divided into two groups: those that specialized in information sharing within the institution (No. 7 and 12) and those that specialized in collaboration with outside the institution (No. 3). Among these, No. 3 and 7 used *Cybozu Office*, and No. 12 used *Cybozu Kintone*. In the case of No. 3, groupware was used to run the project and design the course for local older adults. Their groupware usage was not only for internal communication but also for communication with the sponsors, including local companies and government. In the case of No. 7, since the representative of the group had a hearing impairment, they started using groupware six years ago to share and consolidate the digitalized text information. From the beginning, they thoroughly shared their opinions and support status on older adults to eliminate the staffs situation of "not knowing" or "not understanding." Furthermore, they shared photos and videos as well as text on their smartphones, and shared not only nursing-care situations but also videos of training sessions. This introduction process resulted in a faster decision-making process, according to the participant (No. 3 and 7).

Kintone, which was used in case No. 12, has advanced functions such as highly customizable groupware functions and the capability to create web applications easily, but it is a challenging system to learn how to use. They have a full-time medical information technician in the institution to update and manage the system. Specific applications of the system include a sub-calculus to record complementary information of the electrical medical records (the users can attach PDF files of various images, referral letters, etc.), sharing of incident reports, a form to report body temperature and physical condition under the COVID-19 pandemic, and a function to share the patient's status with the care manager by fax or email. When the staff members want to modify these functions or add new features, they can request them on the dedicated discussion page. These staff always had a supplied computer with a SIM card installed, and they could browse and post information whenever they liked. As a result, they can share information, including the contents of conversations with patients, and use it for comprehensive support of patients. In addition, to encourage the reporting of incidents that are not well shared, some efforts have been made, such as offering a reward for each piece of information reported. Further, *Moodle* was introduced for eLearning within the institution, so that the staff could study the operation manual. Interestingly, in the latter case, a staff qualified as a medical information engineer was stationed in the hospital. The situation enables agile development regularly.

Therefore, information-sharing ICT systems can benefit to the organizations that provide care and support with older adults:

1. Smooth communication within and outside the organization
2. Faster decision-making process of support
3. Increase in the amount of various information that can serve as decision criteria of care and support

In particular, Kamesawa et al. reported a similar case as an example of the use of a monitoring sensor system in a nursing home [10]. They found that while excessive sensitivity of the sensors increased the burden on the caregiver, presenting the minimum necessary information led to the optimization of the care plan. In addition, in this study, the participants at No. 2 exhibited a similar phenomenon. Therefore, to realize items 3. and 2., it is necessary to develop a system that enables facility staff members to acquire and present information to the extent that they can handle.

3.3   Using Monitoring IoTs on Workshop for Seniors

At a community exchange center near the nearby terminal station, staff at No. 11 have held a salon for senior citizens, in collaboration with the local government and companies, to motivate them to rethink their way of living and reflect on their lifestyles. This salon could be different from other workshops provided as day services under the nursing-care insurance or other community events.

This salon is a workshop consisting of a series of five sessions. The first session is an ice-breaker for the participants to experience to look back on their life and living, which becomes the basis of the whole workshop. In the second session, participants are asked to verbalize their likes and dislikes, and then they reflect on their lives and share their experiences with each other in the third session. In parallel with these sessions, the staff collected data on their lives using IoTs such as sleep and electricity sensors provided by local companies. In the fourth session, based on these data, the staff ask the participants to share their habits and preferences regarding sleep and living among the other participants. By doing so, the staff situate them as one of the materials for reflecting on themselves, rather than simply confronting or informing them of the data. Through this process, in the fifth final session, the participants are encouraged to look to the future of their lives.

A unique feature of the workshop is that, unlike conventional *ibasho* (places where they belong) organized by nursing-care insurance services or community activities, it created a place that focuses on the individual. It is meaningful to note that to implement the place, they used various sensors which were conventionally used only for monitoring to reflect on the participants' own lives. Previously, local governments have provided various services to those who needed nursing care or support, and local organizations developed places such as salons. However, in many cases, while they have succeeded in connecting older women to such places, it has been difficult to provide such services to residents who tend to be distant from local organizations, especially older males. This workshop activity has successfully attracted a larger number of senior males from a wide area of the city and has also succeeded in motivating them for life. Further, to ensure the sustainability of the program, the staff works with local companies within the framework of the living lab to raise funds for publicity and operation. In this way, they could build a win-win relationship by offering their knowledge to the participating companies.

3.4 General Discussion

The results of Sects. 3.1 and 3.2 together with Tables 1 and 2 indicate that the following factors are likely to increase the need for prompt information sharing that leads to an urgent need to utilize information systems.

- Scope of information sharing
- The number of staff and the size of the establishment
- Daily changes in symptoms of the target person
- Spatial location of the target person

Note, however, that depending on the number of staff and the size of the facility, there may be no room for the cost and effort required to introduce new information systems. Furthermore, the information literacy of individual staff members could also raise the barrier to implementation of such systems. Therefore, it is important to examine an adaptive application strategy to increase the amount of shared information step by step according to the scope of information sharing.

4 Summary and Future Work

By interview surveys based on the holistic multiple case study framework, we collected the remarkable cases that improve their work by using information systems in community-based care. Then, we summarize the needs of ICT and IoT for the support of older adults and introduce the noteworthy use cases of information-sharing systems and IoTs. Our achievements are as follows:

A1. Support needs by ICTs mainly include the followings:
  - Information sharing on the status of seniors in needs of support and care
  - Information on community resources for recreation planning
  - Support for creating work shifts and placing use schedules
  - Automation of standardized paperwork, i.e. care records, and its summarization
  - Converting handwritten maps into digital information

A2. We summarized two actual use cases of the information system and IoTs in the organizations as follows:
  - Information-sharing ICT systems in an organization can contribute to more smooth communication within and outside the organization, a faster decision-making process of support, and an increase in the amount of information that can serve as decision criteria.
  - We introduced the case of the IoT-introduced workshop. We regarded it remarkable that the sensors, which have not been used as mere monitoring sensors so far, were used to reflect on the individual's life. By changing the purpose of using such sensors from "watching over" to "looking back," it may become easy for seniors to accept these sensors and realize their usefulness.

Our future work is as follows:

- Further analysis of the interview data for specifically checks the relationship between the organizations' characteristics and expected effects of ICT/IoT introduction.
- Propose design schemes for ICT/IoT systems that match the characteristics of the organization

Acknowledgment. This work was supported by JSPS KAKENHI Grant Numbers JP15H02282, and JP18K18445. We would also like to thank all those who cooperated in the interview.

References

1. A 2016 Declining Birthrate White Paper. http://www8.cao.go.jp/shoushi/shoushika/whitepaper/measures/english/w-2016/
2. Robotic Care Devices Portal. http://robotcare.jp/en/home/index.php?lang=en
3. Baig, M.M., Afifi, S., GholamHosseini, H., Mirza, F.: A systematic review of wearable sensors and IoT-based monitoring applications for older adults-a focus on ageing population and independent living. J. Med. Syst. **43**(8), 1–11 (2019). https://doi.org/10.1007/s10916-019-1365-7
4. Cabinet Office, J.: Annual Report on the Ageing Society [Summary] FY2020, July 2020. https://www8.cao.go.jp/kourei/english/annualreport/2020/pdf/2020.pdf
5. Creswell, J.W., Poth, C.N.:: Qualitative Inquiry and Research Design: Choosing Among Five Approaches. Sage Publications, Thousand Oaks (2016)
6. Fozard, J.L., Heikkinen, E.: Maintaining movement ability in old age: challenges for gerontechnology. Stud. Health Technol. inform. **48**, 48–61 (1998)
7. Friedman, H.S., Martin, L.R.: Project: Surprising Discoveries for Health and Long Life from the Landmark Eight Decade Study. Hay House, Inc., Carlsbad (2011)
8. Graafmans, J.: The history and incubation of gerontechnology. In: Kwon, S. (ed.) (2016)
9. Ito, K., et al.: Home automation platform using interaction-based sensing. In: 2019 IEEE International Conference on Consumer Electronics (ICCE), pp. 1–2. IEEE (2019)
10. Kamesawa, A., et al.: Acceptance and practical use of assistive technologies for frail seniors and caregivers: interview surveys on nursing homes. In: Zhou, J., Salvendy, G. (eds.) ITAP 2018, Part I. LNCS, vol. 10926, pp. 70–84. Springer, Cham (2018). https://doi.org/10.1007/978-3-319-92034-4_6
11. Kobayashi, M., Arita, S., Itoko, T., Saito, S., Takagi, H.: Motivating multi-generational crowd workers in social-purpose work. In: Proceedings of the 18th ACM Conference on Computer Supported Cooperative Work & #38; Social Computing, CSCW 2015, pp. 1813–1824. ACM, New York (2015). https://doi.org/10.1145/2675133.2675255
12. Krause, N., Liang, J., Bennett, J., Kobayashi, E., Akiyama, H., Fukaya, T.: A descriptive analysis of religious involvement among older adults in Japan. Ageing Soc. **30**(4), 671 (2010)
13. Krick, T., Huter, K., Domhoff, D., Schmidt, A., Rothgang, H., Wolf-Ostermann, K.: Digital technology and nursing care: a scoping review on acceptance, effectiveness and efficiency studies of informal and formal care technologies. BMC Health Serv. Res. **19**(1), 1–15 (2019)

14. Miura, T., Yabu, K.i., Ogino, R., Hiyama, A., Hirose, M., Ifukube, T.: Collaborative accessibility assessments by senior citizens using smartphone application ReAcTS (Real-world Accessibility Transaction System). In: Proceedings of the Internet of Accessible Things on - W4A 2018 (2018). https://doi.org/10.1145/3192714.3192826

15. Nakamura, M., Nihei, M., Kato, N., Inoue, T.: Impact of the introduction of a verbal socially assistive robot on the relationship between older people and their caregivers in a nursing home. SN Appl. Sci. **2**(10), 1–6 (2020). https://doi.org/10.1007/s42452-020-03434-2

16. Organization, W.H., et al.: Priority assistive products list: improving access to assistive technology for everyone, everywhere. World Health Organization, Technical report (2016)

17. Shibata, T., Wada, K.: Robot therapy: a new approach for mental healthcare of the elderly-a mini-review. Gerontology **57**(4), 378–386 (2011)

18. Siewiorek, D.: Generation smartphone. IEEE Spectr. **49**(9), 54–58 (2012)

19. Tun, S.Y.Y., Madanian, S., Mirza, F.: Internet of things (IoT) applications for elderly care: a reflective review. Aging Clin. Exp. Res. 1–13 (2020)

20. Yin, R.K.: Case Study Research and Applications: Design and Methods. Sage Publications, Thousand Oaks (2017)

Numeric Keypads or Character Keyboards for Numeric Entries on Surveys and Forms: Surprising Results from Older Adults Using Mobile Devices

Erica Olmsted-Hawala[✉], Elizabeth Nichols, and Lin Wang

U.S. Census Bureau, Washington, D.C., USA
erica.l.olmsted.hawala@census.gov

Abstract. These days a growing number of adults are using smartphones to fill out online forms or surveys (For a review of recent empirical studies on older adults using smartphone when answering forms see: [2–4]). The touchscreen keyboard that pops open on a smartphone when users must type their answers into the form can be challenging to use. This is due to its small size and the fact that for some smartphones, the initial keyboard that opens has only characters, not numbers. If the form requires a number to be entered, a user must press a small button, located in the far-left corner to change the keyboard so that it displays numbers. Using the small touchscreen is challenging for older adults, whose fine motor skills may have deteriorated with age (Loos and Romano Bergstrom [12]). Survey and form designers face the challenge of creating an interface that is both convenient to use while also leading to accurate data entry. More recently, some survey designers have been using a numeric keypad design on mobile phones when the expected entry is a number. This is based on the idea that the numeric keypad, with its bigger touch areas offering only numbers, would lead to an improved user experience. This paper reports the results of an experiment with older adults, comparing performance when using a numeric keypad to that when using a touchscreen character keyboard for number entries on a smartphone. When entering a number, results indicate that the numeric keypad design did not lead to more accurate data entry over the character keyboard design. While overall efficiency was also no different between the two designs, there was some evidence that the keypad design takes users less time to initially enter the number. While participants across both conditions were equally satisfied with their experience completing the survey, they overwhelmingly preferred to use the numeric keypad to enter numbers. For designers creating interfaces for smartphones, the recommendation is to use a numeric keypad for input fields that require a number as the answer.

Keywords: Mobile survey design · Mobile guidelines · Older adults · Virtual keyboard · Virtual keypad

1 Introduction

A growing number of adults are using smartphones to fill out online forms or respond to online surveys. For example, in the 2020 U.S. Census 30% of all online responses

Q. Gao and J. Zhou (Eds.): HCII 2021, LNCS 12786, pp. 213–227, 2021.
https://doi.org/10.1007/978-3-030-78108-8_16

came in on a smartphone [1]. For a review of recent empirical studies on older adults using smartphone when completing forms see [2–4]. According to the Pew Research Center, in 2019, 53% of adults 65 years and older in the United States had a smartphone [5]. The American Association of Retired Persons (AARP) reported that 81% of older adults between the ages of 60–69 use smartphones, while 62% of those 70 or older use smartphones [6]. The AARP report also documented that more than 50% of older adults are using their mobile devices for socializing, finding information, and entertainment purposes, and around 37% of older adults were using their mobile devices to conduct financial transactions [6]. These different statistics indicate that older adults are using smartphones for a variety of reasons. With older adults increasingly using smartphones for everyday activities [7], it is likely that older adults are already or will soon be using their smartphones to answer online surveys. There are two notable differences when participants use their smartphones instead of their personal computer (PC) to answer a survey: first, it takes longer to answer on smartphones than on PCs [8, 9] and second, the break-off rate when responding using smartphones is higher than when responding using PCs [10, 11]. That is, more people are likely to stop answering the survey before the survey is completed if they are using a smartphone rather than using a PC. While there are many explanations for why responding to surveys on smartphones takes longer, one reason has to do with the size of the device. Entering answers or selecting responses on a small device with limited screen real estate poses significant physical challenges. This research focuses on the design feature of entering numbers into response fields on smartphones and whether there is a more optimal way to facilitate the entering of a number. We also focused on older adults based on the logic that a design that works for older adults would most certainly work for younger users as well.

When a respondent is filling out an online form on a smartphone, certain questions require the use of a touchscreen keyboard. Typically, when a respondent touches into an input field, a touchscreen keyboard pops open which allows the user to enter letters, characters, symbols or numbers without the need for physical keys. The default touchscreen character keyboard is either alphabetical only or alphanumeric depending upon the smartphone device brand. These keyboards work well if the input field requires words. In Fig. 1, the curser is in the email address field and the default touchscreen character keyboard is open.

In Fig. 2 on left, the curser is in the ZIP code field and the touchscreen character keyboard has opened. The letters on the character keyboard are quite small and the numbers are an additional touch away, located behind the button labeled with "123" in the bottom left corner.

If a respondent wanted to enter their ZIP code, for the phone displayed in the left in Fig. 2, the user would have to first touch the "123" button in the bottom left corner of the touchscreen keyboard. Once the respondent makes this action, the keyboard shifts to what is seen on the right of Fig. 2 with both numbers and symbols available.

Still we have noted that if the input field requires numbers, some designers overwrite the default touchscreen keyboard and display the numeric keypad. The advantage of the numeric keypad for number entry is that the keypad takes up the same amount of space as the character keyboard, but only displays numbers. Therefore, the numbers appear larger compared to when they're displayed on the default character keyboard. See Fig. 3.

Fig. 1. Touchscreen character keyboard open with curser in the email address field.

If a field requires only numbers, it follows that the smartphones' onscreen numeric keypad should open. The larger numbers would likely reduce errors. But as the images above show, developers don't always display the numeric keypad when the input field requires numbers. If a user has to tap an additional key to get to the set of numbers, this likely takes longer and if the numbers are smaller there is likely more opportunity to accidently tap an unintended key. And we can imagine older adults might mis-tap more often. There are well documented age-related differences while using technological devices [12]. Older adults may have a harder time using the smartphone to respond to online surveys and forms due to age-related differences of fine motor skills [13]. By fine motor skills we mean the ability to use one's hands to manipulate tools or objects. Numerous studies using tasks that require fine motor skills show diminishing performance in older adults compared to younger adults [14]. Some older adults experience minor tremors while using their hands during such tasks, which can also contribute to poor performance. But even without tremors, older adults experience more challenges with fine motor skills than younger adults [15]. This type of manipulation ability is needed when using a touchscreen keyboard on a smartphone. Due to the small size of a smartphone (as compared to a desktop or laptop computer) the corresponding input field target areas are small, as is the touchscreen keyboard(s). Yet these keyboards must be used to input data (the answers to the survey questions). We know using the touchscreen keyboards are slower and more difficult to use than physical keyboards [16]. Yet when using smartphones, they must be used. Thus, in this paper we investigated whether

Fig. 2. On left, touchscreen character keyboard, on right, touchscreen keyboard after respondent touches the 123 button to show the numbers, symbols, & punctuation options.

older adults performed differently when using a touchscreen character keyboard to enter numbers into an online survey compared to when using a touchscreen numeric keypad.

The three common usability metrics are accuracy, efficiency and satisfaction. For accuracy and efficiency, our hypothesis is that the numeric keypad would perform quicker and more accurately than the character keyboard as the larger numbered buttons would be easier and quicker for older adults to touch. For satisfaction we have seen in many prior usability studies that irrespective of how participants perform during the session, many participants, especially older adults, end up saying they were satisfied with the study [17]. This seems counterintuitive yet it has been consistent across many participants. Thus, we hypothesize that satisfaction ratings will likely skew towards an "easy" rating. For preference, we hypothesize that respondents will prefer to enter numbers using the numeric keypad rather than the default character keyboard.

2 Methods

2.1 Participants

A convenience sample of 30 participants was recruited from senior centers and community centers in the Washington DC metropolitan area in early 2018. The average participant age was 70, with the youngest being 62 and the oldest at 77 years old. To ensure that

Fig. 3. Touchscreen numeric keypad

participants had familiarity with smartphones and would likely be more accustomed to online forms accessed on a small device, all participants were prescreened, confirming that they owned and had used a smartphone for at least 6 months. Seventy-three percent of participants reported using a smartphone for more than 2 years, 10% between 1 and 2 years, and 17% between 6 months and 1 year. Seventy percent of participants reported using a smartphone every day, while the other 30% less than daily. The participants reported their familiarity with smartphone being an average of 3.6 (SD = 0.8) on a scale of 1–5, where higher scores represented more familiarity. Participants were also pre-screened to ensure an 8th-grade level of education or higher, were fluent in English, and had habitual near vision of 20/50 or better (sufficient for reading newspaper). Participant demographics are summarized in Table 1.

All participants received a Privacy Act Statement that stated the purpose of the study, the information to be collected, and the authority under which the information was collected. A written consent to data collection was obtained from all participants. The data collection was approved by the U.S. Office of Management and Budget.

2.2 Data Collection

One-on-one sessions were conducted at senior and community centers. Participants were "walk ups;" that is, they happened to go to the community or senior center and saw the on-site research activity and volunteered that day to participate. They were pre-screened

Table 1. Participants demographics

Sex (number of participants)	
Male	4
Female	26
Age in years	
Mean (SD)	70 (3.6)
Range	62–77
Education (number of participants)	
Completed high school	5
Some college, no degree	7
Associate degree	2
Bachelor degree	9
Post graduate degree	7
Hispanic origin (number of participants)	
Yes	1
No	29
Race (number of participants)	
White	17
Black or African American	8
Asian	5

by a Census Bureau staff member, signed a consent form, and assigned a unique ID. Then each participant worked with a test administrator (TA) and completed between 4 to 6 experiments, only one of which is the subject of this paper. The experiments were loaded as applications (commonly referred to as apps) onto a Census owned iPhone 5S or 6S. Prior to each session, the TA would open the experiment and enter the participants' unique ID into the app. The TA read a set of instructions to the participants. This included instructing participants *not* to talk aloud during the session, and to complete the survey to the best of their ability as though they were answering the survey at home without anyone's assistance. The experiment was video recorded using QuickTime with the phone plugged into a MacBook laptop. The participants performed the task independently, taking 10–20 min for each experiment, depending upon the experimental design. At the end of the session, the participant was given $40 for their time.

2.3 Study Design

This experiment consisted of 15 survey questions (shown in Table 2). Questions were a mix of topics requiring either a monetary or non-monetary answer, and all required a numeric response. Seven of the questions appeared alone on their own screen (Q1–3 and 6–9), two questions appeared together on one screen (Q4–5), and the remaining six questions appeared on a single longer scrolling screen (Q10–15). Participants were instructed to answer the questions as they would if they were at home and with no researcher present. See Table 2 for a list of the questions and the order in which they appeared.

Table 2. List of questions

Question number	Topic	Answer monetary or non-monetary
1	How many hours last week did you spend reading a book or magazine?	Non-monetary
2	In the past week, how many days did you eat the evening meal alone?	Non-monetary
3	How much time did you spend watching TV last week?	Non-monetary
4-5	How many separate rooms are in the place where you live? How many of these room are bedrooms?	Non-monetary
6	Last month what was the cost of electricity for the place where you live?	Monetary
7	How much do you pay in rent or mortgage each month? If you don't pay a rent or mortgage, please enter your monthly property tax.	Monetary
8	How much was your last grocery bill?	Monetary
9	How much money do you spend on haircuts/hair styling in a month?	Monetary
10-15	Opinion rating question from 1 to 100 on a number of different topics such as the courts, labor unions, universities, banks, environmental organizations, etc.	Non-monetary

Using a between-subjects experimental design, this experiment tested two different ways of displaying the touchscreen keyboard. The first was the typical default alphabet keyboard as shown in Fig. 4, which we labeled "ALPHA". For this design, to enter a number into the input field, respondents first touched the 123 button in the lower left-hand side of the keyboard and then selected the number. The second was the numeric keypad as shown in Fig. 5, which we labeled "NUMERIC". For this design, to enter a number in the input field, respondents touched the number. Participants were randomly assigned to one of the two conditions with 15 participants assigned to the Alpha condition and 15 participants assigned to the Numeric condition. The questions were presented in the same order as listed in Table 2, for both conditions.

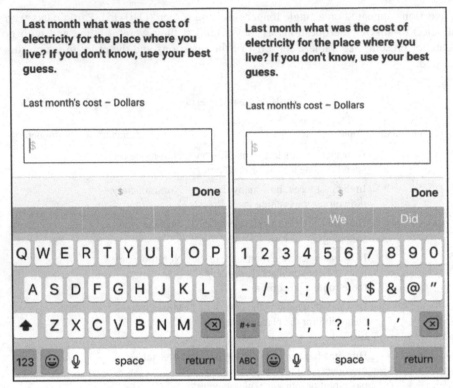

Fig. 4. Question 6 in the ALPHA condition. On the left is the default view of the keyboard with alpha characters only and on the right is the keyboard after the user has touched the 123 button. It displays numbers, symbols & punctuation.

After answering the last survey question, participants answered two self-reported task difficulty questions to assess satisfaction. The first question was, "How easy or difficult was it to complete the survey?" The second question was, "How easy or difficult was it for you to accurately touch your answer?" Both questions used a 5-point rating scale with the endpoints labeled (1 = very easy, 5 = very difficult). Finally, to assess preference, participants where shown an example of the two designs (ALPHA and NUMERIC) side-by-side and asked for their preference when entering a number into a response field.

2.4 Analytic Strategy

In the analyses, we consider significance to be at $p = 0.05$ or less. The primary measures of interest for this experiment were accuracy, efficiency, satisfaction, and user preference. For accuracy, the app counted the number of times the backspace was used. In this study, backspace count was a proxy for accuracy, as it indicates that the participant made an error when entering the answer. A mixed logistic regression model was conducted to determine whether using a backspace key on the question was dependent on condition, while controlling for the participant with a random effect.

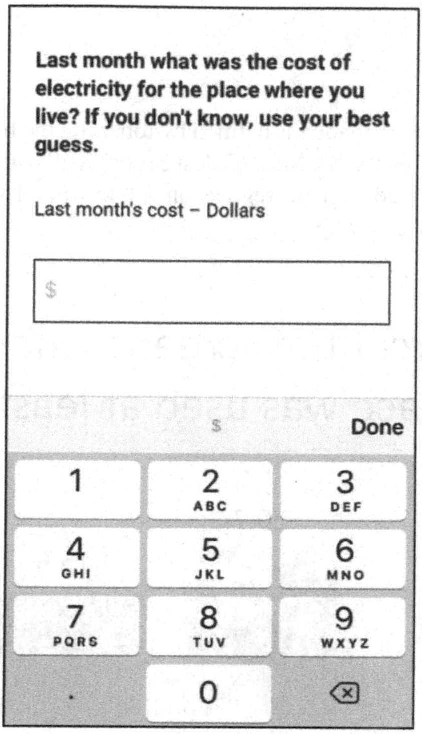

Fig. 5. Question 6 in the NUMERIC keypad condition

For efficiency, the app collected three different time metrics: first, the time between when the participant touched into the input field and when the participant pressed the first number key; second, the amount of time after the number was touched until exiting the input field; and third, the overall time per screen which was calculated from when the survey question first loads onto the smartphone to the time when the participant clicked the "next" button. All efficiency variables were coded at the screen level for each participant. For screens with more than one input field, we summed the time across those input fields. For the efficiency scores we used a mixed linear model of log of time at the question level, controlling for the design condition, the number of fields to answer on the screen and with a random effect for the participant.

For satisfaction, a Chi-square test was used to determine if the self-reported difficulty ratings (e.g., how easy/difficult to complete survey and how easy/difficult to touch answer accurately) were dependent on the condition. There were two Chi-square tests conducted, one for each question. And for preference, we tallied the number of respondents who chose each design when they were shown side-by-side examples of the ALPHA and NUMERIC designs. A test of proportions was conducted to determine if there was a statistically significantly difference in preference between the two designs.

3 Results

3.1 Accuracy

While there were more errors made (as defined by touching the backspace button) using the ALPHA than when using the NUMERIC design across all participants and all screens as shown in Fig. 6, a mixed logistic regression model found the difference was not significant ($F(1,240) = 1.2, p = .3$).

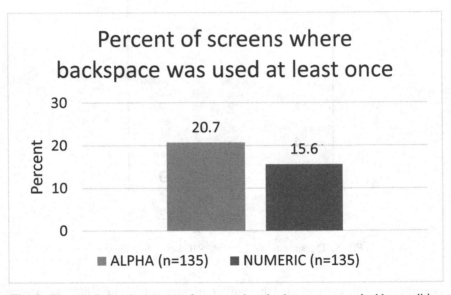

Fig. 6. Chart depicting the percent of screens where backspace was touched by condition

3.2 Efficiency

For the first efficiency metric of time spent between touching into the input field and first touching a number, those in the ALPHA condition spent 9.7 s on average while those in the NUMERIC condition spent 6.9 s, see Fig. 7. Using a mixed linear model modeling log(time) and controlling for condition and number of answer input fields on screen, the difference between conditions was significant at the (F $(1,227) = 25.4$, p < .01). It took respondents more time to enter a number into the input field when in the ALPHA condition than when in the NUMERIC condition.

For the second efficiency metric of time spent after touching a number to exiting the input field, those in the ALPHA condition spent 6.6 s on average while those in the NUMERIC condition spent 8.3 s. Using a mixed linear model modeling log(time) and controlling for condition and number of answer input fields on screen, the condition was not significant ($F (1, 233) = 0.5, p = .5$). There was no significant difference in time after touching a number to exiting the text field between the two conditions as shown in Fig. 8.

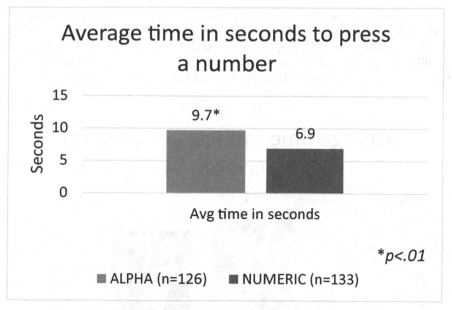

Fig. 7. Average time (in seconds) before pressing a number by condition

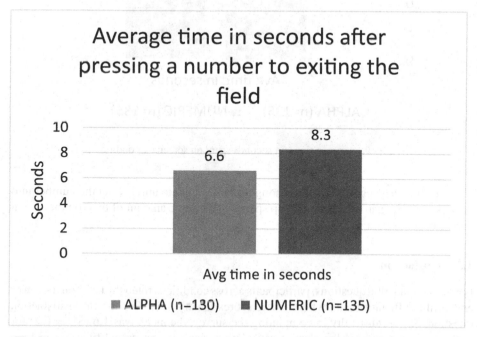

Fig. 8. Average time (in seconds) after touching a number and exiting the field by condition

For the final efficiency measure of overall time spent on the screen, participants in the ALPHA condition took on average 33 s while those in the NUMERIC condition took 30 s on average, see Fig. 9. Using a mixed linear model modeling log(time) and controlling for condition and number of answer input fields on screen, the difference between conditions was not significant in the model (F (1, 238) = 0.8, p = .4).

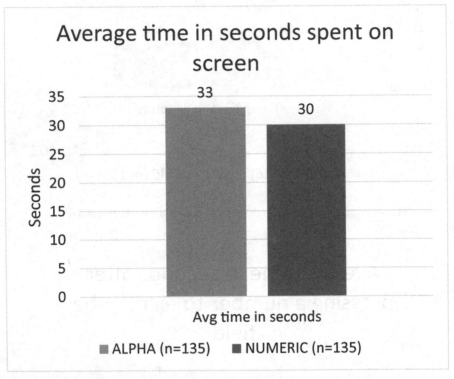

Fig. 9. Average time (in second) spent on screen by condition

The efficiency results show that though it took longer to initially get the number into the answer field, participants ended up spending the same amount of time on the screen regardless of condition.

3.3 Satisfaction

For both satisfaction questions, participants across conditions rated the tasks on the lower end of the difficulty scale, where lower scores mean easier. For the first satisfaction question, on ease/difficulty in completing the survey, the mean was 1.6 (SE = 0.2) for both conditions and for the second satisfaction question, on ease/difficulty touching answers, the mean was 1.7 (SE = 0.3) for NUMERIC and 1.9 (SE = 0.3) for ALPHA. Because there were so few ratings of difficult, we collapse categories 2–5 together to run Chi-square statistics. There was no evidence that satisfaction was dependent on condition for either completing the survey ($\chi 2(1) = 0.1$ $p = 0.7$) or touching answers ($\chi 2(1) = 0.6$ $p = 0.5$).

3.4 Preference

Ninety-three percent of the participants preferred the NUMERIC design when entering numbers into an answer field. A test for proportions showed that a majority of the participants (significantly more than 50%) prefer to have the NUMERIC keypad, ($\chi 2(1) = 22.5$ $p < 0.01$).

4 Discussion

The present study compared accuracy, three different measures of efficiency, two different measures of satisfaction, and preference between two number entry designs: keyboard design (referred to as ALPHA) and keypad design (referred to as NUMERIC). These are common usability metrics that we can use to understand what design features work best for respondents. We opted to work only with older adults in this study. If we could identify the design that worked for older adults, this design would also likely work with adults in other age groups, as the older adults encounter the most difficulty in touch targets of smaller sizes [18, 19].

The most overwhelming finding was on preference, where 93% of the participants preferred the keypad design (NUMERIC) over the keyboard design (ALPHA) for numeric entry. The other significant finding had to do with efficiency. We found that participants took less time to enter the first number using the NUMERIC keypad compared to the ALPHA keyboard. This finding was expected as the respondent had to make an extra step of touching the '123' button in order to bring up the numbers in the keyboard design. However, the overall time spent on the screen shows no time difference by condition. That is, the time saved by not needing to switch keyboards is washed out by the time participants spend reading the questions, considering their answers, entering their answers in the input field and then moving forward in the survey to the next question or screen. That is, the time difference in initially getting the number into the input field does not ultimately lead to significant overall time savings by screen. This was contrary to our hypothesis as we had suspected the NUMERIC keypad design would lead to larger efficiency gains than ALPHA keyboard. It did not.

With respect to the accuracy results, neither the ALPHA keyboard nor the NUMERIC keypad design led to fewer errors. This was unexpected as we had hypothesized that participants would make significantly fewer mistakes with the NUMERIC keypad design. While there were fewer number entry errors in the NUMERIC design, these were not significant. Still it is interesting that given what we know about age-related decline with fine motor skills [15, 18], and that older adults' precision increases with larger target sizes [20], the participants did not make more errors when touching a smaller target area on the ALPHA design. Perhaps this can be understood by the literature on learning acquisition. All participants had used their smartphone for at least six months, with most using it for quite a bit longer. Consequently, they were likely experienced and familiar with the ALPHA design as, when interacting with a smartphone, one must use the ALPHA design often.

Participants in both conditions rated the task as easy to complete and participants in both conditions were equally satisfied with their experiences, yet the NUMERIC was overwhelmingly preferred over the ALPHA for entering numbers. These results are in-line with our hypothesis. The NUMERIC design for entering numbers was significantly preferred by participants, regardless of condition.

5 Conclusion, Limitations, and Implications for Future Research

For designers creating interfaces for smartphones, our recommendation is to use a NUMERIC design for input fields that require a number as the answer. It is the preferred design and while it does not lead to greater efficiency or increased accuracy, it also does not harm performance or satisfaction. If a respondent is pleased or satisfied with a survey, the assumption is completion and submission increases, which is ultimately the goal of all survey designers.

A main limitation of the study is that we only tested with older adults. Though intentional, there may be efficiency differences between the two designs if younger adults were included in the study. We expect it is unlikely that a difference would emerge in a younger population but further testing could confirm this.

Future research could incorporate other measures of accuracy. The use of the backspace button as a proxy measure of accuracy is just one metric, and it assumes the participant notices if they have made a mistake. In addition, it also assumes that backspace always means mistake when in fact, it is possible that people may just want to double check something or reread something and thus use the backspace. One such alternative measure of accuracy could include giving a participant actual numbers to enter, and then measure accuracy based on whether they input the given numbers.

Disclaimer. This report is released to inform interested parties of research and to encourage discussion. The views expressed are those of the authors and not necessarily those of the U.S. Census Bureau. Disclosure avoidance review number: CBDRB-FY21-CBSM002-006.

Acknowledgements. The study was supported by the U.S. Census Bureau's Innovation and Operational Efficiency Program. We thank Russell Sanders, Christopher Antoun, Brian Falcone, Ivonne Figueroa, Alda Rivas, Joanna Lineback, Sabin Lakhe, Kevin Younes, and the MetroStar team. We also thank Eugene Loos, Shelley Feuer and Joanne Pascale for their reviews of an earlier draft of this paper.

References

1. U.S. Census Bureau: Unofficial preliminary para data analysis 2020 Census. Internal email. 4 Nov 2020
2. Olmsted-Hawala, E., Nichols, E., Falcone, B., Figueroa, I.J., Antoun, C., Wang, L.: Optimal data entry designs in mobile web surveys for older adults. In: Zhou, J., Salvendy, G. (eds.) ITAP 2018. LNCS, vol. 10926, pp. 335–354. Springer, Cham (2018). https://doi.org/10.1007/978-3-319-92034-4_26

3. Nichols, E., Olmsted-Hawala, E., Wang, L.: optimal designs of text input fields in mobile web surveys for older adults. In: Zhou, J., Salvendy, G. (eds.) HCII 2019, Lecture Notes in Computer Science, vol. 11592, pp. 463–481 (2019). https://doi.org/10.1007/978-3-030-22012-9_34

4. Nichols, E., Olmsted-Hawala, E., Raim, A., Wang, L.: Attitudinal and behavioral differences between older and younger adults using mobile devices. In: Gao, Q., Zhou, J. (eds.) HCII 2020. LNCS, vol. 12207, pp. 325–337. Springer, Cham (2020). https://doi.org/10.1007/978-3-030-50252-2_25

5. Pew Research Center. Mobile Fact Sheet.https://pewresearch-org-preprod.go-vip.co/internet/fact-sheet/mobile/. For more on age breaks down and smartphones. https://pewresearch-org-preprod.go-vip.co/fact-tank/2019/09/09/us-generations-technology-use/

6. Kakulla, B.N.: Older Adults Keep Pace on Tech Usage: 2020 Tech Trends of the 50 + . American Association of Retired Persons (AARP) Research (2020). https://www.aarp.org/research/topics/technology/info-2019/2020-technology-trends-older-americans.html

7. Fernández-Ardèvol, M., et al.: Methodological strategies to understand smartphone practices for social connectedness in later life. In: Zhou, J., Salvendy, G. (eds.) HCII 2019. LNCS, vol. 11593, pp. 46–64. Springer, Cham (2019). https://doi.org/10.1007/978-3-030-22015-0_4

8. Antoun, C., Couper, M., Conrad, F.: Effects of mobile versus pc web on survey response quality: a crossover experiment in a probability web panel. Public Opin. Q. **81**(S1), 280–306 (2017). https://doi.org/10.1093/poq/nfw088

9. Couper, M., Peterson, G.: Why do web surveys take longer on smartphones? Soc. Sci. Comput. Rev. **35**(3), 357–377 (2015). https://doi.org/10.1177/0894439316629932

10. Mavletova, A., Couper, M.P.: A meta-analysis of breakoff rates in mobile web surveys. In: Toninelli, E., Pinter, R., de Pedraza, P. (eds.) Mobile Research Methods: Opportunities and Challenges of Mobile Research Methodologies, pp. 81–98. Ubiquity Press, London (2015)

11. Nichols, E., Olmsted-Hawala, E., Horwitz, R., and Bentley, M.: Optimizing the decennial census for mobile: a case study. Federal Committee on Statistical Methodology (FCSM) (2015) https://nces.ed.gov/fcsm/pdf/I2_Nichols_2015FCSM.pdf

12. Loos, E.F., Romano Bergstrom, J.: Older adults. In: Romano Bergstrom, J., Schall, A.J. (eds.) Eye Tracking in User Experience Design. pp. 313–329. Elsevier, Amsterdam (2014)

13. Seidler, R.D., et al.: Motor control and aging: links to age-related brain structural, functional, and biochemical effects. Neurosci. Biobehav. Rev. **34**(5), 721–733 (2010). https://doi.org/10.1016/j.neubiorev.2009.10.005

14. Voelcker-Rehage, C.: Motor-skill learning in older adults—a review of studies on age-related differences. Eur. Rev. Aging Phys. Act. **5**, 5–16 (2008)

15. Hoogendam, Y.Y., et al.: Older age relates to worsening of fine motor skills: a population-based study of middle-aged and elderly persons. Front. Aging Neurosci. **6**, 259 (2014)

16. Kim, S., Son, J., Lee, G., Kim, H., Lee, W.: TapBoard: making a touch screen keyboard more touchable. Conference on Human Factors in Computing Systems - Proceedings. pp. 553–562 (2013)

17. Schryer, E., Ross, M.: Does the age-related positivity effect in autobiographical recall reflects differences in appraisal or memory? J. Gerontol.: Seri. B **69**(4), 548–556 (2014)

18. Ketcham, C.J., Stelmach, G.E.: Age-related declines in motor control. Handbook of the Psychology of Aging. 5th edn. pp. 313–348. Academic Press, San Diego (2001)

19. Ketcham, C.J., Stelmach, G.E.: Movement control in the older adult. In: Pew, R.W., Van Hemel, S.B. (eds.) Technology for Adaptive Aging. National Academies Press, Washington, DC (2004)

20. Ketcham, C.J., Seidler, R.D., Van Gemmert, A.W., Stelmach, G.E.: Age-related kinematic differences as influenced by task difficulty, target size, and movement amplitude. J. Gerontol. B Psychol. Sci. Soc. Sci. **57**(1), 54–64 (2002)

The Impact of Ageism on the E-Leisure of Older People in Chile

Javiera Rosell[(✉)] and Alvaro Vergés

Escuela de Psicología, Pontificia Universidad Católica de Chile, Santiago, Chile
{jerosell,ajverges}@uc.cl

Abstract. Empirical studies show that leisure activities are relevant to the well-being of the older population. Thus, online leisure, or E-leisure, can be a useful tool for engagement in leisure activities, providing multiple possibilities. In this way, the study of those factors that promote or hinder E-leisure is relevant, since it will allow the generation of adequate interventions to promote online leisure. Additionally, it has been observed that self-efficacy regarding Internet use is an important aspect for its adoption by older people. Therefore, those who have a greater perception of being capable of using the Internet do it more frequently. Also, ageism is one of the factors influencing the well-being of older adults, especially self-efficacy. In this context, the present study explores the relationship between ageism and E-leisure, considering self-efficacy regarding Internet use as a mediator. For this purpose, a mediation model was performed with the data of 677 Chilean Internet users over 60 years old. Results showed that ageism is negatively related to E-leisure, and self-efficacy plays a mediating role in this relationship. Consequently, those with higher ageism levels reported less self-efficacy for technology use and thus had less involvement in E-leisure activities.

Keywords: Ageism · E-leisure · Self-efficacy

1 Introduction

The use of information and communication technologies (ICT) in the older population is becoming more frequent, so it is particularly important to study the most common activities that older people perform when using ICT, including those aspects that enhance their use, as well as their consequences on well-being. This is essential to ensure that people of all ages can fully participate in a society where the use of technology is rapidly increasing [1, 2].

In Chile, 31.5% of people over 60 report using the Internet [3], and the number of people who have a technological device has increased over the years. For example, from 2013 to 2019 the proportion of older people who have a smartphone increased by almost 40% [4].

The most common uses of ICT by older people have been categorized as information seeking (e.g., information seeking about health or education), communication, productivity or task performance (e.g., banking or shopping), and leisure and entertainment [5].

© Springer Nature Switzerland AG 2021
Q. Gao and J. Zhou (Eds.): HCII 2021, LNCS 12786, pp. 228–239, 2021.
https://doi.org/10.1007/978-3-030-78108-8_17

This shows the substantial heterogeneity in the use of the Internet within the older population [6]. The most frequent use of ICT is for information seeking and communication, which has been reported in different parts of the world [7–9]. In contrast, using ICT for entertainment and leisure activities is one of the least frequent uses among older people. It is relevant to consider that this may be due to the digital literacy and not to a lack of interest in other types of technology uses by the older population [10].

In the study by Vroman et al. [8], only 11% of the participants reported using ICT for playing, whereas 13% referred doing so for participating in hobbies, becoming two of the ten least performed activities. Likewise, Neves et al. [7] found that 19% of the participants informed using the Internet for leisure, in contrast to 81% who reported using it for information seeking. Similar results were obtained by Castro-Rojas et al. [9] in Latin America, where 23.4% of the participants declared playing online, in contrast to 83% who mentioned using the Internet to send emails or 76.6% who use it for contacting friends.

For E-leisure, defined as the leisure through ICT (see Sect. 2.2), the main activities carried out are gaming and engagement in hobbies [11]. However, watching television is also one of the most reported activities among the older population [12]. Also, older people use technological platforms to substitute offline leisure activities, such as reading [11].

Moreover, there is a digital divide that makes age a relevant factor in ICT use inequities. Although many older adults are interested in using technology [10], in general, this age group has a lower use than the younger population, so age is one of the variables that accounts for most of the differences in Internet use [13, 14]. For example, in Chile, 68.5% of people over 60 years reported not using the Internet, compared to only 5.8% of people between 15 and 29 years old [3]. In this context, questions are raised about the impact of leisure activities on the well-being of the older population, and the different factors that influence online and offline leisure.

1.1 Benefits of Leisure in the Older Population

In populations of different ages, leisure has been reported to promote people's subjective well-being through mechanisms such as affiliation, development of mastery, autonomy, and meaning [15].

With regard to the aging population, leisure activities can promote meaning of life in the context of aging-related challenges [16]. From this perspective, leisure can be a central aspect of older people's identity, becoming a protective factor that promotes a good aging [17]. Furthermore, leisure has proved to be an appropriate tool to cope with age-related changes. For example, it allows to replace one activity with another, obtaining the same effects or benefits [18].

Mannell and Snelgrove [19] proposed a theoretical model that explains a direct and positive relationship between leisure and older people's psychological well-being. These include aspects for all ages, such as increasing well-being through keeping busy, coping with stress, having pleasure and fun, personal growth, and affiliation. Also, particular aspects of old age have been highlighted as factors that could enhance the psychological well-being through leisure, such as staying active, a sense of continuity through life, innovation, and adaptation to the aging-related changes.

It is important to note that leisure activities need to be meaningful, motivating, and freely chosen. These characteristics are the ones that will allow positive benefits through leisure, where the person must be able to express him/herself freely and thus experience positive emotions [16]. For example, Yarnal et al. [20] observed that a group of women participating in leisure activities valued the possibility of being entertained, laughing, and having the opportunity to be silly and goofy. Likewise, the connection with others through leisure activities is also appreciated by older people [16]. Furthermore, intergenerational contact has also been highlighted as a benefit of leisure [20].

From a psychopathological perspective, leisure benefits have also been reported, especially relating to depressive symptomatology in the older population. Thus, Fernandez-Fernandez et al. [21] observed a moderating effect of rumination between leisure activities and depressive symptomatology, with those who have less involvement in leisure activities and who engage in more rumination reporting more depressive symptomatology.

1.2 E-Leisure in the Older Population

Regarding the use of ICT to carry out online activities, studies have shown that entertainment and leisure activities are the ones most related to benefits in the well-being of the older people, for example, in the increase of life satisfaction and decrease of depressive symptomatology [22]. In general, those who reported a greater affinity with the Internet showed more satisfaction with leisure activities [23].

Within the different leisure activities that can be carried out through ICT, digital games and video games have been shown to benefit the well-being of older people, especially through the improvement of cognitive functioning [24]. However, it is required to play often enough to perceive these benefits [24], and this could be the reason for the non-significant results in some studies, as those reported in the review of Loos and Kaufman [25]. In addition, the social contact has been reported as a benefit of online gaming, but only a minority of older players do it with others [26].

Despite the benefits, older people tend to decrease their leisure and involvement in novel activities [17]. Just as there is great heterogeneity in the older population, the reasons to engage or not in leisure activities are diverse. Among the main motivations to do so are maintaining autonomy, social contact, self-efficacy, and well-being [16, 27].

In this context, the Internet offers multiple possibilities for personal enhancements, community inclusion, and empowerment [28]. Thus, it is an important tool for adopting a hobby or finding new interests [28]. Also, online communities can contribute to personal growth, strengthen social capital, and expand the type of leisure activities, which will favor the well-being of older people [7, 29]. Furthermore, the frequency of Internet use is positively associated with the number of leisure activities carried out [30, 31].

Despite the opportunities that ICT gives to perform leisure activities, older people's Internet use can be challenging, due to potential difficulties such as keeping up to date, getting help when needed, and being motivated to learn skills for the ICT use [11]. This is also true in the specific case of online leisure, where lack of confidence and the feeling of being pressured to keep up with technological updates are some of the barriers that can diminish its adoption [11].

1.3 Self-efficacy and E-Leisure

In the ICT context, self-efficacy is understood as a person's perception of being capable of using the technology (see Sect. 2.2) and is one of the factors that better predict its use. It has been observed that computer self-efficacy and computer anxiety (i.e., anxiety symptomatology triggered by the ICT use) mediate the association between age and technology adoption [14, 32]. Thus, confidence in using technology and getting help from others when needed are some of the aspects that older people report as more important when making the decision to engage in ICT use [11].

In turn, Internet use can promote older people's psychological well-being and self-efficacy, enhancing their self-esteem [28]. In this regard, online leisure activities improve mental health, allowing access to multiple activities and information [28].

1.4 Ageism and E-Leisure

Older adults' self-efficacy is related to social representations or stereotypes regarding old age and aging, which is known as ageism [33]. In this line, a common ageist conception is that older people cannot learn or are not open to learning new things [34]. It has been observed that prejudices and stereotypes about old age, which are present in the culture as a subjective norm, are internalized and reinforced during life, resulting in people acting in accordance with these beliefs when they reach old age, affecting their mental and physical health [35]. Undoubtedly, these ideas have an impact on older people's relationship with technology, given that it is sometimes assumed that they will have difficulties learning to use new technologies (e.g., "You can't teach an old dog new tricks") [34].

Ageism is also one of the main challenges that older people face with leisure [16]. Certain activities are considered exclusive to young people, for example, high-performance sports. This leaves fewer active leisure activities for the older population, such as watching TV, playing cards or playing bingo [36].

In the online setting, the term game-ageism has been introduced to refer to the belief that belonging to a particular age group implies being inferior or superior to other players, or the idea that being young is appropriate to be a gamer. In contrast, age-gameism refers to the pursuit of pleasure through play regardless of age, promoting social change to overcome age-related constrains [37].

In summary, studies so far have addressed the impact of ageism on older people's well-being and self-efficacy. In addition, there is evidence that self-efficacy is an important predictor of technology adoption by this age group. Less evidence exists of the direct impact of ageism on leisure activities, where particularly its relationship with E-leisure requires further exploration. Also, more information is needed regarding the mechanisms underlying this relationship, for example, aspects involved in mediation or moderation processes.

The present study aims to explore the relationship between ageism and E-leisure in the older population, considering self-efficacy about Internet use as a mediator. It is hypothesized that ageism negatively influences the adoption of online leisure activities through the decrease of self-efficacy related to Internet use.

2 Methodology

2.1 Sample and Procedures

The sample was composed of 677 older Internet users without cognitive impairment living in Chile. A time-oriented question was used as a sensitive indicator to assess cognitive impairment [38]. Therefore, all participants who answered this question incorrectly were excluded from the sample.

Recruitment was done through social networks, targeting people over 60 years old (the age at which a person is considered a senior citizen in Chile). All participants voluntarily accepted their participation before starting the online survey. The Institutional Ethics Committee approved the informed consent used and all the procedures.

2.2 Measures

Ageism. The evaluation of stereotypes about old age and aging was assessed using the revised version of the CENVE (Questionnaire on Negative Stereotypes about Old Age - Cuestionario de Estereotipos Negativos hacia la Vejez) [39]. This is a 15-item questionnaire with a Likert scale format from 1 (strongly disagree) to 4 (strongly agree). The instrument has a unidimensional structure; however, it includes questions on social, cognitive, and personality aspects regarding beliefs about older people, for example, "the vast majority of people 60 years old or older… start to have a considerable deterioration of their memory" or "the vast majority of people 60 years old or older… get angry easily and are grumpy."

Self-Efficacy About Internet Use. This was measured by four items of the Unified Theory of Acceptance and Use of Technology (UTAUT) corresponding to the dimension of "effort expectancy" [40], with a Likert response format ranging from 1 (strongly disagree) to 7 (strongly agree). The instrument includes questions about the perception of being capable of using the Internet smoothly; for example, "I find the Internet easy to use." This instrument was not officially validated in Chile, but a previous translation and application in the country showed a Cronbach's Alpha of .91. Also, all factor loadings were above .5 in the measurement model, and the unidimensional structure of the dimension was supported [41]. Although the instrument used in the current study was based on this translation, the reference to mobile Internet was removed from all the items, leaving only the word 'Internet.'

E-leisure. This aspect was evaluated through four items related to online leisure activities such as gaming, listening to music, watching TV, and reading books or magazines using different electronic devices (e.g., notebook, iPad, tablet, smartphone, and video game console). The item response format, referring to the frequency with which these activities were carried out, included the option "never" and the number of days in a month divided into ranges of 5 days (e.g., from 1 to 5 days, from 6 to 10 days, etc.).

2.3 Data Analysis

The mediation model was assessed using structural equation modeling (SEM). In the first step, the measurement model was evaluated to confirm that all the dimensions included had robust indicators in this sample. The second step fitted the full mediational model, considering ageism as a predictor of E-leisure activities, with self-efficacy as a mediator of this relationship. Also, age and gender were included as covariates in the model.

Thus, this technique gives information about the direct relationship between ageism and E-leisure, and the indirect effect through self-efficacy. Bootstrapping with 2000 replications was used to estimate asymmetric confidence intervals.

Items on ageism and self-efficacy were treated as categorical variables, so the WLSMV estimator was used. The CFI, TLI, RMSEA, and SRMR indices were used to evaluate the model fit, considering cut-off values higher than .95 for CFI and TLI, and values lower than .06 in RMSEA and lower than .8 in SRMR [42].

Mplus 8 was used to fit the structural equation model [43]. Other analyses were performed with R version 4.

3 Results

3.1 Sample Characteristics

The final sample was composed of 577 Internet users over 60 years old. The age mean was 66.57 years, ranging from 60 to 82.

The majority of the sample were females (87.85%). Also, 44.53% of the sample had a college degree or higher. However, 6.75% of participants in the sample did not complete high school education.

3.2 E-Leisure in the Older Population

Table 1 presents the frequency of different E-leisure activities such as gaming, listening to music, watching videos, and reading.

The majority of older adults reported that gaming is one of their most frequent E-leisure activities. Accordingly, 45.6% mentioned playing virtual or digital games between 26 and 30 days a month; however, one fifth of the participants never play.

On the other hand, reading digital books or magazines is one of the least frequent activities reported: only 11.2% indicated doing so between 26 and 30 days a month, and 27.6% never do it.

3.3 The Relationship Between Ageism and E-Leisure with Self-efficacy as a Mediator

The first step to evaluate the mediation effect was to assess the measurement model, considering each item's factorial loading on its corresponding latent factor and the correlation between latent variables.

The fitted model showed good fit indices: $\chi^2(227) = 575.258$, p < .001, CFI = .985, TLI = .984, RMSEA = .052 (95% CI = .046, .057), SRMR = .047.

All the factor loadings were above .50, except for one item of ageism about older persons' interest in sex ($\lambda = .34$) and the item about gaming in the E-leisure latent variable ($\lambda = .32$). Because both items are relevant to each factor and are statistically significant, both of them were retained.

Table 1. Number of people and percentage of E-leisure activities

	Never	1–5 days	6–10 days	11–15 days	16–20 days	21–25 days	26–30 days
Gaming	115 (20.1%)	69 (12.1%)	25 (4.4%)	30 (5.2%)	27 (4.7%)	45 (7.9%)	261 (45.6%)
Listening to digital music	165 (28.9%)	87 (15.3%)	59 (10.4%)	42 (7.4%)	43 (7.5%)	48 (8.4%)	126 (22.1%)
Watching videos, films or series	90 (15.8%)	112 (19.6%)	56 (9.8%)	65 (11.4%)	65 (11.4%)	53 (9.3%)	130 (22.8%)
Reading books or magazines	158 (27.6%)	147 (25.7%)	81 (14.2%)	54 (9.4%)	42 (7.3%)	26 (4.5%)	64 (11.2%)

The full mediation model was estimated considering ageism as a predictor of E-leisure and self-efficacy regarding Internet use as a mediator, with age and gender as covariates. The results showed good fit indices: χ^2 (269) = 582.669, p < .001, CFI = .988, TLI = .986, RMSEA = .045 (95% CI = .04, .05), SRMR = .075. As shown in Fig. 1, all direct paths are significant. The direct relationship between ageism and self-efficacy is negative, which means that people with more ageism reported less self-efficacy regarding Internet use (β = −14, p = .003). Ageism was also negatively associated with E-leisure, so people with more ageism mentioned a lower frequency of E-leisure activities. On the contrary, self-efficacy was positively associated with E-leisure, which implies more reported E-leisure activities in people with higher self-efficacy related to Internet use.

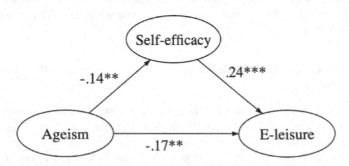

Fig. 1. Path coefficients in the mediation model. All values are standardized. Manifest variables and disturbance terms are not shown to simplify presentation. **p < .01, ***p < .001

The standardized coefficients between the covariates age and gender with self-efficacy and E-leisure are presented in Table 2, in order to simplify Fig. 1.

Table 2. Standardized coefficients between self-efficacy, E-leisure and covariates

	Age	Gender
Self-efficacy	−.03	.019
E-Leisure	−.079	−.30

Note: none of the standardized coefficients were statistically significant

Also, self-efficacy was a significant mediator in the relationship between ageism and E-leisure. The indirect effect coefficient was estimated as −.033 (p = .02), and its asymmetric confidence interval (95%) ranged from −.062 to −.01. Since this range does not include 0, the self-efficacy mediation is statistically significant.

4 Discussion

The impact of leisure activities on the well-being of older people has been studied extensively and, in general, there is a consensus about their benefits [16–19, 22]. Thus, technology as a tool for involvement in leisure activities is becoming a relevant topic that is necessary to study. E-leisure has the advantage of offering multiple possibilities to develop different activities and hobbies [28], with the potential of being a tool for older people to get massively involved in leisure activities. This is especially relevant in this age group, because it has been observed that despite the benefits of leisure, there is a decrease in these types of activities [17].

In this context, the present study explored the hypothesis that ageism is negatively associated with the adoption of E-leisure activities, and that the underlying mechanism of this relationship is the self-efficacy related to Internet use.

Undoubtedly, the adoption of technologies by the older population is highly relevant to E-leisure. In fact, age has been found to be one of the factors that most explains the difference in technology use [13, 14]. This study's results allow to understand some of the obstacles related to technology adoption in this age group. Thus, ageism seems to be an important barrier, because it is related to older people's perception of their own ability to use technology (i.e., self-efficacy). More specifically, those who have higher levels of negative stereotypes about old age and aging believe that they are less capable of using technology and, therefore, perform fewer online leisure activities. This is consistent with previous studies that showed that self-efficacy is an important aspect of technology adoption [11, 14].

It is noteworthy that ageism is also present in technology design. For example, most of the innovations for the older population are focused on health care. Older people are also excluded from design and research in digital technology [44]. This negatively impacts older people's inclusion in the technological world and becomes a barrier to its adoption by this age group [44].

These ageist conceptions are also present in relation to leisure. A distinction is made between those activities for young people and those for older people, which are generally more passive [36]. As mentioned in previous literature [16], the results of this study show a negative relationship between ageism and leisure activities; that is, those with higher levels of ageism are less frequently involved in E-leisure. However, unlike previous evidence, a high percentage of older participants reported gaming through technological devices between 26 and 30 days a month (45.6%). This may be due to the fact that the sample was predominantly a young and highly educated group of older people, who could face fewer barriers for technology use for various activities. Also, we may be facing a phenomenon where the rapid and growing adoption of technology by the older population is accompanied by the development of skills to use different technology functions.

Thus, older people are capable of using technology but are confronted with many ageist ideas that hinder their use. Therefore, interventions that aim to reduce ageism and, in turn, to increase self-efficacy regarding technology use, could favor its adoption by the older population. This would also increase the possibility of their involvement in online leisure activities, which is relevant because telling people that leisure is good for their well-being does not help their engaging in leisure activities [19]. For this reason, to promote leisure, interventions must target potential barriers such as those identified in this study. Likewise, it is necessary to promote instances that show the advantages of using the Internet and its great potential to enhance the well-being of older people [23, 24, 26].

Finally, older persons are interested in participating in leisure activities and are open to discovering new possibilities in this area [16]. Therefore, technology use can be an opportunity to promote leisure and its benefits in the older population.

The limitations in the current study that should be considered include the sample composition, with an age average below 70 years and a high level of education, which limits the generalizability of the findings. This is not surprising because people with these socio-demographic characteristics are the ones who tend to use the Internet the most [4]. Also, it is not possible to establish causality based on the model, due to the cross-sectional design.

Future studies should continue to explore the impact of aging on the adoption of technologies, especially regarding E-leisure, because it is one of the online activities that is most associated with benefits in older people's well-being [22].

Acknowledgments. This work was supported by the National Agency for Research and Development ANID-PFCHA /Doctorado Nacional/2017-21170060; and the ANID Millennium Science Initiative/Millennium Institute for Research on Depression and Personality-MIDAP ICS13_005.

References

1. Loos, E.F., Haddon, L., Mante-Meijer, E.: Introduction. In: Haddon, L., Mante-Meijer, E., Loos, E.F. (eds.) Generational Use of New Media. Routledge (2016)

2. Neves, B.B., Vetere, F. (eds.): Ageing and Digital Technology. Springer, Singapore (2019). https://doi.org/10.1007/978-981-13-3693-5

3. Ministerio de Desarrollo Social de Chile: Encuesta de Caracterización Socioeconómica Nacional. Adultos Mayores. Síntesis de Resultados (2017). http://observatorio.ministeri odesarrollosocial.gob.cl/casen-multidimensional/casen/docs/Resultados_educacion_casen_ 2017.pdf

4. Pontificia Universidad Católica de Chile, Caja Los Andes: Chile y sus mayores: resultados V Encuesta Nacional Calidad de Vida en la Vejez 2019 (2020). http://www.encuestacalidad devidaenlavejez.cl/

5. Wagner, N., Hassanein, K., Head, M.: Computer use by older adults: a multi-disciplinary review. Comput. Hum. Behav. **26**(5), 870–882 (2010). https://doi.org/10.1016/j.chb.2010. 03.029

6. Loos, E.: In search of information on websites: a question of age? In: Stephanidis, C. (ed.) UAHCI 2011. LNCS, vol. 6766, pp. 196–204. Springer, Heidelberg (2011). https://doi.org/ 10.1007/978-3-642-21663-3_21

7. Barbosa Neves, B., Fonseca, J.R.S., Amaro, F., Pasqualotti, A.: Social capital and Internet use in an age-comparative perspective with a focus on later life. PLoS One **13**(2), e0192119 (2018). https://doi.org/10.1371/journal.pone.0192119

8. Vroman, K.G., Arthanat, S., Lysack, C.: "Who over 65 is online?" Older adults' dispositions toward information communication technology. Comput. Hum. Behav. **43**, 156–166 (2015). https://doi.org/10.1016/j.chb.2014.10.018

9. Castro Rojas, M.D., Bygholm, A., Hansen, T.G.B.: Using information and communication technologies to promote healthy aging in costa rica: challenges and opportunities. In: Zhou, J., Salvendy, G. (eds.) ITAP 2016. LNCS, vol. 9755, pp. 194–206. Springer, Cham (2016). https://doi.org/10.1007/978-3-319-39949-2_19

10. Loos, E.F.: Senior citizens: digital immigrants in their own country? Observatorio (OBS*) **6**(1), 1–23 (2012)

11. Genoe, R., Kulczycki, C., Marston, H., Freeman, S., Musselwhite, C., Rutherford, H.: E-Leisure and older adults: findings from an international exploratory study. Ther. Recreation J. **52**(1), 1–18 (2018). https://doi.org/10.18666/trj-2018-v52-i1-8417

12. Kaufman, D., Chang, M.O., Ireland, A.: Leisure time use, meaning of life, and psychological distress: comparing canadian and Korean older adults. J. Educ. Cult. Stud. **2**(4) (2018). https://doi.org/10.22158/jecs.v2n4p327

13. van Deursen, A.J.A.M., van Dijk, J.A.G.M.: The digital divide shifts to differences in usage. New Media Soc. **16**(3), 507–526 (2013). https://doi.org/10.1177/1461444813487959

14. Czaja, S.J., Charness, N., Fisk, A.D., Hertzog, C., Nair, S.N., Rogers, W.A., Sharit, J.: Factors predicting the use of technology: findings from the center for research and education on aging and technology enhancement. Psychol. Aging **21**(2), 333–352 (2006). https://doi.org/10.1037/ 0882-7974.21.2.333

15. Newman, D.B., Tay, L., Diener, E.: Leisure and subjective well-being: a model of psychological mechanisms as mediating factors. J. Happiness Stud. **15**(3), 555–578 (2013). https://doi. org/10.1007/s10902-013-9435-x

16. Dattilo, J., Mogle, J., Lorek, A.E., Freed, S., Frysinger, M.: Using self-determination theory to understand challenges to aging, adaptation, and leisure among community-dwelling older adults. Act. Adap. Aging **42**(2), 85–103 (2017). https://doi.org/10.1080/01924788.2017.138 8689

17. Nimrod, G., Janke, M.C.: Leisure across the later life span. In: Gibson, H.J., Singleton, J.F. (eds.) Leisure and Aging: Theory and Practice, pp. 95–110. L: Human Kinetics, Champaign, (2012)

18. Kleiber, D.A., Genoe, M.R.: The relevance of leisure in theories of aging. In: Gibson, H.J., Singleton, J.F. (eds.) Leisure and Aging: Theory and Practice, pp. 43–66. Human Kinetics, Champaign, IL (2012)

19. Mannell, R.C., Snelgrove, R.: Leisure and the psychological well-being and health of older adults. In: Gibson, H.J., Singleton, J.F. (eds.) Leisure and Aging: Theory and Practice, pp. 143–158. Human Kinetics, Champaign, IL (2012)

20. Yarnal, C.M., Chick, G., Kerstetter, D.L.: "I did not have time to play growing up… so this is my play time. it's the best thing i have ever done for myself": what is play to older women? Leisure Sci. **30**(3), 235–252 (2008). https://doi.org/10.1080/01490400802017456

21. Fernandez-Fernandez, V., Marquez-Gonzalez, M., Losada-Baltar, A., Romero-Moreno, R.: Frequency of leisure activities and depressive symptomatology in elderly people: the moderating role of rumination. Int. Psychogeriatr. **26**(2), 297–305 (2014). https://doi.org/10.1017/s1041610213001877

22. Lifshitz, R., Nimrod, G., Bachner, Y.G.: Internet use and well-being in later life: a functional approach. Aging Ment. Health **22**(1), 85–91 (2018). https://doi.org/10.1080/13607863.2016.1232370

23. Heo, J., Kim, J., Won, Y.-S.: Exploring the relationship between internet use and leisure satisfaction among older adults. Act. Adap. Aging **35**(1), 43–54 (2011). https://doi.org/10.1080/01924788.2010.545975

24. Kaufman, D., Sauvé, L., Renaud, L., Sixsmith, A., Mortenson, B.: Older adults' digital gameplay: patterns, benefits, and challenges. Simul. Gaming **47**(4), 465–489 (2016). https://doi.org/10.1177/1046878116645736

25. Loos, E., Kaufman, D.: Positive impact of exergaming on older adults' mental and social well-being: in search of evidence. In: Zhou, J., Salvendy, G. (eds.) ITAP 2018. LNCS, vol. 10927, pp. 101–112. Springer, Cham (2018). https://doi.org/10.1007/978-3-319-92037-5_9

26. Kaufman, D., Sauve, L.: Digital gaming by older adults: can it enhance social connectedness? In: Zhou, J., Salvendy, G. (eds.) HCII 2019. LNCS, vol. 11593, pp. 167–176. Springer, Cham (2019). https://doi.org/10.1007/978-3-030-22015-0_13

27. Liechty, T., Genoe, M.R.: Older men's perceptions of leisure and aging. Leisure Sci. **35**(5), 438–454 (2013). https://doi.org/10.1080/01490400.2013.831287

28. Forsman, A.K., Nordmyr, J.: Psychosocial links between internet use and mental health in later life: a systematic review of quantitative and qualitative evidence. J. Appl. Gerontol. **36**(12), 1471–1518 (2017). https://doi.org/10.1177/0733464815595509

29. Nimrod, G.: Seniors' online communities: a quantitative content analysis. Gerontologist **50**(3), 382–392 (2010). https://doi.org/10.1093/geront/gnp141

30. Nasi, M., Rasanen, P., Sarpila, O.: ICT activity in later life: internet use and leisure activities amongst senior citizens in Finland. Eur. J. Aging **9**(2), 169–176 (2012). https://doi.org/10.1007/s10433-011-0210-8

31. Zhou, R., Fong, P.S., Tan, P.: Internet use and its impact on engagement in leisure activities in China. PLoS ONE **9**(2), (2014). https://doi.org/10.1371/journal.pone.0089598

32. Berkowsky, R.W., Sharit, J., Czaja, S.J.: Factors predicting decisions about technology adoption among older adults. Innov. Aging **2**(1), igy002 (2018). https://doi.org/10.1093/geroni/igy002

33. Ayalon, L., Tesch-Römer, C.: Introduction to the section: ageism—concept and origins. In: Ayalon, L., Tesch-Römer, C. (eds.) Contemporary Perspectives on Ageism. IPA, vol. 19, pp. 1–10. Springer, Cham (2018). https://doi.org/10.1007/978-3-319-73820-8_1

34. Cutler, S.: Ageism and technology. Generations **29**(3), 67–72 (2005)

35. Robertson, G.: Ageing and ageism: the impact of stereotypical attitudes on personal health and well-being outcomes and possible personal compensation strategies. Self. Soc. **45**(2), 149–159 (2017). https://doi.org/10.1080/03060497.2017.1334986

36. Dionigi, R.A., Horton, S.: The influence of leisure on discourses of aging. In: Gibson, H.J., Singleton, J.F. (eds.) Leisure and Aging: Theory and Practice, pp. 27–40. L: Human Kinetics, Champaign (2012)

37. Vale Costa, L., Veloso, A.I., Loos, E.: Age stereotyping in the game context: introducing the game-ageism and age-gameism phenomena. In: Zhou, J., Salvendy, G. (eds.) HCII 2019. LNCS, vol. 11593, pp. 245–255. Springer, Cham (2019). https://doi.org/10.1007/978-3-030-22015-0_19

38. O'Keeffe, E., Mukhtar, O., O'Keeffe, S.T.: Orientation to time as a guide to the presence and severity of cognitive impairment in older hospital patients. J. Neurol. Neurosurg. Psychiatry **82**(5), 500–504 (2011). https://doi.org/10.1136/jnnp.2010.214817

39. Rosell, J., Verges, A., Torres Irribarra, D., Flores, K., Gomez, M.: Adaptation and psychometric characteristics of a scale to evaluate ageist stereotypes. Arch. Gerontol. Geriatr. **90**, (2020). https://doi.org/10.1016/j.archger.2020.104179

40. Venkatesh, V., Morris, M., Davis, G., Davis, F.: User acceptance of information technology: toward a unified view. MIS Q. **27**(3) (2003). https://doi.org/10.2307/30036540

41. Ramírez-Correa, P., Grandón, E., Painén-Aravena, G.: Efecto de los rasgos de personalidad en el uso de las tecnologías de información. Multidiscip. Bus. Rev. **10**(2), 19–26 (2017)

42. Hu, L.t., Bentler, P.M.: Cutoff criteria for fit indexes in covariance structure analysis: Conventional criteria versus new alternatives. Struct. Eqn. Model.: Multi. J. **6**(1), 1–55 (1999). https://doi.org/10.1080/10705519909540118

43. Muthén, L., Muthén, B.: MplusUser'sGuide, Eighth edn. Muthén & Muthén, Los Angeles, CA (1998–2017)

44. Mannheim, I.: Inclusion of older adults in the research and design of digital technology. Int. J. Environ. Res. Public Health **16**(19) (2019). https://doi.org/10.3390/ijerph16193718

Effects of Text Simplification on Reading Behavior of Older and Younger Users

Fatima Varzgani[✉], Javad Norouzi Nia, Doaa Alrefaei, Mina Shojaeizadeh, and Soussan Djamasbi

Worcester Polytechnic Institute, Worcester, MA 01609, USA
{fvarzgani,jnorouzinia,dalrefaei,minashojaei,djamasbi}@wpi.edu

Abstract. Research shows that simplifying short textual passages to lower reading levels (e.g., lower than 10th grade reading level) can improve the viewing behavior of younger users. However, little work has been done to examine the viewing behavior of younger users for simplified text that are longer in length and are more difficult than specific reading levels such as 10th grade reading level. Similarly, little work has been done to examine whether and how older and younger users differ in viewing such long and complex textual content. In this study, we used eye-tracking to examine older and younger users' viewing behavior for two relatively long and complex text passages with the same content but varying reading difficulty. Our results supported previous research that suggests age-related cognitive difficulties are likely to be mitigated by task experience. Our results also supported previous research that shows text simplification can improve users' viewing behavior. Our results extended the previous research by showing that the positive effects of text simplification continue to hold even when the simplified text is relatively long and still considered to be hard to read.

Keywords: Reading behavior · Eye tracking · Text simplification · User experience · Older and younger users

1 Introduction

The proliferation of sophisticated information technology (IT) products and services make it increasingly possible for people to access vital information online. For example, many decision support systems provide complex information online for making life-changing decisions [1]. Hence, paying close attention to effective communication of online content is both relevant and important to human-computer interaction (HCI) research. Because online information is typically provided through visual displays, many studies have focused on examining the impact of the format and arrangement of visual elements on communication effectiveness [2]. However, little work has focused on textual content, which is an essential part of communication effectiveness [3].

One possible way to improve communication effectiveness and efficiency of textual content is through text simplification [4]. Text simplification refers to modifying readable text passages, i.e., by simplifying their structure, in a way to improve their ease of

© Springer Nature Switzerland AG 2021
Q. Gao and J. Zhou (Eds.): HCII 2021, LNCS 12786, pp. 240–252, 2021.
https://doi.org/10.1007/978-3-030-78108-8_18

processing without changing the meaning of the provided content [5]. Text simplification has been shown to help younger users to read and understand textual information that is lower than 10th grade reading levels in shorter glances [4]. While there has been little research on the effect of text simplification on older users, it is likely that text simplification can also improve communication effectiveness for older users. This improvement can be justified by the cognitive theory of aging which implies that older users tend to take longer time than younger users to process information [6].

In this study we examined whether and how simplifying long and complex passages to a level that still requires advanced reading skills can impact viewing behavior. Based on the above-mentioned studies, we expected to see improved reading experience for both older and younger users. To test this expectation, we used a validated operationalized text simplification methodology [4] to modify a long and complex text passage (18th grade reading level) to a relatively less complex yet advanced reading level (12th grade reading level). We then examined older and younger users' viewing behavior to investigate possible differences in how they process the provided information when reading the two different versions of the same text. Recent technological advances make it possible for researchers to continuously study information processing behavior and unobtrusively by capturing and analyzing users' eye movement data [7–9]. As such, eye tracking can provide insights beyond what users themselves report [10]. In this study, which is part of a larger project examining possible differences in processing complex information between younger and older users, we used eye-tracking to examine whether and how eye movements of older and younger users differ when they read complex text passages.

2 Background

A number of studies suggest that older and younger users are likely to process textual information differently. For example, research indicates that when presented with online information, older users compared to young users, experience more cognitive activity, which in turn can lead to greater attention to the content [11]. Cognitive processing tends to get slower with age, which may be the underlying reason for observed changes in older users' viewing behavior [6], resulting in changes in attention to content, navigation patterns, and/or recall of information, to name a few [11]. Grounded in the cognitive theory of aging [12], studies show that when it comes to website usage, older users tend to take more time to process the same amount of information as compared to younger users [13]. "Website stickiness," or the duration of website visit [13], tend to be shorter for younger users because they process information quicker than their older counterparts. This pattern of behavior is partly because the eyes of younger users move faster, and partly because they tend to use websites more frequently as sources of information. When it comes to reading textual information, younger users do not read the text carefully, or ignore them completely. Djamasbi et al. [3] and Varzgani et al. [14] argued that attention to textual content could be improved by simplifying textual information. In one study, Djamasbi et al. [3] modified relatively short text passages at 10th grade level to examine the impact of text simplification on younger users' task performance. They discovered that participants in the simplified text conditions performed significantly better when it came to answering questions about the text [3]. In another study, Varzgani et al.

[14] examined the impact of text simplification for more complex text passages (18th grade level) on viewing behavior. They showed significantly different cognitive activity (measured as pupillary responses) when participants viewed simplified text compared to when they viewed the original text. They also showed increased attention to the last paragraph in the simplified passage. This behavior is important because attention typically attenuates from top to bottom [15] and because in text passages, the last paragraph often contains important information such as the summary or conclusion of the provided material.

While the studies mentioned above examined the impact of text simplification on performance and viewing behavior, they did not investigate how older and younger users may differ in reaction to text simplification, particularly when the simplified text is still considered to be difficult to read. Because we are interested in communication effectiveness for cognitively complex tasks, in this study, we focus on examining viewing behavior for text passages that even after simplification, still may require higher levels of reading skills (e.g., medical or legal information). In particular, we examine whether and how text simplification for such passages may affect older and younger users' viewing behavior differently.

3 Methodology

We used an eye-tracking experiment to conduct our study. Because we wanted to examine the viewing behavior of older and younger users for passages that required advance reading skills, we recruited participants for our study from a pool of graduate students and employees (faculty and staff) at a university in United States. We chose a text passage at 18th grade level from GRE, a test for graduate admission in US universities. Using a validated set of plain language standards, we then simplified this passage to 12th grade reading level [4, 16], which is still not considered an easy-to-read passage for average readers [17]. From this point on in this current paper, we will refer to the original passage, as OP, and its simplified version as SP.

3.1 Areas of Interest (AOIs)

Areas of Interest (AOI) are used in eye tracking to delineate specific regions of displayed stimulus for gaze analysis [2]. Hence, we used AOIs to investigate whether and how text simplification can impact the behavior of younger and older users differently. To investigate overall differences, the entire passage was considered as one single AOI. Additionally, we divided both passages into three corresponding AOIs. The reason for this delineation was that OP contained three paragraphs; hence, one AOI was designated for each paragraph in OP. The text simplification procedure, however, converted the first paragraph in OP into two paragraphs in SP. Hence, the first AOIs in OP and SP had a different number of paragraphs. The rest of the AOIs in these passages contain the same number of paragraphs [14] (Fig. 1).

a. Original Passage (OP)   **b. Simplified Passage (SP)**

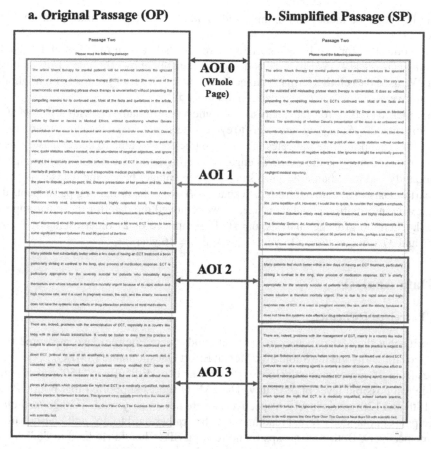

Fig. 1. Areas of Interest (AOIs) in OP and SP

3.2 Participants and Design

We recruited 65 participants from a university located in the northeastern part of the United States. The participants included students, faculty, and university staff, with an age range of 18–70 years. We conducted a between-subject study where the participants were randomly assigned to read one of the two versions of the same passage, either OP or SP. After reading the passage, participants were asked to complete a survey to capture their perceived difficulty of the passage they read.

3.3 Data Collection and Preparation

During the time that participants were viewing the passage, we collected their gaze data using the Tobii TX300 eye-tracking device. This device uses infrared waves to track eye movements and collects gaze data unobtrusively. We used the IVT filter in the Tobii Studio software (version 3.4.8) to process the raw gaze data. As in prior research, we set the IVT saccade identification threshold to 30°/s and fixation duration threshold to 100 ms [18].

We controlled for age by categorizing participants between the ages of 18 and 46 as younger users [19]. We then considered participants above the age of 46 as older users. We used the relative terms "younger" and "older" for user groups to highlight the comparative nature of age categorization in our study.

In order to prepare for data analysis, we removed gaze data sets with less than 80% sampling rate [20]. Sampling rate refers to eye-trackers' success in detecting users' gaze; hence, 80% sampling rate indicates that the eye tracker was able to detect a user's gaze 80% percent of the time the user was engaged in completing the task. Five participants in our study had less than 80% gaze sampling percentage; hence the dataset for these five participants was removed from data analysis. Two of the remaining participants did not provide information about their age, so we removed the data for those participants as well. Therefore, for the analysis, our study comprised of 21 older users (Age > 47 years) and 37 younger users (18 years = <Age <= 46 years).

4 Data Analysis

4.1 Perceived Difficulty

To verify that the text passages used in our study were complex, we measured their perceived difficulty via the Subjective Mental Effort Questionnaire (SMEQ) [21], which ranges from '0' representing the lowest possible level of difficulty to '150' representing the highest possible level of difficulty. The SMEQ scores supported that both OP and SP (18th and 12th grade levels, respectively) were not an easy read. Younger and older participants in our study found reading OP to be "rather hard to do" and "fairly hard to do," respectively. Both user groups found reading SP to be "fairly hard to do." As we expected, these results verified that both text passages used in our study were perceived as harder than average reading material.

The analysis of perceived difficulty provided additional insight. While both user groups rated the perceived difficulty of SP in a similar range ("fairly hard to do," SMEQ-older users = 35.56, SMEQ-younger users = 39.77), they exhibited almost significant differences (p-value = 0.052) in rating the perceived difficulty of OP (SMEQ-older users = 40.00, SMEQ-younger users = 60.33). Additionally, younger users rated SP to be significantly less difficult than OP (p = 0.046) (Table 1). These results indicate that younger users had a more nuanced reaction to text simplification than older users. One possible explanation for these differences in response to text simplification between the two user groups is that older people in our study were recruited from the pool of professionals in a university; hence, they had more exposure to and experience with reading text at the college level. This explanation is consistent with the argument that experience can help people to improve their performance regardless of their age [10, 22, 23]. Another explanation is that younger users tend to exhibit "impatient" viewing behavior; hence, text simplification can help them read text passages more efficiently [3]. We examine the impact of text simplification on viewing behavior in the following sections.

Table 1. Results of SMEQ ratings (Mean, Std. Dev)

	Text passage		
User	OP	SP	OP vs SP
Older	40.00 (18.03)	35.56 (24.85)	t Stat = 0.449, df = 14, P = 0.661
Younger	60.33 (32.10)	39.77 (24.31)	t Stat = 2.103, df = 25, **P = 0.046**
Older vs Younger	t Stat = −2.052, df = 23, P = 0.052	t Stat = −0.432 df = 15, P = 0.672	

4.2 Viewing Behavior

In this section, we report the viewing behavior of older and younger users when they were reading the original or the simplified text passage. We compared user attention to content via three different metrics: average fixation duration, adjusted total fixation duration, and fixation-to-visit duration ratio. Average fixation duration reveals the average lengths of glances with which a stimulus is processed, while total fixation duration reveals the total amount of attention spent on a stimulus. When comparing text passages with different lengths, it is customary to adjust total fixation duration for text length (total-fixation-duration/word-count) [24]. Because simplification typically changes the length of textual passages, we used adjusted fixation duration to examine the viewing behavior of older and younger users for OP and SP.

Visit duration provides information about both fixations and saccades during the time an AOI is processed. Fixation refers to relatively stable gazes that take foveal snapshots of objects that capture our attention. Saccade refers to fast eye movements that change the focus of attention from one fixation to another. Hence visit duration in our study encompasses the total amount of time that is spent to read a passage and to search or change focus during reading. The fixation-to-visit duration ratio reveals the ratio of the AOI visit that was dedicated to reading [1].

Average Fixation Duration. Our analysis showed that older users read both OP and SP with similar average glances (0.219 s for both text passages). The average glance duration for younger users was longer in OP than in SP (0.237 vs. 0.225) but the difference was not significant. On average, younger participants used significantly longer glances when reading OP than their older counterparts (p = 0.041). The differences in average glances between younger and older users were not significant when reading SP (Table 2). Consistent with prior research [3] these results show that younger users processed the simplified passage (SP) with shorter glances. These results also confirm the SMEQ ratings for OP and SP that show younger users found SP significantly easier to read than OP while older users did not.

Adjusted Total Fixation Duration. While our analysis showed lower adjusted values when reading SP (compared to when reading OP) for both younger and older users, these differences between OP and SP were not significant (see OP vs. SP in Table 5).

Table 2. Results of average fixation duration (Mean, Std. Dev) for the entire passage

	Text passage		
User	OP	SP	OP vs SP
Older	0.219 (0.022)	0.219 (0.022)	t Stat = 0.029, df = 17, P = 0.977
Younger	0.237 (0.022)	0.225 (0.021)	t Stat = 1.723, df = 29, P = 0.096
Older vs. Younger	t Stat = −2.164, df = 24, **P = 0.041**	t Stat = −0.713, df = 14, P = 0.487	

Our analysis, however, showed that younger users had significantly higher adjusted fixation duration compared to older users when reading OP (p-value = 0.013). When reading SP, the difference in adjusted fixation duration of both the participant groups was not significant, but close (p-value = 0.066, see Older vs. Younger in Table 3).

Table 3. Results of adjusted total fixation duration (Mean, Std. Dev) for the entire passage

	Text passage		
User	OP	SP	OP vs SP
Older	0.250 (0.051)	0.244 (0.086)	t Stat = 0.161, df = 12, P = 0.875
Younger	0.359 (0.143)	0.330 (0.161)	t Stat = 0.568, df = 33, P = 0.574
Older vs. Younger	t Stat = −2.747, df = 18, **P = 0.013**	t Stat = −1.913, df = 27, P = 0.066	

These results are consistent with younger users' higher perceived reading difficulty for OP captured by SMEQ. It is natural to find a higher cognitive activity (e.g., increased fixation intensity) when a task (in this case, reading OP) is perceived as more difficult to do.

We then refined our analysis by examining the attention that was spent to process each AOI. Our analysis did not show significant differences in attention intensity between corresponding AOIs in OP and SP for younger or older users (see OP vs. SP in Table 4). However, when comparing older and younger users' attention to AOIs, our analysis showed that younger users had significantly longer adjusted fixation duration in all 3 AOIs when reading OP (p-values = AOI1: 0.007, AOI2: 0.039, AOI3: 0.027). When viewing the simplified passage (SP), younger users still had longer adjusted fixation duration than older users; but the difference in adjusted fixation duration between the two user groups was only significant for AOI2 (p-value = 0.043). These results suggest that text simplification had a more pronounced impact on younger users. Younger users viewing behavior become more similar to older user behavior in SP (they differed significantly only in one AOI). Because older users exhibited a more efficient viewing behavior than younger users regardless of which AOI they read, these results indicate that text simplification made younger users' viewing behavior to become more efficient.

Table 4. Results of adjusted total fixation duration (Mean, Std. Dev) for each AOI

AOI 1

User	Text passage		
	OP	SP	OP vs SP
Older	0.261 (0.065)	0.257 (0.112)	t Stat = 0.089, df = 12, P = 0.931
Younger	0.397 (0.159)	0.353 (0.177)	t Stat = 0.784 df = 32, P = 0.439
Older vs. Younger	t Stat = −3.019, df = 19, **P = 0.007**	t Stat = −1.810, df = 23, P = 0.083	

AOI 2

	OP	SP	OP vs SP
Older	0.214 (0.041)	0.184 (0.058)	t Stat = 1.310, df = 14, P = 0.211
Younger	0.281 (0.107)	0.282 (0.197)	t Stat = −0.035, df = 34, P = 0.972
Older vs. Younger	t Stat = −2.212 df = 19, **P = 0.039**	t Stat = −2.125, df = 28, **P = 0.043**	

AOI 3

	OP	SP	OP vs SP
Older	0.212 (0.048)	0.222 (0.067)	t Stat = −0.359, df = 14, P = 0.725
Younger	0.313 (0.152)	0.288 (0.140)	t Stat = 0.504, df = 29, P = 0.618
Older vs. Younger	t Stat = −2.435, df = 17, **P = 0.027**	t Stat = −1.780, df = 28, P = 0.086	

Fixation-to-Visit Duration Ratio. First, we calculated the fixation-to-visit duration ratio for the entire passages. While our analysis did not show significant differences in reading OP vs. SP in each of the two user groups (see OP vs. SP in Table 5), it did show that younger users had a significantly higher fixation-to-visit duration ratio compared to older users when reading OP (p-value = 0.003). Younger and older users' fixation-to-visit duration ratio did not differ significantly when reading SP (p-value = 0.340, see Older vs. Younger in Table 5). Again, these results suggest that text simplification improved younger users reading behavior because it made it to become more like the viewing behavior of older users, who exhibited a more effective reading behavior.

Table 5. Results of adjusted fixation-to-visit duration (Mean, Std. Dev) for the entire passage

	Text passage		
User	OP	SP	OP vs SP
Older	0.830 (0.024)	0.842 (0.035)	t Stat = −0.913, df = 13, P = 0.378
Younger	0.859 (0.021)	0.855 (0.025)	t Stat = 0.511, df = 34, P = 0.613
Older vs. Younger	t Stat = −3.321, df = 22, **P = 0.003**	t Stat = 0.999, df = 11, P = 0.340	

Table 6. Results of adjusted fixation-to-visit duration (Mean, Std. Dev) for each AOI

AOI 1			
User	Text passage		
	OP	SP	OP vs SP
Older	0.834 (0.031)	0.846 (0.039)	t Stat = −0.758, df = 15, P = 0.460
Younger	0.862 (0.021)	0.858 (0.023)	t Stat = 0.522, df = 32, P = 0.605
Older vs. Younger	t Stat = −2.667, df = 19, **P = 0.015**	t Stat = −0.852, df = 10, P = 0.414	
AOI 2			
	OP	SP	OP vs SP
Older	0.843 (0.037)	0.837 (0.034)	t Stat = 0.360, df = 18, P = 0.723
Younger	0.869 (0.027)	0.860 (0.032)	t Stat = 0.894, df = 33, P = 0.378
Older vs. Younger	t Stat = −2.008 df = 20, P = 0.058	t Stat = −1.727 df = 14, P = 0.106	
AOI 3			
	OP	SP	OP vs SP
Older	0.831 (0.026	0.852 (0.031)	t Stat = −1.636, df = 15, P = 0.123
Younger	0.860 (0.024)	0.862 (0.026)	t Stat = −0.279, df = 32, P = 0.782
Older vs. Younger	t Stat = −3.024, df = 23, **P = 0.006**	t Stat = −0.921, df = 13, P = 0.374	

Next, we calculated fixation-to-visit duration ratio for each AOI. We did not find significant differences in fixation-to-visit duration ratio between the two passages' respective AOIs in each user group (see OP vs. SP in Table 6). When comparing fixation-to-visit duration ratio between younger and older users, our analysis showed that younger users had significantly larger fixation-to-visit duration ratios in AOI1 and AOI3 and almost significantly larger ratios in AOI2 when reading OP (p-values = AOI1: 0.015, AOI2: 0.058, AOI3: 0.006). There were no significant differences in reading behavior between the two user groups when they were viewing the simplified passage (SP). These results suggest that text simplification improved younger users' reading behavior by making it more efficient like older users' viewing behavior.

5   Discussion

In this study, we examined older and younger users' viewing behavior when reading text passages that required advanced (college level) reading skills. Hence, we recruited faculty, staff, and students from a university in the United States to participate in our study. We used two text passages that had the same content but were different in grade-level reading. To prepare these text passages for our study, we selected a GRE text passage at 18th grade reading level and simplified it to 12th grade reading level [14]. Our results confirmed that the text passages used in our study were indeed in the difficult reading range for both user groups.

We expected that text simplification would improve the reading experience of both older and younger users in our study. It would improve younger users' viewing behavior because it would help them to read more efficiently. It would improve older users' reading behavior because it would compensate for their age-related cognitive deficits such as slower eye movements [25]. Our results, however, did not show a similar improved reaction to text simplification for both user groups. While younger users found the less complex text passage (SP at the 12th grade reading level) significantly easier to read than the more complex text passage (OP with 18th grade reading level), older users did not perceive SP and OP to be significantly different in reading difficulty. Moreover, younger users perceived the more complex text passage almost significantly harder to read than older users. The differences in reaction to text simplification between younger and older users in our study can be explained by our participants' population. While younger users were recruited from a pool of graduate students, older users were recruited from a pool of faculty and staff, most of whom had masters or doctoral degrees. Hence, the older users in our study were probably more experienced than younger users in reading complex text as part of their daily routine.

Older users' experience in our study can also explain the observed viewing behavior. Our results showed that older users exhibited a more efficient viewing behavior (e.g., shorter average fixation duration, shorter adjusted total fixation duration, shorter fixation-to-visit duration ratio) compared to younger users when reading the more complex passage (OP). When reading the simplified version of the text (SP) viewing behavior of younger users became more like the viewing behavior of older users, more efficient. These results are interesting because they show that compared to younger users, older users have a more efficient reading behavior (read text with shorter glances and spend more time on reading rather than searching) and that younger users (not both user groups) have a more nuanced reaction to text simplification. These results do not support the cognitive theory of aging [12]. Rather, they support the argument that experience is likely to close age-related cognitive gap, such as differences in information processing speed and reaction time, between younger and older users [10]. In other words, the reason, why older users in our study had lower perceived difficulty scores and showed less intense viewing behavior than their younger counterparts, is experience makes people to get better and more comfortable at tasks. The results together suggest that we are likely to improve viewing behavior for complex text passages for older users through training and for younger users through text simplification.

6   Study Limitations and Future Study

Our study is not without limitations. All participants in our study had at least a college degree. Most of the older participants in our study had advanced higher education degrees, such as masters or doctoral degrees. There is a possibility that a population with lower education levels would exhibit different viewing behavior than the one observed in our study. Our study was limited to participants that were recruited from a technical college campus. Future studies, using a population with a more diverse background and expertise, can help make new discoveries. Similarly, a larger sample size is likely to reveal more nuanced reactions to text simplification.

7   Contribution

Studies show that simplifying textual information can have a significant impact on viewing behavior and, thus, the performance of younger users. However, little work has been done to investigate how older and younger users' viewing behavior may differ in reaction to text simplification for more complex passages. Our results suggest that experience (e.g., through frequent use, education, or training) is likely to minimize age-related cognitive deficiencies that can affect older users' viewing behavior. Our results also show that text simplification is likely to improve younger users' viewing behavior to become more efficient and effective in reading.

References

1. Djamasbi, S., Tulu, B., Norouzi Nia, J., Aberdale, A., Lee, C., Muehlschlegel, S.: Using eye tracking to assess the navigation efficacy of a medical proxy decision tool. In: Schmorrow, D.D., Fidopiastis, C.M. (eds.) HCII 2019. LNCS (LNAI), vol. 11580, pp. 143–152. Springer, Cham (2019). https://doi.org/10.1007/978-3-030-22419-6_11
2. Djamasbi, S.: Eye tracking and web experience. AIS Trans. Hum.-Comput. Interact. 6(2), 37–54 (2014). https://doi.org/10.17705/1thci.00060
3. Djamasbi, S., Shojaeizadeh, M., Chen, P., Rochford, J.: Text Simplification and Generation Y: An Eye Tracking Study (2016)

4. Djamasbi, S., Rochford, J., DaBoll-Lavoie, A., Greff, T., Lally, J., McAvoy, K.: Text simplification and user experience. In: Schmorrow, D.D.D., Fidopiastis, C.M.M. (eds.) AC 2016. LNCS (LNAI), vol. 9744, pp. 285–295. Springer, Cham (2016). https://doi.org/10.1007/978-3-319-39952-2_28
5. Siddharthan, A.: Syntactic simplification and text cohesion. Res. Lang. Comput. 4(1), 77–109 (2006). https://doi.org/10.1007/s11168-006-9011-1
6. Glisky, E.L.: Frontiers in neuroscience. In: Riddle, D.R. (ed.) Changes in Cognitive Function in Human Aging, in Brain Aging: Models, Methods, and Mechanisms. CRC Press/Taylor & Francis, Copyright © 2007. Taylor & Francis Group, LLC, Boca Raton, FL (2007)
7. Cyr, D., Head, M., Larios, H., Pan, B.: Exploring human images in website design: a multimethod approach. MIS Q. 33(3), 539–566 (2009). https://doi.org/10.2307/20650308
8. Djamasbi, S.: Eye tracking and web experience. AIS Trans. Hum.-Comput. Interact. 6(2), 16–31 (2014)
9. Tullis, T., Siegel, M.: Does ad blindness on the web vary by age and gender?. In: CHI'13 Extended Abstracts on Human Factors in Computing Systems, pp. 1833–1838. ACM, Paris, France (2013). https://doi.org/10.1145/2468356.2468685
10. Loos, E., Romano Bergstrom, J.: Older adults. In: Eye Tracking in User Experience Design, pp. 313–329 (2014). https://doi.org/10.1016/b978-0-12-408138-3.00012-1
11. Shojaeizadeh, M., Djamasbi, S.: Eye movements and reading behavior of younger and older users: an exploratory eye-tacking study. In: Zhou, J., Salvendy, G. (eds.) ITAP 2018. LNCS, vol. 10926, pp. 377–391. Springer, Cham (2018). https://doi.org/10.1007/978-3-319-92034-4_29
12. Diggs, J.: The cognitive theory of aging, in encyclopedia of aging and public health. In: Loue, S.J.D., Sajatovic, M. (eds.) pp. 216–218. Springer US, Boston, MA (2008). https://doi.org/10.1007/978-0-387-33754-8_92
13. Nguyen, M.H., et al.: Optimising eHealth tools for older patients: collaborative redesign of a hospital website. Euro. J. Cancer Care 28(1), e12882 (2019). https://doi.org/10.1111/ecc.12882
14. Varzgani, F., Norouzi Nia, J., Shojaeizadeh, M., Djamasbi, S.: Viewing Behavior in Complex Passages-An Exploratory Eye-tracking Study (2020)
15. Faraday, P.: Visually Critiquing Web Pages. Springer, Vienna (2000). https://doi.org/10.1007/978-3-7091-6771-7_17
16. Tang, R., Onder, S.B., Hudgins, K.J., Zhou, Z.: Improving Manual and Automated Text Simplification, Business, Editor. Worcester Polytechnic Institute, Boston (2017)
17. Snow, S.: This Surprising Reading Level Analysis That Will Change The Way You Write (2015). https://contently.com/2015/01/28/this-surprising-reading-level-analysis-will-change-the-way-you-write/
18. Shojaeizadeh, M., Djamasbi, S., Chen, P., Rochford, J.: Text simplification and pupillometry: an exploratory study. In: Schmorrow, D.D., Fidopiastis, C.M. (eds.) AC 2017. LNCS (LNAI), vol. 10285, pp. 65–77. Springer, Cham (2017). https://doi.org/10.1007/978-3-319-58625-0_5
19. Gills, J.L., Bott, N.T., Madero, E.N., Glenn, J.M., Gray, M.: A short digital eye-tracking assessment predicts cognitive status among adults. GeroScience (2020). https://doi.org/10.1007/s11357-020-00254-5
20. Kruger, J.-L., Hefer, E., Matthew, G.: Measuring the impact of subtitles on cognitive load: eye tracking and dynamic audiovisual texts. In: Proceedings of the 2013 Conference on Eye Tracking South Africa, pp. 62–66. Association for Computing Machinery, Cape Town, South Africa (2013). https://doi.org/10.1145/2509315.2509331
21. Sauro, J., Lewis, J.R.: Quantifying the user experience. Practical Statistics for User Research, 2nd edn. Morgan Kaufmann Publishers Inc (2016)
22. Hill, R., Dickinson, A., Arnott, J., Gregor, P., McIver, L.: Older web users' eye movements: Experience counts. pp. 1151–1160 (2011). https://doi.org/10.1145/1978942.1979115

23. Loos, E.: In search of information on websites: a question of age? In: Stephanidis, C. (ed.) UAHCI 2011. LNCS, vol. 6766, pp. 196–204. Springer, Heidelberg (2011). https://doi.org/10.1007/978-3-642-21663-3_21
24. Poole, A., Ball, L.: Eye tracking in human-computer interaction and usability research: current status and future prospects, pp. 211–219 (2006)
25. Loos, E., Mante-Meijer, E.: Getting access to website health information: does age really matter? pp. 185–201 (2012)

A Prospective Study of Haptic Feedback Method on a Lower-Extremity Exoskeleton

Yilin Wang[1], Jing Qiu[2($\boxtimes$)], Hong Cheng[1], and Lu Wang[2]

[1] Center for Robotics, School of Automation Engineering, University of Electronic Science and Technology of China, Chengdu 611731, China
[2] Center for Robotics, School of Mechanical and Electrical Engineering, University of Electronic Science and Technology of China, Chengdu 611731, China
qiujing@uestc.edu.cn

Abstract. Medical lower-limb exoskeleton (LLE) has been developed for rehabilitation and walking assistance. However, it lacked feedback on current status to the wearer. The patients with perception lost in lower-extremity (for example, elderly people and paraplegia patients) cannot perceive their lower extremities. Therefore, haptic feedback might be necessary for them if they wear a LLE, which might inform them of current gait state. A prospective study was conducted in this paper with a purpose of designing a vibration device for a lower-extremity exoskeleton system to feed back the current walking state of the exoskeleton to wearers. Firstly, the basic tests were conducted to collect the accuracy and reaction time of subjects based on two vibration modes (strength change and position change vibration mode). Then, the subjects wore an exoskeleton with the two vibration devices to complete walking tasks and the task completion time was recorded. The accuracy of the two vibration devices can both reach about 90%, and there was no significant difference in the reaction time. It indicated that the feedback of the two devices can be well perceived by most subjects. The results of the subjective questionnaires showed that subjects prefer the strength change mode. Although there was no significant of completion time in no-feedback and vibration-feedback modes, the questionnaires showed that exoskeleton with haptic feedback can inform the wearers current state of exoskeleton and made the subjects feel safer. In the future design, LLE with vibration devices can be considered for rehabilitation and walking assistance for the elder people and the patients with motor dysfunction in lower limbs.

Keywords: Haptic device · Exoskeleton · Haptic feedback · Rehabilitation · Walking assistance · The elder people

1 Introduction

With the advancement of haptic and robotic technology, more researchers focused on the combination of rehabilitation haptic device and exoskeletons. The range of haptic and robotic devices used for rehabilitation is from simple gloves to full-arm exoskeletons [1]. Most exoskeleton systems used haptic feedback for force reflection and teleoperation.

© Springer Nature Switzerland AG 2021
Q. Gao and J. Zhou (Eds.): HCII 2021, LNCS 12786, pp. 253–261, 2021.
https://doi.org/10.1007/978-3-030-78108-8_19

The EXOSKELETON project aimed to build a haptic control station, which allowed the operator wearing an exoskeleton-based haptic interface to remotely control a virtual slave robot [2]. X-arm-2 exoskeleton uses force reflection device on its right arm of its operators [3]. Marco Fontana et al. designed a robotic hand exoskeleton conceived for haptic interaction in the context of virtual reality and teleoperation applications [4]. Exoskeletons with haptic devices was also used for rehabilitation. A common point of view is that robotic rehabilitation and assistive technologies have the potential of changing older people's lives and improving quality of life of patients with motor deficiencies [5]. The haptic robotic devices can provide a patient with motor dysfunction a particular feedback that makes the patients understand the environment clearly [6]. In the past decade, most researches developed exoskeleton with haptic devices for arm-rehabilitation training and tasks [7, 8]. In recent years, haptic devices combined with visual enhance-based brain computer interface for rehabilitation lower-limb exoskeleton was developed [9]. However, mobility and vision are two of the human faculties that can be largely affected by age [10]. Elderly with vision and gait impairments may appear anxiety, especially when navigating in an unknown facility [11], such as exoskeleton. They may focus on their feet to confirm current state if wearing an exoskeleton, which may make them ignore other environment information such as traffic or other emergencies. In addition to this, cervical spondylosis is a potential hazard if keeping head down for a long time. Therefore, the feedback of motion status is necessary for the old wearer of exoskeleton. This paper conducted an experiment, aiming to test the efficiency of walking with an exoskeleton equipped with haptic devices.

2   Methods

2.1   Subjects

Ten subjects (seven males and three females, average age: 21 ± 1.6, average height: 167.2 ± 7.6 cm, average weight: 58 ± 6.4 kg) took participant in this study, who were students of University of Electronic Science and Technology. Informed consent was signed prior to the study.

2.2   Materials and Equipment

The exoskeleton named AIDER used in this study was developed by Center for Robotics, University of Electronic Science and Technology. AIDER was designed for the old and patients with motor dysfunction in lower limbs, which can assist them sitting-to-standing, standing and keeping balance, and walking.

Two kinds of self-made vibration devices were used, which was separately designed as the change of strength and position. The button oscillator was used for the vibrator, which has a diameter of 12 mm and a thickness of 2.7 mm. The operating voltage range was 1–5 V, the rated voltage was 3.7 V, and the rated speed was 12000 ± 2500 RPM.

The response mechanism of human skin surface to vibration frequency and amplitude is very complex, which is related to the position of individual's skin constitution and vibrator structure [12]. Demain et al. proposed that hands can detects more information through tactile perception than any other part of human body [13]. Karuei et al. [14] argued that the wrist and spine are the best places to feel vibrations and touch, and then arms. Verrillo et al. [15] found that the most sensitive vibration frequency of human arms was 200 to 300 Hz. What's more, the duration of vibration from 200 to 500 ms is suitable for humans and the vibration interval of a single vibrator is better set to 200 to 300 ms, which will not affect perception or cause discomfort [16].

Hence, the current study was based on the exoskeleton AIDER with two kinds of vibration modules, strength-change vibration (SCV) and position-change vibration (PCV). The duration time and interval time of each PCV vibrator was set at 240 ms and 200 ms respectively. The duration time and interval time of each PCV vibrator was set at 240 ms and 640 ms respectively. And each SCV vibrator's duration time and interval time was 240 ms and 55 ms respectively, which consistent with the step of exoskeleton.

The vibration devices were put on the subjects' back and forearm, as shown in Fig. 1. The back-vibrators represented the step height information, and left/right vibrators stood for left/right step height. The forearm-vibrators feed the step length information back, and left/right vibrators stood for left/right step length.

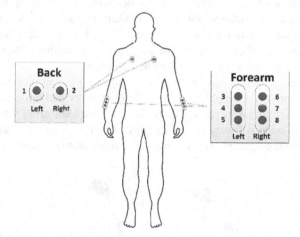

Fig. 1. Position of vibrators (For the strength-change vibration device: the back-vibrators began to vibrate and enhanced as the step height increased. And the vibration of "1" represented left step height, "2" stood for right step height. For the position-change vibration device: the forearm-vibrators began to vibrate from "3" to "5" with the left step length increased, and "5" to "3" with the left step length decreased.)

2.3 Procedure

The whole experiment was divided into four sessions.

In session 1, SCV was used to familiarize the subjects with the vibration mode. A single strength-change vibrator was pasted on the subject's arm in session 1, as Fig. 2(a) showed. The subjects needed to click the "enhanced" or "weakened" buttons soon as

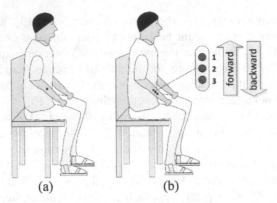

Fig. 2. The position of vibrators. (a) SCV device of session 1 (b) PCV device of session 2

they felt the intensity changes. Each trial last 20 min, and a subject needed complete 3 trails within 5 days.

In session 2, three vibrators were pasted on the subject's arm, as shown in Fig. 2(b). A single test consisted of three vibrators in a random vibration sequence. The subject chose an option of the vibration sequences, such as "1-2-3, forward". A trial included 40 times vibration, and last about 10 min. The accuracy and reaction time were recorded. The subjects were required to complete 3 trials in 5 days.

In session 3, the subjects were required to recognize the gait phase of exoskeleton according to SCV or PCV. Gait phase of exoskeleton was divided into 4 states, as shown in Fig. 3. And the vibrators were pasted on the subject's back and arms, which was shown in Fig. 1. The self-made software randomly played a vibration mode, and the subjects chose the corresponding gait phase. Accuracy and reaction time were recorded.

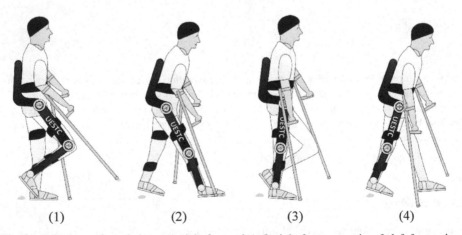

Fig. 3. Gait phase of exoskeleton (1: right foot swing, 2: right foot supporting, 3: left foot swing, 4: left foot supporting)

In session 4, the subjects were required to wear AIDER to walk for 5 meters. The completion time was recorded. The tasks included two mode: no-feedback and with haptic feedback. After walking, the subjects filled the questionnaire which was designed according to Likert scale.

2.4 Data Collection and Analysis

The vibrator strength was divided into 9 levels with a range of 1–5 V, and the voltage increment of each level was 0.5 V. Therefore, the corresponding voltage of level 1 was 1 V, and the level 9 was 5 V. A single trail lasted for 1 s and the strength change interval was set 1 s. Level 1 was removed from this study because 1 V was too feeble to perceive. Therefore, the total combination mode was $A_8^2 = 56$. The reaction time and accuracy were collected by a computer. The subjects selected the options and then the results were recorded. The questions of questionnaires for the comparison of SCV and PCV were set as "easy to master and adapt", "can clearly recognize the step height increase or decrease"/"can clearly recognize the step length increase or decrease", "don't affect walking", "has good effectiveness". The subjects rated each question from "1" to "5" according to Likert scale, which indicated "strongly disagree" and "strongly agree" respectively. *IBM SPSS 22* was used to analyze the statistical results. The reaction time and accuracy were analyzed according to t-test. The result of questionnaires was based on the Wilcoxon test. The significant level was set on 5%.

3 Results

In session 1, Fig. 4 showed the accuracy and reaction time of SCV mode on different patterns, in which negative numbers on x-axis represented vibration decrease and positive numbers were vibration increase. The results indicated that the subjects could perceive large span of vibration combination clearer than small span. When strength grade leap was more than 2 levels, the subjects could clearly perceive the change. The subjects could perceive vibration increase clearer than decrease according to Fig. 4(a), however, there was no significant difference ($t = -1.573$, $P = 0.144$). Reaction time had the same conclusion that no significant difference was observed between vibration increase and decrease ($t = 0.302$, $p = 0.768$). When the strength grade leap was 1 or -1, the subjects could hardly perceive the change of vibration strength.

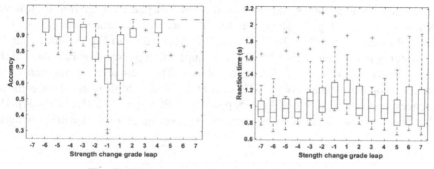

Fig. 4. The accuracy and reaction time of SCV mode

In session 2, the accuracy of 10 position-change vibration mode was shown in Fig. 5. Low accuracy appeared in "3-1-2" and "2-1-3" mode. What's more, the Fig. 6 showed that the accuracy and reaction time of two-vibrator mode has more advantages than three-vibrator mode, and there was a significant difference on accuracy according to t-test (t = 3.402, p = 0.005). No significant difference was observed on reaction time (t = −0.861, p = 0.408).

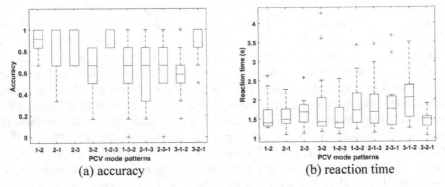

(a) accuracy   (b) reaction time

Fig. 5. The accuracy and reaction time of PCV mode

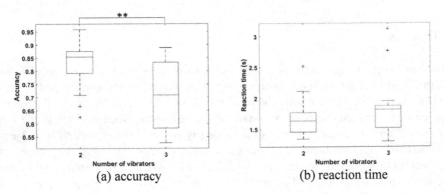

(a) accuracy   (b) reaction time

Fig. 6. The accuracy and reaction time of different patterns

In session 3, the accuracy and reaction time of gait phase recognition in different modes was shown in Fig. 7. There was no difference on accuracy (t = 1.004, P = 0.339) and reaction time (t = 0.373, P = 0.717). According to Fig. 3, phase 1 and 3 were swinging phases, and phase 2 and 4 were supporting phases. Figure 8 showed the accuracy and reaction time of different gait phases. The accuracy of swing phase was lower than supporting phase both in SCV and PCV mode, and there existed significant difference on accuracy (SCV: t = −4.775, p = 0.000; PCV: t = −3.281, p = 0.004). The results indicated that the subjects can perceive supporting phase easier than swinging phase.

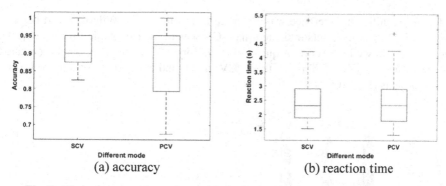

(a) accuracy   (b) reaction time

Fig. 7. The accuracy and reaction time of gait phase recognition in different mode

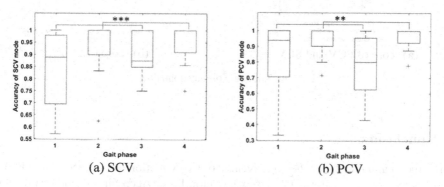

(a) SCV   (b) PCV

Fig. 8. The accuracy of SCV mode

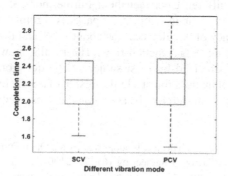

Fig. 9. The completion time of no-feedback mode and haptic feedback mode

In session 4, the subjects were required to wear the exoskeleton AIDER to walk 5 meters. According to the results of session 1 to 3, the SCV mode had more advantages than PCV mode. Therefore, the comparison of no-feedback mode and SCV mode was made in session 4. The results indicated no significant difference in completion time between the no feedback and haptic feedback mode according to t-test ($t = -1.031$, $p = 0.315$). Figure 10(a) showed the average score of the questionnaires of SCV and PCV mode, and significant difference was observed according to the Wilcoxon test (Z = − 5.34, p = 0.000). The results indicated that SCV was more acceptable for the subjects. Figure 10(b) showed the score of questionnaires for SCV mode. The results indicated that the subjects prefer SCV mode than PCV mode, and SCV mode was more trusted for the subjects (Fig. 10(a)).

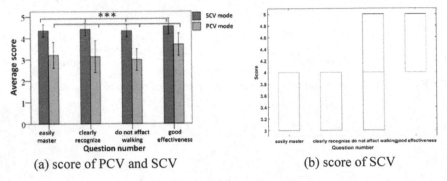

(a) score of PCV and SCV   (b) score of SCV

Fig. 10. The score of questionnaires

4   Conclusions

This paper mainly analyzed the effectiveness of two vibration devices (SCV and PCV) used for feed the gait information of exoskeleton back. According to the results, the accuracy and reaction time of SCV mode had more advantages than PCV mode. However, there was no significant difference between them. Furthermore, 35 kinds of SCV patterns could be perceived more clear than other 21 patterns. From the results, it could be observed that the accuracy of two devices was about 90%, and there was no significant difference between the subjects' reaction time. The results showed that two kinds of devices could be well perceived by most subjects. The questionnaires indicated that SCV was easier to accept by the subjects. In the design of exoskeleton feedback system, the SCV device could be considered to be added on the exoskeleton in order to feed the step information back.

Acknowledgements. This research project is supported by the Open Funding Project of National Key Laboratory of Human Factors Engineering (6142222190308), the Fundamental Research Funds for the Central Universities, University of Electronic Science and Technology of China (ZYGX2019Z010), and the Key research and development project of Sichuan science and technology plan (2018FZ0053).

References

1. Wagner: Haptic and exoskeleton devices for neurorehabilitation of upper limb paralysis: a state of art and a night landing task. Northern Michigan University, NMU Commons, pp. 1–106 (2014)

2. Letier, P., Motard, E., Verschueren, J.-P.: EXOSTATION: haptic exoskeleton based control station. In: IEEE International Conference on Robotics and Automation, pp. 1840–1845 (2010)
3. Haptic Exoskeleton. https://www.haptic.ro/exoscheletul-haptic/. Accessed 28 Oct 2020
4. Fontana, M., Fabio, S., Marcheschi, S., Bergamasco, M.: Haptic hand exoskeleton for precision grasp simulation. ASME. J. Mech. Rob. 5(4), 041014 (2013)
5. Ajayi, M.O., Djouani, K., Hamam, Y.: Interaction control for human-exoskeletons. J. Control Sci. Eng. 2020(10053), 1–15 (2020)
6. Chiasson, J., McGrath, B.J., Rupert, A.H:. Enhanced situation awareness in sea, air and land environments. In: RTO HFM Symposium on "Spatial Disorientation in Military Vehicles: Causes, Consequences and Cures" (2003)
7. Lugo-Villeda, L.I., Frisoli, A., Sandoval-Gonzalez, O., et al.: Haptic guidance of Light-Exoskeleton for arm-rehabilitation tasks. In: The 18th IEEE International Symposium on Robot and Human Interactive Communication, Roman. IEEE (2009)
8. Gupta, A., O'Malley, M.K.: Design of a haptic arm exoskeleton for training and rehabilitation. IEEE/ASME Trans. Mech. 11(3), 280–289 (2006)
9. Duan, S., Wang, C., Li, M., Long, X., Feng, W.: Haptic and visual enhance-based motor imagery BCI for rehabilitation lower-limb exoskeleton. In: 2019 IEEE International Conference on Robotics and Biomimetics (ROBIO). IEEE (2019)
10. Pirker, W., Katzenschlager, R.: Gait disorders in adults and the elderly: a clinical guide. Wien. Klin. Wochenschr. 129(3–4), 81–95 (2017)
11. Crews, J.E., Campbell, V.A.: Vision impairment and hearing loss among community dwelling older americans: implications for health and functioning. Am. J. Public Health 94(5), 823–829 (2004)
12. Verrillo, R.T: Age related changes in the sensitivity to vibration. J. Gerontol. 35(2) (1980)
13. Demain, S., Metcalf, C.D., Merrett, G.V., Zheng, D., Cunningham, S.: A narrative review on haptic devices: relating the physiology and psychophysical properties of the hand to devices for rehabilitation in central nervous system disorders. Disabil. Rehabil. Assist. Technol. 8(3), 181 (2013)
14. Karuei, I., Maclean, K.E., Foleyfisher, Z., et al: Detecting vibrations across the body in mobile contexts. In: Proceedings of the SIGCHI Conference on Human Factors in Computing System, Vancouver, Canada, pp. 3267–3276 (2011)
15. Wilska, A.: On the vibrational sensitivity in different regions of the body surface. Acta Physiol. 31(2–3), 285–289 (2010)
16. Fei, H., Li-Juan, C., Wei, L.U., Ai-Guo, S.: Short-term memory characteristics of vibration intensity tactile perception on human wrist. Acta Physiol. Sinica 66(6), 683–690 (2014)

Understanding the Acceptance of Robo-Advisors: Towards a Hierarchical Model Integrated Product Features and User Perceptions

Man Wu and Qin Gao[✉]

Department of Industrial Engineering, Tsinghua University, Beijing, People's Republic of China
gaoqin@tsinghua.edu.cn

Abstract. Robo-advisors have recently become increasingly accessible and gaining interest among consumers. However, there still exist problems in acceptance of robo-advisors among consumers. In this study, we have identified influential factors of robo-advisor acceptance, conducting an online survey involving 207 participants to examine their relationship with use intention. A hierarchical model of robo-advisor acceptance was built that integrated product features, user perceptions, and use intention. The model showed that the competence and expected earnings of a robo-advisor contribute to users' perception of its usefulness. Furthermore, the customization and competence of a robo-advisor decreases users' perceived risk. Additionally, better designed account management and more authority for users increase perceived control over a robo-advisor. Moreover, although usefulness was regarded as the most important factor, only perceived risk (negatively) and perceived control (positively) were significantly associated with the intention to use robo-advisors. Based on the acceptance model, implications for the robo-advisor design were discussed.

Keywords: Technology acceptance · Robo-advisor · Financial technology

1 Introduction

Managing assets and investment requires financial knowledge and consumes time. Some people seek help from personal financial advisors, but at a high fee. Robo-advisors, as a technology-enabled means, are digital platforms to provide automated financial services at a lower cost than human advisors. Based on advanced analytics capacities such as data science techniques and artificial intelligence, robo-advisors assist users to make decisions regarding portfolio management and investment by considering their goals and preferences. Besides, robo-advisors require very low opening balances, so that nearly everybody can benefit from a robo-advisor if they choose. Robo-advisors are increasingly accessible and gaining interest among consumers.

The process of using a robo-advisor includes three phases: configuration, matching and customization, and maintenance [1]. In the first phase (configuration), the platforms

© Springer Nature Switzerland AG 2021
Q. Gao and J. Zhou (Eds.): HCII 2021, LNCS 12786, pp. 262–277, 2021.
https://doi.org/10.1007/978-3-030-78108-8_20

create accounts by collecting users' personal information and their financial situation in terms of private assets. Users can link their bank accounts directly for quick and easy funding of their robo-advisor accounts. In the second phase (matching and customization), an online survey is conducted on the platforms to ascertain users' risk tolerance, investment goals, needs, and time horizon for financial management. Based on the results of the survey, robo-advisors will automatically compute recommendations and create personalized portfolios to allocate the assets to different financial products, including exchange-traded funds, mutual funds, individual stocks, bonds, futures, or commodities [1]. In the third phase (maintenance), robo-advisors continue to monitor the performance of portfolios and respond to changes in financial products by rebalancing the portfolio.

Although robo-advisors automatically offer advice on financial management with low fees, consumers' adoption of robo-advisors is still slow [2]. In a survey conducted by LendEDU in 2017, 62% of respondents said that they had not used a robo-advisor because they had never heard of a robo-advisor [3]. Another survey conducted by NerdWallet in 2020 found that 84% of respondents would rather work with a human financial advisor to invest their assets, compared with 16% who would prefer to use a robo-advisor [4]. Additionally, the survey found that 68% of respondents thought a human advisor would get them a better return on their investments than robo-advisors [3]. Overall, these surveys show that robo-advisors are less popular than human advisors. Many consumers do not know about robo-advisors and they are doubtful as to whether robo-advisors can manage their assets well. There still exist problems in the acceptance and adoption of robo-advisors among consumers.

There has been limited research exploring the factors for acceptance of robo-advisors. One study found that people with more financial experience were more willing to use robo-advisors [5]. However, the study only focused on individual factors and did not consider factors related to features of robo-advisors. A couple of studies have explored the effects of perceived usefulness, perceived control, and perceived risk on robo-advisor acceptance [6, 7]. Their results showed that perceived usefulness and perceived control were positively associated and perceived risk negatively associated with the intention to use robo-advisors, whereas perceived risk had a negative relationship with use intention. Their studies shed some light on factors of robo-advisor acceptance, but these factors are limited because they only focused on user perceptions of robo-advisors. The impact of robo-advisor features on use intention is unknown, and so it is unclear how to design a robo-advisor.

Our study aims to build an acceptance model of robo-advisors to cover factors relevant to users, technology, and the social environment. We first collected four aspects of influential factors from literature: factors affecting technology acceptance, factors affecting robot acceptance, factors affecting the acceptance of recommender agents, and factors affecting financial behaviors. These influential factors were classified into three categories: individual difference, user perceptions, and product features. Then, we conducted interviews to supplement the product features of robo-advisors that may influence acceptance. Finally, a survey was conducted to examine the importance of influential factors and investigate the relationships between influential factors and use intention. Through the survey, an acceptance model of robo-advisors was formulated. Based on the model, implications were discussed for robo-advisor design.

2 Related Work

2.1 Factors Affecting Technology Acceptance

There are many well-known models and theories of acceptance of technologies. The theory of reasoned action (TRA) [8] is one of the most fundamental theories of human behavior. The TRA model suggests that a person's behavior is determined by their intention to perform the behavior, and that this intention is determined by their attitude toward the behavior and the subjective norm. The subjective norm refers to the person's perception that most people who are important to him think he should or should not perform the behavior. The technology acceptance model (TAM) [9], adapted from TRA, focuses on information technology acceptance. In this model, in addition to the subjective norm, perceived usefulness and perceived ease of use are two main factors that affect acceptance behaviors. The theory of planned behavior (TPB) [10] extends TRA by adding perceived behavioral control as a determinant of intention and behavior. The innovation diffusion theory (IDT) [11] explains the acceptance of technology innovations, in which relative advantages, compatibility, and voluntariness of use are involved.

The unified theory of acceptance and use of technology (UTAUT) [12] offers an overview of these technology acceptance models and incorporates the most reliable constructs into a unified model. This model explains user intentions to use an information system by three key constructs: performance expectancy, effort expectancy, and social influence. In this model, performance expectancy encompasses a broader definition of perceived usefulness, effort expectancy is more broadly defined from perceived ease of use, and social influence encompasses a broader definition of subjective norm. The UTAUT model suggests that individual factors, including gender, age, experience, and voluntariness of use, also influence the acceptance of information technology.

2.2 Factors Affecting Robot Acceptance

Some studies have extended the UTAUT model to the acceptance of social robots, a kind of robot that can interact with users by following social behaviors and rules [13, 14]. In addition to the factors from the UTAUT model (i.e., performance expectancy, effort expectancy, social influence), factors related to users (e.g., attitude toward using technology, self-efficacy, computer experience) and factors related to robots (e.g., perceived sociability, perceived adaptiveness, perceived enjoyment) were added as influential factors in the context of robot agents. Similarly, some studies have discussed influential factors of robot acceptance, including individual factors and robot factors [15, 16]. Individual factors of robot acceptance include users' age, gender, education, and experience with technology/robots, whereas robot factors are adaptability, attractiveness, and appearance.

Furthermore, some studies have focused on robot factors and divided influential factors of robot acceptance into three categories: robot social capability, robot function, and robot appearance [17–19]. The social capability of robots refers to the perceived ability of the robot to perform sociable behavior, such as expressing emotions and using natural cues (e.g., gaze, gestures). The functionality of robots includes the autonomy level, perceived usefulness, perceived ease of use, perceived control, and user preference.

The robot appearance refers to human likeness, animal likeness, or machine likeness. In particular, Young et al. [20] posited the importance of perceived control and perceived safety in robot acceptance. When a user believes that a robot is under his control and safe in a worst-case scenario, he starts to consider whether to adopt the robot.

2.3 Factors Affecting Recommender Agent Acceptance

Recommender agents are software agents that make personalized recommendations according to the interests or preferences of consumers. The design features of recommender agents have been discussed as factors to facilitate system acceptance [21–25]. Recommendation accuracy is the most important factor to affect the acceptance of personality-based recommender systems [22]. A user will feel the system useful when the recommendation is accurate in accordance with the user's preferences, and thus become willing to adopt the system. Explanation and justification for how the recommendation was generated is another important factor when users evaluate recommender systems [23–25]. Providing explanations of the system's reasoning process can strengthen a user's belief in the recommender system's competence and benevolence, and thereby enhance the user's trust and acceptance in the system. In addition, transparency, or increasing a user's understanding of how the system works, is an important factor in acceptance of the recommender system [21, 22, 25]. A recommender system can increase its transparency by explaining how it operates through displaying steps in its process with information necessary to users. Moreover, user control over the system is regarded as an influential factor in users' acceptance of a recommender agent [22, 23, 25]. Giving more authority to users can increase the degree of users' active involvement and promote their trust and satisfaction with the system.

2.4 Factors Affecting Financial Behaviors

Some studies have examined factors that influence financial management and investment behaviors [26, 27]. In one study exploring individual factors affecting retirement saving behaviors, financial knowledge and financial risk tolerance were found to be associated with retirement saving behaviors [27]. Another study explored a number of factors affecting investment behaviors in respect of investor, product, and firm [26]. Among these factors, expected earnings and past performance were found to be the most influential, followed by firm status in the industry and word of mouth. Additionally, a couple of studies investigated factors affecting adoption behaviors of online banking applications [28, 29]: they found that relative advantages had a positive impact on adoption and that perceived risk had a negative impact. Lee [29] further indicated that perceived financial risk (i.e., potential for monetary loss) and perceived security risk (i.e., potential risk of transaction information) had significantly negative effects on adoption intention.

2.5 Summary of Influential Factors

A total of nineteen factors that potentially influence robo-advisor acceptance were collected from literature (see Table 1). These influential factors were categorized into three groups: individual differences, user perceptions, and product features. User perceptions are general factors that influence the acceptance of various types of information technology products, whereas product features are specific factors related to functions and features of robo-advisors.

Table 1. Summary of influential factors collected from literature

Factors	Definition
Individual difference	
Age [12, 15, 16]	The user's age
Gender [12, 15, 16]	The user's gender (e.g., male, female)
Education background [15, 16]	The user's educational background (e.g., Bachelor's, Master's)
Financial experience [5, 12, 15, 16, 20, 23]	Previous experience of financial management
Risk tolerance [27]	The degree of uncertainty someone is willing to accept
Attitude toward technology [13, 14, 19]	Positive or negative feelings about the appliance of the technology
User perceptions	
Perceived usefulness [7, 9, 10, 12–14, 18, 20, 29]	The user's perception that the system is useful
Perceived control [6, 7, 20, 22, 23, 25]	The user's perception that the process of the system is in his control
Perceived risk [7, 20, 28, 29]	The user's perception of the possibility and importance of loss when using the system
Social influence [8, 9, 12–14, 16, 20]	The user's perception that people who are important to him think he should or should not use the system
Product features	
Robot autonomy [6, 7, 17]	The robot's ability to plan and make decisions autonomously
Recommendation accuracy [22]	The degree to which a recommendation meets users' preferences
Explanation/justification [23–25]	The capacity to provide explanation and justification for how the recommendation was generated
Relative advantages [12, 28, 29]	The degree to which the system is perceived as being better than its predecessor
Past performance [26]	How something has performed in the past
Process transparency [6, 21, 22, 25]	The degree to which the user understands how the system operates
Firm status in industry [26]	The firm's position relative to other companies that produce similar products or services
Expected earnings [26]	The amount of money that is expected to earn by the user
Word of mouth [26]	Consumer opinions on a firm's product or service reflected in their daily dialogues

3 Phase One: Interviews

To investigate the factors contributing to robo-advisor acceptance, we conducted a two-phase study. Due to the limited research on robo-advisors, the influential factors were obtained from the fields relevant to robo-advisors, such as robots and financial behaviors, not the robo-advisors themselves. In the first phase, we carried out an interview to explore whether there were new product features of robo-advisors regarded as factors that may affect robo-advisor acceptance that had not been involved in the literature. The second phase was a survey to examine the importance of these factors and their relationships. The current section introduces the method and results of the interview.

3.1 Interview Method

We invited eleven participants, nine males and two females, with ages ranging from 22 to 35 (M = 28.27, SD = 4.00), to participate in the interview. All participants had experience with investment ranging from one to six years but had not used robo-advisors. After being informed about the interview purpose, participants were asked about demographic information (e.g., gender, age, education background, and job) and risk attitudes. Then they were introduced to the functions of robo-advisors. To explore influential factors of robo-advisor acceptance, open-ended explorative questions were asked: 1) How do you feel about robo-advisors? 2) What factors will you consider when you decide whether to use robo-advisors? 3) What factors will encourage you to use robo-advisors? The interview time for each participant was about 30 min.

3.2 Interview Results

The qualitative interview data were analyzed to extract the factors influencing acceptance of robo-advisors. Following the Long Table approach [30], transcripts of the interviews were printed out and cut into strips. Such strips were then categorized into thirteen factors, seven of which were in accordance with those derived from literature, including: 1) recommendation accuracy; 2) explanation/justification; 3) relative advantages; 4) past performance; 5) process transparency; 6) firm status in industry; and 7) expected earnings. Six factors were new factors that were different from those in the literature. They were:

1. Personal information: This represents the management of personal information. Examples are: "...whether the robo-advisor needs to know my privacy information, such as ID number, name and address" and "...whether I can set the visible status of my personal information (e.g., public, visible to my friends, or only visible to myself)",
2. Personal assets: This represents the management of personal assets. An example is: "...whether I can manage my assets at any time".
3. Cash withdrawals: This refers to the authority to withdraw cash from a robo-advisor. Examples are: "...whether I can withdraw cash from the robo-advisor when I want" and "how much withdrawal fee I should pay".

4. Disinvestment: This refers to the authority of disinvestment from a robo-advisor. An example is "...whether I can cancel an investment decided by the robo-advisor".
5. Timely reaction: This refers to whether a robo-advisor can react to changes in financial markets timely. An example is: "...whether the robo-advisor can monitor my invested products and adjust my investment timely according to changes in financial markets".
6. Preference set: This refers to whether users can set their preferences. An example is: "...whether I can set my investment preference in the robo-advisor—for example, a certain stock I prefer to invest in".

It should be noted that robot autonomy and word of mouth were not mentioned in the interview. Due to the limited sample size, the two factors were nevertheless retained and studied in phase two. In total, twenty-five factors were derived.

4 Phase Two: Survey

4.1 Questionnaire Design

To examine the importance of influential factors and their relationships, an online survey was conducted. Individual differences were measured as control variables, and the importance of user perceptions and product features were measured as independent variables. The use intention of robo-advisors was measured as a dependent variable of acceptance. In the first section of the questionnaire, participants' background information, including gender, age, and educational background, were collected. Then, individual differences in financial experience with investment, risk tolerance, and attitudes toward technology were measured. Financial experience with investment was asked using a single item, "what is your previous experience regarding financial investment?" with three levels (i.e., "a novice with a little investment experience," "have certain experience," and "an expert with rich experience"). Risk tolerance was measured by thirteen items (Cronbach's alpha = 0.72) adopted from [31]. Attitude toward technology was assessed using a single item, "what is your attitude toward new technology" with four levels (i.e., "do not trust at all", "reserving opinion and just watching", "relatively willing to try", and "really want to use").

At the beginning of the second section of the questionnaire, a brief introduction to robo-advisors was provided to explain their main functions. The importance of user perceptions was then measured using a seven-point Likert scale. Participants were asked to rate their agreement or disagreement with each item. Perceived usefulness was measured using three items (sample question: "The usefulness of robo-advisors is important to me", Cronbach's alpha = 0.82), adapted from [12]. Social influence was measured using three items (sample question: "It is important to me that people who are important to me think that I should use robo-advisors", Cronbach's alpha = 0.79), adapted from [12]. Perceived control was measured using three items (sample question: "It is important to me that robo-advisors are entirely within my control", Cronbach's alpha = 0.76), adapted from [32]. Perceived risk was measured by four items (sample question: "It is important to me that using robo-advisors has no potential monetary loss", Cronbach's alpha = 0.80), adapted from [29]. Given the negative relationship between perceived risk and technology acceptance found in literature, the items of perceived risk were changed to the reverse statement.

In the third section of the questionnaire, the importance of fifteen product features of robo-advisors were measured, each product feature having an item. Sample questions are "It is important to me that robo-advisors can provide explanation and justification for how they generate recommendation" and "Understanding how robo-advisors operate is important to me". At the end of the questionnaire, two questions were used to measure the use intention of robo-advisors: "I am willing to use robo-advisors" and "I intend to use robo-advisors in the future" (Cronbach's alpha = 0.81).

4.2 Participants

The link to the questionnaire was distributed via online social networks. The screening criterion was that a person should have had investment experience in the past. Of the 215 returned questionnaires, 207 were valid. There were 116 (56%) male respondents and 91 (44%) females. Participants' ages ranged from 18 to 53 years (M = 26.78, SD = 4.82). Among them, 80 (39%) had bachelor's degrees, 86 (42%) had master's degrees, and 41 (20%) had doctoral degrees. Furthermore, 114 (55%) were novices with a little investment experience, 74 (36%) had certain investment experience, and 19 (9%) were experts with rich experience.

4.3 Survey Results

Descriptive Statistics. Descriptive statistics of the importance of user perceptions were carried out. The results showed that ranking in order of importance was perceived usefulness (M = 5.84, SD = 0.88), perceived risk (M = 5.68, SD = 0.96), and perceived control (M = 5.63, SD = 1.01), all with mean values above five on a seven-point scale. Social influence (M = 4.66, SD = 1.10) is less important than the other three factors. Additionally, descriptive statistics were carried out of the importance of product features. As shown in Table 2, all product features of robo-advisors were important, with all mean values higher than five on a seven-point scale. Account management (M = 6.51, SD = 0.78) and authority (M = 6.13, SD = 0.86) were the most important features of robo-advisors.

Factor Analysis. To identify the major dimensions of product features of robo-advisors, principal component factor analysis with varimax rotation was conducted on fifteen items. A threshold of 0.45 loading was used to conclude when an item belonged to a certain factor. Table 2 shows the results of a seven-factor structure. Altogether, 78% of the total variance was explained by the seven factors, indicating a good fit of the model. Three single-item factors remained, because the single item may reflect a different influencing factor from other items. The Cronbach's α coefficients for multiple-item factors were 0.83, 0.76, 0.78, and 0.71 respectively for customization, account management, competence, and authority.

Factor 1, labeled customization, consists of four items and explains 19% of the total variance. It covers both customized features of robo-advisors (e.g., providing a customized recommendation in accordance with personal investment goals and user preference, and acting with an appropriate degree of autonomy consistent with personal needs), and giving explanation and justification for its customized recommendation. Factor 2, labeled accounts management, explains 15% of the total variance and describes the management of personal accounts, including individual information and assets. Factor 3, labeled competence, consists of four items and accounts for 12% of the total variance. It comprises items related to relative advantages of robo-advisors (e.g., managing investment more efficiently and effectively), timely reaction to the financial market, past performance of robo-advisors, and process transparency of robo-advisors. Overall, it describes the competitive competence of robo-advisors. Factor 4, labeled authority, explains 11% of the total variance and refers to the authority of users to withdraw cash and disinvest from robo-advisors.

Table 2. Factor loadings (principal components, varimax rotation)

Factors and their items	M	SD	Loadings of factors						
			1	2	3	4	5	6	7
Customization	5.75	0.89							
Recommendation accuracy	5.86	1.11	0.84	0.29	0.06	−0.04	0.07	0.00	0.11
Preference set	5.76	1.15	0.79	0.09	0.23	0.14	0.04	0.05	0.11
Explanation/justification	5.84	1.16	0.78	0.33	0.08	0.02	0.19	−0.09	−0.01
Robot autonomy	5.44	1.22	0.67	−0.12	0.22	0.31	−0.16	0.25	0.11
Account management	6.51	0.78							
Personal information	6.45	0.93	0.20	0.82	0.09	0.16	0.13	0.05	0.03
Personal assets	6.60	0.79	0.15	0.69	0.21	0.23	−0.04	0.28	0.23
Competence	5.98	0.78							
Past performance	5.79	0.98	0.16	0.05	0.86	0.04	0.15	0.01	0.18
Relative advantages	6.18	0.95	0.32	0.27	0.59	0.24	0.02	0.20	−0.04
Timely reaction	6.11	0.99	0.26	0.31	0.53	0.20	−0.04	0.20	0.07
Process transparency	5.88	1.05	0.13	0.36	0.51	0.15	0.22	−0.05	0.16
Authority	6.13	0.86							
Cash withdrawals	5.95	1.08	0.05	0.08	0.05	0.91	0.03	0.06	0.06
Disinvestment	6.28	0.97	0.18	0.43	0.07	0.71	0.14	0.04	−0.03
Firm status in industry	5.36	1.22	0.08	0.04	0.14	0.09	0.91	0.14	0.11
Expected earnings	5.99	0.95	0.04	0.22	0.08	0.08	0.14	0.92	−0.03
Word of mouth	5.94	1.04	0.36	0.27	0.21	0.10	0.21	−0.05	0.70
Proportion variance			0.19	0.15	0.12	0.11	0.08	0.07	0.05
Cronbach's α			0.83	0.76	0.78	0.71			

Hierarchical Regression. To explore relationships between product features and user perceptions, hierarchical regressions were conducted, as summarized in Table 3. Given that perceived risk was measured with the reversed statement, the scores of items were converted to negative values in the regression analysis. In stage one, control factors explained 5% of variance of perceived usefulness ($F(6,200) = 1.81$, p = .100), 5% of variance of perceived control ($F(6,200) = 1.81$, p = .098), 7% of variance of perceived risk ($F(6,200) = 2.62$, p = .018), and 3% of variance of social influence ($F(6,200) = 0.86$, p = .527). Attitude toward new technology was positively associated with perceived usefulness ($\beta = 0.15$, p = .041) and negatively associated with perceived risk ($\beta = -0.25$, p = .001). People with more positive attitudes toward new technology reported lower importance of perceived risk impeding their intention to use robo-advisors. Educational background was negatively associated with perceived control ($\beta = -0.16$, p = .026). People with higher educational backgrounds reported lower importance of perceived control when using robo-advisors.

In stage two, the introduction of feature factors (i.e., customization, account management, competence, authority, firm status in industry, expected earnings, and word of mouth) explained an additional 22% of variance of perceived usefulness ($F(7,193) = 8.12$, p < .001), 21% of variance of perceived control ($F(7,193) = 7.92$, p < .001), 17% of variance of perceived risk ($F(7,193) = 6.37$, p < .001), and 10% of variance of social influence ($F(7,193) = 3.25$, p = .003). Competence ($\beta = 0.25$, p = .012) and expected earnings ($\beta = 0.14$, p = .036) of robo-advisors were positively related to perceived usefulness. Account management ($\beta = 0.20$, p = .021) and users' authority ($\beta = 0.18$, p = .017) in robo-advisors were positively associated with perceived control. Customization ($\beta = -0.22$, p = .010) and competence ($\beta = -0.20$, p = .042) of robo-advisors were negatively associated with perceived risk. Word of mouth ($\beta = 0.22$, p = .009) had a positive impact on social influence. The final model explained 27% of the total variance of perceived usefulness, 26% of the total variance of perceived control, 24% of the total variance of perceived risk, and 13% of the total variance of social influence.

Multiple Regression. Multiple linear regressions were carried out to investigate how the four user perceptions affect the intention to use robo-advisors. As shown in Table 4, perceived risk ($\beta = -0.36$, p < .001) was negatively related to the intention to use robo-advisors, whereas perceived control ($\beta = 0.16$, p = .014) was positively associated with the use intention. However, perceived usefulness ($\beta = 0.13$, p = .134) and social influence ($\beta = 0.10$, p = .123) were not significantly related to the intention to use robo-advisors. This model explained 24% of the total variance of use intention ($F(4,202) = 15.68$, p < .001).

Table 3. Hierarchical regressions predicting user perceptions

	Perceived usefulness			Perceived control			Perceived risk			Social influence		
	ΔR²	β	p	ΔR²	β	p	ΔR²	β	p	ΔR²	β	p
Stage 1	0.05			0.05			0.07*			0.03		
Gender		0.04	.531		−0.09	.187		0.04	.603		−0.03	.668
Age		−0.03	.627		−0.05	.479		−0.01	.836		0.08	.271
Education background		−0.08	.284		−0.16	.026*		0.12	.101		0.05	.471
Financial experience		0.10	.231		0.13	.094		−0.06	.414		−0.06	.473
Risk tolerance		0.05	.554		0.04	.568		0.05	.529		−0.07	.376
Technology attitudes		0.15	.041*		−0.09	.210		−0.25	<.001***		−0.05	.486
Stage 2	0.22***			0.21***			0.17***			0.10**		
Gender		0.11	.102		−0.04	.573		−0.01	.905		−0.001	.987
Age		−0.03	.663		−0.07	.278		−0.01	.880		0.07	.320
Education background		0.01	.879		−0.06	.327		0.04	.499		0.09	.199
Financial experience		0.01	.850		0.06	.447		0.003	.963		−0.12	.137
Risk tolerance		0.05	.452		0.04	.546		0.04	.550		−0.05	.542
Technology attitude		0.10	.117		−0.15	.024*		−0.20	.003**		−0.09	.211
Customization		0.07	.401		0.06	.489		−0.22	.010*		0.08	.361
Account management		0.12	.163		0.20	.021*		0.01	.927		−0.05	.586
Competence		0.25	.012*		0.08	.442		−0.20	.042*		0.10	.333
Authority		−0.05	.501		0.18	.017*		−0.02	.816		0.02	.780
Firm status in industry		0.05	.482		0.01	.828		−0.05	.433		−0.03	.680
Expected earnings		0.14	.036*		−0.002	.980		−0.07	.322		0.04	.554
Word of mouth		0.05	.545		0.11	.158		0.001	.986		0.22	.009**

Notes: Female – 1, male – 2. *p < .05, **p < .01, ***p < .001.

Table 4. Multiple regressions predicting the intention to use robo-advisors

Scale	M	SD	β	p
Perceived usefulness	5.84	0.88	0.13	.134
Perceived control	5.63	1.01	0.16	.014*
Perceived risk	5.68	0.96	−0.36	<.001***
Social influence	4.66	1.10	0.10	.123

Note: *p < .05, **p < .01, ***p < .001.

5 Discussion

5.1 Acceptance Model of Robo-Advisors

This study identified influential factors and built a hierarchical acceptance model of robo-advisors that integrated product features as the first level, user perceptions as the second level, and use intention as the third level, with individual differences as control variables (see Fig. 1). Between the first level and the second level, the model explained how specific features of robo-advisors affect user perceptions. The competence of a robo-advisor was the strongest positive predictor of perceived usefulness, and expected earnings were the second most important predictor. In terms of the usefulness of a robo-advisor, this study indicated that relative advantages, timely reaction to the financial market, process transparency, past performance, and expected earnings were influential features of robo-advisors. Customization of a robo-advisor was the strongest negative predictor of users' perceived risk. This study showed that customized features were beneficial to decrease users' perceived risk of a robo-advisor. The customized features of a robo-advisor included providing a customized recommendation in accordance with personal risk attitudes, investment goals, and user preference, giving an explanation and justification for the customized recommendation, and acting with an appropriate degree of autonomy, consistent with personal needs. In addition to perceived usefulness, competence was found to be the second most important predictor of perceived risk. The results revealed that the competence of a robo-advisor could not only improve perceived usefulness, but also reduce perceived risk.

Account management and authority of users were the two positive predictors of perceived control over a robo-advisor. This study showed that control over a robo-advisor lay in two aspects: personal information and assets. Control over personal information included the management of privacy information and the visible status of personal information to others, whereas control over assets consisted of the authority to manage assets in a robo-advisor at any time, the authority to withdraw cash from a robo-advisor, and the authority to disinvest from a robo-advisor. In addition, word of mouth was a positive predictor of social influence. Good word of mouth can help attract more customers.

According to participants' self-reported scores, ranking in order of importance was perceived usefulness, perceived risk, and perceived control. As a type of technology-enabled financial product, usefulness and security of a robo-advisor are vital requirements for consumers. As a product with automation capabilities, consumers emphasize

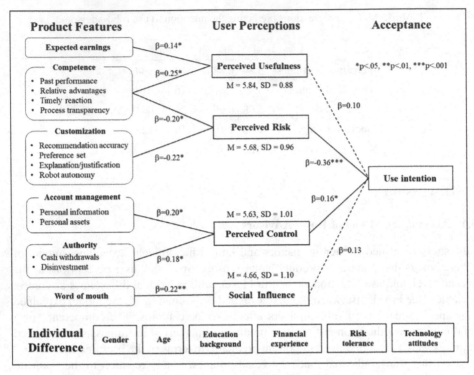

Fig. 1. Acceptance model of robo-advisors

the importance of control over the robo-advisor. However, only perceived risk (negatively) and perceived control (positively) had significant relationships with the intention to use robo-advisors. Although perceived usefulness was the most important factor, it did not decide participants' use intention. This may be because almost all participants regarded the usefulness of robo-advisors as an important but fundamental factor. On the basis of this factor, differences in perceived risk and perceived control of robo-advisors caused differences in use intention.

5.2 Implications for Robo-Advisor Design

The findings from this study can help designers to better understand users' perceptions and acceptance of robo-advisors, thereby improving the design to foster their acceptance and adoption. The acceptance model shows that robo-advisors' competence is helpful to improve perceived usefulness and reduce perceived risk. Therefore, designers should pay attention to enhancing robo-advisors' competence to increase their acceptability. Below are nine suggestions for promoting the competence of robo-advisors.

- At the beginning of use, inform the user of all steps of the process.
- During the process of use, display the current step.
- The interface should be clear and readable enough to show the manipulations and information.

- Provide simple but effective help and demonstration.
- Allow users to view past performance, preferably in the form of graphs.
- Summarize the past performance of the portfolio regularly, such as monthly reports.
- Display the status of the monitoring market on the interface.
- If the portfolio is adjusted due to market changes, inform users of the reasons and how to respond.
- Predict future returns and corresponding probabilities when users decide among candidate portfolios.

Given that robo-advisors can provide a personalized financial service for users, the customized features should be carefully designed to increase products' adaptability. Below are six suggestions for improvement of the customization of robo-advisors.

- Standardize some of the questions that are used to gather information about individual consumers, including risk profile, investment goals, investment experience, etc.
- Provide users with trials before they decide on a portfolio.
- During the trial process, users can change their financial information, such as investment goals, to view different recommended portfolios.
- Provide an explanation and justification for a recommendation, preferably based on users' individual information.
- Allow users to set personalized investment preferences.
- Set the degree of automation to the lowest level at the beginning. When users become familiar with robo-advisors, they can set some operations to be automated.

Given that account management and authority of users are the two most important features to influence the adoption of robo-advisors, we also have five suggestions for the management of personal information and assets.

- Provide clear signs to show the visibility status of personal information and asset information—for example, "only visible to myself".
- Allow users the right not to give some private information.
- Inform users how and when assets can be managed before they transfer their assets to robo-advisors.
- Before assets are transferred, inform users of withdrawal information, including withdrawal conditions, withdrawal fees, etc.
- Before confirming the portfolio, inform users of disinvestment information, such as whether the portfolio can be disinvested after confirmation, disinvestment conditions, disinvestment fees, etc.

6 Conclusion

In this research, we identified influential factors of robo-advisor acceptance and built an acceptance model to demonstrate relationships between influential factors and use intention. To the best of our knowledge, our work is the first study to combine product features of robo-advisors with user perceptions. The comprehensive model of robo-advisor acceptance, involving factors of users, technology, and social environment, sheds additional light on the process of technology adoption, which is a new contribution to technology acceptance theories. Based on the acceptance model, twenty design suggestions for robo-advisors were generated.

This study is also subject to limitations. In the online survey, a brief description of robo-advisors was provided to establish a basic knowledge of the concept. However, participants may have varied understandings of the description of robo-advisors due to their different backgrounds and experience. A possible way to ensure participants' understanding in future research is to use a series of questions to test participants' understanding of the descriptions of robo-advisors presented to them. Another possible direction of future research is to provide a visual aid or an interactive example to describe the functions of robo-advisors.

References

1. Jung, D., Dorner, V., Glaser, F., Morana, S.: Robo-advisory. Bus. Inf. Syst. Eng. **60**, 81–86 (2018). https://doi.org/10.1007/s12599-018-0521-9
2. Jung, D., Dorner, V., Weinhardt, C., Pusmaz, H.: Designing a robo-advisor for risk-averse, low-budget consumers. Electron. Mark. **28**, 367–380 (2018). https://doi.org/10.1007/s12525-017-0279-9
3. Brown, M.: Millennials: Robo-Advisors or Financial Advisors? https://lendedu.com/blog/robo-advisors-vs-financial-advisors/. Accessed 19 July 2020
4. Issa, E.E.: Humans vs. Robots: Americans Prefer Financial Advisors Over Algorithms. https://www.nerdwallet.com/blog/investing/robo-advisor-survey/. Accessed 18 July 2020
5. Hohenberger, C., Lee, C., Coughlin, J.F.: Acceptance of robo-advisors: effects of financial experience, affective reactions, and self-enhancement motives. Financ. Plann. Rev. **2**, (2019). https://doi.org/10.1002/cfp2.1047
6. Rühr, A.: Robo-advisor configuration: an investigation of user preferences and the performance-control dilemma. In: ECIS (2020)
7. Rühr, A., Berger, B., Hess, T.: Can i control my robo-advisor? Trade-offs in automation and user control in (digital) investment management. In: AMCIS 2019 Proceedings (2019)
8. Fishbein, M., Ajzen, I.: Belief, attitude, intention, and behavior: an introduction to theory and research (1977)
9. Davis, F.D.: A technology acceptance model for empirically testing new end-user information systems: theory and results (1985)
10. Ajzen, I., et al.: The theory of planned behavior. Organ. Behav. Hum. Decis. Processes **50**, 179–211 (1991)
11. Rogers, E.M.: Diffusion of Innovations, 4th edn. Simon and Schuster (2010)
12. Venkatesh, V., Morris, M.G., Davis, G.B., Davis, F.D.: User acceptance of information technology: toward a unified view. MIS Q. **27**, 425–478 (2003). https://doi.org/10.2307/30036540
13. Heerink, M., Krose, B., Evers, V., Wielinga, B.: Studying the acceptance of a robotic agent by elderly users. Int. J. Assist. Rob. Mech. **7**, 11 (2006)
14. Heerink, M., Kröse, B., Evers, V., Wielinga, B.: Assessing acceptance of assistive social agent technology by older adults: the almere model. Int, J. Soc. Rob. **2**, 361–375 (2010). https://doi.org/10.1007/s12369-010-0068-5
15. Broadbent, E., Stafford, R., MacDonald, B.: Acceptance of healthcare robots for the older population: review and future directions. Int. J. Soc. Rob. **1**, 319 (2009). https://doi.org/10.1007/s12369-009-0030-6

16. Flandorfer, P.: Population ageing and socially assistive robots for elderly persons: the importance of sociodemographic factors for user acceptance. Int. J. Popul. Res. **2012** (2012)
17. Beer, J.M., Prakash, A., Mitzner, T.L., Rogers, W.A.: Understanding robot acceptance (2011)
18. Gaudiello, I., Zibetti, E., Lefort, S., Chetouani, M., Ivaldi, S.: Trust as indicator of robot functional and social acceptance. An experimental study on user conformation to iCub answers. Comput. Hum. Behav. **61**, 633–655 (2016) https://doi.org/10.1016/j.chb.2016.03.057
19. Looije, R., Cnossen, F., Neerincx, M.A.: Incorporating guidelines for health assistance into a socially intelligent robot. In: ROMAN 2006-The 15th IEEE International Symposium on Robot and Human Interactive Communication, pp. 515–520. IEEE (2006)
20. Young, J.E., Hawkins, R., Sharlin, E., Igarashi, T.: Toward acceptable domestic robots: applying insights from social psychology. Int. J. Soc. Rob. **1**, 95 (2009)
21. Cramer, H., et al.: The effects of transparency on trust in and acceptance of a content-based art recommender. User Mod. User-Adapt. Interact. **18**, 455 (2008)
22. Hu, R., Pu, P.: Acceptance issues of personality-based recommender systems. In: Proceedings of the Third ACM Conference on Recommender systems, pp. 221–224. Association for Computing Machinery, New York (2009). https://doi.org/10.1145/1639714.1639753
23. Xiao, B., Benbasat, I.: E-commerce product recommendation agents: use, characteristics, and impact. MIS Q. **31**, 137–209 (2007)
24. Ye, L.R., Johnson, P.E.: The impact of explanation facilities on user acceptance of expert systems advice. MIS Q. **19**, 157–172 (1995). https://doi.org/10.2307/249686
25. Yoo, K.-H., Gretzel, U.: Creating more credible and persuasive recommender systems: the influence of source characteristics on recommender system evaluations. In: Ricci, F., Rokach, L., Shapira, B., Kantor, P.B. (eds.) Recommender Systems Handbook, pp. 455–477. Springer, Boston, MA (2011). https://doi.org/10.1007/978-0-387-85820-3_14
26. Al-Tamimi, H.A.H.: Factors influencing individual investor behavior: an empirical study of the UAE financial markets. Bus. Rev. **5**, 225–233 (2006)
27. Jacobs-Lawson, J.M., Hershey, D.A.: Influence of future time perspective, financial knowledge, and financial risk tolerance on retirement saving behaviors. Financ. Serv. Rev.-Greenwich **14**, 331 (2005)
28. Al-Jabri, I.M., Sohail, M.S.: Mobile banking adoption: application of diffusion of innovation theory. J. Electron. Commer. Res. **13**, 379–391 (2012)
29. Lee, M.-C.: Factors influencing the adoption of internet banking: an integration of TAM and TPB with perceived risk and perceived benefit. Electron. Commer. Res. Appl. **8**, 130–141 (2009). https://doi.org/10.1016/j.elerap.2008.11.006
30. Krueger, R.A., Casey, M.A., et al.: A practical guide for applied research. In: A Practical Guide for Applied Research (2000)
31. Grable, J., Lytton, R.H.: Financial risk tolerance revisited: the development of a risk assessment instrument☆. Financ. Serv. Rev. **8**, 163–181 (1999). https://doi.org/10.1016/S1057-081 0(99)00041-4
32. Ghani, J.A., Supnick, R., Rooney, P.: The experience of flow in computer-mediated and in face-to-face groups. In: ICIS, pp. 229–237 (1991)

Evaluation of IoT-Setting Method Among Senior Citizens in Japan

Daisuke Yoshioka[1]([⊠]), Hiroki Kogami[2], SooIn Kang[3], Reina Yoshizaki[2], Yuriki Sakurai[1], Koki Nakano[4], Jiang Wu[1], Mahiro Fujisaki-Sueda-Sakai[5], Ikuko Sugawara[6], Takahiro Miura[7], Ken-ichiro Yabu[8], Kenichiro Ito[9] [iD], and Tohru Ifukube[8]

[1] Graduate School of Frontier Sciences, The University of Tokyo, 7-3-1 Hongo, Bunkyo-ku, Tokyo 113-8656, Japan
9821514068@edu.k.u-tokyo.ac.jp
[2] Graduate School of Engineering, The University of Tokyo, 7-3-1 Hongo, Bunkyo-ku, Tokyo 113-8656, Japan
[3] Graduate School of Interdisciplinary Information Studies, The University of Tokyo, 7-3-1 Hongo, Bunkyo-ku, Tokyo 113-8656, Japan
[4] Graduate School of Humanities and Sociology, The University of Tokyo, 7-3-1 Hongo, Bunkyo-ku, Tokyo 113-8656, Japan
[5] School of Medicine, Tohoku University, Sendai, Japan
[6] Institute of Gerontology, The University of Tokyo, 7-3-1 Hongo, Bunkyo-ku, Tokyo 113-8656, Japan
[7] Human Augmentation Research Center, National Institute of Advanced Industrial Science and Technology, Kashiwa, Japan
[8] Research Center for Advanced Science and Technology, The University of Tokyo, 7-3-1 Hongo, Bunkyo-ku, Tokyo 113-8656, Japan
[9] Virtual Reality Educational Research Center, The University of Tokyo, 7-3-1 Hongo, Bunkyo-ku, Tokyo 113-8656, Japan

Abstract. To develop methods for supporting senior citizens is critical because the number of senior citizens is growing globally. Recently, the focus is on supporting senior citizens using information technology (IT), including the Internet of Things (IoT). In the IoT system, IoT tools such as cameras and sensors are connected and interacted by the Internet. Furthermore, we can customize their function easily using smartphones to modulate the function we want. Therefore, senior citizens should customize IoT products and help themselves. However, it is challenging to customize IoT product functions for senior citizens because they had fewer chances to use smartphones or computers than young people. Therefore, other customizing methods for IoT products are needed for senior citizens. In this study, we design a workshop to test, where the setting of the user interface (UI) is suitable for senior citizens. We develop three UIs, namely, voice, touch, and camera. To explore which method is suitable for senior citizens, we evaluate the setting time for each method. Consequently, the setting time of the voice interface is shorter than the others. Furthermore, the system usability scale (SUS) score was higher than 68, indicating that the setting method using the voice interface is acceptable for senior citizens. These results indicate that the voice interface is a suitable setting method for senior citizens.

© Springer Nature Switzerland AG 2021
Q. Gao and J. Zhou (Eds.): HCII 2021, LNCS 12786, pp. 278–292, 2021.
https://doi.org/10.1007/978-3-030-78108-8_21

Keywords: IT literacy and competency of older adults · Natural language user interfaces for older adults · Daily living activity support · Gerontechnology · Internet of Things

1 Introduction

In Japan, where the population is aging, using the IoT to support the lives of senior citizens is becoming essential. Although many people support the lives of senior citizens, a shortage of specialized support providers is becoming an issue because of increasing proportion of senior citizens [1]. Also, one of the reasons is that the number of senior citizens living alone are increasing [2], which requires new resources for daily life support originally provided by family members who lived together. Besides, changes in the senior citizen population, who are the recipients of daily life support, also raise expectations for the IoT. In the past, senior citizens who received support were considered weak. However, it has been reported that the physical and mental functions of today's senior citizens have become 5–10 years younger over the past 20 years [3]. Under these changes, senior citizens have come to be recognized as one-way recipients of support and individuals who live independently, constructing the necessary support according to their needs and protecting their privacy. Therefore, there is a need for a system that allows senior citizens to construct their care without relying on human help, and IoT technology is an attractive tool to meet this need.

The system of IoT can literally implement almost any functions by combining various devices such as sensors, applications, and smart-home appliances [4]. Currently, the devices of IoT can be customized using smartphones and personal computers. Internet usage for people over 80 years old in Japan has increased, although only about 20% of people over 80 own a smartphone or personal computer in 2019 [5]. Thus, we consider that other configuration methods without using smartphones is in need in order to expand the use of the IoT system among senior citizens. However, it is not elucidated what kind or which configuration method is suitable for senior citizens. Therefore, we propose and tested simple user interfaces to configure and construct an IoT system. In this study, we evaluate the setting time and assess the SUS score for three UIs, namely, voice, touch, and camera.

2 Related Works

2.1 Using IoT to Care for Senior Citizens

IoT technology has been applied to support senior citizens. One example is smart home. In smart home, variable devices, such as motion sensors and wearable devices are used to detect the fall and health conditions of senior citizens. When accidents happen, these sensors call for help on behalf of senior citizens [6–8]. Also, Suzuki et al. developed a system of sensors that record the daily log of senior citizens and making it available to their family members using social networking services such as LINE [9]. These examples show that IoT devices are mainly used to watch over senior citizens. However, the self-configuration of IoT systems by the senior citizens was not elucidated in the studies.

2.2 IoT Configuration Method

Natural UIs (NUIs) employ speech, touch, body language, and gestures for users to control applications. Because most senior citizens have difficulties using a mouse and keyboard, NUIs attract senior citizens to use information and communication technology devices [10].

Many configuration methods exist for IoT. Among them, we chose voice, camera, and touch interfaces. The touch interface was adopted as the conventional method for smartphones and tablets. Recently, smart speakers, such as Google Echo and Amazon Alexa, which are controlled by voice interfaces, are spreading widely throughout all generations. Finally, studies showed that a card-based configuration is suitable for senior citizens [11]. Thus, we devised the configuration method to read the cards using the camera. Therefore, we evaluated configuration methods using these UIs in this study.

3 Methods

In this study, we experimented and obtained data from 12 participants (7 males and 5 females, average age of 72.1 ± 3.4 years). The user rates of smartphones, tablets, personal computers, and smart speakers were 75.0%, 50.0%, 91.7%, and 0%, respectively. The process of this experiment was as follows. First, participants were divided into four groups of three participants each. A workshop was conducted for each group at a time. The workshop consisted of four procedures: (1) introduction, (2) making ideas with cards using IoT, (3) experiencing three types of UIs to configure IoT, (4) IoT demonstration and closing. In the procedure of UI experience, we administrated the order of experience (Table 1) to assess effects within the experimental. Table 1 shows the table of administrated order of UI experience.

Table 1. The order of UI experience

ID	First	Second	Third
1A	Camera	Voice	Touch
1B	Voice	Touch	Camera
1C	Touch	Camera	Voice
2A	Camera	Touch	Voice
2B	Voice	Camera	Touch
2C	Touch	Voice	Camera
3A	Camera	Voice	Touch
3B	Voice	Touch	Camera
3C	Touch	Camera	Voice
4A	Camera	Touch	Voice
4B	Voice	Camera	Touch
4C	Touch	Voice	Camera

Each experiment lasted for a maximum of 2 h. Figure 1 shows the laboratory layout in the experiment. Two rooms were used with sufficient distance between to avoid voice input confusion. Each room was equipped with a Wi-Fi network with sufficient speed, and each device was connected to the network. A video camera and voice recorder recorded each device experience. The experimenter measured the time taken for the operation using a stopwatch and wrote it on a recording sheet. The entire experiment was photographed for the purpose of keeping a record.

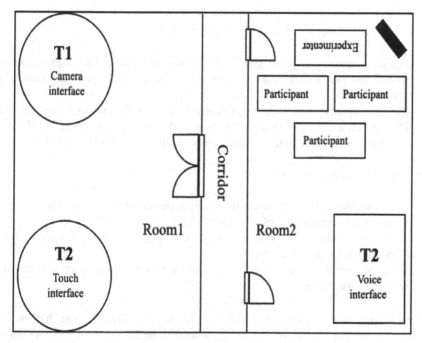

Fig. 1. Laboratory environment

The overall flow of the experiment was as follows.

1. Introduction

   a. The participants were registered and assigned IDs in order of arrival.
   b. After all the participants were present, the purpose of the experiment and managing personal information were explained, and they filled out the consent form for the experiment.
   c. After the participants consented to participate in the experiment, the procedure of the experiment was explained to each participant.

2. Making ideas with cards using IoT

    a. A staff member showed two scenarios of an IoT system represented by combining a Trigger card and an Action card.
    b. The participants used the cards to pick a combination of Trigger and Action cards for a certain scenario of an IoT system. Two combinations were made from a life scenario informed by the staff, and two more combinations were made from two scenarios that the participants idealized based on their daily life. Four scenarios were then carried to each table where the participants used the UI to configure IoT.

3. Experiencing three types of the UI to configure IoT

    a. The participants moved to one of the tables (1–3), where the equipment was placed, and performed the first experiment. The details of each experiment are described later.
    b. The participants evaluated the equipment using a SUS-compliant questionnaire.
    c. The participant moved to the next table and repeated the process (4–5). This process was repeated until all three types of equipment had been tested.

4. IoT demonstration and closing

    a. After completing the experiment using all the devices, the participants were asked to watch a demonstration of staff using the devices.
    b. An overall evaluation of the three types of equipment was conducted using a SUS-complaint questionnaire.
    c. After the work was completed, the participants signed the documents for payment and were dismissed.

The procedure of the experiment for each device was as follows. For each device, we first showed participants a video showing the workflow of the experiment and explained the system used in the experiment. Then, a staff member demonstrated the procedure of the work to be done. Details of the procedures and configuration of each UI are shown below.

The Procedure of the UI Experiment

Voice Interface (Fig. 2). First, participants asked the smart speaker, "Open Voice Settings," to launch the settings application for the voice interface. Then, the speaker asked, "What is the Trigger you selected?" and the participants read out the Trigger card. The speaker then asked, "What is the Action you selected?" and the participants read out the Action card. The information of the combination of cards was saved in the cloud after the speaker's recognition. Then, the speaker asked, "You selected Trigger and Action. Is that correct?" After the participant replied "Yes," the data were sent to the sheet in the cloud. Finally, the speaker said, "Setup complete!".

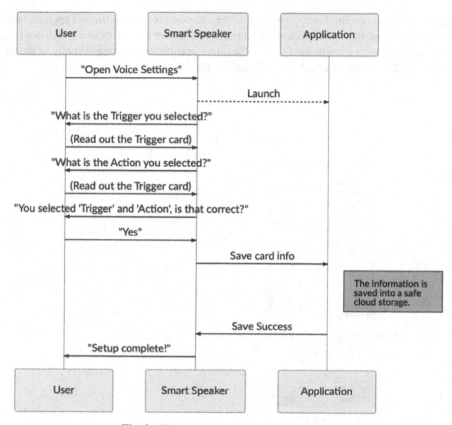

Fig. 2. The procedure of the voice interface

Touch Interface (Fig. 3). First, a function-setting screen, which asked participants to select Trigger and Setting, was displayed on the tablet. In the function-setting screen, there was a blue card with the words "Not selected" written below "Please select 'Trigger,'" and further down, there was a green card with the words "Not selected" written below the "Please select 'Action.'" By touching the card marked "Not selected," the participants were taken to the Trigger and Action selection screens, respectively. The Trigger selection is described in detail below. On the Trigger selection screen, a list of pre-presented cards showing all trigger options was displayed. The participant selects a Trigger by touching the card. The content of the selected card was displayed as a sentence on the screen, where it could be checked, and the participant could confirm whether he or she had selected the intended choice. By pressing the decision button next to the displayed text, the trigger selection is decided, and the screen returns to the function-setting screen. On the function-setting screen, the set trigger text and card were displayed where the "Please select 'Trigger'" and "Not selected" cards were, respectively. This operation could be repeated as many times as necessary until the intended selection was made, and the Action was selected similarly. Finally, when the intended Trigger and Action were selected on the function-setting screen, the participant presses the decision button on the function-setting screen to complete the setting. This information was automatically stored in a sheet in the cloud. After the information was sent to the cloud, the screen transitioned to the "Settings completed" screen. Finally, a smart speaker told them "Setup with 'Trigger' and 'Action'!".

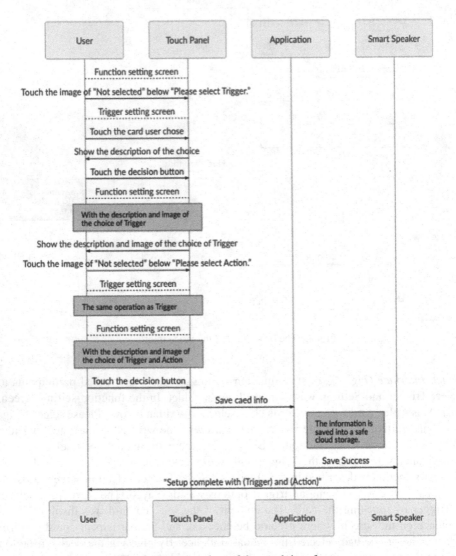

Fig. 3. The procedure of the touch interface

Camera Interface (Fig. 4). To operate the camera interface, participants were asked to say, "Start the setting by camera." A pile of cards was prepared for the participants and they chose the setting as they wish to do. The card has quick-response (QR) codes on the front and back of the card, and by flipping the card, the microprocessor connected with the camera will recognize that the participants have selected a card. The camera was placed facing downward so that it viewed the area where the QR code would be placed. As soon as the system could recognize both the Trigger and Action cards, the information would be sent to the cloud. Finally, the speaker confirmed to the participants, "You registered 'Trigger' and 'Action', right?" In the end, the system tells the subject, "Setup complete!" and the configuration was complete.

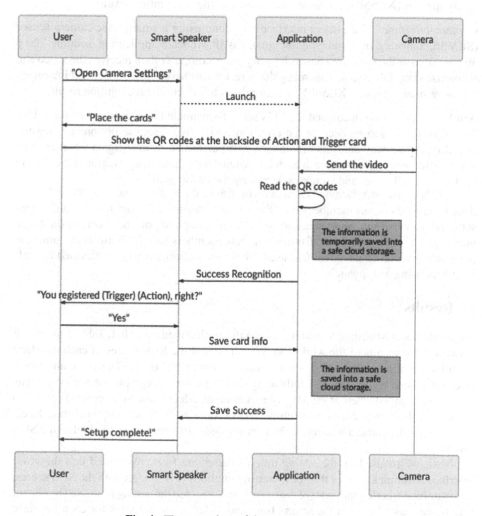

Fig. 4. The procedure of the camera interface

Configuration of UI

Voice Interface. For the voice interface, Echo Dot 3rd generation (B07PFFMQ64, Amazon Inc.) was used. The voice configuration was developed using the Alexa Skills Kit as a beta test. The recognition result was saved in a sheet in the cloud (s 3, Amazon Inc.) provided by the cloud service (Amazon Web Service).

Touch Interface. The touch interface used the iPad (A1893 32 GB Gold, Apple Inc.), running a simple web application developed using Bubble. io. This application was launched on a browser and collected data following the procedure above. The data were sent to a sheet via a mail server. The addition of the data in the sheet instructed a nearby smart speaker (XC56PY, Amazon Inc.) to inform the recognition result.

Camera Interface. The camera interface was done using a smartphone camera sensor (SCV36, Samsung Inc.), relaying the image as IP Webcam application, sending 720 p 30 fps video to the local area network by Wi-Fi. A computer then receives the video and recognizes two QR codes. This recognition result was saved in the sheet and instructed a nearby smart speaker (XC56PY, Amazon Inc.) to inform the recognition result.

Analysis. This study measured the SUS score to evaluate the acceptance of three UIs. The SUS score is composed of ten questions, with five response options to measure usability. A one-way analysis of variance was performed to investigate whether there was a difference in SUS between each UI. Additionally, this study measured the time to set two cards, Trigger and Action, selected by the participants.

For the voice interface and camera recognition, the setting time was defined as the time from when a staff member said, "Please start" before the experimenter said, "open settings" to when the smart speaker said, "setup complete" on the sheet. In the touch interface, the time was taken from when staff members said, "Please start" until the participants received the email was used. These measurements were performed by staff members using a stopwatch.

4   Results

We conducted a workshop to evaluate the configuration method of IoT. Table 2 shows the questionnaire results of the workshop. We calculated the SUS scores of each interface from the questionnaire results to assess user acceptance (Fig. 5). The voice and touch interfaces were higher than 70, indicating that these are acceptable for senior citizens [12]. We examined whether the order of experiments affected the SUS scores (Fig. 6). No significant difference exists between the SUS scores of the voice and touch interfaces. However, in the camera interfaces, the later the order of experience, the higher the SUS scores.

Next, we focused on the setting time of these interfaces. We found that the voice interface was much shorter than other setting methods (Fig. 7). As with the SUS scores, we examined whether the order of the experiment affected the setting time. No significant difference exists between the setting time and order of experiments for each interface (Fig. 8). Because the setting time of the voice interface is shorter than other interfaces, we assumed that the SUS scores would be inversely proportional to the length of the setting time.

Table 2. Individual averaged scores for SUS question items

	Camera interface	Touch interface	Voice interface
q1	4.08	3.92	4.67
q2	2.75	2.50	2.67
q3	3.83	4.25	4.50
q4	3.00	2.58	2.75
q5	4.42	4.08	4.25
q6	2.08	2.17	1.83
q7	3.75	4.00	3.92
q8	2.25	2.17	1.92
q9	4.00	4.25	4.42
q10	3.42	2.92	2.83

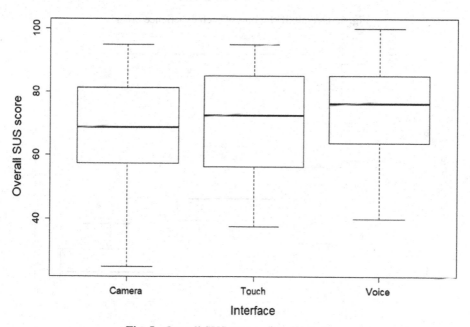

Fig. 5. Overall SUS scores of each interface

To test this hypothesis, we verified the correlation between the SUS scores and setting times ($R = -0.37$, $p = 0.025$). To investigate the effect of the setting time on the SUS scores, we plotted the SUS scores and setting times of the camera, touch, and voice interfaces in red, green, and blue, respectively. No correlation exists between the setting times and SUS scores of the touch interface ($R = -0.13$, $p = 0.690$) and voice

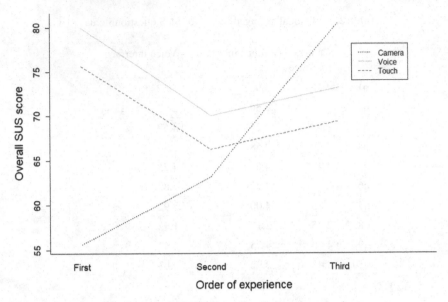

Fig. 6. Overall SUS scores of each experience order

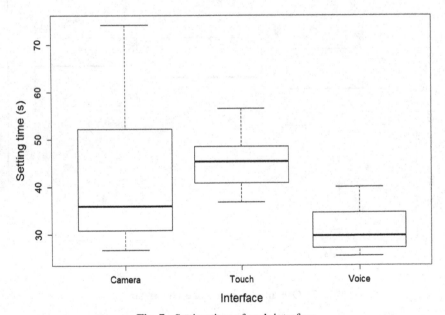

Fig. 7. Setting time of each interface

interface ($R = 0.11$, $p = 0.730$) (Fig. 9). However, we confirmed a negative correlation in the camera interface ($R = -0.61$, $p = 0.036$). These results indicate that the high SUS scores of the voice and touch interfaces are not only because of the setting time of the interfaces.

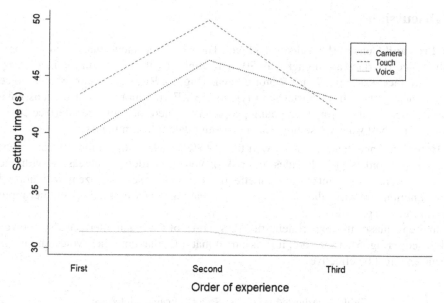

Fig. 8. Setting time of each order of experience

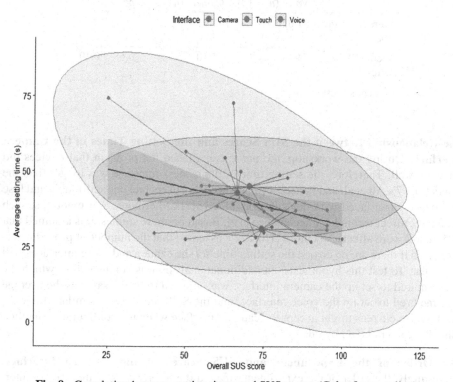

Fig. 9. Correlation between setting times and SUS scores (Color figure online)

5 Discussion

The Pros and Cons of the Voice Interface. The workshop shows that the SUS scores of the voice interface are higher than 70, indicating that the configuration method by voice interface is acceptable for senior citizens (Fig. 5). Ruan et al. showed that voice input is nearly three times faster than typing [13]. Furthermore, senior citizens have more frequent typing errors than young people [14]. Therefore, a voice interface could be one of the best ways for senior citizens to enter data into computers.

However, Applebaum et al. showed that 19.8% to 29.1% of senior citizens (≥65) have voice disorders [15]. Besides, the risk of voice disorders is increasing with age [16]. Therefore, a voice interface is an effective method for senior citizens with normal vocal function, but when they have difficulty speaking because of aging, another input method must be provided.

In the results of this experiment, the SUS scores of the touch interface also showed a high score (Fig. 5). Therefore, it is assumed that a UI that combines voice and touch interfaces might be effective.

Table 3. Adjusted overall SUS score of camera interface

	Voice ($n = 12$)	Camera ($n = 7$)	p^*	d
Average setting time	31.02	31.91		
Overall SUS score	74.38	77.50	0.68	0.19

*Student's t-test

The Relationship Between the SUS Scores and the Setting Times in the Camera Interface. During the workshop, the participants faced the problem that devices did not work well. Therefore, the setting time of the camera interface was longer than the others (Fig. 7). Ali et al. and Panëels et al. showed that users feel uncomfortable and lose confidence when faced with device errors [17, 18]. Furthermore, user emotions, such as anxiety, affect technology acceptance [19]. Based on these studies, it is assumed that SUS scores were affected by those errors. We assumed that the number of procedures is similar, so if there are no errors, the setting time for the camera and voice interfaces will be similar. To test this hypothesis, an additional analysis was conducted, in which the time required to set up the camera interface was adjusted to be the same as the average time required to set up the voice interface, and the SUS scores were similar (Table 3). Thus, senior citizens might accept the camera interface when the configuration method using the camera is improved.

The Order of the Experiment and SUS Scores of the Camera Interface. Interestingly, the order of the experiment affected the SUS scores of the camera interface, unlike the other two (Fig. 8). Participants who experienced other UIs show a high

SUS score for the camera interface. We assumed that the camera interface is more user-friendly than other interfaces. To test this hypothesis, we must compare the SUS score of the camera interface with people using various UIs and those who do not. Because SUS scores increased significantly when the camera interface was used after experiencing other instruments, continued daily use of the instrument might increase the acceptability of the instrument. Therefore, further verification of SUS in the case of long-term use is necessary for future studies.

6 Conclusion

In this study, we designed and evaluated three IoT-setting interactions, including voice, touch, and camera-based interfaces for healthy senior citizens. The results of this research indicate that senior citizens can use both touch panels and the voice interface to configure the IoT device. By developing the IoT devices, which can be customized using voice and touch interfaces, we expect that IT device usage and the quality of life for senior citizens can be improved.

Acknowledgments. The research was partially supported from the following funds: JSPS Program for Leading Graduate Schools (Graduate Program in Gerontology, Global Leadership Initiative for an Age Friendly Society, The University of Tokyo), Foundatiossn of Support Center for Advanced Telecommunications Technology Research (SCAT), JSPS KAKENHI Grant Numbers JP19K14028, JP20H01753, and JP20K20494.

References

1. Ministry of Health, Labor and Welfare Homepage. https://www.mhlw.go.jp/wp/hakusyo/kousei/19/dl/all.pdf. Accessed 25 Feb 2021
2. Cabinet Office, Government of Japan. https://www8.cao.go.jp/kourei/whitepaper/w-2020/zenbun/02pdf_index.html. Accessed 25 Feb 2021
3. Ouchi, Y., et al.: Joint Committee of Japan Gerontological Society (JGLS) and Japan Geriatrics Society (JGS) on the definition and classification of the elderly. Redefining the elderly as aged 75 years and older: Proposal from the Joint Committee of Japan Gerontological Society and the Japan Geriatrics Society. Geriatr. Gerontol. Int. **17**(7), 1045–1047 (2017)
4. Čolaković, A., Hadžialić, M.: Internet of Things (IoT): A review of enabling technologies, challenges, and open research issues. Comput. Netw. **144**, 17–39 (2018)
5. Ministry of Internal Affairs and Communications of Japan Homepage. https://www.soumu.go.jp/johotsusintokei/statistics/statistics05a.html. Accessed 25 Feb 2021
6. Allet, L., Knols, R.H., Shirato, K., de Bruin, E.D.: Wearable systems for monitoring mobility-related activities in chronic disease: a systematic review. Sensors **10**(10), 9026–9052 (2010)
7. Lepri, B., Mana, N., Cappelletti, A., Pianesi, F., Zancanaro, M.: What is happening now? detection of activities of daily living from simple visual features. Pers. Ubiquit. Comput. **14**(8), 749–766 (2010)
8. Hagler, S., Austin, D., Hayes, T.L., Kaye, J., Pavel, M.: Unobtrusive and ubiquitous in-home monitoring: a methodology for continuous assessment of gait velocity in elders. IEEE Trans. Bio-Med. Eng. **57**(4), 813–820 (2010)

9. Suzuki, H., et al.: An updated watch-over system using an IoT device, for elderly people living by themselves. In: IEEE 3rd International Conference on System Reliability and Safety (ICSRS), Barcelona, Spain, pp. 115–119. IEEE (2018)

10. Loureiro, B., Rodrigues, R.: Multi-touch as a natural user interface for elders: a survey: In: 6th Iberian Conference on Information Systems and Technologies (CISTI 2011), Chaves, Portugal, pp. 1–6. IEEE (2011)

11. Kang, S.I., et al.: Design and implementation of age-friendly activity for supporting elderly's daily life by IoT. In: Zhou, J., Salvendy, G. (eds.) HCII 2019. LNCS, vol. 11593, pp. 353–368. Springer, Cham (2019). https://doi.org/10.1007/978-3-030-22015-0_28

12. Bangor, A., Kortum, P., Miller, J.: Determining what individual SUS scores mean: adding an adjective rating scale. J. Usability Stud. **4**(3), 114–123 (2009)

13. Ruan, S., Wobbrock, J.O., Liou, K., Ng, A., Landay, J.: Speech is 3x faster than typing for English and mandarin text entry on mobile devices. arXiv Preprint arxiv:1608.07323 (2016)

14. Kalman, Y.M., Kavé, G., Umanski, D.: Writing in a digital world: self-correction while typing in younger and older adults. Int. J. Environ. Res. Public Health **12**(10), 12723–12734 (2009)

15. Applebaum, J., Harun, A., Davis, A., Hillel, A.T., Best, S.R., Akst, L.M.: Geriatric dysphonia: characteristics of diagnoses in age-based cohorts in a tertiary voice clinic. Ann. Otol. Rhinol. Laryngol. **128**(5), 384–390 (2019)

16. Kojima, H.: Special Issue of the Bronchoesophageal Region in the Elderly Review. Laryngeal function in the speech of aged persons. Nihon Kikan Shokudoka Gakkai Kaiho **45**(5), 360–364 (1994)

17. Abdolrahmani, A., Easley, W., Williams, M., Branham, S., Hurst, A.: Embracing errors: examining how context of use impacts blind individuals' acceptance of navigation aid errors. In: Proceedings of the 2017 CHI Conference on Human Factors in Computing Systems, Colorado, USA, pp. 4158–4169. Association for Computing Machinery (2017)

18. Panëels, S.A., Olmos, A., Blum, J.R., Cooperstock, J.R.: Listen to it yourself! Evaluating usability of what's around me? For the blind. In: Proceedings of the SIGCHI Conference on Human Factors in Computing Systems, Paris, France, pp. 2107–2116 (2013)

19. Lee, Y., Kozar, K.A., Larsen, K.R.: The technology acceptance model: past, present, and future. Commun. Assoc. Inf. Syst. **12**(1), 752–780 (2003)

Building Trust in Mobile Medical Consultations: The Roles of Privacy Concerns, Personality Traits, and Social Cues

Jiaxin Zhang[1,3], Qingchuan Li[2(✉)], and Yan Luximon[3]

[1] School of Innovation Design, The Guangzhou Academy of Fine Arts, Guangzhou, China
[2] School of Humanity and Social Science, Harbin Institute of Technology, Shenzhen, China
liqingchuan@hit.edu.cn
[3] School of Design, The Hong Kong Polytechnic University, Hong Kong, China
jx.zhang@connect.polyu.hk, yan.luximon@polyu.edu.hk

Abstract. It is increasingly popular to access health professionals through mobile medical consultations (MMCs). However, few studies on trust building during MMCs were found. To fill this gap, this study conducted an online survey study with 108 users of MMCs in China. We investigated the predictors of two types of trust (i.e., trust in physicians and trust in MMCs) by examining the influences of privacy concerns, personality traits, social presence of interaction, and social validation. The results indicated that intellect, privacy concerns, social presence of interaction, and social validation are the predictors of trust in physicians, while neuroticism, privacy concerns, and social presence of interaction are the predictors of trust in applications. The findings provided suggestions about how to build trust by considering privacy concerns and personality traits and highlighted the effects of social presence of interaction and social validation, which are interface features, on trust. Practically, this study also implied that practitioners and designers can apply different strategies to enhance trust in physicians and trust in applications in relation to MMCs.

Keywords: Mobile medical consultations · Trust · Privacy concerns · Personality traits · Social cues

1 Introduction

Professional medical consultations are vital to patients' health and wellbeing. With advances in technology, online medical consultation services increasingly help people reach professionals and receive health advice [1]. Various types of online medical services, such as website consultations, online forums, and mobile health applications, help patients manage their health and make treatment decisions [1–4]. Among them, mobile medical consultations (MMCs) could be the most promising method for providing online medical services. MMCs, which allow for immediate communication between patients and physicians through various interaction methods, such as text-, figure-, audio-, and video-based chats, represent one of the functions provided by mobile health applications.

© Springer Nature Switzerland AG 2021
Q. Gao and J. Zhou (Eds.): HCII 2021, LNCS 12786, pp. 293–304, 2021.
https://doi.org/10.1007/978-3-030-78108-8_22

MMCs not only provide more accessible health consultations and diagnoses compared with traditional medical services requiring in-person visits [1, 5], but they also allow for the possibility of tracking patients' combined physical or mental data by wearable devices for diagnoses [4].

While mobile medical services offer opportunities to reach health professionals without geographical constraints, their adoption is facing challenges of trust during consultations [4, 6]. Regarding trust in the adoption of MMCs can involve two aspects: trust in physicians and trust in applications. Trust in physicians plays a fundamental role in medical consultations [7]. It can influence users' willingness to seek mobile medical services, disclose personal information, and follow physicians' advice about treatment [7]. Unlike traditional medical consultations, in which trust is built through face-to-face communications and prior experience with the physicians, MMCs users are more likely to access unknown physicians in a virtual environment. Therefore, building trust between users and physicians in MMCs can be critical to the users' decisions and behaviors in relation to medical treatments. While trust in physicians focuses on the relationship between users and physicians, trust in applications emphasizes users' attitudes towards the service providers. Trust in applications has been widely studied as a vital predictor of technology adoption [5, 8, 9]. In MMCs, users can disclose sensitive information and conduct payment transactions through the applications. Therefore, users' trustworthiness toward the applications can influence their decisions on using MMCs platforms [8].

Although many studies have been conducted to understand the determinants of trust in mobile services [5, 8, 10], there is little knowledge about how to build trust in MMCs. Building trust in MMCs can be quite different from other services because MMCs emphasize immediate communications between patients and physicians. The interaction features involved in the communications can be vital determinants of trust. Previous studies indicated the role that social cues (e.g., social presence and social validation) play in enhancing trust in the healthcare context [2, 11]. In addition, patients' privacy concerns and personality traits can influence relationships between individuals in interactions that specifically involve the transmission of sensitive information [12, 13]. Presently, there is still a lack of evidence to support the effect of social cues, privacy concerns, and personality traits on two types of trust (trust in physicians and trust in applications) in MMCs. Therefore, this study aimed to investigate the relationships associated with privacy concerns, personality traits, social cues, and trust in physicians and trust in applications in MMCs by proposing the following research question: How do privacy concerns, personality traits, and social cues affect patients' trust in mobile medical consultations (MMCs)? To address the research question, this research conducted a survey study to collect empirical data regarding users' privacy concerns, personality traits, attitudes toward the social presence of interaction with physicians, attitudes toward the functions of social validation in MMCs, trust in physicians, and trust in applications. The findings reveal the effects of individual differences related to privacy concerns and personality traits on trust and provide insights into the application of social cues in facilitating trust in MMCs.

2   Literature Review and Hypotheses Development

In this study, we investigated the predictors of two types of trust in relation to MMCs: trust in physicians and trust in applications. Trust is essential to maintain the relationships between different parties [14]. Trust describes the degree to which an individual or a group is willing to rely on or to be vulnerable to other parties [7, 14]. In this study, we define trust in physicians as users' expectations and beliefs in the reliability of physicians' services and advice in MMCs. Trust in applications reflects users' expectations and beliefs in the reliability of the applications providing MMCs. Given the limitation of previous research in identifying the effects of privacy concerns, personality traits, and social cues on trust in physicians and trust in applications, this study attempted to explore these relationships.

Privacy concerns refer to a patient's concerns about disclosing personal information without authority [5, 15]. Specifically, it is an "individual's subjective views of fairness within the context of information privacy" [16 p. 337]. In MMCs, users could be anxious about the unauthorized access or collection of their personal information while sharing their health information with physicians for online diagnoses [17, 18]. Both physicians and applications could present potential risks for privacy disclosures in MMCs; therefore, we propose:

H1. Privacy concerns have a negative effect on trust in physicians and trust in applications in MMCs.

Comprising a set of specific characteristics, an individual's personality can influence differences in thoughts and behaviors toward an information system [19]. Prior work has employed five dimensions to describe an individual's personality traits, including extraversion, agreeableness, conscientiousness, neuroticism, and openness to experience/intellect [19–21]. Extraversion refers to the level of sociability and optimism; agreeableness represents the willingness to be cooperative, sympathetic, and helpful; conscientiousness describes a tendency toward dutifulness and organization; neuroticism indicates a tendency to be anxious, nervous, and emotional; and openness to experience/intellect refers to an individual who is innovative, creative, and curious [19–21]. Trust reflects a disposition to believe in and rely on others [22]. It can be deduced that some personality traits can be positively related toward a disposition to trust, while others can be negatively associated with the disposition to trust. Since few studies have explored the effects of personality traits on trust in MMCs, we propose:

H2. Personality traits have an influence on trust in physicians and trust in applications in MMCs.

Since MMCs involve communication between users and physicians, social cues are critical to the interactions. Social presence is a social cue found to be positively associated with trust in health contexts [2]. Social presence represents the "feeling of being with another" [23 p. 456], usually being measured with perceived warmth, a sense of human contact, and sociality in the interactions. Rather than studying the feeling of social presence, Lu, Fan, and Zhou [24] proposed investigating how interaction methods, such as the use of chat tools, wording styles, figures, or emotional icons, convey the sense of social presence. They defined it as the social presence of interaction, which they found has a positive effect on trust in sellers in online commerce [24]. Although communications in MMCs would be conducted in a more rigorous manner than those in online commerce, it also employs various interaction methods, such as text-, figure-, audio-, or video-based communications [5]. The interaction methods between users and physicians should be able to convey a sense of human warmth and contact, which could influence users' trust in physicians. Also, social presence of interaction would be a possible predictor of trust in applications, as users can rely more on applications that support communications with various interaction methods. Therefore, we hypothesize that:

H3. Social presence of interaction has a positive effect on trust in physicians and trust in applications.

Social validation, defined as the opinions and verifications towards the services provided by other users, is another social cue that influences trust in the online health context [11]. Currently, mobile health applications enable users to share and receive information regarding unknown physicians from other users with the functions and interface features embedded in the interfaces. The recommendations, ratings, and forums in the applications generate a word of mouth of a physician and help to build trust in MMC [25]. Thus, we hypothesize that the users require functions of social validation to build trust in physicians:

H4. Social validation has a positive effect on trust in physicians and trust in applications.

3   Method

3.1   Instrument Development

To test the hypotheses and investigate the relationships among privacy concerns, personality traits, social presence of interaction, social validation, and two types of trust in MMCs, this study applied a survey to collected empirical data, and a questionnaire was designed with three parts. The first part aimed to collect participants' demographic information, including age, gender, city of residence, and education level. The second part measured the participants' personality traits and asked them to report on their usage experience with MMCs, such as applications used, year of use, frequency of use, the registered department, and the interaction methods. Finally, we asked participants to recall their most recent experience with MMCs and to respond to items regarding their attitudes toward privacy concerns (PC), social presence of interaction (SPI) and social validation (SV), trust in physicians (TP), and trust in applications (TA).

Personality traits of extraversion (E), conscientiousness (C), neuroticism (N), and intellect (I) were measured by the adapted Mini-IPIP for the Chinese context. N was constructed by three items; E, C, and I was measured by two items with a five-point Likert scale ranging from 1 (strongly disagree) to 5 (strongly agree) [20]. The measurement items PC, SPI, SV, TP, and TA were adapted from previous studies. To be specific, PC is measured with four items adapted from Li [5]; SPI is measured with four items adapted from Lu, Fan, and Zhou [24], Gefen and Straub [26], Verhagen, van Nes, Feldberg [27]; three items for SV were generated based on the definition of social validation and dimensions of word of mouth Jucks and Thon [11], Hajli, Lin, Featherman, and Wang [25]; and TP and TA were measured with four items adapted separately from Li [5]. A seven-point Likert scale ranging from 1 (strongly disagree) to 7 (strongly agree) was used to measure each item regarding participants' attitudes toward MMCs. To improve the data quality, we inserted an attention filter to detect careless responses. Participants were required to select the designated option in the attention filter. If they failed to do so, the responses were deemed invalid. Table 1 lists the items and constructs utilized in this survey.

Table 1. The measurement scale.

Constructs	Items	Questions	References
Extraversion	E1	I don't talk a lot. (R)	[20]
	E2	I keep in the background. (R)	
Conscientiousness	C1	I often forget to put things back in their proper place. (R)	
	C2	I make a mess of things. (R)	
Neuroticism (N)	N1	I have frequent mood swings	
	N2	I get upset easily	
	N3	I seldom feel blue. (R)	
Intellect (I)	I1	I am not interested in abstract ideas. (R)	
	I2	I have difficulty understanding abstract ideas. (R)	
Privacy concerns	PC1	Using MMC services would make me lose control over the privacy of my information	[5]
	PC2	Using MMC services would not cause any privacy problems	
	PC3	Signing up for and using MMC services would lead to a loss of privacy for me because my personal information could be used without my knowledge	
	PC4	Others might take control of my information if I use MMC services	
Social presence of interaction	SPI1	I can make sense of the attitude of physicians by interacting with them in MMC	[24, 26, 27]
	SPI2	I can imagine how physicians may look like by interacting with them in MMC	
	SPI3	There is a sense of human touch to communicate with physicians in MMC	

(*continued*)

Table 1. (*continued*)

Constructs	Items	Questions	References
	SPI4	Communication in MMC was warm	
Social validation	SV1	I need to know the reputation of the physician when I use this MMC services	[11, 25]
	SV2	I need to know the ratings of the physician from others when I use this MMC service	
	SV3	I need to know the official information about the physician when I use this MMC service	
Trust in physicians	TP1	This MMC service is trustworthy	[5]
	TP2	This MMC service provider provides reliable information	
	TP3	The physicians in this MMC service keeps promises and commitments	
	TP4	The physicians' behaviors in this MMC service meets my expectations	
Trust in applications	TA1	This MMT service provider is trustworthy	[5]
	TA2	This MMT service provider provides reliable information	
	TA3	This MMT service provider keeps promises and commitments	
	TA4	This MMT service provider's behavior meets my expectations	

3.2 Recruitment and Data Collection

We collected empirical data through Wenjuanxing (https://www.wjx.cn), an online Chinese survey platform. Users experienced in using MMCs were selected to participate in this study. Additionally, participants were required to be over 18 years old. Before filling in the questionnaire, participants were asked if they had experienced in consulting physicians about their diseases, their family members' diseases, or their friends' diseases in mobile applications.

The survey was conducted in December 2020. It took one week to collect a total of 182 responses. A reward was offered to our respondents on the survey platform. By examining the attention filter and reversed questions, we deleted 74 careless responses. Thus, 108 valid responses were used for data analysis.

3.3 Data Analysis

The descriptive analysis was applied to show participants' demographic features and usage experience with MMCs. Then, we conducted a Pearson's correlation test to examine the relationships among social cues, user characteristics, and trust. To further test the hypotheses, multiple regression was applied.

This study tested the reliability of all constructs using Cronbach's alpha. A value of above 0.6 is considered an acceptable reliability [28, 29]. We removed the constructs (i.e., extraversion and conscientiousness) with a value lower than 0.6 using Cronbach's alpha. Therefore, the Cronbach's alpha values for the retained constructs ranged from 0.620 to 0.897 in this study. Table 2 presents the results, suggesting that all constructs are accepted in reliability (>0.6). The constructs used in previous studies for the Chinese context suggested good convergent validity and discriminant validity [5, 20, 24]. Thus, the constructs used in this study could be considered reliable and valid.

Table 2. Results for reliability test.

Constructs	Number (N) of items	Cronbach's alpha
Extraversion	2	0.455
Conscientiousness	2	0.512
Neuroticism	3	0.780
Intellect	2	0.620
Privacy concerns (PC)	4	0.897
Social presence of Interaction (SPI)	4	0.802
Social validation (SV)	3	0.620
Trust in Physicians (TP)	4	0.745
Trust in Applications (TA)	4	0.818

4 Results

4.1 Participants

Of the 108 valid respondents, 38 (35.2%) were male and 70 (64.8%) were female. The age distribution was as follows: 18 to 25 years old (32.4%), 26 to 35 years old (46.3%), 36 to 45 (20.4%), and 46 and above (0.9%). All participants had at least a high school education. Table 3 shows the demographic characteristics of the participants.

Participants reported various usage experiences with MMCs. Our participants used 12 types of applications for medical consultations. Among these applications, Ping An Good Doctor had the greatest usage among respondents (63.0%), followed by Wexin Smart Hospital (54.6%), Good Doctor Online (48.1%), Chunyu Doctor (41.7%), and Yilu (Ali Health) (40.7%). Some participants had also used Jingdong Health (14.%) and WeDoctor (10.2%). Other platforms, such as Miaoshou Doctor, Health 160, Medlinker, Weimai, and Baidu Doctor, were less popular; less than 6.5% of participants had used them. Around half of participants (53.7%) had been using MMCs for less than one year, and 46.3% of respondents had been using MMCs for two years or more. Almost half (48.1%) of participants had consulted doctors through mobile applications from two to five times, followed by five times and above (29.6%), and from one to two times (13.0%). Ten participants were not sure how many times they had used MMCs. These

Table 3. Demographic characteristics.

		Frequency	Percentage (%)
Gender	Male	38	35.2
	Female	70	64.8
Age	18–25	35	32.4
	26–35	50	46.3
	36–45	22	20.4
	46 and above	1	0.9
Education level	High school degree/Polytechnic	5	4.6
	Diploma/Bachelor degree	92	85.2
	Master degree and above	11	10.2

results indicate that although mobile medical services are still in the initial phase of adoption, they could have a promising future, since a considerable percentage of participants have accepted MMCs and have used them continuously for years. To be specific, respondents mostly consulted the dermatology (63.0%) and internal medicine (51.9%) departments through MMCs. E.N.T (34.4%), surgery (32.4%), and stomatology (32.4%) departments were also frequently contacted by our respondents. Although various interaction methods were provided by MMCs to support the communication between users and physicians, text messages (92.6%) and image messages (70.4%) were mostly preferred by our respondents. Some respondents also used less popular interaction methods, such as voice message (29.6%), telephone call (21.3%), audio chat (21.3%), video chat (12.0%), and chat groups in QQ or WeChat (14.8%) to communicate with physicians.

4.2 Hypotheses Testing

Table 4 shows the Pearson correlation (r) values among user characteristics, social cues, and trust. The correlation values revealed significant negative relationships between N and TP ($r = -0.196, p < 0.01$), N and TA ($r = -0.305, p < 0.001$), PC and TP ($r = -0.461, p < 0.001$), and PC and TA ($r = -0.406, p < 0.001$). Significant positive relationships were found between I and TP ($r = 0.281, p < 0.01$), SPI and TP ($r = 0.492, p < 0.001$), SPI and TA ($r = 0.428, p < 0.001$), SV and TP ($r = 0.275, p < 0.01$), and SV and TA ($r = 0.190, p < 0.01$).

To further examine the relationships among user characteristics, social cues, and trust, we applied a multiple regression analysis. Based on the correlation results, we utilized N, I, PC, SPI, and SV as the independent variables of TP, and we utilized N, PC, SPI, and SV as the independent variables of TA. The results are shown in Table 5. They show that I, PC, SPI, and SV significantly affect TP, accounting for 42.6% of the variance. Consistent with the correlation results, PC has a negative impact on TP, and I, SPI, and SV have a positive effect on TP. The standardized coefficient Beta indicates that PC was the most important predictor of TP ($\beta = -0.354$), followed by SPI ($\beta = 0.315$), I ($\beta = 0.182$), and SV ($\beta = 0.171$). N, PC, and SV are the predictors for TA, accounting for 32.0% of the variance. N ($\beta = -0.191$) and PC ($\beta = -0.276$) affect TA

Table 4. Pearson correlation (r) values among variables.

	N	I	PC	SPI	SV	TP
I	−0.029					
PC	0.200*	0.000				
SPI	−0.139	0.236*	−0.282*			
SV	−0.178	0.138	−0.055	0.162		
TP	−0.196*	0.281*	−0.461**	0.492**	0.275*	
TA	−0.305**	0.116	−0.406**	0.428**	0.190*	0.612**

** refer to a significant level at the 0.001 (2 tailed)
* refer to a significant level at the 0.01 (2 tailed)

negatively, and SPI ($\beta = 0.309$) influences TA positively. Therefore, H1, H2, H3, and H4 were supported.

Table 5. Standardized coefficient beta (β) of the multiple regression analysis with N, I, PC, SPI, and SV as independent variables and TP and TA as dependent variables.

	TP	TA
N		−0.191*
I	0.182*	
PC	−0.354**	−0.276*
SPI	0.315**	0.309**
SV	0.171**	
R^2	0.426	0.320

** refer to a significant level at the 0.001 (2 tailed)
* refer to a significant level at the 0.01 (2 tailed)

5   Discussion

With the aim of understanding the effects of privacy concerns, personality traits, social presence of interaction, and social validation on trust in MMCs, this study applied a survey method. The multiple regression analysis revealed that the predictors of trust in physicians and trust in applications are different. Regarding the user characteristics, the findings revealed that N negatively affects TA, while it has no effect on TP.

Neuroticism refers to holding a negative attitude (e.g., fear or nervous feelings) about the situation [30]; therefore, users with a higher level of neuroticism could find it more difficult to build trustworthiness with the applications. Previous research also indicated that neuroticism negatively affects trustworthiness toward the service provider in mobile commerce [31]. This research confirmed the effect of neuroticism in MMCs. Although Zhou and Lu [31] revealed a positive relationship between openness to experience and trust in service providers, our study found intellect affects TP only. Intellect describes an individual who is knowledgeable and intelligent. People with a high level of intellect might find it easier to trust people who hold professional knowledge. This might explain why intellect positively influences trust in physicians.

Privacy concerns hinder trust in both physicians and applications. Previous research suggested that privacy concerns can negatively affect trust in mobile medical treatment services [5], and this study also confirmed its effect on trust in MMCs. People have to share sensitive information when consulting physicians about their health problems. Even after the consultation has taken place, users can have concerns about whether their personal information is well protected by the physicians and platforms. Concerns about personal information disclosures hamper users' trust in physicians and applications based on their doubts about the physicians' and applications' integrity and ability to protect their information.

Both SPI and SV are the interaction features in MMCs. Previous work has highlighted the important role of social presence in online communication, particularly in the context of health [2]. Consistent with past findings, the present study also found that social presence conveyed by interaction methods in MMCs can help to build trust in physicians and applications. Respondents in this study reported that text messages (92.6%) and image messages (70.4%) were the main interaction methods used in MMCs. Various interaction methods, such as voice messages, video chats, or chat groups, might enhance media richness by increasing social presence in online communications (ref). Future studies could consider how to integrate this interaction method to increase social presence and enhance trust. Additionally, we confirmed that the functions of social validation can facilitate trust in physicians, revealing that the ratings and comments provided by other users are needed in MMCs. The result is consistent with research about the effect of word of mouth on trust in social commerce [25]. However, we found that the effect of SPI on TA is almost twice as strong as SV in MMCs. This implies that interactions between patients and physicians with warmth and perceived human touch are more important than ratings and comments about physicians shown in MMCs when considering how to enhance trust in physicians.

6 Conclusion

People can easily reach health professionals and receive health advice through mobile medical consultations (MMCs). When using MMCs, trust is a critical issue, as it can not only affect users' behaviors in medical treatments, but also influence adoption behaviors. However, there is still insufficient knowledge about how to build trust in MMCs. This study attempted to examine the effects of privacy concerns, personality traits, social presence of interaction, and social validation on trust in physicians and trust in applications. The findings reveal that intellect, privacy concerns, social presence of interaction, and social validation are the predictors of trust in physicians and neuroticism, privacy concerns, and social presence of interaction are the predictors of trust in applications, indicating that practitioners should apply different strategies to build trust in physicians and trust in applications. Additionally, the results can assist physicians to better communicate with patients in MMCs by considering to improve the social presence of interaction during the consultation. However, this study only discusses the general effects of social presence of interaction and social validation on trust in MMCs. Also, although we found personality traits and privacy concerns related to trust in MMCs, it is possible that these two factors could moderate the influences of social presence of interaction and social validation. Future studies could attempt to examine what type of specific design features of social presence of interactions and social validation can facilitate trust and investigate the moderated effects of privacy concerns and personality traits in MMCs.

Acknowledgement. This research was supported by The First Batch of 2020 MOE Industry-University Collaborative Education Program (Program No. 202002035010, Kingfar-CES "Human Factors and Ergonomics" Program), Shenzhen Educational Science Planning Project (Program No. zdfz20015) and Foundation for Young Talents in Higher Education of Guangdong, China [Project Batch No. 2020WQNCX061].

References

1. Ma, X., Gui, X., Fan, J., Zhao, M., Chen, Y., Zhang, K.: Professional medical advice at your fingertips: an empirical study of an online 'Ask the doctor' platform. In: Proceedings of the ACM on Human-Computer Interaction, vol. 2, no. CSCW (2018)
2. Lazard, A.J., Brennen, J.S., Troutman Adams, E., Love, B.: Cues for increasing social presence for mobile health app adoption. J. Health Commun. **25**(2), 136–149 (2020). https://doi.org/10.1080/10810730.2020.1719241
3. Xing, W., Hsu, P.Y., Chang, Y.W., Shiau, W.L.: How does online doctor–patient interaction affect online consultation and offline medical treatment? Ind. Manag. Data Syst. **120**(1), 196–214 (2019). https://doi.org/10.1108/IMDS-05-2019-0261
4. Blandford, A.: HCI for health and wellbeing: Challenges and opportunities. Int. J. Hum. Comput. Stud. **131**(June), 41–51 (2019). https://doi.org/10.1016/j.ijhcs.2019.06.007
5. Li, Q.: Healthcare at your fingertips: the acceptance and adoption of mobile medical treatment services among Chinese users. Int. J. Environ. Res. Public Health **17**(18), 1–21 (2020). https://doi.org/10.3390/ijerph17186895
6. Chellappa, R., Sin, R.: Personalization versus privacy: an empirical examination of the online consumer's dilemma. Inf. Technol. Manag. **6**, 181–202 (2005)
7. Hall, M.A., Camacho, F., Dugan, E., Balkrishnan, R.: Trust in the medical profession: conceptual and measurement issues. Health Serv. Res. **37**(5), 1419–1439 (2002). https://doi.org/10.1111/1475-6773.01070
8. Shao, Z., Zhang, L., Li, X., Guo, Y.: Antecedents of trust and continuance intention in mobile payment platforms: the moderating effect of gender. Electron. Commer. Res. Appl. **33**, 1 (2019). https://doi.org/10.1016/j.elerap.2018.100823
9. Nilashi, M., Ibrahim, O., Reza Mirabi, V., Ebrahimi, L., Zare, M.: The role of security, design and content factors on customer trust in mobile commerce. J. Retail. Consum. Serv. **26**, 57–69 (2015). https://doi.org/10.1016/j.jretconser.2015.05.002
10. Li, Y.-M., Yeh, Y.-S.: Increasing trust in mobile commerce through design aesthetics. Comput. Hum. Behav. **26**(4), 673–684 (2010). https://doi.org/10.1016/j.chb.2010.01.004
11. Jucks, R., Thon, F.M.: Better to have many opinions than one from an expert? Social validation by one trustworthy source versus the masses in online health forums. Comput. Hum. Behav. **70**, 375–381 (2017). https://doi.org/10.1016/j.chb.2017.01.019
12. Korzaan, M.L., Boswell, K.T.: The influence of personality traits and information privacy concerns on behavioral intentions. J. Comput. Inf. Syst. **48**(4), 15–24 (2008). https://doi.org/10.1080/08874417.2008.11646031

13. Junglas, I.A., Johnson, N.A., Spitzmüller, C.: Personality traits and concern for privacy: an empirical study in the context of location-based services. Eur. J. Inf. Syst. **17**(4), 387–402 (2008). https://doi.org/10.1057/ejis.2008.29
14. Sutcliffe, A.G., Wang, D., Dunbar, R.I.M.: Modelling the role of trust in social relationships. ACM Trans. Internet Technol. **15**(4), 16–24 (2015). https://doi.org/10.1145/2815620
15. Gao, L., Waechter, K.A., Bai, X.: Understanding consumers' continuance intention towards mobile purchase: a theoretical framework and empirical study - a case of China. Comput. Hum. Behav. **53**, 249–262 (2015). https://doi.org/10.1016/j.chb.2015.07.014
16. Malhotra, N.K., Kim, S.S., Agarwal, J.: Internet users' information privacy concerns (IUIPC): the construct, the scale, and a causal model. Inf. Syst. Res. **15**(4), 336–355 (2004)
17. Sun, Z., Reani, M., Li, Q., Ma, X.: Fostering engagement in technology-mediated stress management: a comparative study of biofeedback designs. Int. J. Hum. Comput. Stud. **140**, 102430 (2020). https://doi.org/10.1016/j.ijhcs.2020.102430
18. Zhang, X., Liu, S., Chen, X., Wang, L., Gao, B., Zhu, Q.: Health information privacy concerns, antecedents, and information disclosure intention in online health communities. Inf. Manag. **55**(4), 482–493 (2018). https://doi.org/10.1016/j.im.2017.11.003
19. McElroy, J.C., Hendrickson, A.R., Townsend, A.M., DeMarie, S.M.: Dispositional factors in internet use: personality versus cognitive style. MIS Q. **31**(4), 809 (2017). https://doi.org/10.2307/25148821
20. Zhang, J., Luximon, Y.: A quantitative diary study of perceptions of security in mobile payment transactions. Behav. Inf. Technol. 1–24 (2020). https://doi.org/10.1080/0144929X.2020.1771418
21. Xu, R., Frey, R.M., Fleisch, E., Ilic, A.: Understanding the impact of personality traits on mobile app adoption - insights from a large-scale field study. Comput. Hum. Behav. **62**, 244–256 (2016). https://doi.org/10.1016/j.chb.2016.04.011
22. Zhou, L., et al.: La2O2CN2:Yb3+/Tm3+ nanofibers and nanobelts: novel fabrication technique, structure and upconversion luminescence. J. Mater. Sci. Mater. Electron. **28**(21), 16282–16291 (2017). https://doi.org/10.1007/s10854-017-7534-x
23. Biocca, F., Harms, C., Burgoon, J.K.: Toward a more robust theory and measure of social presence: review and suggested criteria. Presence Teleoperators Virtual Environ. **12**, 456–480 (2003). https://doi.org/10.1162/105474603322761270
24. Lu, B., Fan, W., Zhou, M.: Social presence, trust, and social commerce purchase intention: an empirical research. Comput. Hum. Behav. **56**, 225–237 (2016). https://doi.org/10.1016/j.chb.2015.11.057
25. Hajli, N., Lin, X., Featherman, M., Wang, Y.: Social word of mouth: how trust develops in the market. Int. J. Mark. Res. **56**(5), 673–689 (2014). https://doi.org/10.2501/ijmr-2014-045
26. Gefen, D., Straub, D.W.: Consumer trust in B2C e-Commerce and the importance of social presence: experiments in e-Products and e-Services. Omega **32**(6), 407–424 (2004). https://doi.org/10.1016/j.omega.2004.01.006
27. Verhagen, T., van Nes, J., Feldberg, F., van Dolen, W.: Virtual customer service agents: using social presence and personalization to shape online service encounters. J. Comput.-Mediat. Commun. **19**(3), 529–545 (2014). https://doi.org/10.1111/jcc4.12066
28. Hair, J.F., Ringle, C.M., Sarstedt, M.: PLS-SEM: Indeed a silver bullet. J. Mark. Theory Pract. **19**(2), 139–151 (2011). https://doi.org/10.2753/MTP1069-6679190202
29. Nunnally, J.C.: Psychometric Theory. McGraw-Hill, New York (1978)
30. Halevi, T., Lewis, J., Memon, N.: A pilot study of cyber security and privacy related behavior and personality traits. In: The 22nd International Conference on World Wide Web, pp. 737–744. ACM, New York. (2013). https://doi.org/10.1145/2487788.2488034
31. Zhou, T., Lu, Y.: The effects of personality traits on user acceptance of mobile commerce. Int. J. Hum.-Comput. Interact. **27**(6), 545–561 (2011). https://doi.org/10.1080/10447318.2011.555298

Research on Influencing Factors of Elderly Wearable Device Use Behavior Based on TAM Model

Jin Zhou(✉) and Meiyu Zhou

School of Art Design and Media, East China University of Science and Technology, Shanghai 200237, China

Abstract. In recent years, the development of information technology brings new opportunities for home-based care from the technical level. As a new generation of high-tech products, wearable devices can be used as an effective supplement to home-based care facilities and provide efficient help for home-based care services. In this study, qualitative and quantitative methods are used to study the factors of the elderly adopting wearable devices. The research is based on the technology acceptance model (TAM), and expands it. On the basis of perceived usefulness and perceived ease of use, adding perceived enjoyment and self-efficacy into the subjective internal factors, adding perceived accessibility and perceived risk into the objective external factors, and adding a subjective external factor, perceived sociality to form a matrix model. Through reliability and validity analysis, hypothesis test, structural equation model analysis and so on, the model and hypothesis are verified to make up for the deficiency of subjective factors and exogenous factors in the original TAM model.

Keywords: TAM · Elderly · Wearable devices · Attitude towards using · Behavior intention

1 Introduction

1.1 Research Background

In the reality of deep aging and increasing pension pressure, the number of elderly people suffering from diseases or even loss of living ability is increasing, which brings great pressure to the pension security system, institutions and facilities. In recent years, intelligent application has become a new trend in the development of elderly care, which brings new opportunities for home-based elderly care from the technical level. As a new generation of high-tech products, wearable devices have many advantages, such as environmental intelligent perception, service continuity, real-time and portability, which become an important aspect of the development of new technology in the "silver economy", and provide efficient help for home-based elderly care services [1]. Unfortunately, the market share of wearable products for the elderly is obviously insufficient, and the utilization rate is also very low. Therefore, for wearable device manufacturers, it is very important to have a deeper understanding of the factors that affect the adoption of wearable devices by elderly users.

© Springer Nature Switzerland AG 2021
Q. Gao and J. Zhou (Eds.): HCII 2021, LNCS 12786, pp. 305–320, 2021.
https://doi.org/10.1007/978-3-030-78108-8_23

1.2 Research Status

According to the world population trend report, the global population over 65 is expected to reach 1.5 billion in 2050, accounting for 16% of the total population. Compared with 2017, when the proportion of the elderly population is about 1/11, the aging process is further accelerated [2]. The convenience of wearable devices has high social and technological value in the context of the aging population. Intelligent devices can monitor the health status of the elderly in real time and provide long-term health management. It can solve many problems about providing for the aged, such as "empty nesters", sudden diseases, chronic diseases and so on, and reduce the burden of elderly families and integrated society. On the other hand, as a special consumer group, the elderly's huge population base, increasing material and cultural needs and changing consumption concept will in turn promote the technological innovation of wearable devices and become the next economic growth point of wearable devices market [3].

1.3 Purpose and Significance

We use qualitative and quantitative research methods to study the factors that affect the elderly's adoption of wearable devices. Seeking how wearable devices can provide services for the elderly and make due contributions to the contemporary aging society, maximize the social value and scientific and technological value of wearable devices at the same time, so that the elderly can truly realize the well-being and life convenience brought by the development of society and science and technology.

2 Theoretical Background

Foreign scholars' researches on the influencing factors of the elderly's willingness to use wearable devices mainly refer to the theory of planned behavior (TPB), the theory of Technology Acceptance Model (TAM) and the unified theory of technology acceptance and use (UTAUT). Through these models and combined with the characteristics of wearable devices, the selected models are improved and supplemented to build a more explanatory model of the influencing factors of wearable device behavior intention. Then, through the questionnaire, the data are analyzed to prove whether each path of the new model is effective. At present, the literature rarely combines subjective and objective, internal and external aspects to explore the impact of elderly wearable device use intention. For example, Eunil Park discussed users' perception of intelligent wearable devices, and introduced a comprehensive research model, which adopted factors extracted mainly through expectation confirmation, technology acceptance and process model [4]; Farivar et al. focused on the factors influencing the elderly's intention to use wearable devices, and established a research model to study the effects of cognitive age, perceived complexity and subjective well-being on the elderly's intention to use wearable devices [5]. Another common theory is the integration of Theory of Acceptance and Use of Technology (UTAUT), for example, Talukder et al. established a new theoretical model, namely resistance to change, technology anxiety and self realization, to explore the key predictors of wearable device adoption in the elderly [6].

Domestic research on wearable devices for the elderly mostly focuses on the mapping relationship between wearable devices and home-based care for the elderly, seeking a set of development process in line with the characteristics of the elderly. For example, by summarizing the general design and development process of wearable devices, Liu Yi introduced the design method of designer's situational experience and the participation of the elderly, This paper put forward a complete design and development process and method of wearable devices for the elderly [7]; Xu Juanfang found out the service mode of wearable devices for home-based care by analyzing the function of wearable devices and the demand of home-based care [8]; Luo et al. combined the advantages of wearable devices, the behavior characteristics of the elderly, the status quo of pension and other aspects to build a new O2O intelligent pension community model. Wang et al. elaborated the basic situation of the elderly and the development situation and Prospect of wearable devices in China, analyzed the role of wearable devices in the health care of the elderly, and found out the connection between wearable devices and the needs of the elderly in the field of home-based care, so as to seek wearable devices to make due contributions to the aging society.

Through the analysis of literature, we can find that most of the existing researches on the influencing factors of wearable devices are based on TAM model, and most of the research models are based on the TAM model to modify the characteristics of wearable devices and the characteristics of research objects.

3 Research Hypothesis and Model Design

3.1 Definition of Research Variables

Technology Acceptance Model (TAM) is a model proposed by Davis using rational behavior theory (TRA), absorbing the reasonable core of expectation theory model, self-efficacy theory and other related theories, to study the user's acceptance of information system [9]. Although TAM model is simple and easy to operate, TAM also has its own defects. TAM can only explain 40%–60% of user behavior intention, and nearly half of the related influencing factors can not be explained from the model. Some important control problems are ignored, such as the influence of external variables such as personal factors and social factors on technology acceptance.

Therefore, this study will add four variables from the subjective point of view, one is the user's psychological cognition variable, perceived enjoyment and self-efficacy, the other is the social influence variable, namely perceived sociality. From an objective point of view, two variables are added: perceived accessibility and perceived risk. Meanwhile, perceived usefulness, perceived ease of use, perceived enjoyment and perceived self-efficacy are relative internal variables, while perceived sociality, perceived accessibility and perceived risk are relative external variables. By adding the above variables, the original TAM model makes up for the lack of attention to subjective factors and exogenous factors. The definitions of each research variable are shown in Table 1.

Table 1. Definition of each research variable.

Variable	Definition	Source
Perceived usefulness (PU)	The elderly's subjective perception of the benefits of using wearable devices	TAM
Perceived ease of use (PEU)	Subjective feelings of the elderly on the complexity of using wearable devices	TAM
Perceived enjoyment (PE)	The sense of pleasure and flow experience of the elderly when using wearable devices	Davis (1992)
Perceived sociality (PS)	It includes the influence of subjective norms, social influence and network externality on the audience's acceptance and adoption of wearable devices	Dishaw and Strong (1999)
Perceived risk (PR)	It is used to explain consumers' risk-taking caused by purchasing behavior	Stone and Gronhaug (1993)
Perceived accessibility (PA)	Meet the elderly's basic needs	Wixom and Todd (2005)
Self efficacy (SE)	The elderly's perception of their ability to control and use wearable technology	Hsu and Chiu (2004)
Attitude toward using (ATU)	The positive or negative feelings of the elderly in the process of mobile learning	TAM
Behavioral intention (BI)	The subjective will of the elderly to adopt or accept something or behavior	TAM

3.2 Research Hypothesis and Model

In a large number of studies based on technology acceptance model, the usefulness and ease of use of technology acceptance model has been strongly verified. Therefore, this paper proposes the following assumptions based on the technology acceptance model.

H1: The elderly's perceived usefulness of wearable devices has a positive impact on their attitude towards using wearable devices;
H2: The elderly's perception of wearable device ease of use has a positive impact on their attitude towards using wearable devices;
H3: The elderly's perceived usefulness of wearable devices has a positive impact on their behavioral intention to use wearable devices;
H4: The attitude of the elderly to use wearable devices has a positive impact on their behavioral intention to use wearable devices;

Davis, Ye et al. have proved that perceived enjoyment has a positive impact on users' attitude towards use [10]. They believe that when users feel that wearable devices are a way to make them feel happy, this pleasant feeling will motivate them to choose wearable devices. Therefore, there is a high correlation between perceived enjoyment and users' use attitude. Based on previous studies, this paper proposes the following hypotheses.

H5: The elderly's perceived enjoyment of wearable devices has a positive impact on the use attitude.

Hsu et al. applied the theory of planned behavior (TPB) to the context of IS continuous use, and theoretically derives the model of continuous use of electronic services [11]. The results show that users' continuous use intention is determined by Internet self-efficacy and satisfaction. This paper argues that the perceived self-efficacy of users in the process of using wearable devices will have a positive impact on their willingness to use.

H6: The self-efficacy of the elderly on wearable devices has a positive impact on the use attitude.

According to the theory of sociality, individuals will change more or less under the influence of others. An important phenomenon of social theory is conformity. When an individual is lack of understanding of new things and unable to make accurate judgment, he or she will often extract information by observing the behavior of people around him or her. In this case, many information will tend to be similar and assimilate with each other, resulting in conformity. Similarly, users will be more or less affected by the surrounding crowd when they choose wearable devices as a new learning method. Based on this, this paper puts forward the following hypothesis.

H7: The elderly's perceived sociality of wearable device has a positive impact on the use attitude.

Perceived accessibility, including the accessibility of wearable device content, has a positive impact on the audience's acceptance and adoption of wearable devices. Based on this, this paper proposes the following hypotheses.

H8: The elderly's perceived accessibility of wearable devices has a positive impact on their use attitude.

Jacoby et al. divided perceived risk into five aspects: financial risk, functional risk, psychological risk, social risk and physical risk [12]. Perceived risk has a negative impact on users' willingness to use. Therefore, this paper makes the following assumptions:

H9: The elderly's perceived risk of wearable devices has a negative impact on the use attitude.

This study takes TAM model as the framework, summarizes the previous research results, improves TAM model, and proposes the model construction of elderly wearable device adoption behavior as shown in Fig. 1 according to the corresponding research assumptions.

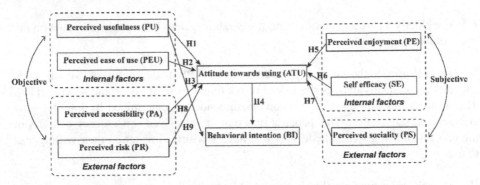

Fig. 1. Model construction of elderly wearable device adoption behavior.

3.3 Research Scale Design

The research variables are: perceived usefulness (PU), perceived ease of use (PEU), perceived enjoyment (PE), perceived accessibility (PA), perceived risk (PR), perceived sociality (PS), self-efficacy (SE), attitude toward using (ATU), behavioral intention (BI). The detailed observation variables are shown in Table 1, covering subjective and objective factors. This paper discusses the influencing factors of elderly people's willingness to use wearable devices from the perspective of "environment-people-influence".

(1) Perceived usefulness

Davis defined perceived usefulness as the degree to which users can improve their performance by accepting a technology. Venkatesh defined perceived usefulness as consumers' subjective feeling of something, which will affect consumers' future behavior. In this study, perceived usefulness is defined as the user's subjective evaluation of the wearable device after use, including the evaluation of the wearable device's body detection ability, the timeliness of obtaining information, and whether it can meet the personalized needs. The design of the scale refers to the research results of Davis, Venkatesh and other scholars, and combined with the characteristics of wearable devices, there are four items, as shown in Table 2.

(2) Perceived ease of use

The perceived ease of use defined by Davis is the user perceived ease of use of an information system, which can be understood as the time and effort that the user perceives from the beginning of accepting and using a new technology to skillfully using it. In this study, perceived ease of use is defined as the user's perception of the difficulty of

Table 2. Items of perceived usefulness scale.

Variable	Scale questions
Perceived usefulness	PU1: It can let me know more about my physical condition
	PU2: It's useful in my work or life
	PU3: It makes my work more efficient or my life more convenient
	PU4: It allows me to receive and view information in real time

wearable device's learnability, operability and portability. The scale items of perceived ease of use are shown in Table 3.

Table 3. Items of perceived ease of use scale.

Variable	Scale questions
Perceived ease of use	PEU1: It's easy to operate and effortless to monitor
	PEU2: Easy to carry, easy to use anytime, anywhere
	PEU3: User friendly interface design, simple interaction, easy to understand
	PEU4: It won't take me a lot of time to learn how to operate it

(3) Perceived enjoyment

MariosKoufaris defined perceived enjoyment as the corresponding emotional response in a pleasant environment [13]. The pleasant flow experience of users in the process of using wearable devices will promote them to continue to use the product, so the perceived enjoyment will affect the wearable devices. This study defines perceived enjoyment as the degree of pleasure users get when using wearable devices. The scale items of perceived enjoyment are shown in Table 4.

Table 4. Items of perceived enjoyment scale.

Variable	Scale questions
Perceived enjoyment	PE1: It can make me feel the joy of high technology
	PE2: It's a good way of entertainment
	PE3: I like the spiritual enjoyment it brings me
	PE4: It can make my spiritual life more colorful

(4) Perceived sociality

Dishaw believed that TAM model should also consider subjective norms, mainly because users of information systems will feel the influence of social pressure and cultural atmosphere in the organizational environment. In reality, people are social, and their decisions are often influenced by family, friends and other people. The scale items of perceived sociality are shown in Table 5.

Table 5. Items of perceived sociality scale.

Variable	Scale questions
Perceived sociality	PS1: It's widely used by people around me
	PS2: People around me recommend its, which will make me think about buying it
	PS3: If I refuse it, others may think I am out of date
	PS4: Everyone around me has it. I can't have none
	PS5: Advertising will make me think about using it

(5) Perceived risk

Jacoby et al. divided perceived risk into five aspects: financial risk, functional risk, psychological risk, social risk and physical risk. According to the characteristics of wearable devices, the questionnaire items of perceived risk dimension are designed according to the above five dimensions, as shown in Table 6.

Table 6. Items of perceived risk scale.

Variable	Scale questions
Perceived risk	PR1: It may cause me time and financial losses in the process of using it
	PR2: It may cause losses due to my personal mistakes or negligence
	PR3: It may reveal my privacy
	PR4: It reduces personal space and brings trouble to my work life
	PR5: It hasn't strict security monitoring

(6) Perceived accessibility

Wixom et al. divided accessibility into information accessibility and purchase accessibility [14]. According to the characteristics of wearable devices, the scale items of perceived accessibility are shown in Table 7.

Table 7. Items of perceived risk scale.

Variable	Scale questions
Perceived accessibility	PA1: I know where to get its content
	PA2: It's very convenient to get its content
	PA3: I can get the body data I want quickly by searching
	PA4: I can easily buy it through a variety of channels

(7) Self efficacy

Self efficacy refers to the individual's speculation and judgment on whether he has the ability to complete a certain behavior. According to Hsu et al., the self-efficacy scale was designed from the following three aspects, as shown in Table 8.

Table 8. Items of self efficacy scale.

Variable	Scale questions
Self efficacy	SE1: Based on my personal ability, I can use it skillfully
	SE2: I know how to use it even without the help of others
	SE3: I believe I have the ability to describe how to use it

(8) Attitude toward using

In the questionnaire design of this study, reference is made to the questionnaire design of the attitude towards use adopted by Davis in the TAM model study. In this paper, the attitude toward using is defined as a clear activity or behavior tendency that users will take in the use of wearable devices. The scale items of attitude toward using are as shown in Table 9.

Table 9. Items of attitude toward using.

Variable	Scale questions
Attitude toward using	ATU1: In the digital age, I think it's a wise choice to use it
	ATU2: I support it and would like to use it often

(9) Behavioral intention

The behavioral intention defined by Davis refers to the judgment of individual's subjective probability of taking a particular behavior, which reflects the individual's willingness to take a particular behavior. The design of the scale is shown in Table 10.

Table 10. Items of behavioral intention.

Variable	Scale questions
Behavioral intention	BI1: In the digital age, I would like to use it for body monitoring
	BI2: When I buy a good wearable device, I am willing to share it with my friends
	BI3: I'd like to recommend a good wearable device to my friends

4 Data Collection and Analysis

4.1 Questionnaire Survey

A total of 446 questionnaires were collected, including 181 online questionnaires and 265 paper questionnaires. After deleting the abnormal answers by SPSS22.0, 342 valid questionnaires were obtained.

4.2 Sample Descriptive Statistics

In the effective sample, the proportion of male wearable device users was 69.3%, which was significantly higher than that of female 30.7% It indirectly reflects that men are more inclined to use wearable devices; in terms of age, the utilization rate of 65–74 years old is 87.1%, and that of 75 years old and above is 12.9%; in terms of health status, the utilization rate of the elderly with chronic diseases is higher, accounting for 58.8%, which is in line with the market positioning of wearable devices, aiming at the health monitoring function needs of the elderly; in terms of living environment, the utilization rate of the elderly living alone is higher The utilization rate was 68.4%. The utilization rate of the elderly living with their spouses was 19.6%, followed by 9.4% living in nursing homes and 2.6% living with their children. In terms of geographic use, the utilization rate of 83.9% in urban areas was significantly higher than that of 16.1% in rural areas. The demographic data of the sample are shown in Table 11.

Table 11. Sample information.

Item	Category	Number	Percentage
Gender	Male	237	69.3%
	Female	105	30.7%
Age	65–74	298	87.1%
	≥ 75	44	12.9%
Health	Good	91	26.6%
	General	50	14.6%
	Poor (with chronic disease)	201	58.8%
Living with	Spouse	67	19.6%
	Children	9	2.6%
	Alone	234	68.4%
	Beadhouse	32	9.4%
Residence	Countryside	55	16.1%
	City	287	83.9%

4.3 Reliability and Validity Analysis of the Questionnaire

Reliability and validity test is usually an important standard to test whether the questionnaire meets the requirements, but also the premise of hypothesis test. In this paper, we first use SPSS22.0 to test the data by kmo and Bartlett test. The results show that the kmo value of the sample is 0.901, the chi square value of Bartlett sphericity test is 4700.081, and the significance level is 0.000, which indicates that this scale is suitable for factor analysis.

Confirmatory factor analysis (CFA) can be used to test the reliability and validity of the scale. The results are shown in Table 12 and Table 13. It can be seen from Table 12 that Cronbach's alpha of each variable is higher than 0.70, and the combined reliability (CR) is higher than 0.80, which shows that the reliability of the scale is high; all items have a standard load greater than 0.7 on the corresponding factors, and the average variance extraction (AVE) of each latent variable is higher than 0.50, which indicates that the convergence validity is good; It can be seen from Table 13 that the square root (diagonal bold value) of ave value of each latent variable is higher than the correlation coefficient between latent variables, indicating good discriminant validity. In conclusion, it can be considered that the samples adopted in this study have high reliability and validity.

Table 12. Loading of indicator variables.

Construct	Items	Factor loading	Cronbach's α (>0.7)	CR (>0.6)	AVE (>0.5)
PU	PU1	0.750	0.868	0.862	0.610
	PU2	0.785			
	PU3	0.790			
	PU4	0.797			
PEU	PEU1	0.762	0.854	0.835	0.559
	PEU2	0.729			
	PEU3	0.770			
	PEU4	0.729			
PE	PE1	0.802	0.862	0.835	0.537
	PE2	0.784			
	PE3	0.770			
	PE4	0.729			
PS	PS1	0.794	0.797	0.846	0.647
	PS2	0.806			
	PS3	0.753			
	PS4	0.729			
	PS5	0.765			
PR	PR1	0.872	0.781	0.836	0.647
	PS2	0.910			
	PR3	0.879			
	PR4	0.782			
	PR5	0.882			
PA	PA1	0.802	0.873	0.861	0.644
	PA2	0.818			
	PA3	0.712			
	PA4	0.812			
SE	SE1	0.818	0.856	0.822	0.606
	SE2	0.802			
	SE3	0.712			
ATU	ATU1	0.876	0.815	0.889	0.727
	ATU2	0.882			
BI	BI1	0.812	0.849	0.895	0.742
	BI2	0.806			
	BI3	0.814			

Table 13. Correlations of the constructs and square root of AVE.

	PU	PEU	PE	PS	PR	PA	SE	ATU	BI
PU	**0.781**								
PEU	0.289	**0.777**							
PE	0.574	0.270	**0.778**						
PS	0.128	0.201	0.196	**0.861**					
PR	−0.163	−0.146	−0.158	−0.132	**0.854**				
PA	0.208	0.268	0.269	0.136	−0.007	**0.825**			
SE	0.328	0.317	0.321	0.257	−0.365	0.157	**0.804**		
ATU	0.235	0.206	0.134	0.248	−0.047	0.243	0.238	**0.852**	
BI	0.604	0.593	0.580	0.230	−0.205	0.353	0.332	0.556	**0.804**

4.4 Hypothesis Testing

In this study, AMOS24.0 was used to test the hypothesis of the model. The results of goodness of fit indicators are shown in Table 14, which are all within the recommended value range, indicating that the research model and sample data have good goodness of fit. The hypothesis test results of structural equation model are shown in Table 15 and Fig. 2.

Table 14. Fit indices.

Indices	X^2/df	RMSEA	CFI	GFI	AGFI	NNFI
Recommendation	≤3	≤0.1	≥0.9	≥0.9	≥0.8	≥0.9
Fitted values	2.51	0.059	0.972	0.923	0.895	0.947

Table 15. Results of the research model.

Hypothesis	Standardized coefficient	P vaule	Result
H1 PU-> ATU	0.516	***	Supported
H2 PEU-> ATU	0.645	***	Supported
H3 PU-> BI	0.514	***	Supported
H4 ATU-> BI	0.426	***	Supported
H5 PE-> ATU	0.290	0.003	Supported
H6 SE-> ATU	0.343	***	Supported
H7 PS-> ATU	0.247	0.033	Supported
H8 PA-> ATU	0.224	0.038	Supported
H9 PR-> ATU	0.216	0.025	Supported

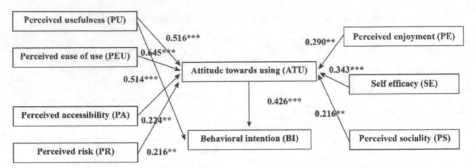

Fig. 2. Research model analysis results (***p < 0.001, **p < 0.01, *p < 0.05).

5   Conclusion

5.1   Conclusion and Discussion

The perceived usefulness and perceived ease of use in TAM model are still important explanatory variables that affect the audience's behavioral intention and actual use behavior of accepting and adopting wearable devices. Therefore, TAM can be said to be a basic model, which can study the user's intention and behavior of accepting or adopting a new technology.

In this paper, we introduce perceived enjoyment, perceived sociality, perceived accessibility, perceived risk and self-efficacy as new potential variables to expand the TAM model. On the one hand, it makes up for the deficiency of endogenous variables in the original TAM model, which focuses on users' psychology, and considers the influence of individual emotion and psychological factors on their attitude and behavior intention The exogenous variables are improved.

Research shows that perceived sociality, that is, social influence has a positive impact on the user's acceptance and adoption of wearable devices. With the decline of the physical function of the elderly, more and more users use wearable devices. When elderly users decide whether to use wearable devices, they are often affected by the people around them and social environment. Positive or negative evaluation will affect the user's adoption behavior. Perceived accessibility, has a positive impact on users' attitude. On the one hand, in the e-commerce era, the convenience of wearable device acquisition, purchase and after-sales maintenance helps users to actively adopt the attitude and behavior of wearable devices; on the other hand, in the Internet era, the convenience of wearable device content acquisition, sharing and feedback has a positive impact on the attitude and behavior of elderly users. Perceived risk, including financial risk, functional risk, psychological risk, social risk and physical risk, has a negative impact on users' attitude. Elderly users' daily health information, such as heart rate and blood pressure, can be monitored by wearable devices. If the user in the process of using improper operation or other unexpected conditions, or will be leaked by the manufacturer or used for other purposes and other potential security risks, it will cause personal information leakage, time and capital loss and other problems. Perceived enjoyment, has a positive impact on the use attitude. Self efficacy refers to the elderly's perception of their ability to control and use wearable technology, which has a positive impact on users' attitude towards using wearable technology.

5.2 Suggestions

Through the research results of this paper, we can see that there is room for further improvement in many aspects of elderly wearable devices, mainly including the following points:

(1) Perceived ease of use will directly or indirectly affect the elderly's attitude. Considering the degradation of the physical function of the elderly, the design should reduce the difficulty of operation, so that users can achieve extremely simplified operation. So as to ensure that they use the function very smoothly, will not produce any psychological burden.

(2) As the user's self-efficacy will continue to change with the accumulation of experience, device operators can try to enhance the elderly's confidence in self-efficacy by means of easy to understand operating instructions, and can also use intuitive publicity methods to make users obtain reliable information, so as to improve the sense of self-efficacy and the possibility of continuous use of it.

(3) What the elderly users are most worried about is the loss of personal time and money caused by the leakage of personal privacy. Today's Internet enterprises have a large amount of personal data of users. If they lose the trust of users, it will not only affect users' choice of products, but also make users lose the trust of enterprises. Therefore, the design of wearable devices should make users feel that the positive benefits outweigh the negative losses caused by privacy information.

(4) Take the differentiation competition as the breakthrough point, and constantly enhance the quality of wearable devices. Although the elderly are willing to accept wearable devices, the utilization rate and retention rate are not very high. The main problems of the existing wearable devices include poor independence, lack of in-depth functional application, poor data analysis user experience, short battery life, high price, etc. These are common problems that continue to plague the industry, and are also bottlenecks that need to be solved urgently.

(5) Users' attitude towards wearable devices will be affected by the people around them. Therefore, manufacturers can adopt a variety of incentives to encourage them to share the information about the devices with others, do a good job in word-of-mouth marketing, and enhance the reputation of enterprises.

References

1. Luo, X.L., Fan, W.G.: Research on urban intelligent pension service mode based on medical and health wearable devices. Lanzhou Acad. J. **10**, 199–208 (2017)
2. SOHU Homepage. https://www.sohu.com/a/311822567_753682. Accessed 10 Feb 2021
3. Wang, Y.J., Yang, L.N., Li, M.Z.: Design requirements of wearable equipment introduced into the field of pension. China Health Ind. **16**(15), 180–182 (2019)

4. Park, E.: User acceptance of smart wearable devices: an expectation-confirmation model approach. Telemat. Inform. **47**, 101318 (2020)
5. Farivar, S., Abouzahra, M., Ghasemaghaei, M.: Wearable device adoption among older adults: a mixed-methods study. Int. J. Ind. Manag. **55**, p10220918 (2020)
6. Talukder, M.S., Sorwar, G., Bao, Y., Ahmed, J., Palash, M.A.S.: Predicting antecedents of wearable healthcare technology acceptance by elderly: a combined SEM-neural network approach. Technol. Forecast. Soc. Change **150**, 119793 (2020)
7. Liu, Y.: Research on wearable device design based on aging society (2016)
8. Xu, J.F.: Design strategy of wearable devices in home care service. Packag. Eng. **37**(12), 125–128 (2016)
9. Davis, F.D., Bagozzi, R.P., Warshaw, P.R.: Extrinsic and intrinsic motivation to use computers in the workplace. J. Appl. Soc. Psychol. **22**(14), 1111–1132 (1992)
10. Ye, H.Z., Li, R., Geng, M.L.: Research on the factors of affecting the mobile learning. In: 3rd International Symposium on Knowledge Acquisition and Modelling (2010)
11. Hsu, M.H., Chiu, C.M.: Predicting electronic service continuance with a decomposed theory of planned behaviour. Behav. Inf. Tech. **23**(5), 59–373 (2004)
12. Jacoby, J., Kaplan, B.: The Components of Perceived Risk and Association for Consumer Research (2004)
13. Koufaris, T., Hampton-Sosa, W.: The development of initial trust in an online company by new customers. Inf. Manag. **41**, 377–397 (2004)
14. Wixom, M., Hampton-Sosa, W.: A theoretical integration of user satisfaction and technology acceptance inform. Syst. Res. **16**(1), 85–102 (2005)

Study on the Control-Display Gain of Touch Zoom Gestures for Older Adults

Ziyao Zhou[1] and Jia Zhou[2(✉)]

[1] Department of Industrial Engineering, Chongqing University, Chongqing, China
[2] School of Management Science and Real Estate, Chongqing University, Chongqing, China

Abstract. Pinch-to-zoom is a common touch gesture used by older adults to see the details of photos, maps or web pages. However, older adults have many difficulties with the use of zoom gesture. The aim of this study was to examine the effect of touch sensitivity on the execution of pinch-to-zoom gestures in older adults. Sensitivity of touch screens to user input depends primarily on the control-display gain (CD). In this study, the larger the CD, the faster the content scales and the more sensitive the zooming; the smaller the CD value, the slower the content changes and the more sluggish the zooming. However, the effect of CD on zooming sensitivity also depends on the triggered finger distance (TD). The larger the TD value, the harder the zooming is triggered and the less sensitive it is. 27 older adults (Age: Mean = 68.56, SD = 5.15) participated in an experiment containing a basic zooming task, which examined various CDs (CD < 1, CD > 1, CD = 1) and TDs (0dp, 100dp, 200dp). The results show that older adults perform best under the condition of CD > 1 and TD = 200dp. CD and TD constrain each other and work together to modulate sensitivity. Increasing the control-display gain and setting the appropriate trigger finger distance can improve task performance. The results of this study can provide a reference for the design of touch gestures for older users from the perspective of interaction sensitivity.

Keywords: Human-computer interaction · Aging · Touch gestures · Control-display gain · Interaction design

1 Introduction

Multi-touch technology, which enables gesture recognition, has been widely adopted by handheld devices. People use touch gestures to operate smartphones, and touch gesture interaction has become an important part of the user experience. For example, users can "pinch" two fingers on the screen to zoom in or out on an area of interest. The pinch-to-zoom gesture allows continuous input compared to another method of zooming by double tapping the content [1]. However, older adults have difficulty using this gesture [2–5]. When tasks involving grasping and continuous movement, older adults have slower motor speed, reduced motor coordination, and less ability to control force [6–8]. This results in older adults tending to make mistakes more often than younger adults when using zoom gestures on smart handheld devices. The existing solution to the difficulty of executing touch gestures for the elderly have mainly been to adopt alternative gestures

© Springer Nature Switzerland AG 2021
Q. Gao and J. Zhou (Eds.): HCII 2021, LNCS 12786, pp. 321–332, 2021.
https://doi.org/10.1007/978-3-030-78108-8_24

[1, 2, 5]. However, the feasibility of replacing frequently used gestures in daily life is limited.

We found two main types of difficulties in executing pinch-to-zoom gesture in older adults: (I) low finger joint flexibility and effortful pinching of two fingers, which resulted in the zooming command not being activated; (II) unexpected and uncontrolled zooming movements, which resulted in not knowing where the target of interest had moved with the fingers. Both are related to sensitivity, while the sensitivity of the touch screen to user input depends mainly on the control display gain. Therefore, we propose that by applying the concept of the control display gain to zooming gestures, the effectiveness and experience of older adults operating zooming gestures can be improved. Decreasing the gain means controlling the sensitivity of the zoom gesture, which may be effective in cases where zooming is unexpected. Increasing the gain means increasing the sensitivity of the zoom gesture, which may alleviate the problems caused by inflexible fingers. If the gain is too large, it has the disadvantage of being difficult to control the accuracy [9, 10]. We therefore introduced a technique, zooming triggered finger distance (TD), for coordinating sensitivity. TD was originally set as a safety threshold to prevent accidental touching. The initial distance between the index finger and thumb when zooming needs to be greater than this value in order to trigger the zoom command. Therefore, the larger the TD value, the harder the zooming is triggered and the less sensitive it is.

Considering these two sensitivity parameters, this study focuses on the effect of touch sensitivity on the zooming performance of older adults. The roles of CD and TD were tested in an experiment involved 27 older adults. The results of this study can provide a reference for the design of touch zoom gestures for older users from the perspective of interaction sensitivity.

2 Related Work

For touch-screen devices, the zoom function may be particularly important for older adults. Due to impaired vision, they often need to zoom in on photos, text, maps or web pages to see details [11]. Pinch-to-zoom gesture is a widely used way to zoom in on touch screens. Older adults, however, do not always perform it effectively, and it is necessary to understand the difficulties they have using this gesture [4, 5, 12–14].

Lepicar et al. [12] found that older adults have more difficulties performing multi-touch gestures than younger adults, and the zoom gesture is one of them. They discussed that the hand dexterity required for the zooming gestures exceeded the abilities of older adults. Kobayash [13] noted that the diffusion motion of the finger (zooming in) is more difficult than the pinching motion (zooming out) when older users perform zooming operations on touch surfaces. Considering that the mobile map interface supports a relatively comprehensive range of gesture types, Harada et al. [14] observed the use of gestures in a map application on smartphones of older adults. When told to find a route between two specific locations, older adults were observed to be unable to flexibly switch between the drag and zoom gestures. Some participants were still dragging content based on two fingers after zooming. There were even participants who subconsciously used four fingers to zoom the interface. These phenomena reflect the meticulous and specific difficulties of older adults in the execution of pinch-to-zoom gestures. Tsai et al. [2]

redesigned the "slide down" to zoom gesture for older adults to replace the pinch-to-zoom gesture. Although the improved gesture was subjectively preferred by older adults, the objective measure of zoom performance was not as good as before the improvement.

In addition to developing alternative gestures, another approach is to make targeted adjustments for input sensitivity. Control-display ratios are related to the sensitivity of the input to the output. There have been some studies of control-display ratios corresponding to mouse-cursor [15–17], but not many have applied this concept to touch gestures [9, 10, 18]. Kwon et al. [9] explored the effect of control-display gain on the usability of tap-n-drag gestures for younger adults, when the information space is too large relative to the screen. To investigate whether increasing the control-display gain could solve problems such as excessive dragging and fatigue, the gain of tap-n-drag is set to 1, 3, 5, 7, 9. The results showed that increasing control-display gain could improve tap-n-drag performance, but excessive gain could have negative effects on task completion time, ease of use, and overall preference. The curve of control-display gain on performance is u-shaped or inverted u-shaped. Zhang et al. [18] investigated the control-display gain design for sliding the slide bar on a phone's touchscreen. The optimal sensitivity of sliding was 2 and 3, in both horizontal and vertical sliding directions. Tao et al. [10] explored the effect of control-to-display gain on some typical touch tasks for young people, with the task deployed on a 23.8-inch touch display. For the dragging, rotating, and zooming tasks, the study all set five gain values:0.75, 1, 2, 3, and 4. The results also showed a u-shaped curve of increasing gain corresponding to task completion time. The optimum gain for both dragging and rotating gestures is 1. For zooming tasks, the best performance was shown when gain = 2. The limitation of existing studies is that there are no studies on pinch-to-zoom gestures for older adults. Therefore, the effect of control-display gain on touch zoom gestures for older adults is still unknown.

3 Hypothesis

The reduced dexterity of finger joints causes difficulties in pinch-to-zoom gesture execution for older adults. This study proposed to improve the sensitivity of touch control by increasing the control-display gain. Therefore, the first hypothesis of this study was as follow.

- H1: Adjusting the control display gain greater than 1 will improve the performance of older adults performing pinch-to-zoom gestures.

The high sensitivity may cause increased control difficulty. Triggered finger distance can reduce sensitivity without changing the control-display gain. So the second hypothesis of this study was as follow.

- H2: Setting the zooming triggered finger distance will further improve the performance of older adults in performing pinch-to-zoom gestures.

4 Method

4.1 Independent Variables

The independent variables were control-display gain and zooming triggered finger distance. Their levels and technical description were as follow:

- Control-display gain (CD < 1, CD = 1, CD > 1)
- Zooming triggered finger distance (TD = 0dp, 200dp, 300dp)

Control-Display Gain (CD). Control-to-display ratio is an important design parameter for interactive interfaces, originally used to describe the mapping relationships between mouse movement and cursor movement on the display [16], and its value is equal to the ratio of mouse movement distance to cursor movement distance.

This study uses the concept of gain to reflect the mapping relationship between control and display. The larger gain is, the more sensitive the response of output to input is. The mouse movement corresponds to the pinching of the finger, and the cursor movement corresponds to the scaling of the content on the screen.

The value of control-display gain in this study is equal to the inverse of the ratio of the change in the distance between the two fingers to the change in the scale of contents on the display (See Fig. 1 and Eq. (1)). The original gain value of the zoom gesture is 1, which means that the display is scaled exactly in proportion to the change in finger distance. When the gain > 1, if the distance between two fingers doubles, the content will be scaled more than twice, which means the more sensitive the scaling is. In the case of gain < 1, the content will be scaled slower than the pinch of fingers, which means the more sluggish the scaling is. The exact values of gain in this study are 0.5(CD < 1), 1 and 2(CD > 1), which were determined based on the user feedback of controllability in the pre-experiment.

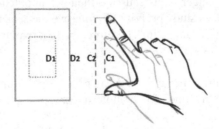

Fig. 1. Parameter information for control-display gain in pinch-to-zoom gesture ($\Delta C = \frac{C_2}{C_1}$, $\Delta D = \frac{D_2}{D_1}$)

$$CD_{gain} = \frac{1}{\Delta C / \Delta D} \tag{1}$$

Zooming Triggered Finger Distance (TD). The zooming triggered finger distance is initially a safety threshold set to prevent accidental touch. In pinch-to-zoom gesture, we take the distance between the user's two fingers at the moment of touching the screen as the initial finger distance. Once the initial distance reaches TD, the scaling command is triggered. In other words, if a user's initial finger distance is greater than or equal to TD, the zoom command is valid the moment the finger touches the screen. However, if the initial distance is less than TD, the zoom command will not be triggered immediately, and the zoom will be valid only after the finger continues to pinch and stretch to make the finger distance meet the TD requirement. Based on its characteristics, we believe that setting an appropriate distance between the two fingers for triggered scaling can help stabilize the touch sensitivity.

The three levels of TD were determined after the pre-experiment. We collected the initial finger distance of participants around 180dp (SD = 5.63), so 0dp, 200dp and 300dp were determined in order to test the role of TD.

4.2 Dependent Variables

The dependent variables and their descriptions were as follows:

- Task completion time: the time between when the participant pressed the "Start" button and when the "Finish" button was pressed.
- Task success rate: the task was considered successful when the participant scaled the target to meet the task zooming accuracy requirements.

4.3 Experimental Design

The study used a 3 × 3 within-subjects design. Each participant was required to perform the zooming task for all 9 combinations of variables, with each combination containing 3 trials. To offset learning effects, the order of the nine conditions was counterbalanced for each participant. There were 27 participants, so a total of $27 \times 9 \times 3 = 729$ trials were collected.

4.4 Participants and Apparatus

Twenty-seven older adults, ranging in age from 60 to 80 years (Mean: 68.56, SD: 5.146), were recruited to participate in this study. Demographic information or experience with technology use was collected. The participants all volunteered to participate in this experiment and will receive some financial compensation after the experiment.

This experimental task is deployed on a Huawei Honor CUN-TL00 smartphone. The operating system of the smartphone is Android 5.1, the screen size is 5 inches and its resolution is 720 × 1280. The application software carrying the zooming task is developed in Java through Android Studio. Task success and task completion time will be automatically saved to the phone's internal storage.

4.5 Task

The task is to scale an object to a specified size by a pinch-to-zoom gesture. A square object of size 150 pixels (green background, movable and zoomable) and a wireframe of size 450 pixels (orange background, red border, fixed) were placed in the center of the screen as shown in Fig. 2, with the square object coinciding with the center of the frame. The participant needs to perform scaling and panning operations on the object to adjust it to match the size and position of the target wireframe. The border width of the target wireframe is 20 pixels, which represents the allowed error for the scaling operation. Therefore, for a successful scaling task, the final object size can vary from 440 pixels to 460 pixels, and the error in its position with respect to the wireframe in any direction is not allowed to exceed 10 pixels.

Fig. 2. Screenshot of the initial state of the zoom task

4.6 Procedure

All experimental procedures in this study were conducted indoors, and the overall environment of the experiments was quiet, with one experimenter and one participant present.

Before the formal experiment, two pre-experiments were conducted. The first pre-experiment was primarily designed to debug and determine the parameters of the experimental prototype. In response to the participants' feedback on their perceptions of using the experiment, we determined the levels of each of the two independent variables and set the target box color to a more striking red. The second pre-experiment was conducted to verify whether the problems identified in the first pre-experiment were effectively addressed and to further refine the experimental process.

In the formal experiment, the experimenter first introduced the background, purpose and content of the experiment to the participants. Participants signed the "informed consent" form after knowing the basic information of the experiment. The participants were then instructed by the experimenter to fill out a questionnaire with basic personal information and information about their daily touch technology use. The experimenter then explained and demonstrated to the participants how to complete the experimental task by pinch-to-zoom gestures on the prototype software. Before officially starting the timing task, the participant performed some practice trials until they were ready to complete the task without any help. The practice time was limited to about 3 min.

The formal experiment began after the participant signaled that he or she was ready to start the timed task (see Fig. 3). The participant clicked the "Start" button on the screen and the timing began. The object was then zoomed to match the size and position of the target wireframe, and the participant clicked the "Finish" button to stop the timing. Between each set of tasks, the participant could take a short break according to his/her condition.

Fig. 3. A participant was performing the zooming task

5   Result

The data obtained from the experiment were analyzed using a 3×3 repeated measurement ANOVA. Greenhouse-Geisser was used to correct the violation in the spherical test. For post hoc comparisons, all p-values were Bonferroni adjusted.

5.1   Success Rate

The task was considered successful when the size and position of the scaled object was within plus or minus 10 pixels of the target wireframe. The success rate was obtained by dividing the number of successful tasks for each participant by the total number of tasks in the corresponding condition. Figure 4 shows the task success rate for each condition.

In the analysis of variance on the success rate, no significant differences were found. Since the experimental task did not have a time limit for participants to complete, the goal was to scale the object to the target size and location as much as possible.

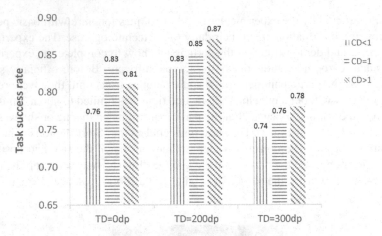

Fig. 4. The success rate for each sensitivity condition.

5.2 Task Completion Time

Figure 5 shows the task completion time for each condition. The ANOVA revealed that the completion time differed depending on control-display gain ($F_{(2,24)} = 29.05$, $p < 0.001$). The result showed that CD > 1 corresponded to the shortest task completion time (Mean = 9.86s, SD = 4.53), CD = 1 was centered (Mean = 11.07s, SD = 4.78), and CD < 1 had the longest task completion time (Mean = 13.90s, SD = 6.42). In terms of zooming triggered finger distance, there was also a significant difference in task completion time ($F_{(2,24)} = 33.23$, $p < 0.001$). The longest time it takes to complete the task with TD = 300dp (Mean = 14.14s, SD = 6.83), then with TD = 0dp (Mean = 10.75s, SD = 4.49) The shortest time for TD = 200dp (Mean = 9.93s, SD = 4.06) There was an interaction effect between control-display gain and zooming triggered finger distance ($F_{(4,24)} = 4.37$, $p = 0.002$).

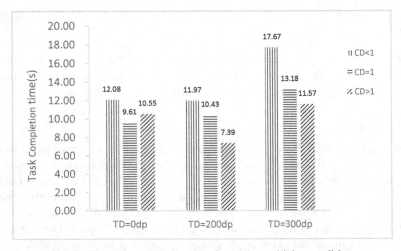

Fig. 5. The task completion time for each sensitivity condition.

Pairwise comparisons of control-display gain and zooming triggered finger distance were further conducted and the result was shown in Table 1.

Table 1. Pairwise comparisons of control-display gain and zooming triggered finger distance

Comparison	Mean$_{(diff)}$	Adj.p
CD > 1 vs. CD = 1	−1.24s	0.024*
CD = 1 vs. CD < 1	−2.83s	<0.000***
CD > 1 vs. CD < 1	−4.07s	<0.000***
TD = 0dp vs. TD = 200dp	0.82s	0.163
TD = 200dp vs. TD = 300dp	−4.21s	<0.000***
TD = 0dp vs. TD = 300dp	−3.39s	<0.000***

Note: * Denotes that Significant at 0.05 level, ** Denotes that Significant at 0.01 level, *** Denotes that Significant at 0.001 level

We then fixed CD or TD at a certain level of interest for a further comparative analysis, and the results are shown in Table 2.

Table 2. Post hoc comparisons fixing independent variable at a certain level

Fixed level	Comparison	Mean$_{(diff)}$	Adj.p
TD = 0dp	CD > 1 vs. CD = 1	0.94s	0.267
	CD = 1 vs. CD < 1	−2.47s	0.004**
	CD > 1 vs. CD < 1	−1.53s	0.074
TD = 200dp	CD > 1 vs. CD = 1	−2.34s	0.001**
	CD = 1 vs. CD < 1	−1.54s	0.024*
	CD > 1 vs. CD < 1	−3.88s	<0.000***
TD = 300dp	CD > 1 vs. CD = 1	−1.61s	0.190
	CD = 1 vs. CD < 1	−4.50s	<0.000***
	CD > 1 vs. CD < 1	−6.10s	<0.000***
CD > 1	TD = 0dp vs. 200dp	3.16s	<0.000***
	TD = 200dp vs. 300dp	−4.18s	<0.000***
	TD = 0dp vs. 300dp	−1.02s	0.211

Note: * Denotes that Significant at 0.05 level, ** Denotes that Significant at 0.01 level, *** Denotes that Significant at 0.001 level

6 Discussion

In order to improve the performance of older adults using pinch-to-zoom gestures, this study attempts to find solutions from control-display gain. And the effect of control-display gain on gesture execution depends on another parameter related to touch sensitivity, zooming triggered finger distance.

For control-display gain, hypothesis 1 was verified. Compared to CD < 1, task completion time was generally reduced by 29% for CD > 1. This demonstrated that improving the sensitivity of touch input could alleviate pinch-to-zoom difficulties caused by inflexible knuckles in older adults [11, 14]. For zooming triggered finger distance, hypothesis 2 was partially confirmed. Under the condition of TD = 200dp, the task corresponded to the highest success rate and the shortest completion time. However, when TD = 300dp, the zooming performance became the worst. The role of zooming triggered finger distance needed to be discussed in more detail under a fixed level of control-display gain.

Figure 6 showed the effect of zooming triggered finger distance on task completion time grouped by control-display gain. Fixing control-display gain at CD > 1, setting the trigger finger distance to a length of 200dp resulted in the best zooming performance, reducing the task completion time by 30% and 36% (p < 0.000 for both) compared to setting no trigger finger distance and setting it to 300dp, respectively. Therefore, we found the optimal configuration of two parameters related to zooming sensitivity for this experiment. With the enhanced control-display gain, setting a 200dp zooming triggered finger distance is helpful for pinch-to-zoom gestures for older adults.

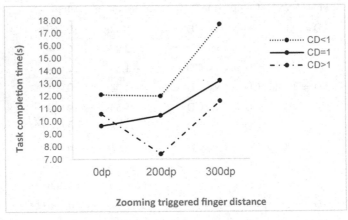

Fig. 6. The effect of TD on task completion time grouped by CD.

There were two possible reasons for this result. Firstly, the control display gain setting (CD = 1), which was commonly used for younger adults, might not be sensitive enough for older adults. The pre-experimental questionnaire showed that 20 of the 27 older participants had experience with smartphones, and 16 of them felt "hard to zoom in" when using the pinch-to-zoom gesture in their daily lives. Therefore, increasing the control display gain to greater than 1 could alleviate this difficulty. Secondly, with higher sensitivity, setting a zooming triggered finger distance actually provided buffering. It avoided the uncontrolled situation where the content is unconsciously zoomed in or out. The initial finger distance of older adults during each zooming task was around 180dp, and this distance was less than but close to 200dp. The two parameters regulating sensitivity influenced each other as a check and balance, contributing the best zooming efficiency at CD > 1 and TD = 200dp.

7 Conclusion

When older adults use pinch-to-zoom gestures to enter zoom commands in the touch screen, the control-display gain value has an impact on zoom performance. Increasing the control display gain and the sensitivity of touch commands can improve task completion performance for older users. However, high sensitivity may compromise controllability. After enhancing the control display gain, setting the trigger scaling two-finger distance to 200dp can act as a buffer to help older users have controlled and effective zooming.

References

1. Farhad, M., MacKenzie, I.S.: Evaluating tap-and-drag: a single-handed zooming method. In: Kurosu, M. (ed.) HCI 2018. LNCS, vol. 10903, pp. 233–246. Springer, Cham (2018). https://doi.org/10.1007/978-3-319-91250-9_18
2. Tsai, T.H., Tseng, K.C., Chang, Y.S.: Testing the usability of smartphone surface gestures on different sizes of smartphones by different age groups of users. Comput. Hum. Behav. **75**(C), 103–116 (2017). https://doi.org/10.1016/j.chb.2017.05.013
3. Wulf, L., Garschall, M., Klein, M., Tscheligi, M.: Young vs old–landscape vs portrait: a comparative study of touch gesture performance. J. Assist. Technol. **9**(3), 136–146 (2015). https://doi.org/10.1108/JAT-10-2014-0029
4. Gao, Q., Sun, Q.: Examining the usability of touch screen gestures for older and younger adults. Hum. Factors **57**(5), 835–863 (2015). https://doi.org/10.1177/0018720815581293
5. Menghi, R., Ceccacci, S., Gullà, F., Cavalieri, L., Germani, M., Bevilacqua, R.: How older people who have never used touchscreen technology interact with a tablet. In: Bernhaupt, R., Dalvi, G., Joshi, A., Balkrishan, D.K., O'Neill, J., Winckler, M. (eds.) INTERACT 2017. LNCS, vol. 10513, pp. 117–131. Springer, Cham (2017). https://doi.org/10.1007/978-3-319-67744-6_8
6. Krehbiel, L.M., Kang, N., Cauraugh, J.H.: Age-related differences in bimanual movements: a systematic review and meta-analysis. Exp. Gerontol. **98**, 199–206 (2017)
7. Hoogendam, Y.Y., van der Lijn, F., Vernooij, M.W., et al.: Older age relates to worsening of fine motor skills: a population-based study of middle-aged and elderly persons. Front. Aging Neurosci. **6**, 259 (2014). https://doi.org/10.3389/fnagi.2014.00259
8. Smith, C.D., Umberger, G.H., Manning, E.L., et al.: Critical decline in fine motor hand movements in human aging. Neurology **53**(7), 1458 (1999). https://doi.org/10.1212/WNL.53.7.1458
9. Kwon, S., Choi, E., Chung, M.K.: Effect of control-to-display gain and movement direction of information spaces on the usability of navigation on small touch-screen interfaces using tap-n-drag. Int. J. Ind. Ergon. **41**(3), 322–330 (2011). https://doi.org/10.1016/j.ergon.2011.02.012

10. Tao, D., Zeng, J., Liu, K., Qu, X.: Effects of control-to-display gain and operation precision requirement on touchscreen operations in vibration environments. Appl. Ergon. **91**, 103293 (2021). https://doi.org/10.1016/j.apergo.2020.103293
11. Claypoole, V.L., Bradford, L.S., Ada, D.M.: Keeping in touch: tactile interface design for older users. Ergon. Des. **24**(1), 18–24 (2016). https://doi.org/10.1177/1064804615611271
12. Lepicard, G., Vigouroux, N.: Comparison between single-touch and multi-touch interaction for older people. In: Miesenberger, K., Karshmer, A., Penaz, P., Zagler, W. (eds.) ICCHP 2012. LNCS, vol. 7382, pp. 658–665. Springer, Heidelberg (2012). https://doi.org/10.1007/978-3-642-31522-0_99
13. Kobayashi, M., Hiyama, A., Miura, T., Asakawa, C., Hirose, M., Ifukube, T.: Elderly user evaluation of mobile touchscreen interactions. In: Campos, P., Graham, N., Jorge, J., Nunes, N., Palanque, P., Winckler, M. (eds.) INTERACT 2011. LNCS, vol. 6946, pp. 83–99. Springer, Heidelberg (2011). https://doi.org/10.1007/978-3-642-23774-4_9
14. Anne, M.P., Ross C., James, D.H.: Exploring the accessibility and appeal of surface computing for older adult health care support. In: Proceedings of the SIGCHI Conference on Human Factors in Computing Systems, pp. 907–916. Association for Computing Machinery, New York (2010). https://doi.org/10.1145/1753326.1753461
15. Géry, C., Daniel, V., Ravin, B., Andy, C.: The impact of control-display gain on user performance in pointing tasks. Hum.-Comput. Interact. **23**(3), 215–250 (2008). https://doi.org/10.1080/07370020802278163
16. Bohan, M., Thompson, S.G., Samuelson, P.J.: Kinematic analysis of mouse cursor positioning as a function of movement scale and joint set. In: Proceeding of the 8th Annual International Conference on Industrial Engineering – Theory, Applications and Practice, Las Vegas, Nevada, USA, November 2003
17. Blanch, R., Guiard, Y., Beaudouin-Lafon, M.: Semantic pointing: improving target acquisition with control-display ratio adaptation. In: Conference on Human Factors in Computing Systems – Proceedings, pp. 519–526 (2008). https://doi.org/10.1145/985692.985758
18. Zhang, Y., Chen, H., Li, W., Wang, Z., Xin, X.: Research on the optimal control-display ratio of smart phone touch screen. In: Rebelo, F., Soares, M.M. (eds.) AHFE 2018. AISC, vol. 777, pp. 382–386. Springer, Cham (2019). https://doi.org/10.1007/978-3-319-94706-8_42

Aging and Social Media

Digital Aging: Reinforcing Normative Masculinities on Instagram

Inês Amaral[1,2]([✉]), Sofia José Santos[3,4], Rita Basílio Simões[1,5], and Maria José Brites[6]

[1] Faculty of Arts and Humanities, University of Coimbra, Coimbra, Portugal
ines.amaral@uc.pt
[2] Communication and Society Research Centre of the University of Minho, Braga, Portugal
[3] Faculty of Economics, University of Coimbra, Coimbra, Portugal
sjs@ces.uc.pt
[4] Centre for Social Sciences, University of Coimbra, Coimbra, Portugal
[5] NOVA Institute of Communication, Lisbon, Portugal
rbasilio@fl.uc.pt
[6] Lusófona University, CICANT, Porto, Portugal
mariajosebrites@ulp.pt

Abstract. Age and gender intersect within power relations dynamics from which arise social hierarchies. Ageist and patriarchal systems perform power within an institutionalization of normative gendered hierarchy, validated by the media and legitimized through the hegemonic social culture. Aging masculinities have been mainly studied in health and social sciences' scientific domains, without the gendered focus. By stemming from a feminist approach, this paper proposed the analysis of co-hashtag networks on Instagram to assess if these digital collective narratives perpetuate or challenge gendered and aging normative perspectives of masculinities. Results show that the semantic structure analyzed intercross age and normative masculinities anchor to soft-porn and patriarchal imaginaries. The data reveal expressions of multiple masculinities such as toxic and hybrid as central to the network. Nevertheless, these hashtags also convey normative understandings of what a man should be by opposition to femininities.

Keywords: Hashtag networks · Gendered digital practices · Hegemonic masculinities · Collective narratives

1 Introduction

Aging is one of the main challenges facing contemporary societies. Its significance and social importance has been leveraged into national and international political discourses and into the domain of public opinion. A growing body of literature highlights the heterogeneity of individual paths of aging. However, media tend to misleadingly depict older people as a homogeneous group, regardless of evident differences considering gender, activity, health, among others [1].

As a result of shared social construction, age and gender are fluid concepts [2–4], intersecting with cultural and social constructions instituted within relational and binary

Q. Gao and J. Zhou (Eds.): HCII 2021, LNCS 12786, pp. 335–348, 2021.
https://doi.org/10.1007/978-3-030-78108-8_25

systems [5]. Feminist scholarship states that there are "multiple intersecting systems of oppression" [3] that conditions people's lives [6]. Discriminatory systems such as patriarchy and ageism intersect with other hierarchical social categories [7], promoting masculinities and femininities ideals that are culturally imagined and validated by the media. These ideals are social representations of what a man or a woman should be [1]. Social facts result from the construction of symbolic representations shared by social systems members inhabiting a universe of specific sociability [8]. Concomitantly, social representations result from socialization and socialization processes directly associated with the collective identity [9]. The "other" is a formal concept [10] that explains social representations validated by society. Therefore, as a shared social construction, social representations classify and categorize phenomena—the objectification of aging as a societal problem associated with stereotypes and anchored in negative social representations [11].

Media and social media narratives co-constitute the social constructions of identities [12]. Therefore, social representations of age gender legitimated by media and social media may narrow or widen stereotypes on specific individuals and groups. Studies show the potential that mainstream media [1, 13, 14], and social media [7, 15], hold in molding society's perceptions and understandings of older people. This article aims to understand how and if digital collective narratives on Instagram perpetuate or challenge gendered and aging normative perspectives of masculinities. Stemming from a feminist approach, this article explores how the intersection of age and gender in digital collective narratives depict aging non-normative masculinities.

1.1 Intersecting Age and Gender: Aging Masculinities

Visibilities and invisibilities are actively produced through political and public discourses. Empirical evidence has demonstrated the invisibility of the gendering of the aging process [9, 16] as opposed to a highlight of normativity in the hegemony of older men considered by society on mostly political stages [1]. For example, in media discourses, older people are underrepresented, and older men are portrayed in line with traditional conceptions of manhood when allowed to be represented [1].

Age and gender intercross disputes within power relations systems, which mold social hierarchies. Patriarchal systems display power dynamics and asymmetric relations within an institutionalization of normative male domination in a gendered hierarchy, legitimized by a hegemonic social culture [7].

Meanings of masculinity and femininity are associated with cultural and geographic diversity. Therefore, "practices and behaviors change as a function of space and time" [2]. As gender is a social construct [17], masculinities are not natural, spontaneous, fixed, or immutable. They stem from dynamic social and cultural processes, being susceptible to being challenged, (re)constructed, and transformed [18]. Considering the patterns of practices through which men and women take a position within the gender hierarchy [5], masculinities can be multiple and even contradictory [2].

As Connell [19] argues, masculinities can be 'multiple'. Even though there is a hegemonic understanding of masculinity, complicit, subordinate, marginal, or subaltern masculinities are structured concerning patriarchal and binary gender hierarchies [20]. There are multiple conceptions and expressions of masculinities, all of which vary according to time, culture, and the individual. Among multiple masculinities, there are four particularly relevant categories of analysis to reflect on gender inequality: hegemonic masculinities [5], toxic masculinities [21], subordinate masculinities [19], and subaltern masculinities [22].

Hegemonic masculinity is associated with rationality, toughness, dominance, strength, power, and leadership. As Connell and Messerschmidt [5] point out, hegemonic masculinity is normative and a socially constructed ideal, which creates a reference from which all men must identify themselves in a relative logic. Complicit masculinities are identified with hegemonic masculinities within a patriarchal system [2].

Toxic masculinity portrays male traits that encourage the legitimacy of violence, domination, devaluation of women, and condemnation of homosexuality [2, 21]. This concept can be interpreted as a declination of hegemonic masculinity since it includes aspects of hegemonic masculinity that are socially destructive and not culturally accepted and, above all, valued [21].

Connell [23] defined subordinate masculinity through gender domination between men's groups, namely (hetero)normative domination. Subordination and domination practices have micro and macro dimensions, with violence and economic and social discrimination as prevalent issues [24].

Subaltern masculinities arise from an unbalanced relation between hegemonic masculinities and those who do not identify with them, frequently identified with characteristics classified as 'feminine' such as sensitivity, emotion, and passivity [24]. Subaltern masculinities arise in a mutual interaction with hegemonic masculinities, although this interplay is uneven in the social order [22]. Subaltern masculinities are also defined as marginalized, including male individuals who are not in line with hegemonic masculinity's normativity [24]. The marginality to which other masculinities are subordinated derives from social and power relations negotiated with hegemonic masculinities [24]. Therefore, "this form of masculinity is discriminated against due to the subordinate condition of social class or ethnicity. Marginalization is produced in exploited or oppressed groups that may share many of the characteristics of hegemonic masculinity, but that are socially unauthorized" [24].

Hearn [25] argues that studies on older people have remained ungendered or focused on older women. The author states that "a focus on older men needs to be considered in the context of a change of and about men and has been occurring in the full range of social awareness, from the global to the societal, local, domestic, and personal, as well as in cultural, media and academic sites and forums". Thompson and Langendoerfer [26] contend "the gendered order of the time urged each man to adopt the arrangement of the separate spheres resonant within the nation's patriarchal culture".

Aging masculinities have been understudied in different scientific domains [25, 26]. The main studies on aging masculinities focus on health and social sciences' scientific domains, frequently converging on the body and sexuality [27]. Studies on older people and digital are mostly ungendered and have focused on access and use [28, 29], practices [30], active aging [31], intergenerational uses [32–35], gaming [36], mobile devices [37] and apps [38].

1.2   (Re)Negotiating Age and Gender Through Mediated Interfaces

Contemporary digital cultures promote media reconfigurations from which the technology shapes and are shaped by society [39]. Within social media mediated interfaces, people become nodes connected by information. New social objects that derive from technological affordances promote complex interactions based on content and metadata. Therefore, social practices result from the (re)construction of objects and subjects. New bonds are materialized in connecting nodes, edges, and networks based on metadata, content, and affordances. Social networks formed in social media are means of circulating content and conversation, depending on technical platforms' appropriation. A social network can be interpreted as a structure composed of individuals connected by one or more interdependence types. Facebook's like or Twitter retweet, for example, can be seen as an expression of interest but, essentially, as a social sign. There are standards of connectivity on and in the network that have transformed digital culture. Content is the new relational bond of communities and networks, replacing symmetrical social relations as in networks of friends.

Furthermore, individuals are not connected only by social relationships but by context, shared experiences, and shared interests. The new ties focus on content and conversation, highlighting the graphs of friendship networks' interest and activity [40]. Hence, it can be inferred that the content and appropriation of this content can also translate bonds of social relationships established online and are carried out in networks and communities.

Hashtag networks in social media (e.g. on Twitter or Instagram) describe structures that allow the analysis of conversational interactions as networks of users that produce sociability - interaction phenomena or the capacity for the foundation of groups and the construction of networks supported in social relations [41]. Asymmetric social networks whose relational link is the content and not the structure of following, such as hashtag networks, maximize the idea of "individualism in a network" [42, 43] and isolate social properties from digital communication. The appropriation of the network by social networks of content outlines a critical barometer from global audiences' perspective. New social ties focus on content and conversation. Therefore, metadata and content replace reciprocity or intention as a tie, considering the centrality of the appropriation of technological affordances in creating social networks that go beyond the mere technical potential of platforms, such as following or friends networks.

Socio-technical spheres are organized in large-scale action networks that shed light on institutionalized collective actions [44, 45], which challenge the nature of collective action [46] within micro and macro politics [47]. Collective narrative processes on social media arise from this framework. Through a hashtag structure, social media aggregate individual expressions and statements into a networked collective narrative, enabling streaming of (re)negotiations of meanings of gender identities.

Users engage with social media's technicity and imaginaries, embodying them into their daily lives. As mediated interfaces, digital platforms operate a "reconfiguration of socio-technical practices" [48] through users' engagement with their technicity and imaginaries by the (re)negotiation of gender and sexual identities. Social media enhances

cultures and subcultures of sociability, where intimacy and sexuality are imagined, reproduced, and reconstructed on cultural and ideological grounds. By stemming from rein-
vented structures and social hierarchies, social media challenges normative and hegemonic masculinities by re-engendering digital social spaces. Social media uses and
imaginaries rely on collective narratives across hashtags streaming.

Considering that masculinities are "context-dependent and culturally constrained"
[49], a growing body of literature has focused on the (re)negotiation of masculinities in
digital environments [50–54].

Men's gendered practices and identities are mediated through interfaces across social
media platforms and mobile apps of dating, lifestyle, fitness and health, and gaming.
Technological affordances of social media and apps may enhance 'toxic technocultures' across the manosphere [54] as well as challenge hegemonic masculinities [55].
According to Light [51], social media platforms facilitate spaces for "non-normative,
queer masculinities and relations". Rodriguez, Huemmer, and Blumell [55] argue that
the digital ecosystem may "deconstruct and understand masculinities within heteronormative digital media". Networked masculinities have been studied to understand how
masculinities are produced, reproduced, and coopted in the digital realm. Through analyzing YouTube comments to Gillette's short film We Believe, Trott [56] found out that
"several mechanisms of digital hegemony are identified as strategies utilized by a collective of men (and in some cases, women) that work to reassert masculine and patriarchal
power in the digital sphere". Nevertheless, research on gendered identities and practices
in mediated interfaces has not focused on older men.

Santos, Amaral, and Brites [7] studied how men and masculinities' representations
interact with age and ageism in hashtag networks on Twitter. Results reveal that "the patriarchal discourses intersect with ageism, perpetuating stereotypes". Amaral, Santos, and
Brites [2] analyzed hashtag networks on Instagram to understand how collective narratives represent masculinities and intergenerational identities and relations. The analysis
revealed that power relations tend to be anchored in discourses of heteronormativity,
although multiple and hybrid masculinities are also present in the analyzed stream.

2   Method

This article aims to understand if digital collective narratives may continue or challenge
gendered and aging normative perspectives of masculinities by exploring the intersection of age and gender on a semantic structure of hashtags on Instagram. "How does
the intersection of age and gender in digital collective narratives depict aging non-
normative masculinities?" is the research question that guides this paper. The study
relies on a dataset of posts indexed with the hashtag #fashiongrandpas, used in different appropriations of Instagram's affordances to (re)negotiate gendered practices and
male identities in an intergenerational perspective. Data was gathered through the tool
Instagram Scrapper. Dataset was collected from the public Instagram stream consists
of randomly selected 1068 media items with 3500 co-hashtags of #fashiongrandpas
published between 2011-12-18 and 2019-11-23.

The methodological approach is social network analysis combined with content
analysis, aiming to 1) identify the leading hashtags and categories of #fashiongrandpas

streaming, and 2) map semantic structures by examining if age and gender may intersect in the co-hashtag network to assess if aging normative perspectives of masculinities are perpetuated or challenged in the dataset. It is considered a co-hashtag when two hashtags appear in the same post. Therefore, on this type of network, a node is a hashtag and an edge is a co-occurrence. Conducting a co-hashtag analysis based on a specific hashtag provides data on how subjects are related to others.

The co-hashtag network was analyzed using Gephi software to generate an undirected graph to explore relations between hashtags, identify communities, visually represent them and identify bridging nodes.

3   Results and Discussion

The dataset consists of 1068 Instagram posts (1052 images and 16 videos) indexed with the hashtag #fashiongrandpas. 3500 co-hashtags from the main hashtag were identified. The data were first analyzed using the content analysis methodology using the MAXQDA software to identify hashtags' frequencies and categories.

Table 1 shows the ten most common co-hashtags. It has been found that hashtags are used to index content to streaming from three different categories: fashion (#style, n = 222, #fashion n = 216, #menswear n = 163), Instagram (#instadaily n = 114, #instamood n = 108, #followme n = 107, #nofilter n = 103) and soft porn (#samatized n = 105, #budapestsam n = 104).

Table 1. Top 10 co-hashtags.

Hashtags	Frequency
#style	222
#fashion	216
#mewswear	163
#instadaily	114
#instamood	108
#followme	107
#samatized	105
#budapestsam	104
#nofilter	103
#lifeassam	103

Content analysis of the media items was carried out using the MAXQDA software to assess which hashtags were most frequent (>50). Through this analysis, a sample of 46 hashtags with 3931 co-occurrences was identified. Hashtags were categorized into 11 categories, as shown in Fig. 1. The least frequent hashtags (<50) are 3454 with 2319 co-occurrences.

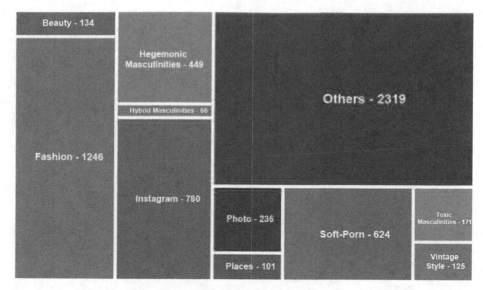

Fig. 1. Categories of co-hashtags.

#fashiongrandpas streaming is associated with fashion issues but also with an intergenerational approach to male identity. Co-hashtags categories reveal that the dominant discourses on this streaming are about fashion, soft-porn, and hegemonic masculinities. Instrumental categories such as Instagram, photo, and places aim to index content to multiple streams and gather broader audiences. It was also found discourses on toxic masculinities and hybrid masculinities, specifically transgender identities. Beauty and vintage categories are closely related to fashion and connected to multiple and hybrid masculinities.

The co-hashtag network was analyzed using Gephi software to generate an undirected graph to explore relations between hashtags, identify communities, visually represent them and identify bridging nodes. The undirected graph is a network that has 3501 distinct nodes (hashtags) with 6250 edges (co-occurrences). The collected data show an interesting image of the network's macrostructure, as shown in Fig. 2. The network representation reveals a nucleus of small, highly clustered groups in the center of the graph and nodes with less connectivity at the borders.

Diameter is the maximum geodesic distance of an entire connected network. This measure allows us to get a sense of the structure's size and list how many steps are necessary to cross the system: how far away are the most distant nodes. As Table 2 shows, the network's diameter under analysis is 4, which means that the social system's dimension is not significant and that four paths are needed to connect the two most distant nodes. The average path length in this co-hashtag network is 2,016.

The modularity of a network measures the strength of a community, taking into account the degree distribution. This agglomerative method detects communities, which are defined as groups of nodes that, internally, are densely more connected than the rest of the network. Each node is included in a single community. Granovetter [57] showed that the communities' connections tend to be strong and that the ties between these

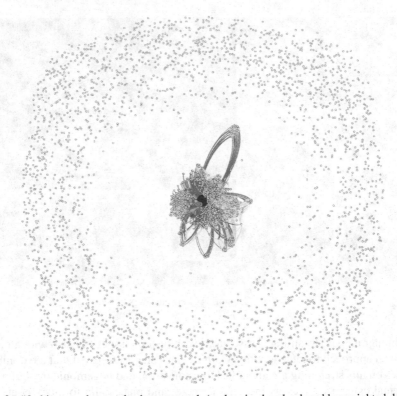

Fig. 2. #fashiongrandpas co-hashtag network (nodes sized and colored by weighted degree).

Table 2. Network metrics.

Metric	
Average degree	3,57
Average weight degree	26,219
Diameter	4
Average path length	2,016
Density	0,0001
Modularity	0,378
Communities	2693

groups are mostly weak. The network's modularity (0,378) is significant because it is close to 0,4 [40]. This data reveals that the measured value (0,377) indicates a complex internal structure organized in 2693 communities. Although there have been identified eleven qualitative categories for the co-hashtags, the co-hashtag network analysis allows observing that these categories merged into five major semantic communities when considered their modularity properties. Results show that community 1 aggregates fashion, places, and Instagram's hashtags. In community 2 it is possible to observe a merging of fashion, beauty, vintage, and hybrid masculinities. Community 3 assembles toxic masculinities and Instagram hashtags into one semantic stream quite central in the network. The larger community (4) comprehends semantic indexation focused on places, photo, and Instagram's hashtags. Community 5 is the more complex as it evidences direct connections between discourses around toxic masculinities, hegemonic masculinities, soft porn, fashion, and Instagram's hashtags. The use of Instagram's hashtags in almost all communities allows identifying these hashtags' potential to aggregate content to exponentiate audiences. Figure 3 visually represents the communities found in the network following a visual parameter of range weighted degree.

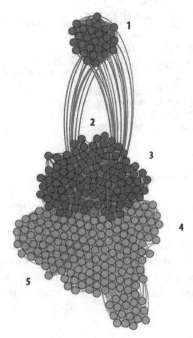

Fig. 3. Network's communities (nodes colored by community).

Density is very low (0,001), which shows high fragmentation and potential for dividing hashtags into subgroups. The comparison between this measure and density allows inferring that there are central hashtags. By correlating the data on density and diameter with the average path length and number of short paths (598150), the main conclusion is that the network is fragmented, and the interactions are not established in an adjacency logic. The potential for expanding audiences lies in hashtags that are common to several subgroups and can be identified as bridging nodes.

The eigenvector's centrality seeks to find the most central nodes in terms of the network's overall structure. Each node's location concerning each dimension is defined as eigenvalue and the collection of these values is called eigenvector [40]. Calculating the eigenvector centrality distribution of the network's centrality in Gephi, we find 28 nodes with higher centrality, as shown in Fig. 4. Among the 28 nodes, there are 377 edges, which corresponds to 6.03% of the total network connections.

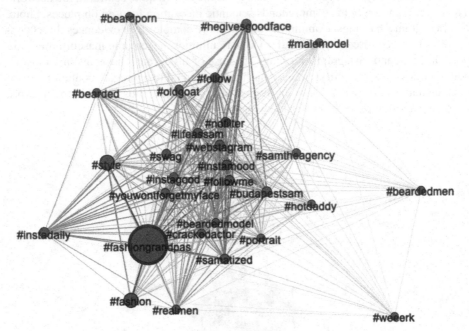

Fig. 4. Bridging nodes (nodes sized and colored by eigenvector centrality).

The eigenvector centrality distribution enabled the bridging nodes of this semantic network to be identified and, consequently, the nodes that are central to this network. In a clear intersection between age and gender, the network is organized around hashtags that refer to soft porn, hegemonic masculinities, toxic masculinities, hybrid masculinities, and Instagram hashtags.

4   Conclusions

This paper aimed to analyze digital collective narratives to examine if co-hashtag networks perpetuate or challenge gendered and aging normative perspectives of masculinities. Stemming from a feminist approach and by exploring intersections of age and gender in a co-hashtag network, the study aimed to answer the research question: "How does the intersection of age and gender in digital collective narratives depict aging non-normative masculinities?".

Through the combination of content analysis and social network analysis, results show that the analyzed semantic structure is centered on an intersection between age and patriarchy evident in dominant discourses anchored to imaginary about soft-porn (#hegivesgoodface, #budapestsam, #hotdaddy), toxic (#oldgoat, #realmen) and hegemonic masculinities (#bearded, #beardporn, #beardmen). There are also prevalent hashtags about fashion (#style, #fashion, #malemodel), beauty (#samtheagency), vintage

(#crackedactor), and hybrid masculinities (#weeerk). The analysis shows that online expressions of male identities tend to perpetuate hegemonic masculinity. Therefore, power relations are perpetuated in images that support discourses of heteronormativity as an aggregating element of male group identity.

Data allows to conclude that hashtags associated with Instagram, photo, and places are merely instrumental in the analyzed structure. In addition to the main hashtag #fashiongrandpas, the center of the network are expressions that perpetuate the stereotyping associated with masculinities, contributing to the manosphere within a triangulation between hegemonic, toxic, and hybrid masculinities aggregated around soft porn and fashion.

It was found that the frequency and relevance of hashtags that challenge the normative perspective of gender and aging are reduced. Although expressions of hybrid masculinities are found, data show their connection to soft porn. However, it should be emphasized that the data defies the logic of the 'real man', associating multiple masculinities with issues of fashion and beauty. Still, these associations are heteronormative and do not challenge the gendered perspective of aging associated with how a man should be and behave.

Future studies should consider analyzing intersections between age and masculinity discourses across digital platforms to assess how connective actions are incorporated into the manosphere.

Acknowledgments. We acknowledged the support of the project "(De) Coding Masculinities: Towards an enhanced understanding of media's role in shaping perceptions of masculinities in Portugal" (Reference PTDC/COM-CSS/31740/2017) in retrieving the data.

References

1. Amaral, I., Santos, S.J., Daniel, F., Filipe, F.: (In)visibilities of Men and aging in the media: discourses from Germany and Portugal. In: Zhou, J., Salvendy, G. (eds.) HCII 2019. LNCS, vol. 11593, pp. 20–32. Springer, Cham (2019). https://doi.org/10.1007/978-3-030-22015-0_2
2. Amaral, I., Santos, S.J., Brites, M.J.: Mapping intergenerational masculinities on instagram. In: Gao, Q., Zhou, J. (eds.) Human Aspects of IT for the Aged Population. Technology and Society. HCII 2020, Lecture Notes in Computer Science, vol. 12209, pp. 3–16 (2020)
3. Edström, M.: Visibility patterns of gendered ageism in the media buzz: a study of the representation of gender and age over three decades. Feminist Media Stud. 18(1), 77–93 (2018)
4. Lorber, J., Farrell, S.A.: The Social Construction of Gender. Sage, Newbury Park (1991)
5. Connell, R.W., Messerschmidt, J.W.: Hegemonic masculinity: rethinking the concept. Gend. Soc. 19(6), 829–859 (2005)
6. Crenshaw, K.: Demarginalizing the intersection of race and sex: a black feminist critique of antidiscrimination doctrine, feminist theory and antiracist politics. Univ. Chicago Legal Forum 139, 139–167 (1989)
7. Santos, S.J., Amaral, I., Brites, M.J.: Masculinities and ageing: deconstructing online representations among portuguese speaking users. In: Gao, Q., Zhou, J. (eds.) HCII 2020. LNCS, vol. 12209, pp. 89–100. Springer, Cham (2020). https://doi.org/10.1007/978-3-030-50232-4_7

8. Durkeim, É.: The Rules of Sociological Method. The Free of Glenco, New York (1964)
9. Daniel, F., Caetano, E., Monteiro, R., Amaral, I.: Representações sociais do envelhecimento ativo num olhar genderizado. Análise Psicol. **34**(4), 353–364 (2016)
10. Moscovici, S.: Social Cognition: Perspectives on Everyday Understanding. Academic Press, London (1981)
11. Daniel, F., Antunes, A., Amaral, I.: Representações sociais da velhice. Análise. Psicológica **33**(3), 291–301 (2015)
12. Woodward, K.: Identidade e diferença: uma introdução teórica e conceitual. In: Silva, T.T. (ed.) Identidade e diferença: a perspectiva dos estudos culturais, pp. 7–71. Vozes, Petrópolis (2000)
13. Gerbner, G., Gross, L., Signorielli, N., Morgan, M.: Aging with television: images on television drama and conceptions of social reality. J. Commun. **30**, 37–47 (1980)
14. Vernon, J.A., Williams, J.A., Phillips, T., Wilson, J.: Media stereotyping: a comparison of the way elderly women and men are portrayed on prime-time television. J. Women Aging **2**(4), 55–68 (1991)
15. Makita, M., Mas-Bleda, A., Stuart, E., Thelwall, M.: Ageing, old age and older adults: a social media analysis of dominant topics and discourses. Ageing Soc. **41**(2), 1–26 (2019)
16. Amaral, I., Daniel, F., Abreu, S.G.: Policies for gender equality in Portugal: contributions to a framework for older women. Revista Prisma Soc. **22**, 346–363 (2018)
17. Butler, J.: Gender Trouble: Feminism and the Subversion of Identity. Routledge, New York (1990)
18. Boni, F.: Framing media masculinities: men's lifestyle magazines and the biopolitics of the male body. Euro. J. Commun. **17**(4), 465–478 (2002)
19. Connell, R.W.: Masculinities. University of California Press, Berkeley (1995)
20. Hopkins, P., Noble, G.: Masculinities in place: situated identities, relations and intersectionality. Soc. Cult. Geogr. **10**(8), 811–819 (2009)
21. Kupers, T.A.: Toxic masculinity as a barrier to mental health treatment in prison. J. Clin. Psychol. **61**(6), 713–724 (2005)
22. Kimmel, M.S.: A produção simultânea de masculinidades hegemônicas e subalternas. Horizontes Antropológicos **4**(9), 103–117 (1998)
23. Connell, R.W.: Masculinities, 2nd edn. University of California Press, Berkeley (2005)
24. Januário, S.B.: Masculinidades em (re) construção: Gênero. Corpo e Publicidade. LabCom. IFP, Covilhã (2016)
25. Hearn, J.: Imaging the aging of men. In: Featherstone, M., Wernick, A. (eds.) Images of Aging: Cultural Representations of Later Life, pp. 97–114. Routledge, London (1995)
26. Thompson Jr., E.H., Langendoerfer, K.B.: Older men's blueprint for being a man. Men Masculinities **19**(2), 119–147 (2016)
27. Jackson, D.: Exploring Aging Masculinities: The Body, Sexuality and Social Lives. Palgrave MacMillan, New York (2016)
28. Loos, E.: Generational use of new media and the (ir)relevance of age. In: Colombo, F., Fortunati, L. (eds.) Broadband Society and Generational Changes, pp. 259–273. Peter Lang, Berlin (2011)
29. Loos, E.: Senior citizens: digital immigrants in their own country? Observatorio (OBS*) **6**(1), 01–023 (2012)
30. Fernández-Ardévol, M., Rosales, A.: Older people, smartphones and whatsApp. In: Vicent, J., Haddon, L. (eds) Smartphone Cultures, pp. 55–68. Routledge, Abingdon (2018)
31. Amaral, I., Daniel, F.: The use of social media among senior citizens in Portugal: active ageing through an intergeneration approach. In: Zhou, J., Salvendy, G. (eds.) ITAP 2018. LNCS, vol. 10926, pp. 422–434. Springer, Cham (2018). https://doi.org/10.1007/978-3-319-92034-4_32

32. Aroldi, P.: Generational belonging between media audiences and ICT users. In: Colombo, F., Fortunati, L. (eds.) Broadband Society and Generational Changes, pp. 51–68. Peter Lang, Frankfurt am Main (2011)
33. Bolin, G., Skogerbø, E.: Age, generation and the media. Northern Lights **11**, 3–14 (2013)
34. Amaral, I., Brites, M.J.: Trends on the digital uses and generations. In: Proceedings of INTED2019 Conference, pp. 5109–5115. Valencia (2019)
35. Brites, M.J., Amaral, I., Santos, S.J.: Intergenerational perspectives on audiences studies: from youth to senior representations. In: Gao, Q., Zhou, J. (eds.) HCII 2020. LNCS, vol. 12208, pp. 579–588. Springer, Cham (2020). https://doi.org/10.1007/978-3-030-50249-2_41
36. Loos, E., Kaufman, D.: Positive impact of exergaming on older adults' mental and social well-being: in search of evidence. In: Zhou, J., Salvendy, G. (eds.) ITAP 2018. LNCS, vol. 10927, pp. 101–112. Springer, Cham (2018). https://doi.org/10.1007/978-3-319-92037-5_9
37. Rosales, A., Fernández-Ardèvol, M., Comunello, F., Mulargia, S., Ferran-Ferrer, N.: Older people and smartwatches, initial experiences. El Profesional de la Información **26**(3), 457–463 (2017)
38. Sharma, A., Samanta, T.: Crafting "youthful" desire, "doing" masculinity: narratives of middle-aged to older men in grindr grid and offline spaces in Mumbai. India. Ageing Int. **45**(4), 361–379 (2020)
39. Livingstone, S.: Critical debates in internet studies: reflections on an emerging field, London: LSE Research Online (2025). http://eprints.lse.ac.uk/1011. Accessed 22 Feb 2021
40. Amaral, I.: Redes Sociais na Internet: Sociabilidades Emergentes. LabCom. IFP, Covilhã (2016)
41. Ferréol, G.: Sociologia: Léxico das Ciências Sociais. Porto Editora, Porto (2007)
42. Wellman, B., Gulia, M.: Net Surfers don't ride alone: virtual communities as communities. In: Wellman, B. (ed.) Networks in the Global Village, pp. 331–366. Westview, Boulder (1999)
43. Recuero, R.: Redes Sociais na Internet. Sulina Editora Meridional, Porto Alegre (2009)
44. Bennett, W.L., Segerberg, A.: The logic of connective action: digital media and the personalization of contentious politics. Inf. Commun. Soc. **15**(5), 739–768 (2012)
45. Kavada, A.: Social movements and political agency in the digital age: a communication approach. Media Commun. **4**(4), 8–12 (2016)
46. Bimber, B.: Three prompts for collective action in the context of digital media. Polit. Commun. **34**(1), 6–20 (2017)
47. Murru, M.F., Amaral, I., Brites, M.J., Seddighi, G.: Bridging the gap between micro and macro forms of engagement: three emerging trends in research on audience participation. In: Das, R., Ytre-Arne, B. (eds.) The Future of Audiences, pp. 161–177. Springer, Cham (2018)
48. boyd, D.: Social media: a phenomenon to be analyzed. Soc. Media + Soc. **1**(1) (2015)
49. Springer, K.W., Mouzon, D.M.: One step toward more research on aging masculinities: operationalizing the hegemonic masculinity for older men scale (HMOMS). J. Men's Stud. **27**(2), 183–203 (2019)
50. Lohan, M., Faulkner, W.: Masculinities and technologies: Some introductory remarks. Men Masculinities **6**(4), 319–329 (2004)
51. Light, B.: Networked masculinities and social networking sites: a call for the analysis of men and contemporary digital media. Masculinities Soc. Change **2**(3), 245–265 (2013)
52. Schmitz, R.M., Kazyak, E.: Masculinities in cyberspace: an analysis of portrayals of manhood in men's rights activist websites. Soc. Sci. **5**(18) (2016)
53. Bonner-Thompson, C.: 'The meat market': production and regulation of masculinities on the Grindr grid in Newcastle-upon-Tyne, UK. Gen. Place Cult. **24**(11), 1611–1625 (2017)
54. Ging, D.: Alphas, betas, and incels: Theorizing the masculinities of the manosphere. Men Masculinities **22**(4), 638–657 (2017)
55. Rodriguez, N.S., Huemmer, J., Blumell, L.E.: Mobile masculinities: an investigation of networked masculinities in gay dating apps. Masculinities Soc. Change **5**(3), 241–267 (2016)

56. Trott, V.A.: 'Gillette: The best a beta can get': Networking hegemonic masculinity in the digital sphere. New Media Soc. 1461444820978293 (2020)

57. Granovetter, M.: The strength of weak ties. Am. J. Soc. **78**(6), 1360–1380 (1973)

Generational Perspectives on EU Documents Tackling Disinformation

Maria José Brites[1]([⊠]) [iD], Inês Amaral[2,3] [iD], Rita Basílio Simões[2,4] [iD],
and Sofia José Santos[5] [iD]

[1] Lusófona University, CICANT, Porto, Portugal
mariajosebrites@ulp.pt
[2] Faculty of Arts and Humanities, University of Coimbra, Coimbra, Portugal
ines.amaral@uc.pt, rbasilio@fl.uc.pt
[3] Communication and Society Studies Centre, University of Minho, Braga, Portugal
[4] Nova Institute of Communication, Lisboa, Portugal
[5] Faculty of Economics, Centre for Social Studies, University of Coimbra, Coimbra, Portugal
sjs@ces.uc.pt

Abstract. The last decade witnessed great transformations concerning the internet with the perils of disinformation becoming key concerns among political actors. Within this framework, the EU has developed efforts to approach these digital challenges taking into account the political challenges. These challenges are related with elections and trust in information campaigns and media coverage. However, they don't take in consideration a generational approach. This has an impact on effective and valuable relationships between citizens and the EU demands. This chapter intends to shed light on Europe's efforts to address disinformation from a generational-driven perspective, focusing on five key documents that the EU has created in 2018 to tackle disinformation as, for political reasons, 2018 was a strategic year to engage citizens in the democratic process anticipating EU parliament elections. By means of document and thematic analysis, this chapter points to the poor achievement of this objective, given that the analyzed documents weakly address different generational groups, their specific problems, and needs. It thus calls for more generational-oriented communication policies.

Keywords: Disinformation · Generations · Media literacy · EU

1 Introduction

The last decade was of great transformations in regard to the overwhelming uses of the internet, its connections to our daily life and the growing awareness of the impossibility to control all digital environments. Within this context, disinformation has been one of the key concerns among political decision-makers, namely the EU. Indeed, as a key player and norm-diffuser actor, the EU has developed strategies, reports [1–4] and recommendations [2–4] in order to approach digital information challenges taking into account different circumstances and perspectives but leaving somehow unattended citizens' generational specific needs [5].

Q. Gao and J. Zhou (Eds.): HCII 2021, LNCS 12786, pp. 349–360, 2021.
https://doi.org/10.1007/978-3-030-78108-8_26

The way one produces accesses and interprets information depends on one's own subjectivity, being age one of its main features. As age is relevant in one's identity and specificity, generations both synthesis and perform specific collective identities [6], with media contributing to these constructions [7]. That is why, according to Mannheim [8], media environments can be identified as "generational contexts", following the argument that age-based groups similarly manage their experience. Therefore, generations should be seen as something situational and contextual, i.e., diverse in terms of their definition and depending on their own context. Therefore, as Amaral and Brites [7] argue based upon Mannheim [9], This continuing character of generational changes amplifies the notion of a "generational situation", which refers to key terms such as "generational site" or "generation status", "generational actuality" or "generational context", and "generational units" or groups of people from the same age with similar contexts.

Stemming from the idea that generational perspectives and understandings are key to produce, engage and interpret information, this chapter analyses EU's efforts to address disinformation through looking specifically into the generational language of five key documents produced by the EU in 2018 (see 4. Results) - a key year, because of the political environment with Brexit referendum, Trump election and upcoming European Parliament elections, concerning engaging citizens in European politics - to tackle disinformation. To put the analysis forward, this chapter is structured into three sections. The first one gives a glimpse on the existing literature review on these topics, addressing the digital realm, (dis)information, and generational contexts. The second part explains methods and showcases analysed data. Finally, the last section discusses the results and proposes a generational-oriented approach.

2 Literature Review

The digital realm opened the floor to different new actors and dynamics, offering new ways of connection. Indeed, the current media ecosystem's configuration encourages more participants to the gatekeeping process [9], opening citizens' possibility to give their testimony influencing public debate and political action [5]. However, contrary to the traditional gatekeepers, most of these new actors are not attached to consensually established professional codes of conduct. Instead, they follow non-professional criteria for engaging and (re)producing content-based mostly upon personal preferences, emotions [9], and ideologies. Within this environment, the value of the information disseminated turns out to be determined not necessarily by the product's value but rather by the interactions a given content generates [9]. Therefore, emotional, and personal logics of consumption, production, and content sharing emerge [10].

On par with the democratisation of the capacity to produce and disseminate content, there has been an increase of news that purposely distorts information - which is commonly labelled as 'disinformation' - constituting a growing problem for the functioning of modern democracies [1].

According to the European Commission (EC) [2] disinformation is defined as "false, inaccurate, or misleading information designed, presented and promoted to intentionally cause public harm or for profit" with the danger of harm comprising "threats to democratic political processes and values, which can specifically target a variety of sectors, such as health, science, education, finance and more". Malevolence and malpractice are of course part of this equation. Malevolence indicates provocations and speechmaking of the fakers and malpractice denotes to the altered and devious business circuits of advertising online and the profiling power of algorithms [3]. When considering malware, it is related to the robotized tools available for hacking and capturing information systems unbeknownst of their users [11].

"This forward-looking definition places malinformation in the whole ecosystem of information disorders (including radicalization, hate speech, surveillance...) and other risks of harm (harassment, addiction...). They are part of the digital citizenship issue, associated with online and offline freedoms, especially freedom of expression. They relate to this "grey zone" of harms that are not illegal or illegitimate in most countries but that affect human rights and threaten quality education (...) since the integrity of information is altered and the integrity of elections since peace and democracy (...) are undermined" [11].

One of the central pieces that sustain 'disinformation' is fake news -, the buzz word imposed by Donald Trump during the 2016 elections [11]. Despite the intuitive nature of the concept, it is relevant to take note that.

"While the term fake news has emerged as a key signifier for the larger challenges facing journalism and news organizations today, it has obscured key factors-namely the commodification of platforms, the blending of personal and public information in social networks, and the masking of advertising and data extraction online-that are contributing to a so-called crisis in news" [12].

"Fake news" is an oversimplification of the multifaceted problem of information disorders. One of the problems that this idea of "fake news" comprises is that journalists' main actors are at the heart of the problem. However, "disinformation does not include journalistic errors, satire, or parody. Fake news and online disinformation are not per se illegal and thus are not covered by existing legislation or self-regulation although some member states are looking into legislative actions" [3]. Existing discussions about 'fake news' incorporate a range of information categories.

"This includes relatively low-risk forms such as honest mistakes made by reporters, partisan political discourse, and the use of clickbait headlines, to high-risk forms such as for instance foreign states or domestic groups that would try to undermine the political process in European Member States and the European Union, through the use of various forms of malicious fabrications, infiltration of grassroots groups, and automated amplification techniques" [2]

Media and Information Literacy [4] is one form of addressing the problem of disinformation, in association with transparency, enhanced practices of accountability and trust, and algorithm changes [2]. In the short and long term, the role of platforms, news media and fact-checking organizations and the role of public authorities are also pivotal to these efforts [2]. Brites and colleagues [13], after a wide range of stakeholder's consultation (from school libraries to media regulators) on audiences and forms of participation, considered that a combination of prescriptive regulatory approaches and media literacy activities grounded in the society are relevant and potentially successful approaches to the subject.

As a normative global power, the EU sees itself as a promoter of universal norms and principles in its relations with non-members [14], but also within its own borders. Indeed, human rights and democracy are cornerstones of the EU's identity [15], with the media and the digital realm performing a key role. In this sense, the escalation of disinformation "and the gravity of the threat have sparked growing awareness and concerns in civil society" crosscutting different continents and with particular attention from the EU [3]. In 2018, the European Commission proposed a series of measures to tackle disinformation online, with the aim of "Ensuring transparency about sponsored content, in particular political advertising, as well as restricting targeting options for political advertising and reducing revenues for purveyors of disinformation" [3].

The new environment has brought into the equation the skills and dispositions, or literacies, that are most desirable to engage citizens in media literacy in the current ubiquitous media age [12]. Agreeing to Paul Mihailidis [12], "literacies associated with critical news engagement have emerged from the broader field of media literacy, which focuses on critical inquiry, analysis, reflection and production". These aptitudes related to news, are concentrated on "assessing credibility, accuracy, and bias of news stories, and the role of the journalist as a storyteller and reporter of facts" [12].

As literacy skills are discussed, issues and studies on generational uses of the media and the digital realm also emerge. As the definition of generation is not static [6, 8], Bolin and Skogerbø [16], Aroldi [17], Colombo and Fortunati [18], and Loos, Haddon and Mante-Meijer [19] showed that media experiences in an intergenerational perspective surpass the traditional labels of "digital natives" and "digital immigrants" [20, 21] with an impact on media literacy. In fact, as Amaral and Brites [7] argue, "older people have experienced many societal and technological changes, adults follow technology since they were young in the perspective of living with digital media". There is a fluid process of generational identity-making backed by media experiences [22]. In this sense, media education cannot be focused exclusively on one generation and must be addressed in lifelong learning as well as an intergenerational approach" [7].

3   Context and Method

The last decade was of great transformations in regard to the overwhelming uses of the internet and its connections to our daily life on par with a growing understanding of the impossibility to control all digital environments. At the European level, the Digital Single Market strategy (created on May 2015) was created based upon three fundamental pillars: better digital access (consumers and businesses) across Europe; the creation of accurate conditions to improve digital networks and innovative services; and the maximization of the growing offers and perspectives the digital economy is believed to entail. While promises on the digital realm were burgeoning, the Brexit referendum (2016) and the US presidential campaign (2016) on par with the Cambridge Analytica scandal started to shed light on the perils of the digital realm concerning politics, pointing to the need to pay particular attention to disinformation and information disorders as well as to the data-driven complex dynamics. Political preoccupations entered, then, in an explicit way into the EU media literacy and (dis)information agendas.

The beginning of the road of the EU towards a consistent disinformation plan dates back to 2015 when the European Council invited the High Representative to develop an action plan to address Russia's ongoing disinformation campaigns. It also started to improve and indicate that social networks and digital platforms must ensure transparent practices and protection of citizens' privacy and personal data. These efforts were done bearing in mind the challenges that the cross borders and country specificities differences entailed, and considering at the same time that these contingencies implied the need for a European approach and coordinated actions. This was one of the reasons EC created in 2017 the High-Level Expert Group to recommend policies and guidelines on this matter. They delivered a report on the 12th of March 2018. At the same time, the EC also attempted to listen to European citizens in a large consultation process whose results were presented in the Eurobarometer.

Recurring to document analysis combined with thematic analysis [23], this article examines five documents that the European Union created in 2018 to tackle disinformation (see Table 1). For political reasons, 2018 was a strategic year to engage citizens in the democratic process anticipating EU parliament elections.

In order to identify the presence/absence of a generational perspective in regard to EU disinformation policies, it explored the following research questions: 1) Is there any generational perspective that these documents include?; 2) If they so, what type of generational perspectives are put forward?; and 3) How are the main topics of concern articulated with the different generational contexts?

In line with these questions and in order to put forward our analysis, we begin by searching for words/expressions in each document that could lead us to the notion of a specific subject/person/group and his/her/its generation. This allowed us to focus on whether there is or is not a generational approach (meaning that different generations are considered with their diversities and needs) towards disinformation and media literacy; and, whenever a generational approach emerged, to explore what type of generational perspectives are put forward. We, then, thematically identified the topics and the contexts referred to when invoking those words/expressions in order to identify the terms and the meaning of the use of a generational perspective. This allowed us to explore how the different topics of concerns address different generational actors, their specific related problems and what is conceived as appropriate solutions for them. Finally, we problematized the results achieved in order to draw a research and intervention agenda that can successively approach disinformation.

Data and results are presented below. First, we list the analyzed documents identifying words/expressions in each document that implies a specific subject/person/group and his/her/its generation. Afterwards, we draw conclusions of these identifications while also combining them with the issues that are under analysis in the documents and which take into account the context (Brexit, Trump election, European politics) in which they were produced. Examples of the trends are showcased in quotations and particular attention should be paid to the statements we underlined for emphasis purposes.

Table 1. List of analyzed documents

Year	Document	Identifications
2018	Tackling online disinformation: a European Approach [3]	"Younger users", "young people", "adults", "child" + "citizens", "users"
2018	Commission Recommendation of 14.2.2018 on enhancing the European nature and efficient conduct of the 2019 elections to the European Parliament [24]	"citizen"
2018	EU Code of Practice on Disinformation [25]	"stakeholders", "citizens", "consumers"
March 2018	A multi-dimensional approach to disinformation Report of the independent High-level Group on fake news and online disinformation [2]	"children and young people", "schoolchildren", "young generations", young public", "older generations", "adults" + "as teachers", "media professionals", "journalists", "stakeholder"
April 2018	Flash Eurobarometer 464 [1]	"Younger users", "Younger respondents (15 to 24 years old)" + "Students", "Respondents", "Europeans"

4 Results

Table 1 clearly points to a lack of generational perspectives, identifications and contexts, privileging an uncharacterized identification of citizens. Specifically, analysed texts point to 1) an approach focused on adults in working positions and/or in general identifications, to 2) an absence of old people and, finally, 3) a limited identification of young audiences which are mostly cornered in the school context. When reading these documents through a generational lens, results are not necessarily uplifting as it is hard to identify this notion - it appears mostly in contexts where authors are addressing for instance disinformation in general terms - and also to perceive specific related problems and solutions, namely direct policies.

4.1 Responsibility of Citizens (Part of the Solution)

The responsibility of the citizens, of the European citizens, is something that we can find in the analyzed documents. They are considered as part of the solution and there is both an identification of the need to create solutions where they can fit and that can provide them with better tools to fight disinformation. At the same time, they are identified as part of the solution, because they are considered as active subjects that have the duty to participate and engage in the democratic sphere. Two examples of this trend are illustrated in the quotations below (the underlining is ours for emphasis purposes).

- "Our open democratic societies depend on public debates that allow well-informed citizens to express their will through free and fair political processes. <u>Media have traditionally played a key role in holding public authorities to account and in providing the information that enables citizens to form their own views on societal issues and actively and effectively participate in democratic society.</u>" [3]
- "Right to participate in the democratic life of the Union and that decisions shall be taken as openly and as closely as possible to the citizen" [24]

Lifelong processes of learning and also the internet and new and reinforced possibilities also make it possible that citizens are more aware of current civic and digital environments and also have increased possibilities of getting more skilled to act. This trend is showcased in the quotations below (the underlining is ours for emphasis purposes).

- "Today, the Internet has not only vastly increased the volume and variety of news available to citizens but has also profoundly changed the ways citizens access and engage with news. <u>Younger users, in particular, now turn to online media as their main source of information. The easy availability of diverse quality information has the potential to make democratic processes more participatory and inclusive.</u>" [3]
- "The life-long development of critical and digital competences, in particular for young people, is crucial to reinforce the resilience of our societies to disinformation" [3]

4.2 Responsibility of Citizens (Part of the Problem)

Citizens are also considered as part of the problem, because of acts that contribute to spreading information disorders, even if without intention. Social networks may play an important role in increasing the problem. One example of this trend is illustrated in the quotations below. (the underlining is ours for emphasis purposes).

- "Users themselves are also playing a role in disseminating disinformation, which tends to travel more quickly on social media due to the propensity of users to share content without any prior verification. The ever-increasing volume and speed of content flowing online increases the risk of indiscriminate sharing of disinformation." [3]

4.3 Policies

European preoccupations are also targeting future improvements, for citizens and namely to young people. New policies can present sudden changes in Europeans attitudes and practices and can also promote a better knowledge of the political processes and consequently forms of avoiding disinformation. Policies towards disinformation are central to the mitigation of the problem, however, they are considered difficult to implement. The documents indicate a lack of generational marks, even if it is implicit in the idea of "adulthood". Young people are also identified in relation to policies to improve forms of safer navigation in digital environments. Three examples of this trend are showcased in the quotations below. Particular attention should be paid to the statements we underlined for emphasis purposes (the underlining is ours for emphasis purposes).

- "The spread of disinformation also affects policy-making processes by skewing public opinion. Domestic and foreign actors can use disinformation to manipulate policy, societal debates and behaviour in areas such as climate change, migration, public security, health5, and finance. Disinformation can also diminish trust in science and empirical evidence." [3]
- "The Commission supports a number of initiatives, including through the Erasmus + programme, on Internet safety, digital well-being and, digital skills that aim at fostering a critical awareness of citizens – in particular, young people – of the digital environment, which in turn helps strengthen digital media literacy." [3]
- "Consistently with Article 10 of the European Convention on Human Rights and the principle of freedom of opinion, Signatories should not be compelled by governments, nor should they adopt voluntary policies, to delete or prevent access to otherwise lawful content or messages solely on the basis that they are thought to be 'false'." [25]

4.4   Schools, News Media and Other Stakeholders

Even if the documents analyzed have few signs about age groups and generations, there are several indications about schools that target especially children and young people, and also allusions to adults such as journalists, academia, schools, civil society organizations that can foster citizens skills in dealing with disinformation and better understand digital spaces. Four examples of this trend can be seen in the quotations below (the underlining is ours for emphasis purposes).

- "Educational institutions, news media, and public authorities should invest in independently run digital media and information literacy (MIL) efforts to increase awareness and understanding of media and information, digital technology, and data analytics. These efforts should be differentiated for different demographics, including not only children and young people, but also the adult population, and working to counter inequalities in how well equipped different European citizens are to make full use of digital media." [2]
- "Cooperate with CSOs and academia to formulate and implement skill and age-specific media and information literacy approaches, and for all ages, while pursuing their media literacy projects in cooperation with schools and other educational institutions that target younger generations;" [2]
- "Civil society organisations are very active in developing media literacy actions and programmes including via experimental collaborations with other stakeholders, to help the younger generations to become conscious consumers of news within the new digital ecosystems. Moreover, many interesting initiatives are already undertaken to help older generations improve their media literacy skills" [2]
- "transparency should reflect the importance of facilitating the assessment of content through indicators of the trustworthiness of content sources, media ownership and verified identity. These indicators should be based on objective criteria and endorsed by news media associations, in line with journalistic principles and processes." [25]

4.5 (Critical) Media Literacy

Media literacy and critical views on the processes that can ensure that citizens have better skills to deal with the complexities of the information society [26]. However, it is not healthy to consider that this is placing the solutions on the audience's shoulders. Media literacy processes imply much more than that idea. Three examples of this trend can be found in the quotations below (the underlining is ours for emphasis purposes).

- "The EU should make this a stated priority with the aim of integrating critical media literacy into the core literacies guaranteed to all schoolchildren in Europe, with formal status in national school curricula. This can engage libraries as well. The HLEG recommends the EU to transmit this recognition beyond Europe via membership of OECD and Unesco." [2]
- "Media literacy cannot therefore be limited to young people but needs to encompass adults as well as teachers and media professionals who often cannot keep the pace of the digital transformation induced by fast-evolving media technologies." [2]
- "Disinformation is a multifaceted problem, does not have one single root cause, and thus does not have one single solution. Some forms of disinformation have clearly been enabled by the development of specific digital media, including platform products and services, but the problem also involves some political actors, news media, and civil society actors. Problems of disinformation are thus connected with wider political, social, civic and media issues in Europe" [2]

We need to highlight that it is needed to demystify the preponderant role of citizens in the process. The Fake News and Disinformation Online: Flash Eurobarometer 464 [1] indicated some intriguing answers. When asked which institutions and media actors should act to stop the spread of *fake news*, journalists are the top answer in 22 countries, with the highest proportions seen in France (56%) and the Netherlands (55%), and the lowest in Hungary (23%) and Italy (33%). Respondents in France, Austria and Portugal (all 38%) are most likely to say that citizens themselves should act to stop the spread of *fake news*, while those in Bulgaria (23%), Belgium, Italy and Finland (25%) are the least likely to choose this response.

5 Discussions and Conclusions

This article aimed to analyze five important EU instruments on disinformation from 2018 in order to document the level of the importance attached to a generational-oriented perspective in the European policy regarding this critical domain. As the results reported above show, two weak generational imageries are put forward in the analyzed documents: *adults* and *children and young people*, both constructed mainly by a general and unspecific identification of citizens. With the exception of references to adults in working positions and to schoolchildren, there are no robust efforts in identifying and addressing different generational groups, their specific problems nor needs. Also, we observed the lack of articulation of the main topics made relevant regarding the prevention and combating of disinformation with the specificities of the various generational contexts. More significantly, despite the presence of recurrent mentions to the idea of "adulthood", and also to the universe of the younger people, the analyzed documents are far from promoting a generational perspective in approaching disinformation and, thus, from fostering generational-specific policies with a loop impact on media literacy.

The intergenerational perspective is only explicitly mentioned in the analyzed documents when emphasizing lifelong learning and young people's digital media literacy training. This one size fits all approach that takes 'adulthood' as a rule for all citizens removes specificities for different generations and their needs and does not promote intergenerational policies. The idea of citizens' responsibilization incurs a logic that considers citizen participation in the media, neglecting that digital platforms call everyone to the public debate. The general idea that a democratic society has all its citizens well-informed also forgets that disadvantaged and excluded groups [27] do not have access to Education, a central pillar for democracy and the promotion of media literacy.

The analyzed documents focus on the engagement with the news and the need for quality information, highlighting critical and civic literacies as ways to combat disinformation. However, European citizens' media diets vary by age, gender, socio-cultural and socio-economic contexts, and country.

The documents also show an aggregation of generations in a homogeneous group, not recognizing their heterogeneity [28–30]. The homogenization of different age groups leads to the difficulty of reading different generations' needs in their different life stages and their concrete learning possibilities arising from community public policies that consider European citizens attending at the macro level and the various micro-levels. Concerning specifically the process of ageing, scientific literature has shown that is not homogeneous, rather diverse and asymmetries [31]. Nonetheless, generalizations of this process are denounced by studies that show that differences [32]. Moreover, inequalities are often hidden, defining young and old adults in the process of 'adulthood'.

The generalization found in documents is worrying, as public policies must emanate useful discourses and actions capable of changing democratic societies through Education.

In order to appropriately fight disinformation, we argue, it is needed to adopt a generational-oriented approach in all the relevant domains at stake. This requires a broader view of communication as a situated practice shaped by cultural and identity aspects. Future research thus needs to create more shreds of evidence of how the new mediatic ecosystem is offering far-reaching opportunities for personalized dynamics of content production, uses and consumption, demanding generational-oriented communication policies.

Acknowledgements. This article results from research undertaken within two projects: Social Media Resilience Toolkit - SMaRT-EU (LC-01563446; http://smart-toolkit.eu) is funded by the European Commission/Media Literacy for All; "DeCodeM (De)Coding Masculinities: Towards an enhanced understanding of media's role in shaping perceptions of masculinities in Portugal", which is supported by the Foundation for Science and Technology (Portugal) under Grant PTDC/COMCSS/31740/2017.

References

1. European Commission: Fake News and Disinformation Online: Flash Eurobarometer 464. European Commission, Brussels (2018)
2. European Commission: A multi-dimensional approach to disinformation: Report of the independent High level Group on fake news and online disinformation. European Commission, Brussels (2018)
3. European Commission: Tackling online disinformation: a European Approach. European Commission, Brussels (2018)
4. European Audiovisual Observatory: Mapping of media literacy practices and actions in EU. Strasbourg (2016)
5. Loos, E., Nijenhuis, J.: Consuming fake news: a matter of age? The perception of political fake news stories in Facebook ads. In: Gao, Q., Zhou, J. (eds.) HCII 2020. LNCS, vol. 12209, pp. 69–88. Springer, Cham (2020). https://doi.org/10.1007/978-3-030-50232-4_6
6. Corsten, M.: The time of generations. Time Soc. **8**(2–3), 249–272 (1999)
7. Amaral, I., Brites, M.J.: Trends on the digital uses and generations. In: Proceedings of INTED2019 Conference, Valencia (2019)
8. Mannheim, K.: The problem of generation. In: Mannheim, K. (ed.) Essays on the Sociology of Knowledge, pp. 276–320. Routledge & Kegan Paul, London (1952)
9. Singer, J.B.: User-generated visibility: secondary gatekeeping in a shared media space. New Media Soc. **16**(1), 55–73 (2013)
10. Amaral, I., Santos, S.J.: Algoritmos e redes sociais: a propagação de fake news na era da pós-verdade. In: Figueira, J., Santos, S.C. (eds.) As fake news e a nova ordem (des)informativa na era da pós-verdade: manipulação, polarização, filter bubbles, Coimbra, pp. 63–85 (2019)
11. Frau-Meigs, D.: Notícias falsas e desordens informativas. In: Brites, M.J., Amaral, I., Silva, M.T. (eds.) Literacias cívicas e críticas: refletir e praticar, pp. 77–80. CECS, Braga (2019)
12. Mihailidis, P.: Literacia para as notícias. In: Brites, M.J., Amaral, I., Silva, M.T. (eds.) Literacias cívicas e críticas: refletir e praticar, pp. 69–72. CECS, Braga (2019)
13. Brites, M.J., Chimirri, N.A., Amaral, I., Seddighi, G., Torres da Silva, M., Murru, M.F.: Stakeholder discourses about critical literacies and audience participation. In: Das, R., Ytre-Arne, B. (eds.) The Future of Audiences, pp. 179–195. Springer, Cham (2018). https://doi.org/10.1007/978-3-319-75638-7_10
14. Manners, I.: Normative power Europe: a contradiction in terms? J. Common Market Stud. **40**(2), 235–258 (2002)
15. Lucarelli, S.: Introduction: values, principles, identity and European Union foreign policy. In: Lucarelli, S., Manners, I. (eds.) Values and Principles in European Foreign Policy, pp. 1–18. Routledge, Londra and New York (2006)
16. Bolin, G., Skogerbø, E.: Age, generation and the media. Northern Lights **11**, 3–14 (2013)
17. Aroldi, P.: Generational belonging between media audiences and ICT users. In: Colombo, F., Fortunati, L. (eds.) Broadband Society and Generational Changes, pp. 51–68. Peter Lang, Frankfurt am Main (2011)
18. Colombo, F., Fortunati, F.: Broadband Society and Generational Changes. Peter Lang, Frankfurt am Main (2011)
19. Loos, E., Haddon, L., Mante-Meijer, E.: Generational Use of New Media. Routledge, Farnham (2012)
20. Prensky, M.: Digital natives, digital immigrants. Horizon **9**(5), 1–6 (2011)
21. Helsper, E.J., Eynon, R.: Digital natives: where is the evidence? Br. Edu. Res. J. **36**(3), 503–520 (2010)
22. Brites, M.J., Amaral, I., Santos, S.J.: Intergenerational perspectives on audiences studies: from youth to senior representations. In: Gao, Q., Zhou, J. (eds.) HCII 2020. LNCS, vol. 12208, pp. 579–588. Springer, Cham (2020). https://doi.org/10.1007/978-3-030-50249-2_41

23. Bowen, G.A.: Document analysis as a qualitative research method. Qual. Res. J. **9**(2), 27–40 (2009)
24. European Commission: Commission Recommendation of 14.2.2018 on enhancing the European nature and efficient conduct of the 2019 elections to the European Parliament. European Commission, Brussels (2018)
25. European Commission: EU Code of Practice on Disinformation. European Commission, Brussels (2018)
26. Loos, E., Ivan, L., Leu, D.: "Save the Pacific Northwest tree octopus": a hoax revisited. Or. Inf. Learn. Sci. **119**(9, 10), 514–528 (2018)
27. Simões, R.B., Amaral, I., Santos, S.: Media education and digital inclusion: tackling the social exclusion of disadvantaged groups in Europe. In: Proceedings of INTED2020 Conference, Valencia (2020)
28. Nelson, E.A., Dannefer, D.: Aged heterogeneity: Fact or fiction? The fate of diversity in gerontological research. Gerontologist **32**(1), 17–23 (1992)
29. Stone, M.E., Lin, J., Dannefer, D., Kelley-Moore, J.A.: The continued eclipse of heterogeneity in gerontological research. J. Gerontol. Ser. B **72**(1), 162–167 (2017)
30. Loos, E.: Senior citizens: digital immigrants in their own country? Observatorio (OBS*) **6**(1) (2012)
31. Amaral, I., Daniel, F., Abreu, S.: Policies for gender equality in Portugal: contributions to a framework for older women. Prisma Social **22**, 347–363 (2018)
32. Amaral, I., Daniel, F.: The use of social media among senior citizens in Portugal: active ageing through an intergeneration approach. In: Zhou, J., Salvendy, G. (eds.) ITAP 2018. LNCS, vol. 10926, pp. 422–434. Springer, Cham (2018). https://doi.org/10.1007/978-3-319-92034-4_32

Smartphone Overuse in the Old Age: A Qualitative Exploration on Actual Smartphone Use and Perceptions Among Italian Older Heavy Users

Alessandro Caliandro[1]($\boxtimes$) (iD), Marco Gui[2], Alice Di Leva[3], and Valentina Sturiale[2]

[1] Department of Political and Social Sciences, University of Pavia, Pavia, Italy
alessandro.caliandro@unipv.it
[2] Department of Sociology and Social Research, University of Milano-Bicocca, Milan, Italy
[3] Department of Philosophy and Education Sciences, University of Torino, Turin, Italy

Abstract. This article investigates the phenomenon of smartphone overuse among a group of Italian older users. Drawing on the analysis of 20 qualitative interviews and smartphone log data of the same group, the article explores the actual use of smartphone in older people everyday life against their perceptions about permanent connection and digital overuse. The article concludes that, notwithstanding a limited use of smartphones, overuse is an important cultural topic in their narrations about everyday use of such a device. Specifically, interviewees feel trapped within unwanted forms of sociality (especially related messaging apps) that they perceive artificial and shallow. This condition leads participants to use smartphones as less as possible and only to accomplish practical and instrumental tasks. This article aims at contributing to studies on media ideologies, which are still limited regarding older people's smartphone ideologies.

Keywords: Smartphone · Older people · Overuse · Log data · Perceptions

1 Introduction

Since the diffusion of smartphones in industrialized countries, digital media experience has entered a new phase where users are permanently connected [1]. Public debate has grown about the undesired side effect of such pervasive digital connection. A diffuse perception of being overwhelmed by digital stimuli has emerged among Internet users: according to an Ofcom study, half of all British Internet users feel they are spending too much time browsing the Internet each day [2]. A large majority of Americans feel that the use of mobile phones frequently or occasionally hurts their conversations [3]. As far as Italy is concerned, a survey on 2000 web users of all ages [6], respondents were asked how much they agreed with the following statements: "I spend more time on the Internet than I would like" (*overconsume*), "I often try to do too many things at the same time when I am online" (*multitask*), and "when I use the Internet, I lose time

© Springer Nature Switzerland AG 2021
Q. Gao and J. Zhou (Eds.): HCII 2021, LNCS 12786, pp. 361–378, 2021.
https://doi.org/10.1007/978-3-030-78108-8_27

for more important things" (*displace*). The respondents agreed or strongly agreed with such statements in percentages between 26% to 43%.

Research has addressed these feelings through different concepts such as internet and smartphone addiction [4], or the concept of Permanently online– Permanently connected (PO-PC) [5]. Most of the studies about digital overuse focus on young people or the adult population.

We know that the perception of overusing digital media affects young people more than adults (especially older users) [6] and also that social media use seems to have more collateral effects on young than on older people [7]. Nonetheless, older people make a large use of smartphones too [8]. They customarily employ smartphones in their everyday life to accomplish strategic tasks [9] as well as develop their own ideas on how smartphones work and their impact on themselves and society at large [10]. As far as we know, no evidence exists about how older internet users feel and live the flipsides of constant connectivity. In this paper we investigate the habits and perceptions of a group of Italian smartphone heavy digital users aged 65+ , through log data analysis and qualitative interviews, to describe how this particular population perceives hyper-connectivity and digital overuse. This article aims at contributing to studies on media ideologies, intended as "beliefs about how a medium communicates and structures communication [11], which guide decisions on the use of available digital communication tools" (p. 4) [12]. To our knowledge, only few researches studied older people's smartphone ideologies drawing on an empirical exploration on the mutual effects between actual and perceived use.

2   Digital Overuse and Italian Digital Context

Qualitative studies have investigated the problems users perceive when it comes to digital communication's ubiquitous presence in daily life. Salo et al. [13] used narrative interviews and identified the following aspects of 'technostress' related to social networking sites: concentration, sleep, identity, and social relation problems. Stephens et al. [14] use a Q-method[1] to capture people's perceptions of communication overload. They find seven dimensions that form communication overload: compromising message quality, having many distractions, using many information and communication technologies, pressuring for decisions, feeling responsible to respond, overwhelming with information, and piling up of messages.

The quantitative literature on digital overuse perception shows that this feeling decreases with age [6]. So far, research has not tried to disentangle the reasons behind this less sensitivity to digital overuse perception.

Regarding the use of digital media within the specific context of Italy, the older population has limited digital access compared to other age groups. In Italy only the 27% of people aged 65–74 access the Internet and 7% use social media- (consider instead that in Europe the 48% of older people (65–74) access the Internet and 16% use social

---

[1] Q Methodology is a research method created by William Stephenson (1902–1989) to study people's viewpoint on specific subjects. Q methodology makes use of factor analysis to look for correlations between subjects across a sample of variables. In this way, it reveals and describes divergent views as well as consensus in a group [56].

media) [15]. However, wealthier older people with greater cultural and social capital, who started to use computers during their qualified working career, are characterized by increased possession and use of ICTs [16]. In fact, among the few older Italian Internet users, 91% access the Internet daily, at least three times a day [17]: this datum put older Italian internet users well above the European (EU 28) average (77%), making them, de facto, heavy Internet users [18].

A similar trend can be seen if we look at smartphone use. Smartphones had an exceptional diffusion worldwide: 45% of the World population owns a smartphone [19]. In Italy the diffusion of smartphones is particularly pronounced too, since 94% of the population owns a smartphone, which is mainly used to access social media applications [20]. Italian older people seem to have a keen interest in smartphones, since 44% of older users aged 65–74 access the Internet regularly using the smartphone [21]. Moreover, when they access the Internet via smartphones, they seem to prefer social media applications, and in particular WhatsApp, which, according to an Ipsos' study [22], has been downloaded by 87% of people aged 55+ .

All these data suggest that older Italian internet users are a population worthy of being studied more deeply as well as they can be an appropriate population within which exploring the smartphone overuse phenomenon.

3 Smartphones and Older People

Although smartphones appear to play an important role in the life of older people, research in this area is still underdeveloped [8]. Anyway, several notable contributions are starting to emerge [57]. In particular, scholars stress the key role played by instant messaging apps within older people's everyday life practices [9], where WhatsApp takes the lion share. As a matter of fact, WhatsApp amounts to be the most diffused Instant messaging application among older people in western countries [8], which, they perceive as an "user-friendly messaging app with a clean and simple to use design" [23].

Thanks to the possibility of micro-coordination [24] afforded by WhatsApp, older people are able to create and join, in nearly real-time, social groups composed by different relevant actors, such as peers, relatives, children and grandchildren [25]. This is an important outcome, since the empowerment of social relations by means of digital media is deemed to have positive effects on older people's well-being [26, 27]. Research demonstrated that older people using digital media for curating their social networks show higher levels of self-esteem [28], feel less lonely and more autonomous [29] as well as perform better in managing intergenerational relations [30, 31] and leisure activities [32].

Nevertheless, research so far has focused more on the positive effects that smartphones exert on older people's sociality, overlooking the exploration of their possible negative impacts. Studies on ITCs and social media have broadly investigated the different kinds of risks older people perceive in the use of such technologies- which include exposure to obscene content and hate speech [33], privacy issues [34], and fear of wasting time [35]. Therefore, more studies of the kind are needed on the topic of smartphones and older people. Specifically, scholars urge to develop more research on older people's media ideologies [18], intended as "beliefs about how a medium communicates and structures communication [11], which guide decisions on the use of available digital communication tools" (p.4) [12]. Regarding smartphone use, it would be important to develop more research on older people's perception on smartphones' disadvantages, criticalities and drawbacks [58]. Research of the kind is also important to contrast ageist and techno-deterministic views [36] on smartphone use. In fact, most of the studies on smartphones' negative social and physiological impact tend to focus on younger people [37]. Perhaps, teens and younger adults are considered, by default, heavy smartphone users and so as populations that are more exposed to smartphones' negative effects as well as endowed with more information to provide regarding smartphone culture. Nonetheless, older people are social actors endowed with a full agency. They too employ smartphones in their everyday life to accomplish strategic tasks [10] (and not necessarily to seek support from others [9]) as well as develop their own ideas on how smartphones work and their impact on themselves and society at large. For example, in a qualitative research on grandmothers, Colombo et al. [38], highlight the older people's discourse on the "correct" use of technology, which is wise and moderate - in contrast with that of the younger generations, which they perceive as antisocial and excessive. Similarly, in a comparative study involving groups of Italian and Spanish older and younger people, Fernández-Ardèvol et al. [12] observed the same rhetoric at work. Although older and young participants use the smartphone in quite distinctive ways (e.g. the formers are much more inclined to make phone calls than the latters), each group claims to use the smartphone correctly, in contrast with the habits of other (abstract) social categories, who are deemed to use the smartphone immoderately, incorrectly and ineffectively.

Whereas these kinds of studies are scarce, there is a proliferation of research focusing on physical impairments that hamper a correct use of smartphones by older people [39, 40]. This research has the noble objective to urge developers to design smartphones' interfaces that would be more 'older people friendly' [41]. Nevertheless, we must not forget that older people are not a homogeneous group of individuals, and most of them are perfectly at ease with smartphone technologies and functionalities currently available. Social research on ICTs and aging has amply demonstrated that being old is not, by itself, a barrier in accessing digital media as well as does not mean lacking digital skills [42, 43]. On the contrary, strategies of ICTs use appear to be significantly influenced by factors related to personal and generational biographies (e.g. previous jobs or familiar context) [44, 45].

Given the above-mentioned gaps of and challenges posed by social research on aging and smartphone use, this article tries to explore both the older people actual use of smartphone and their perception of smartphone overuse. The ultimate scope is to understand how actual smartphone practices interact with smartphone ideologies, and vice versa. Specifically, regarding the Italian context, the article aims at answering the follow research questions:

RQ1: How much and for what do Italian older people use smartphone in their everyday life?

RQ2: How do Italian older smartphone users perceive constant connectivity? Do they perceive digital overuse?

RQ3: Which dimensions of perceived overuse are particularly relevant for this population? Which ones are less relevant?

RQ4: How do Italian older users talk about other people's digital overuse?

4   Methods

To answer the above research questions, we set a qualitative explorative study based on the analysis of 75089 smartphone log data and face-to-face interviews conducted with Italian individuals aged over 65[2]. We recruited our participants thanks to the support of Auser Monza-Brianza, a civic association promoting active aging in the north-east area of Milano (Italy). Most Auser's members are 65 years old or over; the majority of them is aged 65 to 75 - (in fact we recruited only 3 volunteers aged –65). In particular, Auser Monza-Brianza was pivotal to put us in contact with older people who were already acquainted with ICTs and, especially, who customarily use smartphones within their everyday life activities – (in particular our participants use a lot the smartphone to manage Auser's activities they are involved in). Since we were interested in studying smartphone overuse among older people, it was crucial for us to get in touch with persons who could be considered as 'heavy' users.

30 Auser's members accepted to participate the first phase of log data collection; 20 of them also accepted to be interviewed (10 males and 10 females, aged 62-76, with different educational qualifications, see Appendix).

The log data were collected through RescueTime, a tracking device meant to monitor smartphone users' activities [46]. The app was installed on the smartphones of 30 volunteers and remained on from January 24 to February 24, 2019. The app is by default respectful of users' privacy, since it only allows to trace users' activities but not their content (e.g. it is possible to know if a person used Gmail and for how long, but not the content of her emails). Anyhow, all participants singed an informed consent before having the app installed on their devices.

Since RescueTime releases only quantitative data, qualitative interviews were necessary to answer comprehensively our research questions. The interviews were conducted from September to December 2019 and involved only 20 participants - because 10 volunteers did not agree to be interviewed. Each interview lasted, on average, two hours and was audio-recorded. We conducted the interviews by employing a semi-structured interview format [47], which allowed the interviewees to freely express themselves while touching all the topics listed in the researcher's interview schedule [48]. The interview schedule was structured around three main themes of discussion, which were designed to answer our research question; that is: 1) perception of constant connectivity; 2) perception of digital overuse; 3) perception of digital overuse concerning other social groups.

After transcription, interviews were analyzed separately by the four authors through a process of open and axial coding, which permitted to generate codes and categories by following an interactive and grounded approach [49]. Conflicts in the construction of categories and data interpretation were addressed and eventually resolved in ad hoc sessions of discussion. The interpretation of results drew on a grounded-theory approach [50], that is, we tried to build new theoretical knowledge out of our qualitative data and not to test prefabricated hypotheses or obtain generalizable results [51].

---

[2] There are different ways of defining older people, according to the World Health Organization older people in developed World economies are usually defined as individual aged 65 years or more [59].

5   Findings

RQ1: How much and for what do Italian older people use smartphone in their everyday life?

The analysis of log data provides a comprehensive overview of our participants daily use of smartphone. Over 31 days, on average, participants accessed their smartphones 127 times per day, spending 1 h and 8 min daily on them. Each access lasts on average 32 s. If we look at the time spent on the smartphone during the day, we can observe an interesting fluctuating trend. Figure 1 shows that the use of smartphone is quite stable during the day (from 8 am to 8 pm), with a decline from 1 pm to 5 pm and at 7 pm. The highest picks of use are registered at 8 am and 8 pm. The subsequent interviews have been very useful to make sense of this data. Participants explain that the smartphone is "the first thing [they] check in the morning and the last before sleeping" (P3); a statement that explains the 8 am and 8 pm picks. Usually, in the morning they check the news and/or whish good morning to their contacts; in the evening, before going to sleep, they check the latest news and/or wish goodnight to people. Also, participants explain that they avoid using smartphone during lunch (1 pm) and dinner time (7 pm), because they are either engaged in eating and conversing or explicitly ban the use of smartphone as a 'family rule'. Lastly, the down pick around 4 pm is due to the fact that some of the participants usually, at the time, are busy in the caring of their grandchildren.

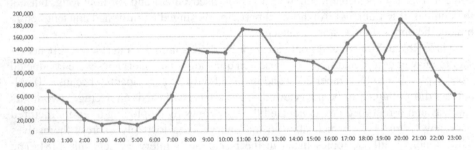

Fig. 1. Overall use per duration (in seconds) over the 24 h

The chart illustrates the time spent on smartphone by participants per each hour daily. The variable hour has been constructed summing all the seconds registered each day for each hour.

Figure 2 provides a general overview on what participants do when they are on the smartphone. As it is immediately evident, the vast majority of applications and websites accessed fall into the category Communication & Scheduling. As a matter of fact, Communication & Scheduling means WhatsApp, which counts for the 50% of the category. (The other functions accessed are residual or totally physiological when one uses a smartphone: 'Voice Chat' (22%) (that is phone calls) 'General Activities' (21%) (mainly checking the contact list), 'Email' (6%), 'Calendars' (1%)). Although largely used, the time of presence on WhatsApp is limited: on average 13,5 s per access. Again, interviews were crucial to make sense of this pattern of usage. As participants stressed multiple times, they use WhatsApp principally to organize work actives related to Auser, in which they use very brief and concise communications, as P7 explains:

"I work a lot on the Auser [WhatsApp] group. I send messages, I do not make calls, I send messages for asking about the availability of the members. They reply: "I am free that day, ok", and I say: "thank you for your help." Because for coordinating people you must do like this, because it is voluntary work".

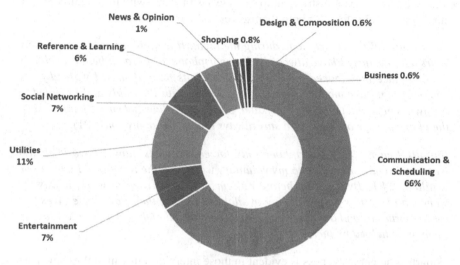

Fig. 2. Access per category

RQ2: How Do Italian Older Smartphone Users Perceive Constant Connectivity? Do They Perceive Digital Overuse?

Very often participants declare to feel sometimes 'oppressed by' smartphones, which force them into unwanted and undesired social interactions. Especially, WhatsApp and social media notifications seem to suck our participants in such form of 'forced sociality'. To this purpose, P5 clearly explains:

I have some friends who bother me, because every morning they send me WhatsApp messages with jokes, photos, good morning, etcetera, notifications chime all the time, but I can't follow all this nonsense, it is exhausting. So, I just reply 'good morning', nothing more (P5).

Such 'bothering' is not exclusively related to the 'quantity' of notifications received, but also to the 'quality' of social relations the notifications point to. Participants perceive such smartphone-mediated forms of sociality as useless and shallow. P10 is explicit about this:

I have 3 o 4 WhatsApp groups, which I use for work... for coordinating the vol- untary initiatives I am into. Anyway, sometimes people use these groups to send stupid messages, jokes, photos, etc. ... then the stream of this nonsense starts and never stops... it is crazy! .... I mean, if I send you messages, just reply to that message, period! don't start with nonsense! it is useless!

Anyhow, the constant connectivity favoured by smartphones has positive aspects too. First, some of the participants report to be used to constant connectivity, because they have been socialized to it in their previous work environments (where they were used to being constantly connected to phones, cellular phones, faxes, PCs). Second, they see the smartphone as an instrument to stay always in touch with their family and close friends, and so feel safer - for both themselves and their beloved ones.

I don't turn off the smartphone during the night. It is a habit I took many, many years ago; because I have always had a smartphone, or to say it better a cellular phone - since they looked more like baseball bats than phones. I worked for a company that gave me Motorola. I was a widow with little kids and I needed to be always in contact with the babysitter. Since then, I have taken the habit to keep the phone always on. I use it to stay always in touch with my sons (P1).

Initially I carried the smartphone only for emergencies, now I have it always with me, because now, due to my voluntary work with the red cross, I need to be available 24 h. By the way, before retirement, when I used to work, it was the same, so I kept this habit of being available 24 h. So, the smartphone gives you this opportunity, and it is cool because you can immediately reach people and help them or be helped by them" (P16).

Smartphone pervasiveness is evident in those interviews in which the same person, who shortly before claimed to use the smartphone rarely, soon after gets to admit that s/he starts to suspect that his/her screen time is out of control; as in the case of P2:

I use the smartphone, but not constantly. I try not to be too much tethered to it, I think I stay on my smartphone half an hour per day, so very rarely, that's it ... then, during the day I receive some messages from WhatsApp, from both voluntary work and family. After lunch I check the news to see what is going on in the World. Then I read some books with an ad hoc smartphone application ... and that's it...Well now that I hear myself talking, I start thinking that maybe I need to take a break from the smartphone. As a matter of fact, every time one has a little bit of spare time, s/he turns on this box and checks if a message has arrived.

The ability to use the smartphone in a consistent and moderate way throughout the day is highly praised by our participants. In general participants stress that, when they don't have to use the smartphone for work purposes, they prefer to check it during those peaceful moments of relaxation (e.g. after lunch or breakfast), which are more frequent and longer in the life of retired people. This obviously put less pressure on smartphone use habits. Participants appear to use their smartphones less in the moments of clipping, less in a hurry, and more in some 'dedicated' moments of the day.

"When I wake up in the morning, I immediately check the news on the smartphone, it is like reading the newspaper, isn't it?" (P20).

"Well, when I wake up in the morning, as a first thing I check my agenda to see what it is scheduled for the day" (P14).

The pensioner condition seems to give our participants the opportunity to plan time with the tool in a more conscious and organized way. This could explain at least partially the less pressure and the less perception of overuse that emerges among older people in quantitative research [6]

RQ3: Which Dimensions of Perceived Overuse are Particularly Relevant for this population? Which ones are Less Relevant?

Responses of participants in several cases highlight the presence of stressors and discomfort in relation to smartphone usage. In particular, we may connect some recorded descriptions to some of the dimensions described by Stephens et al. [14]. Several interviewees point out how the very presence of the smartphone, and the constant availability that comes from it, is a source of constant distraction. In the following quote, for example, P12 declares to use little WhatsApp because the unregulated use of other users makes it a source of distraction.

[I use it] very little, some news [I receive] some messages, I am connected with the local CGIL group and the regional SPI groups if a piece of news comes along I take a look at it... then I don't look at it anymore because then they [every other person in the group] all answer ok ok. [I use it] if something important happens, for example when the USB office was bombed.

Messaging apps often get cited in the descriptions of participants as an example of something causing communication overload, especially in connection to constant notifications, which, in turn, is attributed more to a lack of competence and technical prowess in using the smartphone rather than to an intrinsic characteristic. This is made clearer in this interview by P6:

WhatsApp, in my opinion, especially when using groups, should be used to transmit information: "there is a meeting at this time" and period... there is this exaggerated mania to answer, "There is a meeting", "ok I'm coming", "ok that other one", "no, I can't", it becomes something that to get that information you have to scroll through forty, fifty, one hundred messages... that according to me it is an incorrect use of the medium. It is important because with a single communication you put yourself in communication with a certain number of people, but the communication should be targeted, for example in small Facebook groups made, say, of 30 people. often those thirty people are forced to look at things that have nothing to do with the motivation for which the group was created.

Another element that occurs a lot in descriptions, both in personal and collective terms, is a feeling of inadequacy and inability to manage the wide range of information conveyed by the use of the smartphone. On a collective side, many participants are aware, for example, of the phenomenon of fake news and are developing a series of information verification tactics, as described by P8:

Yes, I run into fake news, at least I saw them twice… you think that it is true but then you discover that it is crap… I do not respond immediately to a conversation, because I think twice, maybe I go search for the source, to understand. So, I don't want to give an answer right away and then maybe I give it wrong because maybe the news is a hoax.

Along with these normative discourses, participants tend to articulate a narrative on the (wrong) smartphone use of 'others'. As already mentioned, the focus of the stress generated by smartphones lies in the misuse of other users (e.g. friends and contacts), who do not follow a proper netiquette or spam the interviewees with numerous useless messages. The issue of privacy is also often linked to this subject: the constant displaying of people's private life that participants encounter is digital venues (especially in WhatsApp groups), often generates a sense of annoyance and stress, as described by P9:

I would use privacy as a filter. So, you want privacy, but then why you are sharing things that are truly yours, intimate… That is, we want privacy so much and then instead you throw into an [online] group. "First you want privacy but then you feed [online] groups of intimate news, in my opinion you are wrong."

Another source of distress is the overload of information caused by constant (internet) connectivity enabled by smartphones, which participants fear of not being able to control. P17, for example, declares himself overwhelmed by the stimulus and the constant presence of information, which in his case are a complete nuisance:

I am concerned about the information overload that all of us poor mortals have. I probably have to be close to that threshold there because then some kinds of information begin to appear more and more frequently and than I reject that information, it is quite worrisome to me

The last element that contributes to the distrust of this population towards the instrument is the perception of the quality of the message. The conversation mediated by smartphones precludes a series of contextual elements that are precious in reading the content.

Probably because writing has a much more important mental involvement than dialogue, because you have to form an opinion on far fewer elements… Now I talk to you and I see your eyes, your gestures, the light… which are 70% of the things you say. While with WhatsApp I only read "sure", whether it's an assertive expression, like you did, or an ironic expression… then I have to mentally organize myself to respond to something that I don't know what the hell it means and it makes it difficult for me (P15).

RQ4: How do Italian Older Users Talk About Other People's Digital Overuse?

The way in which a social group relates to 'generalized others' [52], tells us a lot about their cultural point of view on the world. In our interviews, participants very often compare their correct use of the smartphone with the incorrect one of (abstract) others.

Therefore, such narratives amount to be very important for having a comprehensive understanding of our participants' perception on smartphone overuse.

In general, our participants seem to bestow upon themselves the role of 'controller' of other people (and other generations) digital overuse, ready to notice all the red flags in their digital behaviour. However, the reported phenomenon seems to be transgenerational and not only related to young people:

During meals, business meetings, a ceremony in the church or moments... instead sometimes at the funeral I saw people open their purse and peek... oh my good! wait! Wait (P11).

Such judgment on the overuse and use of smartphones in inappropriate times, it is not only reported about other generations. In fact, also their peers seem to be, for some respondents, unable to properly manage their phone, implementing behaviours defined as 'incorrect':

But even some of my friends have this phone at the table, I tried to eat there and you have it there, call the daughter, come on, you can call your daughter even after half an hour! I personally find it incorrect (P2).

Another kind of bad habit our participants deem their (peer) friends culprit of a sort of excessive 'self-promotion'. Our participants usually run into this behavior within the many WhatsApp and Facebook groups they belong to, which their peers clog with pictures of themselves, their grandchildren, pets, meals, etc.:

People constantly share their private pictures: look at my nephew how he's beautiful; look at me! I am so beautiful, I am blonde... come on, I don't care, it is stupid (P4).

I don't like people who put -I went to lunch here-, -I went to lunch there...-communions, sharing... maybe because I'm not part of that kind of person not having family, not having anything so particular [...] for what? For me they are not useful (P9).

Participants perceive this constant showing of as an incompressible breach into one's own privacy:

No, my photos, I already do not look well... my photos NEVER, please... but not even my granddaughter... no, no, no, it is private stuff... what is the point of making these things public (P1).

Surprisingly younger generation are not so frequently mentioned in the interviews. Anyway, when younger generations are mentioned, they tend to be portrayed as the most affected by smartphone overuse. In general, younger people, and especially teenagers, are considered not reflexive and educated enough to understand, and thus contrast, the negative effects of smartphones. In particular they seem not having enough cultural resources for filtering the overload of content, information, and notification coming from their mobile devices. As a result, teenagers are sucked into their screen and find themselves isolated from the real world. This narrative is well exemplified by the following reflection of P18, in which he comments the use of the smartphone by his grandson:

Until 13 years old, my nephew didn't own a smartphone (now he's 14 and we got him one) … of course, when one is little s/he can run into some information s/he has not the capacity to control and process. In fact, often, when I see my nephew on the smartphone I say: "now you put down that damn appliance" … because, I noted that for him the smartphone is the main tool, he isolates himself with it and it occupies all of his life. For example, Instagram – I don't use it, but I paid attention when he used it – I saw he gave harts to anyone and I said "ok, but before giving hearts try to think if it is worth … because, if you give hearts to anyone it's like to give them to no one. I tried to make him understand that he must use the tool, and not the other way around.

To our participants, this state of constant self-isolation in which teenagers live had a negative impact on family bonds - which participants perceive as weakened as since smartphones came along. The bitterness of this situation is well described by P13:

I am disheartened when I see how my family relations are now. We [he and his children and grandchildren] continuously exchange messages, photos, information but we don't interact face to face as we were used to doing once.

In general, participants concur in observing that smartphones are having a global nefarious impact on the cohesiveness of the social fabric, and are exactly the teenagers those who are paying the higher price. Teenagers are now condemned to live artificial social relations, which are empty of stimuli and meanings, as P2 efficaciously explains:

The smartphone has changed many things, because with it one does anything, see everything (even too much). To me this is scary, because in this way the younger people have no more special moments in which see and know each other, they just stand still. To me smartphones steal union, companionship, human contact. Another thing I heard is that now people fall in love via smartphone, I was baffled. They say in China one basically falls in love via smartphone, there is no more human contact, one stays with a man/woman no more, but with a smartphone.

In conclusion, we can see that our participants articulate a well-defined ideology of the smartphone, which emerges very clearly when they compare their own use of smartphone with that of other social categories (less educated peers or teenagers). To our participants, there clearly exists a good and a bad way of using the smartphone. The good way is that one they carry out, that is, moderate and aimed to accomplish practical and useful tasks. Vice versa, the bad way of using the smartphone consists in overusing it. Such overuse is perceived even more dangerous when it is aimed at playful purposes (such as killing the time or seeking new friends online).

6 Conclusions

The present analysis shows that our participants' actual use of smartphone in daily life is limited. On average they use the smartphone for 1 h & 8 min every day (32 s per access) and mainly to access WhatsApp, which is principally employed to accomplish practical tasks. Moreover, it seems that they develop a series of tactics (such as banning the use of smartphone during meals as a family rule or texting only brief messages in group chats in order to limit the time spent within them) to defended themselves from the negative consequences of an excessive use of the smartphone. Nevertheless, the topic of overuse seems to be central in their narrations on smartphone use in everyday life. Participants often report to feel overwhelmed by smartphones, and specifically by the state of constant connectivity smartphones expose them to. There are two main sources of distress related to constant connectivity: an informational and social overload. On the one hand, participants feel that smartphones inundate them with a deluge of (bad) information, of which they lack the right instruments and skill to filter. On the other hand, smartphones (with the complicity of notifications systems embedded in the many Instant Messaging groups they participate in) tend to suck participants into unwanted social relations that they perceive as artificial and shallow. To our participants the blame for these two forms of overload is not on the smartphone per se, but rather on the misuse of smartphone carried out by other social groups. In general, participants believe that there is a correct way of using the smartphone that is moderate and instrumental, which is their way. While there exist an incorrect one that is immoderate and playful, which is mainly played out by their less educated peers, but it is culturally epitomized by teenagers' behaviours. In our opinion this particular smartphone ideology can be responsible for the limited and moderate actual use, testified both by log data and some participants statements – or at least it helps us to better make sense of it.

Obviously, these results must be considered as preliminary and descriptive, since they stem from an explorative qualitative analysis developed on an understudied topic, and so by no means generalizable. In fact, the older users interviewed in our study belong to a well-educated and active segment of older people in northern Italy. Therefore, many of these results must be read by taking into consideration the composition of our 'sample'. Anyhow, comparing our results with the existing literature can offer some interesting point of reflection.

Some of our participants refer to plan specific 'moments for the smartphone' during the day, showing that they have the possibility of time, and perhaps also the skills, to organize the time to use the tool in a planned way. This possibility of more programmed times dedicated to media use could explain why quantitative research indicates that older people suffer less from perceived overuse [6].

Notwithstanding their pervasive and limited use of mobile media, they condemn compulsive and annoying use carried out by generalized others. Our interviewees emphasize the importance of a wise and moderate use of smartphones. Comparing these results with the literature, we can highlight the dimensions of overuse that are relevant for our participants and those which are not. Considering the study by Salo et al. [13], which identifies four major aspects of technostress (concentration, sleep, identity, and social relation problems), we can say that only the first and the last seem to be relevant for our interviewees, while sleep and identity problems were not referred to in the interviews.

Also, we have seen that self-promotion on social media is a practice that is almost absent in the behaviours of our interviewees. This eliminates a reason for the intensive use of the media but also a source of technostress. If we consider the Stephens et al. [14] typology of communication overload (compromising message quality, having many distractions, using many information and communication technologies, pressuring for decisions, feeling responsible to respond, overwhelming with information, and piling up of messages) we find that among our interviewees the dimensions of distraction and overwhelming are present, while there are no clear mentions of pressure for decision, less responsibility to respond quickly. It is likely that the more relaxed time schedule retired people have (although they could be involved in many activities), implies a lower manifestation of those problems connected with multitasking between working and private life issues in a condition of time pressure.

Overall, this research shows that the issue of problematic smartphone use is relevant also in the world of older people; smartphone management skills also concern them, but this population has specificities with respect to the literature on overuse by young people. Specifically, our participants use their smartphones less as a tool of identity construction and social promotion. Also, the greater availability of time removes those kinds of 'pressure' that are critical in the overuse of younger people and, especially, adults. Anyhow, further quantitative research can better analyze the differences between age groups [10, 58] as well as confirm some of the insights emerged in this exploratory study.

Acknowledgements. This work was supported by the Fondazione Cariplo (Bando 2017, ricerca scientifica: Ricerca sociale sull'invecchiamento: persone, luoghi e relazioni. Project name: "Aging in a networked society. Older people, social networks and well-being") – No Grant Number.

Appendix

Participant	Gender	Age	Marital status	Education	Last occupation
1	M	71	Married	High school degree	Director
2	M	71	Married	High school degree	Manager
3	M	75	Widow	High school degree	Technician
4	M	72	Married	High school degree	Clerical worker
5	M	70	Married	High school degree	Clerical worker
6	M	70	Married	Middle school degree	Director
7	M	65	Married	High school degree	Manager
8	M	72	Married	University degree	Director
9	M	62	Married	High school degree	Clerical worker
10	M	75	Married	High school degree	Manager
11	M	74	Married	High school degree	Clerical worker

(continued)

(*continued*)

Participant	Gender	Age	Marital status	Education	Last occupation
12	F	66	Single	Middle school degree	Clerical worker
13	F	71	Married	HIGH school degree	Clerical worker
14	F	70	Married	Middle school degree	Plant operator
15	F	70	Married	Elementary school degree	Plant operator
16	M	68	Married	University degree	Manager
17	M	76	Widow	High school degree	Clerical worker
18	F	70	Married	Elementary school degree	Plant operator
19	M	71	Widow	University degree	Free Lance worker
20	M	73	Married	High school degree	Technician
21	M	63	Married	High school degree	Director
22	F	68	Married	Middle school degree	Plant operator
23	F	72	Widow	High school degree	Clerical worker
24	M	61	Married	University degree	Manager
25	M	76	Married	Middle school degree	Craft worker
26	M	73	Single	University school degree	Director
27	F	69	Married	High school degree	Sales worker
28	M	74	Married	High school degree	Clerical worker
29	F	75	Married	Elementary school degree	Clerical worker
30	F	70	Married	High school degree	Manager

References

1. Chayko, M.: Superconnected: The Internet, Digital Media, and Techno-Social Life. Sage, London (2020)
2. Internet use and attitudes: 2016 Metrics Bulletin. Ofcom, London (2016). https://www.ofcom. org.uk/__data/assets/pdf_file/0023/63950/Internet-use-and-attitudes-2016.pdf
3. Rainie, L., Zickuhr, K.: Americans' views on mobile etiquette. Pew Res. Center **26**, 948–958 (2015). https://www.pewresearch.org/internet/wp-content/uploads/sites/9/2015/08/2015-08-26_mobile-etiquette_FINAL.pdf
4. Kwon, M., Lee, J.Y., Won, W.Y., Park, J.W., Min, J.A., Hahn, C., et al.: Development and validation of a smartphone addiction scale (SAS). PLoS ONE **8**, (2013). https://doi.org/10.1371/journal.pone.0056936
5. Vorderer, P., Krömer, N., Schneider, F.M.: Permanently online–permanently connected: explorations into university students' use of social media and mobile smart devices. Comp. Hum. Behav. **63**, 694–703 (2016). https://doi.org/10.4324/9781315276472-1
6. Gui, M., Büchi, M.: From use to overuse: digital inequality in the age of communication abundance. Soc. Sci. Comp. Rev. **39**, 3–19 (2019). https://doi.org/10.1177/0894439319851163

7. Turkle, S.: Reclaiming Conversation: The Power of Talk in a Digital Age. Penguin, New York (2015)
8. Miller, D.: These tools help older people connect digitally while isolating. The Conversation (2020). https://theconversation.com/these-tools-help-older-people-connect-digitally-while-isolating-134860
9. Marston, H.R., Musselwhite, C., Hadley, R.A.: COVID-19 vs Social Isolation: the impact technology can have on communities, social connections and citizens. Ageingissues (2020). https://ageingissues.wordpress.com/2020/03/18/covid-19-vs-social-isolation-the-impact-tec hnology-can-have-on-communities-social-connections-and-citizens/?fbclid=IwAR30zMJ ujZfWFBImQR6V_wLJWlnHBrUYq21_SgTBS9qQ7Hgl9jkQ-_BU9kg
10. Rosales, A., Fernández-Ardèvol, M.: Smartphone usage diversity among older people. In: Sayago, S. (ed.) Perspectives on Human-Computer Interaction Research with Older People. Springer, Cham (2019). https://doi.org/10.1007/978-3-030-06076-3_4
11. Gershon, I.: The Breakup 2.0: Disconnecting Over New Media. Cornell University Press, New York (2010)
12. Fernández-Ardèvol, M., Belotti, F., Ieracitano, F., Mulargia, S., Rosales, A., Comunello, F.: I do it my way: Idioms of practice and digital media ideologies of adolescents and older adults. New Med. Soc. 1–19 (2020). https://doi.org/10.1177/1461444820959298
13. Salo, J.T., Tan, T.M., Kumar, A.J.: The mediating role and main effects of self-brand presentation strength. In: European Marketing Academy Conference: Leaving Footprints. Groningen, Netherlands (2017)
14. Stephens, K.K., Mandhana, D.M., Kim, J.J., Li, X., Glowacki, E.M., Cruz, I.: Reconceptualizing communication overload and building a theoretical foundation. Comm. Theory. **27**, 269–289 (2017). https://doi.org/10.1111/comt.12116
15. Sala, E., Gaia, A.: Older people's use of 'information and communication technology' in Europe: the italian case. Aut. Loc. Ser. Soc. **42**, 163–183 (2019). https://doi.org/10.1447/95863
16. Colombo, F., Aroldi, P., Carlo, S.: New elders, old divides: ICTs, inequalities and well being amongst young elderly Italians. Comunicar. **23**, 47–55 (2015). https://doi.org/10.3916/C45-2015-05
17. Eurostat: Individuals - frequency of internet use (2019). https://ec.europa.eu/eurostat/databr owser/view/isoc_ci_ifp_fu/default/table?lang=en&fbclid=IwAR3DhIEYYO4yUBUA8LN YanrWXuEUQo8z1w3XpgH6zyLivsyAsXPTiEHvlWY
18. Carlo, S.: Invecchiare Online. Vita e Pensiero, Milano (2017)
19. Statista: Number of smartphone users worldwide from 2016 to 2021. Statista (2020). https://www.statista.com/statistics/330695/number-of-smartphone-users-worldwide/
20. WeAreSocial: Digital in 2020. WeAreSocial.com (2020). https://wearesocial.com/digital-2020
21. Istat: Internet@Italia 2018 Domanda e offerta di servizi online e scenari di digitalizzazione (2018). https://www.istat.it/it/files/2018/06/Internet@Italia-2018.pdf
22. Ipsos: Gli over 55 sono inseparabili dallo smartphone (2018). https://www.ipsos.com/it-it/eve nto-ipsos-al-wired-nextfest-2018-firenze
23. ASSA: Anthropology of Smartphones and Smart Ageing: About the Project. Ucl.Ac.Uk (2020). https://www.ucl.ac.uk/anthropology/assa/
24. Humphreys, L.: Mobile social media: future challenges and opportunities. Mob. Med. Comm. **1**, 20–25 (2013). doi.org/20-25.0.1177/2050157912459499
25. Taipale, S., Farinosi, M.: The big meaning of small messages: the use of whatsapp in intergenerational family communication. In: Zhou, J., Salvendy, G. (eds.) ITAP 2018. LNCS, vol. 10926, pp. 532–546. Springer, Cham (2018). https://doi.org/10.1007/978-3-319-92034-4_40

26. Hutto, C.J., Bell, C., Farmer, S., Fausset, C., Harley, L., Nguyen, J., Fain, B.: Social media gerontology: understanding social media usage among older adults. Web Intell. **1**, 69–87 (2015). https://HICSS.2014.223

27. Amaral, I., Daniel, F.: The use of social media among senior citizens in Portugal: active ageing through an intergeneration approach. In: Zhou, J., Salvendy, G. (eds.) ITAP 2018. LNCS, vol. 10926, pp. 422–434. Springer, Cham (2018). https://doi.org/10.1007/978-3-319-92034-4_32

28. Damant, J., Knapp, M., Freddolino, P., Lombard, D.: Effects of digital engagement on the quality of life of older people. Heal. Soc. Care Comm. **25**, 1679–1703 (2017). https://doi.org/10.1111/hsc.12335

29. Sourbati, M.: On older people, internet access and electronic service delivery: a study of sheltered homes. In: Loos, E., Mante-Meijer, E., Haddon, L. (eds.) The Social Dynamics of Information and Communication Technology, pp. 95–104. Ashgate, Aldershot (2008)

30. Harley, D., Howland, K., Harris, E., Redlich, C.: Nearer to being characters in a book: how older people make sense of online communities and social networking sites. In: 48th Hawaii International Conference on System Sciences, pp. 2023-2032. IEEE Press, Hawaii (2015). https://doi.org/10.1109/hicss.2015.242

31. Jung, E.H., Walden, J., Johnson, A.C., Sundar, S.S.: Social networking in the aging context: why older adults use or avoid Facebook. Tel. Info. **34**, 1071–1080 (2017). https://doi.org/10.1016/j.tele.2017.04.015

32. Doyle, C., Goldingay, S.: The rise of the silver surfer: online social networking and social inclusion for older adults. Jour. Soc. Inc. **3**, 40–54 (2012). https://doi.org/10.36251/josi.54

33. Ivan, L., Hebblethwaite, S.: Grannies on the net: Grandmothers' experiences of Facebook in family communication. Rom. Jour. Comm. Pub. Rel. **18**, 11–25 (2016). https://doi.org/10.21018/rjcpr.2016.1.199

34. Arjan, R., Pfeil, U., Zaphiris, P.: Age differences in online social networking. In: Conference on Human Factors in Computing Systems, pp. 2739–2744. ACM Press, New York (2008). https://doi.org/10.1145/1358628.1358754

35. Carlo, S., Vergani, M.: Risk and benefit perceptions: resistance, adoption and uses of ICT among the italian elderly. In: Zhou, J., Salvendy, G. (eds.) ITAP 2016. LNCS, vol. 9754, pp. 155–166. Springer, Cham (2016). https://doi.org/10.1007/978-3-319-39943-0_15

36. Loos, E., Haddon, H., Mante-Meijer, E.: Generational Use of New Media. Ashgate Publishing, Farnham (2012)

37. Turkle, S.: Alone Together: Why We Expect More from Technology and Less from Each Other. Hachette, London (2017)

38. Colombo, F., Aroldi, P., Carlo, S.: I use it correctly!: the use of ICTs among Italian grandmothers in a generational perspective. Hum. Tech. **14**, 343–365 (2018). https://doi.org/10.17011/ht/urn.201811224837

39. Smith, A. L., Chaparro, B.S.: Smartphone text input method performance, usability, and preference with younger and older adults. Hum. Fac. **57**, 1015–1028 (2015). http://doi.org/0.1177/0018720815575644

40. Wildenbos, G.A., Peute, L., Jaspers, M.: Aging barriers influencing mobile health usability for older adults: a literature framework (MOLD-US). Inter. J. Med. Info. **114**, 66–75 (2018). https://doi.org/10.1016/j.ijmedinf.2018.03.012

41. Petrovčič, A., Taipale, S., Rogelj, A., Dolničar, V. (2018). Design of mobile phones for older adults: an empirical analysis of design guidelines and checklists for feature phones and smartphones. Inter. Jour. Hum. Comp. Inter. **34**, 251–264 (2018). https://doi.org/10.1080/10447318.2017.1345142

42. Millward, P.: The 'grey digital divide': Perception, exclusion and barriers of access to the Internet for older people. Fir. Mon. **8**, (2003). https://firstmonday.org/ojs/index.php/fm/article/view/1066

43. Rosales, A., Fernández-Ardèvol, M.: Generational comparison of simultaneous internet activities using smartphones and computers. In: Zhou, J., Salvendy, G. (eds.) Human Aspects of IT for the Aged Population: Design for Aging, pp. 478–489. ITAP 2016. Lecture Notes in Computer Science, vol 9754. Springer, Cham (2016). https://doi.org/10.1007/978-3-319-39943-0_46

44. Colombo, F., Carlo, S.: Access and use of ICTs among the italian young elderly: a field study. In: Zhou, J., Salvendy, G. (eds.) ITAP 2015. LNCS, vol. 9193, pp. 166–176. Springer, Cham (2015). https://doi.org/10.1007/978-3-319-20892-3_17

45. Rosales, A., Fernández-Ardèvol, M.: Beyond whatsapp: older people and smartphones. Rom. Jour. Comm. Pub. Rel. **18**, 27–47 (2016). https://doi.org/10.21018/rjcpr.2016.1.200

46. Stier, S., Breuer, J., Siegers, P., Thorson, K.: Integrating survey data and digital trace data: key issues in developing an emerging field. Soc. Sci. Comp. Rev. **38**, 503–516 (2020). https://doi.org/10.1177/0894439319843669

47. McCracken, G.: The Long Interview. Sage, London (1988)

48. Denzin, N.K., Lincoln, Y.: S: The Sage Handbook of Qualitative Research. Sage, Thousand Oaks (2011)

49. Charmaz, K.: Grounded theory: objectivist and constructivist methods. grounded theory: objectivist and constructivist methods. In: Denzin, N., Lincoln, Y. (eds.) The Sage handbook of qualitative research, pp. 509–535. Sage, Thousand Oaks (2011)

50. Glaser, B.G., Strauss, A.L.: The Discovery of Grounded Theory: Strategies for Qualitative Research. Transaction Publishers, Piscataway (2009)

51. Burawoy, M.: The extended case method. Soc. Theory. **16**, 4–33 (1998). https://doi.org/10.1111/0735-2751.00040

52. Mead, G.H.: (C. W. Morris ed.): Mind, Self, and Society from the Standpoint of a Social Behaviorist. University of Chicago Press, Chicago (1934)

53. Bryant, A.: The Effect of Social Media on the Physical, Social Emotional, and Cognitive Development of Adolescents. Merric Scholar Works (2018). https://scholarworks.merrimack.edu/honors_capstones/37/

54. Marston, H.R.: Millennials and ICT - findings from the technology 4 young adults (T4YA) project: an exploratory study. Societies **9**(4), 80 (2019). https://doi.org/10.3390/soc9040080

55. Sims, T., Reed, A.E., Carr, D.C.: Information and communication technology use is related to higher well-being among the oldest-old. J. Geron. **72**, 761–770 (2017). https://doi.org/10.1093/geronb/gbw130

56. Stephenson, W.: Introduction to Q-methodology. Operant subjectivity **17**, 1–13 (1993). https://doi.org/10.15133/j.os.1993.006

57. Fernández-Ardèvol, M., Rosales, A.: Older people, smartphones and whatsApp. In: Vincent, J., Haddon, L. (eds.) Smartphone cultures, pp. 55–68. Routledge, New York (2017)

58. Fernández-Ardèvol, M., et al.: Methodological strategies to understand smartphone practices for social connectedness in later life. In: Zhou, J., Salvendy, G. (eds.) HCII 2019. LNCS, vol. 11593, pp. 46–64. Springer, Cham (2019). https://doi.org/10.1007/978-3-030-22015-0_4

59. European Commission: Aging Europe: Looking at the lives of older people in the EU. Publications Office of the European Union (2019). https://ec.europa.eu/eurostat/documents/3217494/10166544/KS-02-19%E2%80%9691681-EN-N.pdf/c701972f-6b4e-b432-57d2-91898ca94893

How Do Older Adults Learn Informally via Social Media? A Pilot Study of Chinese Urban Older Adults

Yue Chen and Qin Gao[✉]

Tsinghua University, Beijing 100084, China
gaoqin@tsinghua.edu.cn

Abstract. With the prevalence of social media among older adults, informal learning via social media has become a common and effective approach for lifelong learning and successful aging. However, little research has summarized older users' specific needs and behaviors during learning. Especially, little attention has been paid to the need for self-worth, which is crucial to health and well-being but decreases in old age. Therefore, this study conducted interviews with eight older adults in China to understand their needs and behaviors adopted during informal learning via social media. The results revealed four major needs satisfied by informal learning, i.e., practical needs, enjoyment needs, self-worth needs, and social-connectedness needs. We also identified older adults' cognitive and social behaviors during learning. Especially, the participants emphasized the need for self-worth, but it has not been well satisfied by current social media platforms or much discussed in previous relevant research. Finally, we proposed implications for design and future research about older adults' informal learning via social media.

Keywords: Older adults · Informal learning · Social media · Self-worth

1 Introduction

To promote active and healthy aging, older adults need social connections, self-contentment, and self-growth [1]. An effective approach is lifelong learning. Learning can be either formal or informal [2]. Formal learning, such as learning courses in a third-age university, is only available for a small number of older adults due to the limited educational resources. In China, there were 250 million older adults but only 76 thousand third-age universities [3]. Informal learning is the noninstitutionalized and unstructured learning that occurs in daily life [4]. This self-paced way fits older adults' needs for a leisure style of learning [5]. Informal learning resources are also available on smart devices and social media. Therefore, it becomes more prevalent for older adults to learn informally.

Social media provide a great opportunity for older people's informal learning. A survey in Netherland suggests that 76 percent of 65 to 74-year-olds used social media [6]. In China, WeChat has become a major social media platform for older adults. In

© Springer Nature Switzerland AG 2021
Q. Gao and J. Zhou (Eds.): HCII 2021, LNCS 12786, pp. 379–392, 2021.
https://doi.org/10.1007/978-3-030-78108-8_28

2020, a WeChat mini program for video editing and sharing, named Xiao Nian Gao, attracted more than 500 million users, of whom most were older or middle-aged users [7]. Over 65% of senior users use WeChat as a source for content consumption, such as reading articles and watching videos [8]. Besides content consumption, some older adults also produce and share their knowledge with online learning communities on social media [9, 10].

Some research identified themes, needs, and social interaction when older adults learned informally on mobile devices (e.g., a literature review [11]). However, some problems remain unsolved and thus hinder better designs of ICT for older adults' informal learning. First, little research has summarized older users' specific needs satisfied by informal learning via social media. Second, informal learning can increase learners' competence and bring a feeling of accomplishment. It potentially enhances self-worth, which is crucial to successful aging [1] but generally decreases with increasing age [12]. However, most previous studies devoted to providing tangible and social support better to older learners [e.g., 14, 15] but paid little attention to their needs for self-worth or self-esteem during informal learning. Third, older adults may take cognitive learning behaviors and interact with others during informal learning via social media, but little research has identified these behaviors and their associations with the feelings such as self-worth and social connectedness.

To better understand older adults' needs and design ICT for informal learning, this study aims to identify (1) the current sources and topics of older adults' daily informal learning and the overall impact on their life, (2) their needs and barriers of informal learning, and (3) their cognitive and social behaviors to learn and interact with others. We conducted a qualitative semi-structured interview with eight Chinese urban older adults (aged 64 to 90 years old) to obtain in-depth and detailed information about relevant phenomena during informal learning.

2 Literature Review

2.1 Older Adults' Needs for Informal Learning and Social Media Using

Researchers have identified older adults' needs for formal and informal learning, including cognitive, emotional, and social needs, by bottom-up methods such as surveys and interviews [11, 13–16]. Some studies suggested differences between older and younger adults. Older adults were motivated more by the needs of knowledge, self-growth, and belongingness but less by the needs of competitions [13, 14]. They had a stronger interest in daily-life topics, e.g., healthcare, hobbies, and cooking [13–16]. They had more experience and wisdom, but their cognitive and physical capacities declined and they were generally less familiar with ICT [17, 18].

Older adults used social media to satisfy their needs for information and social connection. They used social media to receive news and information in time [19]. They interacted with not only family members and friends but also other users online with the same hobbies for a sense of social connectedness [20, 21]. They also created content and expressed themselves on social media to increase self-worth and self-identity and engage in a more meaningful life [22]. However, little research identified what motivated older adults to learn informally via social media.

2.2 Self-worth

Self-worth, or self-esteem, has been found strongly associated with the feeling of social connectedness, well-being, and decreasing death anxiety [23–25]. Self-worth involves two components, i.e., positive self-regard and perceived usefulness [26, 27]. Positive self-regard is the belief that oneself is good. Positive self-regard was seen almost equal to self-worth in some research [28], whereas perceived usefulness or competence was discussed less frequently.

However, perceived usefulness, or subjective usefulness, has been found beneficial to older adults. In long term (several years), perceived usefulness can promote mental health and quality of life and further decrease mortality [29–31]. For Chinese older adults, physical and mental health may be affected more by perceived usefulness than by overall self-esteem measured by Rosenberg self-esteem scale [32], in which most items ask about positive self-regards.

People in the East Asia culture were also found to report lower self-worth measured by Rosenberg self-esteem scale than people in the North American culture [33–35] because of the following reasons. First, self-reported self-worth may be decreased by modesty, a social norm in East Asia [34]. Second, East Asians emphasize and value continued self-improvement and hard working to future goals and thus feel tolerant to a low level of self-worth [36, 37]. Third, East Asians tend to see a person as a member in a community or society, and thus self-evaluation depends more on whether they meet the standards of their social roles [35]. All these phenomena suggest that in East Asian culture, perceived usefulness needs to be studied more.

2.3 Behaviors During Informal Learning

Because of the broad and various definitions of informal learning, it is hard to synthesize the forms and typical activities of informal learning. One of the most widely used frameworks [38, 39] classified informal learning into four forms based on the dimensions of consciousness and intentionality: (1) self-directed learning (both conscious and intentional), (2) incidental learning (conscious but not intentional, e.g., a by-product of other activities), (3) integrative learning (nonconscious but intentional, and can result in sudden insights and "aha" moments), and (4) tacit learning (neither conscious nor intentional, usually during socialization). Similarly, researchers categorized 12 learning behaviors in the workplace according to three dimensions, named intentionality, developmental relatedness (by oneself or with others), and learning competence (mental or actional) [4, 40].

For informal learning via social media, relatedness (individual or interpersonal) may be concerned most among different dimensions. For example, to describe informal learning with mobile devices, researchers developed a survey instrument with two dimensions, i.e., information seeking and sharing [41] based on theoretical models of information searching process and social learning. However, little research explored and summarized the social media-based informal learning behaviors of older adults.

3 Method

3.1 Participants

The participants were recruited by snowball sampling of three types of sources: (1) the authors' social networks, (2) the older adults living in the same community where one of the authors lived, and (3) the older adults who participated in the previous research of the authors' department. We interviewed eight urban older adults living in four communities in two cities in China. Table 1 presents the information of the participants. Six of them were female, and two were male. They aged from 64 to 90 (M = 74, SD = 11). They all had more or fewer health problems but could deal with most activities of daily living independently. They all retired and had education levels at least junior secondary education (middle school). Seven of them lived with their partner or children, whereas P1 lived alone and her children lived close to her community. All of them had been using smart devices with social media for more than two years and spent more than one hour per day on smart devices.

Table 1. Sociodemographic, health status, and behavioral variables of participants.

ID	Age	Gender	Health problems	Education	Household composition	Time on smart devices
P1	85	F	Poor waist, high blood pressure, presbyopia	SV[a]	Lives alone. Her children live near her community in the same city	>1 h/day
P2	64	F	Minor problems, presbyopia	Bachelor	Lives with her husband and children	>1 h/day
P3	64	F	None	LS[b]	Lives with her husband	>1 h/day
P4	68	F	Poor knees and waist, slight presbyopia	LS	Lives with her husband. Her children live in the same city	Most of the day time
P5	68	M	High blood pressure, presbyopia, poor hearing	SV	Lives with his wife. His children live in the same city	Most of the day time
P6	68	M	High blood pressure, presbyopia, poor hearing and one deaf ear	SV	Lives with his wife and children	>1 h/day
P7	86	F	Had a tumor before but recovered, presbyopia	Bachelor	Lives with her husband. Her children live in the US	>3 h/day
P8	90	F	Macula and presbyopia	Master	Lives with her children	>3 h/day

[a]SV: Secondary Vocational School
[b]LS: Lower Secondary School

3.2 Data Collection and Analysis

P1 was interviewed via the video chatting function of WeChat, whereas others were interviewed face to face. P7 and P8 were interviewed together, whereas other participants were interviewed individually. In each interview, we asked questions in the following four major themes:

1. Sources and topics of informal learning: What informal learning topics are you interested in? What sources do you learn these topics from?
2. Motivation, needs, and barriers: Why do you learn these topics? Why do you learn from these sources? What problems did you ever encounter? How did you solve the problems?
3. Behaviors during learning:

   a. How do you search, organize, store, and review the information? How do you practice and apply the knowledge?
   b. Do you interact with others during learning? How and why do you interact with others during learning? Do you share or produce knowledge with others and how?

4. Current physical and psychological status and impacts of informal learning: How healthy are you in general? Generally, are you happy and satisfied with your life, and why? In your daily life, what is changed by the knowledge and relevant technologies?

Each interview lasted for around one hour and was audio-recorded and transcribed to texts later. The interview scripts were analyzed by a thematic approach based on grounded theory [42]. An interview was analyzed as soon as possible. For each theme, data were coded iteratively. Then the codes were categorized as findings inductively, which can be explained and supported by the relevant coded transcripts.

4 Results

4.1 Sources and Topics of Older Adults' Daily Informal Learning

Sources of Informal Learning. Participants obtained information from various ways both online and offline. Social media on smart devices had been one of the most frequently adopted information sources for them. All of them used WeChat every day to connect with others and get information from, e.g., WeChat Moment, articles of WeChat channels, and short videos in WeChat mini programs. Besides WeChat, the participants also got information from news aggregator applications popular in China, such as TouTiao. P2 and P7 also listened to audio-based lectures via applications of audiobooks and radio streaming. Besides smart devices, the participants also got information from traditional sources such as televisions (all the participants), newspapers and books (P7 and P8), community workshops or lectures (P4 and P6), and the third age university (P2, P4, and P7).

Noted that even some non-formal courses of the third age university were offered via WeChat during the COVID-19 pandemic. For example, P7 took a painting course via WeChat group, where the instructor gave step-by-step painting instructions in photos or videos and assigned and commented on every student's homework. Similarly, P2 and P3 participated in the free lectures about piano playing via WeChat.

Topics of Informal Learning. First, most participants wanted to learn about necessary or useful knowledge relevant to their daily life. All the participants learned healthcare knowledge through informal learning, such as diet and Chinese medicines mentioned by six participants, medical knowledge mentioned by four participants, and physical work-outs mentioned by P1 and P4. All the participants also learned useful daily-life skills, such as cooking and garbage classification. Second, most participants learn knowledge that can help them better connect with society. All the participants were interested in news and politics from smart devices. P2 and P7 were interested in learning new IT skills for better living. P7 also learned oral English to better communicate with her grandchildren who lived abroad. Third, all the participants learned their hobbies via social media, such as art, music, sports, planting, history, geography, and psychology.

4.2 Needs and Barriers

Practical Needs. All the participants learned for practical needs, such as to get healthcare information (mentioned by all the participants), to solve daily life problems (P2, P3, P6, P7, and P8), and to keep cognitive functions (P1, P3, and P4). Some participants (P1, P5, and P6) said that they only wanted to learn a minimum level of ICT skills that were necessary for their daily life.

Needs for Enjoyment. All the participants learned for leisure, enjoyment, and curiosity about new things. All of them learned to enjoy their hobbies. Five of them said they learned to feel free and autonomous. Three participants (P2, P3, and P7) learned because they were curious and interested in education, new knowledge, and new technologies. Learning is one of P7's hobbies. She even took courses from the third age university for almost thirty years. Because the educational resources for were limited in China several decades ago, some participants were interested in education for compensational reasons:

> *"Our generations had little opportunities of education when we were young. I finished formal education after the graduation of middle school and did not learn much in my childhood. However, now new technologies provide me free and easy access to new knowledge. Meanwhile, I am retired and have a lot of free time. Therefore, I must grasp this good chance to keep updated." [P3, 64 years old]*

Most of them were leisure learners and cared more about positive feelings than learning performance. Therefore, they preferred more flexible ways to learn. They would give up if there were too many complex requirements (mentioned by P1, P3, P7, and P8). Though interested in new technologies, P2 would give up learning if she cannot handle it. P3 said a major reason that she did not take formal courses was that she did not like a strict schedule. Therefore, she preferred learning fragmentedly via social media.

Needs for Self-worth. Third, most participants learned for a sense of self-esteem, self-worth, or values. On the one hand, learning itself can provide promote positive self-regard. Four participants (P1, P3, P4, and P8) said they learned to get busy and avoid a feeling of emptiness. Three participants (P3, P4, and P7) learned to lead a fulfilling life and feel a sense of self-improvement and accomplishment. For example, P7 was proud of getting certifications of completing courses:

"I can get full marks on the exams of the courses I take." [P7, 86 years old]

On the other hand, the participants wanted to become more useful to others. They wanted to learn the trends in society (mentioned by P1, P7, and P8). If they were outdated, they would feel that they were useless and troubling other people. Three participants (P2, P4, and P7) also mentioned that they learned to promote grandchildren's growth:

"I am learning piano playing to feel a sense of accomplishment... Another reason is that my grandson is learning fluting. I want to demonstrate to him that his grandma is still working hard to learn music even though her functions and flexibility have been declined." [P4, 68 years old]

The need to keep self-esteem and be useful to others sometimes hindered participants from learning. P1 and P7 said they gave up learning some ICT skills from their young family members because they did not want to bother their young family members. P4 and P7 also said they hoped to be respected, not ignored or underestimated by others. For example, P4 shared her experience of dropping out of a painting course in the third age university. In a lecture, the instructor commented on the homework of all the students except her, and thus she felt ignored and hurt.

Needs for Social Connectedness. Fourth, most participants learned new things for connections with others and the society. They consumed news and learned politics to keep updated with the society (mentioned by five participants). P2 reposted useful and knowledgeable content on WeChat Moment to help and interact with others. P4 also shared useful content with her friends and family members who could not meet offline.

Other Needs and Barriers. They also needed suitable information display for learning. Almost every participant complained that the small font size on their smart devices. They preferred paper-based assistance for learning, such as manuals for new devices or notebooks (mentioned by P5, P7, and P8). They also preferred multimodal input channels because of their declined vision or audition.

Some factors hindered the participants to learn. First, offline educational resources were limited, but they needed to learn some subjects face to face, such as art, music, and ICT. Second, P6 and P8 had little time for learning because they were busy taking care of their grandchildren or partner. Third, they stopped learning due to physical impairments. For example, P3 used to take a dancing course but quitted it after she got arthritis.

4.3 Behaviors to Learn and Interact with Others

Cognitive Learning Behaviors. The participants obtained and internalized knowledge and skills by searching, browsing, storing, and reviewing the relevant content. Most participants obtained new knowledgeable content from subscribed channels or reposted by their friends on social media. Some of them (P2, P4, P7, and P8) used search engines to find specific knowledge they were interested in, but in most cases, the participants just read or watched what they encountered. Some of them (P1, P3, P4, and P5) relied on the information flow customized based on their view history on WeChat mini programs or other content feeding applications.

Nearly all participants mentioned that they stored or recorded knowledge during learning by smart devices and paper-based notebooks. On the one hand, half of them used the "adding to my favorites" function of social media platforms to store useful articles and videos (P2, P3, P4, and P6). P2 and P4 also used laptops to store and organize the lecture videos of piano playing. However, P3 and P4 also mentioned that it was hard to find something from their "favorites" later for review and practice. On the other hand, most participants relied on paper-based notetaking (P1, P3, P4, P5, and P7). P5 said he kept writing a diary every day and may search for information later by dates. P1, P3, and P7 recorded knowledge on their notebooks chronologically, but P1 and P3 said they wanted to reorganize their notebooks according to the topics.

Social Interaction During Learning. All the participants interacted with others during learning, including their friends, family members, neighbors, past schoolmates, and past colleagues. The participants who took courses online or in the third age university also interacted with their classmates and instructors of the courses (P2, P3, P4, and P7). The forms of interaction include: (1) liking or commenting on others' posts, (2) reposting valuable, interesting, or useful content, (3) discussing homework and Q&A with instructors in WeChat groups (P2, P4, and P7), and (4) posting original content to others by the targeted or directed conversation among users (P2 and P3). When the participants had technical problems during learning online, all of them tend to ask family members or neighbors for face-to-face help first.

The participants rarely produced and broadcasted knowledgeable content on e.g., WeChat moments, or shared their feelings online during learning. There were three possible reasons. First, most participants felt a low self-efficacy in ICT skills and domain knowledge, and thus they thought their experience was not useful or valuable to others (P1, P3, P4, P7, and P8). They kept lurking to avoid bothering others with the overwhelming information. Second, some of them felt it hard to find someone with similar interests, experience, and knowledge background to communicate deeply (P1, P3, and P4). As P1 said:

> "I always keep silent after reading an article or watching a video... I felt hard to find someone to talk about the content after my husband passed away... but it is not a big problem for me, because I am an introvert. I keep busy by doing handcrafts and I feel fulfilled." [P1, 85 years old].

Third, some participants (P2, P3, and P6) worried about privacy and Internet fraud, and therefore tended to generate less but consume more content.

4.4 Impacts of Informal Learning on Their Life

From a pragmatic view, most participants suggested that they lead a better, healthier, and more convenient life after beginning to learn anything via social media. From a socioemotional perspective, informal learning via social media made all the participants happier. They could learn more about the world and keep connected with society. Some of them also said informal learning made their life more meaningful and valuable (P1, P3, P4, P6, and P7).

5 Discussion

5.1 Findings

We gave an overview of information sources and topics that Chinese urban older adults were interested in. The three major topics were pragmatic knowledge/skills (e.g., healthcare), knowledge/skills for social inclusion (e.g., ICT skills), and knowledge/skills of their hobbies for leisure, which were consistent with the previous research (e.g., the review [11]).

Echoing these major topics, **we identified older adults' major needs during informal learning**, including practical needs (e.g., obtaining healthcare knowledge), enjoyment needs, self-worth needs, and social-connectedness needs. Among the identified needs, practical, enjoyment, and connected needs have been addressed in previous research [e.g., 7, 9], but self-worth needs are seldomly discussed in the current literature about older adults' informal learning or social media using.

In detail, we found that informal learning via social media may have satisfied older adults' needs for self-worth in the following aspects. First, as mentioned by five of the eight participants, informal learning was an approach to continuous self-improvement, which could promote self-worth especially for East Asians [36, 37]. Second, informal learning of useful knowledge (such as ICT skills) made older adults feel autonomous, competent, and useful to others [43]. It is a major reason why they learned to use ICT and keep updated with trends. Third, during informal learning, a few older adults may share useful knowledge with others and thus promote the feeling of self-worth.

We identified specific cognitive and social behaviors adopted by older adults during informal learning via social media. Regarding cognitive behaviors, older adults may browse and search for new content, store knowledge, practice skills, and apply them in their life, in line with previous research about mobile informal learning [41]. Regarding social behaviors, older adults may like, comment, or repost content useful to others.

However, the participants seldom generated new content or shared their knowledge and feelings with others. A major reason was that they felt low self-efficacy in ICT skills and thus worried that their content might be useless and bother others. Another reason was that older people had fewer needs for identity but more needs for generativity (contributions to younger generations) than young adults [44], whereas self-identity and self-expression were one of the major motivations for generating content on social media [45, 46]. Therefore, older adults seldomly post their knowledge or feelings during learning on social media.

The results of posting were different from some previous studies suggesting that older adults were willing to produce and share their knowledge with online learning communities [9, 10]. The difference may result from two possible reasons. First, these previous studies [9, 10] were conducted in Western cultures, which emphasize the enhancement of self-images more. The participants in our study were all older adults in East Asian cultures, which emphasize one as a member of a community [33, 36]. It may hinder older adults from posting their feelings and knowledge on social media. Second, previous studies was conducted on platforms only for older adults or online networks for hobby learning [9, 10]. However, the participants in our study mainly used WeChat and some of them had difficulty finding people with similar interests. Older adults are probably more willing to share their feelings with peers and people with similar interests, but in China, there is a lack of social media platforms specifically designed for older adults with similar interests.

5.2 Implications for Design and Future Research

First, future design and research for older adults need to pay more attention to increasing the feelings of self-worth and generativity. This study suggests that older adults have strong needs for perceived usefulness to others and the feeling of generativity, but most of them lurk and worry about whether the information they shared is useful or valuable to others. A lack of self-worth even decreased their knowledge sharing behaviors and further hindered older adults' social connectedness and contributions to society.

Some empirical studies have designed workshops or intergeneration communication programs to support older adults' informal learning and the sense of self-worth [47–49]. However, there still lacks knowledge about how to design ICT platforms for older adults' informal learning and enhancement of self-worth. The interviews in this study suggests that older adults' self-worth can be potentially increased by, for example, presenting learning progress or improvement, highlighting their contributions to others, and matching older users with peers who have similar interests. Future research is needed to better enhance older adults' self-worth during informal learning.

Second, future design for older adults may emphasize better user experience more than better cognitive performance. Overall, we found that older adults pursue positive feelings (including self-worth) more. Therefore, to support older adults' informal learning, future design may, for example, design mechanisms or procedures for more flexible and self-paced participation in learning and social interactions.

Third, though we identified several cognitive and social behaviors during informal learning, it remained unclear about the impacts of these behaviors on positive feelings such as self-worth. Identifying the impacts of different behaviors can guide the design of platforms to promote specific behaviors. Therefore, future research may adopt quantitative methods to investigate the actual impacts of different informal learning behaviors on those positive feelings.

5.3 Limitations

First, this study only interviewed eight participants. They were more educated than the current elderly population in urban China. Therefore, they were probably more interested in informal learning and had better ICT skills than the average elderly population in China. Second, learning behaviors were recalled and self-reported by the participants in interviews. To trace their learning behaviors and experience more accurately, future research may adopt other methods such as observations and diary study in long term.

6 Conclusion

This study conducted interviews with eight Chinese older adults to understand their needs and behaviors adopted during informal learning via social media. First, the interviews identified sources and topics in which Chinese urban older adults were interested. Second, it revealed four major types of needs satisfied by informal learning, i.e., practical needs, enjoyment needs, self-worth needs, and social-connectedness needs. Especially, the participants emphasized the need for self-worth, but it has not been well satisfied by current social media platforms or much discussed in previous relevant research. Third, the interviews identified older adults' cognitive and social behaviors during learning. We also proposed design implications and suggestions for future research about older adults' informal learning via social media.

Acknowledgement. This study was supported by China Postdoctoral Science Foundation No. 2020M670362. We thank all those who participated.

References

1. Reichstadt, J., Sengupta, G., Depp, C.A., Palinkas, L.A., Jeste, D.V.: Older adults' perspectives on successful aging: qualitative interviews. Am. J. Geriatr. Psychiatry **18**, 567–575 (2010)
2. Ainsworth, H.L., Eaton, S.E.: Formal, Non-Formal and Informal Learning in the Sciences. ERIC (2010)
3. Xinhua News (新华社): The Central Committee of the Communist Party of China and the State Council issued the "Medium and Long-term Plan for the State to Actively Respond to Population Aging" (中共中央国务院印发《国家积极应对人口老龄化中长期规划》). http://www.gov.cn/xinwen/2019-11/21/content_5454347.htm
4. Jeong, S., Han, S.J., Lee, J., Sunalai, S., Yoon, S.W.: Integrative literature review on informal learning: antecedents, conceptualizations, and future directions. Hum. Resour. Dev. Rev. **17**, 128–152 (2018)
5. Brockett, R.G.: The relationship between self-directed learning readiness and life satisfaction among older adults. Adult Educ. Q. **35**, 210–219 (1985)
6. Statistics Netherlands: More elderly active on social media. https://www.cbs.nl/en-gb/news/2020/04/more-elderly-active-on-social-media. Accessed 02 Feb 2021
7. Sohu: Analysis Report of "Short Video Mini Programs" for Middle-aged and Elderly People (中老年「短视频小程序」分析报告: 小年糕&早安看看的对比分析_产品). www.sohu.com/a/381003584_114819

8. Tencent Research Institute (腾讯研究院): 吾老之域: 老年人微信生活与家庭微信反哺. Zhejiang Publishing Group Digital Media Co., Ltd. (浙江出版集团数字传媒有限公司) (2018)

9. Morrison, D., McCutheon, J.: Empowering older adults' informal, self-directed learning: harnessing the potential of online personal learning networks. Res. Pract. Technol. Enhanc. Learn. **14**(1), 1–16 (2019). https://doi.org/10.1186/s41039-019-0104-5

10. Burmeister, O.K.: What seniors value about online community. J. Community Inform. **8**, 1–12 (2012)

11. Jin, B., Kim, J., Baumgartner, L.M.: Informal learning of older adults in using mobile devices: a review of the literature. Adult Educ. Q. **69**, 120–141 (2019). 0741713619834726

12. Orth, U., Robins, R.W., Widaman, K.F.: Life-span development of self-esteem and its effects on important life outcomes. J. Pers. Soc. Psychol. **102**, 1271 (2012)

13. Kim, A., Merriam, S.B.: Motivations for learning among older adults in a learning in retirement institute. Educ. Gerontol. **30**, 441–455 (2004)

14. Leen, E.A., Lang, F.R.: Motivation of computer based learning across adulthood. Comput. Hum. Behav. **29**, 975–983 (2013)

15. Xiong, J., Zuo, M.: Older adults' learning motivations in massive open online courses. Educ. Gerontol. **45**, 82–93 (2019). https://doi.org/10.1080/03601277.2019.1581444

16. Liyanagunawardena, T.R., Williams, S.A.: Elderly learners and massive open online courses: a review. Interact. J. Med. Res. **5**, e1 (2016)

17. Pappas, M.A., Demertzi, E., Papagerasimou, Y., Koukianakis, L., Voukelatos, N., Drigas, A.: Cognitive-based e-learning design for older adults. Soc. Sci. **8**, 6 (2019)

18. Zhou, J., Rau, P.-L., Salvendy, G.: Age-related difference in the use of mobile phones. Univ. Access Inf. Soc. **13**(4), 401–413 (2013). https://doi.org/10.1007/s10209-013-0324-1

19. Quinn, K.: Cognitive effects of social media use: a case of older adults. Soc. Media + Soc. **4**, 2056305118787203 (2018)

20. Coelho, J., Duarte, C.: A literature survey on older adults' use of social network services and social applications. Comput. Hum. Behav. **58**, 187–205 (2016). https://doi.org/10.1016/j.chb. 2015.12.053

21. Hope, A., Schwaba, T., Piper, A.M.: Understanding digital and material social communications for older adults. In: Proceedings of the SIGCHI Conference on Human Factors in Computing Systems, pp. 3903–3912. Association for Computing Machinery, Toronto (2014). https://doi.org/10.1145/2556288.2557133

22. Brewer, R., Piper, A.M.: "Tell It Like It Really Is": a case of online content creation and sharing among older adult bloggers. In: Proceedings of the 2016 CHI Conference on Human Factors in Computing Systems, pp. 5529–5542. Association for Computing Machinery, San Jose (2016). https://doi.org/10.1145/2858036.2858379

23. Deci, E.L., Ryan, R.M.: Human autonomy: the basis for true self-esteem. In: Kernis, M. (ed.) Efficacy, Agency, and Self-esteem . The Springer Series in Social Clinical Psychology, pp. 31–49. Springer, Heidelberg (1995). https://doi.org/10.1007/978-1-4899-1280-0_3

24. Murphy, D., Joseph, S., Demetriou, E., Karimi-Mofrad, P.: Unconditional positive self-regard, intrinsic aspirations, and authenticity: pathways to psychological well-being. J. Humanist. Psychol. **60**, 258–279 (2020)

25. Zhang, J., et al.: Relationship between meaning in life and death anxiety in the elderly: self-esteem as a mediator. BMC Geriatr. **19**, 1–8 (2019). https://doi.org/10.1186/s12877-019-1316-7

26. Ranzijn, R., Keeves, J., Luszcz, M., Feather, N.T.: The role of self-perceived usefulness and competence in the self-esteem of elderly adults: confirmatory factor analyses of the Bachman revision of Rosenberg's Self-Esteem Scale. J. Gerontol. B Psychol. Sci. Soc. Sci. **53**, P96–P104 (1998)

27. Tafarodi, R.W., Swann, W.B., Jr.: Two-dimensional self-esteem: theory and measurement. Personality Individ. Differ. **31**, 653–673 (2001)
28. Rosenberg, M.: Conceiving the Self. RE Krieger (1986)
29. Gruenewald, T.L., Karlamangla, A.S., Greendale, G.A., Singer, B.H., Seeman, T.E.: Feelings of usefulness to others, disability, and mortality in older adults: the MacArthur study of successful aging. J. Gerontol. B Psychol. Sci. Soc. Sci. **62**, P28–P37 (2007). https://doi.org/10.1093/geronb/62.1.P28
30. Gu, D., Brown, B.L., Qiu, L.: Self-perceived uselessness is associated with lower likelihood of successful aging among older adults in China. BMC Geriatr. **16**, 1–12 (2016)
31. Okamoto, K., Tanaka, Y.: Subjective usefulness and 6-year mortality risks among elderly persons in Japan. J. Gerontol. B Psychol. Sci. Soc. Sci. **59**, P246–P249 (2004)
32. Yang, Y., Wen, M.: Parental dissatisfaction, health, and well-being among older Chinese adults: the mediating role of self-esteem and feeling useless. J. Fam. Issues **40**, 2456–2477 (2019). https://doi.org/10.1177/0192513X19860182
33. Heine, S.J., Lehman, D.R., Markus, H.R., Kitayama, S.: Is there a universal need for positive self-regard? Psychol. Rev. **106**, 766 (1999)
34. Cai, H., et al.: Tactical self-enhancement in China: is modesty at the service of self-enhancement in East Asian culture? Soc. Psychol. Pers. Sci. **2**, 59–64 (2011)
35. Heine, S.J., Hamamura, T.: In search of East Asian self-enhancement. Pers. Soc. Psychol. Rev. **11**, 4–27 (2007)
36. Heine, S.J., et al.: Divergent consequences of success and failure in Japan and North America: an investigation of self-improving motivations and malleable selves. J. Pers. Soc. Psychol. **81**, 599 (2001)
37. Steger, M.F., Kawabata, Y., Shimai, S., Otake, K.: The meaningful life in Japan and the United States: levels and correlates of meaning in life. J. Res. Pers. **42**, 660–678 (2008). https://doi.org/10.1016/j.jrp.2007.09.003
38. Schugurensky, D.: The forms of informal learning: towards a conceptualization of the field (2000)
39. Bennett, E.E.: A four-part model of informal learning: extending Schugurensky's conceptual model (2012)
40. Doornbos, A.J., Simons, R.-J., Denessen, E.: Relations between characteristics of workplace practices and types of informal work-related learning: a survey study among Dutch Police. Hum. Resour. Dev. Q. **19**, 129–151 (2008)
41. Mills, L.A., Knezek, G., Khaddage, F.: Information seeking, information sharing, and going mobile: three bridges to informal learning. Comput. Hum. Behav. **32**, 324–334 (2014). https://doi.org/10.1016/j.chb.2013.08.008
42. Glaser, B.G., Strauss, A.L., Strutzel, E.: The discovery of grounded theory; strategies for qualitative research. Nurs. Res. **17**, 364 (1968)
43. Brandt, Å., Samuelsson, K., Töytäri, O., Salminen, A.-L.: Activity and participation, quality of life and user satisfaction outcomes of environmental control systems and smart home technology: a systematic review. Disabil. Rehabil. Assist. Technol. **6**, 189–206 (2011)
44. Sheldon, K.M., Kasser, T.: Getting older, getting better? Personal strivings and psychological maturity across the life span. Dev. Psychol. **37**, 491 (2001)
45. Pierce, J.L., Kostova, T., Dirks, K.T.: The state of psychological ownership: integrating and extending a century of research. Rev. Gen. Psychol. **7**, 84–107 (2003)
46. Kietzmann, J.H., Hermkens, K., McCarthy, I.P., Silvestre, B.S.: Social media? Get serious! Understanding the functional building blocks of social media. Bus. Horiz. **54**, 241–251 (2011)
47. Andreoletti, C., Howard, J.L.: Bridging the generation gap: intergenerational service-learning benefits young and old. Gerontol. Geriatr. Educ. **39**, 46–60 (2018). https://doi.org/10.1080/02701960.2016.1152266

48. Cucinelli, G., Davidson, A.-L., Romero, M., Matheson, T.: Intergenerational learning through a participatory video game design workshop. J. Intergener. Relatsh. **16**, 146–165 (2018)
49. Carucci, K., Toyama, K.: Making well-being: exploring the role of makerspaces in long term care facilities. In: Proceedings of the 2019 CHI Conference on Human Factors in Computing Systems, pp. 1–12 (2019)

Observing Social Connectedness in a Digital Dance Program for Older Adults: An EMCA Approach

An Kosurko[1]($\boxtimes$), Ilkka Arminen[1], Rachel Herron[2], Mark Skinner[3], and Melisa Stevanovic[4]

[1] University of Helsinki, Helsinki, Finland
{an.kosurko,ilkka.arminen}@helsinki.fi
[2] Brandon University, Brandon, Canada
HerronR@brandonu.ca
[3] Trent University, Peterborough, Canada
markskinner@trentu.ca
[4] Tampere University, Tampere, Finland
melisa.stevanovic@helsinki.fi

Abstract. Sustainable societies require healthy populations that are inclusive of all ages in meaningful social engagement. Given the digital nature of contemporary social life, there is substantial interest in how older adults interact with information communication technology (ICT) and new media. For ageing rural populations, ICT is considered opportune to address increasing social isolation and loneliness by connecting older people in digital society. Understanding how older adults experience and achieve social connectedness through ICT is important to inform the development of programs and services designed for their meaningful engagement in social activities. More data is needed, particularly for people living with cognitive challenges, and in rural areas. But there are methodological challenges for this type of research involving this demographic. People living with dementia, for example, may depend on third party support to participate in programs and to articulate experience using verbal language. This paper introduces an international expansion of a study "Improving social inclusion for Canadians with dementia and their carers through Sharing Dance," [1] a digitally-delivered dance program. The expansion study will examine the impact of the program for social connectedness in an international context, using similar data collection methods to the Canadian study, while adding an additional layer of analysis using ethnomethodology and conversation analysis (EM/CA). This paper will both share findings from the Canadian study and introduce the conceptualization of the international study that builds on its foundation. A sample EM/CA analysis is provided, illustrating observable behaviour for comparison in different contexts, reducing dependence upon verbal language.

Keywords: Aging · Social connectedness · Digital · Dance

Q. Gao and J. Zhou (Eds.): HCII 2021, LNCS 12786, pp. 393–404, 2021.
https://doi.org/10.1007/978-3-030-78108-8_29

1 Introduction

Assistive technology to enable an ageing population to age in place is developing rapidly [2] while at the same time institutions are adopting information communication technology (ICT) approaches in a general "mediatization" of services and programs [3]. People, along with technologies of different generations adapt and develop as they increasingly interact through digital connections and pathways [4]. If older people are not participating in the development of digital technology in everyday interaction, how effectively can that digital technology be used to address their social exclusion? ICT is often touted as a solution to the problem of connecting older adults in rural areas to services and programs, but often using a top-down, interventionist approach. Focusing on social connectedness, ICT may be used to enhance older adult social connectedness according to their preferences for meaningful engagement at interpersonal, community, and societal levels [5]. For many older people and people living with dementia, access to digital resources for basic services and programs requires assistance from informal and formal caregivers and facilitators. Meanwhile, isolated individuals face decline in health and meaningful participation in society with no access to digital supports or their development, a phenomenon made more apparent during the COVID-19 Pandemic.

Understanding digital social connectedness for older adults via their participation in its development will, from a social sciences perspective, serve to critically inform and evaluate the effectiveness of digital programs designed to address the social inclusion of an ageing population, with implications for an entire network of formal and informal health, economy, care, and support at local, national, and global levels. The Sharing Dance Seniors program has demonstrated its potential to enhance older adult social inclusion, including people living with dementia through embodied expression [6] but how it is delivered remotely via ICT mediates its effectiveness by either enhancing or creating barriers to social inclusion [7]. The thematic analysis of the CIHR study [8] provided a foundation for a deeper analysis, pointing to social interactions of various dynamics through digital means. Further study of the digital delivery of this program using an EM/CA analysis will help to identify and articulate more specific affordances and constraints [9] for older people to meaningfully participate in and potentially reconstruct conditions to make sense of and contribute to the digital sphere.

Understanding social connectedness for older adults in digital contexts will critically inform the evaluation of such programs designed to address social inclusion for an ageing population [10]. Building on a previous study, "Improving social inclusion for Canadians with dementia and their carers through Sharing Dance" [1], this paper introduces a new study to systematically examine the social connectedness of older adults living with dementia, through their interactions in a digitally delivered dance program, Sharing Dance Seniors. Specifically, comparisons will be drawn between the program's digital mode of delivery to experiences of in-person dance instruction. Using an ethnomethodology and conversation analysis (EM/CA) approach, digital vs. in-person interactions will be compared in observations of older adults living with dementia in online vs. in-person dance instruction. Data will be collected through participant observation and video ethnography. Video recordings of the dance sessions will be analyzed using EM/CA to compare digital vs. in-person interactions of participants and draw comparisons between international contexts. Understanding how older people living with dementia interact in digital vs. in-person settings will provide insights into the affordances and constraints involved in providing digital services and programs across borders, along with a deeper understanding of impact. This will contribute to best practices and policy guidelines for digital program and service delivery and provide opportunities for older people and people living with dementia to contribute to technology development.

This paper introduces the international extension of the study "Improving social inclusion for Canadians with dementia and their carers through Sharing Dance" [1]. First, the Canadian study will be presented including a description of the Sharing Dance program; research methods; and findings related to digitally mediated social connectedness, with a discussion on limitations of the qualitative methods. This will lead to the introduction of the international extension project with proposed research questions and a sample of the proposed EM/CA method.

2 International Expansion Research Design

2.1 The Canadian Study: Improving Social Inclusion for Canadians with Dementia and Their Carers Through Sharing Dance

The Improving Social Inclusion for Canadians with Dementia and Carers through Sharing Dance [1] study evaluated a specialized dance program for older people created by Canada's National Ballet School (NBS) in partnership with Baycrest Health Sciences, in its expansion through remote delivery from an urban centre to remote and rural areas across Canada. The four-year study (2017–2021) involved two regional pilot studies of three phases each in non-metropolitan regions of two Canadian provinces, Peterborough, Ontario (seven sites), and Brandon (Westman), Manitoba (six sites).

About the Baycrest NBS Sharing Dance Seniors Program. Sharing Dance Seniors aims to make dance accessible to older people with a range of physical and cognitive abilities, including people living with dementia. Developed by Canada's National Ballet School (NBS) and Baycrest Health Sciences, the program is offered in terms (e.g., Fall, Winter, Spring). Terms are designed to build weekly from class to class. Each dance within a class includes physical and artistic goals such as physical awareness and mobility; coordination; strength; confidence; eye focus; storytelling through movement and gesture; joy; and engagement with music. The program was developed and is delivered in-person but also has a suite of remotely-led (through video streaming) dance sessions available for participants in institutional and community settings with on-site facilitators supporting participants. The program was piloted for nation-wide expansion under the Public Health Agency of Canada's Multi-Sectoral Partnerships to Promote Healthy Living and Prevent Chronic Disease approach, in collaboration with long-term (residential) care homes, regional home care providers, and community support agencies. During the study, the Sharing Dance Seniors program was delivered digitally (via live-stream video, pre-recorded videos for download, or pre-recorded video stream) and in-person during special events. Sharing Dance Seniors is produced as a weekly video series for streaming to multiple remote settings from a studio at NBS in Toronto, Ontario. Facilitators are identified locally for each site (in both community and institutional settings) and are integral to the digital delivery of the program. The facilitator welcomes and organizes participants; participates in and models the program for participants; monitors safety of participants and encourages interactions; and collects and provides feedback to NBS after sessions via an online form. Program orientation and training was provided for facilitators via online course modules through NBS' online learning platform.

Data Collection. With ethics approval from Trent University in Peterborough, Ontario, and Brandon University in Brandon, Manitoba, data was collected through observations, interviews, focus groups, diaries, and researcher reflections. Observations focused on participants' experiences of social inclusion at weekly sessions in each pilot at every site, recorded in writing in a semi-structured guide that developed over the two-year period. Researchers were encouraged to participate during the sessions, to enhance participation in the program and to help participants feel less 'observed'. Data collected through observations included descriptions of settings and participants; details of activity sequences and interactions; gestures, facial expressions, and reactions to other participants and on-screen instructors. Some sites provided informed consent for video to be recorded for later analysis to supplement in-situ field notes. All participants were given the option of keeping a diary of their experiences of the program to complete after each dance session through a semi-structured questionnaire in a provided journal or tablet to record their experiences. Data collected through diaries was limited in many cases due to the need for third-party support in completing entries. Focus groups were held with participants, their carers, facilitators, administrators, staff, and volunteers at the end of the eight-week sessions for each site in each pilot and data collected was to provide deeper insights for use in and analysis of interviews. Semi-structured interviews were conducted with interested participants, carers, facilitators, administrators, staff, and volunteers upon completion of the eight-week sessions. Interviews conducted prior to and after program sessions provided insights into participants' characteristics and attitudes towards dance as well as personal reflections into their experiences of the dance program. For some participants living with dementia, post-session interviews were deemed inappropriate due to limited memory of participation in the dance program and these were discontinued to avoid potentially stressful situations for these participants [1].

Research Participants. Research participants were originally recruited in partnership with community organizations, Community Care in Peterborough, Ontario, for the three phases of Peterborough pilots (P1, P2, P3), and the Alzheimer Society of Canada Westman Region office in Brandon, Manitoba, for the Brandon pilots (B1, B2, B3). The Sharing Dance Seniors pilot program and research project was also advertised in both regions using local radio and newspaper channels along with word of mouth and referrals by the partner agency support groups. As the pilot studies expanded, returning participants recommended the program to others who joined sessions in the community settings. In institutional settings, recreation directors promoted the program internally to wider audiences and purposively selected participants based on whom they thought would be ideal participants, including persons living with dementia and their carers. Information sessions were held at each site and open to residents' families and local community members. There were 23 participants in P1, 54 in P2, 40 in P3 (including eight people living with dementia), 16 in B1 (including seven people living with dementia), 36 in B2 (including 15 people living with dementia), and 140 in B3 (including 68 people living with dementia), for a total of 289 participants in the three phases in both regions. Research participants included older adult participants between the ages of 66 and 96; persons living with dementia; administrators and staff in both community and institutional settings; facilitators; volunteers; and carers.

Data Analysis. The qualitative data analysis began with an initial round of inductive thematic analysis [6] identifying emerging thematic codes through detailed analysis using Nvivo software. As data collection progressed, the research team reflected on the evolving thematic code book to resolve coding differences between investigators, and examined new and emerging codes with each pilot. To be attentive to different dimensions of social inclusion within the data [11], conceptualization of social exclusion was incorporated into the coding to look for themes of potential exclusion or inclusion related to financial resources; social connections and resources; services; transport and mobility; safety; macro-economic; place & community; individual capacity; life-course trajectories. These themes, along with other themes generated from analysis of the pilots, were organized by the three research objectives of the original Canadian research project which were: to explore older persons' experiences; to assess program delivery effectiveness; and to identify the challenges of scaling up the program [1].

Findings. The following qualitative findings from the original study will demonstrate how people living with dementia received support from carers in participating in the program. During the second half of the study, there was a shift of setting from the community centre to institutional personal care homes, and participants included more people living with dementia. In response to local feedback in this context, the research team invited caregivers to attend, explained by a community administrator below:

> I think more caregivers should be encouraged to attend the session – I think it would pull families closer together because the people I talk to – they're lost. They'll say their family member or their friend – they say "I don't know what to do with them" but if they come together it might be that cohesiveness that they need. (Community Centre Administrator, B2).

Staff and volunteers were also added at some sites, that created a network of people around participants to support their meaningful participation in the program. One carer described the effect.

> I was really impressed at how the [staff and volunteers] had assisted the residents and how positive reinforcement allowed them to engage and enjoy movement which is obviously going to be promoting good stimulation. I was really quite impressed when everybody had a partner that was kind of positively motivated. It was fabulous. (B3, Neepawa Carer)

One volunteer shared how surprised she was that participants in the institutional setting, people living with dementia participated even though the on-screen instructor (OSI) was not in the room. They also indicated that participants required assistance with instructions.

You could see that they were trying – listening - and they were doing it. When [the OSI] would say [to] put their arms on the arms of the chair or their seat and they would do that - they were listening and they were doing it. That surprised me. And [the instructor is] not even in the room. ... Sometimes it seemed that they would do [the dance] but they needed more cuing or more instructions (Volunteer, Interview Transcript, Institutional Setting, B2).

One example of this was E, who would often follow the screen movements, but needed reminding to focus on the screen.

E almost misses the start of the music, but [staff] cues her to look at the screen, so she turns and catches on immediately to following the opening moves of the sequence, her wrists turning for the snail movements demonstrated by the OSI (Field Notes, Institutional Setting, B2).

Screen focus was one of the challenges of the digital delivery for many participants [5] and they would often look to others for cues of what to do, rather than the screen. One volunteer reflected in a diary that, "It would seem that when others in the group commenced the dance movements, participants would then look at other participants to follow the instructed movements (Volunteer, Diary Transcript, B2).

The series of quotes in the qualitative data above draw a picture of how participants, particularly people living with dementia were in some cases dependent upon third-party support to participate in the digitally-delivered instruction of the Sharing Dance Seniors program. Further, their experience of the effectiveness of the digital delivery of the program was articulated by third parties, such as in the quote below:

I was curious to see, to tell you the truth if, how they would respond via television, because I do exercise programs regularly – I was curious to see how technology would play a part – I thought it was great – I thought that some really latched on to the fact that it was via tv, but some still watched me – think there was a good mix of that– lots were on me because that's something they look for regularly, they're looking at me regularly – but a great combination because they had the music as well right – it was powerful in that sense because they got it all.

The understanding of how people living with dementia are responsive to the digital delivery of programs like Sharing Dance Seniors is limited to the subjective interpretation of carers and volunteers of their familiar interaction. This presents a limitation in the data to speak to the effectiveness of the digital delivery of the program from the perspective of some participants. For example, one institutional carer described a moment that she did not enjoy when it seemed that the resident she was supporting was not enjoying herself.

I think there was maybe one time – I felt like I was sitting beside the one lady who didn't seem to be enjoying the program. I was trying really hard to make it better when she seemed to become agitated. I had to remind myself that she was enjoying it in her own way ... (Staff Interview Transcript, B2).

A volunteer also described how they were unsure of how best to support participants:

As a volunteer, we were the ones they could see what we were doing if they couldn't get all the instructions we could help. I didn't know how much we were meant to help them – you know we just let them do things and obviously they would look at us, but sometime you know – with S – I would help him uncross his legs and say, "your legs" or you know get their arm and move it, so if I wasn't supposed to do that I imagine someone would stop me. Sometimes it seemed that they would do it but they needed more cuing or more instructions. Some of them could really do with more with one-on-one.

In each of the described scenarios above, carers who were present during the program to support participants were focused on providing the necessary cues for them to participate and were unsure of their interpretation of what they were supposed to be doing. One the one hand, the staff member articulated that she had to allow the participant to experience the program in their own way, while the volunteer felt that the participant needed more cuing and instructions.

Discussion. Uncertainty of the volunteers in knowing how best to support participants indicates a need for greater understanding of how to read different participants' level of participation or how well they are connecting to each other in interactions for the intended purpose of the program, to enhance social inclusion.

The next section of this paper introduces a new study to address this methodological challenge of reading levels of interaction by expanding on the analysis in the methods to use EM/CA as a tool to observe interactions and compare them in different contexts.

2.2 International Expansion

Building on this work that used a qualitative, thematic analysis with implications for social inclusion, the unique contribution of this proposed project will be in the international expansion of the program evaluation, with a more detailed analysis of social interactions in digital vs. in-person contexts using EM/CA research tools. To articulate observable social connectedness for people living with dementia using ICT, this analysis will focus on detailed observations of older adults and people living with dementia in social interactions through the digital dance program. EM/CA will provide the theoretical framework and method for data collection and analysis to study older adult social connectedness. The assumption is that older peoples' and their carers' everyday methods create order in their joint social activities, which has implications for older peoples' experiences of social connectedness. Emphasis will be placed on observable behavioral aspects of human experience, rather than introspection as its primary mode of inquiry [12]. Objectives of the research are: 1) To contribute to understanding of digital social connectedness for older people, including older people from rural areas and people living with dementia, through remotely-delivered dance instruction; iii) To critically assess the effectiveness of digital delivery for social connectedness of people living with dementia.

Ethics. Informed consent will include anonymity of subjects and obtained well in advance of the program due to the need for third-party consent of older participants in institutional settings. Sensitivity to the inclusion of persons living with dementia

(PWD) will require ongoing verbal consent and appropriate inclusion in methods such as interviews and focus groups in consultation with carers. (i.e. we found previously that interviews caused anxiety for PWD to remember participating in the program for some who did not recall it.) If in-person delivery is not possible (due to COVID-19), permission is granted to access data from the CIHR study within the parameters of the original ethics agreement that will allow analysis of data from the previously completed study.

Data Collection. Participants will be recruited through outreach to personal care settings and community-centre/dementia-care administrators in a purposive sampling of older adults aged 75 and up, including persons living with dementia. Data will be collected through video recordings of eight weekly dance sessions. In the home delivery of the program, 5 individuals will be observed during 8 weeks of 25 min-sessions (40 × 25 = 1000 min of recorded video); in institutional settings, 3 groups will be observed over 8 weeks (1 digital international, 1 in-person, 1 mixed digital/in-person delivery) (24 × 45 = 1080 min); (group maximum of 10 people including participants, (5) carer, volunteer and staff facilitators (5)). A total of approximately 35 h of video recordings will take approximately 105 h in which to view, select and analyze. In week seven for group settings, a focus group will be conducted (digitally or in-person) with questions about their experiences and to seek contributions of their own gestures to incorporate in the final 8th session). Field notes will be conducted to provide context, (est 60 days @ 1–2 pages) Short interviews will be conducted after weekly sessions with selected individual participants in both home and institutional settings (approximately 5 min weekly with 5 individuals = 30 interviews for a total of 150 min of transcripts).

EMCA Analysis. Using EM/CA will enhance the qualitative methods used in the CIHR study that provided reflective accounts of participants and their carers (including family, staff, community volunteers). Conversation analysis of data collected through video recordings and observations in the previous Canadian study will also be possible through articulated data sharing agreements in accordance with ethics guidelines and approvals governed by Canada's Tri-Council Policy Statement. The following sample of EMCA analysis conducted on existing data from the previous project demonstrates the potential for observable participant connectedness in response to the digital delivery of the program.

Sample EM/CA Analysis: Dancing Her Way. The following excerpt has been adapted from a field note for the purpose of this paper. It demonstrates an interaction between two older adults living with dementia (L and D), in a dance class that is delivered digitally via an on-screen instructor (OSI) to the group they are part of. The focus is on the interaction between L and D who are meant to follow along with the OSI as they call out and demonstrate movements such as kicking their legs in time with the music. In this example, L expresses concern that D is not participating in the dance class by shaking a fist at D (see Line 04), while D deviates from the instruction and follows only the final kick.

01. OSI: So we're going to kick our one leg straight out as far
             as comfortable,

02. L: [((L kicks legs out, Looks over at D
                            who does not move, D is looking at L.))

03. OSI: So that might be on the floor or just off the floor, I'm
             going to take it off the floor (.) so I'm going, (.) Out,
             (.) In, (.) Out. (.)   In, (.05) Kick, (.) and kick.

04.   [((L shakes a fist at D, who looks away, D lifts chin
                         up high briefly then lets head relax and turns face
                         away from L and looks ahead.))]

05. OSI: So there we have our legs and our arms and then we're
             going to put them all together.

06. OSI: [((Motions to piano player))

07. OSI: Thanks

                  ((Music Starts, L watches D, neither move))

12. OSI: Out in, Here come the legs, Kick. (.) In. (.) Out, (.05)
             Out, (.05) In. (.) >Really kick=Out.<

15.→D: [((D kicks one leg out in a
                           high kick and then lowers leg. Lifts chin)).

16.→ L: [((L watches this with mouth open in
                           amazement expression and smiles))

18. OSI: And we're going to pause at the end of this phrase

             ((Music stops))

Discussion. What is interesting about this excerpt is that at first glance it seems as
though D is not participating in the program because they are not following the dance
as instructed by the OSI (line 02). D watches L as the OSI explains the moves for the
next dance sequence. L, who is following the moves, responds to D's lack of movement
by shaking a fist at D (a gesture of communication that is individual to L), (line 04),
to which D responds by turning away and looking forward. Once the music begins, D
does not move until the final kick, on the OSI cue and does one large kick (line 15)

and then stops as L watches with a look that expresses amazement (line 16). There is a performativity about D's interaction with L that denotes a flourish in creativity and self-expression, rather than non-participation, as had been described by a carer in the qualitative findings of the previous study. D's semi-compliance with the instruction on D's own terms indicates a strengthening of deontic status [13] that problematizes the nature of simply following instruction for some participants. This case illustrates the complexity of facilitating social connectedness remotely, as participants need to negotiate their sense of self and agency. This sample of EMCA demonstrates how providing the opportunity to connect remotely through a common goal to participate is simply a starting point. Facilitators and carers providing support for participants also need to be sensitive to individuals' sense of agentic acquiescence.

3   Conclusion

This paper introduced the international extension of the study "Improving social inclusion for Canadians with dementia and their carers through Sharing Dance" [1]. We presented findings from the Canadian study that demonstrated how people living with dementia received support from carers to participate in the digitally delivered dance program. The data revealed a need for greater understanding of participants' level of participation and connectedness to other participants, to inform carer practices of support. The understanding of how people living with dementia were responsive to the digital delivery of Sharing Dance Seniors was limited to the subjective interpretation of carers and volunteers. A deeper analysis of the interactions of participants in different contexts may speak to the effectiveness of the digital delivery of the program.

We then introduced the international extension project with research objectives that focus on understanding digital social connectedness through remotely-delivered dance instruction; and to critically assess the effectiveness of digital delivery for social connectedness of people living with dementia, along with a sample of the proposed EM/CA method using previously collected data.

The international study proposes to address the methodological challenge of reading levels of interaction by expanding on the analysis in the methods to use EM/CA as a tool to observe interactions and to compare them in different contexts (in-person vs. digital, international, etc.).

Using EM/CA analysis to make explicit the factors that influence older adult social connectedness in digital settings will contribute to multidisciplinary calls for measuring effectiveness of ICT for social connectedness [14]; social health and social participation [15]; effectiveness research in quality and evidence of acceptance of ICT [16]; with better methodological quality [17]; with minimal risk of bias [18]; and in groups such as in people with cognitive impairments, and people living in rural areas [19]. Data will include observations and reflections of older people and people living with dementia as co-creators of knowledge and relevant contributors to social research in a participatory approach in the assessment and influence of digital technology design for social inclusion/connectedness and further, facilitate the use of such evidence in monitoring and evaluation.

EM/CA uses video as its basis for analysis. Ethnography employing in-person field notes and interviews with participants may enrich the video observations for understanding how people living with dementia interact with digital programs and their co-participants. EM/CA will provide a sensitive method to address how people articulate understandings and emotions as we observe their behaviour in situations and environments that influence their interactions in relation to digital technology. Comparisons drawn between in-person and digital delivery of dance interactions may allow affordances and constraints for digital social connectedness to be observed. Participants will be observed as they interact with instructors and others around and through digital technology in activities designed to encourage interactions through movement and dance. An in-depth study of the program's delivery modes, particularly the mediated interaction of the digital delivery in comparison to its in-person delivery using an EM/CA approach will theoretically allow the affordances and constraints that influence interactions to emerge [9]. Identifying details in interactions and their role in social connectedness may contribute to our understanding of how to best support interaction for social inclusion in multiple contexts and raise discussion about the limits of observability and measurability of human connectedness. This project will emphasize the important contributions that older people and people living with dementia make to the development of effective ICT-delivered programs.

Acknowledgements. The Improving Social Inclusion for Canadians with Dementia and Carers through Sharing Dance study was funded by a Canadian Institutes of Health Research/Alzheimer Society of Canada Operating Grant: Social Inclusion of Individuals with Dementia and Carers (CIHR/ASC grant no. 150702). The study is also funded, in part, by the Canada Research Chairs program (Mark Skinner, Trent University; Rachel Herron, Brandon University). The study evaluated a specialized dance program for older people created by Canada's National Ballet School (NBS) in partnership with Baycrest Health Sciences, in its expansion through remote delivery from an urban centre to remote and rural areas across Canada. (See Skinner et al., 2019; www.sdseniorsresearch.com).

References

1. Skinner, M.W., Herron, R.V., Bar, R.J., Kontos, P., Menec, V.: Improving social inclusion for people with dementia and carers through sharing dance: a qualitative sequential continuum of care pilot study protocol. BMJ Open **8**(11), e026912 (2018)
2. Gallistl, V., Wanka, A.: Representing the 'older end user'? Challenging the role of social scientists in the field of 'active and assisted living.' Int. J. Care Caring **3**(1), 123–128 (2019)
3. Sawchuk, K.: Tactical mediatization and activist ageing: pressures, push-backs, and the story of RECAA. MedieKultur J. Media Commun. Res. **29**(54), 18 (2013)
4. Loos, E.F., Haddon, L., Mante-Meijer, E.A. (eds.) Generational Use of New Media. Farnham: Ashgate, Farnham (2012)
5. Waycott, J., Vetere, F., Ozanne, E.: Building social connections: a framework for enriching older adults' social connectedness through emerging information and communication technologies. In: Neves, B., Vetere, F. (eds.) Ageing and Digital Technology: Designing and Evaluating Emerging Technologies for Older Adults, pp. 58–74. Springer, Berlin (2019)

6. Kontos, P., Grigorovich, A., Kosurko, A., Bar, R.J., Herron, R.V., Menec, V.H., Skinner, M.W.: Dancing with dementia: exploring the embodied dimensions of creativity and social engagement. The Gerontologist (2020)
7. Kosurko, A., et al.: Opportunities and challenges of digital delivery of sharing dance seniors for social inclusion. Romanian J. Commun. Public Relat. **22**(2), 23–37 (2020)
8. Braun, V., Clarke, V.: What can "thematic analysis" offer health and wellbeing researchers? Int. J. Qual. Stud. Health Well-being 9 (2014)
9. Arminen, I., Licoppe, C., Spagnolli, A.: Respecifying mediated interaction. Res. Lang. Soc. Interact. **49**(4), 290–309 (2016)
10. Silva, P.A.: Are we ready to dance at home? A review and reflection of available technologies. In: Zhou, J., Salvendy, G. (eds.) HCII 2019. LNCS, vol. 11593, pp. 216–231. Springer, Cham (2019). https://doi.org/10.1007/978-3-030-22015-0_17
11. Walsh, K., O'Shea, E., Scharf, T.: Rural old-age social exclusion: a conceptual framework on mediators of exclusion across the lifecourse. Ageing Soc. **40**(11), 2311–2337 (2020)
12. Moore, R.J.: Ethnomethodology and conversation analysis: Empirical approaches to the study of digital technology in action. The SAGE handbook of digital technology research. Sage (2013)
13. Stevanovic, M., Monzoni, C.: On the hierarchy of interactional resources: embodied and verbal behavior in the management of joint activities with material objects. J. Pragm. **103**, 15–32 (2016)
14. Khosravi, P., Rezvani, A., Wiewiora, A.: The impact of technology on older adults' social isolation. Comput. Hum. Behav. **63**, 594–603 (2016)
15. Pinto-Bruno, Á.C., García-Casal, J.A., Csipke, E., Jenaro-Río, C., Franco-Martín, M.: ICT-based applications to improve social health and social participation in older adults with dementia. A systematic literature review. Aging Ment. Health **21**(1), 58–65 (2017)
16. Van der Heide, L.A., Willems, C.G., Spreeuwenberg, M.D., Rietman, J., de Witte, L.P.: Implementation of CareTV in care for the elderly: the effects on feelings of loneliness and safety and future challenges. Technol. Disab. **24**(4), 283–291 (2012)
17. Poscia, A., Stojanovic, J., La Milia, D.I., Duplaga, M., Grysztar, M., Moscato, U., Magnavita, N.: Interventions targeting loneliness and social isolation among the older people: an update systematic review. Exper. Gerontol. **102**, 133–144 (2018)
18. Chen, Y.R.R., Schulz, P.J.: The effect of information communication technology interventions on reducing social isolation in the elderly: a systematic review. J. Med. Internet Res. **18**(1) (2016)
19. Stojanovic, J., et al.: Decreasing loneliness and social isolation among the older people: systematic search and narrative review. Epidemiol. Biostat. Public Health **14**(2), suppl.1, (2017)

Online News and Gamification Habits in Late Adulthood: A Survey

Francisco Regalado$^{(\boxtimes)}$ [iD], Liliana Vale Costa [iD], and Ana Isabel Veloso [iD]

DigiMedia, Department of Communication and Art, University of Aveiro, Aveiro, Portugal
{fsfregalado,lilianavale,aiv}@ua.pt

Abstract. Older adults are part of a significant proportion of the global population and given the rapid advancements of a digital society, the use of technologies by this age group is growing at a fast pace. However, technological products still overlook the older adults' physiologic, psychologic, and social needs. In the journalism sector, World's *cyberization,* current demands to have access to the latest updated news, and information overload have led to an interest in gamification to draw the readers' motivations and engagement with the news. The purpose of this paper is to describe a survey conducted from June 1st of 2020 until July 9th of 2020 to a total of 248 older adults aged 50 and over from sixteen different countries. During this study, researchers intended to assess older adults' context in terms of social media, online news, and games' usage, as well as their familiarity with gamification strategies. The results suggest that respondents are online news consumers to stay up-to-date on societal occurrences. In the context of a gamified online news' community, they would like to be valued for the following: groups' activity; frequency with which they talk to other people; and debate, shareability, and reaction to news.

Keywords: Ageing · Online news · Gamification · Survey · miOne

1 Introduction

As the World population ages [1], the consumption of technology by all age cohorts increases [2], despite the barriers presented and the perceived preconceptions by older adults [3–5]. Furthermore, there is a gradual need to develop technology products that take into account age impairments, whether they are psychological, physiological, and/or social.

Alongside technological developments, a growing digitalization has affected many sectors, including journalism [6]. Digital versions of printed publications have, therefore, emerged [6] and a change in the interaction paradigms has also been observed – *e.g.* multimedia, interactivity and hypertext [7]. Additionally, older adults started to adopt online journalism as a complementary source of news [8]. During this process, social media started to play an important role in the creation and dissemination of user-generated content [9] – forming a new type of end-users: *prosumers* (both consumers and producers of information) [10].

© Springer Nature Switzerland AG 2021
Q. Gao and J. Zhou (Eds.): HCII 2021, LNCS 12786, pp. 405–419, 2021.
https://doi.org/10.1007/978-3-030-78108-8_30

Meanwhile, the use of mobile technologies in news consumption and ubiquity of news in both domestic and mobility spaces was accompanied by an increase in the sources of distraction, making it necessary to constantly find innovative strategies to grab the readers' attention [8] to the news. The use of game elements and techniques for contexts that go beyond entertainment purposes – *i.e.* gamification [11] is suggested to engage readers and attract attention [12] while driving the newspapers' businesses [8].

This paper presents the survey results relative to the older adults' context in terms of social media, online news, and games' usage, as well as familiarity with gamification strategies. In specific, a questionnaire was applied, and a total of 248 responses from participants aged 50 and over from 12 different countries were obtained. The results allowed, *inter alia*, the characterization of the technological devices used by the respondents to access the Internet and consume news, preferred activities to perform online, means of news' consumption, activities, and motivations that can be targeted to design a gamification system for online news.

2 Theoretical Background

2.1 An Ageing Population

It is a well-known fact that the world's population is getting older and progressively living longer [4]. As a matter of fact, European countries such as Italy, Germany, Belgium, Spain, Greece, United Kingdom, and France, and Japan are on the top of countries with more than 10 million inhabitants and with the highest percentage of people aged over 60 years old [1]. Many reasons could contribute to this demographic change – *e.g.* better health conditions, decrease in fertility rates, and longer lifespan [1]. In fact, this fraction of the world's population is very heterogeneous [13], despite the well-known changes that occur during the ageing process [4, 5, 14–18]:

- Physiologic: The older adults' movements tend to be 1.5 to 2 times slower than the young adults. Moreover, earing losses are very likely to occur, as well as changes in the visual system. Extra time is needed to shift the attention focus, and there is also a general decrease in spatial cognition, and the ability to understand written and spoken language;
- Psychologic: Depressive symptoms are very frequent, strongly motivated by physiological deficiencies;
- Social: Social media may have a great impact on older adults' longevity and health since social isolation can accelerate the ageing process.

In view of all that was mentioned, it is important to develop technological solutions that consider the limitations, context of use, motivations, and needs of older adults.

2.2 Older Adults and Information Communication Technologies

The use of digital technology has been growing at a fast pace, having major implications in the way people produce, distribute, access, and consume information. The way technological products work, their aspect, performance, and the reaction to users' actions have been suffering constant changes [4].

However, there is a fairly common and entrenched stereotype that older adults do not and will not use technology. In fact, there are many barriers that can be pinpointed to affect older adults' use of digital media [3–5]. These are: (i) intrapersonal (*e.g.* believing to be too old to use technologies); (ii) structural (*e.g.* the cost of owning a personal computer); (iii) interpersonal – the non-existence of people to teach how to use; (iv) the age-related wage disparity; (v) the lack of perception to the need to use technological products; (vi) the difficulty to use the technological products; and (vii) the usability problems that can lead to distrust of the accessed information. Although these barriers are still present, the use of Internet has been gaining significant popularity among older adults, being this age group one with the most accentuated growth in Internet usage [19]. Moreover, Internet is a leisure activity for older adults in two distinct ways: a tool to learn, plan and buy leisure; and an activity *per se* [19].

According to PORDATA [2], a data bank of certified statistics on Portugal, there is also a growing trend of Internet use among Portuguese older adults. In the same vein, the benefits that Internet and computer usage can bring are very likely to outweigh the challenges and costs of change - *e.g.* enhancing the sense of independence and empowerment; lower levels of depression; improvements on self-image and self-confidence; and decreasing feelings of loneliness while promoting social connectivity [19].

Since Information and Communication Technologies (ICT) are increasingly more used in the most diverse contexts, older adults must be prepared to adopt these technologies and take advantage of their capabilities [20]. The Web has also changed over the years with different implications for online journalism. In the next section, the evolution of the web, as well as its impact on digital media, will be explored.

2.3 The Evolution of Digital Media

In 1989, Tim Berners-Lee invented the World Wide Web – a space where information sharing is privileged, in which hypermedia and hypertext systems have been used [21]. The first iteration of the Web – Web 1.0, was mainly characterized by a mono-directional sharing of information, being, therefore, a read-only technology [21].

The second iteration of the Web – Web 2.0, came a few years later in 2004, characterized for being more participative, people-centered and allowing the formation of online communities [21]. This way, users were empowered to interact with each other, and incentivized to be part of the process of making media, instead of just consuming it [22]. Thus, a new type of end-users was formed – the ones who create and diffuse information [23], hence becoming *prosumers* [10].

The Web evolution has also brought some changes in the terminology adopted over the years, *i.e.* terms like 'cyber' started to be common in the most varied contexts. Based on the definition of the prefix 'cyber' in the Cambridge Dictionary [24], it refers to the act of "involving, using, or relating to computers, especially the Internet." The industry of journalism used this mentioned prefix to characterize a new form of journalism in which there is a change in the interaction paradigm and news' consumption patterns – *cyberjournalism* [6].

The urge to shift to this new digital world was felt more intensely by newspapers' owners when compared to other media – it was a "digital gold rush" [6], and nobody wanted to be left behind [25]. At the beginning of this new era, newspapers adopted a strategy where the printed version was similar to the online one, making it difficult to see the economic value in having two forms of publishing [6]. As time progressed, newspapers' sites adopted web features, such as multimedia, interactivity and hypertext [7].

Additionally, technologically-qualified youngsters want to choose their source of information, since they consider traditional media (*e.g.* radio, TV) to be controlled by an anonymous authority [25]. Therefore, the Internet is becoming progressively their primary source of information, not only because it receives faster updates, but also because they can control the information they get and are able to confront the different sources [25]. This trend of online news adoption is not only registered among the younger population, since "older generations have adopted digital media as a complementary source of news", as highlighted by Conill and Karlsson [8, p.14].

Journalism plays a major role in democracies, *i.e.* it is "responsible for a free flow of information, criticism and control of the powerful, bringing transparency into society and its institutions" [26, p. 433]. In fact, modern societies are from the early stages information societies [27] in the sense that the term 'information society' is used to characterize an attribute of societal formation, as information is highly present at all stages of societal development [28]. In an information society, the flow of information is crucial, and, as stated by Lenstra, "the information society is also an ageing society" [29, p. 76].

Social media are an example of a communal space that fosters user-generated content [9] and as such, they may reinforce the interconnection between journalists and citizens, not only being news sources, but also news sensors [22]. Many terms have been used to describe the readers' participation in news production, "such as citizen journalism, user-generated content, and participatory journalism" [22, p. 312]. Being this new phase the point of contact between journalism and social media, it can be called *social journalism*, a more networked side of journalism [22].

Despite all of the previously mentioned, there are some reservations regarding the strengthening of the relationship between consumers and journalists through an online channel, since the institutional power of the latter can be questioned when it comes to deciding what is newsworthy or credible [22]. According to Siapera and Veglis [7], newspapers' websites were reticent to join social media, but recently every major and respectful newspaper has some type of presence in social media – whether it is Facebook, Twitter, or a blog. Additionally, Allan [25] identified immediacy[1] as one of the characteristics of online journalism, as well as the introduction of more information about a given subject and the ability to benefit from the interactivity potential of the web. Notwithstanding the previously mentioned reservations regarding the adoption of a close online relationship with consumers, research from the Pew Research Center [30] states that the majority of adults from the studied countries uses at least one social media or messaging application, suggesting that their use is deep-rooted in the population.

In conclusion, social media can be a great ally to online journalism. The act of sharing news always happened in the most different social contexts, but social media only came to accelerate and extend the access and dissemination of information [22].

---

[1] An advantage that the site has over its press and television competitors.

Moreover, it offers innovative means to promote content, and increase the audience reached, potentially bringing loyal consumers [22].

2.4 Gamification in Journalism

Due to mobile technologies' ubiquity and subsequent increase in the usage of sources of distractions, the media landscape has been characterized by a constant fight for audiences' attention [8]. In order to grab readers' attention, newspapers have adopted new strategies such as spawning notifications related to headlines and activities with more fun and even playable side [31].

In fact, journalism has been using a different number of ways to potentially capture one's attention: (i) *storytelling* - "telling a story which is exciting or dramatic enough to engage presumptive viewers" [32, p. 467]; (ii) *immersive journalism* - "the production of news in a form in which people can gain first-person experiences of the events or situation described in news stories" [33, para. 1], having great help from Virtual Reality (VR) technologies, by allowing users to feel like they are experiencing what happened [34]; and (iii) *newsgames* – "a genre that is currently emerging: videogames based on news events." [35, para. 2].

Gamification, defined by Werbach and Hunter [11] as "the use of game elements and game-design techniques in non-game contexts" (p. 26), is also a great way to increase users' engagement, motivation, and fidelity, leading them to spend more time on the system [12]. This is important not only to engage older adults with online newspapers but also to motivate them to overcome their difficulties with technology. According to Conill and Karlsson [8], the reason behind gamifying news is related to the fact that it is a powerful tool to engage users to be informed, empowering them with information, and making them responsible for the information they choose to consume.

Moreover, there are two great advantages of news' gamification [8]: (i) benefiting businesses' logic by boosting users news' consumption; and (ii) boosting users' engagement to read the news, increasing their intrinsic motivation, and creating a desirable habit.

In order to successfully implement a gamified strategy in any system, it is necessary to track users' behaviors [8]. To do so, there is a set of metrics that can be defined [8, 31, 36]: (i) page views, (ii) time on pages, (iii) shareability – in order to measure the audience's interest; (iv) news accessed; (v) unique visits and (vi) users' returns.

In conclusion, gamification can be a great addition to online news. Not only because it can engage the audience and boost the consumption of news, but also because it can promote the collaboration of readers with the process of news' production, making social journalism something that can appeal to readers' motivations. As pointed out by Salwen *et al.* [6], the newspaper industry has great difficulty in making profits and, thus, it is important to establish a well-bonded relationship with the audience - in which gamification can be a great help.

3 Method and Sample

This research relied on a survey method per questionnaire. This approach allowed more direct analysis of data and an easier distribution of the questionnaire. The study was carried out, following the Ethics and Deontology Council of the University of Aveiro Ethical Approval for the SEDUCE 2.0 project - use of Communication and Information in the miOne online community by senior citizens (Project FCT POCI-01–0145-FEDER-031696).

3.1 Procedures

The mentioned questionnaire was distributed by email to a total of 2782 contacts from Universities of the Third Age located in sixteen different countries (Australia, Austria, Brazil, Canada, Czech Republic, France, Germany, Netherlands, New Zealand, Poland, Portugal, Slovakia, Spain, Sweden, United Kingdom and the United States of America). The questionnaire was applied, and data was collected using an online survey hosted on the FormsUA[2] platform. The mentioned instrument had an English and a Portuguese version due to the different distribution zones and is constituted as being cross-sectional, *i.e.* applied during a specific point in time – from June 1st of 2020 to July 9th of the same year.

3.2 Questionnaire Design

A survey method was used, applying a questionnaire as a data collection tool. The mentioned questionnaire was administered in order to assess older adults' context in terms of social media, online news, and games usage, as well as their familiarity with gamification strategies.

Demographic information included age, gender, level of education, and country of residence. Table 1 summarizes the questions asked and goals for data analysis.

On questions 1, 4, 5, 6, 10.1, and 10.2 multiple answers were allowed. SPSS[3] was used to perform data analysis and data management.

3.3 Participants

Of the 279 responses, 248 were considered valid since they fitted in the age criteria defined by Lee and their colleagues [38], *i.e.* youngest-old, aged between 65 and 74 years old; middle-old, aged between 75 and 84; and oldest-old, aged over 85 years. Moreover, an additional younger age group was added – *i.e.* pre-seniors, aged between 50 and 64 years old.

Demographics. Table 2 Provides an Overview of the sample's Demographic Characterization. The Majority of Respondents (57%; N = 140) Are Male, Whereas 43% (N = 107) Are Female and 1 Person with Other Gender.

The average age of the sample was, approximately, 67 years old (SD = 8,369; minimum = 50; maximum = 91). In order to standardize the age distribution, a readjustment

---

[2] Available at: http://forms.ua.pt/ (Date accessed: 06-01-2021). A service offered by the University of Aveiro using the LimeSurvey software – https://www.limesurvey.org/pt/ (Date accessed: 06-01-2021).

[3] Available at: https://www.ibm.com/analytics/spss-statistics-software (Date accessed: 06–01-2021).

Table 1. Summary of the questions asked in the questionnaire. Retrieved from *Gamifying News for the miOne Online Community* [37].

Data collection questions	Goals for data analysis
1. Which devices do you usually use to access the Internet?	Identify the main activities performed by older adults in the digital context.
2. Please indicate the frequency in which you perform the following activities (Access to the Internet/Social media/Online banking or other financial products, Read/Share/Discuss online news, Try to avoid news, Online search/shopping, Send and read emails, Use entertainment media)	Identify the main activities performed by older adults in the digital context.
2.1. If you try to avoid the news... What is the reason? 3. What interests you the most in the following types of news? 4. What is/are the reason(s) for consuming news?	Identify the motivations for news' consumption.
5. Which means do you usually use to consume news? 6. Which activities do you usually do when you access the news?	Identify the means used to consume news.

7. Do you use any points/card/coupon or discount mechanisms in your daily life?
    7.1. If yes, which one(s)?
    7.2. If yes, does the use of these mechanisms encourage you to use the service(s) more and more?
	Understand the familiarity with gamification mechanisms in daily life.

8. In an online social network/community, please indicate the importance of the following activities you would like to be valued for.	Identify what adult learners like to be valued for online communities.

9. Do you use any mobile application in your everyday life that rewards you with challenges, badges, levels, points, or leaderboards?
    9.1. If yes, which?
    9.2. If yes, what motivates you to continue using the application?
	Understand the familiarity with gamification mechanisms in mobile applications contexts.

10. Do you usually play games?
    10.1. Who do you usually play with?
    10.2. What motivates you to play games?
	Identify the familiarity with games and the context in which they are played.

11. What is your motivation for using social networks? 12. What activities do you usually do when you access social networks?	Identify the motivations for using social media and the type of activities carried out in these contexts.

and adaptation of the previously defined criteria were made, *i.e.* pre-senior, aged between 50 and 64 years old; young-old – aged between 65–74 years old; and old – aged over 75 years old. The predominant respondents' age group was young-old (44%; N = 110), followed by pre-seniors (38%; N = 93), and old (18%; 45%). Residence countries included America, Europe, and Oceania continents, with Portugal (60%; N = 146) and United Kingdom (29%; N = 72) being the predominant ones. Five percent (N = 13) of respondents were from Australia, and the remaining 6% (N = 14) were from other countries – *e.g.* United States of America, Canada, Sweden, and Slovakia. It is worth noting that there were three non-answer in this question.

Regarding the level of education, there were also three non-answers, and the majority had higher academic degrees. 36% (N = 89) of respondents had a College/University degree, whereas 35% (N = 86) had a Graduate University degree. A considerable number of respondents had a High School degree – 19% (N = 46), and a Primary School degree – 9% (N = 22).

Table 2. Demographic characterization of the sample.

Gender	N	%
Total	248	100
Male	140	57
Female	107	43
Other	1	0
Age	N	%
Total	248	100
Pre-senior	93	38
Young-old	110	44
Old	45	18
Country of residence	N	%
Total	245	100
Portugal	146	60
United Kingdom	72	29
Australia	13	5
Other	14	6
Education level	N	%
Total	245	100
Primary School	22	9
High Scholl	46	19
College/University	89	36
Graduate University	86	35
Other	2	1

4   Results

When surveyed about the devices used to access the Internet, most of the respondents elected PC/Notebook (80, 20%; N = 199) as the most preferred, followed by the smartphone/iPhone (69%; N = 171), and, lastly, the tablet/iPad, used by 46,80% (N = 116) of the considered sample.

Regarding the perceived frequency relative to the most performed online activities, using a 5 item-scale (ranging from *never* to *always*), it is possible to conclude that 'Send and read emails' is the most perceived performed activity (118 always and 93 often), followed by 'Access the Internet' (111 always and 120 often), and 'Read online news' (60 always and 106 often). Moreover, respondents are also interested in activities such as 'Online search', 'Access social media', and 'Online banking or other financial products'.

Concerning the means to consume news, respondents ascertained to prefer traditional means of communication, *i.e.,* television (87,50%; N = 217) and radio (53,63%; N = 133) are the most preferred ones. Mobile devices with internet access are also on the top three, with 50,40% (N = 125) of respondents using this medium. Immediately after, there are search engines (47,58%; N = 118) and websites/app of news in newspapers (39,92%; N = 99).

Figure 1 illustrates respondents' main reasons to consume news. As shown in the graph, keeping up with world's (85,77%; N = 211), country's (83,33%; N = 205), and region's (71,54%; N = 176) news are the most important reasons among respondents. Nonetheless, they also value having different perspectives on different events (67,07%; N = 165), having info about everyday life (58,13%; N = 143), and consuming news as a part of their routines (36,59%; N = 90).

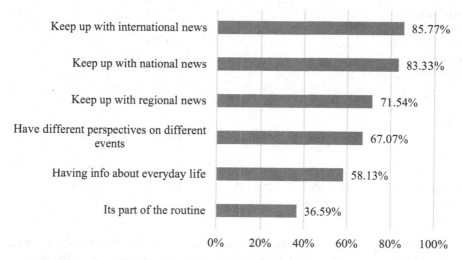

Fig. 1. Respondents' main reasons to consume News (N = 248).

In response to *What interests you the most in the following types of news?* respondents revealed their most preferred types of news. Using a 5 item-scale of interest (ranging from *not at all interested* to *very interested*), and corroborating what was previously perceived, national (95 very interested and 92 somewhat interested), regional (65 very interested and 122 somewhat interested), and international (64 very interested and 86 somewhat interested) news are the respondents' preferred types of news. Moreover, political news, breaking news, and science and technology news also arouse older adults' interest. Lastly on this list is health news, a topic that is so close to the target audience.

When the subjects were asked to indicate which activities they usually do when accessing the news, the majority elected 'read news' (89,11%; N = 211), followed by 'share news' (34,68%; N = 86), and 'react to news' (32,66%; N = 81) with similar percentage. Lastly, on the same question, commenting on news is also an activity selected by respondents, as part of their self-expression.

Moreover, in response to the question that assessed the main activities that respondents like to be value for, through a 5 item-scale of importance (ranging from *not at all important* to *extremely important*), they demonstrated to give great importance to activity in groups (7 extremely important and 40 very important), followed by the frequency with which they talk to other people in the community (6 extremely important and 33 very important), debate news (3 extremely important and 32 very important), share news (5 extremely important and 31 very important), and react to news (6 extremely important and 26 very important) – see Table 3.

Table 3. Main activities respondents like to be valued for (N = 248).

	Not at all important		Slightly important		Moderately important		Very important		Extremely important	
	N	%	N	%	N	%	N	%	N	%
Activity in Groups	64	25,8	59	23,8	78	31,5	40	16,1	7	2,8
Frequency with which you talk to other people in the community	64	25,8	55	22,2	90	36,3	33	13,3	6	2,4
Debate news	85	34,3	61	24,6	67	27,0	32	12,9	3	1,2
Share news	71	28,6	71	28,6	70	28,2	31	12,5	5	2,0
React to news	74	29,8	66	26,6	76	30,6	26	10,5	6	2,4

After assessing the respondents' motivations and most performed activities when accessing news, a couple of questions related to gamification were posed. The first one, related to the use of points, cards, coupons, or discounts, in order to assess the use of gamification in the respondents' daily life; whereas the second one intended to perceive the subjects' perception of gamification in strategies in the various contexts. The results show that 65,32% (N = 162) of respondents recognize the use of systems with points, cards, coupons, or discounts – see Fig. 2. However, only 10,89% (N = 27) acknowledged using gamified mobile apps.

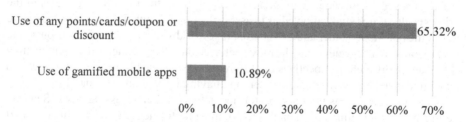

Fig. 2. Respondents' contact with gamification systems (N = 248).

To assess a possible familiarity to game elements by games themselves, respondents were asked "Do you usually play games?". 42,7% (N = 106) stated playing games on a usual basis.

Lastly, 79,25% (N = 84) of the respondents who play games (N = 106) affirms playing alone, whereas 16,98% (N = 18) play games with relatives, and 33,02% (N = 35) play with friends. When asked "What motivates you to play games?", 73,58% (N = 78) of respondents reported to be motivated by progress the game, 27,36% (N = 29) by the competition with others that arises in the context of game-playing, 25,47% (N = 27) by the provided learning experience, 18,87% (N = 20) by the possibility of socializing and making friends, and 13,21% (N = 14) of respondents feel motivated by being possible to play as a team.

5 Discussion

After the results of the questionnaire have been presented and analyzed, it is possible to discuss them.

Despite the poor digital literacy that characterizes older adults, and a certain resistance to use digital devices, more than 80% of the respondents use a personal computer to access the Internet. Mobile devices, such as smartphones, are also making significant progress, as 69% of the sample use them to *surf* the Internet.

Interpersonal communication is something that older adults value much [3], being also a way to prevent mental diseases, such as depression that can lead to suicidal thoughts in more extreme cases of social isolation [15]. This fact is supported by the respondents' answers relative to their preferred activity, *i.e.* send and read emails. Accessing social media, communication and establish a contact space *par excellence*, is also quite valued, being the fifth most performed activity by older adults. Staying up to date is, clearly, a priority, as reading online news and online searching are the third and fourth most performed activities, respectively. Accessing online banking or other financial products, which frequently offers some resistance to use, is also featured in this 6 item-list of the most performed activities when accessing the Internet, social media, and/or news' consumption.

Despite these advances in technology use, news' consumption is still very traditional, as television and radio are the most preferred means. However, more than half of respondents use mobile devices with Internet access to keep up with the news.

The products of journalism are great to keep up with the most recent events in the world. Results of this study allowed us to assess the main motivations to consume online news of the questioned older adults, showing that worldwide news is simultaneously the main reason to consume news and the most preferred ones. Respondents also demonstrate to like having different perspectives on different events, possibly because it is a way to engage in debates in an informed manner; and having info about everyday life.

Expectably, reading is the most performed activity when accessing news. Sharing, reacting, and commenting are all on this top of most performed activities, which are part of self-expression, which is crucial to self-growth, change, openness, and self-revelation [19].

Lastly, as already discussed, gamification plays a major role in captivating one's attention. The subjects of this study revealed to have a moderate familiarity with this mechanism, as more than a half use them on daily basis – through the use of points, cards, coupons, or discounts; and a little less than a half claims to play games, which is good evidence that respondents are familiar with game elements. The sense of progress is highly valued, but the same does not happen with the social side of game-playing, since the vast majority of respondents who play games claim to do it alone, and don't have a great sense of team or socialization while playing.

To sum up, identifying which activities must be valued and targeted is important in order to develop a gamification strategy that involves older adults and online communities or online news. In this sense, the study's results revealed that older adults like to be valued the most by: (i) activity in groups; (ii) frequency with which they talk to other people in the community; (iii) debate news; (iv) share news; and (v) react to the news.

6 Conclusion

In conclusion, this paper assesses some of the main contexts of the use of online news and games. The study allowed the characterization of the technological devices used, what type of activities the respondents perform on the Internet, means used during the news' consumption, type of news preferred, and familiarity with games and elements in entertainment or non-entertainment purposes. Moreover, the main activities and motivations that can be targeted to construct a gamification system were identified.

The limitations of this study are twofold. Firstly, a convenience sample was used, and as such, caution must be applied when extrapolating results and findings to other contexts. Thus, throughout this study, it was only possible to make a descriptive data analysis.

Secondly, this study's questionnaire is cross-sectional, *i.e.* applied during a specific point in time. During this period of time, due to the COVID-19 outbreak, the massification of the use of technologies and news' consumption occurred, which may have interfered in the respondents' perception of the usual reality.

To minimize these limitations, the following guidelines for future research should be considered: (a) random sample should be selected from the students at the Universities of the Third Age from the different countries; and (b) applying a questionnaire in a different period of time should also be considered.

The mentioned pandemic has changed everyone's lives, and it may be interesting to realize the impact that this technological transition is having on the use of technological products and the consumption of online news.

Acknowledgments. This work was supported by the research project SEDUCE 2.0 - Use of Communication and Information in the miOne online community by senior citizens. This project is funded by FCT – Fundação para a Ciência e a Tecnologia, I.P., COMPETE 2020, Portugal 2020 and European Union, under the European Regional Development Fund, POCI-01–0145-FEDER-031696 SEDUCE 2.0.

References

1. WHO: Active Ageing: A Policy Framework. A Contribution of World Health Organization to the Second United Nations World Assembly of Ageing, Madrid (2002). https://doi.org/10.1080/713604647
2. PORDATA: PORDATA - Indivíduos com 16 e mais anos que utilizam computador e Internet em % do total de indivíduos: por grupo etário. https://www.pordata.pt/Portugal/Ind ivíduos+com+16+e+mais+anos+que+utilizam+computador+e+Internet+em+percentagem+do+total+de+indivíduos+por+grupo+etário-1139. Accessed 09 Jan 2020
3. Leist, A.K.: Social media use of older adults: a mini-review. Gerontology. **59**, 378–384 (2013). https://doi.org/10.1159/000346818
4. Fisk, A.D., Rogers, W.A., Charness, N., Czaja, S.J., Sharit, J.: Designing for Older Adults: Principles and Creative Human Factors Approaches, Second Edition. CRC Press, Boca Raton (2009). https://doi.org/10.1201/9781420080681
5. Pak, R., McLaughlin, A.: Designing Displays for Older Adults. CRC Press, Boca Raton (2011)
6. Salwen, M.B., Garrison, B., Driscoll, P.D.: Online News and the Public. Lawrence Erlbaum, New Jersey (2005)
7. Siapera, E., Veglis, A.: Introduction: the evolution of online journalism. In: Siapera, E., Veglis, A. (eds.) The Handbook of Global Online Journalism. Wiley-Blackwell, New Jersey (2012). https://doi.org/10.1002/9781118313978.ch1
8. Conill, R.F., Karlsson, M.: The gamification of journalism. In: Davis, D.Z., Gangadharbatia, H. (eds.) Emerging Research and Trends in Gamification, pp. 356–383. IGI Global, Pennsylvania (2015). https://doi.org/10.4018/978-1-4666-8651-9.ch015
9. Kaplan, A.M., Haenlein, M.: Users of the world, unite! The challenges and opportunities of Social Media. Bus. Horiz. **53**, 59–68 (2010). https://doi.org/10.1016/j.bushor.2009.09.003
10. Toffler, A.: The Third Wave. Bantam Books, New York (1981)
11. Werbach, K., Hunter, D.: For the Win: How Game Thinking can Revolutionize Your Business. Wharton School Press, Pennsylvania (2012)
12. Sotirakou, C., Mourlas, C.: Designing a gamified news reader for mobile devices. In: Proceedings of 2015 International Conference on Interactive Mobile Communication Technologies and Learning, IMCL 2015, pp. 332–337. Institute of Electrical and Electronics Engineers Inc., Thousand Oaks, California (2015). https://doi.org/10.1109/IMCTL.2015.7359614
13. Bjursell, C.: Inclusion in education later in life: Why older adults engage in education activities. Eur. J. Res. Educ. Learn. Adults. **10**, 215–230 (2019). https://doi.org/10.3384/rela.2000-7426.rela20192

14. Ferreira, S., Veloso, A.I.: Older adults in ICT contexts: recommendations for developing tutorials. In: Zhou, J., Salvendy, G. (eds.) HCII 2019. LNCS, vol. 11592, pp. 376–387. Springer, Cham (2019). https://doi.org/10.1007/978-3-030-22012-9_27

15. Forsell, Y., Jorm, A.F., Winblad, B.: Suicidal thoughts and associated factors in an elderly population. Acta Psychiatr. Scand. **95**, 108–111 (1997). https://doi.org/10.1111/j.1600-0447.1997.tb00382.x

16. Jorm, A.F., Henderson, A.S., Scott, R., Korten, A.E., Christensen, H., Mackinnon, A.J.: Factors associated with the wish to die in elderly people. Age Ageing. **24**(5), 389–392 (1995). https://doi.org/10.1093/ageing/24.5.389

17. Leon, C.F.M., Glass, T.A., Beckett, L.A., Seeman, T.E., Evans, D.A., Berkman, L.F.: Social networks and disability transitions across eight intervals of yearly data in the New Haven EPESE. J. Gerontol. Ser. B Psychol. Sci. Soc. Sci. **54B**, S162–S172 (1999). https://doi.org/10.1093/geronb/54b.3.s162

18. Eng, P.M., Rimm, E.B., Fitzmaurice, G., Kawachi, I.: Social ties and change in social ties in relation to subsequent total and cause-specific mortality and coronary heart disease incidence in men. Am. J. Epidemiol. **155**, 700–709 (2002). https://doi.org/10.1093/aje/155.8.700

19. Nimrod, G.: The benefits of and constraints to participation in seniors' online communities. Leis. Stud. **33**, 247–266 (2014). https://doi.org/10.1080/02614367.2012.697697

20. Pappas, M.A., Demertzi, E., Papagerasimou, Y., Koukianakis, L., Voukelatos, N., Drigas, A.: Cognitive-based E-learning design for older adults. Soc. Sci. **8** (2019). https://doi.org/10.3390/socsci8010006

21. Aghaei, S., Nematbakhsh, M.A., Farsani, H.K.: Evolution of the world wide web: from Web 1.0 to Web 4.0. Int. J. Web Semant. Technol. **3**, 1–10 (2012). https://doi.org/10.5121/ijwest.2012.3101

22. Hermida, A.: Social journalism: exploring how social media is shaping journalism. In: The Handbook of Global Online Journalism, pp. 309–328. Wiley-Blackwell (2012). https://doi.org/10.1002/9781118313978.ch17

23. Vázquez-Herrero, J., Negreira-Rey, M., Pereira-Fariña, X.: Interactive documentary contributions to the renewal of journalistic narratives: realities and challenges. Revista Latina de Comunicación Social **72**, pp. 397–414 (2017). https://doi.org/10.4185/RLCS-2017-1171en

24. Cambridge Dictionary: CYBER- | Significado, definição em Dicionário Inglês. https://dictionary.cambridge.org/pt/dicionario/ingles/cyber. Accessed 26 Dec 2019

25. Allan, S.: Online News: Journalism and the Internet. Open University Press, McGraw-Hill International, Berkshire (2006)

26. Meier, K.: Journalism meets games: Newsgames as a new digital genre. Theory, boundaries, utilization. J. Appl. J. Med. Stud. **7**, 429–444 (2018). https://doi.org/10.1386/ajms.7.2.429_1

27. Giddens, A.: Contemporary Critique of Historical Materialism, vol. 2: The Nation State and Violence. Polity Press, Cambridge (1995)

28. Elyakov, A.D.: The nature of the modern information society. Sci. Tech. Inf. Process. **37**, 60–73 (2010). https://doi.org/10.3103/S0147688210010090

29. Lenstra, N.: The community-based information infrastructure of older adult digital learning: a study of public libraries and senior centers in a medium-sized city in the USA. Nord. Rev. **38**, 65–77 (2017). https://doi.org/10.1515/nor-2017-0401

30. Pew Research Center: Use of smartphones and social media is common across most emerging economies | Pew Research Center. https://www.pewresearch.org/internet/2019/03/07/use-of-smartphones-and-social-media-is-common-across-most-emerging-economies/. Accessed 27 Aug 2020

31. Foxman, M.: Play the news: fun and games in digital journalism. Tow Cent. Digit. J. Columbia Univ. (2015). https://doi.org/10.7916/D8J67V59

32. Ekström, M.: Information, storytelling and attractions: TV journalism in three modes of communication. Media Cult. Soc. **22**, 465–492 (2000). https://doi.org/10.1177/016344300 022004006

33. de la Peña, N., et al.: Immersive journalism: Immersive virtual reality for the first-person experience of news. Presence Teleoper. Virtual Environ. **19**, 291–301 (2010). https://doi.org/ 10.1162/PRES_a_00005

34. Kool, H.: The ethics of immersive journalism: A rhetorical analysis of news storytelling with virtual reality technology. Intersect **9**(3) (2016)

35. newsgaming.com: newsgaming.com – faq. http://www.newsgaming.com/faq.html. Accessed 03 Jan 2020

36. Wojdynski, B.: Games and quizzes in online journalism: reaching users via interactivity and customization. In: RMA - Information Resources Management Association (Eds.) Emerging Research and Trends in Gamification, pp. 667–693. IGI Global (2015). https://doi.org/10. 4018/978-1-4666-8651-9

37. Regalado, F.: Gamifying News for the miOne Online Community [Master Dissertation in Multimedia Communication] (2021, in press)

38. Lee, S.B., Oh, J.H., Park, J.H., Choi, S.P., Wee, J.H.: Differences in youngest-old, middle-old, and oldest-old patients who visit the emergency department. Clin. Exp. Emerg. Med. **5**, 249–255 (2018). https://doi.org/10.15441/ceem.17.261

Debunking the #Manosphere: An Exploratory Analysis on Patriarchy and Ageism Within the Digital Realm

Sofia José Santos[1,2(✉)], Inês Amaral[3,4], Rita Basílio Simões[1,5], and Maria José Brites[6]

[1] Faculty of Economics, University of Coimbra, Coimbra, Portugal
sjs@ces.uc.pt
[2] Centre for Social Sciences, University of Coimbra, Coimbra, Portugal
[3] Faculty of Arts and Humanities, University of Coimbra, Coimbra, Portugal
ines.amaral@uc.pt
[4] Communication and Society Research Centre of the University of Minho, Braga, Portugal
[5] NOVA Institute of Communication, Lisboa, Portugal
rbasilio@fl.uc.pt
[6] Lusófona University, CICANT, Porto, Portugal
mariajosebrites@ulp.pt

Abstract. Online and offline realms are not detached one from the other but are rather convergent and mutually reinforcing. Over the past decade, as the so-called "digital era" emerged and expanded, expressions of misogynist beliefs started to burgeon within the online realm. On par with male misogynist individualised agency, there has also been a growth of what has been labelled the manosphere. Although mainly revolving around gender identities and roles, the manosphere is profoundly tied to conservative imaginaries of race, nationality, sexuality, religion and, we argue, age. Taking into account the feminist argument the personal is political, that age and gender are intersecting categories, and that the digital is a central realm in collective and connective action, this paper draws an exploratory study on how patriarchy and ageism inform the politics of the #manosphere, exploring at the same time how the digital realm makes this convergence and result prolific concerning manosphere's agenda and mobilisation.

Keywords: Technology · Age · Masculinities · Intersectionality

1 Introduction

Burgeoning and continually expanding in the past decade, the "manosphere" represents today one of the most visible faces of online misogyny, holding a boom in both its activity, agency and engagement. Supported by an anti-feminist political agenda that aims to "reassert or redefine a particular throwback vision of masculinity that is in conflict with feminist ideals and the shifting roles of women" [1], the manosphere, its members and the values they say to represent are also profoundly tied to conservative imaginaries of race, nationality, sexuality, religion [1, 2] and, we argue, age.

© Springer Nature Switzerland AG 2021
Q. Gao and J. Zhou (Eds.): HCII 2021, LNCS 12786, pp. 420–429, 2021.
https://doi.org/10.1007/978-3-030-78108-8_31

Existing literature on the "manosphere" has focused primarily on how patriarchy and subsequent hegemonic and toxic masculinities sustain these online formations, their discourses, their agendas and their practices. As a significant part of the manosphere feeds on and disembogues in Alt-Right movements - indeed misogyny and anti-feminism are compelling mobilising rhetorics for white nationalism [4] - intersectional perspectives have also been emerging, mainly crosscutting gender, race and nationality. However, patriarchy is also intimately interwoven with ageism.

As power structures, ageism and patriarchy intersect toward constructed imaginaries and symbolic representations that produce and reproduce relations of privilege and discrimination concerning gender, race, class and age [5, 6]. According to Wilinska [7] "discourses of gender and ageing have a political character: they define relations between different groups of people, establish a power structure and play a determining role in assigning certain societal spaces to individuals". However, "whereas ageism discriminates people on the grounds of age, [and] patriarchy privileges men aligned with the ideal of 'hegemonic masculinity'" [5], they have been mutually reinforced [8]. Older men and older women tend to be depicted in line with normative and hegemonic conceptions of masculinities and femininities. Within this matrix, older people tend to be perceived and represented in line with asexuality, heteronormativity, and the concepts of heteronormative family and inactive life [9]. Homogenisation and gendered invisibility of the ageing process within media and public discourses has been contributing to this trend [10, 11]. The fact that old men are usually labelled and stigmatised as "asexual" or "dirty old men" illustrates patriarchal prejudices on age [12].

This immanent articulation renders "age" and "ageing" pivotal analytical categories to critically explore and understand the manosphere, particularly if taking the fact that the digital realm is vital in the manosphere's formation, participation and mobilisation. Also, whereas digital technologies may represent an opportunity for inclusion and improve citizens' quality of life, especially concerning senior individuals, demographic and socio-cultural changes tend to push the older citizens toward digital and social exclusion. Increased age is also associated with decreased digital access levels, limited modes of use, and connecting patterns. Digital practices of older people depend on the country, socioeconomic status, education, family structure, race, gender, geographic location, and cultural and social participation [13]. The digital divide between younger and older generations can be deemed more a social than a technological gap, as it involves dimensions such as competences, skills, practices, and informed choices [14].

Not only the manosphere, as a digital community, tends to exclude older people but its agenda, practices and ultimately politics contribute to the perpetuation of ageism by means of patriarchy. The centrality of the digital real when discussing the manosphere made us for the purpose of this paper to identify the manosphere as "#manosphere". Taking into account the feminist argument that the personal is political, that age and gender are intersecting categories [15], and that the digital is a central realm in collective action, this paper intends to draw an exploratory study on how patriarchy and ageism inform the politics of the #manosphere and how the digital realm allows it to be particularly effective concerning agenda's consolidation and political mobilisation. For that purpose, the paper is structured into three sections. The first section characterises and maps the #manosphere, exploring how patriarchy and ageism, as two intersecting oppressive systems, inform #manosphere politics, and shedding light on the specificities of the digital realm in this context. Finally, the third presents an exploratory analysis of a small sample that intends to provide concrete examples of the articulation between ageism, patriarchy and the digital realm so that it illustrates the research agenda this paper sets.

1.1 The #Manosphere

Manosphere appeared for the first time in 2009 in a blog post to "describe an online network of men's interest communities" and was later rendered popular by means of Ian Ironwood through its book on "The Manosphere: A new hope for masculinity" [2]. Today, the "manosphere" is a loose online network constituted by blogs, podcasts, videos, websites and social media accounts where the belief that men are victims of women and that the ongoing "feminist delusion" [2] and the "politically correct" needs to be halted and reversed.

Misogyny has always been present in patriarchal societies and the phenomena of sexist discourses circulating within the public sphere are no novelty [16]. However, this so-called "toxic brand of anti-feminism" has gained momentum and visibility in the last decade, particularly in the West. The possibilities the digital opened to network collective participation and action were pivotal to the relevance the #manosphere gained. Indeed, "the internet gives the manosphere qualities that distinguish it from offline movements. It is heterogeneous and nebulous, constantly changing and without a central establishment. It is read, written, contested, added on and replied to, by thousands of contributors, each with their own understandings and intentions" [1]. Also, as far-right political parties increased their political participation in national and european parliaments, and political leaders and representatives, such as Donald Trump, Jair Bolsonaro or Janusz Korwin-Mikkemade - to name but a few - validated misogynist discourses and practices, the #manosphere agenda left the margins and started to burgeon at the centre of established institutions and was, thus, legitimised by their agenda and practices.

Although its structure is loose and organic, four broad groups or subcultures can be identified within the #manosphere: Men's right's activists" (MRAs) "Men going their own way" (MGTOW), Pick-up artists" (PUAs) and the Incels [1, 3, 4, 17, 18].

The MRAs are the oldest and main subculture of the #manosphere. They can be described as "a loosely defined, but largely retrograde, collection of activists and internet talkers who fight for what they see as "men's rights" [19]. The MGTOW, in turn, share the radical stand that the perfect option for men is to steer clear of relationships with women. Accordingly, as society is set up against men and the system is impossible to change, the only way out is to "go your own way" [18]. Not surprisingly, they perceive their group as "a statement of self-ownership, where the modern man preserves and protects his own sovereignty above all else" [20]. At the beginning of 2021, their website had almost 33,000 members; its forums enclosed more than 50,000 topics, and their videos had been viewed 130 million times [20]. The PUAs focus on sharing techniques that allow men to successfully pick-up women. They share the idea that men are oppressed and "conceptualizes the masculinity crisis in terms of the femininization of the man" [18]. It often involves a "game" rationale, within which women are reduced "to sexual targets, rating their attractiveness on a scale of 1 to 10, and deploying techniques like before 'negging' to get a girl to notice you" [21]. Finally, the Incels share a deep feeling of rejection, placing the blame for their celibate on women who do not date them. They "feel that women owe them sex", "and that women are cruel and oppressive for denying them their wont" [1]. Subreddits like r/ForeverAlone or forums, such as LoveShyl or SlutHate are examples of Incels communities [1].

1.2 #Manosphere (Ageing and Gendered) Politics

Despite internal tensions and conflicts, the different #manosphere groupings are generally united in their subscription to the what is commonly coined as the "Red Pill philosophy/ideology which sustains the #manosphere politics and which, we argue, is informed, by both patriarchy and ageism. The term is used based upon the plot of the film "Matrix", where the protagonist is offered a choice: "You take the blue pill – the story ends, you wake up in your bed and believe whatever you want to believe. You take the red pill – you stay in Wonderland and I show you how deep the rabbit hole goes". The metaphor of the red pills encloses the idea of opposition, choice, and awakening. Within the manosphere, the 'red pill' represents accepting the harsh reality that men (and not women) are the ones being harmed and oppressed in today's societies and not the other way around as feminists and the "politically correct" groups state [22]. While mainly revolving around gender identities and roles anchored in traditional, heteronormative, and gendered sexual performances of men and women, this philosophy is also informed by ageism impacting, in turn, age identities.

To make our argument, three concepts are pivotal: patriarchy, hegemonic and toxic masculinities and ageism. Patriarchy embodies the institutionalization of male domination in a gendered hierarchy that is hegemonically legitimised [23]. At the centre of patriarchy as an oppressive system lies the concept of "hegemonic masculinity" which represents a culturally ideal of what it means to be a "real man" [24] and "goes in line with notions of rationality, leadership, courage, endurance, strength, heteronormativity, and sexual drive [5]. Men who adopt features and attributes consistent with the ideal of "hegemonic masculinity" affirm their alleged superiority over women - and also over men who do not comply with the aforementioned ideals [25]. In turn, toxic masculinity is built upon the specific elements of hegemonic masculinity "that foster domination of others" [26]. As a behaviour and attitude, it is expressed namely through "a strong need to dominate and control others", "a readiness to resort to violence, and the stigmatisation and subjugation of women, gays, and men who exhibit feminine characteristics" [26]. Domestic violence, harassment, gender-based rhetorical violence or sexual violence are concrete expressions of toxic masculinity. Ageism is a system of privilege and discrimination that is based upon "the understanding of age as a pivotal signifier concerning subjects, ranking them considering what is conceived as more and less desired ages" [5].

Patriarchy and ageism intersect in the central point of "hegemonic" and "toxic masculinities". In fact, concerning the masculine heteronormative ideal of sexual endurance, male seniority is not seldom times represented and perceived in line with one of the two options - either an asexual or a dirty old men [12]. Also, as men get older, they tend to lose physical endurance and strength. As such, within patriarchal and ageist societies, age identities perform an active role in gendered representations - and the opposite is also true. Within patriarchy, as men get closer to seniority, characteristics that are hegemonically attributed to being "a real man" (e.g. physical strength and sexual dominance) might decrease, making men (and patriarchal societies) perceive their (man) power as declining [5].

The way patriarchy and ageism inform the #manosphere holds profound political implications as the #manosphere proposes and legitimates power relations and proposes a specific gendered and age-based hierarchical distribution of resources and status in society. The #manosphere politics, by subscribing to hegemonic [25] and toxic masculinities [26], embodies misogynist and ageist beliefs.

1.3   The Digital Grammar of Participation and Mobilization

Media and social media is a way to engage citizens. Media practices, mediated engagement and social participation in the digital era have generalised informed audiences, massive media use, and users engagement. Participation stems from the civic agency, which involves citizens' civic engagement in public and political life [27]. This allows for both macro and micro participation: the former relates to participation in the social and political imagined community, while the latter refers to private life's spheres. #Manosphere politics crosscuts both. As Soon explains, "macro-level and micro-level approaches have been used to determine conditions that influence successful mobilisation, collective action participation and the threshold or tipping point when one crosses from non-participation to participation" [28]. In fact, #manosphere ideas "circulate through YouTube videos, anonymous message boards such as 8Chan, Facebook groups, and Twitter accounts", making its discourses and the practices they promote and legitimate to "be chopped up and recirculated in more palatable forms" [4]. The cyberspace is, indeed, a repository for collective cultural memory where a networked society is built upon a fragmented collective identity [29]. In an approach to the Internet as a space for participatory and collective culture, Cavanagh [30] argues, "the theme of hyper-identity comes to the fore insofar as it is inherently tied to the Internet's functionality as a 'social network'".

As connection is pivotal both for the digital realm and for the widespread of #manosphere politics, the Bennett and Segerberg's [31] 'logic of connective action', i.e., that proceeds from personal actions framed in digital social networks and that stands in opposition to the "logic of collective action", applies. Accordingly, "this shift from group-based to individualised societies is accompanied by the emergence of flexible social 'weak tie' networks [32] that enable identity expression and the navigation of complex and changing social and political landscapes" [31]. According to Granovetter's [32], weak ties are much more important for social network maintenance and influence than strong ties as the actors who share strong bonds are usually part of the same social circle, while the actors with weaker ties were significant in establishing the connection between different social groups [33]. Provided by technology, individuals' interconnection enhances individual actions on a collective scale through weak ties. Internet connectivity allows for the "smart networks" advocated by Albert Barabási [34] and the "intelligent collectives" postulated by Rheingold [35], summarising a problematic asymmetry between the individual and the collective empowered by digital cultures and subcultures. As such, and following Chadwick's [36] theory on media hybridity, the

#manosphere should be analysed as a "context of participation" [37] where a specific political agenda is cumulatively built, consolidated and able to mobilise.

In fact, the digital environment have fundamentally increased the surge and widespread of anti-feminism discourses as the interaction and dissemination logic of online media, particularly social media, has created unparalleled conditions to intensify the flow and efficiency of misogyny and toxic masculinity [2, 18]. Based upon a "facebook disclosure" logic [38], social media promote contents and information diets increasingly guided and endorsed by personal beliefs and emotions [38, 39], and the feeling of belonging to a group with similar opinions appears as mobilizing element [40]. As Ging [2] highlights, the "technological affordances of social media, such as speed, anonymity, platform algorithms, and social disembodiment, facilitate new and different ways in which to assert male hegemony", having "radically increased the flow of antifeminist ideas and information across groups, platforms and geographical boundaries. Hyperlinking to and reposting articles, blog entries, memes, and videos have enabled the rapid spread and homogenization of MRA rhetoric throughout the Anglophone world and beyond" [2].

2 Exploratory Analysis

This section presents an exploratory analysis of a small sample of data in order to illustrate the research agenda this paper sets. Computational methods were used to extract data within a medium-specific approach [41]. Data was selected and extracted from Twitter in the form of tweets using the network analysis and visualization software NodeXL. Textual data was collected from Twitter feeds using the word "manosphere". Retrieved tweets focused on a 8 days timelapse - from the 19th February to the 26th February 2021. The 1064 tweets from 697 users were first grouped according to three specific categories (see Table 1) and then grouped according to the topic that framed the tweet. Quantitative content analyses (Table 2) combined with critical discourse analysis was put forward to explore how patriarchy and ageism inform the politics of the #manosphere, and how the digital realm favours the consolidation of #manosphere's agenda and mobilisation .

Table 1. Codebook used in the exploratory analysis of tweet texts.

Number	Category	Description
1	Age and gender reinforce #manosphere politics	When terms referring to both age and gender identities and roles reinforce misogyny, incivility and discrimination in a mutually reinforcing logic
2	Age or gender reinforce #manosphere politics	When terms referring to age or gender identities and roles reinforce misogyny, incivility and discrimination
3	Others	Tweets whose message does not relate to any of the above or was unclear

Table 2. Quantitative exploratory analysis taking into account codebook.

Number	Category	Tweets	Frequency ($N = 1064$)
1	Age and gender reinforce #manosphere politics	18	1,69%
2	Age and/or gender reinforce #manosphere politics	92	8,65%
3	Others	954	89,66%

Data showed that the vast majority of the tweets including the term "manosphere" were not openly misogynist, even if subscribing - implicitly or explicitly - to the #manosphere politics. However, the usage of terms referring to age and/or gender identities and roles to reinforce misogyny, incivility and discrimination is more than 8%, corresponding to 92 tweets. Among these tweets, two examples can be used as illustrations of this discourse. The first - "The red pill manosphere made me embrace my manhood, I have grasped a better understanding of what a man is capable of doing on this earth. I am by nature oozing testosterone staved off by a feminine upbringing that constantly shames masculinity." - sheds light on how #manosphere politics is informed by patriarchal understandings of societies an, most importantly, how openly toxic elements of patriarchy, such as misogyny and uncivility inform and validate the #manosphere. The second - "The red pill manosphere made me embrace my manhood, I have grasped a better understanding of what a man is capable of doing on this earth. I am by nature oozing testosterone staved off by a feminine upbringing that constantly shames masculinity" - highlights a binary and hierarchical understanding of gender relations with clear benefit for "hegemonic masculinities". Finally, 18 tweets, corresponding to almost 2% of the total tweets, used terms referring to both age and gender identities and roles, in a mutually reinforcing logic, to successfully put forward the #manosphere politics. Among these, three examples are worth being analysed. The first one illustrates the different expectations the politics of the #manosphere hold concerning gender and age: "Manosphere guys be like "damn this 50 year old man is so HOT. Look how sexy and hot he is. So much hotter than gross disgusting 50 year old women. Oh I'm straight btw". The two others, in a record of criticism of the manosphere (and not subscribing to its rationale), foresee how the association of a certain age with successful notions of femininity and masculinity are proposed and validated by manosphere policies. The first one states "@hallangerhans @EtherealVg @FWPlayboy Key question is how many kids. You could do worse than a 40something fitness fanatic with some tasteful plastic surgery and mega millions. Manosphere heresy I realize. I know that we should only go for 24 and younger"; while the other one, adopting an intersectional lens towards the manosphere politics, intersects age, gender and class in the irony placed: "@GwendolynKansen I'm 27 now. I'm already an old maid according to the manosphere."

While the digital is pervasive in everyday practices and in sustaining discourses, so is the #manosphere, emerging in conversations of a wide palette of topics, making its agenda to be able to engage a growing number of people in #manosphere conversations.

Although the #manosphere can reach more and more people through social media affordances - even people who are not interested in the topic - it makes the fight for gender equality to happen also in this disseminated, networked and connected actions.

3 Conclusions

Online and offline realms are not detached one from the other but somewhat convergent and mutually reinforcing. Over the past decade, as the so-called "digital era" emerged and expanded, expressions of misogynist beliefs started to burgeon within the online realm. On par with male misogynist individualised agency, there has also been a growth of the #manosphere.

Taking into account the feminist argument that the personal is political, that age and gender are intersecting categories, and that the digital is a central realm in collective and connective action, this paper intended to draw an exploratory study on the politics of the #manosphere with the intent to shed light on how ageism and patriarchy sustain each other and how the digital is prolific in setting the floor for this convergence. As such, by means of literature review and an exploratory analysis, it explored how patriarchy and ageism inform the politics of the #manosphere and how the digital realm allows it to be particularly effective concerning its agenda's consolidation and political mobilisation.

The paper concluded that ageism and patriarchy are pivotal in the politics of the #manosphere, with a harmful impact on age and gender identities. The intersection between both in this analytical context is particularly challenging as discriminatory subtexts are more common than explicit texts. This sheds light on the pervasiveness of ageist and patriarchal imaginaries in contemporary societies and on the need for an enhanced research agenda on intersectionality concerning ageism and patriarchy in the current "cultural backlash" western societies have been facing.

Acknowledgments. This article was financed by national Portuguese funds through FCT (Fundação para a Ciência e a Tecnologia) in the framework of the project "(De)Coding Masculinities: Towards an enhanced understanding of media's role in shaping perceptions of masculinities in Portugal" (Reference PTDC/COM-CSS/31740/2017).

References

1. Lilly, M.: 'The world is not a safe place for men': the representational politics of the manosphere. Doctoral dissertation. University of Ottawa (2016)
2. Ging, D.: Alphas, betas, and incels: theorizing the masculinities of the manosphere. Men Masculinities **22**(4), 638–657 (2019)
3. Wiklund, M.: The Misogyny within the manosphere: a discourse analysis in a Swedish context. Master thesis. Malmo University (2020)
4. Lewis, H.: To Learn about the Far Right, Start With the "Manosphere." The Atlantic **7**, 1–5 (2019)
5. Santos, S.J., Amaral, I., Brites, M.J.: Masculinities and ageing: deconstructing online representations among portuguese speaking users. In: Gao, Q., Zhou, J. (eds.) HCII 2020. LNCS, vol. 12209, pp. 89–100. Springer, Cham (2020). https://doi.org/10.1007/978-3-030-50232-4_7

6. Barrett, A.E., Naiman-Sessions, M.: 'It's our turn to play': performance of girlhood as a collective response to gendered ageism. Ageing Soc. **36**(4), 764–784 (2016)
7. Wilinska, M.: Because women will always be women and men are just getting older: intersecting discourses of ageing and gender. Current Soc. **58**(6), 879–896 (2010)
8. Hearn, J., Melechi, A.: The Transatlantic Gaze: Masculinities, Youth and the American Imaginary. age, Thousand Oaks (1992)
9. Amaral, I., Daniel, F., Abreu, S.G.: Policies for gender equality in Portugal: contributions to a framework for older women. Revista Prisma Soc. **22**, 346–363 (2018)
10. Amaral, I., Daniel, F.: The use of social media among senior citizens in Portugal: active ageing through an intergeneration approach. In: Zhou, J., Salvendy, G. (eds.) ITAP 2018. LNCS, vol. 10926, pp. 422–434. Springer, Cham (2018)
11. Amaral, I., Santos, S.J., Daniel, F., Filipe, F.: (In)visibilities of men and aging in the media: discourses from Germany and Portugal. In: Zhou, J., Salvendy, G. (eds.) HCII 2019. LNCS, vol. 11593, pp. 20–32. Springer, Cham (2019). https://doi.org/10.1007/978-3-030-22015-0_2
12. Sandberg, L.: In lust we trust? Masculinity and sexual desire in later life. Men Masculinities **19**(2), 192–208 (2015)
13. Amaral, I., Daniel, F.: Ageism and IT: social representations, exclusion and citizenship in the digital age. In: Zhou, J., Salvendy, G. (eds.) ITAP 2016. LNCS, vol. 9755, pp. 159–166. Springer, Cham (2016)
14. Amaral, I.: Senior citizens and the internet. In: Merskin, D. (ed.) The SAGE International Encyclopedia of Mass Media and Society, pp. 1549–1551. Sage Publications, Thousand Oaks (2020)
15. Hearn, J.: Imaging the aging of men. In: Featherstone, M., Wernick, A. (eds.) Images of Aging: Cultural Representations of Later Life, pp. 97–114. Routledge, London (2005)
16. Coston, B.M., Kimmel, M.: White men as the new victims: reverse discrimination cases and the men's rights movement. Nevada Law J. **13**(2), 368–385 (2013)
17. Basu, T.: The "manosphere" is getting more toxic as angry men join the incels. MIT Technology Review (2021). https://www.technologyreview.com/2020/02/07/349052/the-manosphere-is-getting-more-toxic-as-angry-men-join-the-incels/. Accessed 21 Feb 2021
18. Ribeiro, M.H., et al.: The Evolution of the Manosphere Across the Web. Icwsm (2020)
19. Futrelle, D.: WTF is a MGTOW? A Glossary. http://www.wehuntedthemammoth.com/wtf-is-a-mgtow-a-glossary/. Accessed 12 Feb 2021
20. Bates, L.: The rise of a toxic male separatist movement who hate women. The Irish Times. https://www.irishtimes.com/life-and-style/the-rise-of-a-toxic-male-separatist-movement-who-hate-women-1.4339250. Accessed 12 Feb 2021
21. Dewey, C.: Inside the 'manosphere' that inspired Santa Barbara shooter Elliot Rodger. The Washington Post. https://www.washingtonpost.com/news/the-intersect/wp/2014/05/27/inside-the-manosphere-that-inspired-santa-barbara-shooter-elliot-rodger/. Accessed 12 Feb 2021
22. Cohen, R.: Welcome to the manosphere: a brief guide to the controversial men's rights movement. Mother Jones. https://www.motherjones.com/politics/2015/01/manosphere-mens-rights-movement-terms/. Accessed 12 Feb 2021
23. Galtung, J.: Peace by Peaceful Means: Peace and Conflict, Development and Civilization, vol. 14. Sage, Thousand Oaks (1996)
24. Connell, R.W.: Masculinities. University of California Press, Berkeley (1995)
25. Connell, R.W.: Masculinities, 2nd edn. University of California Press, Berkeley (2005)
26. Kupers, T.A.: Toxic masculinity as a barrier to mental health treatment in prison. J. Clin. Psychol. **61**(6), 713–724 (2005)
27. Dahlgren, P., Alvares, C.: Political participation in an age of mediatisation: towards a new research agenda. Javnost-The Public **20**(2), 47–65 (2013)

28. Carpentier, N.: Media and Participation: A Site of Ideological-Democratic Struggle. Intellect (2011)
29. Fernback, J.: The individual within the collective: virtual ideology and the realization of collective principles. In: Jones, S. (ed.) Virtual Culture. Identity & Communication in Cybersociety. Sage, London (1997).
30. Cavanagh, A.: Sociology in the Age of the Internet. Open University, UK (2007)
31. Bennett, W.L., Segerberg, A.: The logic of connective action: digital media and the personalization of contentious politics. Inf. Commun. Soc. **15**(5), 739–768 (2012)
32. Granovetter, M.: The strength of weak ties. Am. J. Sociol. **78**(6), 1360–1380 (1973)
33. Amaral, I.: Redes Sociais na Internet: Sociabilidades Emergentes. LabCom.IFP, Covilhã (2016)
34. Barabási, A.-L.: Linked. Perseus Publishing, Cambridge (2003)
35. Rheingold, H.: A Comunidade Virtual. Gradiva, Lisboa (1996)
36. Chadwick, A.: The Hybrid Media System: Politics and Power. Oxford University Press, Oxford (2017)
37. Bimber, B.: Three prompts for collective action in the context of digital media. Polit. Commun. **34**(1), 6–20 (2017)
38. Rochlin, N.: Fake news: belief in post-truth. Library Hi Tech **35**(3), 386–392 (2017)
39. Giuliani, G., Santos, S.J., Garraio, J.: Online social media and the construction of sexual moral panic around migrants in Europe. Socioscapes. Int. J. Soc. Politics Cult. **1**(1), 161–180 (2019)
40. Bakardjieva, M.: Do clouds have politics? Collective actors in social media land. Inf. Commun. Soc. **18**(8), 983–990 (2015)
41. Rogers, R.: Digital Methods. MIT Press, Cambridge (2013)

New Media, Old Misogyny: Framing Mediated Madonna on Instagram from an Ageing Perspective

Rita Basílio Simões[1,2]([✉]), Inês Amaral[1,3], Sofia José Santos[4,5], and Maria José Brites[6]

[1] Faculty of Arts and Humanities, University of Coimbra, Coimbra, Portugal
rbasilio@fl.uc.pt
[2] NOVA Institute of Communication, Lisboa, Portugal
[3] Communication and Society Research Centre of the University of Minho, Braga, Portugal
[4] Faculty of Economics, University of Coimbra, Coimbra, Portugal
sjs@ces.uc.pt
[5] Centre for Social Sciences, University of Coimbra, Coimbra, Portugal
[6] Lusófona University, CICANT, Porto, Portugal
mariajosebrites@ulp.pt

Abstract. From a feminist perspective, mainstream media representations have always performed disciplinary functions. Particularly, regarding ageing women. On digital platforms, individuals would have a greater agency to perform and shape gender norms and sexual roles. However, scholarship has been expressing scepticism with the liberatory promise of the online realm, as well as cautions with digital network harassment and the so-called nanosphere. Yet, little is known about how exactly misogynistic rhetoric operates on popular social media to discipline ageing women's feminity. This paper extends the feminist scholarship to the field of Instagram, focusing specifically on representations of the pop star Madonna. It presents an analysis of how ageing women femininities representations are mobilised on Instagram through a case study of posts indexed with hashtags. Applying computational methods and drawing on the insights of Feminist Critical Discourse Analysis, it approaches these networked representations by exploring the interplay between sexism and ageism within the misogynistic driven forces targeting Madonna and her ageing feminity.

Keywords: Social media · Online misogyny · Ageism

1 Introduction

Popular representations are a battlefield for competing discourses towards gender and age, and ageing bodies. The ageing female body is highly invisible when women no longer perform reproductive functions. Differently, when it is visible, it is mostly devalued or positioned as an object of antipathy and disgust. It is as the ageing female body doesn't meet a linguistic and visual repertory capable of giving a valuable meaning to age and ageing [1, 2]. While, now, there is undoubtedly a greater diversity of middle-aged and older women's visual representations, there is also a considerably increased chance of misrepresenting women in digitally images [3]. Also, despite the promise of democratic renewal of the Internet and of online sociability, critical feminist work highlights the interplay between a post-feminist discourse of free will and choice-making and more subtle or blatant forms of sexism and misogyny [4, 5] and ageist trolling [6].

As social media platforms have gained more users, celebrities have recurred to these sites to establish their brand and interact with fans [7–9]. Pop stars, female actresses, singers have found in social media new opportunities to connect with fans and establish their brand. However, evidence of being routinely suffering online harassment in various forms has posed new challenges to celebrities' online persona. Media coverage indicates that celebrities who use their sexual allure for publicity deserve their victimisation [10]. Notably, public attitudes toward celebrity bashing differ based on the type of perpetrator and the celebrity-victim likability [11].

Moreover, women celebrities who once were sex symbols at popular imaginaries are particularly vulnerable to ageist abuse [2]. Now over 60, Madonna is an interesting case of study because her artistic brand has always expressed a sexual nature. Her sexualised performances seen in the past as inspiring young generations "are now deemed grotesque, and this repulsion seems to lie in knowledge of Madonna's real age rather than in the body she displays" [2].

This paper presents an analysis of how ageing women femininities representations are mobilised on Instagram through a case study of posts indexed with hashtags within a digital collective narrative process that intersects ageing and patriarchal paradigms. Applying computational methods to extract data within a medium-specific approach [12] and drawing on the insights of Feminist Critical Discourse Analysis [13], we approach these representations by exploring the interplay between sexism and ageism within the misogynistic driven forces targeting Madonna and her ageing feminity.

1.1 Media, Ageism and Female Body

There is a great deal of literature that explores the traditional media's role in reproducing and maintaining ideologies that assert dominant power in society. From mainstream news to fictional depictions, media can reproduce and perpetuate inequality by demanding conformity to particular hegemonic discourses [14–17]. While there may always be room for resistance, gender, sexuality, age, and other identity constructs and their combined impact can only be acknowledged through the broad cultural framework that gives them meaning. Including, and foremost, mainstream media representations, which are in the hands of the small group of media producers and, nevertheless, provide for larger audiences the "preferred readings" [18], often in favour of the narrative thrust. Through this process, the media produce and convey social knowledge by referencing an unavoidable field of pre-existing meanings. Hence, events are always "coded" at a certain level of consensuality, established by the "repertoire of dominant ideologies" that give plurality a certain degree of cohesion [19].

Media culture is saturated with tensions and contradictions with which identity imageries and performances are ruled. Among the range of contradictory depictions is the femininity of older women, mainly celebrated when restricted to women who do not look older. The interplay between gender and age reflects a complex set of structuring power forces, rendering the older female body, "both hypervisible and invisible" [1]. To be visible, ageing women have to seem young. However, based on youth/beauty/sexual desirability, the prevailing normative femininity model hardly accommodates the ageing women's bodies. Often, ageing representations convey how women should hide the signs of ageing and even be afraid of looking old. Indeed, when women look at their age and show, without make-up or digital filters, their body, their visible ageing is often depicted as deliberate neglect. At the same time, though, women who do not behave according to their age are frequent targets of abusive commentary and repulse [2]. This youth-oriented mass culture explains the contemporary growth of anti-ageing products and services and the ever-expanding markets of 50+ consumer goods and lifestyle-products targeting an "increasingly growing minority" of middle-aged and older individuals [20]. Moreover, the celebration of youth and beauty "heralded an increasing medical discursive interest in the pathologisation of age, resulting in menopause becoming more closely associated with decline and decay, and ageing represented as linked to loss: of power, beauty and sexuality" [2].

Shaped by prejudice and bias against older people, different forms of ageism spread across mainstream media content. While ageing's physical signs are frequently stereotyped, traditionally and still most of the time, they are simply hidden from view [2, 3, 21–24]. On the big screen, despite ageing stars interpreting older women for an ever-growing mature women audience, age is not only pathologised but also essentialised. This process happens "through a foregrounding of biological functions, and a linking of such functions to behavioural and emotional norms" [2]. On the small screen, ageing female presenters fade in the air "as programmes get 'refreshed'" [23]. In the news media globally, "women beyond 65 years of age are more likely representing ordinary persons, whereas older men serve as experts or spokespersons more commonly" [24]. When in the news, the ageing population is often depicted as a societal threat, responsible for what some gerontology scholars [57] label "apocalyptic demography". In tandem with the longer life spans and the lower fertility rates, the large generation of people reaching retirement age is, according to the mainstream's hegemonic narrative, pushing societies to a dead-end [22, 25, 26]. Additionally, despite the evidence of more diverse media contents in the contemporary landscape, there are few certainties regarding the emancipatory potential of these more varied representations [27].

1.2 Online Femininity and Misogyny

It was against this backdrop that we saw being raised optimistic visions of the new media platforms' liberatory potential. In the early days of the Internet, new media scholars saw individuals' agency opportunities to perform and shape gender norms and sexual roles. Some pointed to the chance to explore multiple identities and, by doing that, to develop more empathy for other groups and identity performances [28].

The digital environment would also allow the exploration of positive online sociability through disembodied and fragmented identities. Technology's visions as helping to change expressions of self allow seeing beyond the identity structuration [29]. Notably, users may act independently of their bodies on which gender and sexual discipline have been exercised [30]. Thus, while old media are the loci of naturalisation of normative representations, digital platforms would favour the liberation from gender, sexuality, and age prejudices and constraints.

However, offline embodied constraints followed us online. Scholarship on the Internet's evolution shows that digital media technologies often help replicate and perpetuate offline social inequalities by inviting limited types of social identity construction and negotiation. Mediated interfaces and their affordances and the very architecture of the Internet may reproduce normative patterns already dominant within offline social, political, and economic contexts [31–36]. As the algorithms that govern online experiences can favour normative and prescriptive rationales to make sense of self and others, platforms design and policies may be based upon and replicate harmful stereotypes and behaviours. Indeed, scholars have been studying digital platforms as suitable spaces for the creation of politically homogenous and polarising realms that can serve as breeding grounds for sexism, as well as for white supremacy, homophobia, transphobia and sexist speech [37]. To date, the most severe expression of online sexist hatred is the politics known as the "manosphere". As a product of the geekier and more extreme Internet spaces, such as 4/Chan, and Reddit, and sites of men's rights groups, this deeply misogynistic phenomenon has been characterised as highly personalised politics of anti-feminism [38, 39], toxic masculinity [40] and alt-right sensibilities [41].

Along with these deeply misogynistic practices, digital platforms have been facilitating new modalities of direct violence. Interpersonal violence is widely recognised as a globally significant human rights problem. According to estimates by the World Health Organization [58], 35% of women worldwide report having experienced either physical or sexual violence by a partner or sexual violence by a friend, family member, acquaintance or stranger. National studies and police data in a range of countries indicate the highly gendered pattern of domestic and sexual violence, with women continuing to represent the majority of victims and men overwhelmingly, although not exclusively, the perpetrators. Research demonstrates the persistent nature and prevalence of harassment, domestic and sexual violence [59–61]. Moreover, it shows that these harms are disturbingly common, highly gendered and most often relational [62, 63].

With the rapid uptake of Internet-enabled devices, as well as digital communication services such as social media networks, it is perhaps unsurprising that digital technologies might also be used as tools to facilitate gender-based harms. Thus, concerns with digital technologies' potential to facilitate a wide range of harmful behaviours already known or entirely new targeting women have also emerged. Evidence of these harmful practices being outward across digital platforms is being gathered worldwide. It is telling a story of slurs and harassment, nonconsensual photographic, doxing, trolling, defamation, death or rape threats, mob attacks or stalking [42–46].

Far from finding in digital technologies a way for individual liberation and democratic renewal, women are frequently online violence targets. In this context, digital platforms reproduce offline dominant gender norms and facilitate new ways of practising gender violence. Moreover, suppose violence across the lifespan has a cumulative effect, resulting in a high lifetime rate for older women increasing the overall disadvantages these women experience [47].

Online abuse may also take the form of indirect speech acts across a wide range of mainstream online platforms, such as Instagram, Twitter, Facebook memorial pages or Tinder. From a racialised perspective, these types of expressions of hatred practices have been seen as "racially loaded toxic comments" [48]. These commentaries devalued and dehumanised those targeted, normalising their exclusion or their "othering", as Harmer and Lumsden [49] put it. Likewise, misogynist content legitimises sexism, favouring women chilling, silencing, and self-censorship [50, 51]. Frequently, older women's bodies are harmfully labelled as 'MILF' and 'cougar' to validate the way they express "the standards of inducing a hetero-sexual desire-reaction in an average man, and 'soccer-mom' or 'granny' for the truly invisible ones, whose bodies do not" [64].

Notably, misogyny also spans online as a form of popular culture, what Banet-Weiser [5] calls "popular misogyny". Linked to the increasing visibility of women and feminism, both being networked through all types of media, popular misogyny functions as a reaction to the increasing popularity and acceptance of feminist issues. As in other historical moments, when feminism comes out from its niches, the artillery of "the status quo position it as a peril, and skirmishes ensue between those determined to challenge the normative and those determined to maintain it" [5].

The popular feminism with which popular misogyny interplays is situated within cultural practices and believes that mask forms of gender oppression under the guise that gender equality is achieved and feminist is no longer necessary. Under this postfeminist ethos about which several feminist scholars have been reflecting [4, 52, 53], women are socialised to believe that undergoing strict diets or being submitted to risky plastic surgeries means to have a free choice [4]. Also, as postfeminist subjects, women, especially young women, are encouraged to engage in typical masculine behaviours as a way of emancipation. Ultimately, far from meaning that equality is achieved, these behaviours, with which women engage, reify heteropatriarchal norms and female objectification [53].

Moreover, postfeminist sensibility [4] is ageist in its nature. Within this culture, as Rasmussen [54] contends, "even very youthful women are pressured to respond to what has been referred to as 'time panic'". In this vein, as "every woman inevitably grows older, ageism is the ultimate method through which a woman is disciplined and silenced and eventually stripped of those gains she may have been able to achieve as a youthful postfeminist subject".

Furthermore, as a reactionary response to recent cultural shifts, popular misogyny stands for a more subtle range of forms of gender policing in the face of, for instance, the 2008 economic-recession and a crisis of masculinity [52]. Just as "the second-wave feminism was redundant in a more contemporary social order, so now could the empowered postfeminist subject also be dismissed, particularly when she could be connected to the disruption of patriarchal security by taking up to much space in the workplace" [54].

Within this feminist framework, popular misogyny can be seen in most of the interstices of media representations and online performances and sociability, from mobile dating apps such as Tinder [55] to sites of user-generated content like Urban Dictionary [51]. However, little is known about how exactly misogynistic rhetoric operates on popular social media to discipline ageing women's feminity. This research is aimed to extend the feminist scholarship to the field of Instagram, focusing specifically on representations of the singer Madonna. The research questions that guided our analysis are: 1) What are the visibility patterns of misogynistic rhetoric targeting Madonna?; and 2) How do these patterns intersect with dominant ideologies to discipline ageing femininity?

2   Method

Digital grammars display human-machine-platform actions and multivalent syntaxes, namely hashtags, which provide different networks and approaches to track digital collective narratives in real-time [56]. This paper aims to analyse how ageing women femininities representations are mobilised on Instagram through a case study of posts indexed with hashtags within a digital collective narrative process that intersects ageing and patriarchal paradigms.

Following the assumption of technological affordances [33], we conducted a study that relied on misogynistic hashtags and ageists focused on the singer Madonna. The empirical study applied computational methods to extract data within a medium-specific approach [12]. The dataset was collected through the tool DMI Instagram Scraper and randomly selected 1380 media items from the public stream of Instagram indexed with selected hashtags. Data were analysed through feminist critical discourse analysis [13] using the MAXQDA software. The visual and textual discourses conveyed by the images collected in the mentioned streams and their respective captions and hashtags were open coded by the authors. Once stabilised, the coding scheme was applied to the sample.

3   Results

Representations of women and feminism on the Internet fit in a post-feminist context in which new forms of violence emerge, anchored in hate speech and misogynistic rhetoric that seeks to legitimise micro gender-based violence as mere freedom of expression. In a post-feminist logic, social media have framed discursive spaces in which misogyny and ageist prejudices are perpetuated in public spheres that are often anonymised. The case study focuses on misogynistic rhetoric mobilised against the singer Madonna through posts indexed with seven hashtags, as shown in Table 1.

Table 1. Dataset.

Hashtag	Frequency
#oldmadonna	57
#oldonna	171
#madonnaisold	44
#madonnaisover	208
#madonnaisdead	10
#madonnawhore	654
#fuckmadonna	236

The posts were coded in four dominant rhetorical misogynistic forces: disgusting ageing sexuality, abjected ageing body, sexist hate, and anti-feminist hatred, which will be briefly illustrated and described in what follows (Figs. 1–4).

4 Discussion

4.1 Disgusting Ageing Sexuality

Fig. 1. Example of images coded as disgusting ageing sexuality.

Misogynistic rhetoric targeting Madonna sexuality highlights its disgusting, ageing nature. Ridicularising her sexual agency and humiliating it by using blasting comparison with younger pop stars more is a way of shame Madonna, "not just as an older woman but also as a woman who has historically used her body as a sexualised commodity" [12]. As Whelehan [2] contends, "ageing stars are implicitly exhorted to leave their 'sexiness' at the door of menopause or face ageist slurs". This is the case of this pop star of the old media economy of the controlled image market, for whom sexuality was always used to sell herself as a cultural product. Thus, there are no meanings capable of reconciling post-menopausal women to sexuality in the post-feminist and supposedly liberatory context. At the same time, this type of misogynistic rhetoric functions as a form of policing ageing women's sexuality, reminding them that they are too old to express a sexual agency. The price to pay it is severe public scrutiny (Fig. 1).

4.2 Abjected Ageing Body

Fig. 2. Example of images coded as abjected ageing body.

Another form of misogynistic rhetoric and ageing women policing networked across Instagram is manifested in posts that abjects Madonna's ageing body. As with other digital platforms, this popular social media is a site where pop stars are often subject to a new media economy of smash-and-grab image wars. Slurs targeting Madonna body express strong emotion by abjecting how she looks and abjecting how she shamelessly pursues youthfulness. Images of her aged body and misogynistic comments also reveal how Madonna is rejected in the context of a culture dominated by market values, in which the pop star is no longer valuable [12] (Fig. 2).

4.3 Sexist Hate

Different forms of gendered abuse targeting high profile women have thrived online. They comprise a diverse set of conduct, such as sexually graphic invites to look at Madonna as an object deserving to be "fucked" (or raped), as we saw in the analysed sample. Overall, these types of insults certainly have a direct impact. Moreover, they favour female objectification and the normalising of violence against women. Likewise, different forms of gendered abuse targeting common women have thrived online. However, online gender-based abuse is never a mere attack on an individual subject: it addresses the person's identity. Thus, it may typically aim at a certain high profile woman, as in this case, but its consequences can be traced to all that happens with women in the public sphere. As above mentioned, misogynist content legitimises sexism and is keen on perpetuating women chilling, silencing, and self-censorship [50, 51] (Fig. 3).

Fig. 3. Example of images coded as sexist hate.

4.4 Anti-Feminism Hatred

Madonna representations on Instagram are also fulled of misogynist rhetoric supporting extreme anti-feminist and anti-women's rights attitudes and beliefs. Reminding us to consider both the digital opportunities afforded by digital practices as well as the challenges it faces, these discourses point to a concerted set of attacks targeting feminism as redundant, ridiculous and intrinsically prejudicial and threatening toward men. Madonna is the best scapegoat to revalidate misogynistic topes about how feminist ideas are no longer necessary to have a high profile and privilege.

Fig. 4. Example of images coded as anti-feminist hatred.

5 Conclusions

This paper departed from a case study to gather evidence on how ageing femininities representations are mobilised on Instagram. Using posts indexed with hashtags focusing on Madonna's pop star, we analysed misogynistic rhetoric patterns targeting this celebrity and the interplay between those patterns and dominant ideologies in post-feminist online and offline realms. Overall, we documented that while interactivity might produce a different kind of social connections, namely, between celebrities, users, and fans, it does not remove these relationships from the broader influence of hegemonic culture. Notably, the interplay between the visible patterns and the dominant ideologies is twofold: it disciplines ageing femininity by constructing bounded subject positions and normalises the nanosphere's political logics. As others [6], we framed Madonna's mediated representations on Instagram as presenting micro-discursive displays of long-held disapproval of ageing femininity. By articulating these imaginaries with systemic slurs and abuse, we further show that, as other loci of the nanosphere, Instagram's conspicuous consumption culture is also governed by toxic masculinity. Future studies on digital representations of ageing feminity should gather more evidence on popular misogyny and the visual economy for ageing women online.

Acknowledgements. Financial support from Portuguese national funds through FCT (Fundação para a Ciência e a Tecnologia) in the framework of the project "Online Violence Against Women: preventing and combating misogyny and violence in a digital context from the experience of the COVID-19 pandemic" (Reference GENDER RESEARCH 4 COVID-19–058).

References

1. Woodward, K.: Performing age performing gender. NSWA J. **18**(1), 162–186 (2006)
2. Whelehan, I.: Ageing appropriately: postfeminist discourses of ageing in contemporary hollywood. In: Gwynne, J., Muller, N. (eds.) Postfeminism and Contemporary Hollywood Cinema, pp. 78–95. Palgrave Macmillan UK, London (2013). https://doi.org/10.1057/978113730 6845_6
3. Hurd Clarke, L.: Facing Age: Women Growing Older in Anti-Aging Culture. Rowman & Littlefield Publishers, Lanham (2011)
4. Gill, R.: Postfeminist media culture: elements of a sensibility. Eur. J. Cult. Stud. **10**(2), 147–166 (2017)
5. Banet-Weiser, S.: Empowered: Popular Feminism and Popular Misogyny. Duke University Press (2018)
6. Gorton, K., Garde-Hansen, J.: From old media whore to new media troll: the online negotiation of Madonna's ageing body. Fem. Media Stud. **13**(2), 288–302 (2013)
7. Marwick, A., Boyd, D.: To see and be seen: celebrity practice on Twitter. Convergence **17**(2), 139–158 (2011)
8. Ingleton, P., York, L.: From Clooney to Kardashian: reluctant celebrity and social media. Celebrity Stud. **10**(3), 364–379 (2019)
9. Jorge, A.: Celebrity bloggers and vloggers. In: Ross, K. (ed.) The International Encyclopedia of Gender, Media, and Communication, pp. 1–7. Wiley (2020)
10. Lawson, C.E.: Innocent victims, creepy boys: discursive framings of sexuality in online news coverage of the celebrity nude photo hack. Fem. Media Stud. **18**(5), 825–841 (2018)

11. Ouvrein, G., Pabian, S., Machimbarrena, J.M., De Backer, C.J., Vandebosch, H.: Online celebrity bashing: wrecking ball or good for you? Adolescent girls' attitudes toward the media and public bashing of Miley Cyrus and Selena Gomez. Commun. Res. Rep. **35**(3), 261–271 (2018)
12. Rogers, R.: Digital Methods. MIT Press, Cambridge (2013)
13. Lazar, M. (ed.): Feminist Critical Discourse Analysis: Gender, Power and Ideology in Discourse. Palgrave MacMillan, Basingstoke (2005)
14. Fairclough, N.: Media Discourse. Arnold, London (1995)
15. Macdonald, M.: Exploring Media Discourse. Arnold, London (2003)
16. Kress, G., van Leeuwen, T.: Reading Images: The Grammar of Visual Design. Routledge, London (2006)
17. Simões, R.B.: Crime, Castigo e Género nas Sociedades Mediatizadas: Políticas de (In)justiça no Discurso dos Media. Media XXI, Porto (2016)
18. Hall, S.: Encoding/Decoding. In: Durham, M., Kellner, D. (eds.) Media and Cultural Studies: Keywords, pp. 163–173. Blackwell Publishing, Oxford (1980)
19. Hall, S.: Culture, the media and the 'ideological effect.' In: Curran, J., Gurevitch, M., Woollacott, J. (eds.) Mass Communication and Society, pp. 315–348. Arnold, London (1977)
20. Ylänne, D.V.: Representing Ageing. Palgrave Macmillan, London (2012)
21. Greer, G.: The Change: Women Aging and the Menopause. Hamish Hamilton, London (1996)
22. Lundgren, A.S., Ljuslindr, K.: 'The baby-boom is over and the ageing shock awaits': populist media imagery in news-press representations of population ageing. Int. J. Ageing Later Life **6**(2), 39–71 (2011)
23. Warren, L., Richards, N.: 'I don't see many images of myself coming back at myself': representations of women and ageing. In: Ylänne, D.V. (ed) Representing Ageing, pp. 149–168. Palgrave Macmillan, London (2012)
24. Edström, M.: Visibility patterns of gendered ageism in the media buzz: a study of the representation of gender and age over three decades. Fem. Media Stud. **18**(1), 77–93 (2018)
25. Cruikshank, M.: Learning to be Old. Gender, Culture, and Aging. Rowman & Littlefield Publishers, Oxford (2003)
26. Fealy, G., McNamara, M.: Constructing Ageing and Age Identity: A Case Study of Newspaper Discourses. National Centre for the Protection of Older People, Dublin (2009)
27. Amaral, I., Santos, S.J., Daniel, F., Filipe, F.: (In)visibilities of men and aging in the media: discourses from Germany and Portugal. In: Zhou, J., Salvendy, G. (eds.) HCII 2019. LNCS, vol. 11593, pp. 20–32. Springer, Cham (2019). https://doi.org/10.1007/978-3-030-22015-0_2
28. Turkle, S.: Life on the Screen: Identity in the Age of the Internet. Touchstone, New York (1995)
29. Haraway, D.: A manifesto for cyborgs: science, technology, and socialist feminism in the 1980s. Aust. Fem. Stud. **2**(4), 1–42 (1987)
30. Stone, A.: The War of Desire and Technology At the Close of the Mechanical Age. MIT Press, Cambridge (1995)
31. Lupton, D.: Quantified sex: a critical analysis of sexual and reproductive self-tracking using apps. Cult. Health Sex. **17**(4), 440–453 (2015)
32. De Ridder, S., Vesnić-Alujević, L., Romic, B.: Challenges when researching digital audiences: mapping audience research of software designs, interfaces and platforms. Participations J. Aud. Recep. Stud. **13**(1), 374–391 (2016)
33. Butcher, T., Helmond, A.: The Affordances of Social Media Platforms. In: Burgess, J., Marwick, A., Poell, T. (eds.) The SAGE Handbook of Social Media, pp. 233–253. SAGE, London (2017)
34. Massanari, A.: # Gamergate and the fappening: how reddit's algorithm, governance, and culture support toxic technocultures. New Media Soc. **19**(3), 329–346 (2017)

35. Noble, S.U.: Algorithms of Oppression: How Search Engines Reinforce Racism. NYU Press, New York (2018)
36. Simões, R. B., Amaral, I.: Sexuality and self-tracking apps: Reshaping gender relations and sexual and reproductive practices. In: Rees, E. (ed.) The Routledge Companion to Gender, Sexuality and Culture. Routledge, London (2021). (Forthcoming)
37. Yardi, S., Boyd, D.: Dynamic debates: An analysis of group polarisation over time on twitter. Bull. Sci. Technol. Soc. **30**(5), 316–327 (2010)
38. Marwick, A., Caplan, R.: Drinking male tears: language, the manosphere, and networked harassment. Fem. Media Stud. **18**(4), 543–559 (2018)
39. Ging, D.: Memes, masculinity and mancession: love/hate's online metatexts. Ir. Stud. Rev. **25**(2), 170–192 (2017)
40. Banet-Weiser, S., Miltner, K.M.: # MasculinitySoFragile: culture, structure, and networked misogyny. Fem. Media Stud. **16**(1), 171–174 (2016)
41. Marwick, A., Lewis, R.: Media Manipulation and Disinformation Online. Data & Society Research Institute, New York (2017)
42. Citron, D.K.: Hate Crimes in Cyberspace. Harvard University Press, Cambridge (2014)
43. Powell, A., Henry, N.: Policing technology-facilitated sexual violence against adult victims: police and service sector perspectives. Polic. Soc. **28**(3), 291–307 (2016)
44. Jane, E.A.: 'You're a ugly, whorish, slut': understanding e-bile. Fem. Media Stud. **14**(4), 531–546 (2014)
45. Mantilla, K.: Gendertrolling: How Misogyny Went Viral. Praeger, Santa Barbara (2015)
46. McGlynn, C., Rackley, E., Houghton, R.: Beyond 'revenge porn': the continuum of image-based sexual abuse. Feminist Legal Stud. **25**(1), 25–46 (2017)
47. Mears, J.: Violence against older women: activism, social justice, and social change. J. Elder Abuse Negl. **27**(4–5), 500–513 (2015)
48. Siapera E., Moreo, E., Zhou, J.: Hate Track: Tracking and Monitoring Racist Speech Online. Irish Human Rights and Equality Commission, Dublin (2018)
49. Lumsden, K., Harmer, E.: Online Othering. Palgrave MacMillan, New York (2019)
50. Ging, D., Siapera, E.: Special issue on online misogyny. Fem. Media Stud. **18**(4), 515–524 (2018)
51. Ging, D., Lynn, T., Rosati, P.: Neologising misogyny: urban dictionary's folksonomies of sexual abuse. New Media Soc. **22**(5), 838–856 (2010)
52. Negra, D., Tasker, Y. (eds.): Gendering the Recession: Media and Culture in an Age of Austerity. Duke University Press (2014)
53. McRobbie, A.: The Aftermath of Feminism: Gender, Culture and Social Change. Sage, London (2009)
54. Rasmussen, L.: Tracking the relationship between postfeminism, representations of ageing women, and the rise of popular misogyny as portrayed in FX's *Sons of Anarchy* (2014–2018). In: Haas, M., Pierce, N. A., Busi, G. (eds.) Antiheroines of Contemporary Media: Saints, Sinners, and Survivors, pp. 41 56. Lexington Books, Lanham (2020)
55. Lee, J.: Mediated superficiality and misogyny through cool on tinder. Social Media+Society **5**(3), 1–11 (2019).
56. Omena, J.J., Amaral, I.: Sistema de leitura de redes digitais multiplataforma. In: Omena, J.J. (ed.) Métodos Digitais: Teoria-Prática-Crítica, pp. 121–140. iNOVA Media Lab   ICNOVA, Lisboa (2019)
57. Gee, E., Gutman, G.M.: The Overselling of Population Aging: Apocalyptic Demography, Intergenerational Challenges, and Social Policy. Oxford University Press, Oxford (2000)
58. WHO. Violence against women (2013). https://www.who.int/news-room/fact-sheets/detail/violence-against-women. Accessed 21 Feb 2021
59. Kearl, H.: Stop Global Street Harassment: Growing Activism around the World. Praeger, Santa Barbara (2015)

60. Logan, L.: Street harassment: current and promising avenues for researchers and activists. Sociol. Compass **9**(3), 196–211 (2015)
61. Fileborn, B., Vera-Gray, F.: 'I Want to be able to walk the street without fear': transforming justice for street harassment. Feminist Legal Stud. **25**(2), 203–227 (2017)
62. Bates, L.: Everyday Sexism. Simon and Schuster, London (2014)
63. Kelly, L: Preface. Standing the test of time? Reflections on the concept of the continuum of sexual violence'. In: Brown, J., Walklate, S. (eds.) Handbook on Sexual Violence, pp. xvii–xxvi. Routledge, Oxon (2012).
64. Tiidenberg, K.: Visibly ageing femininities: women's visual discourses of being over-40 and over-50 on Instagram. Fem. Media Stud. **18**(1), 61–76 (2018)

Digital Social Interactions in Later Life: Effects of Instant Messaging on Situational Mood of Older Smartphone Users

Friedrich Wolf[1](✉) ⓘ, Johannes Naumann[2], and Frank Oswald[1] ⓘ

[1] Goethe University, Frankfurt, Germany
fr.wolf@em.uni-frankfurt.de
[2] Bergische Universität Wuppertal, Wuppertal, Germany

Abstract. Over the last few years, it has been observed that new digital technologies are gaining acceptance among the over-60s, who are increasingly catching up in terms of the use of smartphones, tablets and notebooks. Particularly the so-called instant messaging apps that are used for everyday communication between family and friends are prevalent. Specific data on the effect of smartphone use in later life, particularly for social interaction via instant messaging, are scarce. Especially with respect to a differentiated and situational in-situ assessments and the inclusion of affective components of well-being outcomes, such as situational mood. In scientific discourse, instant messaging apps are often ascribed the role of stressors that can have a negative impact on well-being. Still, there are no studies examining this for smartphone use in later life. First, findings show that smartphone use as well as instant messaging use in later life not only varies between individuals, but also shows very large intraindividual differences. Second, multilevel analyses show that there is a negative effect of instant messaging on the extent of situational tension, independently of how the social situation was evaluated. These results indicate that the relationship between ICT use and subjective well-being should be considered more situationally and domain-specifically in further research.

Keywords: Smartphone use · Older adults · Situational mood · Instant messaging · Log data · Ambulatory assessment · Social interactions

1 Introduction

Over the last few years especially in Western societies new digital technologies are gaining acceptance also among the over-60s, who are increasingly catching up in terms of the use of smartphones, tablets and notebooks. The figures indicate two trends: first, that increasing numbers of older adults are using digital technologies in different countries, and second, that ICT use particularly in this group is very diverse. The fact that in later life different digital devices and services are being used makes it both worth and necessary to monitor ICT use closely in this age group [1, 7, 13]. Particularly those 60 and over, are interesting on the one hand as they have not grown up with digital technologies and

© Springer Nature Switzerland AG 2021
Q. Gao and J. Zhou (Eds.): HCII 2021, LNCS 12786, pp. 443–458, 2021.
https://doi.org/10.1007/978-3-030-78108-8_33

have to learn how to use them in later life. On the other hand, after retirement this group may no longer feel the pressure to keep pace with new technologies required in the labor market.

Especially the smartphone stands out. Due to its portability, and the direct and individualized relationship to the consumer's body, this device is relatively unique in the technological development of recent years and has changed and influenced everyday life like no other device in recent years. Although the smartphone is a multifunctional tool, it is mainly used for social exchange. Particularly the so-called instant messaging apps that are used for everyday communication between family and friends are prevalent [1, 7, 13]. These apps enable various forms of social interaction via video, photos, voice and text messages.

Despite the assumption that (extensive) smartphone use is negatively related to health and well-being in general [e.g., 23], specific data on the effect of smartphone use in later life, particularly for specific purposes, such as social interaction via instant messaging, are scarce. This is even more so regarding a differentiated and situational in-situ assessments and the inclusion of affective components of well-being outcomes, such as situational mood. In public discourse, instant messaging apps and other social media are often ascribed the role of stressors that can have a negative impact on well-being [24, 29]. Currently, there are no studies examining these effects in later life. Findings on the use and impact of digital technologies in later life usually take a very general view of the phenomenon by assessing the statistical relationship between Internet use and subjective well-being or feelings of loneliness [e.g., 6, 20, 32].

Another phenomenon in existing studies is that they attempt to measure the effects of ICT use in later life primarily derive from cross-sectional data [e.g., 8, 9]. However, especially in the case of the use of digital technologies and instant messaging, measures for the immediate assessment of situational effects on well-being outcomes–such as facets of mood–are needed to detect differentiated relationships between ICT use and well-being. In contrast, links between general evaluations of social contacts and well-being may draw another picture.

This paper is aiming to empirically analyze (1) to what extent the use of instant messaging apps influences the situational mood of older technology users and (2) whether technology use alone may serve to predict of mood and whether the number and evaluation of social contacts are relevant as well.

2   Digital Social Interactions in Later Life

2.1   Social Interaction, Well-Being and Mood in Later Life

Some studies on age differences showing that older adults are more satisfied with their social contacts than younger age groups and that social connectedness is linked to better well-being and lower levels of loneliness [e.g., 20, 22]. However, it has also been shown that although many older adults report high satisfaction with their social ties, some experience conflicts as well [12, 18, 19, 22]. Thus, to better understand the complex links between social relationships and well-being in later life it is important to dig deeper into the dynamic of indicating and maintaining social interaction in the face of digital communication. That includes a differentiated approach to address facets of social connectedness, for instance in terms of general awareness and evaluation of existing relationships as well as concrete interaction in terms of using Information and Communication Technologies (ICTs) and Social Networking Sites (SNSs) or widespread Instant Messaging Apps [e.g., 33], and to empirically analyze their effects on outcomes of well-being.

Among the many facets of well-being in psychological research (e.g., the appraisal theories of psychology [10, 14], there has been a long tradition of analyzing emotional components and mood in later life as well [e.g., 18]. Despite different definitions, mood is particularly important with respect to digital social interactions as it has a strong time-sensitive component. Moreover, it is subject to intraindividual variability due to various influencing factors [15]. One may assume that not only the use of instant messaging has an effect on mood, but also the general evaluation of social contacts can influence the situational mood. This paper is based on a three-dimensional model of mood. According to Thayer, two main factors, tense arousal and energetic arousal, are the basis for positive mood [27]. Following this approach, the focus of this paper is mainly on tense arousal.

2.2   Digital Social Interaction in Germany

In Germany, the vast majority of older adults today regularly use smartphones in their daily lives. In the 60–69 age group, 73% of older adults regularly used a smartphone in 2019, while not quite half of older adults in the 70+ age group were smartphone users (43%) [30]. At the same time, the growth rates in this age group are particularly high, raising about 13% per year (from 2018 to 2019), representing ca. 1,5 million new users. [1].

A representative survey of smartphone use in Germany based on objective log files protocols showed that the use of digital communication offerings, especially instant messaging, is widespread even among older adults and is independent of gender. The instant messaging app WhatsApp is particularly dominant in this area in Germany. WhatsApp accounts for approximately 54% of all communication via instant messaging and e-mail combined [1]. The prominent position of WhatsApp and thus of instant messaging in the digital everyday life of older adults is also demonstrated by the fact that approx. 92% of online users over the age of 65 use the app at least occasionally [1]. Considering that WhatsApp only entered the market only 11 years ago and that mobile instant messaging had until then primarily taken place via SMS or MMS, it becomes clear how far-reaching the change in the everyday lives of older adults is as a result of this new medium.

2.3   Social Interaction via Instant Messaging

In addition to its high prevalence instant messaging can be seen as an individual form of digital social interaction. On the level of pure functionality, instant messaging offers a variety of different forms of communication, which can all be combined in a single communication channel. Communication can assume the following forms: Messages in the form of texts, voice recordings, images or videos. These formats enable asynchronous or synchronous communication. In addition, telephony or video telephony can be used as direct real-time interaction. Communication can be bidirectional with one communication partner or multidirectional in groups with several communication partners. In both cases, all the functions mentioned above can be used. In addition, some instant messaging apps also offer features via profile pictures and status messages that are more commonly attributed to digital social networks. The distinction between communication platform and social media service is thus blurred. Another special feature is that active and passive use alternate and, depending on the communication channel, can also result in purely passive use. Integration on the smartphone and the possibility of notification of new messages of all kinds enable social contact to reach the user at any time in everyday life in all situations. The sum of these functions show that the phenomenon of instant messaging represents a completely new form of social interaction and can only be hardly compared with other media.

As noted earlier, most studies regarding social interactions via instant messengers do not specifically address older adults but rather mostly mixed-age groups of adults.

A qualitative study by O'Hara et al. was able to show that adult users of instant messengers used them primarily for close social relationships and that the use was part of regular relationship care [14]. A study by Taipale et al. supports these findings and also showed that instant messaging has a central role in family exchanges between multiple generations [26].

This also makes instant messaging a genuinely intergenerational application that is not only used by different generations likewise, but also enables intergenerational exchange. Taking these findings into account, it is evident that instant messaging has the potential to affect well-being and situational mood, since communication with significant others is the primary aspect of instant messaging.

2.4 Instant Messaging and Well-Being

Beside general links between social exchange and well-being only few studies examine the effect of instant messaging on subjective well-being or mood in later life [2, 5, 24, 28]. Although this age-group is of special interest, as mentioned earlier, studies on instant messaging are often not specifically aimed towards the 60+ age group, but rather unspecific addressing samples in middle adulthood. In 2019, a study of adult Taiwanese found a positive statistical association between instant messaging use and loneliness and depressed mood. In particular, negatively experienced communication via instant messaging apps led to a reduction in subjective well-being [28]. These findings are supported by a study by Blabst et al., who were able to show a relationship between active WhatsApp use and an increased perception of stress, even when the social exchange itself was rated as positive overall [5]. A study by Shin et al. also fits into this pattern. They found different and very individual factors, mainly related to the design and functionality, which can trigger stress when using instant messengers [24]. In contrast, a study by Bano et al. with adolescents and younger adults showed a positive relationship between WhatsApp use and subjective well-being [2].

Even though the available studies are still rather scattered and partly contain contradictory findings, it is clear that on a cross-sectional level there are statistical associations between instant messaging and stress or tense arousal. It is unclear whether this is age-specific or whether these findings can also be found in older adults.

2.5 Research Aims and Hypotheses

In sum, this study has a two-fold aims, that is:

(1) To monitor smartphone use in later life based on objective situational data over a period of seven days in order to detect inter- and intra-individual differences and stability.
(2) To objectively assess features of instant messaging in close link to situational mood as well as general evaluations of social contacts to detect immediate effects of instant messaging on facets of mood–as well as to detect basic stable relationships between ICT use and well-being.

The following hypotheses shall be derived from these aims, based on data from a German sample:

(1) Differentiated assessment of smartphone use in situational terms provides evidence for inter- and intra-individual differences and stability.
(2) There are statistically significant effects of both, the situational instant messaging use as well as the general evaluation of social contacts on the situational mood of the participants.

3 Methods

3.1 Design

The present study consists of two central components. The first is a micro-longitudinal assessment of smartphone use and accompanying factors of everyday life [21]. The second is a cross-sectional survey to determine general attitudes and experiences regarding digital technologies. The micro-longitudinal assessment covered a total of 7 consecutive days. During this period, active smartphone use was automatically recorded in the form of a logfile protocol using the Android app movisensXS [11]. At the same time, the participants were asked to provide information about their daily routine, their personal situation and the evaluation of their smartphone use 4 times a day, i.e., up to 28 times in total during the entire period. The questions of the ambulatory assessment always referred to the situation in the past hour. The individual questionnaires of the ambulatory assessment were triggered randomly between 9 a.m. and 9 p.m. and could be answered directly on the participant's own smartphone. This approach created an authentic impression of smartphone use on the one hand and everyday life and personal perceptions on the other. The cross-sectional survey enables a more precise classification of the group in terms of socio-demographic variables, as well as attitudes, knowledge and experience with regard to digital technologies.

3.2 Sample

The sample consists of a total of 42 German older adults over the age of 60, with more detailed sociodemographic information available from 40 people. Information sheets and

Table 1. Descriptive statistics on sociodemographic variables.

	All (N = 40)	Male (N = 16)	Female (N = 24)
Age			
M (SD)	70.24 (5.38)	70.64 (5.24)	69.95 (5.6)
Min-Max	61–82	65–82	61–79
Marital status N (%)			
Married, partnered	25 (62)	14 (88)	11 (46)
Unpartnerd	15 (38)	2 (12)	13 (54)
Educational attainment N (%)			
University degree	21 (54)	8 (50)	13 (57)
Non university degree	18 (46)	8 (50)	10 (43)
Housing situation N (%)			
Living alone	16 (40)	4 (25)	12 (50)
Living not alone	24 (60)	12 (75)	12 (50)

Note: N = 40. Including criteria for sample were that participants were at least 60 years old and retired. All participants lived in urban areas and in their own households.

events were used to draw attention to the study in various institutions of organized work with older adults. At the same time, the project was advertised through the Frankfurt Community College (Volkshochschule) and the University of the Third Age (Universität des 3. Lebensalters), two local colleges with courses for older adults. Participation was voluntary and no incentives were given. A prerequisite for participation was to own an Android smartphone. During data collection, the subjects were already retired, privately residing, and living in urban areas. Participants were recruited between September 2019 to August 2020. The sample includes primarily younger older adults and approximately 60% of the sample is female. Overall, it is a sample that has a comparatively high level of formal education, as well as the majority being married or partnered and living with at least one other person in the household. However, there are slight differences here between the surveyed men and women. The latter were more likely to live alone and were neither married nor partnered.

3.3 Instruments

Smartphone Use. The Variable smartphone use is based on the log files protocols of the participants. Permission for data collection was obtained after a face-to-face meeting and a detailed explanation of the nature and form of the data to be collected. To ensure anonymity, no person-related data like names or addresses were collected. The Ethics Committee of the Department of Education at Goethe University gave permission for the project. Smartphone usage was defined as the frequency of interactions with the smartphone. All actions performed on the smartphone between switching the display on and off are summarized as one session. A session can thus have different durations, depending on how the smartphone is used. The actual duration of smartphone use is strongly influenced by factors that cannot be controlled and are difficult to compare between different users - e.g., competence in handling, motor skills, eyesight, variety of apps used, display time-out, etc. Smartphone use in the form of frequency of interaction with the device is a good indicator of regular use in everyday life.

Instant Messaging. The variable Instant messaging is based on the logfiles protocol of the participants. Instant messaging includes all interactions with WhatsApp, Threema, Telegram, Samsung Messenger, and Google Messenger. No other instant messaging apps were used during the survey period. To be categorized as an instant messaging app, the following criteria had to be present: At a minimum, the functionality must enable text and picture messaging. In addition, it had to be possible to address a group as well as individuals. Two different measures are used as indicators. For the intensity of use over the entire survey period (see Fig. 2), the instant messaging sessions are counted. A session is defined as one or more consecutive interactions with an instant messaging app within a smartphone session. The frequency of smartphone interaction was preferred over the actual duration of use, as this can be influenced by many other factors that cannot be controlled - e.g., experience with the smartphone, typing speed, navigation ability, eyesight, etc. For instant messaging use as a predictor of calmness, the variable was adjusted to look at whether instant messaging was used (1) or not (0) at the respective measurement time point of the ambulatory assessment. The measure thus indicates the presence vs. absence of instant messaging use in the last hour of smartphone use.

Positive and negative evaluation of social interactions was measured by two items on a 7-point Likert scale. Participants were able to evaluate the social contacts of the past hour (on- and offline) as either very pleasant to very unpleasant or as very comfortable to very uncomfortable. The scale is based on the work of Bernstein et al. [3]. They had measured the rating of social contacts with only one item (very pleasant to very unpleasant). In order to capture more nuances in the evaluation, the scale was supplemented by an additional item. The multilevel reliability is based on the concept of Shrout et al. based on generalizability theory [25]. Multilevel reliability showed a very good reliability of the two items. The reliability of average of all rating across all items and timepoints R_{kF} was 0.98 and the generalizability of change R_c was 0.70. Individuals accounted for 24% of the variance in different ratings (ID). 39% of the variance was due to individuals' response behavior at different measurement time points (ID × MTP) and 3% was due to different responses to questions per individual (ID × items). 34% of the variance was from unknown sources (residual variance). For the multilevel model, each value was group-mean-centered. In the present case this means that each measurement time point was centered at the participant's mean. Positive values thus mean that the social contacts of the past hour were evaluated higher than this person's average over all measurement time points of the person and negative values mean that the evaluation was lower than the average over all measurement time points.

Number of Social Contacts. The number of social contacts represents all on- and offline contacts of the past hour. The question asked was: with how many people (approximately) did you have personal contact in the past hour? (Including contacts via smartphone or telephone).

Tension. Mood is assessed based on the concept of Wilhelm et al. [31] according to which mood can be divided into three different dimensions - calmness, valence and energetic arousal. Each dimension is measured with two items on a 7-point Likert scale. Tension is part of the calmness factor. For the present multilevel model, tension is represented by the item very relaxed - very tense. The item very calm - very restless was omitted from the present analysis. Even though the multilevel reliability between both items was good, the correlation on the L1 level was quite low. For this reason, and because other studies and public discourse tend to discuss tension as being related to instant messaging, the factor of calmness has not been completely included in the model.

3.4   Software

Random intercept models were estimated with the R-package lme4 1.1-23 [4]. Multilevel reliability, correlations and descriptive statistics were conducted with R-package psych 1.9.12 [17]. For all analysis R version 4.0.2 [16] was used.

4   Results

4.1   Instant Messaging in Daily Life of Older Adults

First, descriptive statistics on smartphone and instant messaging use in the daily lives of older adults will be reported. The focus is on inter- as well as intra-individual differences in daily smartphone use. All data refer to a period of 7 consecutive days.

As can be seen in Table 1, smartphone use differs quite substantially between the observed participants. Within the complete survey period of seven days, a total of 9029 sessions, i.e., interactions with the smartphone, were registered for 41 subjects. On average, this is 220 sessions per day with a standard deviation of 115. A look at the scatter of the data shows that the person with the fewest interactions had only 64 sessions, while the person with the highest usage had a total of 481 sessions over 7 days. In other words, this person picks up his/her smartphone 7.5 times as often. If we look at instant messaging use in comparison, we see a similar picture. Over 7 days, the participants used instant messaging applications an average of 51 times, although the standard deviation is also high here at 36 sessions. A look at the range also reveals large differences. The person with the lowest instant messaging use has only two interactions with an instant messaging app over 7 days, while the person with the highest frequency of use has 151 sessions. In total, 2119 instant messaging uses were registered by all 41 persons. In relation to total smartphone use, this means that 23% of all smartphone interactions are associated with instant messaging use.

Figure 1 uses individual boxplots to show inter- as well as intra-individual differences between participants with regard to their smartphone use. Each person is represented by a boxplot, where each boxplot contains the number of smartphone sessions per day. Based on the medians, it is evident that there are noticeable differences in terms of average usage between the participants. For example, frequent users use their smartphone almost three times as often as infrequent users. At the same time, the boxplots show clear differences in the number of smartphone sessions per day. Many boxplots show variations of 30 or

Table 2. Smartphone use and instant messaging (N = 41)

Variable	Mean (SD)	Min-Max (Range)	Total Sessions (%)
Smartphone use	220.22 (115.04)	64–481 (417)	9029 (100)
Instant messaging	51.68 (36.06)	2–151 (149)	2119 (23)

Note: Recorded Smartphone Sessions. A smartphone session is defined as every action happens while the display is turned on. Recorded time: 7 consecutive days

40 sessions between the different days in the observation period. Correlation between median and standard deviation of daily smartphone usage frequency is very high with r = 0.69 (95%-CI = 0.45; 0.81). The more the smartphone is used daily, the higher the intraindividual variance of usage. For details see Fig. 1.

Figure 2 shows individual boxplots in terms of the number of instant messaging sessions per day. As in Fig. 1, there are also considerable interindividual differences. The low-volume users, who use instant messaging apps less than 5 times a day, contrast with the high-volume users, who use instant messaging an average of 10 times a day. At the same time, however, substantial upward and downward variations can be observed. Daily instant messaging use therefore varies considerably from day to day.

Looking again at the relationship between median and standard deviation, we see the same pattern as for smartphone use only. Individuals with a higher average daily usage also show a higher intraindividual variance. Correlation between median and standard deviation of daily use frequency is r = 0.7 (95%.CI = 0.5; 0.83). For details see Fig. 2.

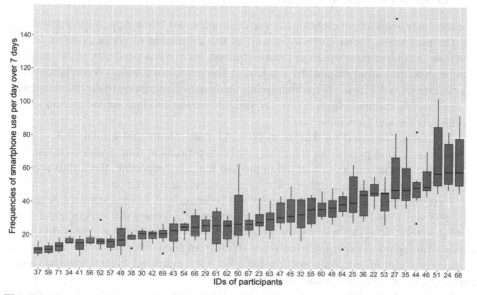

Fig. 1. Boxplots for smartphone sessions for each participant. Each boxplot contains the sum of smartphone sessions per study day per participant.

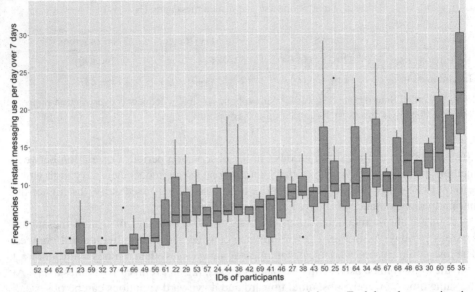

Fig. 2. Boxplots for instant messaging sessions for each participant. Each boxplot contains the sum of smartphone sessions per study day per participant.

4.2 Effects of Instant Messaging, Number of Social Contacts and Evaluation of Social Contacts on Calmness

For the analysis of the relationship between calmness and WhatsApp usage, controlling for the number of social contacts as well as the evaluation of social contacts in the last hour, a random intercept model was estimated. First, the dependency of the variable calmness on the cluster variable ID was tested. The intraclass correlation coefficient ICC was 0.256 (CI = 0.176; 0.374), which speaks against the assumption of the independence of the variable calmness from the cluster variable person and thus for the calculation of a multilevel model (see Table 3).

The model is based on data from N = 41 participants and a total of K = 789 measurement time points. For the model, only measurement time points were used in which smartphone use was observed in the last hour. All reported effects thus refer to situations in which the smartphone was used in some form in the past hour.

First, the random effects of the model will be examined. Here, a standard deviation of 0.698 was found for calmness with regard to between-person differences and a standard deviation of 1.102 with regard to within-person variance. Thus, the participants differ with regard to experienced calmness both from each other and depending on the respective situation. In comparison, the latter is larger, indicating greater intraindividual differences than interindividual differences.

Looking at the fixed effects of the model, we first find a statistically significant positive effect due to the positive evaluation of social contacts in the past hour (b = 0.261; t = 5.901). The more positively the social contacts of the past hour were rated

Table 3. Random intercept model: effects of instant message use, number of social contacts in the last hour and the evaluation of these contacts on situational calmness (N = 41)

Random effects	VAR	SD	95%-CI	
Tension (between)	0.488	0.698	0.522; 0.873	
Tension (within)	1.2148	1.102	1.046; 1.159	
Fixed effects	b	SE b	95%-CI	t
Intercept	5.564	0.123	5.319; 5.803	45.160
Positive evaluation of social contacts	0.261	0.044	0.176; 0.345	5.901
Number of social contacts	−0.001	0.006	−0.012; 0.009	−0.211
Instant messaging use	−0.188	0.089	−0.367; −0.015	−2.096

Note: N = 41; K = 789. CI were conducted with bootstrapping from 10000 samples. R^2-marginal was 0.034, R^2-conditional was 0.31

Table 4. Correlation matrix for all variables on between (L2) and within (L1) person levels

	M (SD)	Median (R)	1	2	3
1 Tension (L1)	5.49 (1.32)	6 (1–7)			
2 Positive evaluation of social contacts (L1)	5.83 (1.11)	6 (1–7)	0.36***		
3 Number of social contacts (L1)	2.95 (7.09)	2 (−)	0.00	0.1***	
4 Instant messaging (L1)	0.37 (0.48)	− (0–1)	−0.02	0.08*	0.03
1 Tension (L2)	5.5 (0.72)	5.56 (1–7)			
2 Positive evaluation of social contacts (L2)	5.87 (0.68)	5.83 (1–7)	0.68***		
3 Number of social contacts (L2)	2.96 (2.16)	2.48 (−)	0.14	−0.34*	
4 Instant messaging (L2)	0.38 (0.22)	− (0–1)	0.05	−0.03	0.28

Note: N = 41; K = 789. *p < .05; **p < 0.01; ***p < .001
Range is the theoretical range of the scale. (3) Scale has no limits. (4) Dichotomous scale, therefore, no median.

in comparison to the average rating of the respective participant, the higher was the reported calmness of the person. The more positive the evaluation, the more relaxed the participant was. In contrast, the number of on- and offline social contacts in the past hour showed no significant effect on situational calmness (b = −0.001; t = −0.211). Whether instant messaging was used in the past hour showed a negative significant effect on situational calmness (b = −0.188; t = −2.096). If the participants used an instant messaging app in the past hour, they reported feeling slightly more tense on average than if they did not use instant messaging. In terms of variance explained, the fixed effects as a whole were only able to explain about 3% of the variance (R2-marginal = 0.034) in situational calm, while the entire model including random effects was able to explain 31% of the variance (R2-conditional = 0.31. Significance testing was performed with 95% bootstrapping confidence intervals with N = 10000 samples (see Table 3).

Since it must be assumed that the effects of instant messaging use on situational calmness can vary from person to person, a random slope model was conducted in addition to the random intercept model. However, this did not show a statistically significantly better model fit than the random intercept model ($X^2(2, N = 41) = 0.373$, p > 0.05), which is why the latter was retained.

Table 4 shows the distribution of variables appearing in the random intercept model, including correlations. The coefficients are given separately for between (L2) and within (L1) person levels. No floor or ceiling effects were observed for any of the variables, either at the L1 or L2 level. Therefore, it can be assumed that the different items are sensitive to changes.

5 Discussion

First, the descriptive analyses showed that smartphone use as well as instant messaging use in later life not only varies between individuals, but also shows very large intraindividual differences. While the assumption that the daily smartphone use intensity is very steady over time is true for those in the sample who showed a comparatively low smartphone or instant messaging use, it was possible to show that especially high frequency users show very large day-specific differences in use. In the future, the question of how these fluctuations can be explained or come about will have to be answered. It is possible that frequent users also use a higher number of different apps that satisfy various everyday needs. This could be an indicator for the differences found.

Second, the results of the descriptive analyses show that smartphone use in later life is strongly associated with digital social activities. Almost a quarter of the total smartphone interactions also include the use of an instant messenger. No other usage category was used as frequently. For older adults, as well as for younger adults, the smartphone is primarily used for a variety of social interactions.

Third, the results of the random intercept model seem to confirm previous studies according to which the use of digital technologies can have negative effects on variables associated with subjective well-being [5, 24, 28]. The present study was able to show that across different individuals, the use of instant messaging apps was generally associated with greater tension, regardless of whether social contacts were positively evaluated and how much contact one had with other people. Alternative models revealed no significant effects of instant messaging on valence or energetic arousal, while at the same time the positive effect of the evaluation of social contacts remained unchanged. Future empirical research should therefore focus more on the influence of instant messaging on subdimensions of mood.

In addition, the present analyses have shown that the integration of log files as an objective measure of smartphone use, which is independent of the recall performance of the participants, can be successfully used in social science analyses and can also uncover new and interesting phenomena.

The relationship between instant messaging and situational mood also shows that it is not just the technology that should be taken into account, but also other factors that might influence the situational mood. The example of instant messaging in particular illustrates that technology serves as a mediator for social interaction and should therefore never be considered independently of other social and environmental influences.

6 Conclusion, Limitations and Implications for Future Research

6.1 Conclusion

The first Hypothesis was that the differentiated assessment of smartphone use in situational terms provides evidence for inter- and intra-individual differences and stability. The results in Table 2 and Figs. 1 and 2 confirm this assumption. Some of the participants differed substantially in terms of their average usage, with frequent users using the smartphone 3 times as often as infrequent users on a daily average. In parallel, it was found that smartphone use could vary considerably from one day of the week to the next. This pattern of high intraindividual variability was also related to the average variety of usage. The more frequently the smartphone was used on average, the more the individual days of the week differed from each other in frequency. The same pattern was also found with regard to instant messaging use.

The second Hypothesis was that there are statistically significant effects of both, the situational instant messaging use as well as the general evaluation of social contacts on the situational mood of the participants. This hypothesis was also confirmed by the data. It could be shown (see Table 4) that both the use of instant messaging in the past hour and the evaluation of social contacts had a significant influence on the situational tension resp. relaxedness. While a more positive evaluation of social contacts than the individual average tended to lead to higher relaxation ratings, the use of instant messaging had the opposite effect. In situations in which the participants had used an instant messaging app, they tended to report higher tension. This effect was relatively constant across all participants. A random slopes model did not show a significantly better model fit. In contrast, the number of social contacts in the past hour showed no effect on situational tension. Overall, however, the factors instant messaging and evaluation of social contacts could only explain a small part of the variance in situational tension.

6.2 Limitations

The sample of our study is not representative of the older population in Germany. Due to the required voluntariness and the sensitive data that were collected, it was not possible to realize a random sample. Thus, participants have relatively high levels of formal education. Therefore, one might assume that smartphone use is different in other groups, e.g., among people with lower levels of formal education or among those who refused to participate because of data protection concerns. Also, due to technical reasons, it was not possible to interview iOS users, although the authors would not expect a systematic influence on situational mood and related variables.

In addition, the study only covers a single week of digital data usage. To what extent exactly this week is representative for the everyday life of the participants is debatable. At the same time, attention was paid to the fact that there were no special events such as birthdays or vacations during the week of the survey.

Finally, one need to consider that half the data was collected during the Covid-19 pandemic. However, during the summer months of 2020 Germany was not subject to a lockdown or travel restrictions to other European countries.

6.3 Implications for Future Research

An objective of future research could be a more precisely differentiated definition and assessment of instant messaging. It is quite conceivable that specific usage patterns of instant messaging, e.g., the number of messages sent, the type of interaction via text or voice, or activities in group chats, as well as a more active or passive style of use might have an influence on situational mood.

Moreover, it would be interesting to see to what extent cross-device use can also have an influence on situational mood. It is conceivable that the smartphone in particular can act as a stressor, while instant messaging on a non-portable device that does not draw attention to itself when new messages are received could have no negative effect on situational mood.

In addition, future research should take a more differentiated look at the evaluation and nature of (digital) social contacts and not focus solely on the intensity and duration of instant messaging use. The technical systems should be understood as a medium that can influence the reception of a message, but cannot be held solely responsible for it.

References

1. Andree, M., Thomsen, T.: Atlas der digitalen Welt (2020)
2. Bano, S., Cisheng, W., Khan, A.N., Khan, N.: WhatsApp use and student's psychological well-being: role of social capital and social integration. Child Youth Serv. Rev. **103**, 200–208 (2019)
3. Bernstein, M.J., Zawadzki, M.J., Juth, V., Benfield, J.A., Smyth, J.M.: Social interactions in daily life. J. Soc. Pers. Relat. **35**(3), 372–394 (2018)
4. Bates, D., Mächler, M., Bolker, B., Walker, S.: Fitting linear mixed-effects models using lme4. J. Stat. Softw. **67**(1), 1–48 (2015)
5. Blabst, N., Diefenbach, S.: WhatsApp and wellbeing: a study on WhatsApp usage, communication quality and stress. In: Proceedings of the 31st International BCS Human Computer Interaction Conference, England (2017)
6. Elliot, A.J., Mooney, C.J., Douthit, K.Z., Lynch, M.F.: Predictors of older adults' technology use and its relationship to depressive symptoms and well-being. J. Gerontol. Ser. B Psychol. Sci. Soci. Sci. **69**(5), 667–677 (2014)
7. European Commission. Statistical office of the European Union. Ageing Europe: Looking at the lives of older people in the EU: 2020 edition. Publications Office (2020)
8. Fernández-Ardèvol, M., et al.: Methodological strategies to understand smartphone practices for social connectedness in later life. In: Zhou, J., Salvendy, G. (eds.) HCII 2019. LNCS, vol. 11593, pp. 46–64. Springer, Cham (2019). https://doi.org/10.1007/978-3-030-22015-0_4
9. Huang, C.: Internet use and psychological well-being: a meta-analysis. Cyberpsychol. Behav. Soc. Netw. **13**(3), 241–249 (2010)
10. Moors, A.: Appraisal theory of emotion. In: Zeigler-Hill, V., Shackelford, T.K. (eds.) Encyclopedia of Personality and Individual Differences, pp. 1–9. Springer, Heidelberg (2017). https://doi.org/10.1007/978-3-319-28099-8_493-1

11. movisens GmbH. Experience sampling—MovisensXS. https://www.movisens.com/en/pro ducts/movisensxs/. Accessed 15 Jan 2021
12. Mund, M., et al.: Loneliness is associated with the subjective evaluation of but not daily dynamics in partner relationships. Int. J. Behav. Dev. (2020). https://doi.org/10.1177/016502 5420951246
13. Nelson Kakulla, B.: 2020 Tech Trends of the 50+. AARP Research, Washington DC (2020)
14. O'Hara, K.P., Massimi, M., Harper, R., Rubens, S., Morris, J.: Everyday dwelling with What- sApp. In: Proceedings of the 17th ACM Conference on Computer Supported Cooperative Work and Social Computing, pp. 1131–1143 (2014)
15. Ong, A.D., Zautra, A.J.: Intraindividual variability in mood and mood regulation in adulthood. In: Diehl, M., Hooker, K., Sliwinski, M.J. (eds.), Handbook of Intraindividual Variability Across the Life Span, pp. 198–215. Routledge/Taylor and Francis Group (2015)
16. R Core Team: R: A Language and Environment for Statistical Computing. R Foundation for Statistical Computing (2020). https://www.R-project.org/
17. Revelle, W.: Psych: procedures for psychological, psychometric, and personality research. Northwestern University (2020). https://CRAN.R-project.org/package=psych
18. Rook, K.S.: Social networks in later life: weighing positive and negative effects on health and well-being. Curr. Dir. Psychol. Sci. 24(1), 45–51 (2015)
19. Rook, K.S., Charles, S.T.: Close social ties and health in later life: strengths and vulnerabilities. Am. Psychol. 72(6), 567–577 (2017)
20. Scrutton, J., Creighton, H.: The links between social connections and wellbeing in later life. ILC report (2015)
21. Seifert, A., Harari, G.M.: Mobile data collection with smartphones. In: Gu, D., Dupre, M.E. (eds.) Encyclopedia of Gerontology and Population Aging, pp. 1–3. Springer, Heidelberg (2019)
22. Shankar, A., Rafnsson, S.B., Steptoe, A.: Longitudinal associations between social connec- tions and subjective wellbeing in the english longitudinal study of ageing. Psychol. Health 30(6), 686–698 (2015)
23. Shaw, H., Ellis, D.A., Geyer, K., Davidson, B.I., Ziegler, F.V., Smith, A.: Quantifying smart- phone "use": choice of measurement impacts relationships between "usage" and health. Technol. Mind Behav. 1(2), 15 (2020)
24. Shin, I., Seok, J., Lim, Y.: Too close and crowded: understanding stress on mobile instant messengers based on proxemics. In: Proceedings of the 2018 CHI Conference on Human Factors in Computing Systems, pp. 1–12 (2018)
25. Shrout, P.E., Lane, S.P.: Psychometrics. In: Mehl, M.R., Conner, T.S. (eds.) Handbook of Research Methods for Studying Daily Life, pp. 302–320. Guilford Press (2012)
26. Taipale, S., Farinosi, M.: The big meaning of small messages: the use of WhatsApp in inter- generational family communication. In: Zhou, J., Salvendy, G. (eds.) ITAP 2018. LNCS, vol. 10926, pp. 532–546. Springer, Cham (2018). https://doi.org/10.1007/978-3-319-92034-4_40
27. Thayer, R.E.: The Biopsychology of Mood and Activation. Oxford University Press, New York (1989)
28. Tsai, H.S., Hsu, P.-J., Chang, C.-L., Huang, C.-C., Ho, H.-F., LaRose, R.: High tension lines: negative social exchange and psychological well-being in the context of instant messaging. Comput. Hum. Behav. 93, 326–332 (2019)
29. Vahedi, Z., Saiphoo, A.: The association between smartphone use, stress, and anxiety: a meta-analytic review. Stress Health 34(3), 347–358 (2018)
30. VuMA (Arbeitsgemeinschaft Verbrauchs- und Medienanalyse): Anteil der Smartphone- Nutzer in Deutschland nach Altersgruppe im Jahr 2019 [Graph]. https://de.statista.com/statis tik/daten/studie/459963/umfrage/anteil-der-smartphone-nutzer-in-deutschland-nach-alters gruppe. Accessed 15 Jan 2021

31. Wilhelm, P., Schoebi, D.: Assessing mood in daily life. Eur. J. Psychol. Assess. **23**(4), 258–267 (2007)
32. Wilson, C.: Is it love or loneliness? Exploring the impact of everyday digital technology use on the wellbeing of older adults. Ageing Soc. **19**, 1–25 (2017)
33. Zaccaria, D., et al.: Assessing the impact of social networking site use on older people's loneliness and social isolation. A randomized controlled trial: the aging in a networked society-social experiment study (ANS-SE). Contemp. Clin. Trials Commun. **19**, 100615 (2020)

Online Representations of Older People Generated by Public Sector Organizations

Wenqian Xu[✉]

Linköping University, Bredgatan 32, 602 21 Norrköping, Sweden
`wenqian.xu@liu.se`

Abstract. This article investigates the generation of online representations of older people by institutions. Specifically, it discusses the ways in which public sector organizations generate online representations of older people from a production perspective. This article uses the following questions to frame its analysis: What do we know about online representations of older people generated by public sector organizations? What do we know about the way in which public sector organizations generate online representations of older people? And, how can public sector organizations improve online representations of older people from a production perspective? The analysis primarily draws on secondary data (i.e., existing literature and examples of public sector organizations) to address these questions. After summarizing existing research examining online representations of older people generated by public sector organizations, this article offers a specific example of a public sector organization generating online representations of older people (i.e., a Swedish municipality). A discussion of the approaches public sector organizations takes to generating online representations of older people is provided, and the argument is made that public sector organizations have a convergent position where they must take care of older people while presenting this care online. Moreover, this article discusses the generation of online representations of older people in the public sector concerning accountability, calling for greater accountability in representations of older people online.

Keywords: Ageism · Content production · Digital media · Media logic · Older people · Online representation · Power structure · Public sector

1 Introduction

The Madrid International Plan of Action on Ageing (MIPAA), as the most influential United Nations document on population ageing since 2002, encourages mass media to move beyond the portrayal of stereotypes and showcase the diversity of older people, while presenting positive images of older people that highlight their wisdom, strengths, contributions, courage and resourcefulness [1]. Mass media plays a crucial role in shaping images of older people. Specifically, mass media generates images of older people and reproduces social and cultural constructions of old age [2]; Additionally, mass media serves to reproduce age relations and justify inequalities between age groups [3]. Media representations of older people may have significant social consequences. For instance,

© Springer Nature Switzerland AG 2021
Q. Gao and J. Zhou (Eds.): HCII 2021, LNCS 12786, pp. 459–470, 2021.
https://doi.org/10.1007/978-3-030-78108-8_34

the perpetuation of age stereotypes may impact perceptions and attitudes toward older people and the ageing process [4]. Negative images of older people in mass media can adversely affect the health and well-being of older people [5]. With an interest in representations of older people in visual media, Loos and Ivan introduced the concept of "visual ageism," referring to the social practice of visually underrepresenting older people or misrepresenting them in a prejudiced way [6]. Given the ways that digital media (i.e., social networking sites) offers ease and convenience to users in terms of producing and distributing content depicting older people, online representations of older people should be more diverse and act to destabilize age stereotypes [7, 8]. Existing empirical studies have examined digital media content generated by personal accounts, suggesting that digital media served as both a generator and distributor of age stereotypes (see e.g., [9–11]). In this sense, the aforementioned potential for the role of digital media appears to remain unfulfilled.

Technological developments have facilitated digitalization of the media industry, whereby all media content is effortlessly digitalized, produced and distributed through technologically convergent communication channels [12]. This media environment creates opportunities for institutions (e.g., public sector organizations, for-profit organizations, volunteer sector organizations) to deliver targeted messages to specific audiences. Various types of institutions appropriate and manage digital media (often termed "new media") to produce and deliver information about older people. As Jensen envisioned, institutions at local, regional and international levels are expected to increasingly depend on networked digital media. Additionally, they will turn to digitally processed forms of representation and interaction with the potential to shape our understanding of society and culture [13] (p. 59). With the use of digital media platforms, institutions can play a role in the ongoing process of defining social conditions and societal problems. It has been recognized by the United Nations and national governments that public sector digitalization has the potential to improve delivery of public services and ensure transparency, participation and collaboration in decision-making processes. Amid recent COVID-19 lockdowns, the pursuit of digitalization in the public sector can be clearly seen at the national and municipal levels [14]. Public sector organizations have appropriated and made use of digital media to improve management and administration of resources, procedures and policymaking. Given the strong presence and social implications of digital media usage in the public sector, attention should be paid to the role of public sector organizations in generating online representations of older people.

This article uses the following questions to frame its analysis: What do we know about online representations of older people generated by public sector organizations? What do we know about the ways in which public sector organizations generate online representations of older people? And, how can public sector organizations improve online representations of older people from a production perspective? The structure of this article is as follows: The following section summarizes existing research examining online representations of older people generated by public sector organizations, highlighting issues with online representations of older people (especially those living in supportive care) as being idealistically independent and vital. Next, the article provides an example of a public sector organization (i.e., a Swedish municipality) generating online representations of older people. This article goes on to discuss the convergence in public sector organizations of the notion of taking care of older people (acting as a caretaker) and the notion of showing their care for older people (profiling as a caretaker). The final section discusses generation of online representations concerning accountability, proposing greater accountability in generating online representations of older people in the public sector as a possible means of improving online representations of older people.

2   Online Representations of Older People Generated by Public Sector Organizations

Media representation is often understood as the ways in which media portrays a social group or individual. The media relies on a manufactured process of selecting ideas that determine content [15]. Media representation of older people refers to how the media portrays older people, being mediated by content producers. In this sense, the media's version of "reality" is understood as a re-presentation, rather than presentation. Media representations of older people can be seen as a rich resource for cultural gerontologists, serving as context-specific cultural constructs that offer versions of the "reality" of older people for highly specific purposes [16]. Existing studies on media representations of older people often define older people as those aged 50 and above [17]. Online representations of older people generated by institutions are purposefully produced and envisaged to target a specific audience, potentially shaping the audience's knowledge of older people. From the perspective of institutions, representations of older people may be based on an integration of certain values, meanings and ideas. To explore the possibilities for representing older people in alternative ways, identifying online representations of older people and the ways in which they are generated by institutions is essential.

With a focus on online representations of older people generated by institutions, there is a body of existing research drawing attention to online representations generated by public sector organizations in Western societies which represent and/or protect the interests of older people (e.g., those living in supportive care), including authorities, senior citizen organizations, and others. Empirical studies found that older people were being increasingly represented in digital media managed by public sector organizations as being sociable, joyful, happy and relatively healthy in later life (see e.g., [2, 11, 18–20]). These online representations serve to promote positive images of older people highlighting their independence, autonomy and engagement. For example, one study found that older people were visually represented as happy, socially involved and extroverted on the website of a Danish advocacy group for older people in the period of April 2016 to October 2018. This failed to reflect the reality of many older people suffering from loneliness, frailty or dependence on others for assistance [2]. Another study out of the United Kingdom found that older people were increasingly represented in a diversified manner in terms of ethnic background, fitness levels, physical abilities and vitality on public sector websites between 2013 and 2019 [21]. Yet another study from 2018 found that older people were predominantly represented through municipal Facebook pages as remaining socially engaged and moderately physically capable, failing to reflect the actual conditions facing older people in residential care settings [22].

Representations of older people generated by public sector organizations can be seen as a counter-narrative to negative representations of older people in various media (e.g., as a homogeneous, disempowered, dependent and fragile group). Nevertheless, there is a risk of typecasting older people as remaining socially active and vital, while homogenizing the older population regardless of heterogeneity in later life. From this perspective, these representations of older people become cases of visual ageism. Furthermore, extremely positive representations of older people were found to reduce downstream memory performance and attract decreased attention from older people [23]. In this sense, online representations of older people appear problematic, despite the fact that they counteract representations of all older people as being fragile, vulnerable and dependent. From a critical point of view, online representations of older people generated by these institutions have failed to contribute to our knowledge of older people and growing old, while also leading to visual ageism.

Online representations of older people in the public sector are much in alignment with typical third-age representations found in cultural discourse on ageing. Old age has been re-framed into two distinct yet interconnected concepts: the third age and fourth age [24, 25]. The third age (60–79 years old) is seen as a life phase where engagement and independence are sustained, while the fourth age (80+ years old) is associated with negative characteristics (e.g., infirmity, decline and death) [26]. From the perspective of cultural gerontology, the fourth age is characterized by an unfavorable "cultural imaginary," given the concentration of infirmity within long-term care [27]. The third age is considered to define post-retirement life [28], and through a process of antagonistic reciprocity, the cultural and structural boundaries of the third age may provide the structural boundaries for the fourth age [29] (p. 122). Consumption practices are the governing logic of this cultural field, while the socializing influences of mass consumer society determine much of the habitus of the third age [29, 30]. Despite negative representations of older people remaining dominant in print media [31], a shift toward more "positive" representations of older people can be seen in Western visual media over the last decade of the twentieth century [6]. Similarly, dominant representations of older people in entertainment media appear to be "positive" and associated with "a denial of old age" [17]. These identified "positive" representations of older people were aligned with stereotype research on a typology of older people [16, 32]. Considering the dichotomy of positivity and negativity reflected in representations of older people, Hannah and Steeden noted that there is a deficiency of balanced representation of older adults that mirrors their actual life experiences [31]. Representations of idealistic third-agers in the media are often linked with very specific intentions or ideological constructions. For instance, a Canadian magazine for older people put forth an aspirational identity for third-agers as being fit, fashionable, functional and flexible, constructed to foster a particular perspective on successful ageing [33]. Magazine representations of older people's consumer lifestyles are driven by the commercial purpose of facilitating an image of being "youthful," active and successful [2]. Another study focusing on visual representations of older people argued that using the "third age" concept enabled public authorities to disseminate a positive image of ageing (living longer and being healthier), while stressing a sense of self-responsibility for remaining active and compensating loss of resources in later life, serving to keep the myth of "eternal youth alive" [34]. These media representations result in social expectations toward older people in terms of having or pursuing socially active and healthy lifestyles, regardless of whether they are able to do so.

Therefore, this article highlights problems with online representations of older people as being "youthful" third-agers (especially when it comes to representing health and social care users as ideally independent and well-functioning), as they are associated with neglecting the possible declines of very old age and of the highly specific purposes which do not fully represent the interests of older people.

3 Public Sector Organizations Generating Online Representations of Older People: Case of a Swedish Municipality

This section makes use of an example of a Swedish public sector organization (municipality) generating online representations of older people (reinforcing typical third-age representations). The following findings are primarily concerned with the practices of institutional practitioners and the power structure related to generating online representations of older people at the municipal level. The findings also draw attention to the role that media logic plays in generating representations of older people in the public sector from the perspectives of media production and media effects.

The empirical study introduced in this section is a study investigating the production process for digital photos of older people within a municipality (as a rule-based public administration). This is a follow-up to research examining typical third-age representation in the municipality's digital media [22]. This study attempted to explore municipal officers' beliefs and work practices when it came to generating online representations of older people. Semi-structured interviews with municipal officers were conducted, with a primary focus on how municipal officers obtained, selected, published and evaluated online photos of older people. The findings revealed that typical third-age representations were a result of municipal officials striving to create a positive image of the municipality and its services, while following municipal policy and EU laws regarding data protection, obtaining photos through particular external and internal sources, adjusting to and developing photographic standards, and endeavoring to promote citizen engagement through these photos. From an institutional logic perspective, this study indicated that municipal officers' work practices and beliefs were guided by both the logic of bureaucracy and the logic of social media. Specifically, empirical results revealed that the logic of bureaucracy, especially in terms of routines, was found to directly influence the gathering and selection of photos of older people by municipal officers. For instance, it was found that officers endeavored to follow a set of municipal policies and instructions, complied with formal procedures for obtaining informed consent from individuals, and performed photo-taking and photo-searching tasks with consideration given to efficiency. Additionally, social media logic was found to direct municipal officers to make use of social media platforms to establish networks of content, faculties, field professionals, locations and digital media platforms, as well as to increase the prominence of particular photos of older people. This translation of institutional logic served to select and publish photos representing older people as maintaining engagement and independence.

This study spotlights the role of media logic in generating online representations of older people in the public sector. Altheide and Snow introduced the concept of media logic as a form of communication and highlighted the influence of media formats in constructing messages within a particular medium [35] (p. 10). Media logic refers to "the organizational, technological, and aesthetic determinants of media functioning, including the ways in which they allocate material and symbolic resources and work through formal and informal rules" [36]. From a media sociology perspective, media logic is associated with the ideas of media content production and media effects. From the perspective of content production, media logic may function as a formatting logic for determining "the classification of materials, the choice of mode of presentation, and the selection of social experience" [36]. Despite the fact that media logic initially referred to the logic of traditional mass media (e.g., print media, television and radio), the conceptualization of media logic has been broadened to encompass digital media (for instance, social media logic [37]). As illustrated previously, social media logic plays a role in directing municipal officers to select and publish digital photos which show sociable, active and healthy older people. In this sense, social media logic plays an important role in the municipality's generation of online representations of older people, as it mediates the way in which the municipality represents older people online. From the perspective of media effects, media logic is a key concept of mediatization research examining media-related impacts on other social institutions. Media serves as an independent institution with a media logic that other social institutions are forced to adapt to, while also becoming an integrated part of other institutions, given the ways that many institutional activities are conducted through the media [38]. Previous mediatization studies substantiated the mediatization process of rule-based administrative public sector organizations at the organizational and individual levels where the logic of bureaucracy and social media logic play a role in institutional activities (see e.g., [39–44]). For instance, one study found that social media logic led public agencies to invest resources in channels that involved relatively few citizens who were favorably inclined to the agency, increase communicative and image-building power, as well as participate in more personalized communication (e.g., exposure of individual employees, use of informal communication styles) [44]. In the municipality under examination, the translation of social media logic highlights the impacts of social media on the production process of digital photos of older people within the municipality, which can be seen as a specific case of the mediatization of public sector organizations. The mediatization of the municipality has important ramifications in cultural discourse of the third age in terms of contributing to online representations of older people as maintaining engagement and independence.

4 Public Sector Organizations in a Convergent Position

Public sector organizations are associated with having a legitimate and formal duty to act in the interests of senior citizens. This section discusses the position of public sector organizations when generating online representations of older people, emphasizing the role that public sector organizations play in taking care of older people (acting as a caretaker) and simultaneously showing their care for older people through digital media (profiling as a caretaker).

Public sector organizations have a social responsibility to serve the interests of older people. For instance, it is essential to respect the dignity of older people and prevent violations of ethical responsibilities regarding the protection of older people. Furthermore, these organizations are expected to follow the lead of international social policy when it comes to tackling age discrimination, given that online representations of older people have implications for the well-being of older people, while also affecting societal attitudes toward older people and the concept of growing old [45]. As a specific and pertinent example, municipalities in Sweden have a legitimate responsibility to care for older people in certain areas, such as in residential care settings [46]. In this sense, public sector organizations are unlikely to generate offensive and negative online representations of older people. However, they also may not strive to generate any "revolutionary" representations of older people, rather providing representations likely echoing prevalent social stereotypes of older people, as they do not have an official duty to challenge societal views and attitudes regarding older people in digital media.

Public sector organizations are expected to show their care and highlight available services for older people with the support of digital media, driven by longstanding values. One of the most important of these values is transparency, conceptualized as comprising the visibility of information and the ability to infer conclusions from data [47]. Given varying levels of access to information, there is potential for transparency in the public sector to be achieved, given "the fuller transparency, the nominal transparency, the conditional transparency and the transparency in the allocation and management of sensitive information" [48]. Additionally, from a postmodernist perspective, various forms of computer-mediated transparency are needed to amplify positive effects on societal trust [49]. Thus, there is a need for public sector organizations to share digital information concerning public services for senior citizens as a means of enhancing transparency. Digital media use by public sector organizations is often associated with concerns over improving public perception of these institutions. For instance, digital media has allowed public sector organizations to bypass traditional mass media and reach out to citizens directly, while also inspiring these organizations to promote positive images of these institutions, especially when it comes to crisis communication (see e.g., [44, 50, 51]). In this sense, public sector organizations are likely to provide effective services for senior citizens through the use of digital media.

The convergent position can be seen in studies examining the intentions of public sector organizations when generating online representations of older people. For example, a study exploring nursing home staff perspectives on Instagram representations illustrated an online representation of a fun, social and active nursing-home life, finding that this was a result of a marketing motive to attract adult children to place senior relatives in such institutions, as well as an assurance motive to provide evidence of resident participation in social activities as promised [52]. As public sector organizations mediate the manner in which older people are represented online, the convergent position could explain why older people are represented in line with typical third-age representations. This convergence may lead to the marginalization of the oldest populations from the power structure of representations of older people online, resulting in misleading information concerning care provided to citizens (as taxpayers). Hence, it is necessary for public sector organizations in the convergent position to assess fulfillment of their responsibilities in terms of caring for and representing older people online.

5   Accountability in the Public Sector When Generating Online Representations of Older People

The production of digital content addressing older people by public sector organizations must be viewed in the context of digitalization and the use of digital media. Digitalization has the power to improve the delivery of services, ensure transparency, participation and collaboration in the decision-making process [53]. It is hoped that digitalization can have positive impacts in terms of cost reduction, productivity improvement, information-sharing, full-scale citizen participation and realizing decision-making that is more open and transparent [54] (p. 19). Digital media usage in the public sector is one of the digitalization strategies aimed at advancing transparency and public participation. Still, there are differing results, with one example being researched finding that digital media usage by the majority of EU municipalities did not substantially promote accountability and citizen participation [55]. Digital media offers opportunities for facilitating public participation and improving public administration. For instance, innovative forms of participation in digital media have been seen to empower citizens in terms of control of public administration, including through forming new public services and reshaping existing services [56]. In this respect, social expectations regarding the fostering of e-governance by digitalization and requirements for successful implementation serve as a fundamental basis for public sector organizations when generating digital content representing older people.

It has been seen that e-governance in the public sector can "support public services, government administration, democratic processes, and relationships among citizens, civil society, the private sector, and the state" [57]. Yet, there is evidence that the expected benefits of e-governance are yet to be attained in countries where it has been implemented, strengthening calls for enforcing effectiveness (not purely efficiency) and achieving desirable impacts (not merely producing output) [58]. As one of the core institutional principles of e-governance, accountability is defined as the "social relationship in which an actor feels an obligation to explain and to justify his or her conduct to some significant other" [59] (p. 184). Accountability has undoubtedly positive attributes associated with greater transparency and fair governance. Additionally, assessing the actual conduct of institutions is highly desirable [60]. When it comes to representing older people online, improvements to accountability in the public sector are expected to be seen.

The production of digital content concerning older people can be seen as an accountability task for public sector organizations who have the responsibility to offer services to older people and protect their rights. Accountability requires the implementation of e-governance initiatives to facilitate communication between citizens and public sector organizations [61]. This communication is emphasized in existing research as a prerequisite for the realization of citizen participation in the public sector. However, this communication remains underdeveloped in most instances [62].

Accountability in the public sector entails increased participation of older people and other civil society actors (e.g., viewers' and pensioners' associations) in generating and evaluating digital content about older people, while also enhancing public sector communication with citizens. In this way, older people can directly participate in creating content agendas, generating online representations of older people, and evaluating posted digital content to meet citizens' informational needs. By advocating for the visual communication rights of older people, collaborative means can be realized for involving older people in the creation of digital visual content and enhancing older people's power to meaningfully influence their representations [63]. In this regard, the participation of older people has the potential to strengthen their position within the power structure of representations of older people online. Citizen e-participation can come in the forms of political, policy and social participation [64], and it can be achieved through the acts of obtaining information, engaging in deliberation and participating in decision-making [65]. Given the various forms and levels of e-participation, public sector organizations have the power to encourage and facilitate older people and other civil society actors to better engage in generating online representations of older people. This can have positive effects in terms of formulating media policy, encouraging dialogue and acting to improve services and the representations of older people.

6 Concluding Remarks

Online representations of older people generated by public sector organizations have emphasized the brighter side of later life while failing to reflect actual conditions experienced by older people (e.g., those living in supportive care). These representations have contributed to forming a new norm of ageing and creating a model for what defines an older person, leading to visual ageism [6]. These representations may also have the result of homogenizing older people as being a wholly active and healthy group, regardless of heterogeneous lifestyles, living situations and personal pursuits [66]. Additionally, these representations risk making older people feel responsible for compensating loss of resources in later life [34]. These online representations marginalize older people by showing limited functions and neglecting to highlight the ways in which older people contribute to society. There is an essential need to explore the possibilities of generating alternative representations by examining how public sector organizations generate online representations of older people (see e.g., [21]). Research examining the ways in which a Swedish municipality (as an example of a public sector organization) produced digital photos of older people indicates that certain work beliefs and municipal practices resulted in typical third-age representations. From an institutional logic perspective, social media logic and the logic of bureaucracy both factored into the production process of digital photos of older people. When considering the guiding role of institutional logic in the municipal production process, media representations of older people in the public sector are at risk of being further reinforced as an idealistic image of third-agers. It has been found that the institutionalization of an active ageing image can lead to insufficient alternative images and a failure to foster public recognition of diversity in later life [67]. Therefore, this article has addressed the convergent position of public sector organizations to protect the interests of older people, while simultaneously acting as a caretaker for older people and showing their care for older people through digital media. This article also calls for greater accountability in the public sector when it comes to the process of producing digital content concerning older people.

Acknowledgements. This project has received funding from the European Union's Horizon 2020 research and innovation programme under the Marie Skłodowska-Curie grant agreement No 764632. This study was accomplished within the context of the Swedish National Graduate School for Competitive Science on Ageing and Health (SWEAH) funded by the Swedish Research Council.

References

1. United Nations: The Madrid International Plan of action on ageing and the political declaration, New York (2002)
2. Christensen, C.L.: Visualising old age: photographs of older people on the website of the DaneAge association. Nord. Rev. **40**, 111–127 (2019)
3. Angus, J., Reeve, P.: Ageism: a threat to "aging well" in the 21st century. J. Appl. Gerontol. **25**, 137–152 (2006)
4. Zhang, Y.B., Harwood, J., Williams, A., Ylänne-McEwen, V., Wadleigh, P.M., Thimm, C.: The portrayal of older adults in advertising. J. Lang. Soc. Psychol. **25**, 264–282 (2006)
5. Bai, X.: Images of ageing in society: a literature review. J. Popul. Ageing. **7**, 231–253 (2014)
6. Loos, E., Ivan, L.: Visual ageism in the media. In: Ayalon, L., Tesch-Römer, C. (eds.) Contemporary Perspectives on Ageism, pp. 163–176. Springer, Cham (2018)
7. Oró-Piqueras, M., Marques, S.: Images of old age in YouTube: destabilizing stereotypes. Continuum (N. Y) **31**, 257–265 (2017)
8. Lazar, A., Diaz, M., Brewer, R., Kim, C., Piper, A.M.: Going gray, failure to hire, and the ick factor. In: Proceedings of the 2017 ACM Conference on Computer Supported Cooperative Work and Social Computing - CSCW 2017, pp. 655–668. ACM Press, New York (2017)
9. Levy, B.R., Chung, P.H., Bedford, T., Navrazhina, K.: Facebook as a site for negative age stereotypes. Gerontologist **54**, 172–176 (2014)
10. Makita, M., Mas-Bleda, A., Stuart, E., Thelwall, M.: Ageing, old age and older adults: a social media analysis of dominant topics and discourses. Ageing Soc. **41**, 1–26 (2019)
11. Ylänne, V., Williams, A., Wadleigh, P.M.: Ageing well? Older people's health and well-being as portrayed in UK magazine advertisements. Int. J. Ageing Later Life. **4**, 33–62 (2010)
12. Jenkins, H.: Convergence? I diverge. Technol. Rev. **104**, 93 (2001)
13. Jensen, K.B.: Media Convergence: The Three Degrees of Network, Mass and Interpersonal Communication. Routledge, New York (2010)
14. United Nations DESA: 2020 United Nations E-Government Survey, New York (2020)
15. Stewart, C., Kowaltzke, A.: Media: New Ways and Meanings. Wiley, Milton (2007)
16. Ylänne, V.: Representations of ageing in the media. In: Twigg, J., Martin, W. (eds.) Routledge Handbook of Cultural Gerontology, pp. 369–376. Routledge, London and New York (2015)
17. Centre for Ageing Better: Doddery but dear?: examining age-related stereotypes, London (2020)
18. Loos, E.: Designing for dynamic diversity: representing various senior citizens in digital information sources. Obs. (OBS *) **7**, 21–45 (2013)
19. Carlstedt, E.: A fun, active and sociable life on display – nursing home presentations on Instagram. Ageing Soc. **39**, 2109–2132 (2019)

20. Loos, E.: The organizational use of online stock photos: the impact of representing senior citizens as eternally youthful. Hum. Technol. **14**, 366–381 (2018)
21. Sourbati, M., Loos, E.F.: Interfacing age: diversity and (in)visibility in digital public service. J. Digit. Media Policy **10**, 275–293 (2019)
22. Xu, W.: (Non-)Stereotypical representations of older people in Swedish authority-managed social media. Ageing Soc. https://doi.org/10.1017/S0144686X20001075
23. Fung, H.H., Li, T., Zhang, X., Sit, I.M.I., Cheng, S.-T., Isaacowitz, D.M.: Positive portrayals of old age do not always have positive consequences. J. Gerontol. Ser. B Psychol. Sci. Soc. Sci. **70**, 913–924 (2015)
24. Higgs, P., Gilleard, C.: The ideology of ageism versus the social imaginary of the fourth age: two differing approaches to the negative contexts of old age. Ageing Soc. **40**, 1–14 (2019)
25. Laslett, P.: A Fresh Map of Life: The Emergence of the Third Age. Harvard University Press, Cambridge (1991)
26. Kydd, A., Fleming, A., Gardner, S., Hafford-Letchfield, T.: Ageism in the third age. In: Ayalon, L., Tesch-Römer, C. (eds.) Contemporary Perspectives on Ageism. International Perspectives on Aging, pp. 115–130. Springer, Cham (2018) https://doi.org/10.1007/978-3-319-73820-8_8
27. Gilleard, C., Higgs, P.: Studying dementia: the relevance of the fourth age. Qual. Ageing Older Adults **15**, 241–243 (2014)
28. Gilleard, C., Higgs, P.: Contexts of Ageing: Class, Cohort and Community. Polity Press, Cambridge (2005)
29. Gilleard, C., Higgs, P.: Third and fourth ages. In: The Wiley Blackwell Encyclopedia of Health, Illness, Behavior, and Society, pp. 2442–2448. Wiley, Chichester (2014)
30. Gilleard, C., Higgs, P.: The third age as a cultural field. In: Carr, D., Komp, K. (eds.) Gerontology in the Era of the Third Age: Implications and Next Steps, pp. 33–50. Springer, New York (2011). https://doi.org/10.1007/978-3-319-73820-8_8
31. Hannah, J.S., Steeden, B.: Exploring representations of old age and ageing, London (2020)
32. Williams, A., Wadleigh, P.M., Ylänne, V.: Images of older people in UK magazine advertising: toward a typology. Int. J. Aging Hum. Dev. **71**, 83–114 (2010)
33. Marshall, B.L., Rahman, M.: Celebrity, ageing and the construction of 'third age' identities. Int. J. Cult. Stud. **18**, 577–593 (2015)
34. Loos, E.: Visual representation of senior citizens: the role of discourse coalitions for identification with images and accessible information delivery. Online J. Commun. Media Technol. **3**, 87–100 (2013)
35. Altheide, D., Snow, R.: Media Logic. Sage Publications, Beverly Hills (1979)
36. Mazzoleni, G., Splendore, S.: Media logic. In: Communication. Oxford University Press (2015)
37. Van Dijck, J., Poell, T.: Understanding social media logic. Media Commun. **1**, 2 (2013)
38. Hjarvard, S.P.: The Mediatization of Culture and Society. Routledge, London (2013)
39. Thorbjørnsrud, K.: Mediatization of public bureaucracies: administrative versus political loyalty. Scan. Polit. Stud. **38**, 179–197 (2015)
40. Thorbjornsrud, K., Ustad Figenschou, T., Ihlen, Ø.: Mediatization in public bureaucracies: a typology. Communications **39**, 3–22 (2014)
41. Fredriksson, M., Schillemans, T., Pallas, J.: Determinants of organizational mediatization: an analysis of the adaptation of Swedish government agencies to news media. Pub. Adm. **93**, 1049–1067 (2015)
42. Sandén, J., Turunen, J.: Public servants' values and mental mediatization – an empirical study of Swedish local government. Scand. J. Public Adm. **24**, 3–28 (2020)
43. Fredriksson, M., Pallas, J.: Public sector communication and mediatization. In: Luoma-aho, V., Canel, M. (eds.) The Handbook of Public Sector Communication, pp. 167–179. Wiley (2020)

44. Olsson, E.-K., Eriksson, M.: The logic of public organizations' social media use: toward a theory of 'social mediatization.' Pub. Relat. Inq. **5**, 187–204 (2016)
45. Carrigan, M., Szmigin, I.: The ethical advertising covenant: regulating ageism in UK advertising. Int. J. Advert. **19**, 509–528 (2000)
46. Beck, I., Törnquist, A., Broström, L., Edberg, A.-K.: Having to focus on doing rather than being—nurse assistants' experience of palliative care in municipal residential care settings. Int. J. Nurs. Stud. **49**, 455–464 (2012)
47. Michener, G., Bersch, K.: Identifying transparency. Inf. Polity **18**, 233–242 (2013)
48. Rodrigues, K.F.: Unveiling the concept of transparency: its limits, varieties and the creation of a typology. Cad. EBAPE BR **18**, 237–253 (2020)
49. Meijer, A.: Understanding modern transparency. Int. Rev. Adm. Sci. **75**, 255–269 (2009)
50. Fredriksson, M., Pallas, J.: Much ado about media: public relations in public agencies in the wake of managerialism. Pub. Relat. Rev. **42**, 600–606 (2016)
51. Wæraas, A.: Communicating identity: the use of core value statements in regulative institutions. Adm. Soc. **42**, 526–549 (2010)
52. Carlstedt, E., Jönson, H.: Online representations of nursing-home life in Sweden: perspectives from staff on content, purpose and audience. Ageing Soc. **40**, 1–17 (2019)
53. Blanc, D.L.: E-participation: a quick overview of recent qualitative trends, New York (2020)
54. Milakovich, M.E.: Digital governance: new technologies for improving public service and participation. Routledge (2012)
55. Bonsón, E., Torres, L., Royo, S., Flores, F.: Local e-government 2.0: social media and corporate transparency in municipalities. Gov. Inf. Q. **29**(2), 123–132 (2012). https://doi.org/10.1016/j.giq.2011.10.001
56. Luoma-aho, V., Canel, M.: The Handbook of Public Sector Communication. Wiley (2020)
57. Dawes, S.S.: The evolution and continuing challenges of e-governance. Pub. Adm. Rev. **68**, S86–S102 (2008)
58. Saxena, K.B.C.: Towards excellence in e-governance. Int. J. Pub. Sect. Manag. **18**, 498–513 (2005)
59. Bovens, M.: Public accountability. In: Ewan, F., Lawrence Jr., L., and Pollitt, C. (eds.) The Oxford Handbook of Public Management. Oxford Handbooks, Oxford (2009)
60. Bovens, M.: Two concepts of accountability: accountability as a virtue and as a mechanism. West Eur. Polit. **33**, 946–967 (2010)
61. Pina, V., Torres, L., Acerete, B.: Are ICTs promoting government accountability?: a comparative analysis of e-governance developments in 19 OECD countries. Crit. Perspect. Account. **18**, 583–602 (2007)
62. Piqueiras, P., Canel, M., Luoma-aho, V.: Citizen engagement and public sector communication. In: Luoma-aho, V., Canel, M. (eds.) The Handbook of Public Sector Communication, pp. 277–287. Wiley (2020)
63. Ivan, L., Loos, E., Tudorie, G.: Mitigating visual ageism in digital media: designing for dynamic diversity to enhance communication rights for senior citizens. Societies **10**, 76 (2020)
64. Meijer, A.J., Burger, N., Ebbers, W.: Citizens4Citizens: mapping participatory practices on the internet. Electron. J. E-Gov. **7**, 99–112 (2009)
65. Oates, B.J.: The potential contribution of ICTs to the political process. Electron. J. E-Gov. **1**, 31–39 (2003)
66. van Dyk, S., Lessenich, S., Denninger, T., Richter, A.: The many meanings of "active ageing" confronting public discourse with older people's stories. Rech. Sociol. Anthropol. **44**, 97–115 (2013)
67. Enßle, F., Helbrecht, I.: Understanding diversity in later life through images of old age. Ageing Soc. 1–20 (2020). https://doi.org/10.1017/S0144686X20000379.

Author Index

Printed in the United States
by Baker & Taylor Publisher Services